Weight Watchers®

New 365 DAY MENU COOKBOOK

Weight Watchers®

New

365 DAY MENU COOKBOOK

MACMILLAN • USA

Weight Watchers

Since 1963, Weight Watchers has grown from a handful of people to millions of enrollments annually. Today, Weight Watchers is the recognized leading name in safe and sensible weight control. Weight Watchers members form a diverse group, from youths to senior citizens, attending meetings virtually around the globe.

Weight-loss and weight-management results vary by individual, but we recommend that you attend Weight Watchers meetings, follow the Weight Watchers food plan and participate in regular physical activity. For the Weight Watchers meeting nearest you, call 1-800-651-6000.

MACMILLAN
A Simon & Schuster Macmillan Company
1633 Broadway
New York, NY 10019

Copyright © 1996 by Weight Watchers International, Inc.

Library of Congress Cataloging-in-Publication Data

Weight Watchers new 365-day menu cookbook.

p.   cm.
Includes index.
ISBN 0-02-861015-6 (alk. paper)
1. Reducing diets—Recipes.   I. Weight Watchers International.
II. Title: Weight Watchers new three hundred and sixty five-day
menu cookbook
RM222.2.W3224   1996
641.5'635—dc20   96-11094
                                      CIP

Manufactured in the United States of America

10 9 8 7 6 5 4 3 2 1

Designed by Nick Anderson

Cover photo by Martin Jacobs

Cover photo: Paella, page 174

CONTENTS

INTRODUCTION

Ask anyone who has lost weight: Maintaining the new weight requires as much vigilance as losing it in the first place. It's an ongoing adventure in which healthful eating habits are used and strengthened every day.

Whether you're seeking to lose weight or maintain a weight goal—and really, isn't that all of us?—planning sensible meals is always a challenge. In *Weight Watchers New 365-Day Menu Cookbook*, we've done the hard work for you: We've devised a year's worth of menus—not just for dinner, but for the whole day. The result is an all-new collection of 365 recipes and menus that points the way to nutritionally sound yet incredibly tempting eating.

Weight Watchers New 365-Day Menu Cookbook includes 365 recipes for Breakfasts and Brunches, Light Meals and Main Meals, plus a menu specially designed to complement the recipe for the day. Oriental Seafood–Pasta Salad, for example, is served with Stir-Fried Vegetables, a pineapple wedge, and Chinese Tea. Have a yen for burger and fries but don't think you should indulge? Fast-Food–Style Turkey Burgers are served with Baked Potato Sticks—and a chocolate shake. Every recipe has complete nutrition information, and each day's menu is nutritionally balanced and comes with Weight Watchers Selection™ Information as well as counts for fat and fiber grams.

In addition to 365 recipes, there are hundreds of menu ideas—mini-recipes for the meals that aren't featured, complete with specific ingredient amounts and cooking times. You'll also find a snack—sometimes two!—in every day's menu. And we've taken your busy life into account: Some days actually include fast-food or deli-counter fare, and nearly all feature easy-to-brown-bag Light Meals.

Organized by type of entrée—Meat, Fish, Poultry and Meatless—*Weight Watchers New 365-Day Menu Cookbook* is *not* a plan for day-by-day, week-by-week eating. Instead, use it as you would any other cookbook: If you have leftovers after feasting on Lemon-Thyme Roast Chicken, use them up later that week in Chicken–Wheat Berry Sauté or Macaroni and Chicken Salad, or use them in a mini-recipe. If the weather forecast is for cold and snow, how about hearty Individual Shepherd's Pies or Spicy Black Bean Stew; if it's the dog days of August, wouldn't Crab in Canteloupe Baskets or Thai Beef Salad be refreshing?—or look in the index for something else that strikes your fancy. Your options are as endless as they are delicious.

Whether your goal is to lose or maintain weight, or simply to expand your repertoire of easy, nutritious meals, *Weight Watchers New 365-Day Menu Cookbook* is the cookbook you'll turn to again and again.

BREAKFAST
Cooked Oatmeal, 1 cup, with $^3/_4$ cup blueberries
Skim Milk, 1 cup
Coffee or Tea (optional)

LIGHT MEAL
French Dip Roast Beef Sandwich, 1 serving
  (see recipe)
Carrot Sticks, $1^1/_2$ cups
Broccoli Florets, $^1/_2$ cup
Dill Pickles, 2 medium
Frozen Seedless Green Grapes, 20 small or 12 large
Unsweetened Raspberry-Flavored Seltzer

MAIN MEAL
Spinach 'n' Bean Salad (In medium bowl, combine
  2 cups torn spinach leaves, $^1/_2$ cup *each* sliced
  mushrooms and red onion, 2 ounces drained
  cooked white beans, 1 tablespoon imitation bacon
  bits and 1 tablespoon ranch salad dressing.)
Rice Cakes, 2, with 2 teaspoons reduced-calorie tub
  margarine
Iced Tea

SNACK
Reduced-Calorie Chocolate Dairy Shake, 1 serving

This menu provides: 2 Milks, 3 Fats, 2 Fruits,
14 Vegetables, 4 Proteins, 5 Breads, 40 Optional
Calories.

Per serving: 28 g Fat, 22 g Fiber.

FRENCH DIP ROAST BEEF SANDWICH

Makes 4 servings

One 8-ounce loaf French bread, cut in half horizontally, then vertically into
  4 equal slices to make 8 pieces
12 ounces cooked lean boneless roast beef, thinly sliced
2 cups hot low-sodium beef broth

1. Onto each of 4 warm plates, place 2 bread pieces, cut-side up.

2. Top each bread piece with $1^1/_2$ ounces roast beef, then $^1/_4$ cup broth.
Cover each plate tightly with foil; let stand 1–2 minutes, until heated
through.

Serving (1 sandwich) provides: 3 Proteins, 2 Breads, 10 Optional Calories.

Per serving: 326 Calories, 8 g Total Fat, 2 g Saturated Fat, 66 mg Cholesterol,
436 mg Sodium, 29 g Total Carbohydrate, 2 g Dietary Fiber, 32 g Protein,
47 mg Calcium.

MEATS

ROAST BEEF SANDWICH WITH HORSERADISH MAYONNAISE

Makes 4 servings

2 tablespoons + 2 teaspoons reduced-calorie mayonnaise
2 tablespoons prepared horseradish
8 slices reduced-calorie multi-grain bread
8 ounces cooked lean boneless roast beef, thinly sliced
2 medium tomatoes, sliced
2 cups arugula leaves
$^1/_4$ teaspoon salt
Freshly ground black pepper, to taste

1. In small cup or bowl, combine mayonnaise and horseradish.

2. Spread each bread slice with one-fourth of mayonnaise mixture.

3. To assemble sandwiches, place 4 bread slices, spread-side up, onto work surface; top each with 2 ounces roast beef, then one-fourth of tomato slices, arugula, salt and pepper and 1 remaining bread slice, spread-side down. Cut sandwiches diagonally into halves.

Serving (1 sandwich) provides: 1 Fat, 2 Vegetables, 2 Proteins, 1 Bread.

Per serving: 226 Calories, 8 g Total Fat, 2 g Saturated Fat, 48 mg Cholesterol, 386 mg Sodium, 18 g Total Carbohydrate, 3 g Dietary Fiber, 20 g Protein, 59 mg Calcium.

BREAKFAST
Orange, 1 small
Reduced-Calorie Whole-Wheat Bread, 2 slices, toasted, with 1 teaspoon peanut butter and 2 teaspoons apricot jam
Skim Milk, 1 cup
Coffee or Tea (optional)

LIGHT MEAL
Roast Beef Sandwich with Horseradish Mayonnaise, 1 serving (see recipe)
Cauliflower Florets, 1 cup
Diet Root Beer

MAIN MEAL
Onion and Zucchini Frittata (Spray medium non-stick skillet with nonstick cooking spray; heat. Add 1 cup *each* chopped onions and zucchini; cook over medium heat, stirring constantly, until tender. In small bowl, beat 1 egg with 1 tablespoon skim milk, $^1/_4$ teaspoon salt and pinch freshly ground black pepper; stir into vegetable mixture. Cook, covered, until mixture is firm.)
Tossed Salad Greens, 1 cup, with 1 cup cooked sliced beets and 1 teaspoon *each* olive oil and wine or cider vinegar
Breadsticks, 4 long
Pear, 1 small
Unsweetened Seltzer with Lemon Wedge

SNACK
Aspartame-Sweetened Peach Nonfat Yogurt, 1 cup

This menu provides: 2 Milks, 3 Fats, 2 Fruits, 12 Vegetables, 3 Proteins, 4 Breads, 35 Optional Calories.

Per serving: 29 g Fat, 23 g Fiber.

BREAKFAST

Papaya, $^1/_2$ medium
Bran Flakes Cereal, $1^1/_2$ ounces
Skim Milk, 1 cup
Coffee or Tea (optional)

LIGHT MEAL

Braised Beef and Red Onion Sandwich, 1 serving
  (see recipe)
Sliced Radishes, $^1/_2$ cup, with 2 teaspoons
  reduced-calorie mayonnaise
Raspberries, $^3/_4$ cup
Diet Ginger Ale

MAIN MEAL

Skillet Rice and Beans (In medium saucepan, heat
  1 teaspoon olive oil; add $^1/_2$ cup *each* chopped
  onion and red and green bell peppers. Cook over
  medium-high heat, stirring frequently, until vegetables are softened. Add 1 cup tomato juice,
  2 ounces *each* drained cooked red kidney beans
  and black beans and $^1/_2$ teaspoon dried basil;
  cook, stirring frequently, until heated through.
  Serve over 1 cup cooked brown rice.)
Lettuce Wedge with Russian Dressing (In small cup
  or bowl, combine $1^1/_2$ teaspoons *each* reduced-
  calorie mayonnaise and ketchup; spoon over
  1 iceberg lettuce wedge.)
Diet Cola

SNACK

Aspartame-Sweetened Vanilla Nonfat Yogurt, 1 cup
Mini Rice Cakes, 6

This menu provides: 2 Milks, 3 Fats, 2 Fruits,
$8^1/_2$ Vegetables, $3^1/_2$ Proteins, 6 Breads, 25 Optional
Calories.

Per serving: 20 g Fat, 22 g Fiber.

BRAISED BEEF AND RED ONION SANDWICH

Makes 4 servings

8 slices reduced-calorie rye bread
2 tablespoons prepared country-style mustard
2 servings Beef Braised in Red Wine (page 24), chilled
1 cup sliced red onions

1. Spread 4 of the bread slices with one-fourth of the mustard.

2. To assemble sandwiches, place mustard-spread bread slices, spread-side up, onto work surface; top each with one-fourth of the Beef Braised in Red Wine, onion slices and 1 remaining bread slice. Cut sandwiches diagonally into halves.

Serving (1 sandwich) provides: $^1/_4$ Fat, $1^1/_2$ Vegetables, $1^1/_2$ Proteins, 1 Bread, 15 Optional Calories.

Per serving: 232 Calories, 5 g Total Fat, 1 g Saturated Fat, 32 mg Cholesterol, 449 mg Sodium, 29 g Total Carbohydrate, 2 g Dietary Fiber, 17 g Protein, 69 mg Calcium.

PITA PIZZA WITH GROUND BEEF

Makes 4 servings

4 small (1-ounce) whole-wheat pitas, split horizontally to make 8 rounds
4 ounces extra-lean ground beef (10% or less fat)
1 garlic clove, minced
1 cup tomato sauce (no salt added)
1 teaspoon dried oregano leaves
3 ounces skim-milk mozzarella cheese, grated
1/4 teaspoon salt
Freshly ground black pepper, to taste

1. Preheat oven to 425° F.

2. Place pita rounds onto nonstick baking sheet; bake 5–10 minutes, until toasted. Remove pitas from oven; leave oven on.

3. Meanwhile, spray small nonstick skillet with nonstick cooking spray; heat. Add beef and garlic; cook over medium-high heat, stirring to break up meat, 2–3 minutes, until no longer pink. Remove from heat; set aside.

4. Spread each toasted pita round with 2 tablespoons tomato sauce. Sprinkle sauce with equal amounts of oregano, then cheese; top cheese with equal amounts of reserved beef, then sprinkle evenly with salt and pepper. Bake 5 minutes, until sauce is bubbling and cheese is melted.

Serving (2 pita pizzas) provides: 1 Vegetable, 1 3/4 Proteins, 1 Bread.

Per serving: 202 Calories, 7 g Total Fat, 3 g Saturated Fat, 30 mg Cholesterol, 418 mg Sodium, 21 g Total Carbohydrate, 3 g Dietary Fiber, 15 g Protein, 150 mg Calcium.

BREAKFAST

Blueberries, 3/4 cup
Breakfast Rice Pudding (In small saucepan or microwavable bowl, combine 1/2 cup cooked long-grain rice, 1/2 cup skim milk and 1/4 teaspoon cinnamon; cook over low heat, stirring frequently, or microwave on Medium [70% power], stirring once or twice during cooking, until warm. Stir in sugar substitute to equal 2 teaspoons sugar.)
Coffee or Tea (optional)

LIGHT MEAL

Pita Pizza with Ground Beef, 1 serving (see recipe)
Marinated Artichoke Hearts (In medium bowl, combine 1 1/2 cups cooked artichoke hearts, 1 tablespoon minced fresh flat-leaf parsley, 2 teaspoons wine vinegar, 1 teaspoon olive oil and 1 garlic clove, minced; refrigerate, covered, at least 1 hour.)
Peach Sundae (Top 4 ounces sugar-free vanilla nonfat frozen yogurt with 1 medium peach, pitted and sliced.)
Mineral Water with Lime Wedge

MAIN MEAL

Grilled Swordfish Salad (In small bowl, combine 1 tablespoon *each* reduced-sodium soy sauce and fresh lemon juice and 1 garlic clove, minced. Brush one 4-ounce boneless swordfish steak with soy sauce mixture; grill or broil, turning once, 8–10 minutes, until fish flakes easily when tested with fork. On plate, arrange 1 cup *each* mixed salad greens, cucumber slices and green bell pepper strips and 6 cherry tomatoes; top with cooked swordfish. Drizzle fish and vegetables with 1 teaspoon olive oil and 2 teaspoons red wine or rice wine vinegar.)
Sugar Snap Peas, 1 1/2 cups, sprinkled with minced fresh mint leaves
Flatbreads, 3/4 ounce
Aspartame-Sweetened Strawberry Nonfat Yogurt, 3/4 cup
Diet Lemonade, 1 cup

SNACK

English Muffin, 1 (2 ounces), split and toasted, with 2 teaspoons *each* reduced-calorie tub margarine and strawberry jam
Skim Milk, 1/2 cup

This menu provides: 2 Milks, 3 Fats, 2 Fruits, 14 Vegetables, 3 1/4 Proteins, 5 Breads, 85 Optional Calories.

Per serving: 31 g Fat, 21 g Fiber.

BREAKFAST
Grapefruit, $^1/_2$ medium
Cornflakes, $^3/_4$ ounce
Skim Milk, $^1/_2$ cup
Coffee or Tea (optional)

LIGHT MEAL
Hamburger Club Sandwich, 1 serving (see recipe)
Celery and Carrot Sticks, 1 cup *each*
Aspartame-Sweetened Strawberry Nonfat Yogurt,
   1 cup
Diet Cherry Cola with Lemon Wedge

MAIN MEAL
Baked Cod, 4 ounces, with 2 teaspoons reduced-
   calorie tub margarine and lemon wedges
Baked Potato, 6 ounces, with 1 tablespoon nonfat
   sour cream and $^1/_4$ cup chopped scallions
Steamed Broccoli, 1 cup, with 1 teaspoon olive oil
   and chopped fresh garlic
Apple, 1 small, cored and sliced, drizzled with
   1 teaspoon honey
Herbal Tea

SNACK
Milk Shake (In blender, combine $^1/_2$ cup skim milk,
   2 ice cubes, sugar substitute to equal 1 teaspoon
   sugar and 1 teaspoon instant decaffeinated coffee
   powder; purée until smooth.)

This menu provides: 2 Milks, 3 Fats, 2 Fruits,
8 Vegetables, $3^1/_2$ Proteins, 4 Breads, 45 Optional
Calories.

Per serving: 23 g Fat, 21 g Fiber.

5
HAMBURGER CLUB SANDWICH
Makes 4 servings

8 ounces extra-lean ground beef (10% or less fat)
12 slices reduced-calorie multi-grain bread
3 tablespoons reduced-calorie mayonnaise
8 medium iceberg lettuce leaves
1 tablespoon + 1 teaspoon imitation bacon bits
2 medium tomatoes, sliced
$^1/_4$ teaspoon salt
Freshly ground black pepper, to taste

1. Spray rack in broiler pan with nonstick cooking spray. Preheat broiler.

2. Form beef into four 4" patties; place onto prepared rack. Broil 4" from heat, turning once, 8 minutes, until cooked through.

3. Slice burgers into halves horizontally, making 8 thin burgers; set aside.

4. Lightly toast bread; spread each toast slice with $^3/_4$ teaspoon mayonnaise.

5. To assemble sandwiches, place 4 toast slices, spread-side up, onto work surface; top each with 2 lettuce leaves, 1 thin beef burger, 1 teaspoon bacon bits, another toast slice, another thin beef burger, one-fourth of the tomato slices, the salt and pepper and 1 remaining toast slice, spread-side down. Cut sandwiches diagonally into halves.

Serving (1 sandwich) provides: 1 Fat, $1^1/_2$ Vegetables, $1^1/_2$ Proteins, $1^1/_2$ Breads, 15 Optional Calories.

Per serving: 261 Calories, 11 g Total Fat, 3 g Saturated Fat, 39 mg Cholesterol, 512 mg Sodium, 25 g Total Carbohydrate, 4 g Dietary Fiber, 18 g Protein, 53 mg Calcium.

6
GRILLED HAMBURGER WITH FRESH TOMATO SALSA

Salsa is great on burgers! Make the salsa at the last minute for the freshest possible taste.

Makes 4 servings

³/₄ cup diced tomato
¹/₄ cup diced red onion
¹/₄ cup minced fresh cilantro
1 tablespoon fresh lime juice
1 teaspoon minced deveined seeded jalapeño pepper
   (wear gloves to prevent irritation)
¹/₄ teaspoon freshly ground black pepper
10 ounces extra-lean ground beef (10% or less fat)
¹/₂ teaspoon ground cumin
¹/₂ teaspoon onion powder
¹/₂ teaspoon salt

1. Preheat outdoor barbecue grill according to manufacturer's directions, or preheat broiler and spray rack in broiler pan with nonstick cooking spray.

2. To prepare salsa, in medium bowl, combine tomato, onion, cilantro, juice, jalapeño pepper and black pepper; set aside.

3. In large bowl, combine beef, cumin, onion powder and salt; form into 4 equal patties. Grill patties over hot coals or place onto prepared rack in broiler pan and broil 4" from heat, turning once, 8 minutes, until beef is cooked through. Serve with salsa.

Serving (1 burger, ¹/₄ cup salsa) provides: ¹/₂ Vegetable, 2 Proteins.

Per serving: 136 Calories, 7 g Total Fat, 3 g Saturated Fat, 44 mg Cholesterol, 329 mg Sodium, 3 g Total Carbohydrate, 1 g Dietary Fiber, 15 g Protein, 12 mg Calcium.

BREAKFAST
Grapefruit, ¹/₂ medium
Reduced-Calorie Whole-Wheat Bread, 2 slices, toasted, with 1 tablespoon peanut butter
Skim Milk, 1 cup
Coffee or Tea (optional)

LIGHT MEAL
Grilled Hamburger with Fresh Tomato Salsa, 1 serving (see recipe)
Hamburger Roll, 1 (2 ounces)
Nonfat Tortilla Chips, 1 ounce, with Yogurt-Cilantro Dip (In small bowl, combine ¹/₂ cup plain nonfat yogurt, 1 tablespoon minced fresh cilantro and pinch garlic powder.)
Cucumber and Jicama Spears, 1 cup *each*
Root Beer Float (In tall glass, combine 1 cup diet root beer and ¹/₃ cup skim milk; add enough ice cubes to fill glass.)

MAIN MEAL
Broiled Halibut, 4 ounces
Baked Sweet Potato, 3 ounces, with 2 teaspoons reduced-calorie tub margarine and 1 teaspoon firmly packed light or dark brown sugar
Steamed Italian Green Beans, 1 cup, with Garlic "Butter" (In small cup or bowl, combine 2 teaspoons reduced-calorie tub margarine and pinch garlic powder.)
Iceberg Lettuce Wedge, 1, with 1 tablespoon fat-free blue cheese dressing
Mango, ¹/₂ small
Unsweetened Lemon-Lime–Flavored Seltzer

SNACK
Plain Popcorn, hot-air popped, 3 cups, with 1 teaspoon freshly grated Parmesan cheese
Diet Cherry Cola

This menu provides: 2 Milks, 3 Fats, 2 Fruits, 7¹/₂ Vegetables, 5 Proteins, 6 Breads, 45 Optional Calories.

Per serving: 35 g Fat, 24 g Fiber.

SLICED STEAK SALAD WITH HERB VINAIGRETTE

Makes 4 servings

BREAKFAST

Aspartame-Sweetened Strawberry-Banana Nonfat Yogurt, 1 cup, with $^1/_2$ medium banana, sliced, and 1 tablespoon wheat germ
Graham Crackers, 3 ($2^1/_2$" squares)
Coffee or Tea (optional)

LIGHT MEAL

Sliced Steak Salad with Herb Vinaigrette, 1 serving (see recipe)
Flatbreads, $^3/_4$ ounce
Iced Herbal Tea

MAIN MEAL

Skinless Roast Turkey Breast, 2 ounces
Cooked Wild Rice, $^1/_2$ cup, sprinkled with $^1/_2$ packet low-sodium instant chicken broth and seasoning mix
Maple-Glazed Acorn Squash (Preheat oven to 450° F. In small cup or bowl, combine 2 teaspoons reduced-calorie tub margarine, melted, and 1 teaspoon maple syrup; brush onto 7-ounce baked acorn squash half. Bake 10 minutes, until golden brown.)
Steamed Brussels Sprouts, 2 cups, sprinkled with fresh lemon juice
Cranberry Relish (In small bowl, combine 1 cup cranberries, chopped, $^1/_2$ cup chopped celery and sugar substitute to equal 4 teaspoons sugar.)
Unsweetened Mandarin Orange–Flavored Seltzer

SNACK

Bagel, $^1/_2$ small (1 ounce), with 1 teaspoon peanut butter
Skim Milk, 1 cup

This menu provides: 2 Milks, 3 Fats, 2 Fruits, 8 Vegetables, 4 Proteins, 6 Breads, 55 Optional Calories.

Per serving: 15 g Fat, 25 g Fiber.

2 cups arugula leaves
2 cups radicchio leaves
2 cups Belgian endive leaves
1 pound boiled new potatoes, cooled and sliced
8 ounces lean boneless beef sirloin, thinly sliced
1 tablespoon + 1 teaspoon olive or vegetable oil
1 tablespoon + 1 teaspoon wine or cider vinegar
1 tablespoon minced fresh thyme, oregano, marjoram or tarragon leaves or 1 teaspoon dried
$^1/_2$ fluid ounce (1 tablespoon) dry white wine
$^1/_2$ teaspoon prepared mustard
Pinch salt
Freshly ground black pepper, to taste

1. To prepare salad, divide arugula, radicchio and Belgian endive evenly among 4 plates; top each with 4 ounces potato slices and 2 ounces steak.

2. To prepare dressing, in small jar with tight-fitting lid or small bowl, combine oil, vinegar, thyme, wine, mustard, salt and pepper; cover and shake well or, with wire whisk, blend until combined.

3. Just before serving, pour one-fourth of dressing over each portion of salad.

Serving (2 cups salad, 1 tablespoon dressing) provides: 1 Fat, 3 Vegetables, 2 Proteins, 1 Bread, 5 Optional Calories.

Per serving: 266 Calories, 9 g Total Fat, 2 g Saturated Fat, 50 mg Cholesterol, 97 mg Sodium, 26 g Total Carbohydrate, 3 g Dietary Fiber, 20 g Protein, 62 mg Calcium.

THAI BEEF SALAD

This fabulous salad is great for lunch or dinner and can be served over any combination of greens.

Makes 4 servings

10 ounces lean boneless beef loin, cut into $^1/_4$" strips

$^1/_2$ cup finely diced onion

3 tablespoons reduced-sodium soy sauce

2 tablespoons minced deveined seeded jalapeño pepper
   (wear gloves to prevent irritation)

2 garlic cloves, minced

1 teaspoon minced pared fresh ginger root

1 cup bean sprouts

$^1/_4$ cup minced fresh cilantro

2 teaspoons oriental sesame oil

8 cups packed trimmed washed spinach leaves, dried and torn
   into bite-size pieces

1. Spray large nonstick skillet with nonstick cooking spray; heat. Add beef; cook over medium-high heat, stirring constantly, 30 seconds, until no longer pink. Add onion, soy sauce, jalapeño pepper, garlic and ginger; cook, stirring frequently, 5 minutes, until onion is softened. Remove from heat. Add bean sprouts, cilantro and oil; toss to combine.

2. Divide spinach evenly among 4 bowls; top each portion of spinach with one-fourth of the beef mixture.

Serving (2 cups spinach, $^1/_2$ cup beef mixture) provides: $^1/_2$ Fat, 4$^3/_4$ Vegetables, 2 Proteins.

Per serving: 187 Calories, 7 g Total Fat, 2 g Saturated Fat, 42 mg Cholesterol, 628 mg Sodium, 11 g Total Carbohydrate, 5 g Dietary Fiber, 22 g Protein, 184 mg Calcium.

BREAKFAST

Unsweetened Applesauce, $^1/_2$ cup

Frozen Pancakes, 2, heated, with 1 tablespoon maple syrup and 1 teaspoon reduced-calorie tub margarine

Skim Milk, 1 cup

Coffee or Tea (optional)

LIGHT MEAL

Thai Beef Salad, 1 serving (see recipe)

Breadsticks, 2 long

Orange, 1 small

Iced Tea with Lemon Wedge

MAIN MEAL

Broiled Halibut, 4 ounces

Cooked Couscous, 1 cup, with 2 teaspoons reduced-calorie tub margarine

Steamed Brussels Sprouts, 1 cup, with 2 teaspoons *each* reduced-calorie tub margarine and fresh lemon juice

Aspartame-Sweetened Blueberry Nonfat Yogurt, 1 cup

Sparkling Mineral Water

SNACK

Reduced-Fat Cheddar Cheese, $^3/_4$ ounce

Fat-Free Crackers, 7

This menu provides: 2 Milks, 3 Fats, 2 Fruits, 6$^3/_4$ Vegetables, 5 Proteins, 6 Breads, 45 Optional Calories.

Per serving: 30 g Fat, 20 g Fiber.

Thai Beef Salad

BEEF AND VEGETABLE SOUP

This soup is both light and flavorful, and adapts well to any combination of vegetables.

Makes 4 servings

2 teaspoons reduced-calorie tub margarine
1 cup diced onions
1 cup diced celery
1 cup diced carrot
10 ounces lean boneless beef loin, cut into $^1/_2$" cubes
1 cup low-sodium beef broth
1 cup coarsely chopped green beans
1 cup thawed frozen corn kernels
$^1/_4$ cup chopped scallions
$^1/_4$ cup minced fresh flat-leaf parsley
$^1/_4$ teaspoon freshly ground black pepper

1. In large saucepan, melt margarine; add onions, celery and carrot. Cook over medium-high heat, stirring frequently, 5 minutes, until vegetables are softened.

2. Add beef, broth, green beans, corn, scallions, parsley, pepper and 2 cups water to vegetable mixture; bring liquid to a boil. Reduce heat to low; simmer, stirring occasionally, 20 minutes, until beef is cooked through and vegetables are tender.

Serving (1$^1/_2$ cups) provides: $^1/_4$ Fat, 2$^1/_4$ Vegetables, 2 Proteins, $^1/_2$ Bread, 5 Optional Calories.

Per serving: 194 Calories, 5 g Total Fat, 2 g Saturated Fat, 42 mg Cholesterol, 120 mg Sodium, 19 g Total Carbohydrate, 4 g Dietary Fiber, 19 g Protein, 53 mg Calcium.

BREAKFAST
Cantaloupe, $^1/_4$ small
English Muffin, $^1/_2$ (1 ounce), toasted, with 1 teaspoon raspberry jam
Skim Milk, 1 cup
Coffee or Tea (optional)

LIGHT MEAL
Beef and Vegetable Soup, 1 serving (see recipe)
French Bread, 1 slice (1 ounce), with 1$^1/_2$ teaspoons reduced-calorie tub margarine
Tossed Green Salad, 2 cups, with Raspberry Vinaigrette (In small jar with tight-fitting lid or small bowl, combine 1 tablespoon raspberry vinegar and 1 teaspoon olive oil; cover and shake well or, with wire whisk, blend until combined.)
Diet Ginger Ale

MAIN MEAL
Skinless Roast Chicken Breast, 3 ounces
Garlic Potatoes (In small bowl, with electric mixer, combine 6 ounces hot cooked potato, peeled and cubed, 2 tablespoons nonfat sour cream, 2 teaspoons reduced-calorie tub margarine and 1 garlic clove, minced.)
Steamed Broccoli, 8 spears, with $^1/_2$ cup sliced roasted red bell pepper
Unsweetened Applesauce, $^1/_2$ cup, with pinch cinnamon
Light Wine Spritzer (In wineglass, combine $^1/_2$ cup *each* unsweetened seltzer and dry light white wine [4 fluid ounces].)

SNACK
Yogurt Crunch (In small bowl, combine $^3/_4$ cup plain nonfat yogurt and 1 (1-ounce) reduced-calorie granola bar, crumbled)

This menu provides: 2 Milks, 3 Fats, 2 Fruits, 11$^1/_4$ Vegetables, 5 Proteins, 5 Breads, 110 Optional Calories.

Per serving: 29 g Fat, 20 g Fiber.

LAMB AND VEGETABLE SANDWICH WITH GARLIC MAYONNAISE

Makes 4 servings

LIGHT MEAL
Lamb and Vegetable Sandwich with Garlic
    Mayonnaise, 1 serving (see recipe)
Pickled Beets (In medium bowl, combine 1 cup
    cooked sliced beets, $^1/_2$ cup sliced onion, $^1/_4$ cup
    cider vinegar, sugar substitute to equal 2 teaspoons
    sugar, pinch salt and freshly ground black pepper,
    to taste; refrigerate, covered, at least 1 hour.)
Aspartame-Sweetened Cherry Nonfat Yogurt, 1 cup
Mint Tea

MAIN MEAL
Cream of Mushroom Soup (In blender, combine
    1 cup cooked mushrooms, $^1/_2$ cup skim milk and
    pinch *each* salt, ground white pepper and ground
    nutmeg; transfer to small saucepan or microwav-
    able bowl. Cook over low heat, stirring frequently,
    or microwave on Medium (70% power), stirring
    once or twice during cooking, until warm.)
Broiled Red Snapper, 6 ounces
Baked Potato, 4 ounces, with 2 teaspoons reduced-
    calorie tub margarine
Julienned Zucchini and Carrots (Spray medium non-
    stick skillet with nonstick cooking spray; heat.
    Add 1 cup *each* julienne-cut zucchini and carrots;
    cook over medium-high heat, stirring frequently,
    until vegetables are tender. Sprinkle with salt and
    freshly ground black pepper to taste.)
Kiwi Fruit, 1 medium
Non-Alcoholic White Wine, 4 fluid ounces ($^1/_2$ cup)

SNACK
Reduced-Fat Cheddar Cheese, $^3/_4$ ounce
Fat-Free Crackers, 7

This menu provides: 2 Milks, 3 Fats, 2 Fruits,
$10^3/_4$ Vegetables, 5 Proteins, 5 Breads, 50 Optional
Calories.

Per serving: 27 g Fat, 26 g Fiber.

Twelve $^1/_4$"-thick eggplant slices
2 tablespoons + 2 teaspoons reduced-calorie mayonnaise
1 garlic clove, minced
8 slices whole-grain bread
4 ounces lean boneless roast lamb, thinly sliced
2 medium tomatoes, sliced

1. Preheat oven to 425° F. Spray nonstick baking sheet with nonstick cooking spray.

2. Place eggplant slices in a single layer onto prepared baking sheet; bake 15 minutes, until golden brown.

3. In small cup or bowl, combine mayonnaise and garlic.

4. Spread 4 of the bread slices with one-fourth of the mayonnaise mixture each.

5. To assemble sandwiches, place mayonnaise-spread bread slices, spread-side up, onto work surface; top each with 1 ounce lamb, one-fourth *each* of the tomato and eggplant slices and 1 remaining bread slice. Cut sandwiches diagonally into halves.

Serving (1 sandwich) provides: 1 Fat, $1^3/_4$ Vegetables, 1 Protein, 2 Breads.

Per serving: 253 Calories, 8 g Total Fat, 2 g Saturated Fat, 28 mg Cholesterol, 358 mg Sodium, 33 g Total Carbohydrate, 5 g Dietary Fiber, 14 g Protein, 73 mg Calcium.

LAMB BURGERS WITH FETA CHEESE

*Lamb burgers are a flavorful change from beef burgers;
if you don't see ground lamb at your supermarket,
ask the butcher to grind some for you.*

Makes 4 servings

9 ounces lean ground lamb
$^1/_2$ teaspoon salt
$^1/_4$ teaspoon garlic powder
$^1/_4$ teaspoon dried rosemary leaves, crumbled
Pinch freshly ground black pepper
$^3/_4$ ounce feta cheese, crumbled

1. In medium bowl, combine lamb, salt, garlic powder, rosemary, and pepper; form into 4 equal patties.

2. In medium nonstick skillet, cook patties 3 minutes; turn over. Top each patty with one-fourth of the cheese; cook, covered, 3 minutes, until cheese is melted and patties are cooked through.

Serving (1 burger) provides: 2 Proteins.

Per serving: 119 Calories, 6 g Total Fat, 3 g Saturated Fat, 51 mg Cholesterol, 374 mg Sodium, 0 g Total Carbohydrate, 0 g Dietary Fiber, 14 g Protein, 39 mg Calcium.

BREAKFAST
Broiled Grapefruit (Sprinkle $^1/_2$ medium grapefruit with 1 teaspoon firmly packed light or dark brown sugar; place on nonstick baking sheet. Broil 2–3 minutes, until topping is bubbling.)
Corn Flakes, $^3/_4$ ounce
Skim Milk, 1 cup
Coffee or Tea (optional)

LIGHT MEAL
Lamb Burgers with Feta Cheese, 1 serving (see recipe)
Hamburger Roll, 1 (2 ounces)
Carrot and Celery Sticks, 1 cup *each*
Dill Pickle, $^1/_2$ medium
Greek Olives, 6 large
Corn and Red Pepper Salad (In medium bowl, combine $^1/_2$ cup cooked corn kernels, $^1/_4$ cup diced red bell pepper, 1 tablespoon minced fresh flat-leaf parsley and 1 tablespoon fat-free Italian dressing.)
Diet Cola

MAIN MEAL
Tomato Juice Cocktail (In tall glass, combine $^1/_2$ cup low-sodium tomato juice, 1 tablespoon fresh lemon juice and pinch *each* freshly ground black pepper and celery salt; add enough ice cubes to fill glass. Serve with celery stick stirrer.)
Steamed Striped Bass, 4 ounces, with 2 teaspoons reduced-calorie tub margarine and 1 lemon wedge
Baked Potato, 8 ounces, with 3 tablespoons plain nonfat yogurt and 1 tablespoon chopped scallion
Steamed Broccoli Florets and Carrot Slices, $^1/_2$ cup *each*, with 2 teaspoons reduced-calorie tub margarine
Reduced-Calorie Vanilla-Flavored Pudding (made with skim milk), $^1/_2$ cup
Iced Decaffeinated Coffee

SNACK
Peach Melba (Scoop 4 fluid ounces sugar-free vanilla nonfat frozen yogurt into small dish. Pare, pit and slice $^1/_2$ medium peach. Surround frozen yogurt with peach slices; top with $1^1/_2$ teaspoons raspberry spreadable fruit.)

This menu provides: 2 Milks, 3 Fats, 2 Fruits, $9^1/_4$ Vegetables, 4 Proteins, 6 Breads, 110 Optional Calories.

Per serving: 34 g Fat, 22 g Fiber.

BREAKFAST
Mango, $^1/_2$ small
Frozen Waffle, 1, heated, with 1 teaspoon *each*
    reduced-calorie tub margarine and maple syrup
Skim Milk, $^3/_4$ cup
Coffee or Tea (optional)

LIGHT MEAL
Lamb Hash, 1 serving (see recipe)
Celery and Carrot Sticks, 1 cup *each*, with 1 table-
    spoon fat-free ranch dressing
Flatbreads, $^3/_4$ ounce
Sugar-Free Chocolate Nonfat Frozen Yogurt, 4 fluid
    ounces
Unsweetened Black Cherry–Flavored Seltzer

MAIN MEAL
Grilled Swordfish, 4 ounces
Boiled New Potatoes, 6 ounces, with 1 teaspoon *each*
    reduced-calorie tub margarine and minced fresh
    flat-leaf parsley
Steamed Asparagus, 6 spears, with 1 teaspoon *each*
    reduced-calorie tub margarine and fresh lemon
    juice
Torn Romaine and Iceberg Lettuce Leaves, 2 cups,
    with 6 cherry tomatoes, $^1/_2$ cup cucumber slices
    and 1 tablespoon balsamic vinegar
Baked Apple (Preheat oven to 350° F. Pare 1 small
    apple halfway down from stem end; core and
    place in small baking dish. Sprinkle apple with
    1 teaspoon granulated sugar and $^1/_4$ teaspoon
    cinnamon; add $^1/_4$" water to pan. Bake, covered,
    30 minutes, until tender.)
Diet Lemonade, 1 cup

SNACK
Graham Crackers, 3 ($2^1/_2$" squares)
Skim Milk, 1 cup

This menu provides: 2 Milks, 3 Fats, 2 Fruits,
$11^1/_2$ Vegetables, 4 Proteins, $5^1/_2$ Breads,
105 Optional Calories.

Per serving: 26 g Fat, 26 g Fiber.

12
LAMB HASH

*This hash makes a great breakfast or
brunch entrée as well as a hearty supper.*

Makes 4 servings

1 tablespoon + 1 teaspoon reduced-calorie tub margarine
1 pound 4 ounces all-purpose potatoes, pared and cut into $^1/_4$" cubes
2 cups chopped onions
10 ounces lean boneless loin of lamb, cut into $^1/_2$" cubes
$^1/_2$ teaspoon salt
$^1/_2$ teaspoon freshly ground black pepper
2 tablespoons minced fresh flat-leaf parsley

1. In large nonstick skillet, melt margarine; add potatoes. Cook over medium-high heat, stirring frequently, 12 minutes, until potatoes are softened. Add onions; cook, stirring frequently, 5 minutes, until onions are softened.

2. Increase heat to high; add lamb, salt and pepper. Cook, stirring frequently, 3 minutes, until lamb is no longer pink and potatoes and onions are tender. Add parsley; cook, stirring constantly, until combined.

Serving ($^1/_2$ cup) provides: $^1/_2$ Fat, 1 Vegetable, 2 Proteins, 1 Bread.

Per serving: 262 Calories, 6 g Total Fat, 2 g Saturated Fat, 47 mg Cholesterol, 370 mg Sodium, 33 g Total Carbohydrate, 4 g Dietary Fiber, 19 g Protein, 40 mg Calcium.

GREEK GRILLED LAMB SALAD

For a speedy lamb salad, cook the meat the day before and use packaged lettuce blends available in the produce section of the supermarket.

Makes 4 servings

2 tablespoons minced fresh oregano, or 1 teaspoon dried	1 teaspoon Dijon-style mustard
1 teaspoon grated lemon zest*	1/4 teaspoon salt
1/2 cup minus 1 tablespoon fresh lemon juice	Pinch freshly ground black pepper
2 garlic cloves, minced	8 cups torn assorted tender lettuce leaves
8 ounces lean boneless loin of lamb	2 medium tomatoes, each cut into eight wedges
1 tablespoon olive oil	1 1/2 ounces feta cheese, crumbled
1 tablespoon tomato sauce (no salt added)	6 large Greek olives, pitted and finely chopped

1. To prepare marinade, in gallon-size sealable plastic bag, combine oregano, zest, 1/4 cup of the juice and half the garlic; add lamb. Seal bag, squeezing out air; turn to coat lamb. Refrigerate at least 1 hour or overnight, turning bag occasionally.

2. Preheat outdoor barbecue grill according to manufacturer's directions, or preheat broiler and spray rack in broiler pan with nonstick cooking spray.

3. Drain marinade into small saucepan; bring to a boil. Remove from heat. Grill lamb over hot coals or place onto prepared rack in broiler pan and broil 4" from heat, turning once and brushing frequently with marinade, 12 minutes, until cooked through.

4. Meanwhile, to prepare dressing, in small jar with tight-fitting lid or small bowl, combine oil, tomato sauce, mustard, the remaining garlic, the salt, pepper and remaining 3 tablespoons juice; cover and shake well or, with wire whisk, blend until combined.

5. Transfer lamb to cutting board; slice thinly.

6. Divide lettuce among 4 bowls; top each portion with 4 tomato wedges, one-fourth of the cheese, one-fourth of the olives and 2 ounces of the cooked lamb, then drizzle each portion with one-fourth of the dressing.

Serving (1 salad) provides: 1 Fat, 5 Vegetables, 2 Proteins.

Per serving: 206 Calories, 12 g Total Fat, 4 g Saturated Fat, 47 mg Cholesterol, 583 mg Sodium, 10 g Total Carbohydrate, 2 g Dietary Fiber, 16 g Protein, 159 mg Calcium.

BREAKFAST

Papaya, 1/2 medium, with lime wedge
Reduced-Calorie Rye Bread, 2 slices, toasted, with 2 teaspoons reduced-calorie tub margarine
Skim Milk, 1 cup
Coffee or Tea (optional)

LIGHT MEAL

Low-Sodium Beef Broth, 1 cup, with 20 oyster crackers
Greek Grilled Lamb Salad, 1 serving (see recipe)
Celery and Carrot Sticks, 1 cup *each*
Breadsticks, 2 long
Honeydew Melon, 2" wedge
Unsweetened Seltzer with Lemon Wedges and Mint Leaves

MAIN MEAL

Broiled Shrimp, 4 ounces, with Lemon "Butter" (In small cup or bowl, combine 1 teaspoon *each* reduced-calorie tub margarine, melted, and fresh lemon juice.)
Steamed Butternut Squash, 7 ounces, with 1 teaspoon firmly packed light or dark brown sugar
Steamed Sugar Snap Peas, 1 cup, with 1 teaspoon reduced-calorie margarine
Tossed Green Salad, 2 cups, with 1 tablespoon fat-free creamy Italian dressing
French Bread, 1 slice (1 ounce)
Iced Herbal Tea

SNACK

Pudding Parfait (In stemmed glass, layer 1/2 cup *each* reduced-calorie chocolate- and vanilla-flavored pudding [made with skim milk].)

This menu provides: 2 Milks, 3 Fats, 2 Fruits, 15 Vegetables, 4 Proteins, 5 Breads, 135 Optional Calories.

Per serving: 31 g Fat, 23 g Fiber.

The zest of the lemon is the peel without any of the pith (white membrane). To remove zest from lemon, use a zester or the fine side of a vegetable grater.

Greek Grilled Lamb Salad

SCOTCH BROTH

Makes 4 servings

1 1/2 ounces pearl barley
1 tablespoon + 1 teaspoon vegetable oil
2 cups diced celery
2 cups diced carrots
1 cup diced onions
4 ounces cooked lean boneless lamb, diced
8 cups low-sodium beef broth

1. In large bowl, combine barley and 2 cups water; let soak at least 1 hour. Drain barley, discarding liquid; rinse. Drain again; set aside.

2. In large saucepan, heat oil; add celery, carrots and onions. Cook over medium-high heat, stirring frequently, 5 minutes, until vegetables are softened. Add lamb; cook, stirring constantly, 1 minute. Add broth and drained barley; bring liquid to a boil. Reduce heat to medium-low; cook, stirring occasionally, 45–60 minutes, until barley is tender.

Serving (2 cups) provides: 1 Fat, 2 1/2 Vegetables, 1 Protein, 1/2 Bread, 40 Optional Calories.

Per serving: 227 Calories, 8 g Total Fat, 2 g Saturated Fat, 27 mg Cholesterol, 238 mg Sodium, 19 g Total Carbohydrate, 5 g Dietary Fiber, 21 g Protein, 56 mg Calcium.

BREAKFAST

Grapefruit Sections, 1/2 cup
Raisin French Toast (In shallow bowl, combine 1 beaten egg, 1/4 cup skim milk and 1/4 teaspoon vanilla extract; add 1 1/2 slices cinnamon-raisin bread, turning until egg mixture is absorbed. Spray small nonstick skillet or griddle with nonstick cooking spray; heat. Cook bread over medium heat, turning once, 5 minutes, until golden brown on both sides. Serve with 2 teaspoons maple syrup.)
Coffee or Tea (optional)

LIGHT MEAL

Scotch Broth, 1 serving (see recipe)
Spinach Salad (In medium bowl, combine 2 cups torn spinach leaves, 2 teaspoons balsamic vinegar and 1 teaspoon imitation bacon bits.)
Aspartame-Sweetened Raspberry Nonfat Yogurt, 1 cup
Herbal Tea

MAIN MEAL

Macaroni and Two Cheeses (In medium saucepan, combine 1 cup hot cooked elbow macaroni, 1/4 cup skim milk, 3/4 ounce *each* grated skim-milk mozzarella cheese and reduced-fat cheddar cheese and ground white pepper to taste; cook over low heat, stirring constantly, 5 minutes, until cheeses are melted.)
Steamed Carrot and Celery Slices, 1 cup *each*
Green Beans with Tomatoes and Onions (In medium nonstick skillet, heat 1 teaspoon olive oil; add 1 cup *each* blanched cut green beans, coarsely chopped tomato and chopped onions, 1 teaspoon minced fresh flat-leaf parsley and pinch *each* salt, freshly ground black pepper. Cook over medium-high heat, stirring frequently, until vegetables are tender.)
Mixed Dried Fruit, 3/4 ounce
Sparkling Mineral Water with Twist of Lime

SNACK

French Bread, 1 slice (1 ounce), toasted, with 1 teaspoon peanut butter
Skim Milk, 1/2 cup

This menu provides: 2 Milks, 3 Fats, 2 Fruits, 16 1/2 Vegetables, 4 Proteins, 5 Breads, 80 Optional Calories.

Per serving: 27 g Fat, 21 g Fiber.

LIGHT MEAL

Open-Face Reuben Sandwich, 1 serving (see recipe)
Veggies 'n' Mustard-Yogurt Dip (In small bowl, combine $^1/_4$ cup plain nonfat yogurt and 2 tablespoons prepared mustard; serve with 1 cup *each* carrot sticks and cauliflower florets.)
Sugar-Free Cherry-Flavored Gelatin, $^1/_2$ cup
Diet Cream Soda

MAIN MEAL

Grilled Chicken Cutlet, 2 ounces
Vegetable Pasta (Spray medium nonstick skillet with nonstick cooking spray; heat. Add $^1/_2$ cup *each* diced zucchini, diced green bell pepper and cubed pared eggplant. Cook over medium-high heat, stirring frequently, until vegetables are softened. Add 1 cup tomato sauce [no salt added]; cook, stirring frequently, until heated through. Pour over 1 cup cooked fusilli pasta; sprinkle with 1 teaspoon freshly grated Parmesan cheese.)
Mixed Green Salad, 2 cups, with 1 teaspoon *each* vegetable oil and red wine vinegar
Garlic-Herb Bread (Spread 1-ounce slice Italian bread with 1 fresh garlic clove, minced or the pulp of 1 roasted garlic clove and $^1/_2$ teaspoon *each* minced fresh basil and oregano leaves; drizzle with 1 teaspoon olive oil. Place onto baking sheet; broil until lightly browned.)
Yogurt-Apricot Parfait (In small cup or bowl, combine $^1/_2$ cup plain nonfat yogurt and sugar substitute to equal 2 teaspoons sugar. In stemmed glass, spoon half of the yogurt mixture; top with 3 medium apricots, pitted and sliced, then remaining yogurt mixture.)

SNACK

Plain Popcorn, hot-air popped, 3 cups, with 2 teaspoons reduced-calorie tub margarine, melted

This menu provides: 2 Milks, 3 Fats, 2 Fruits, 16 Vegetables, 4 Proteins, 6 Breads, 20 Optional Calories.

Per serving: 32 g Fat, 31 g Fiber.

15

OPEN-FACE REUBEN SANDWICH

Makes 4 servings

8 slices reduced-calorie rye bread
2 tablespoons prepared country-style mustard
4 ounces lean boneless roast pork, thinly sliced
2 cups well-drained sauerkraut
3 ounces reduced-fat Swiss cheese, sliced
Freshly ground black pepper, to taste

1. Preheat broiler.

2. Lightly toast bread; spread each toast slice with $^3/_4$ teaspoon mustard.

3. To assemble sandwiches, place toast slices, spread-side up, onto rack in broiler pan; top each with $^1/_4$ ounce pork, one-fourth sauerkraut, another $^1/_4$ ounce pork and one-fourth of the cheese. Sprinkle evenly with pepper; broil 4" from heat 2 minutes, until cheese is melted and lightly browned.

Serving (2 slices) provides: 1 Vegetable, 2 Proteins, 1 Bread.

Per serving: 250 Calories, 7 g Total Fat, 3 g Saturated Fat, 34 mg Cholesterol, 775 mg Sodium, 26 g Total Carbohydrate, 1 g Dietary Fiber, 19 g Protein, 62 mg Calcium.

16

VEAL AND ROASTED PEPPER SANDWICH

Makes 4 servings

One 8-ounce loaf Italian bread, cut horizontally in half,
    then vertically into 4 equal slices to make 8 pieces
8 ounces lean boneless roast veal, sliced
2 cups drained roasted red bell peppers
20 small pimiento-stuffed green olives, sliced
2 tablespoons red wine or cider vinegar
Freshly ground black pepper, to taste

Place 4 bread slices, cut-side up, onto work surface; top each with 2 ounces
of the veal, one-fourth of the roasted peppers and the olives. Sprinkle
evenly with vinegar and black pepper; top each with 1 remaining bread
slice.

Serving (1 sandwich) provides: $^{1}/_{2}$ Fat, 1 Vegetable, 2 Proteins, 2 Breads.

Per serving: 294 Calories, 8 g Total Fat, 2 g Saturated Fat, 60 mg Cholesterol,
870 mg Sodium, 33 g Total Carbohydrate, 2 g Dietary Fiber, 20 g Protein,
65 mg Calcium.

BREAKFAST

Banana, $^{1}/_{2}$ medium
Fat-Free Muffin, 1 (2 ounces), with 1 teaspoon *each*
    reduced-calorie tub margarine and peach jam
Skim Milk, $^{1}/_{2}$ cup
Coffee or Tea (optional)

LIGHT MEAL

Veal and Roasted Pepper Sandwich, 1 serving
    (see recipe)
Fennel-Orange Salad with Citrus Vinaigrette
    (Arrange 2 cups sliced fennel and $^{1}/_{2}$ cup *each*
    orange sections and red onion slices on plate.
    In small jar with tight-fitting lid or small bowl,
    combine 1 tablespoon fresh orange juice and
    1 teaspoon *each* olive oil, balsamic vinegar and
    red wine or cider vinegar; cover and shake well
    or, with wire whisk, blend until combined. Pour
    dressing over salad; sprinkle with pinch *each* salt
    and freshly ground black pepper.)
Reduced-Calorie Granola Bar, 1 (1 ounce)
Diet Cola

MAIN MEAL

Shrimp Stir-Fry (Spray large nonstick skillet with
    nonstick cooking spray; heat. Add 4 ounces
    peeled and deveined shrimp, 1 cup torn spinach
    leaves, $^{1}/_{2}$ cup *each* broccoli florets, sliced scallions
    and sliced celery, $^{1}/_{4}$ cup low-sodium chicken
    broth and 2 teaspoons reduced-sodium soy sauce.
    Cook over medium-high heat, stirring frequently,
    until shrimp turn pink; sprinkle with dried red
    pepper flakes, to taste.)
Cooked Brown Rice, $^{1}/_{2}$ cup
Cucumber Salad (In small bowl, combine $^{1}/_{2}$ cup
    cucumber slices, 1 teaspoon *each* vegetable oil and
    rice wine vinegar and pinch ground white pepper.)
Aspartame-Sweetened Tropical Fruit Nonfat Yogurt,
    1 cup
Jasmine Tea

SNACK

Cereal Munchies (In small bowl, combine $^{3}/_{4}$ ounce
    bite-size shredded wheat cereal, sugar substitute to
    equal 2 teaspoons sugar and pinch cinnamon; toss
    to combine.)
Coffee "Egg Cream" (In tall glass, combine 1 cup
    diet coffee soda and $^{1}/_{2}$ cup skim milk.)

This menu provides: 2 Milks, 3 Fats, 2 Fruits, 12 Vegetables, $3^{1}/_{2}$ Proteins, 6 Breads, 110 Optional Calories.

Per serving: 27 g Fat, 20 g Fiber.

BREAKFAST
Orange, 1 small
Shredded Wheat Cereal, ³/₄ ounce
Skim Milk, 1 cup
Coffee or Tea (optional)

LIGHT MEAL
Tomato Juice, 1 cup
Tuna Salad Pita (In small bowl, combine 4 ounces
   drained canned water-packed tuna, ¹/₄ cup *each*
   chopped onion and celery, 2 teaspoons reduced-
   calorie mayonnaise and ¹/₄ teaspoon lemon-pepper
   seasoning. Cut 1 large [2-ounce] whole-wheat pita
   in half crosswise; open to form 2 pockets. Fill
   each pocket with half of the tuna salad; top each
   portion of salad with ¹/₄ cup alfalfa sprouts.)
Cucumber and Carrot Sticks, 1 cup *each*
Aspartame-Sweetened Black Cherry Nonfat Yogurt,
   1 cup
Iced Tea with Lemon Wedge

MAIN MEAL
Beefy Mushroom-Barley Soup, 1 serving (see recipe)
Watercress, Arugula and Endive Salad, 2 cups, with
   1 tablespoon fat-free Italian Dressing
Apple, 1 small
Pumpernickel Roll, 1 ounce, with 1¹/₂ teaspoons
   reduced-calorie tub margarine
Sparkling Mineral Water

SNACK
Cinnamon-Raisin Bread, toasted, with 1 teaspoon
   each peanut butter and strawberry jam

This menu provides: 2 Milks, 3 Fats, 2 Fruits,
15 Vegetables, 4 Proteins, 6 Breads, 25 Optional
Calories.

Per serving: 20 g Fat, 29 g Fiber.

17
BEEFY MUSHROOM-BARLEY SOUP

*This hearty soup is a meal in itself. Make a double batch and
freeze the extra portions to have on hand for another meal.*

Makes 4 servings

1¹/₂ ounces dried mushrooms
¹/₂ cup warm water
2 teaspoons reduced-calorie tub
   margarine
2 cups chopped onions
1 cup diced celery
¹/₂ cup diced carrot
1 garlic clove, minced
10 ounces lean boneless beef loin,
   cut into ¹/₂" cubes

2 cups sliced white mushrooms
1 cup low-sodium beef broth
¹/₂ teaspoon salt
¹/₄ teaspoon freshly ground black
   pepper
¹/₄ teaspoon dried thyme leaves
1 bay leaf
3 ounces pearl barley
¹/₄ cup minced fresh flat-leaf
   parsley

1. In medium bowl, combine dried mushrooms and water; let stand
20 minutes. With slotted spoon, remove soaked mushrooms from liquid.
Set mushrooms aside; reserve liquid.

2. Line sieve with medium paper coffee filter; place over small bowl. Pour
mushroom liquid through filter. Reserve liquid; discard coffee filter containing any particles of dirt and sand.

3. In large saucepan, melt margarine; add onions, celery, carrot and
garlic. Cook over medium-high heat, stirring frequently, 5 minutes, until
vegetables are softened.

4. Add beef, white mushrooms and reconstituted dried mushrooms to
vegetable mixture; cook, stirring frequently, 4 minutes, until beef is no
longer pink. Add broth, salt, pepper, thyme, bay leaf, reserved mushroom
liquid and 5 cups water; bring liquid to a boil. Stir in barley. Reduce heat
to low; simmer, stirring occasionally, 1³/₄ hours, until barley and
vegetables are very tender and flavors are blended. Stir in parsley; remove
and discard bay leaf.

Serving (1¹/₄ cups) provides: ¹/₄ Fat, 3 Vegetables, 2 Proteins, 1 Bread,
5 Optional Calories.

Per serving: 351 Calories, 5 g Total Fat, 1 g Saturated Fat, 51 mg Cholesterol,
891 mg Sodium, 37 g Total Carbohydrate, 6 g Dietary Fiber, 41 g Protein,
47 mg Calcium.

BEEF BOURGUIGNONNE

Makes 4 servings

1 tablespoon + 1 teaspoon olive or vegetable oil
1 cup chopped onions
2 garlic cloves, minced
13 ounces lean boneless beef round steak, cut into 1 1/2" cubes
1 pound 4 ounces all-purpose potatoes, pared and cubed
4 cups sliced carrots (1" slices)
8 fluid ounces (1 cup) dry red Burgundy wine
1 bay leaf
1 teaspoon dried thyme leaves
1/4 teaspoon salt
Freshly ground black pepper, to taste
4 cups small whole white mushrooms, woody ends removed
2 cups frozen pearl onions

1. In large saucepan or Dutch oven, heat oil; add chopped onions and garlic. Cook over medium-high heat, stirring frequently, 7 minutes, until lightly browned. Add beef; cook, stirring frequently, 1–2 minutes, until beef is browned on all sides.

2. Add potatoes, carrots, wine, bay leaf, thyme, salt and pepper to beef mixture; bring liquid to a boil. Reduce heat to low; simmer, covered, adding water, a few tablespoons at a time to keep mixture from sticking, 45 minutes, until carrots and potatoes are tender.

3. Add mushrooms and pearl onions to beef mixture; simmer, covered, 15–20 minutes, until pearl onions are tender. Remove and discard bay leaf.

Serving (2 cups) provides: 1 Fat, 5 1/2 Vegetables, 2 1/2 Proteins, 1 Bread, 50 Optional Calories.

Per serving: 439 Calories, 10 g Total Fat, 2 g Saturated Fat, 53 mg Cholesterol, 251 mg Sodium, 53 g Total Carbohydrate, 7 g Dietary Fiber, 27 g Protein, 106 mg Calcium.

BREAKFAST
Tangerine, 1 large
Puffed Wheat Cereal, 3/4 ounce
Skim Milk, 1 cup
Coffee or Tea (optional)

LIGHT MEAL
Waldorf Salad with Cheese (In medium bowl, combine 1 small apple, cored and diced, 1/2 cup chopped celery, 3/4 ounce reduced-fat cheddar cheese, grated, and 2 teaspoons reduced-calorie mayonnaise; serve over 2 cups shredded red cabbage.)
Graham Crackers, 3 (2 1/2" squares)
Diet Cola with Lemon Wedge

MAIN MEAL
Beef Bourguignonne, 1 serving (see recipe)
Steamed Green Beans, 1 cup, with 2 teaspoons *each* fresh lemon juice and reduced-calorie tub margarine
French Bread, 1 ounce
Sugar-Free Berry-Flavored Gelatin, 1/2 cup, topped with 1/4 cup aspartame-sweetened raspberry nonfat yogurt
Unsweetened Seltzer with Lime Wedge

SNACK
Pretzels, 3/4 ounce
Skim Milk, 3/4 cup

This menu provides: 2 Milks, 3 Fats, 2 Fruits, 12 1/2 Vegetables, 3 1/2 Proteins, 5 Breads, 60 Optional Calories.

Per serving: 26 g Fat, 21 g Fiber.

Beef Bourguignonne

19
COUNTRY BEEF STEW

*This wonderful winter meal keeps beautifully
and tastes even better the next day.*

Makes 4 servings

2 teaspoons olive oil

1 cup chopped onions

1 garlic clove, minced

2 teaspoons all-purpose flour

$^3/_4$ teaspoon salt

$^1/_2$ teaspoon freshly ground black pepper

10 ounces lean boneless beef loin, cut into 2" cubes

10 ounces small red potatoes, quartered

1 cup small whole white mushrooms, woody ends removed

1 cup pearl onions

1 cup baby carrots

2 cups low-sodium beef broth

$^1/_4$ cup red wine vinegar

1 tablespoon tomato paste (no salt added)

$^1/_4$ teaspoon dried thyme leaves

$^1/_4$ teaspoon dried tarragon leaves

1 bay leaf

2 tablespoons minced fresh flat-leaf parsley

1. In large saucepan, heat oil; add chopped onions and garlic. Cook over medium-high heat, stirring frequently, 5 minutes, until onions are softened.

2. On sheet of wax paper or paper plate, combine flour, $^1/_4$ teaspoon of the salt and $^1/_4$ teaspoon of the pepper; add beef, turning to coat evenly. Add beef to onion mixture; cook, stirring frequently, 4 minutes, until beef is browned on all sides. Add potatoes, mushrooms, pearl onions and carrots; cook, stirring frequently, 2 minutes.

3. Add broth, vinegar, tomato paste, thyme, tarragon, bay leaf, remaining $^1/_2$ teaspoon salt, remaining $^1/_4$ teaspoon pepper and 5 cups water to beef mixture; bring liquid to a boil. Reduce heat to low; simmer, covered, 40 minutes, until beef is cooked through and vegetables are tender. Stir in parsley; remove and discard bay leaf.

Serving (1 cup) provides: $^1/_2$ Fat, $2^1/_4$ Vegetables, 2 Proteins, $^1/_2$ Bread, 10 Optional Calories.

Per serving: 241 Calories, 6 g Total Fat, 1 g Saturated Fat, 43 mg Cholesterol, 513 mg Sodium, 27 g Total Carbohydrate, 3 g Dietary Fiber, 21 g Protein, 52 mg Calcium.

BREAKFAST

Apple, 1 small

Hard-Cooked Egg, 1

Reduced-Calorie Whole-Wheat Bread, 2 slices, toasted, with 2 teaspoons reduced-calorie tub margarine

Skim Milk, 1 cup

Coffee or Tea (optional)

LIGHT MEAL

English Muffin Pizza (Split and toast one 2-ounce English muffin. Top split side of each muffin half with 2 tablespoons tomato sauce [no salt added], then sprinkle each with $^3/_4$ ounce grated nonfat mozzarella cheese and $^1/_4$ teaspoon dried oregano leaves. Place onto nonstick baking sheet; broil until heated.)

Tomato and Cucumber Slices, 1 cup *each,* with 1 tablespoon fat-free Italian dressing

Diet Cola

MAIN MEAL

Country Beef Stew, 1 serving (see recipe)

Corn Bread, 2" square, with 1 teaspoon reduced-calorie tub margarine

Arugula and Endive Salad, 2 cups, with $1^1/_2$ teaspoons ranch dressing

Banana Parfait (In stemmed glass, layer $^1/_2$ cup reduced-calorie vanilla-flavored pudding [made with skim milk] and $^1/_2$ medium banana, diced.)

Iced Tea

SNACK

Reduced-Calorie Granola Bar, 1 (1 ounce)

Skim Milk, $^1/_2$ cup

This menu provides: 2 Milks, 3 Fats, 2 Fruits, $11^1/_4$ Vegetables, 4 Proteins, $5^1/_4$ Breads, 115 Optional Calories.

Per serving: 31 g Fat, 21 g Fiber.

BREAKFAST

Orange, 1 small
Cornflakes, ³/₄ ounce
Skim Milk, 1 cup
Reduced-Calorie Whole-Wheat Bread, 2 slices,
    toasted, with 1 tablespoon nonfat cream cheese
Coffee or Tea (optional)

LIGHT MEAL

Shrimp Salad Sandwich (In small bowl, combine
    4 ounces peeled and deveined cooked tiny shrimp,
    ¹/₄ cup chopped celery and 1 tablespoon reduced-
    calorie mayonnaise; spread salad between 2 slices
    reduced-calorie multi-grain bread.)
Carrot Sticks and Whole Green Beans, 1 cup *each*
Reduced-Calorie Chocolate-Flavored Pudding (made
    with skim milk), ¹/₂ cup
Diet Cola

MAIN MEAL

Little-Batch Meatballs, 1 serving (see recipe)
Cooked Whole-Wheat Spaghetti, 1 cup, with
    1 teaspoon *each* reduced-calorie tub margarine
    and freshly grated Parmesan cheese
Cooked Italian Green Beans, 1 cup
Torn Iceberg and Romaine Lettuce Leaves, 2 cups,
    with ¹/₂ cup *each* sliced radishes and green bell
    pepper and 1 teaspoon *each* olive oil and balsamic
    vinegar
Raspberries, ³/₄ cup
Sparkling Mineral Water

SNACK

Coffee Milk Shake (In blender, combine ¹/₂ cup skim
    milk, 2 ice cubes, sugar substitute to equal 1 tea-
    spoon sugar and 1 teaspoon instant decaffeinated
    coffee powder; purée until smooth.)

This menu provides: 2 Milks, 3 Fats, 2 Fruits,
14³/₄ Vegetables, 4 Proteins, 5¹/₂ Breads,
105 Optional Calories.

Per serving: 27 g Fat, 37 g Fiber.

20
LITTLE-BATCH
MEATBALLS

Makes 4 servings

One 2-ounce English muffin, crumbled
¹/₂ cup skim milk
10 ounces extra-lean ground beef (10% or less fat)
1 cup grated zucchini
4 fluid ounces (¹/₂ cup) non-alcoholic white wine
2 tablespoons freshly grated Parmesan cheese
2 tablespoons tomato paste (no salt added)
2 teaspoons dried oregano leaves
3 cups crushed tomatoes (no salt added)

1. In large bowl, combine muffin crumbs and milk; let stand 5 minutes.

2. With fork, mash soaked muffin crumbs. Add beef, zucchini, 2 table-spoons of the wine, the cheese, tomato paste and 1 teaspoon of the oregano; mix well. Form into 24 equal meatballs.

3. Spray large nonstick skillet with nonstick cooking spray; heat. Add meatballs; cook over medium-high heat, turning as needed, 10 minutes, until browned on all sides. Remove meatballs from skillet; set aside.

4. In same skillet, cook remaining ¹/₃ cup + 2 teaspoons wine over medium-high heat, scraping up browned bits from bottom of pan. Add tomatoes, remaining 1 teaspoon oregano and 1¹/₂ cups water; bring mix-ture to a boil. Reduce heat to low; add meatballs. Simmer, covered, 30–40 minutes, until meatballs are cooked through and sauce is thickened.

Serving (6 meatballs, ³/₄ cup sauce) provides: 2¹/₄ Vegetables, 2 Proteins, ¹/₂ Bread, 40 Optional Calories.

Per serving: 233 Calories, 9 g Total Fat, 3 g Saturated Fat, 47 mg Cholesterol, 479 mg Sodium, 20 g Total Carbohydrate, 2 g Dietary Fiber, 20 g Protein, 163 mg Calcium.

21

BEEF BRAISED IN RED WINE

This easy-to-prepare and flavorful dish makes a delicious hot entrée, or try it cold as a wonderful filling for Braised Beef and Red Onion Sandwich (see page 3).

Makes 8 servings

1 tablespoon + 1 teaspoon olive oil
4 cups coarsely chopped onions
4 cups coarsely chopped carrots
1 garlic clove, minced
One 1-pound 14-ounce lean boneless beef round roast
$^1/_4$ teaspoon salt
Freshly ground black pepper, to taste
8 fluid ounces (1 cup) dry red wine
1 bay leaf
1 teaspoon dried oregano leaves
1 teaspoon dried thyme leaves

1. In large pot or Dutch oven, heat oil; add onions. Cook over medium-high heat, stirring frequently, 8–10 minutes, until onions are golden brown. Add carrots and garlic; cook, stirring frequently, 5 minutes, until carrots are tender.

2. Sprinkle beef on all sides with salt and pepper; add to vegetable mixture. Cook, turning beef frequently, 5 minutes, until browned on all sides.

3. Add wine, bay leaf, oregano and thyme to beef mixture; bring liquid to a boil. Reduce heat to low; simmer, covered, turning beef occasionally and adding water, a few tablespoons at a time to keep beef from sticking, $1^1/_2$–2 hours, until beef is cooked through and very tender and liquid is thickened. Remove from heat; let stand 10 minutes. Remove and discard bay leaf.

4. Transfer beef to cutting board; slice. Arrange beef slices on serving platter; top with vegetable mixture.

Serving (3 ounces beef, one-quarter of vegetable mixture) provides: $^1/_2$ Fat, 2 Vegetables, 3 Proteins, 25 Optional Calories.

Per serving: 229 Calories, 7 g Total Fat, 2 g Saturated Fat, 64 mg Cholesterol, 157 mg Sodium, 13 g Total Carbohydrate, 3 g Dietary Fiber, 24 g Protein, 46 mg Calcium.

BREAKFAST
Grapefruit Sections, $^1/_2$ cup
White Omelet Sandwich (In small bowl, beat 3 egg whites and pinch *each* salt and ground white pepper until frothy. In small nonstick skillet, melt 2 teaspoons reduced-calorie tub margarine; add egg white mixture. Cook, covered, until mixture is firm. Place omelet between 2 slices reduced-calorie whole-wheat toast.)
Skim Milk, 1 cup
Coffee or Tea (optional)

LIGHT MEAL
Gazpacho (In food processor, combine 1 cup chopped tomato, $^1/_2$ cup *each* chopped green bell pepper, onion and celery, 1 tablespoon fresh cilantro and 2 teaspoons fresh lemon juice; purée. Stir in $^1/_2$ teaspoon celery seeds and freshly ground black pepper, to taste; refrigerate, covered, until chilled. Serve topped with 2 tablespoons nonfat sour cream.)
Nonfat Tortilla Chips, 1 ounce
Mocha Milk Shake (In blender, combine 1 cup skim milk, 3 ice cubes, sugar substitute to equal 2 teaspoons sugar, 2 teaspoons unsweetened cocoa powder and 1 teaspoon instant decaffeinated coffee powder; purée until smooth.)

MAIN MEAL
Beef Braised in Red Wine, 1 serving (see recipe)
Mashed Potatoes (In small bowl, with electric mixer, combine 4 ounces hot cooked potato, peeled and cubed, 1 tablespoon *each* reduced-calorie tub margarine and low-sodium beef broth and ground white pepper, to taste.)
Steamed Cabbage, 2 cups
Baked Apple (Preheat oven to 350° F. Pare 1 small apple halfway down from stem end; core and place in small baking dish. Sprinkle apple with 1 teaspoon granulated sugar and $^1/_4$ teaspoon cinnamon; add $^1/_4$" water to pan. Bake, covered, 30 minutes, until tender.)
Sparkling Mineral Water

SNACK
Roasted Chestnuts, 12 small (Preheat oven to 425° F. Cut X into base of each chestnut. Place on small baking sheet; bake 15–25 minutes, until tender, stirring occasionally. Peel skins while chestnuts are still warm.)

This menu provides: 2 Milks, 3 Fats, 2 Fruits, 11 Vegetables, 4 Proteins, 5 Breads, 90 Optional Calories.

Per serving: 25 g Fat, 42 g Fiber.

22

LIGHT AND EASY BEEF AND VEGETABLE LOAF

*This meatloaf is a new twist on an old favorite. For a great lunch,
serve it cold with mustard and cucumber spears.*

Makes 4 servings

1 cup chopped onions
1 cup shredded carrot
1 cup shredded zucchini
1 garlic clove, minced
One 1-ounce slice white bread, torn into small pieces
2 tablespoons skim milk
10 ounces extra-lean ground beef (10% or less fat)
2 tablespoons egg substitute
1 tablespoon minced fresh flat-leaf parsley
1 teaspoon salt
1 teaspoon freshly ground black pepper
½ teaspoon dried thyme leaves
¼ teaspoon ground sage leaves

1. Preheat oven to 350° F. Spray 1-quart baking dish with nonstick cooking spray.

2. Spray medium skillet with nonstick cooking spray; heat. Add onions; cook over medium-high heat, stirring frequently, 7 minutes, until golden brown. Add carrot, zucchini and garlic; cook, stirring constantly, 3 minutes, until vegetables are softened. Remove from heat; set aside to cool.

3. In small bowl, combine bread and milk; let stand 10 minutes.

4. In large bowl, combine beef, egg substitute, parsley, salt, pepper, thyme, sage, cooled vegetables and soaked bread. Shape beef mixture into oval loaf; place into prepared dish. Bake 1 hour and 15 minutes, until cooked through. Remove from oven; let stand 5 minutes. Cut into 16 equal slices.

Serving (4 slices) provides: 1½ Vegetables, 2 Proteins, ¼ Bread, 10 Optional Calories.

Per serving: 183 Calories, 8 g Total Fat, 3 g Saturated Fat, 44 mg Cholesterol, 668 mg Sodium, 12 g Total Carbohydrate, 2 g Dietary Fiber, 17 g Protein, 52 mg Calcium.

23

PIZZA BURGERS

*These burgers are a nice change from the
ordinary—the kids will love them, too!*

Makes 4 servings

10 ounces extra-lean ground beef (10% or less fat)
$^1/_2$ teaspoon salt
$^1/_2$ teaspoon freshly ground black pepper
$^1/_2$ teaspoon dried oregano leaves
$^1/_4$ cup tomato sauce (no salt added)
$^1/_4$ cup thinly sliced white mushrooms
$1^1/_2$ ounces skim-milk mozzarella cheese, grated
1 tablespoon minced fresh flat-leaf parsley

1. In large bowl, combine beef, salt, pepper and oregano; form into 4 equal patties.

2. In medium nonstick skillet, cook patties 3 minutes; turn over. Spread each patty with 1 tablespoon tomato sauce; top each with 1 tablespoon mushrooms and one-fourth of the cheese. Cook, covered, 4 minutes, until cheese is melted and patties are cooked through. Serve sprinkled with parsley.

Serving (1 pizza burger) provides: $^1/_2$ Vegetable, $2^1/_2$ Proteins.

Per serving: 156 Calories, 9 g Total Fat, 4 g Saturated Fat, 50 mg Cholesterol, 377 mg Sodium, 2 g Total Carbohydrate, 0 g Dietary Fiber, 17 g Protein, 76 mg Calcium.

BREAKFAST
Blueberry Yogurt (In small bowl, combine $^3/_4$ cup *each* plain nonfat yogurt and blueberries.)
Cinnamon Toast (Spread 1 slice cinnamon-raisin bread, toasted, with 1 teaspoon reduced-calorie tub margarine; sprinkle with $^1/_2$ teaspoon granulated sugar and pinch cinnamon.)
Coffee or Tea (optional)

LIGHT MEAL
Turkey Salad (Combine 2 ounces skinless boneless cooked turkey breast, diced, $^1/_4$ cup chopped celery, 2 tablespoons *each* chopped red onion and arugula leaves, 1 tablespoon fresh lemon juice and 2 teaspoons reduced-calorie mayonnaise.)
Celery and Carrot Sticks, 1 cup *each*
Tomato and Cucumber Slices, 1 cup *each*, with $1^1/_2$ teaspoons *each* olive oil and balsamic vinegar
Rice Cakes, 2
Chocolate "Egg Cream" (In tall glass, combine 1 cup diet chocolate soda and $^3/_4$ cup skim milk.)

MAIN MEAL
Pizza Burgers, 1 serving (see recipe)
English Muffin, 1 (2 ounces), split and toasted
Steamed Broccoli Rabe, 1 cup
Tossed Green Salad, 2 cups, with 1 tablespoon fat-free creamy Italian dressing
Tutti-Frutti Sundae (Top 4 fluid ounces sugar-free vanilla nonfat frozen yogurt with $^1/_2$ cup fresh fruit salad.)
Diet Black Cherry Soda

SNACK
Whole-Wheat Pretzels, $1^1/_2$ ounces

This menu provides: 2 Milks, 3 Fats, 2 Fruits, $15^1/_2$ Vegetables, $4^1/_2$ Proteins, 6 Breads, 80 Optional Calories.

Per serving: 29 g Fat, 22 g Fiber.

BREAKFAST

Cantaloupe, 1/4 small
Nonfat Cottage Cheese, 1/2 cup, mixed with 1/2 teaspoon cinnamon and sugar substitute to equal 2 teaspoons sugar
Bagel, 1/2 small (1 ounce)
Skim Milk, 1 cup
Coffee or Tea (optional)

LIGHT MEAL

Gazpacho (In food processor, combine 1 cup coarsely chopped tomato, 1/2 cup *each* chopped green bell pepper, onion and celery, 1 tablespoon minced fresh cilantro and 2 teaspoons fresh lemon juice; purée until almost smooth. Stir in 1/2 teaspoon celery seeds and freshly ground black pepper, to taste; refrigerate, covered, until chilled. Serve topped with 2 tablespoons nonfat sour cream.)
Chicken Salad Sandwich (In small bowl, combine 2 ounces skinless boneless cooked chicken breast, chopped, 1/2 cup chopped celery, 2 teaspoons reduced-calorie mayonnaise and pinch freshly ground black pepper; spread salad between 2 slices reduced-calorie rye bread.)
Carrot Sticks, 1 cup
Fresh Fig, 1 large
Herbal Tea

MAIN MEAL

Risotto with Ground Beef, Zucchini and Tomatoes, 1 serving (see recipe)
Steamed Artichoke Hearts, 2 cups, tossed with 1 tablespoon minced fresh flat-leaf parsley and 1 teaspoon *each* olive oil and fresh lemon juice)
Spinach-Vegetable Salad (In medium bowl, combine 2 cups torn spinach leaves, 1/2 cup *each* sliced mushrooms and red onion, 1 tablespoon imitation bacon bits and 1 tablespoon fresh lemon juice.)
Aspartame-Sweetened Strawberry-Banana Nonfat Yogurt, 1 cup
Diet Cola

SNACK

Baked Sweet Potato Sticks, 3 ounces, sprinkled with 1 teaspoon firmly packed light or dark brown sugar

This menu provides: 2 Milks, 3 Fats, 2 Fruits, 21 Vegetables, 4 Proteins, 4 3/4 Breads, 145 Optional Calories.

Per serving: 27 g Fat, 22 g Fiber.

24

RISOTTO WITH GROUND BEEF, ZUCCHINI AND TOMATOES

Makes 4 servings

1 tablespoon + 1 teaspoon olive oil
2 cups chopped onions
2 cups chopped zucchini
5 ounces lean ground beef (10% or less fat)
7 ounces Arborio or other short-grain rice
4 large or 8 small plum tomatoes, chopped
3 1/2 cups hot low-sodium vegetable broth
8 fluid ounces (1 cup) dry white wine
1 tablespoon + 1 teaspoon freshly grated Parmesan cheese
Freshly ground black pepper, to taste
Fresh flat-leaf parsley sprigs, to garnish

1. In medium saucepan, heat oil; add onions and zucchini. Cook over medium-high heat, stirring frequently, 5 minutes, until vegetables are softened. Add beef; cook, stirring to break up meat, 3–4 minutes, until no longer pink.

2. Add rice and tomatoes to beef mixture; stir to combine. Cook, stirring constantly, 1 minute. Add 1/2 cup of the broth and the wine; cook, stirring constantly, until liquid is absorbed.

3. Continuing to stir, add remaining broth, 1/2 cup at a time; cook, stirring constantly after each addition, 18 minutes, until all liquid is absorbed, rice is tender and mixture is creamy. Remove from heat; stir in cheese and pepper. Serve garnished with parsley.

Serving (1 1/2 cups) provides: 1 Fat, 3 Vegetables, 1 Protein, 1 3/4 Breads, 80 Optional Calories.

Per serving: 393 Calories, 10 g Total Fat, 2 g Saturated Fat, 23 mg Cholesterol, 653 mg Sodium, 54 g Total Carbohydrate, 3 g Dietary Fiber, 15 g Protein, 58 mg Calcium.

GROUND BEEF CHILI

Serve this simple chili over rice for an easy and hearty meal.

Makes 4 servings

1 teaspoon vegetable oil
1¹/₂ cups cubed green bell peppers
1 cup chopped onions
2 garlic cloves, minced
1 tablespoon + 1 teaspoon mild or hot chili powder
1 teaspoon ground cumin
¹/₄ teaspoon cinnamon
¹/₄ teaspoon ground red pepper
10 ounces lean ground beef (10% or less fat)
2 cups canned whole Italian tomatoes (no salt added), drained and chopped
1 bay leaf
1 teaspoon dried oregano leaves

1. In large saucepan or Dutch oven, heat oil; add bell peppers and onions. Cook over medium-high heat, stirring frequently, 5 minutes, until onions are softened. Add garlic; cook, stirring frequently, 1 minute. Add chili powder, cumin, cinnamon and ground red pepper; cook, stirring constantly, 30 seconds, until vegetables are well coated.

2. Add beef to vegetable mixture; cook, stirring to break up meat, 4–5 minutes, until no longer pink. Add tomatoes, bay leaf and oregano; bring mixture to a boil. Reduce heat to low; simmer, covered, 1¹/₂ hours, until mixture is thickened. Remove and discard bay leaf.

Serving (1 cup) provides: ¹/₄ Fat, 2¹/₄ Vegetables, 2 Proteins.

Per serving: 195 Calories, 9 g Total Fat, 3 g Saturated Fat, 44 mg Cholesterol, 275 mg Sodium, 14 g Total Carbohydrate, 3 g Dietary Fiber, 17 g Protein, 67 mg Calcium.

BREAKFAST

Strawberries, 1 cup
Whole-Wheat English Muffin, 1 (2 ounces), split and toasted, with 1¹/₂ teaspoons reduced-calorie tub margarine
Skim Milk, ¹/₂ cup
Coffee or Tea (optional)

LIGHT MEAL

Tuna-Vegetable Salad (In medium bowl, combine 1 cup torn iceberg lettuce leaves, 6 cherry tomatoes, halved, ¹/₂ cup cucumber slices, 4 ounces drained canned water-packed tuna, and 2 tablespoons fat-free Italian dressing.)
Roll, 1 ounce, with 2 teaspoons reduced-calorie tub margarine
Reduced-Calorie Chocolate-Flavored Pudding (made with skim milk), ¹/₂ cup
Diet Cream Soda

MAIN MEAL

Ground Beef Chili, 1 serving (see recipe)
Cooked Brown Rice, 1 cup, with 2 tablespoons minced fresh flat-leaf parsley and 2 teaspoons reduced-calorie tub margarine
Red and Green Bell Pepper Strips, 1 cup *each*
Tossed Green Salad, 2 cups, with 1 tablespoon fat-free ranch dressing
Papaya, ¹/₂ medium
Non-Alcoholic Beer, 12 fluid ounces

SNACK

Vanilla Wafers, 3
Skim Milk, 1 cup

This menu provides: 2 Milks, 3 Fats, 2 Fruits, 14¹/₄ Vegetables, 4 Proteins, 5¹/₂ Vegetables, 145 Optional Calories.

Per serving: 28 g Fat, 21 g Fiber.

CHILI CON CARNE

This classic chili is wonderfully beefy; vary it by adjusting the proportions of meat to beans, substituting lean ground lamb, turkey or pork for the beef or by adding a spoonful or two of pureed canned chipotle peppers in adobo sauce. Make it today to enjoy later in the week; it tastes even better a day or so after it's made.

Makes 4 servings

2 teaspoons olive or corn oil
10 ounces lean ground beef (10% or less fat)
1 1/2 cups chopped onions
1 tablespoon mild or hot chili powder, or to taste
1 1/2 teaspoons ground cumin
1 1/4 cups canned tomato purée (no salt added)
1/2 cup low-sodium beef broth
8 ounces drained cooked pinto beans
1 tablespoon unsweetened cocoa powder, dissolved in 2 tablespoons
 hot water
1 teaspoon dried oregano leaves

1. In large nonstick skillet, heat oil; add beef and onions. Cook over medium-high heat, stirring to break up meat, 10–12 minutes, until beef is no longer pink and onions are golden brown.

2. Reduce heat to medium-low; add chili powder and cumin. Cook, stirring occasionally, 5 minutes, until flavors are blended.

3. Add tomato purée and broth to beef mixture; cook, stirring occasionally, 20 minutes, until mixture is thickened. Add beans, dissolved cocoa and oregano; cook, stirring frequently, 5 minutes, until mixture is heated through.

Serving (1 1/4 cups) provides: 1/2 Fat, 2 Vegetables, 3 Proteins, 5 Optional Calories.

Per serving: 287 Calories, 10 g Total Fat, 3 g Saturated Fat, 44 mg Cholesterol, 394 mg Sodium, 29 g Total Carbohydrate, 6 g Dietary Fiber, 22 g Protein, 66 mg Calcium.

BREAKFAST
Strawberries, 1 cup
Frozen Waffle, 1, heated, with 2 teaspoons maple
 syrup
Skim Milk, 1 cup
Coffee or Tea (optional)

LIGHT MEAL
Three-Bean Toss (In small bowl, combine 2 ounces
 each drained cooked chick-peas and red kidney
 beans, 1/2 cup cooked cut green beans and 1 1/2
 teaspoons *each* olive oil and balsamic vinegar.)
Crispbreads, 3/4 ounce
Sugar-Free Grape-Flavored Gelatin, 1/2 cup
Diet Ginger Ale

MAIN MEAL
Chili Con Carne, 1 serving (see recipe)
Cooked Brown Rice, 1 cup
Cooked Sliced Yellow Squash, 1 cup
Tossed Green Salad, 2 cups, with 1/2 cup sliced
 radishes and 1 tablespoon reduced-calorie ranch
 dressing
Mango, 1/2 small
Iced Tea with Lime Slice

SNACK
Whole-Wheat Pretzels, 1 1/2 ounces
Skim Milk, 1 cup

This menu provides: 2 Milks, 3 Fats, 2 Fruits, 10 Vegetables, 5 Proteins, 6 Breads, 65 Optional Calories.

Per serving: 34 g Fat, 30 g Fiber.

CHILI TACOS

Makes 4 servings

1 tablespoon + 1 teaspoon olive oil
1 cup finely chopped green bell pepper
$^1/_2$ cup minced onion
4 garlic cloves, minced
1 teaspoon finely chopped deveined seeded jalapeño pepper
   (wear gloves to prevent irritation)
8 ounces drained cooked red kidney beans
5 ounces lean ground beef (10% or less fat)
4 ounces cooked lean boneless pork, shredded or finely chopped
2 teaspoons ground cumin
1 teaspoon dried oregano leaves
Pinch salt
Freshly ground black pepper, to taste
1 cup canned whole Italian tomatoes (no salt added), chopped
8 taco shells
2 cups shredded Romaine or iceberg lettuce leaves
1 cup mild, medium or hot salsa
$^1/_4$ cup nonfat sour cream
2 tablespoons minced fresh cilantro

1. In medium nonstick skillet, heat oil; add bell pepper, onion, garlic and jalapeño pepper. Cook over medium-high heat, stirring frequently, 6–7 minutes, until vegetables are golden brown. Add beans, beef, pork, cumin, oregano, salt and black pepper; cook, stirring to break up meat, 3–4 minutes, until beef is no longer pink. Add tomatoes; reduce heat to low. Simmer, stirring frequently, adding water, a few tablespoons at a time to keep mixture from sticking, 10 minutes, until thickened.

2. Fill each taco shell with an equal amount of beef mixture; top evenly with lettuce, salsa and sour cream. Serve sprinkled with cilantro.

Serving (2 tacos) provides: 1 Fat, $3^1/_4$ Vegetables, 3 Proteins, 1 Bread, 30 Optional Calories.

Per serving: 399 Calories, 16 g Total Fat, 4 g Saturated Fat, 45 mg Cholesterol, 972 mg Sodium, 40 g Total Carbohydrate, 5 g Dietary Fiber, 25 g Protein, 140 mg Calcium.

BREAKFAST
Banana, $^1/_2$ medium, sliced
Cornflakes, $^3/_4$ ounce
Skim Milk, 1 cup
Reduced-Calorie Whole-Wheat Bread, toasted, 2 slices, with 2 teaspoons reduced-calorie tub margarine
Coffee or Tea (optional)

LIGHT MEAL
Fennel-Shrimp Salad (In small bowl, combine $^1/_2$ cup finely chopped fennel, 2 ounces peeled and deveined cooked small shrimp, 2 teaspoons reduced-calorie mayonnaise and $^1/_2$ teaspoon fresh lemon juice.)
Carrot Sticks, 1 cup
Roll, 1 small (1 ounce)
Grapefruit, $^1/_2$ medium, with 1 teaspoon firmly packed light or dark brown sugar
Iced Herbal Tea

MAIN MEAL
Chili Tacos, 1 serving (see recipe)
Baked Spaghetti Squash, 1 cup
Boiled Corn on the Cob, 1 small ear (5")
Berry Yogurt Parfait (In stemmed glass, layer 1 cup aspartame-sweetened mixed-berry nonfat yogurt and $^1/_4$ cup thawed frozen light whipped topping [8 calories per tablespoon].)
Diet Cola with Lime Wedge

SNACK
Pumpernickel Bread, 1 slice, with 1 tablespoon nonfat cream cheese and 1 teaspoon grape jam

This menu provides: 2 Milks, 3 Fats, 2 Fruits, $8^1/_4$ Vegetables, 4 Proteins, 6 Breads, 115 Optional Calories.

Per serving: 32 g Fat, 21 g Fiber.

Chili Tacos

28

BEEF TACOS WITH TOMATO SALSA

Tacos are fun to eat and a snap to make!
If you are short on time, use store-bought salsa.

Makes 4 servings

1 cup diced tomato
1/2 cup minced fresh cilantro
1/4 cup diced red onion
2 tablespoons fresh lime juice
1 tablespoon minced deveined seeded jalapeño pepper (wear gloves to prevent irritation)
1 cup chopped yellow onions
8 ounces lean ground beef (10% or less fat)
1/4 cup tomato sauce (no salt added)
1 tablespoon mild or hot chili powder
1 teaspoon ground cumin
1 garlic clove, minced
8 taco shells
1 1/2 ounces reduced-fat cheddar cheese
1 cup shredded iceberg lettuce

1. To prepare salsa, in large bowl, combine tomato, cilantro, red onion, juice and jalapeño pepper; set aside.

2. Spray large nonstick skillet with nonstick cooking spray; heat. Add chopped onions; cook over medium-high heat, stirring frequently, 5 minutes, until softened. Remove onions from skillet; set aside.

3. In same skillet, cook beef, stirring to break up meat, 4–5 minutes, until no longer pink. Add tomato sauce, chili powder, cumin, garlic and cooked onions; cook, stirring frequently, 3 minutes, until thickened.

4. Spoon an equal amount of beef mixture into each taco shell; sprinkle evenly with cheese. Top each portion of cheese with 2 tablespoons lettuce and divide salsa evenly among tacos.

Serving (2 tacos) provides: 2 Vegetables, 2 Proteins, 1 Bread, 20 Optional Calories.

Per serving: 276 Calories, 13 g Total Fat, 4 g Saturated Fat, 43 mg Cholesterol, 296 mg Sodium, 25 g Total Carbohydrate, 4 g Dietary Fiber, 18 g Protein, 173 mg Calcium.

BREAKFAST
Cooked Oatmeal, 1 cup, with 2 tablespoons raisins, 2 teaspoons reduced-calorie tub margarine and 1 teaspoon granulated sugar
Skim Milk, 1 cup
Coffee or Tea (optional)

LIGHT MEAL
Broiled Flounder, 4 ounces
Boiled New Potatoes, 4 ounces, with 2 teaspoons *each* reduced-calorie tub margarine and minced fresh flat-leaf parsley
Steamed Zucchini Slices, 1 1/2 cups
Iceberg Lettuce Wedge, 1, with 1 tablespoon fat-free Thousand Island dressing
Sugar-Free Lemon-Flavored Gelatin, 1/2 cup, with 1 tablespoon thawed frozen light whipped topping (8 calories per tablespoon)
Diet Grape-Ginger Ale

MAIN MEAL
Beef Tacos with Tomato Salsa, 1 serving (see recipe)
Yellow Rice (In small saucepan, combine 1 cup cooked long-grain rice, 2 tablespoons water and 1/4 teaspoon *each* ground turmeric and garlic powder; cook, stirring constantly, until liquid is evaporated and mixture is heated through.)
Watercress Salad, 2 cups, with 1/2 cup orange sections and 1 1/2 teaspoons ranch dressing
Aspartame-Sweetened Peach Nonfat Yogurt, 1 cup
Unsweetened Seltzer with Lime Wedge

SNACK
Frozen Orange Pop (Pour 1/2 cup low-calorie orange-flavored drink into small paper cup; freeze until almost firm. Insert ice-cream-bar stick vertically into partially frozen drink; freeze until solid. Unmold.)

This menu provides: 2 Milks, 3 Fats, 2 Fruits, 10 Vegetables, 4 Proteins, 6 Breads, 75 Optional Calories.

Per serving: 32 g Fat, 21 g Fiber.

BREAKFAST

Blueberries, ³/₄ cup
Reduced-Calorie Sourdough Bread, 2 slices, toasted,
  with 2 teaspoons reduced-calorie tub margarine
Skim Milk, 1 cup
Coffee or Tea (optional)

LIGHT MEAL

Broiled Sea Bass, 4 ounces
Cooked Brown Rice, ¹/₂ cup, with 2 teaspoons *each*
  minced fresh flat-leaf parsley and reduced-calorie
  tub margarine
Steamed Asparagus, 6 spears, with 1 teaspoon fresh
  lemon juice
Tomato, 1 medium, sliced, with 1 tablespoon fat-free
  Thousand Island dressing
Diet Lemonade, 1 cup

MAIN MEAL

Beef Enchiladas with Green Sauce, 1 serving
  (see recipe)
Tossed Green Salad, 2 cups, with 1 ounce sliced
  avocado and 1 tablespoon fat-free Italian dressing
Sugar-Free Strawberry Nonfat Frozen Yogurt, 4 fluid
  ounces
Unsweetened Raspberry-Flavored Seltzer

SNACK

Plain Popcorn, hot-air popped, 3 cups, with 2 tablespoons raisins

This menu provides: 2 Milks, 3 Fats, 2 Fruits,
8¹/₂ Vegetables, 4¹/₂ Proteins, 5 Breads, 80 Optional
Calories.

Per serving: 26 g Fat, 24 g Fiber.

**Serving (2 enchiladas, one-quarter of the cilantro
mixture, 3 tablespoons yogurt) provides:** ³/₄ Milk,
1¹/₂ Vegetables, 2¹/₂ Proteins, 2 Breads.

Per serving: 336 Calories, 7 g Total Fat,
3 g Saturated Fat, 54 mg Cholesterol,
328 mg Sodium, 40 g Total Carbohydrate,
4 g Dietary Fiber, 30 g Protein, 493 mg Calcium.

*To roast chile, preheat broiler. Line baking sheet or pie
pan with foil; set whole chile onto prepared baking
sheet. Broil chile 4–6" from heat, turning frequently with
tongs, until skin is lightly charred on all sides. Transfer
chile to bowl; let cool. Wearing surgical gloves, peel, seed,
and devein chile over bowl to catch juices.*

BEEF ENCHILADAS WITH GREEN SAUCE

*These enchiladas are a welcome change
from those cooked in tomato sauce.*

Makes 4 servings

1 cup packed fresh cilantro
¹/₂ cup packed washed trimmed spinach leaves
¹/₄ cup packed fresh flat-leaf parsley
1 garlic clove, minced
1 medium poblano chile, roasted,* peeled and seeded
2 tablespoons fresh lime juice
¹/₂ teaspoon mild or hot chili powder
1 cup evaporated skimmed milk
1 cup chopped Italian sweet green (frying) pepper
1 tablespoon minced deveined seeded jalapeño pepper (wear gloves to
  prevent irritation)
10 ounces lean boneless beef loin, cut into ¹/₄" strips
1 cup diced zucchini
Eight 6" corn tortillas
1¹/₂ ounces reduced-fat white cheddar cheese
³/₄ cup plain nonfat yogurt

1. Preheat oven to 400° F. Spray 1-quart baking dish with nonstick cooking spray.

2. In food processor, combine cilantro, spinach, parsley, and garlic;
process until very finely chopped. Add chile, juice and chili powder; purée
until smooth. Add milk; process until combined. Spread prepared dish
with ¹/₄ cup cilantro mixture; set aside dish and remaining cilantro
mixture.

3. In large nonstick skillet, cook Italian and jalapeño peppers over
medium-high heat, stirring frequently, 5 minutes, until softened; add
beef. Cook, stirring frequently, 3 minutes, until beef is no longer pink.
Add zucchini; cook, stirring frequently, 2 minutes.

4. To assemble enchiladas, place tortillas on work surface; arrange an
equal amount of beef mixture along center of each tortilla. Fold sides of
tortillas over filling to enclose; place, seam-side down, into prepared baking dish. Spread tortillas evenly with remaining cilantro mixture; sprinkle
evenly with cheese. Bake 20 minutes, until bubbling and lightly browned.

5. Place 2 enchiladas on each of 4 plates; top each portion evenly with
one-fourth of the cilantro mixture and 3 tablespoons yogurt.

30
ZESTY BEEF FAJITAS

Fajitas are a fun way to "make your own" dinner.
For best results, use a cast-iron skillet over very high heat.

Makes 4 servings

10 ounces lean boneless beef sirloin, cut into $^1/_4$" strips
1 teaspoon ground cumin
$^1/_2$ teaspoon mild or hot chili powder
$^1/_2$ teaspoon freshly ground black pepper
1 medium green bell pepper, seeded and sliced ($^1/_2$" slices)
1 cup Spanish onion slices ($^1/_2$" slices)
$^1/_4$ cup fresh lime juice
Eight 6" flour tortillas
2 cups finely shredded iceberg lettuce
$1^1/_2$ ounces reduced-fat cheddar cheese, grated
1 cup salsa

1. Sprinkle beef on all sides with cumin, chili powder and black pepper; set aside.

2. Spray large cast-iron skillet with nonstick cooking spray; heat. Add bell pepper and onion; cook over high heat, stirring constantly, 3 minutes, until vegetables are lightly browned. Add seasoned beef; cook, stirring constantly, 3 minutes, until beef is no longer pink. Add juice; toss to combine.

3. Wrap tortillas in wax paper; microwave on High (100% power) 1–2 minutes, until warm.

4. To assemble fajitas, place an equal amount of beef mixture onto center of each warm tortilla; top each portion of beef with $^1/_4$ cup lettuce, an equal amount of cheese and 2 tablespoons salsa; roll tortillas to enclose.

Serving (2 fajitas) provides: 3 Vegetables, $2^1/_2$ Proteins, 2 Breads.

Per serving: 309 Calories, 8 g Total Fat, 3 g Saturated Fat, 51 mg Cholesterol, 966 mg Sodium, 34 g Total Carbohydrate, 3 g Dietary Fiber, 23 g Protein, 191 mg Calcium.

BREAKFAST
Mango, $^1/_2$ small
Fortified Cold Cereal, $^3/_4$ ounce
Skim Milk, $^3/_4$ cup
Coffee or Tea (optional)

LIGHT MEAL
Creamy Zucchini Soup (In food processor, combine $^1/_2$ cup *each* chopped zucchini and low-sodium chicken broth, 2 tablespoons evaporated skimmed milk and 1 tablespoon minced fresh dill; purée until smooth. Transfer mixture to small saucepan; heat.)
Tuna Melt (In small bowl, combine 2 ounces drained canned water-packed tuna, 1 tablespoon chopped onion and 2 teaspoons reduced-calorie mayonnaise. Toast 2 slices reduced-calorie multi-grain bread; top each toast slice with half of the tuna mixture and 1 nonfat process American cheese slice. Place onto nonstick baking sheet; broil until heated.)
Celery and Carrot Sticks, 1 cup *each*
Diet Cream Soda

MAIN MEAL
Zesty Beef Fajitas, 1 serving (see recipe)
Spicy Pinto Beans (In small microwavable casserole, combine 4 ounces drained cooked pinto beans and $^1/_2$ teaspoon *each* mild or hot chili powder and ground cumin, mashing beans with fork to form a chunky paste; microwave on High [100% power] 1–2 minutes, until heated through.)
Cucumber Salad (In small bowl, combine $^1/_2$ cup cucumber slices, 1 teaspoon *each* vegetable oil and rice wine vinegar and pinch ground white pepper.)
Cantaloupe, $^1/_4$ small
Unsweetened Lime-Flavored Seltzer

SNACK
Chocolate-Peanut Butter Shake (In blender, combine $^2/_3$ cup cold water, 3 ice cubes, 1 packet reduced-calorie chocolate-flavored dairy shake mix and 1 teaspoon smooth peanut butter; purée until smooth and thick.)

This menu provides: 2 Milks, 3 Fats, 2 Fruits, $9^1/_4$ Vegetables, $4^1/_2$ Proteins, 6 Breads, 10 Optional Calories.

Per serving: 26 g Fat, 20 g Fiber.

31

CREAMY BEEF AND NOODLES

This is a lighter version of the classic Beef Stroganoff.

Makes 4 servings

3 ounces wide egg noodles

10 ounces lean boneless beef loin, cut into $^1/2$" strips

2 medium onions, thinly sliced

2 cups small whole white mushrooms, woody ends removed

1 tablespoon + 1 teaspoon reduced-calorie tub margarine

1 tablespoon + 1 teaspoon all-purpose flour

1 cup low-sodium beef broth

1 teaspoon prepared mustard

$^1/2$ teaspoon paprika

$^1/2$ teaspoon salt

$^1/4$ teaspoon freshly ground black pepper

$^1/4$ cup light sour cream

4 fresh flat-leaf parsley sprigs, to garnish

1. In large pot of boiling water, cook noodles 5–6 minutes, until tender; drain, discarding liquid. Set aside; keep warm.

2. In medium nonstick skillet, cook beef over medium-high heat, stirring frequently, 3 minutes, until no longer pink. Remove beef from skillet. Wipe skillet clean; set beef aside.

3. Spray same skillet with nonstick cooking spray; heat. Add onions; cook over medium-high heat, stirring frequently, 7 minutes, until golden brown. Add mushrooms; cook, stirring frequently, 6 minutes, until lightly browned. Remove vegetables from skillet. Wipe skillet clean; set vegetables aside.

4. In same skillet, melt margarine; sprinkle with flour. Cook over medium-high heat, stirring constantly, until bubbling. Continuing to stir, gradually add broth, mustard, paprika, salt and pepper; cook, stirring constantly, 4 minutes, until mixture is thickened. Stir in sour cream.

5. Return cooked beef, onions and mushrooms to skillet; stir to coat. Cook, stirring frequently, until mixture is heated through.

6. Divide warm noodles evenly among 4 plates; top each portion of noodles with one-fourth of the beef mixture. Serve garnished with parsley.

Serving ($^3/4$ cup beef mixture, $^1/2$ cup noodles) provides: $^1/2$ Fat, $1^1/2$ Vegetables, 2 Proteins, 1 Bread, 35 Optional Calories.

Per serving: 258 Calories, 9 g Total Fat, 3 g Saturated Fat, 68 mg Cholesterol, 393 mg Sodium, 24 g Total Carbohydrate, 2 g Dietary Fiber, 22 g Protein, 27 mg Calcium.

32

Spaghetti with Herbed Meatballs

Everyone loves spaghetti with meatballs! This version, spiked with the bright flavor of fresh herbs, will become your family's favorite.

Makes 4 servings

1 cup finely chopped onions
1 teaspoon salt
8 ounces lean ground beef (10% or less fat)
$^1/_4$ cup minced fresh flat-leaf parsley
3 tablespoons plain dried bread crumbs
1 tablespoon + 1 teaspoon minced fresh thyme leaves
$^3/_4$ teaspoon dried sage leaves
$^1/_4$ teaspoon freshly ground black pepper
2 cups canned whole Italian tomatoes (no salt added), drained and chopped
6 ounces spaghetti

1. In small bowl, combine onions and $^3/_4$ teaspoon of the salt; let stand 30 minutes.

2. Line medium sieve with medium paper coffee filter; place over small bowl. Add onion mixture; with back of wooden spoon, press onion mixture to extract as much liquid as possible. Transfer solids to medium bowl; discard liquid.

3. Add beef, parsley, bread crumbs, thyme, $^1/_2$ teaspoon of the sage and the pepper to drained onions; mix well. Form into 12 equal meatballs.

4. In large nonstick skillet, cook meatballs over medium-high heat, turning as needed, 10 minutes, until browned on all sides.

5. Stir tomatoes, remaining $^1/_4$ teaspoon salt and the remaining $^1/_4$ teaspoon sage into skillet with meatballs; bring liquid to a boil. Reduce heat to low; simmer, covered, 20 minutes, until meatballs are cooked through and sauce is thickened.

6. Meanwhile, in large pot of boiling water, cook spaghetti 8–10 minutes, until tender. Drain, discarding liquid.

7. Add cooked spaghetti to meatball mixture; cook, tossing constantly, 2 minutes, until mixture is heated through.

Serving (1 cup spaghetti with sauce, 3 meatballs) provides: $1^1/_2$ Vegetables, $1^1/_2$ Proteins, $2^1/_4$ Breads.

Per serving: 317 Calories, 7 g Total Fat, 2 g Saturated Fat, 35 mg Cholesterol, 698 mg Sodium, 45 g Total Carbohydrate, 3 g Dietary Fiber, 19 g Protein, 75 mg Calcium.

BREAKFAST
Mixed-Fruit Yogurt (In small bowl, combine $^3/_4$ cup plain nonfat yogurt and $^1/_2$ cup fresh fruit salad.)
Reduced-Calorie Whole-Wheat Bread, 2 slices, toasted, with 2 teaspoons reduced-calorie tub margarine
Coffee or Tea (optional)

LIGHT MEAL
Tuna Salad Sandwich (In small bowl, combine 4 ounces drained canned water-packed tuna, flaked, $^1/_2$ cup chopped celery, 2 teaspoons reduced-calorie mayonnaise and pinch freshly ground black pepper; spread salad between 2 slices reduced-calorie rye bread.)
Cucumber and Carrot Sticks, 1 cup *each*
Apple, 1 small
Diet Cola with Lemon Wedge

MAIN MEAL
Spaghetti with Herbed Meatballs, 1 serving (see recipe)
Steamed Spinach, 1 cup
Red and Green Leaf Lettuce Salad, 2 cups, with Balsamic Vinaigrette (In small jar with tight-fitting lid or small bowl, combine 2 teaspoons balsamic vinegar, 1 teaspoon olive oil and pinch garlic powder; cover and shake well or, with wire whisk, blend until combined.)
Italian Bread, 1 slice (1 ounce)
Sugar-Free Vanilla Nonfat Frozen Yogurt, 4 fluid ounces
Iced Tea

SNACK
Chocolate "Egg Cream" (In tall glass, combine 1 cup diet chocolate soda and $^3/_4$ cup skim milk.)

This menu provides: 2 Milks, 3 Fats, 2 Fruits, $12^1/_2$ Vegetables, $3^1/_2$ Proteins, $5^1/_4$ Breads, 50 Optional Calories.

Per serving: 24 g Fat, 22 g Fiber.

RIGATONI, BEEF AND VEGETABLE RAGOÛT

Makes 4 servings

1 tablespoon + 1 teaspoon olive oil

$^1/_2$ cup minced onion

$^1/_2$ cup minced carrot

$^1/_2$ cup minced celery

2 garlic cloves, minced

$^1/_2$ cup minced green bell pepper

$^1/_2$ cup chopped pared eggplant

5 ounces lean ground beef (10% or less fat)

2 cups canned whole Italian tomatoes (no salt added), chopped

1 bay leaf

$^1/_2$ teaspoon dried oregano leaves

$^1/_2$ teaspoon dried thyme leaves

$^1/_2$ teaspoon dried basil

$^1/_4$ teaspoon salt

$^1/_4$ teaspoon dried red pepper flakes

6 ounces rigatoni pasta

$^1/_4$ cup minced fresh flat-leaf parsley

1 tablespoon + 1 teaspoon freshly grated Parmesan cheese

1. In medium saucepan, heat oil; add onion, carrot, celery and garlic. Cook over medium-high heat, stirring frequently, 5 minutes, until vegetables are softened. Add bell pepper and eggplant; cook, stirring frequently, 5 minutes, until bell pepper is lightly browned.

2. Add beef to vegetable mixture; cook, stirring to break up meat, 3–4 minutes, until no longer pink. Add tomatoes, bay leaf, oregano, thyme, basil, salt and red pepper flakes; bring liquid to a boil. Reduce heat to low; simmer 15–20 minutes, until mixture is thickened. Remove and discard bay leaf.

3. Meanwhile, in large pot of boiling water, cook rigatoni 13 minutes, until tender. Drain, discarding liquid; place into serving bowl. Keep warm.

4. Top warm rigatoni with beef mixture; toss to combine. Sprinkle rigatoni mixture with parsley and cheese.

Serving (2 cups) provides: 1 Fat, 2$^1/_4$ Vegetables, 1 Protein, 2 Breads, 10 Optional Calories.

Per serving: 318 Calories, 10 g Total Fat, 2 g Saturated Fat, 23 mg Cholesterol, 411 mg Sodium, 43 g Total Carbohydrate, 4 g Dietary Fiber, 15 g Protein, 101 mg Calcium.

BAKED MACARONI AND BEEF CASSEROLE

This casserole can be assembled ahead and baked later; if it's refrigerated, increase baking time to 30 minutes.

Makes 4 servings

3 ounces elbow macaroni
8 ounces lean ground beef (10% or less fat)
$^1/_2$ cup chopped onion
$^1/_2$ cup chopped red bell pepper
1 cup tomato sauce (no salt added)
$^1/_4$ cup minced fresh flat-leaf parsley
$^1/_4$ teaspoon dried basil
$^1/_4$ teaspoon dried thyme leaves
$^1/_4$ teaspoon freshly ground black pepper
$1^1/_2$ ounces skim-milk mozzarella cheese, grated

1. Preheat oven to 350° F.

2. In large pot of boiling water, cook macaroni 8–10 minutes, until tender. Drain, discarding liquid; set aside.

3. In large nonstick skillet, cook beef, stirring to break up meat, 4–5 minutes, until no longer pink. Remove from heat; set aside.

4. Spray medium nonstick skillet with nonstick cooking spray; heat. Add onion and bell pepper; cook over medium-high heat, stirring frequently, 5 minutes, until vegetables are softened. Add tomato sauce, parsley, basil, thyme, black pepper and reserved beef; cook, stirring frequently, 3 minutes, until heated through. Remove from heat.

5. Add cooked macaroni to beef mixture; stir to combine. Transfer mixture to 1-quart baking dish; sprinkle evenly with cheese. Bake 20 minutes, until bubbling and slightly browned on top.

Serving ($1^1/_4$ cups) provides: $1^1/_2$ Vegetables, 2 Proteins, 1 Bread.

Per serving: 238 Calories, 8 g Total Fat, 3 g Saturated Fat, 41 mg Cholesterol, 106 mg Sodium, 23 g Total Carbohydrate, 2 g Dietary Fiber, 18 g Protein, 87 mg Calcium.

BREAKFAST
Banana, $^1/_2$ medium, sliced
Puffed Rice Cereal, $^3/_4$ ounce
Skim Milk, 1 cup
Coffee or Tea (optional)

LIGHT MEAL
Tuna Salad Niçoise (In medium bowl, combine 2 cups shredded Romaine lettuce leaves, 1 medium tomato, quartered, $^1/_2$ cup cooked cut green beans, 2 ounces drained canned water-packed tuna, 6 large pitted black olives and 1 tablespoon *each* rinsed drained capers and fat-free Italian dressing)
Breadsticks, 2 long
Sugar-Free Cherry-Flavored Gelatin, $^1/_2$ cup
Sparkling Mineral Water with Lemon Wedge

MAIN MEAL
Baked Macaroni and Beef Casserole, 1 serving (see recipe)
Steamed Asparagus, 9 spears, with 2 teaspoons reduced-calorie tub margarine
Carrot-Raisin Salad (In small bowl, combine 1 cup shredded carrots, 2 tablespoons raisins and 1 teaspoon *each* granulated sugar, reduced-calorie mayonnaise and fresh lemon juice.)
Roll, 1 ounce, with 1 teaspoon reduced-calorie tub margarine
Sugar-Free Vanilla Nonfat Frozen Yogurt, 4 fluid ounces
Diet Raspberry-Ginger Ale

SNACK
Reduced-Fat Swiss Cheese, $^3/_4$ ounce
Melba Rounds, 12
Skim Milk, $^3/_4$ cup

This menu provides: 2 Milks, 3 Fats, 2 Fruits, 12 Vegetables, 4 Proteins, 6 Breads, 80 Optional Calories.

Per serving: 30 g Fat, 20 g Fiber.

35

ORIENTAL BEEF IN LETTUCE WRAPPERS

*The dipping sauce in this recipe may be made up
to three days ahead and refrigerated; prepare extra
to use as a dipping sauce for cut-up raw vegetables.*

Makes 4 servings

$^{1}/_{4}$ cup rice wine vinegar
1 tablespoon reduced-sodium soy sauce
2 teaspoons minced fresh mint leaves
1 teaspoon minced pared fresh ginger root
1 teaspoon grated orange zest*
1 teaspoon oriental sesame oil
8 large iceberg lettuce leaves
8 ounces cooked lean boneless roast beef, cut into $^{1}/_{4}$" strips
1 cup bean sprouts
1 cup shredded seeded pared cucumber
8 large fresh mint leaves

1. In medium bowl, combine vinegar, soy sauce, minced mint leaves, ginger, zest and oil; set aside.

2. Place lettuce leaves on work surface; top center of each leaf with 1 ounce beef strips, 2 tablespoons bean sprouts, 2 tablespoons cucumber and 1 mint leaf. Fold sides of each lettuce leaf over filling; starting from shortest end, roll leaves to enclose.

3. Place 2 rolls on each of 4 plates, seam-side down; serve with vinegar mixture for dipping.

Serving (2 rolls, $1^{1}/_{2}$ tablespoons dipping sauce) provides: $^{1}/_{4}$ Fat, $1^{1}/_{2}$ Vegetables, 2 Proteins.

Per serving: 136 Calories, 5 g Total Fat, 2 g Saturated Fat, 46 mg Cholesterol, 192 mg Sodium, 4 g Total Carbohydrate, 1 g Dietary Fiber, 18 g Protein, 24 mg Calcium.

The zest of the orange is the peel without any of the pith (white membrane). To remove zest from orange, use a zester or the fine side of a vegetable grater; wrap orange in plastic wrap and refrigerate for use at another time.

36
CABBAGE STUFFED WITH BEEF AND VEAL

This version of an old favorite can be made ahead and kept refrigerated for up to a day or frozen in individual portions for up to 3 months. For variety, try using different herbs and vegetables.

Makes 4 servings

8 large cabbage leaves, ribs removed

2 teaspoons reduced-calorie tub margarine

1 cup chopped onions

1 garlic clove, minced

5 ounces lean ground beef (10% or less fat)

5 ounces lean ground veal

$^1/_4$ cup egg substitute

3 tablespoons plain dried bread crumbs

1 tablespoon minced fresh dill

1 tablespoon minced fresh flat-leaf parsley

$^1/_4$ teaspoon salt

Pinch freshly ground black pepper

$^1/_2$ cup low-sodium chicken broth

$^1/_4$ cup tomato sauce (no salt added)

1. Preheat oven to 350° F. Spray 2-quart baking dish with nonstick cooking spray.

2. Fill a large bowl with ice water; set aside.

3. In large pot of boiling water, cook cabbage leaves 3 minutes, until just tender; with tongs, transfer cabbage to ice water. When cool, drain, discarding liquid; place cabbage leaves onto paper towels to dry.

4. In medium nonstick skillet, melt margarine; add onions. Cook over medium-high heat, stirring frequently, 5 minutes, until softened. Add garlic; cook, stirring frequently, 1 minute. Remove from heat; set aside to cool.

5. In large bowl, combine beef, veal, egg substitute, bread crumbs, dill, parsley, salt, pepper and cooled onion mixture; shape into 8 equal logs.

6. Place 1 log onto center of each cabbage leaf. Fold sides of each leaf over logs; starting from shortest end, roll leaves to enclose. Place rolls, seam-side down, into prepared baking dish. In small bowl, combine broth and tomato sauce; pour over cabbage rolls. Bake, covered, 45 minutes, until filling is cooked through.

Serving (2 cabbage rolls, 3 tablespoons sauce) provides: $^1/_4$ Fat, 1$^3/_4$ Vegetables, 2$^1/_4$ Proteins, $^1/_4$ Bread, 5 Optional Calories.

Per serving: 189 Calories, 7 g Total Fat, 2 g Saturated Fat, 52 mg Cholesterol, 319 mg Sodium, 15 g Total Carbohydrate, 4 g Dietary Fiber, 19 g Protein, 91 mg Calcium.

BREAKFAST
Mango Yogurt (In small bowl, combine $^3/_4$ cup plain nonfat yogurt and $^1/_2$ small mango, pared, pitted and diced.)

Reduced-Calorie Whole-Wheat Bread, 2 slices, toasted, with 2 teaspoons reduced-calorie tub margarine

Coffee or Tea (optional)

LIGHT MEAL
Broiled Flounder, 4 ounces

Cooked Green Lima Beans, $^1/_2$ cup, with 1$^1/_2$ teaspoons reduced-calorie tub margarine

Steamed Spinach, 1 cup

Cherry Tomatoes, 6, with 1 tablespoon fat-free Italian dressing

Aspartame-Sweetened Strawberry-Banana Nonfat Yogurt, 1 cup

Unsweetened Citrus-Flavored Seltzer

MAIN MEAL
Cabbage Stuffed with Beef and Veal, 1 serving (see recipe)

Steamed Green Peas, $^1/_2$ cup, with $^1/_2$ cup steamed Diced Carrot and 1 teaspoon reduced-calorie tub margarine

Caesar Salad (In medium bowl, combine 2 cups torn Romaine lettuce leaves, $^1/_4$ cup packaged croutons and 1 tablespoon fat-free Caesar salad dressing.)

Kiwi Fruit, 1 medium

Sparkling Mineral Water

SNACK
Whole-Wheat Pretzels, 1$^1/_2$ ounces

This menu provides: 2 Milks, 3 Fats, 2 Fruits, 9$^3/_4$ Vegetables, 4$^1/_4$ Proteins, 5$^3/_4$ Breads, 30 Optional Calories.

Per serving: 24 g Fat, 30 g Fiber.

BREAKFAST

Apple, 1 small
Reduced-Calorie Rye Bread, 2 slices, toasted, with
   2 teaspoons grape jam
Skim Milk, $^3/_4$ cup
Coffee or Tea (optional)

LIGHT MEAL

Bean and Salsa Salad (In small bowl, combine
   6 ounces drained cooked red kidney beans,
   $^1/_2$ cup finely chopped red onion, $^1/_4$ cup mild,
   medium or hot salsa and 1 teaspoon fresh lime
   juice. Line plate with 8 lettuce leaves; top with
   bean mixture, 2 tablespoons nonfat sour cream
   and 1 tablespoon minced fresh cilantro.)
Nonfat Tortilla Chips, 1 ounce
Mango, $^1/_2$ small
Root Beer "Float" (In tall glass, combine 1 cup diet
   root beer and $^1/_3$ cup skim milk; add enough ice
   cubes to fill glass.)

MAIN MEAL

Eggplant Niçoise, 1 serving (see recipe)
Cooked Orzo Pasta, $^1/_2$ cup, with 1 tablespoon
   minced fresh flat-leaf parsley
Cucumber Slices, 1 cup, with $^1/_2$ cup plain nonfat
   yogurt and 1 teaspoon minced fresh dill
Baked Butternut Squash, $1^1/_2$ cups
Whole-Wheat Pita, 1 small (1 ounce), toasted, sprin-
   kled with 1 teaspoon olive oil and pinch garlic
   powder
Sugar-Free Chocolate Nonfat Frozen Yogurt, 4 fluid
   ounces
Mineral Water with Lime Wedge

SNACK

Rice Cake, 1, with 1 teaspoon peanut butter

This menu provides: 2 Milks, 3 Fats, 2 Fruits,
$11^1/_2$ Vegetables, 4 Proteins, 6 Breads, 110 Optional
Calories.

Per serving: 23 g Fat, 32 g Fiber.

37
EGGPLANT NIÇOISE

Makes 4 servings

2 medium eggplants
1 tablespoon olive oil
1 cup chopped onions
1 cup chopped green bell pepper
2 garlic cloves, minced
5 ounces lean ground beef (10% or less fat)
3 cups canned whole Italian tomatoes (no salt added), chopped
6 large or 10 small black olives, pitted and chopped
$1^1/_2$ teaspoons minced fresh oregano leaves or $^1/_2$ teaspoon dried
Freshly ground black pepper, to taste
1 tablespoon + 1 teaspoon freshly grated Parmesan cheese

1. Preheat oven to 400° F.

2. Cut eggplants lengthwise into halves. With serrated spoon, scoop out eggplant pulp, leaving $^1/_2$" shells. Chop pulp; set aside.

3. Place eggplant shells, cut-side down, onto nonstick baking sheet. Bake 10 minutes; turn shells over. Bake 10 minutes longer, until shells are just tender. Remove from oven; set aside. Leave oven on.

4. Meanwhile, in large nonstick skillet, heat oil; add onions, bell pepper and garlic. Cook over medium-high heat, stirring frequently, 5 minutes, until vegetables are softened. Add beef; cook, stirring to break up meat, 3–4 minutes, until no longer pink. Add tomatoes, olives, oregano, black pepper and reserved eggplant pulp; bring mixture to a boil. Reduce heat to low; simmer, covered, stirring frequently, 25–30 minutes, until mixture is thickened and flavors are blended.

5. Spoon one-fourth of beef mixture into each eggplant shell; sprinkle evenly with cheese. Bake 15 minutes, until slightly crispy. Serve warm or at room temperature.

Serving (1 stuffed eggplant half) provides: 1 Fat, $5^1/_2$ Vegetables, 1 Protein, 10 Optional Calories.

Per serving: 241 Calories, 9 g Total Fat, 2 g Saturated Fat, 23 mg Cholesterol, 425 mg Sodium, 32 g Total Carbohydrate, 7 g Dietary Fiber, 14 g Protein, 194 mg Calcium.

BEEF-STUFFED PEPPERS

Makes 4 servings

2 medium red bell peppers, halved and seeded
2 medium yellow bell peppers, halved and seeded
8 ounces lean ground beef (10% or less fat)
2 cups finely chopped tomatoes
1 cup finely chopped onions
1 cup finely chopped green bell pepper
3 egg whites
3 tablespoons plain dried bread crumbs
1/4 teaspoon salt
Freshly ground black pepper, to taste
1 cup tomato sauce (no salt added)
Fresh flat-leaf parsley sprigs, to garnish

1. Preheat oven to 400° F. Spray large shallow baking pan with nonstick cooking spray.

2. Place red and yellow bell pepper halves, cut-side up, in large microwavable baking dish with vented cover; microwave on Medium (70% power) 10 minutes, until tender. Uncover; let stand until cool.

3. Meanwhile, in medium bowl, combine beef, tomatoes, onions, green bell pepper, egg whites, bread crumbs, salt and black pepper.

4. Fill each cooked pepper half with an equal amount of beef mixture, pressing mixture down and, with fork, making decorative ridges into top of mixture. Place stuffed pepper halves, stuffed-side up, into prepared baking pan; bake 25–30 minutes, until beef mixture is lightly browned.

5. Pour tomato sauce over stuffed pepper halves; bake 15–20 minutes longer, until sauce is bubbling and browned around edges. Serve garnished with parsley.

Serving (2 stuffed pepper halves) provides: 5 Vegetables, 1 3/4 Proteins, 1/4 Bread.

Per serving: 217 Calories, 7 g Total Fat, 2 g Saturated Fat, 35 mg Cholesterol, 284 mg Sodium, 23 g Total Carbohydrate, 5 g Dietary Fiber, 18 g Protein, 37 mg Calcium.

BREAKFAST
Peach, 1 medium, sliced
Wheat Flakes Cereal, 3/4 ounce
Skim Milk, 1 cup
Coffee or Tea (optional)

LIGHT MEAL
Open-Face Tuna Melt (In small bowl, combine 3 ounces drained canned water-packed tuna, 1/2 cup finely chopped celery and 2 teaspoons reduced-calorie mayonnaise; spread onto 1 slice multi-grain toast. Top tuna with 1 slice nonfat process American cheese. Place onto nonstick baking sheet; broil 1 minute, until cheese is melted.)
Radishes, Cucumber Sticks and Cauliflower Florets, 1 cup *each*
Honeydew Balls, 1 cup
Mint Iced Tea

MAIN MEAL
Beef-Stuffed Peppers, 1 serving (see recipe)
Baked Potato, 1 (4 ounces), with 1 teaspoon freshly grated Parmesan cheese
Steamed Zucchini, 1 cup, with 2 teaspoons reduced-calorie tub margarine and 1 teaspoon dried basil
Sugar-Free Chocolate Nonfat Frozen Yogurt, 4 fluid ounces
Unsweetened Mandarin Orange–Flavored Seltzer

SNACK
Graham Crackers, 3 (2 1/2" squares)
"Hot Toddy" (In small saucepan, combine 3/4 cup skim milk and 2 teaspoons reduced-calorie tub margarine; bring just to a boil. Remove from heat; stir in sugar substitute to equal 2 teaspoons sugar.)

This menu provides: 2 Milks, 3 Fats, 2 Fruits, 14 Vegetables, 3 3/4 Proteins, 4 1/4 Breads, 60 Optional Calories.

Per serving: 24 g Fat, 27 g Fiber.

39

BEEF AND SPINACH ROLLS

*This easy entrée looks beautiful and tastes wonderful—
a perfect dish to serve to company.*

Makes 4 servings

9 ounces lean boneless beef sirloin
3 cups packed trimmed, washed and dried fresh spinach leaves
$^1/_4$ teaspoon salt
Pinch freshly ground black pepper
$^3/_4$ ounce freshly grated Parmesan cheese

1. Preheat oven to 350° F.

2. Slice beef horizontally almost all the way through; spread open butterfly fashion. Place beef between 2 sheets of wax paper; with meat mallet or bottom of heavy saucepan, gently pound until very thin. Remove and discard wax paper; set beef aside.

3. In large nonstick skillet, heat 2 tablespoons water; add spinach. Cook over medium-high heat, stirring occasionally, until wilted. Drain, discarding liquid; set spinach aside to cool.

4. Sprinkle beef on both sides with salt and pepper; place onto work surface. Sprinkle beef evenly with cheese; top with cooled spinach. Starting from shortest end, roll beef to enclose filling.

5. Place medium cast-iron skillet over medium-high heat; add beef roll, seam-side down. Cook, turning as needed, 1 minute, until browned on all sides. Transfer skillet to oven; bake 15 minutes, until cooked through. Remove from oven; let stand 5 minutes.

6. Slice beef roll crosswise into 12 equal pieces; arrange on serving platter.

Serving (3 slices) provides: $1^1/_2$ Vegetables, 2 Proteins.

Per serving: 121 Calories, 5 g Total Fat, 2 g Saturated Fat, 43 mg Cholesterol, 321 mg Sodium, 2 g Total Carbohydrate, 2 g Dietary Fiber, 18 g Protein, 141 mg Calcium.

BEEF WITH ASPARAGUS AND CHERRY TOMATOES

This is a quick and very colorful meal; for a change of pace, substitute sugar snap peas or green beans for the asparagus.

Makes 4 servings

24 asparagus spears, cut diagonally into $^1/_2$" pieces
10 ounces lean boneless beef sirloin, cut into $^1/_4$" strips
$^1/_2$ teaspoon salt
$^1/_4$ teaspoon freshly ground black pepper
$^1/_2$ cup diagonally sliced scallions ($^1/_2$" slices)
1 garlic clove, very thinly sliced
24 cherry tomatoes

1. In large nonstick skillet, combine asparagus and $^1/_4$ cup water; bring liquid to a boil. Reduce heat to low; simmer 2 minutes, until asparagus are just tender and water is evaporated.

2. Sprinkle beef on all sides with salt and pepper; add beef, scallions and garlic to cooked asparagus. Cook, stirring frequently, 4 minutes, until beef is cooked through. Add tomatoes; cook, stirring frequently, 2 minutes, until tomatoes are heated through.

Serving ($^1/_4$ of mixture) provides: $2^1/_4$ Vegetables, 2 Proteins.

Per serving: 129 Calories, 4 g Total Fat, 1 g Saturated Fat, 43 mg Cholesterol, 324 mg Sodium, 7 g Total Carbohydrate, 2 g Dietary Fiber, 18 g Protein, 39 mg Calcium.

BREAKFAST
Raspberries, $^3/_4$ cup
Bagel, $^1/_2$ small (1 ounce), toasted, with 1 teaspoon reduced-calorie tub margarine
Skim Milk, 1 cup
Coffee or Tea (optional)

LIGHT MEAL
Chef's Salad (In medium bowl, combine 2 cups shredded iceberg lettuce, 1 ounce skinless boneless cooked turkey breast, sliced, 1 hard-cooked egg, sliced, $^1/_4$ cup *each* red bell pepper strips, sliced radishes and packaged croutons and 1 tablespoon fat-free ranch dressing.)
Roll, 1 ounce, with 1 teaspoon reduced-calorie tub margarine
Cherries, 12 large
Diet Lemonade, 1 cup

MAIN MEAL
Beef with Asparagus and Cherry Tomatoes, 1 serving (see recipe)
Cooked Brown Rice, 1 cup
Tossed Green Salad, 2 cups, with Ginger Vinaigrette (In small jar with tight-fitting lid or small bowl, combine 2 teaspoons rice wine vinegar, 1 teaspoon vegetable oil and $^1/_2$ teaspoon minced pared fresh ginger root; cover and shake well or, with wire whisk, blend until combined.)
Reduced-Calorie Butterscotch-Flavored Pudding (made with skim milk), $^1/_2$ cup
Iced Tea

SNACK
Plain Popcorn, hot-air popped, 3 cups, with 1 teaspoon reduced-calorie tub margarine, melted
Skim Milk, $^1/_2$ cup

This menu provides: 2 Milks, 3 Fats, 2 Fruits, $11^1/_4$ Vegetables, 4 Proteins, $5^1/_2$ Breads, 65 Optional Calories.

Per serving: 27 g Fat, 20 g Fiber.

BREAKFAST

Banana, $^1/_2$ medium
Cooked Oatmeal, $^1/_2$ cup
Pumpernickel Bagel, $^1/_2$ (1 ounce), toasted, with
    1 teaspoon reduced-calorie tub margarine
Skim Milk, $^3/_4$ cup
Coffee or Tea (optional)

LIGHT MEAL

Tuna-Pasta Salad (In medium bowl, combine $^1/_2$ cup
    cooked shell macaroni, 2 ounces drained canned
    water-packed white tuna, 6 cherry tomatoes,
    halved, $^1/_4$ cup diced red onion and 1 tablespoon
    fat-free Italian dressing.)
Carrot and Celery Sticks, 1 cup *each*
Whole-Wheat Roll, 1 ounce, with 1 teaspoon
    reduced-calorie tub margarine
Peach, 1 medium
Iced Tea

MAIN MEAL

Tournedos of Beef, Hunter's Style, 1 serving (see
    recipe)
Grilled Sliced Potatoes, 4 ounces, with 3 tablespoons
    plain nonfat yogurt
Cooked Broccoli, 4 spears
Cooked Sliced Yellow Squash, 1 cup
Torn Iceberg and Green Leaf Lettuce Leaves, 2 cups,
    with 4 tomato wedges, $^1/_4$ cup sliced red onion
    and 1 teaspoon *each* olive oil and red wine
    vinegar
Low-Calorie Lime-Flavored Gelatin, $^1/_2$ cup
Sparkling Mineral Water

SNACK

Aspartame-Sweetened Nonfat Strawberry Yogurt,
    1 cup

This menu provides: 2 Milks, 3 Fats, 2 Fruits,
17 Vegetables, $3^1/_4$ Proteins, 6 Breads, 45 Optional
Calories.

Per serving: 28 g Fat, 25 g Fiber.

41
TOURNEDOS OF BEEF, HUNTER'S STYLE

*We've cut fat substantially by wrapping the fillets
with lean ham instead of the traditional bacon.*

Makes 4 servings

Four 3-ounce beef tournedos (small
    boneless beef tenderloin steaks)
I ounce lean boiled ham, cut into
    four 6 × $^3/_4$" strips
Four I-ounce slices French bread
    (without crust), toasted
I garlic clove, cut
I tablespoon + I teaspoon stick
    margarine
3 cups sliced mushrooms
I cup chopped shallots
8 fresh thyme sprigs, chopped, or
    $^1/_2$ teaspoon dried
4 fluid ounces ($^1/_2$ cup) dry red
    wine
$^1/_2$ cup low-sodium chicken broth
Freshly ground black pepper, to
    taste
Fresh thyme sprigs, to garnish

1. Wrap each tournedo around its circumference with 1 ham strip; secure
with kitchen string.

2. Rub both sides of each toast slice with cut side of garlic; set aside.

3. In large nonstick skillet, melt 2 teaspoons of the margarine; add mushrooms, shallots and chopped thyme. Cook over medium-high heat, stirring constantly, 5–8 minutes, until vegetables are tender. Remove
vegetables from skillet; set aside.

4. In same skillet, cook beef, turning as needed, 5–8 minutes, until
browned on both sides. Remove beef from skillet; set aside.

5. In same skillet, combine wine and broth; cook, scraping up browned
bits from bottom of pan, until liquid has reduced in volume to about
$^1/_2$ cup. Add remaining 2 teaspoons margarine, swirling skillet until margarine is melted and mixture is slightly thickened.

6. Return mushroom mixture and browned beef to skillet; cook, turning
beef occasionally, 5–9 minutes, until beef is done to taste.

7. Set 1 toast slice onto each of 4 plates. Place 1 cooked tournedo onto
each toast slice; top each with one-fourth of the mushroom mixture.
Sprinkle with pepper; serve garnished with thyme sprigs.

Serving (1 toast slice, 1 tournedo, $^3/_4$ cup mushroom mixture) provides: 1 Fat,
2 Vegetables, 2 $^1/_4$ Proteins, 1 Bread, 30 Optional Calories.

Per serving: 309 Calories, 11 g Total Fat, 3 g Saturated Fat, 51 mg Cholesterol,
361 mg Sodium, 25 g Total Carbohydrate, 2 g Dietary Fiber, 23 g Protein,
54 mg Calcium.

STEAK FRITES

Makes 4 servings

1 pound 4 ounces all-purpose potatoes, pared and cut into ¼" sticks
½ teaspoon freshly ground black pepper
¼ teaspoon salt
Four 3-ounce lean boneless beef sirloin steaks (1" thick)
¼ cup steak sauce
½ cup minced shallots
4 garlic cloves, minced
Fresh flat-leaf parsley sprigs, to garnish

1. Preheat oven to 450° F. Spray nonstick baking sheet with nonstick cooking spray.

2. Place potato sticks in a single layer onto prepared baking sheet; sprinkle evenly with ¼ teaspoon of the pepper and the salt. Bake, turning potato sticks occasionally with spatula, 12–15 minutes, until crisp and golden brown. Transfer potatoes to large serving platter; keep warm.

3. Increase oven temperature to broil. Spray rack in broiler pan with nonstick cooking spray.

4. Brush one side of steaks with half the steak sauce; place onto prepared rack, brushed-side up. Broil 4" from heat 4 minutes.

5. Turn steaks over; brush with remaining steak sauce. With fork, press shallots, garlic and remaining ¼ teaspoon pepper into steaks; broil 3 minutes, until steaks are cooked through.

6. Place steaks onto serving platter with potatoes; garnish with parsley.

Serving (1 steak, 4 ounces potato) provides: ¼ Vegetable, 2 Proteins, 1 Bread, 20 Optional Calories.

Per serving: 259 Calories, 5 g Total Fat, 2 g Saturated Fat, 50 mg Cholesterol, 434 mg Sodium, 33 g Total Carbohydrate, 3 g Dietary Fiber, 21 g Protein, 31 mg Calcium.

BREAKFAST
Raisins, 2 tablespoons
Bran Flakes Cereal, ¾ ounce
Skim Milk, ½ cup
Coffee or Tea (optional)

LIGHT MEAL
Taco-Bean Salad (In medium bowl, combine 2 cups torn Romaine lettuce leaves, 1 cup chopped red and green bell peppers, ½ cup *each* cooked corn kernels and chopped onion and 2 ounces drained cooked black beans. In small jar with tight-fitting lid or small bowl, combine 1 teaspoon *each* vegetable oil, cider vinegar and fresh orange and lemon juices, ½ teaspoon prepared mustard, ½ garlic clove, minced, and ¼ teaspoon ground cumin; cover and shake well or, with wire whisk, blend until combined. Pour over lettuce mixture; toss to combine. Top with ¼ cup mild, medium or hot salsa and 1 ounce broken nonfat tortilla chips.)
Creamy Cucumber Rounds (In small bowl, combine 1 cup cucumber slices, 2 tablespoons nonfat sour cream and 1 tablespoon fresh minced herbs.)
Diet Ginger Ale

MAIN MEAL
Steak Frites, 1 serving (see recipe)
Tomato and Asparagus Salad (In small jar with tight-fitting lid or small bowl, combine 1 teaspoon *each* olive oil and balsamic and red wine or cider vinegars and ½ teaspoon dried herbs; cover and shake well or, with wire whisk, blend until combined. Pour over 1 cup *each* sliced tomatoes and cooked cut asparagus.)
Herbed French Bread (Drizzle 1-ounce slice toasted French bread with 1 teaspoon olive oil; sprinkle with 1 teaspoon minced fresh flat-leaf parsley.)
Fresh Raspberry Coupe (In stemmed glass, layer ¾ cup raspberries and 1 cup aspartame-sweetened vanilla nonfat yogurt.)
Sparkling Mineral Water

SNACK
Decaffeinated Cappuccino, made with skim milk, 5 fluid ounces

This menu provides: 2 Milks, 3 Fats, 2 Fruits, 14¼ Vegetables, 3 Proteins, 5 Breads, 45 Optional Calories.

Per serving: 25 g Fat, 29 g Fiber.

GRILLED MARINATED LONDON BROIL

The piquant flavor in this aromatic entrée comes from three different types of vinegar.

Makes 4 servings

$^1/_2$ cup finely chopped onion

$^1/_4$ cup sherry vinegar

2 fluid ounces ($^1/_4$ cup) dry red wine

2 tablespoons low-sodium soy sauce

4 garlic cloves, coarsely chopped

1 tablespoon balsamic vinegar

2 teaspoons olive oil

Sugar substitute to equal 1 tablespoon + 1 teaspoon sugar

1 teaspoon grated pared fresh ginger root

Freshly ground black pepper, to taste

15 ounces lean boneless beef bottom round steak (1" thick)

8 medium scallions (white portion with some green)

1. In small bowl, with wire whisk, combine onion, sherry and red wine vinegars, soy sauce, garlic, balsamic vinegar, oil, sweetener, ginger and pepper. Transfer to gallon-size sealable plastic bag; add steak. Seal bag, squeezing out air; turn to coat steak. Refrigerate 4 hours, turning bag after 2 hours.

2. Drain marinade into small saucepan; bring to a boil. Remove from heat.

3. Spray rack in broiler pan with nonstick cooking spray. Preheat broiler.

4. Place steak onto prepared rack in broiler pan; broil 4" from heat, turning once and basting with reserved marinade, 5–10 minutes, until beef is done to taste. Let stand 5 minutes; thinly slice.

5. Arrange steak on serving platter; serve with scallions.

Serving (3 ounces steak, 2 scallions) provides: $^1/_2$ Vegetable, 3 Proteins, 35 Optional Calories.

Per serving: 217 Calories, 9 g Total Fat, 2 g Saturated Fat, 66 mg Cholesterol, 360 mg Sodium, 6 g Total Carbohydrate, 1 g Dietary Fiber, 26 g Protein, 27 mg Calcium.

BREAKFAST
Strawberries, 1 cup
Raisin Bran Cereal, $^3/_4$ ounce
Skim Milk, $^1/_2$ cup
Reduced-Calorie Wheat Bread, 2 slices, toasted, with 2 teaspoons reduced-calorie tub margarine
Coffee or Tea (optional)

LIGHT MEAL
Turkey Sandwich (Layer 2 ounces skinless boneless roast turkey breast, sliced, $^1/_2$ medium tomato, sliced, $^1/_2$ cup arugula leaves, 2 teaspoons reduced-calorie mayonnaise and 1 teaspoon prepared mustard between 2 slices reduced-calorie rye bread.)
Cucumber and Carrot Sticks, 1 cup each
Graham Crackers, 3 (2 $^1/_2$" squares)
Skim Milk, 1 cup

MAIN MEAL
Grilled Marinated London Broil, 1 serving (see recipe)
Baked Potato, 8 ounces, with 2 teaspoons reduced-calorie tub margarine
Steamed Asparagus, 6 spears
Spinach Salad (In medium bowl, combine 2 cups torn spinach leaves, 2 teaspoons balsamic vinegar and 1 teaspoon imitation bacon bits.)
Honeydew Melon, 2" wedge
Decaffeinated Cappuccino, made with skim milk, 5 fluid ounces

SNACK
Frozen Fruit Pop, 1 bar

This menu provides: 2 Milks, 3 Fats, 2 Fruits, 11$^1/_2$ Vegetables, 5 Proteins, 6 Breads, 90 Optional Calories.

Per serving: 28 g Fat, 30 g Fiber.

GRILLED TERIYAKI STEAK

This is a quick and easy way to spice up a grilled steak.

Makes 4 servings

$^1/_4$ cup reduced-sodium soy sauce
$^1/_2$ fluid ounce (1 tablespoon) dry white wine
1 tablespoon rice wine vinegar
1 teaspoon honey
$^1/_2$ teaspoon dry mustard
$^1/_2$ teaspoon freshly ground black pepper
10 ounces lean boneless beef sirloin

1. Spray rack in broiler pan with nonstick cooking spray. Preheat broiler.

2. In small bowl, combine soy sauce, wine, vinegar, honey, mustard and pepper; brush beef on both sides with some of the soy sauce mixture.

3. Place beef onto prepared rack in broiler pan; broil 4" from heat, turning once and brushing frequently with remaining soy sauce mixture, 14 minutes, until cooked through. Transfer beef to cutting board; slice thinly.

Serving (2 ounces) provides: 2 Proteins, 10 Optional Calories.

Per serving: 130 Calories, 4 g Total Fat, 2 g Saturated Fat, 50 mg Cholesterol, 638 mg Sodium, 3 g Total Carbohydrate, 0 g Dietary Fiber, 18 g Protein, 11 mg Calcium.

45

BROILED STEAK WITH SHALLOT SAUCE

This easy and elegant sauce can be made in the few minutes it takes to cook the steak.

Makes 4 servings

10 ounces lean boneless beef sirloin
$^1/_4$ teaspoon salt
2 teaspoons reduced-calorie tub margarine
2 tablespoons minced shallots
$^1/_4$ cup red wine vinegar
$^1/_4$ cup low-sodium beef broth
2 teaspoons Worcestershire sauce
$^1/_4$ teaspoon freshly ground black pepper
1 teaspoon arrowroot, dissolved in 1 tablespoon water

1. Spray rack in broiler pan with nonstick cooking spray. Preheat broiler.

2. Sprinkle beef on all sides with salt. Place beef onto prepared rack; broil, turning once, 14 minutes, until cooked through.

3. Meanwhile, to prepare shallot sauce, in small saucepan, melt margarine; add shallots. Cook over medium-high heat, stirring frequently, 2–3 minutes, until softened. Stir in vinegar, broth, Worcestershire sauce and pepper; bring liquid to a boil. Reduce heat to low; simmer, stirring frequently, 2 minutes. With wire whisk, stir in dissolved arrowroot; continuing to stir, simmer 30 seconds, until mixture is thickened.

4. Transfer beef to cutting board; slice thinly. Arrange beef slices on serving platter; top with shallot sauce.

Serving (2 ounces beef, 2 tablespoons sauce) provides: $^1/_4$ Fat, 2 Proteins, 5 Optional Calories.

Per serving: 130 Calories, 5 g Total Fat, 2 g Saturated Fat, 50 mg Cholesterol, 223 mg Sodium, 3 g Total Carbohydrate, 0 g Dietary Fiber, 18 g Protein, 10 mg Calcium.

BREAKFAST
Raisins, 2 tablespoons
Cornflakes, $^3/_4$ ounce
Skim Milk, $^1/_2$ cup
Reduced-Calorie Rye Bread, 2 slices, toasted, with 2 teaspoons reduced-calorie tub margarine
Coffee or Tea (optional)

LIGHT MEAL
Tuna-Rice Salad (In medium bowl, combine $^1/_2$ cup *each* cooked brown rice and chopped celery, 2 ounces drained canned water-packed tuna and 1 tablespoon *each* minced chives and fat-free Italian dressing.)
Jicama and Carrot Sticks, 1 cup *each*
Tomato, 1 medium, sliced, with 1 tablespoon minced fresh basil and 1 teaspoon balsamic vinegar
Breadsticks, 2 long
Unsweetened Mandarin Orange–Flavored Seltzer

MAIN MEAL
Artichoke Soup (In food processor or blender, combine 1 cup low-sodium chicken broth, $^1/_2$ cup drained canned artichoke hearts, 2 tablespoons minced fresh flat-leaf parsley and 1 tablespoon fresh lemon juice; purée until smooth. Transfer to small saucepan; heat.)
Broiled Steak with Shallot Sauce, 1 serving (see recipe)
Boiled New Potatoes, 8 ounces, with 2 teaspoons reduced-calorie tub margarine
Steamed Green Beans, 1 cup, with 1$^1/_2$ teaspoons reduced-calorie tub margarine
Reduced-Calorie Butterscotch-Flavored Pudding (made with skim milk), $^1/_2$ cup
Iced Tea

SNACK
Chocolate-Banana Shake (In blender, combine $^1/_2$ medium banana, sliced, $^2/_3$ cup cold water, 3 ice cubes and 1 packet reduced-calorie chocolate flavor dairy shake mix; purée until smooth and thick.)

This menu provides: 2 Milks, 3 Fats, 2 Fruits, 10 Vegetables, 3 Proteins, 6 Breads, 70 Optional Calories.

Per serving: 25 g Fat, 21 g Fiber.

46
SLICED STEAK WITH SPRING VEGETABLES

*This is a delicious "no-fuss" meal; enjoy it year 'round
by changing the vegetables to fit the season.*

Makes 4 servings

1 cup baby carrots
24 asparagus spears, cut into 2" pieces
1 cup sugar snap peas
1 cup halved small red radishes
$^1/_4$ teaspoon salt
$^1/_4$ teaspoon freshly ground black pepper
1 tablespoon + 1 teaspoon reduced-calorie tub margarine
1 tablespoon fresh lemon juice
10 ounces lean boneless beef sirloin

1. Preheat broiler. Spray rack in broiler pan with nonstick cooking spray.

2. In nonstick skillet, bring $^1/_2$ cup water to a boil; add carrots. Reduce heat to medium; cook, covered, 6 minutes, until just tender. Add asparagus, peas and radishes; cook, covered, 4 minutes. Remove cover; cook 2 minutes, until water is evaporated.

3. Sprinkle vegetables with half of the salt and half of the pepper. Add margarine and juice; toss until margarine is melted and vegetables are coated.

4. Sprinkle beef on both sides with remaining salt and pepper; place onto prepared rack. Broil, turning once, 14 minutes, until cooked through.

5. Transfer beef to cutting board; slice thinly. Arrange beef slices on serving platter; surround with vegetable mixture.

Serving (2 ounces beef, $1^1/_4$ cups vegetable mixture) provides: $^1/_2$ Fat, $2^1/_2$ Vegetables, 2 Proteins.

Per serving: 183 Calories, 6 g Total Fat, 2 g Saturated Fat, 50 mg Cholesterol, 263 mg Sodium, 11 g Total Carbohydrate, 4 g Dietary Fiber, 21 g Protein, 63 mg Calcium.

MIDDLE EASTERN BEEF BROCHETTES

Makes 4 servings

$^3/_4$ cup plain nonfat yogurt

3 tablespoons minced fresh mint leaves

1 tablespoon minced fresh oregano leaves, or 1 teaspoon dried

1 teaspoon grated lemon zest*

1 tablespoon fresh lemon juice

1 teaspoon ground cumin

$^3/_4$ teaspoon salt

$^3/_4$ teaspoon freshly ground black pepper

1 garlic clove, minced

10 ounces lean boneless beef loin, cut into 16 equal cubes

1 medium yellow squash, sliced into 8 equal pieces

8 small white onions

1 medium zucchini, sliced into 8 equal pieces

$^1/_4$ medium eggplant, pared and cut into 8 cubes

8 cherry tomatoes

1. Spray rack in broiler pan with nonstick cooking spray. Preheat broiler.

2. In medium bowl, combine $^1/_2$ cup of the yogurt, 2 tablespoons of the mint, the oregano, zest, juice, cumin, salt, pepper and garlic. Add beef, squash, onions, zucchini, eggplant and tomatoes; toss to coat. Let stand 15 minutes.

3. Thread alternately, onto each of 8 long metal skewers, 2 beef cubes, 1 squash piece, 1 onion, 1 zucchini piece, 1 eggplant cube and 1 tomato; discard remaining yogurt mixture. Place skewers onto prepared rack; broil 4" from heat, turning once, 8 minutes, until beef is cooked through and vegetables are lightly browned.

4. Place 2 filled skewers onto each of 4 plates; gently remove beef and vegetables from skewers. Serve each portion topped with 1 remaining tablespoon yogurt; sprinkle evenly with remaining mint.

Serving (2 skewers) provides: $2^3/_4$ Vegetables, 2 Proteins, 25 Optional Calories.

Per serving: 180 Calories, 4 g Total Fat, 1 g Saturated Fat, 44 mg Cholesterol, 500 mg Sodium, 18 g Total Carbohydrate, 3 g Dietary Fiber, 20 g Protein, 158 mg Calcium.

The zest of the lemon is the peel without any of the pith (white membrane). To remove zest from lemon, use a zester or the fine side of a vegetable grater.

BREAKFAST
Blackberries, $^3/_4$ cup
Frozen Pancakes, 2, heated, with 1 tablespoon maple syrup and 1 teaspoon reduced-calorie tub margarine
Skim Milk, 1 cup
Coffee or Tea (optional)

LIGHT MEAL
Nonfat Cottage Cheese, 1 cup, with $^1/_2$ cup cubed tomato and 2 teaspoons minced fresh dill
Red Bell Pepper Strips and Celery Sticks, 1 cup *each*
English Muffin, $^1/_2$ (1 ounce), with 1 teaspoon reduced-calorie tub margarine
Pear, 1 small
Iced Herbal Tea

MAIN MEAL
Middle Eastern Beef Brochettes, 1 serving (see recipe)
Steamed Spinach, 1 cup, with 1 teaspoon *each* olive oil and balsamic vinegar
Green 'n' Bean Salad (In medium bowl, combine 2 cups mixed salad greens, 2 ounces drained cooked white beans, 10 small Greek olives and 1 tablespoon fat-free Italian dressing
Whole-Wheat Pita, 1 large (2 ounces)
Reduced-Calorie Vanilla-Flavored Pudding (made with skim milk), $^1/_2$ cup
Decaffeinated Coffee or Tea

SNACK
Vanilla "Egg Cream" (In tall glass, combine 1 cup diet cream soda and $^1/_2$ cup skim milk.)

This menu provides: 2 Milks, 3 Fats, 2 Fruits, $13^3/_4$ Vegetables, 5 Proteins, 5 Breads, 115 Optional Calories.

Per serving: 30 g Fat, 28 g Fiber.

48
MEDITERRANEAN LAMB STEW

This wonderful and hearty stew has lots of vegetables. As with most stews, it tastes even better the next day. Make it the day before and refrigerate; simply reheat when needed.

Makes 4 servings

1 tablespoon + 1 teaspoon all-purpose flour
$^1/_4$ teaspoon salt
$^1/_4$ teaspoon freshly ground black pepper
10 ounces lean boneless loin of lamb, cut into 1" cubes
1 tablespoon + 1 teaspoon vegetable oil
1 cup chopped onions
2 cups quartered white mushrooms
1 tablespoon minced fresh oregano leaves or $^1/_2$ teaspoon dried
1 teaspoon grated lemon zest*
1 garlic clove, minced
1 cup pearl onions
1 cup frozen cut okra
1 cup cubed eggplant
1 cup tomato sauce (no salt added)
$^1/_2$ cup low-sodium beef broth
2 tablespoons minced fresh flat-leaf parsley

1. On sheet of wax paper or paper plate, combine flour, salt and pepper; add lamb, turning to coat evenly.

2. In large saucepan, heat oil; add lamb. Cook over medium-high heat, stirring frequently, 4 minutes, until lamb is browned on all sides. Add chopped onions; cook, stirring frequently, 5 minutes, until onions are softened.

3. Reduce heat to medium-low; add mushrooms, oregano, zest and garlic. Cook, stirring constantly, 1 minute, until mushrooms begin to release their liquid. Add pearl onions, okra, eggplant, tomato sauce and broth; cook, covered, stirring occasionally, 40 minutes, until lamb is cooked through and tender. Stir in parsley.

Serving ($1^1/_4$ cups) provides: 1 Fat, 4 Vegetables, 2 Proteins, 15 Optional Calories.

Per serving: 238 Calories, 9 g Total Fat, 2 g Saturated Fat, 47 mg Cholesterol, 215 mg Sodium, 21 g Total Carbohydrate, 4 g Dietary Fiber, 19 g Protein, 94 mg Calcium.

The zest of the lemon is the peel without any of the pith (white membrane). To remove zest from lemon, use a zester or the fine side of a vegetable grater; wrap lemon in plastic wrap and refrigerate for use at another time.

49

INDIVIDUAL SHEPHERD'S PIES

Makes 4 servings

1 pound 4 ounces all-purpose potatoes, pared and quartered
2 tablespoons skim milk
$^1/_2$ teaspoon salt
$^1/_4$ teaspoon freshly ground black
  pepper
1 tablespoon + 1 teaspoon
  reduced-calorie tub margarine,
  melted

1 cup diced onions
$^1/_2$ cup diced red bell pepper
$^1/_2$ cup diced zucchini
10 ounces lean ground lamb
$^1/_2$ teaspoon dried rosemary leaves
$^1/_4$ teaspoon garlic powder

1. Preheat oven to 400° F. Spray four 1-cup baking dishes with nonstick cooking spray.

2. Place potatoes into large pot; add water to cover. Bring liquid to a boil; reduce heat to low. Simmer 15 minutes, until potatoes are tender. Drain, discarding liquid; return potatoes to pot.

3. With electric hand mixer or potato masher, roughly mash potatoes. Add milk, $^1/_4$ teaspoon of the salt and half of the black pepper; mash until as smooth as possible. Set aside.

4. In large nonstick skillet, combine 1 tablespoon of the margarine, onions and bell pepper. Cook over medium-high heat, stirring frequently, 5 minutes, until vegetables are softened. Add zucchini; cook, stirring, 1 minute, until zucchini is softened. Set aside.

5. In large bowl, combine lamb, rosemary, garlic powder, remaining $^1/_4$ teaspoon salt and remaining black pepper.

6. In medium nonstick skillet, cook lamb mixture, stirring to break up meat, 4–5 minutes, until no longer pink; remove from heat. Spoon one-fourth of the lamb mixture into each prepared baking dish; sprinkle evenly with reserved vegetable mixture. Spread one-fourth of the potato mixture over each portion of vegetables; drizzle evenly with remaining margarine. Bake 30 minutes, until heated through and potato topping is lightly browned.

Serving (1 pie) provides: $^1/_2$ Fat, 1 Vegetable, 2 Proteins, 1 Bread, 5 Optional Calories.

Per serving: 257 Calories, 7 g Total Fat, 2 g Saturated Fat, 47 mg Cholesterol, 374 mg Sodium, 31 g Total Carbohydrate, 3 g Dietary Fiber, 18 g Protein, 46 mg Calcium.

BREAKFAST
Orange and Grapefruit Sections, $^1/_2$ cup
Bagel, $^1/_2$ small (1 ounce), with 1 teaspoon *each*
  reduced-calorie tub margarine and peach jam
Skim Milk, 1 cup
Coffee or Tea (optional)

LIGHT MEAL
Broiled Ham and Cheese (Toast 2 slices reduced-
  calorie whole-wheat bread; layer $^1/_2$ ounce thinly
  sliced cooked ham, 2 tomato slices and 1 slice
  nonfat process American cheese onto each toast
  slice. Place onto nonstick baking sheet; broil until
  heated.)
Bean Salad (In small bowl, combine $^1/_2$ cup *each*
  steamed green beans, sugar snap peas and wax
  beans and 1 tablespoon fat-free Italian dressing.)
Pear, 1 small
Diet Lemon-Lime Soda

MAIN MEAL
Individual Shepherd's Pies, 1 serving (see recipe)
Steamed Cauliflower Florets, 1 cup, with 1 teaspoon
  reduced-calorie tub margarine and pinch grated
  lemon zest
Tossed Green Salad, 2 cups, with $^1/_4$ cup *each* sliced
  radishes and red bell pepper and 1$^1/_2$ teaspoons
  Thousand Island dressing
Roll, 1 ounce, with 1 teaspoon reduced-calorie tub
  margarine
Aspartame-Sweetened Strawberry-Banana Nonfat
  Yogurt, 1 cup
Sparkling Mineral Water

SNACK
Oat-Bran Pretzels, 1$^1/_2$ ounces

This menu provides: 2 Milks, 3 Fats, 2 Fruits,
12 Vegetables, 4 Proteins, 6 Breads, 25 Optional
Calories.

Per serving: 25 g Fat, 27 g Fiber.

5 0
FUSILLI WITH LAMB, VEGETABLES AND CHEESE

Makes 4 servings

6 ounces fusilli pasta
1 cup chopped onions
2 garlic cloves, minced
5 ounces lean ground lamb
4 large or 8 small plum tomatoes, chopped
1 tablespoon fresh lemon juice
$^1/_2$ teaspoon dried oregano leaves
$^1/_2$ teaspoon dried thyme leaves
Pinch salt
Freshly ground black pepper, to taste
2 cups warm cooked chopped spinach
3 ounces feta cheese, crumbled

1. In large pot of boiling water, cook fusilli 12 minutes, until tender. Drain, discarding liquid; place into serving bowl. Keep warm.

2. Meanwhile, spray medium nonstick skillet with nonstick cooking spray; heat. Add onions and garlic; cook over medium-high heat, stirring frequently, 6–7 minutes, until onions are golden brown. Add lamb; cook, stirring to break up meat, 3–4 minutes, until no longer pink. Reduce heat to low; add tomatoes, juice, oregano, thyme, salt and pepper. Cook, stirring occasionally, 5 minutes, until tomatoes are soft.

3. Add spinach to warm fusilli; toss to combine. Top fusilli mixture with lamb mixture; sprinkle with cheese.

Serving (2 cups) provides: $2^1/_2$ Vegetables, 2 Proteins, 2 Breads.

Per serving: 318 Calories, 8 g Total Fat, 4 g Saturated Fat, 42 mg Cholesterol, 367 mg Sodium, 43 g Total Carbohydrate, 4 g Dietary Fiber, 19 g Protein, 260 mg Calcium.

LAMB CHOPS WITH MINT GLAZE

Lamb chops and mint are the perfect match! Here, the flavors team up to make a simple yet elegant dinner entrée.

Makes 4 servings

¹/₂ cup distilled white vinegar
2 tablespoons minced fresh mint leaves
1 tablespoon mint jelly
Four 3-ounce rib lamb chops
¹/₄ teaspoon salt
¹/₄ teaspoon freshly ground black pepper

1. Spray rack in broiler pan with nonstick cooking spray. Preheat broiler.

2. To prepare mint glaze, in mini–food processor, combine vinegar, mint and mint jelly; purée until smooth.

3. Transfer vinegar mixture to small saucepan; bring to a boil. Reduce heat to low; simmer 5 minutes, until slightly syrupy.

4. Sprinkle lamb chops on both sides with salt and pepper; place onto prepared rack. Spread twice with some of the mint glaze; broil 4" from heat 2 minutes. Turn chops over. Spread lamb twice with some of the remaining mint glaze; broil 2–3 minutes, until cooked through.

5. Transfer each lamb chop to plate; top evenly with remaining mint glaze.

Serving (1 lamb chop, 2 teaspoons mint glaze topping) provides: 2 Proteins, 10 Optional Calories.

Per serving: 150 Calories, 7 g Total Fat, 3 g Saturated Fat, 52 mg Cholesterol, 185 mg Sodium, 5 g Total Carbohydrate, 0 g Dietary Fiber, 16 g Protein, 12 mg Calcium.

BREAKFAST
Orange Sections, ¹/₂ cup
Frozen Pancakes, 2, heated, with 2 teaspoons maple syrup
Skim Milk, 1 cup
Coffee or Tea (optional)

LIGHT MEAL
Shrimp Salad (In small bowl, combine 2 ounces peeled and deveined cooked shrimp, chopped, 2 teaspoons reduced-calorie mayonnaise and 1 teaspoon *each* fresh lemon juice and minced fresh dill.)
Carrot and Celery Sticks, 1 cup *each*
Watercress Leaves, 2 cups, with 6 cherry tomatoes, 1 cup sliced cucumber and 1 tablespoon fat-free Italian dressing
Roll, 1 ounce, with 1 teaspoon reduced-calorie tub margarine
Iced Decaffeinated Cappuccino, made with skim milk, 5 fluid ounces

MAIN MEAL
Lamb Chops with Mint Glaze, 1 serving (see recipe)
Steamed Wild Rice, ¹/₂ cup
Steamed Snow Peas, 1 cup, with ¹/₄ cup drained canned sliced water chestnuts
Tossed Green Salad, 2 cups, with ¹/₄ cup packaged croutons and 1 teaspoon *each* olive oil and red wine vinegar
Vanilla Pudding Parfait (In stemmed glass, layer ¹/₂ cup reduced-calorie vanilla-flavored pudding [made with skim milk] and 2 tablespoons graham cracker crumbs; top with 1 tablespoon thawed frozen light whipped topping [8 calories per tablespoon].)
Decaffeinated Coffee or Tea

SNACK
Frozen Seedless Green Grapes, 20 small or 12 large

This menu provides: 2 Milks, 3 Fats, 2 Fruits, 17 Vegetables, 3 Proteins, 5¹/₂ Breads, 95 Optional Calories.

Per serving: 28 g Fat, 20 g Fiber.

LIGHT MEAL
Poached Flounder Fillet, 2 ounces, with $1^1/_2$ teaspoons tartar sauce
Pasta Toss (In small saucepan, combine 1 cup cooked rotelle pasta, $^1/_2$ cup canned crushed tomatoes [no salt added], $^1/_4$ cup minced fresh basil and 2 teaspoons freshly grated Parmesan cheese; cook, tossing frequently, until heated through.)
Spinach-Mushroom Salad (In medium bowl, combine 2 cups torn spinach leaves, $^1/_2$ cup *each* sliced mushrooms and sliced red onion, 1 hard-cooked egg, sliced, 2 teaspoons imitation bacon bits and $1^1/_2$ teaspoons Italian dressing.)
Sugar-Free Strawberry Nonfat Frozen Yogurt, 4 fluid ounces
Iced Tea

MAIN MEAL
Lemon-Marinated Lamb Chops, 1 serving (see recipe)
Baked Acorn Squash, 7 ounces, with 1 teaspoon maple syrup
Steamed Spinach, 1 cup, with 2 teaspoons *each* reduced-calorie tub margarine and fresh lemon juice
Iceberg Lettuce Wedge, 1, with 1 tablespoon fat-free Italian dressing
French Bread, 1 slice (1 ounce)
Sparkling Mineral Water with Lemon Wedge

SNACK
Strawberry-Banana Shake (In blender, combine $^1/_2$ medium banana, sliced, $^2/_3$ cup cold water, 3 ice cubes and 1 packet reduced-calorie strawberry-flavored dairy shake mix; purée until smooth and thick.)

This menu provides: 2 Milks, 3 Fats, 2 Fruits, 10 Vegetables, 4 Proteins, 5 Breads, 120 Optional Calories.

Per serving: 31 g Fat, 24 g Fiber.

LEMON-MARINATED LAMB CHOPS

For best flavor, marinate these chops, or any other lean cut of lamb, for at least an hour before cooking.

Makes 4 servings

1 teaspoon grated lemon zest*
$^1/_4$ cup fresh lemon juice
1 teaspoon Dijon-style mustard
$^1/_4$ teaspoon dried rosemary leaves, crumbled
$^1/_4$ teaspoon salt
Pinch freshly ground black pepper
Four 3-ounce loin lamb chops

1. To prepare marinade, in gallon-size sealable plastic bag, combine zest, juice, mustard, rosemary, salt and pepper; add lamb. Seal bag, squeezing out air; turn to coat lamb. Refrigerate 1–3 hours, turning bag occasionally.

2. Preheat broiler. Spray rack in broiler pan with nonstick cooking spray.

3. Drain and discard marinade. Place lamb onto prepared rack; broil 4" from heat, turning once, 4–5 minutes, until cooked through.

Serving (1 lamb chop) provides: 2 Proteins.

Per serving: 125 Calories, 6 g Total Fat, 2 g Saturated Fat, 54 mg Cholesterol, 132 mg Sodium, 1 g Total Carbohydrate, 0 g Dietary Fiber, 17 g Protein, 13 mg Calcium.

The zest of the lemon is the peel without any of the pith (white membrane). To remove zest from lemon, use a zester or the fine side of a vegetable grater.

53

MEDALLIONS OF LAMB WITH OVEN-ROASTED VEGETABLES

Roasted vegetables are wonderful to have on hand; use different combinations, if you like, according to the season.

Makes 4 servings

2 cups thickly sliced carrots
1 cup thickly sliced parsnips
1 cup cubed butternut squash
1 cup cubed beets
1 cup pearl onions
$^1/_2$ teaspoon salt
$^1/_2$ teaspoon freshly ground black pepper
10 ounces lean boneless loin of lamb
1 garlic clove, minced
$^1/_2$ teaspoon dried rosemary leaves

1. Preheat oven to 400° F. Spray large roasting pan with nonstick cooking spray.

2. Spread carrots, parsnips, squash, beets and onions evenly in prepared roasting pan; sprinkle evenly with $^1/_4$ teaspoon of the salt and $^1/_4$ teaspoon of the pepper. Spray vegetables lightly with nonstick cooking spray; roast 35 minutes, until just tender. Remove vegetables from oven; leave oven on.

3. Sprinkle lamb with garlic, rosemary, remaining $^1/_4$ teaspoon salt and remaining $^1/_4$ teaspoon pepper. Move vegetables to sides of roasting pan, making a well in center; place lamb into well. Roast, turning lamb once, 20 minutes, until lamb is cooked through and tender and vegetables are golden brown.

4. Transfer lamb to cutting board, slice thinly. Arrange lamb slices on serving platter; surround with roasted vegetables.

Serving (2 ounces lamb, 1$^1/_4$ cups vegetables) provides: 2 Vegetables, 2 Proteins, $^3/_4$ Bread.

Per serving: 203 Calories, 5 g Total Fat, 2 g Saturated Fat, 47 mg Cholesterol, 375 mg Sodium, 24 g Total Carbohydrate, 4 g Dietary Fiber, 17 g Protein, 81 mg Calcium.

BREAKFAST
Papaya, $^1/_2$ medium, with lime wedge
Reduced-Calorie Multi-Grain Bread, 2 slices, toasted, with 2 teaspoons reduced-calorie margarine and 2 teaspoons grape jam
Skim Milk, 1 cup
Coffee or Tea (optional)

LIGHT MEAL
Crab Salad-Stuffed Tomato (In small bowl, combine 4 ounces drained canned crabmeat, 2 teaspoons *each* reduced-calorie mayonnaise and fresh lemon juice and 1 teaspoon minced fresh dill. Cut 1 medium tomato in half; scoop out seeds and pulp, leaving firm shell. Spoon one-half crabmeat mixture into each tomato half.)
Watercress and Cucumber Salad, 2 cups, with 1 tablespoon fat-free Italian dressing
Flatbreads, $^3/_4$ ounce
Vanilla "Egg Cream" (In tall glass, combine 1 cup diet cream soda and $^1/_2$ cup skim milk.)

MAIN MEAL
Medallions of Lamb with Oven-Roasted Vegetables, 1 serving (see recipe)
Baked Potato, 8 ounces, with 2 tablespoons nonfat sour cream and 1 teaspoon minced chives
Steamed Kale, 1 cup, with 2 teaspoons *each* reduced-calorie tub margarine and fresh lemon juice
Torn Romaine and Bibb Lettuce Leaves, 2 cups, with 1 tablespoon fat-free ranch dressing
Reduced-Calorie Chocolate-Flavored Pudding (made with skim milk), $^1/_2$ cup
Unsweetened Seltzer with Lemon Wedge

SNACK
Plain Popcorn, hot-air popped, 3 cups, with 2 tablespoons raisins

This menu provides: 2 Milks, 3 Fats, 2 Fruits, 10$^1/_2$ Vegetables, 4 Proteins, 5$^3/_4$ Breads, 115 Optional Calories.

Per serving: 22 g Fat, 35 g Fiber.

Medallions of Lamb with Oven-Roasted Vegetables

BROILED MEDALLIONS OF LAMB WITH LEMON-GARLIC CRUST

Medallions of lamb are the tender fillets from loin lamb chops. Here, they team deliciously with a zesty herb and yogurt mixture to make a meal that tastes like you fussed for hours.

Makes 4 servings

1 tablespoon plain nonfat yogurt
2 teaspoons grated lemon zest*
1 tablespoon fresh lemon juice
4 garlic cloves, minced
2 teaspoons dried rosemary leaves
Freshly ground black pepper, to taste
Four 3-ounce lean medallions of lamb
Fresh rosemary sprigs, to garnish

1. Preheat broiler. Spray rack in broiler pan with nonstick cooking spray.

2. In small bowl, combine yogurt, zest, juice, garlic, dried rosemary and pepper.

3. Place lamb onto prepared rack; spread with half the yogurt mixture. Broil 4" from heat 4 minutes; turn lamb over. Spread lamb with remaining yogurt mixture; broil 2 minutes, until cooked through. Serve garnished with rosemary sprigs.

Serving (1 medallion of lamb) provides: 2 Proteins, 2 Optional Calories.

Per serving: 132 Calories, 6 g Total Fat, 2 g Saturated Fat, 54 mg Cholesterol, 51 mg Sodium, 2 g Total Carbohydrate, 0 g Dietary Fiber, 17 g Protein, 32 mg Calcium.

The zest of the lemon is the peel without any of the pith (white membrane). To remove zest from lemon, use a zester or the fine side of a vegetable grater.

BREAKFAST
Orange, 1 small
Cooked Oatmeal, ¹/₂ cup, with 2 teaspoons reduced-calorie tub margarine and 1 teaspoon firmly packed light or dark brown sugar
Skim Milk, 1 cup
Coffee or Tea (optional)

LIGHT MEAL
Pasta with Broccoli and Chick-Peas (In small bowl, combine 1 cup *each* cooked pasta and cooked broccoli florets, 4 ounces drained cooked chick-peas, ¹/₂ cup hot low-sodium chicken broth, 1 teaspoon *each* olive oil and minced fresh garlic and pinch freshly ground black pepper.)
Tomato Slices, ¹/₂ cup
Sugar-Free Cherry-Flavored Gelatin, ¹/₂ cup
Diet Ginger Ale

MAIN MEAL
Broiled Medallions of Lamb with Lemon-Garlic Crust, 1 serving (see recipe)
Minted Peas, Carrots and Rice (In small saucepan, combine ¹/₂ cup *each* cooked green peas, carrots and brown rice and 2 teaspoons *each* reduced-calorie tub margarine and minced fresh mint leaves; cook over medium heat, stirring constantly, until margarine is melted and mixture is heated.)
Steamed Asparagus, 6 spears, with fresh lemon juice
Strawberry Sundae (Top 4 fluid ounces sugar-free vanilla nonfat frozen yogurt with ³/₄ cup sliced strawberries.)
Decaffeinated Espresso

SNACK
Vanilla Milk Shake (In blender, combine ³/₄ cup skim milk, 3 ice cubes, sugar substitute to equal 2 teaspoons sugar and 1 teaspoon vanilla extract; purée until smooth.)

This menu provides: 2 Milks, 3 Fats, 2 Fruits, 5 Vegetables, 4 Proteins, 5 Breads, 85 Optional Calories.

Per serving: 27 g Fat, 26 g Fiber.

55

PORK BURGERS WITH ONIONS

*Pork burgers are a nice change from beef burgers; for a different
taste, substitute minced pared fresh ginger root for the sage.*

Makes 4 servings

10 ounces lean ground pork
1 teaspoon ground sage
1 teaspoon salt
$^1/_2$ teaspoon garlic powder
$^1/_2$ teaspoon freshly ground black pepper
2 cups sliced onions

1. In large bowl, combine pork, sage, salt, garlic powder and pepper; form
into 4 equal patties.

2. Spray large skillet with nonstick cooking spray; heat. Add onions; cook
over medium-high heat, stirring frequently, 7 minutes, until lightly
browned. Remove onions from skillet; set aside.

3. In same skillet, cook patties over medium-high heat, turning once,
10 minutes, until cooked through; serve topped with cooked onions.

Serving (1 burger, $^1/_2$ cup onions) provides: 1 Vegetable, 2 Proteins.

Per serving: 190 Calories, 11 g Total Fat, 4 g Saturated Fat, 60 mg Cholesterol,
300 mg Sodium, 7 g Total Carbohydrate, 1 g Dietary Fiber, 15 g Protein,
27 mg Calcium.

56

PORK AND ANGEL HAIR SOUP

Makes 4 servings

3 ounces angel hair pasta (capellini)
2 teaspoons oriental sesame oil
2 cups low-sodium vegetable broth
2 cups low-sodium chicken broth
2 cups low-sodium beef broth
4 ounces cooked lean boneless pork, cut into $^1/_4$" strips
1 cup sliced scallions

1. In large pot of boiling water, cook pasta 3 minutes, until tender. Drain, discarding liquid. Add oil to pasta; toss to coat. Set aside; keep warm.

2. Meanwhile in medium saucepan, combine vegetable, chicken and beef broths; bring to a boil. Reduce heat to low; add pork. Simmer 1 minute, until pork is heated.

3. Divide warm pasta mixture evenly among 4 soup bowls; add broth mixture. Top each portion with $^1/_4$ cup of the scallions.

Serving (1$^1/_2$ cups) provides: $^1/_2$ Fat, $^1/_2$ Vegetable, 1 Protein, 1 Bread, 30 Optional Calories.

Per serving: 199 Calories, 7 g Total Fat, 2 g Saturated Fat, 22 mg Cholesterol, 241 mg Sodium, 20 g Total Carbohydrate, 1 g Dietary Fiber, 16 g Protein, 35 mg Calcium.

BREAKFAST
Plums, 2 small
Nonfat Cottage Cheese, $^1/_2$ cup, drizzled with 2 teaspoons honey
Reduced-Calorie Multi-Grain Bread, 2 slices, toasted
Skim Milk, 1 cup
Coffee or Tea (optional)

LIGHT MEAL
Grilled Cheese and Tomato Sandwich (Toast 2 slices reduced-calorie rye bread; top each slice toast with $^1/_2$ medium tomato, sliced, and one $^3/_4$-ounce slice nonfat process American cheese. Place onto nonstick baking sheet; broil 1–2 minutes, until heated.)
Green Bell Pepper Strips, 1 cup
Dill Pickle, 1 medium
Unsweetened Mandarin Orange–Flavored Seltzer

MAIN MEAL
Pork and Angel Hair Soup, 1 serving (see recipe)
Scallop Stir-Fry (In large nonstick skillet, heat 1 teaspoon vegetable oil; add 1 cup snow peas, $^1/_2$ cup *each* chopped onion and broccoli florets, 3 ounces scallops, 2 tablespoons reduced-sodium soy sauce, 2 garlic cloves, minced, and $^1/_2$ teaspoon grated pared fresh ginger root. Cook over medium-high heat, stirring frequently, 5–10 minutes, until vegetables are tender and scallops are cooked through.)
Cooked Brown Rice, 1 cup
Tropical Fruit Cup (In small bowl, combine $^1/_4$ large tangerine, sectioned, $^1/_4$ medium kiwi fruit, pared and sliced, $^1/_8$ small mango, pared, pitted and cut into chunks, and 1$^1/_2$ ounces pared pineapple, cut into chunks.)
Green Tea

SNACK
Peanut Butter–Vanilla Milk Shake (In blender, combine 1 cup skim milk, 3 ice cubes, 1$^1/_2$ teaspoons smooth peanut butter, sugar substitute to equal 2 teaspoons sugar and 1 teaspoon vanilla extract; purée until smooth.)

This menu provides: 2 Milks, 3 Fats, 2 Fruits, 10$^1/_2$ Vegetables, 4 Proteins, 5 Breads, 70 Optional Calories.

Per serving: 24 g Fat, 27 g Fiber.

Pork and Angel Hair Soup

PENNE WITH PORK AND VEGETABLES

Makes 4 servings

6 ounces penne pasta
1 tablespoon + 1 teaspoon olive oil
1 cup coarsely chopped onions
$^1/_2$ medium green bell pepper, seeded and cut into $^1/_2$" strips
$^1/_2$ medium yellow bell pepper, seeded and cut into $^1/_2$" strips
5 ounces lean ground pork
4 fluid ounces ($^1/_2$ cup) dry white wine
2 cups canned whole Italian tomatoes (no salt added), drained and chopped
2 tablespoons minced fresh flat-leaf parsley

2 garlic cloves, minced
1 bay leaf
1 teaspoon dried oregano leaves
1 teaspoon dried thyme leaves
1 teaspoon dried basil
$^1/_4$ teaspoon dried red pepper flakes
$^1/_4$ teaspoon freshly ground black pepper
Pinch salt
1 tablespoon + 1 teaspoon freshly grated Parmesan cheese

1. In large pot of boiling water, cook penne 13 minutes, until tender. Drain, discarding liquid; place into serving bowl. Keep warm.

2. Meanwhile in large nonstick skillet, heat oil; add onions. Cook over medium-high heat, stirring frequently, 5 minutes, until softened. Add green and yellow bell peppers; cook, stirring frequently, 2–3 minutes, until bell peppers are softened.

3. Make well in center of vegetables; add pork. Cook, stirring to break up meat, 3–4 minutes, until no longer pink. Stir onion mixture and wine into cooked pork; cook, stirring frequently, 2 minutes, until almost all liquid is evaporated. Add tomatoes, parsley, garlic, bay leaf, oregano, thyme, basil, red pepper flakes, black pepper and salt; cook, stirring frequently, 15–20 minutes, until sauce is thickened and flavors are blended. Remove and discard bay leaf.

4. Top warm penne with pork mixture; toss to combine. Serve sprinkled with cheese.

Serving (2 cups) provides: 1 Fat, 2 Vegetables, 1 Protein, 2 Breads, 35 Optional Calories.

Per serving: 333 Calories, 9 g Total Fat, 2 g Saturated Fat, 25 mg Cholesterol, 294 mg Sodium, 44 g Total Carbohydrate, 3 g Dietary Fiber, 15 g Protein, 106 mg Calcium.

BREAKFAST
Dried Apricots, 3 halves
Apple-Cinnamon Toast (Spread each of 2 slices reduced-calorie multi-grain toast with 2 tablespoons hot unsweetened applesauce; sprinkle each with sugar substitute to equal 1 teaspoon sugar and $^1/_4$ teaspoon cinnamon.)
Skim Milk, 1 cup
Coffee or Tea (optional)

LIGHT MEAL
Poached Salmon, 3 ounces, with Dill Mayonnaise (In small cup or bowl, combine 2 teaspoons reduced-calorie mayonnaise and 1 teaspoon minced fresh dill.)
Steamed Vegetable Medley (Place 1 cup *each* frozen artichoke hearts, cut asparagus and sliced leeks into steamer insert; steam over simmering water until tender. Serve sprinkled with fresh lemon juice.)
Roll, 1 small (1 ounce), with 2 teaspoons reduced-calorie tub margarine
Aspartame-Sweetened Lemon Nonfat Yogurt, $^3/_4$ cup
Iced Herbal Tea

MAIN MEAL
Penne with Pork and Vegetables, 1 serving (see recipe)
Steamed Sliced Zucchini, 1 cup
Arugula and Endive Salad, 1 cup, with 1 tablespoon fat-free Italian dressing
Breadsticks, 2 long
Pear, 1 small

SNACK
Sugar-Free Chocolate Nonfat Frozen Yogurt, 4 fluid ounces

This menu provides: 2 Milks, 3 Fats, 2 Fruits, 12 Vegetables, 4 Proteins, 5 Breads, 90 Optional Calories.

Per serving: 31 g Fat, 31 g Fiber.

CURRIED PORK MEATBALLS WITH BASMATI RICE

Makes 4 servings

Serving (6 meatballs, $^1/4$ cup sauce, $^1/2$ cup rice) provides: $^1/2$ Fat, 1 Fruit, $^3/4$ Vegetable, $2^1/4$ Proteins, 1 Bread, 10 Optional Calories.

Per serving: 333 Calories, 10 g Total Fat, 2 g Saturated Fat, 47 mg Cholesterol, 439 mg Sodium, 46 g Total Carbohydrate, 4 g Dietary Fiber, 20 g Protein, 61 mg Calcium.

1 tablespoon + 1 teaspoon reduced-calorie tub margarine
1 cup finely chopped onions
4 garlic cloves, minced
10 ounces lean ground pork
$^1/4$ cup egg substitute
1 tablespoon plain dried bread crumbs
1 tablespoon minced fresh flat-leaf parsley
1 teaspoon ground cumin
$^1/2$ teaspoon salt
$^1/4$ teaspoon freshly ground black pepper

2 tablespoons mild or hot curry powder
$^1/4$ teaspoon cinnamon
2 small apples, pared, cored and diced
$^1/2$ medium banana, peeled and sliced
$^1/2$ cup apple juice
$^1/4$ cup tomato sauce (no salt added)
$^1/2$ cup low-sodium chicken broth
1 bay leaf
2 cups cooked basmati rice, hot

1. In medium nonstick skillet, heat 2 teaspoons of the margarine; add $^1/2$ cup of the onions and 1 teaspoon of the garlic. Cook over medium-high heat, stirring frequently, 7 minutes, until onions are lightly browned. Remove from heat; let cool.

2. In large bowl, combine pork, egg substitute, bread crumbs, parsley, cumin, salt, pepper and onion mixture; form into 24 equal meatballs.

3. Spray large nonstick skillet with nonstick cooking spray; heat. Add meatballs; cook over medium-high heat, turning as needed, 6 minutes, until browned on all sides and cooked through. Transfer meatballs to plate; keep warm.

4. In same skillet, heat remaining 2 teaspoons margarine; add curry powder, cinnamon, remaining $^1/2$ cup onions and remaining garlic. Cook over medium-high heat, stirring frequently, 5 minutes, until onions are softened. Add apples, banana and juice; cook 4 minutes, until apples are tender. Add tomato sauce, broth, bay leaf and $^1/2$ cup water; bring liquid to a boil. Reduce heat to low; simmer, covered, 8 minutes, until heated through and flavors are blended. Remove and discard bay leaf.

5. Transfer fruit mixture to food processor; purée until smooth.

6. Return fruit mixture to skillet. Add reserved meatballs; bring mixture just to a boil. Reduce heat to low; simmer, covered, 12 minutes, until meatballs are heated through and sauce is slightly thickened. Serve over cooked rice.

CHILI-STUFFED ACORN SQUASH

Makes 4 servings

Two 14-ounce acorn squashes
1 tablespoon + 1 teaspoon olive oil
1/2 cup chopped onion
1/2 cup finely chopped green bell pepper
4 garlic cloves, minced
1/2 minced deveined seeded jalapeño pepper (wear gloves to prevent irritation)
5 ounces lean ground pork

2 bay leaves
1 teaspoon mild or hot chili powder
1 teaspoon ground cumin
1 teaspoon dried oregano leaves
1 pound drained cooked red kidney beans
1 cup low-sodium chicken broth
Freshly ground black pepper, to taste
Minced fresh cilantro, to garnish

1. Pierce squashes in several places and microwave on High (100% power) for 1 minute. Halve and seed squashes. Place halves on microwavable plate; cover with plastic wrap and microwave on High (100% power) for 7 minutes or until tender.

2. Preheat oven to 375° F.

3. In medium nonstick saucepan, heat oil; add onion, bell pepper, garlic and jalapeño pepper. Cook over medium-high heat, stirring frequently, 5 minutes, until vegetables are softened. Add pork; cook, stirring to break up meat, 3–4 minutes, until no longer pink. Add bay leaves, chili powder, cumin and oregano; cook, stirring constantly, 1 minute.

4. Add beans, broth and black pepper to pork mixture; bring liquid to a boil. Reduce heat to low; simmer, stirring occasionally, 30 minutes, until mixture is thickened and flavors are blended. Remove and discard bay leaves.

5. Fill squash cavities with equal amounts of pork mixture; place onto nonstick baking sheet. Bake 10–15 minutes, until heated through and tops are crispy. Serve sprinkled with cilantro.

Serving (1 stuffed squash half) provides: 1 Fat, 3/4 Vegetable, 3 Proteins, 1 Bread, 5 Optional Calories.

Per serving: 335 Calories, 9 g Total Fat, 2 g Saturated Fat, 24 mg Cholesterol, 73 mg Sodium, 49 g Total Carbohydrate, 10 g Dietary Fiber, 20 g Protein, 117 mg Calcium.

BREAKFAST

Fresh Fig, 1 large
English Muffin, 1/2 (1 ounce), toasted, with 1 tablespoon nonfat cream cheese and 1 teaspoon strawberry jam
Skim Milk, 1 cup
Coffee or Tea (optional)

LIGHT MEAL

Turkey Sandwich (Layer 2 ounces skinless boneless roast turkey breast, sliced, 1/2 medium tomato, sliced, 1/2 cup arugula leaves, 2 teaspoons reduced-calorie mayonnaise and 1 teaspoon prepared mustard between 2 slices reduced-calorie rye bread.)
Dill Pickle, 1 medium
Skim Milk, 1 cup

MAIN MEAL

Chili-Stuffed Acorn Squash, 1 serving (see recipe)
Baked Potato, 4 ounces, with 1 tablespoon *each* nonfat sour cream and minced chives
Celery Sticks, 1 cup
Baked Nectarine (Preheat oven to 350° F. Halve and pit 1 small nectarine; place into small baking dish, cut-side up. Add 1/4" water to dish. Top each nectarine half with 1 teaspoon *each* reduced-calorie margarine and firmly packed light or dark brown sugar and 1/4 teaspoon cinnamon; bake 35–45 minutes, until tender and golden.)
Unsweetened Raspberry-Flavored Seltzer

SNACK

Pretzels, 3/4 ounce
Diet Orange Soda

This menu provides: 2 Milks, 3 Fats, 2 Fruits, 6 3/4 Vegetables, 5 Proteins, 5 Breads, 75 Optional Calories.

Per serving: 21 g Fat, 21 g Fiber.

BREAKFAST

Peach, 1 medium
Reduced-Calorie Multi-Grain Bread, 2 slices, with
1 teaspoon peanut butter
Aspartame-Sweetened Strawberry-Banana Nonfat
Yogurt, 1 cup
Coffee or Tea (optional)

LIGHT MEAL

Lobster Roll (In small bowl, combine 2 ounces
cooked shelled lobster, $^1/_2$ cup chopped celery,
2 teaspoons reduced-calorie mayonnaise, 1 teaspoon fresh lemon juice and pinch ground white
pepper; transfer to one 2-ounce frankfurter roll.)
Bell Pepper Confetti (In small bowl, combine $^1/_2$ cup
each diced red, yellow and green bell peppers.)
Iced Tea with Mint Sprig

MAIN MEAL

Oven-Braised Citrus Pork Cubes, 1 serving (see
recipe)
Black Bean and Rice Medley (In small saucepan or
microwavable bowl, combine 1 cup chopped
tomato, $^1/_2$ cup cooked brown rice, 2 ounces
drained cooked black beans, $^1/_4$ cup tomato juice,
$^1/_2$ teaspoon *each* mild or hot chili powder and
ground cumin and freshly ground black pepper,
to taste; cook over low heat, stirring frequently, or
microwave on High [100% power], stirring once
or twice during cooking, until warm.)
Zucchini Salad (In small bowl, combine 1 cup sliced
zucchini, 1 tablespoon minced fresh flat-leaf parsley and 1 teaspoon *each* olive oil and fresh lime
juice.)

SNACK

Strawberry-Kiwi Shake (In blender, combine 1 cup
skim milk, $^1/_2$ medium kiwi fruit, pared and
sliced, $^1/_4$ cup strawberries, sliced, 3 ice cubes and
sugar substitute to equal 2 teaspoons sugar; purée
until smooth.)

This menu provides: 2 Milks, 3 Fats, 2 Fruits,
$8^3/_4$ Vegetables, 5 Proteins, 4 Breads.

Per serving: 23 g Fat, 21 g Fiber.

60
OVEN-BRAISED CITRUS PORK CUBES

Makes 4 servings

$^1/_2$ cup chopped onion
$^1/_2$ cup fresh orange juice
2 teaspoons fresh lemon juice
3 garlic cloves, chopped
1 bay leaf
$^1/_2$ teaspoon dried oregano leaves
$^1/_2$ teaspoon ground cumin
$^1/_2$ teaspoon freshly ground black pepper
15 ounces lean boneless pork loin, cut into 1-inch cubes
Fresh cilantro sprigs, to garnish

1. To prepare marinade, in gallon-size sealable plastic bag, combine
onion, orange and lemon juices, garlic, bay leaf, oregano, cumin and pepper; add pork. Seal bag, squeezing out air; turn to coat pork. Refrigerate at
least 2 hours or overnight, turning bag occasionally.

2. Preheat oven to 325° F. Spray 1-quart baking dish with nonstick cooking spray.

3. Transfer pork mixture to prepared baking dish; bake, covered, 3 hours,
until pork is very tender. Remove and discard bay leaf. Serve pork mixture
garnished with cilantro sprigs.

Serving (3 ounces pork, $^1/_4$ of the juice mixture) provides: $^1/_4$ Fruit,
$^1/_4$ Vegetable, 3 Proteins.

Per serving: 179 Calories, 6 g Total Fat, 2 g Saturated Fat, 67 mg Cholesterol,
72 mg Sodium, 7 g Total Carbohydrate, 0 g Dietary Fiber, 24 g Protein,
42 mg Calcium.

61
HAWAIIAN PORK AND PINEAPPLE BROCHETTES

These brochettes are a snap to prepare,
yet make a fun and special entrée.

Makes 4 servings

10 ounces lean boneless loin of pork, cut into 1" cubes
1/4 teaspoon salt
Pinch freshly ground black pepper
1 cup drained canned pineapple chunks (no sugar added)
3/4 cup drained canned water chestnuts

1. Spray rack in broiler pan with nonstick cooking spray. Preheat broiler.

2. Sprinkle pork on all sides with salt and pepper. Thread, alternating, an equal amount of pork, pineapple and water chestnuts onto 8 long metal skewers. Place skewers onto prepared rack; broil 4" from heat, turning once, 8 minutes, until pork is cooked through and pineapple and water chestnuts are lightly browned.

Serving (2 skewers) provides: 1/2 Fruit, 2 Proteins, 1/4 Bread.

Per serving: 166 Calories, 6 g Total Fat, 2 g Saturated Fat, 45 mg Cholesterol, 176 mg Sodium, 11 g Total Carbohydrate, 0 g Dietary Fiber, 16 g Protein, 19 mg Calcium.

BREAKFAST
Cantaloupe, 1/4 small
Reduced-Calorie Whole-Wheat Bread, 2 slices, toasted, with 2 teaspoons *each* reduced-calorie tub margarine and grape jam
Skim Milk, 1 cup
Coffee or Tea (optional)

LIGHT MEAL
Grilled Tuna, 4 ounces
Roasted New Potatoes, 8 ounces
Steamed Asparagus, 6 spears, with 1 teaspoon *each* reduced-calorie tub margarine and fresh lemon juice
Tomato Salad (In medium bowl, combine 1 medium tomato, diced, 1/4 cup sliced red onion, 3 tablespoons minced fresh flat-leaf parsley and 1 tablespoon fat-free Italian dressing.)
Plum, 1 small
Iced Tea

MAIN MEAL
Hawaiian Pork and Pineapple Brochettes, 1 serving (see recipe)
Cooked Brown Rice, 1/2 cup
Steamed Spinach, 1 cup, with 2 teaspoons reduced-calorie tub margarine
Zucchini and Yellow Squash Spears, 1 cup *each*
Unsweetened Cranberry-Flavored Seltzer

SNACK
Plain Popcorn, hot-air popped, 3 cups, with 1 tablespoon freshly grated Parmesan cheese and 1 teaspoon reduced-calorie tub margarine, melted
Skim Milk, 1 cup

This menu provides: 2 Milks, 3 Fats, 2 Fruits, 9 1/2 Vegetables, 4 Proteins, 5 1/4 Breads, 65 Optional Calories.

Per serving: 33 g Fat, 29 g Fiber.

62
STIR-FRIED PORK WITH THREE PEPPERS AND ONIONS

*This brightly colored dish is not only beautiful
and delicious but also quick to fix!*

Makes 4 servings

2 teaspoons olive oil
1 medium red bell pepper, seeded and cut into ¹/4" strips
1 medium green bell pepper, seeded and cut into ¹/4" strips
1 medium yellow bell pepper, seeded and cut into ¹/4" strips
2 cups sliced Spanish onions (¹/4" slices)
10 ounces lean boneless pork loin, cut into ¹/4" strips
¹/2 teaspoon dried oregano leaves
¹/2 teaspoon salt
¹/4 teaspoon freshly ground black pepper
1 tablespoon white wine vinegar

1. In large skillet, heat oil; add red, green and yellow bell peppers. Cook over medium-high heat, stirring frequently, 5 minutes, until peppers are softened. Add onions; cook, stirring frequently, 5 minutes, until onions are softened.

2. Add pork, oregano, salt and black pepper to vegetable mixture; cook, stirring frequently, 5 minutes, until pork is browned on all sides. Add vinegar; cook, stirring frequently, 1 minute, until pork is cooked through.

Serving (1 cup) provides: ¹/2 Fat, 2¹/2 Vegetables, 2 Proteins.

Per serving: 174 Calories, 6 g Total Fat, 2 g Saturated Fat, 42 mg Cholesterol, 320 mg Sodium, 12 g Total Carbohydrate, 2 g Dietary Fiber, 17 g Protein, 47 mg Calcium.

63
Stir-Fried Pork with Vegetables

Try this colorful and easy entrée using any of your favorite vegetables for a different dish each time you prepare it.

Makes 4 servings

2 teaspoons olive oil
2 medium onions, cut into $^1/_4$" slices
2 cups broccoli florets
1 medium red bell pepper, seeded and cut into 1" pieces
1 medium zucchini, halved lengthwise and cut into 1" pieces
1 cup sugar snap peas
10 ounces lean boneless pork loin, cut into $^1/_4$" strips
1 teaspoon minced fresh thyme leaves or $^1/_4$ teaspoon dried
$^1/_4$ teaspoon salt
Pinch freshly ground black pepper
1 tablespoon white wine vinegar

1. In large nonstick skillet, heat oil; add onions. Cook over medium-high heat, stirring frequently, 5 minutes, until softened. Add broccoli and $^1/_4$ cup water; cook, covered, 4 minutes, until broccoli is tender. Add bell pepper, zucchini and peas; cook, covered, 2 minutes, until bell pepper is tender.

2. Move vegetables to sides of skillet, making a well in center; place pork, thyme, salt and black pepper into well. Cook pork mixture, stirring frequently, 6 minutes, until pork is browned on all sides. Add vinegar; toss pork mixture and vegetables together. Cook, continuing to toss, 3 minutes, until pork is cooked through.

Serving ($1^1/_2$ cups) provides: $^1/_2$ Fat, $2^3/_4$ Vegetables, 2 Proteins.

Per serving: 190 Calories, 7 g Total Fat, 2 g Saturated Fat, 42 mg Cholesterol, 226 mg Sodium, 14 g Total Carbohydrate, 5 g Dietary Fiber, 20 g Protein, 82 mg Calcium.

BREAKFAST
Raspberries, $^3/_4$ cup
Fortified Cold Cereal, $^3/_4$ ounce
Skim Milk, 1 cup
Coffee or Tea (optional)

LIGHT MEAL
Smoked Turkey Sandwich (Layer 2 ounces skinless boneless smoked turkey, sliced, 2 tomato slices, $^1/_4$ cup alfalfa sprouts and 1 tablespoon reduced-calorie mayonnaise between 2 slices reduced-calorie whole-wheat bread.)
Cucumber Salad (In small bowl, combine $^1/_2$ cup cucumber slices, 1 teaspoon *each* vegetable oil and rice wine vinegar and pinch ground white pepper.)
Peach, 1 medium
Iced Herbal Tea

MAIN MEAL
Stir-Fried Pork with Vegetables, 1 serving (see recipe)
Cooked Brown Rice, $^1/_2$ cup
Tossed Green Salad, 2 cups, with 1 tablespoon fat-free creamy Italian dressing
Unsweetened Lemon-Lime Seltzer

SNACK
Crunch Medley (In small bowl, combine 3 cups hot-air popped plain popcorn, $^3/_4$ ounce small pretzel twists and $^3/_4$ ounce multi-grain cereal squares.)
Skim Milk, 1 cup

This menu provides: 2 Milks, 3 Fats, 2 Fruits, $8^3/_4$ Vegetables, 4 Proteins, 6 Breads, 20 Optional Calories.

Per serving: 24 g Fat, 29 g Fiber.

Stir-Fried Pork with Vegetables

64

POTTED PORK CHOPS AND ONIONS

*Good old-fashioned potted meat is homey and delicious;
for the taste you remember from grandma, cook these
chops until the meat is falling off the bone.*

Makes 4 servings

2 teaspoons reduced-calorie tub margarine
3 medium onions, sliced
Four 3-ounce loin pork chops
1/4 teaspoon salt
Pinch freshly ground black pepper
1 cup apple juice
1/2 teaspoon caraway seeds

1. In large saucepan, melt margarine; add onions. Cook over medium-high heat, stirring frequently, 5 minutes, until softened.

2. Sprinkle pork on both sides with salt and pepper. Add pork, juice and caraway seeds to onion mixture; bring liquid to a boil. Reduce heat to low; simmer, covered, 1 hour and 15 minutes, until pork is cooked through and falling off the bone.

Serving (1 pork chop, 1/2 cup onion mixture) provides: 1/4 Fat, 1/2 Fruit, 3/4 Vegetable, 2 Proteins.

Per serving: 184 Calories, 6 g Total Fat, 2 g Saturated Fat, 50 mg Cholesterol, 201 mg Sodium, 13 g Total Carbohydrate, 1 g Dietary Fiber, 19 g Protein, 34 mg Calcium.

BREAKFAST
Nectarine, 1 small
English Muffin, 1/2 (1 ounce), toasted, with 1 teaspoon *each* nonfat cream cheese and peach jam
Skim Milk, 1/2 cup
Coffee or Tea (optional)

LIGHT MEAL
Broiled Scallops, 4 ounces, with lemon wedge
Steamed Brussels Sprouts, 1 cup
Tossed Green Salad, 2 cups, with 1 tablespoon fat-free Italian dressing
French Bread, 2 slices (2 ounces), with 2 1/2 teaspoons reduced-calorie tub margarine
Aspartame-Sweetened Strawberry Nonfat Yogurt, 1 cup
Iced Tea

MAIN MEAL
Potted Pork Chops and Onions, 1 serving (see recipe)
Mashed Potatoes (In small bowl, with electric mixer, combine 4 ounces hot cooked potato, peeled and cubed, 1 tablespoon *each* reduced-calorie tub margarine and low-sodium beef broth and ground white pepper, to taste.)
Steamed Green Beans, 1 cup
Pickled Beets (In medium bowl, combine 1 cup cooked sliced beets, 1/2 cup sliced onion, 1/4 cup cider vinegar, sugar substitute to equal 2 teaspoons sugar, pinch salt and freshly ground black pepper, to taste; refrigerate, covered, at least 1 hour.)
Chocolate-Strawberry Parfait (In stemmed glass, layer 1/2 cup reduced-calorie chocolate-flavored pudding [made with skim milk] and 1/2 cup strawberries, sliced; top with 1 tablespoon thawed frozen light whipped topping [8 calories per tablespoon].)
Decaffeinated Coffee or Tea

SNACK
Graham Crackers, 3 (2 1/2" squares)

This menu provides: 2 Milks, 3 Fats, 2 Fruits, 11 3/4 Vegetables, 4 Proteins, 5 Breads, 75 Optional Calories.

Per serving: 26 g Fat, 25 g Fiber.

PORK CHOPS WITH TOMATOES AND SAGE

Makes 4 servings

1 tablespoon + 1 teaspoon olive oil
1 cup finely chopped onions
1 garlic clove, minced
Four 5-ounce lean loin pork chops
1 cup canned whole Italian tomatoes (no salt added), chopped
4 fluid ounces ($^1/_2$ cup) dry white wine
2 tablespoons minced fresh sage leaves
Pinch salt
Freshly ground black pepper, to taste

1. In large nonstick skillet, heat oil; add onions and garlic. Cook over medium-high heat, stirring frequently, 5 minutes, until onions are softened.

2. Add pork chops to onion mixture; cook, turning once, 4 minutes, until brown on both sides.

3. Add tomatoes, wine, sage, salt and pepper to pork chop mixture; stir gently to combine. Bring liquid to a boil. Reduce heat to medium-low; braise, turning pork chops occasionally and adding water, a little at a time, to keep mixture from sticking, 15 minutes, until pork chops are cooked through. Transfer pork chops to serving platter; keep warm.

4. Increase heat to medium-high; cook tomato mixture, stirring frequently, until reduced in volume and thickened; pour over warm pork chops.

Serving (1 pork chop, one-quarter of the tomato mixture) provides: 1 Fat, 1 Vegetable, 3 Proteins, 25 Optional Calories.

Per serving: 248 Calories, 10 g Total Fat, 3 g Saturated Fat, 71 mg Cholesterol, 208 mg Sodium, 7 g Total Carbohydrate, 1 g Dietary Fiber, 26 g Protein, 56 mg Calcium.

PORK CHOPS WITH CIDER VINEGAR GLAZE

Cider vinegar and sage team up to make a luscious glaze for these pork chops. A cast-iron skillet retains the heat and cooks evenly, but if you don't have one, a nonstick skillet will also work well.

Makes 4 servings

Four 3-ounce loin pork chops
$1/4$ teaspoon ground white pepper
$1/2$ cup low-sodium chicken broth
$1/4$ cup cider vinegar
Pinch ground sage
1 tablespoon minced fresh flat-leaf parsley

1. Sprinkle pork chops lightly on both sides with pepper.

2. Spray large cast-iron skillet with nonstick cooking spray; heat. Add pork; cook over high heat, turning once, 6 minutes, until browned on both sides.

3. Add broth, vinegar and sage to pork; bring liquid to a boil. Reduce heat to low; simmer, turning once, 5 minutes, until pork is cooked through and tender and liquid is slightly reduced. Sprinkle with parsley and serve.

Serving (1 pork chop, 2 tablespoons liquid) provides: 2 Proteins, 5 Optional Calories.

Per serving: 129 Calories, 5 g Total Fat, 2 g Saturated Fat, 50 mg Cholesterol, 59 mg Sodium, 1 g Total Carbohydrate, 0 g Dietary Fiber, 19 g Protein, 19 mg Calcium.

BREAKFAST
Honeydew Melon, 2" wedge
Scrambled Egg with Cheese (In small nonstick skillet, melt 1 teaspoon reduced-calorie tub margarine; add 1 egg, beaten. Cook over medium-high heat, stirring frequently, until egg is just set. Sprinkle egg with $3/4$ ounce reduced-fat cheddar cheese; cook, covered, 1 minute, until cheese is melted.)
Reduced-Calorie Multi-Grain Bread, 2 slices, with 2 teaspoons reduced-calorie tub margarine
Skim Milk, 1 cup
Coffee or Tea (optional)

LIGHT MEAL
Vegetable Soup, canned, 1 cup
Watercress and Cucumber Pita Sandwich (In small bowl, combine 1 cup watercress leaves, $1/2$ cup thinly sliced cucumber and 1 tablespoon reduced-calorie mayonnaise. Cut 1 large [2-ounce] whole-wheat pita in half crosswise; open to form 2 pockets. Fill each pocket with half of the watercress mixture.)
Sugar-Free Vanilla Nonfat Frozen Yogurt, 4 fluid ounces, with 1 teaspoon chocolate syrup
Sparkling Mineral Water

MAIN MEAL
Pork Chops with Cider Vinegar Glaze, 1 serving (see recipe)
Baked Potato, 8 ounces, with 3 tablespoons plain nonfat yogurt and 1 tablespoon minced chives
Steamed Swiss Chard, 1 cup
Red and Green Bell Pepper Rings, 1 cup *each*, with 1 tablespoon fat-free blue cheese dressing
Fruit Salad, $1/2$ cup
Iced Tea with Lemon Wedge

SNACK
Vanilla "Egg Cream" (In tall glass, combine 1 cup diet cream soda and $1/2$ cup skim milk.)

This menu provides: 2 Milks, 3 Fats, 2 Fruits, 10 Vegetables, 4 Proteins, $5^1/2$ Breads, 110 Optional Calories.

Per serving: 31 g Fat, 23 g Fiber.

67
PORK CHOPS WITH CABBAGE AND APPLES

Makes 4 servings

1 tablespoon + 1 teaspoon olive oil
2 cups chopped onions
Four 5-ounce lean loin pork chops
2 cups chopped cabbage
2 cups chopped fennel bulb
2 cups low-sodium chicken broth
2 small apples, pared, cored and chopped
2 tablespoons golden raisins
1 teaspoon fennel seeds
Pinch salt
Freshly ground black pepper, to taste

1. In large nonstick skillet, heat oil; add onions. Cook over medium-high heat, stirring frequently, 5 minutes, until softened.

2. Add pork chops to onion mixture; cook, turning once, 4 minutes, until brown on both sides.

3. Add cabbage, fennel, broth, apples, raisins, fennel seeds, salt and pepper to pork chop mixture; stir gently to combine. Bring liquid to a boil. Reduce heat to low; simmer, covered, turning pork chops occasionally and adding water, a little at a time to keep mixture from sticking, 30 minutes, until cabbage and fennel are tender and pork chops are cooked through.

Serving (1 pork chop, one-quarter of the vegetable mixture) provides: 1 Fat, $^3/_4$ Fruit, 3 Vegetables, 3 Proteins, 10 Optional Calories.

Per serving: 305 Calories, 13 g Total Fat, 3 g Saturated Fat, 67 mg Cholesterol, 213 mg Sodium, 22 g Total Carbohydrate, 4 g Dietary Fiber, 28 g Protein, 97 mg Calcium.

68

PORK MEDALLIONS WITH PINK APPLESAUCE

Applesauce is the perfect accompaniment to pork, and it is so easy to make! Cooking the apples with the skin on gives the applesauce its lovely pink color; make a double batch and save half for dessert another day.

Makes 4 servings

4 small McIntosh apples, cored and cut into eighths
Four 3-ounce lean boneless pork loin cutlets
$1/2$ teaspoon salt
$1/4$ teaspoon ground white pepper

1. In large saucepan, combine apples and $2/3$ cup water; bring liquid to a boil. Reduce heat to low; simmer, covered, 30 minutes, until apples are very tender.

2. Transfer apple mixture to food mill. Purée apple mixture; discard skin. Set aside.

3. Sprinkle pork on both sides with salt and pepper.

4. Spray medium nonstick skillet with nonstick cooking spray; heat. Add pork; cook over medium-high heat, turning once, 12 minutes, until cooked through. Transfer pork to cutting board; slice thinly. Serve sliced pork with applesauce.

Serving (2 ounces pork, $1/4$ cup applesauce) provides: 1 Fruit, 2 Proteins.

Per serving: 177 Calories, 5 g Total Fat, 2 g Saturated Fat, 50 mg Cholesterol, 318 mg Sodium, 14 g Total Carbohydrate, 2 g Dietary Fiber, 18 g Protein, 20 mg Calcium.

BREAKFAST
Blackberry Yogurt (In small bowl, combine $3/4$ cup *each* plain nonfat yogurt and blackberries.)
Cinnamon Toast (Spread 1 slice cinnamon-raisin bread, toasted, with 1 teaspoon reduced-calorie tub margarine; sprinkle with $1/2$ teaspoon granulated sugar and pinch cinnamon.)
Coffee or Tea (optional)

LIGHT MEAL
Steamed Vegetable and Tofu Medley (In medium nonstick skillet, heat 1 teaspoon oriental sesame oil; add 4 ounces firm tofu, cubed, and $1/4$ cup *each* steamed broccoli florets, sliced carrot, cauliflower florets, sugar snap peas and bean sprouts. Cook over medium-high heat, stirring frequently, until heated through. Add 1 tablespoon fresh lemon juice and 2 teaspoons reduced-sodium soy sauce; toss to combine.)
Cooked Brown Rice, $1/2$ cup
Sugar-Free Lime-Flavored Gelatin, $1/2$ cup, with 1 tablespoon thawed frozen light whipped topping (8 calories per tablespoon)
Chinese Tea

MAIN MEAL
Pork Medallions with Pink Applesauce, 1 serving (see recipe)
Cooked Bulgur, 1 cup
Steamed Whole Green Beans, 1 cup, with 2 teaspoons reduced-calorie tub margarine
Red and Green Leaf Lettuce Salad, 2 cups, with $1/2$ cup sliced yellow bell pepper and 1 tablespoon fat-free Italian dressing
Pumpernickel Roll, 1 ounce, with 1 teaspoon reduced-calorie tub margarine
Reduced-Calorie Butterscotch-Flavored Pudding (made with skim milk), $1/2$ cup
Unsweetened Raspberry-Flavored Seltzer

SNACK
Plain Popcorn, hot-air popped, 3 cups
Skim Milk, $1/2$ cup

This menu provides: 2 Milks, 3 Fats, 2 Fruits, $9^{1}/2$ Vegetables, 4 Proteins, 6 Breads, 70 Optional Calories.

Per serving: 34 g Fat, 31 g Fiber.

LIGHT MEAL
Barley and Bean Salad (In medium bowl, combine
1 cup *each* cooked barley, chopped cucumber and
chopped tomato, 2 ounces drained cooked red
kidney beans and 2 teaspoons *each* olive oil and
red wine vinegar.)
Celery and Carrot Sticks, 1 cup *each*
Sugar-Free Strawberry Nonfat Frozen Yogurt, 4 fluid
ounces
Unsweetened Black Cherry–Flavored Seltzer

MAIN MEAL
Molasses-Glazed Ham Steak, 1 serving (see recipe)
Cooked Corn on the Cob, 1 small ear, with 2 teaspoons reduced-calorie tub margarine
Grilled Vegetables (Preheat grill according to manufacturer's directions. Grill $^1/_2$ cup *each* thickly
sliced zucchini, yellow squash, green bell pepper,
pared eggplant, red onion and fennel over hot
coals or on stove top grill, turning as needed, until
lightly browned and tender.)
Watermelon, 3 × 2" wedge
Diet Lemonade, 1 cup

SNACK
Gingersnaps, $^1/_2$ ounce
Skim Milk, $^3/_4$ cup

This menu provides: 2 Milks, 3 Fats, 2 Fruits,
14 Vegetables, 3 Proteins, $4^1/_2$ Breads, 100 Optional
Calories.

Per serving: 24 g Fat, 34 g Fiber.

69
MOLASSES-GLAZED HAM STEAK

*This simple glaze wakes up the taste of ham steak. Try multiplying
the recipe as needed and using it to glaze a whole baked ham.*

Makes 4 servings

1 tablespoon + 1 teaspoon molasses
1 tablespoon firmly packed light or dark brown sugar
2 teaspoons Dijon-style mustard
1 teaspoon cider vinegar
One 8-ounce lean boneless cooked ham steak

1. Preheat outdoor barbecue grill according to manufacturer's directions,
or preheat broiler and spray rack in broiler pan with nonstick cooking
spray.

2. In small bowl, combine molasses, brown sugar, mustard and vinegar.

3. Grill ham over hot coals or place onto prepared rack in broiler pan and
broil 4" from heat, turning once and brushing frequently with molasses
mixture, 6–8 minutes, until lightly browned on both sides.

Serving (2 ounces) provides: 2 Proteins, 25 Optional Calories.

Per serving: 116 Calories, 3 g Total Fat, 1 g Saturated Fat, 30 mg Cholesterol,
746 mg Sodium, 9 g Total Carbohydrate, 0 g Dietary Fiber, 12 g Protein,
22 mg Calcium.

70
SPAGHETTI WITH HERBED VEAL SAUCE

Makes 4 servings

6 ounces spaghetti

1 tablespoon + 1 teaspoon olive oil

1 cup finely chopped onions

14 ounces lean ground veal

4 garlic cloves, minced

2 cups canned whole Italian tomatoes (no salt added), drained and chopped

3/4 cup minced fresh flat-leaf parsley

2 tablespoons minced fresh tarragon leaves or 2 teaspoons dried

2 tablespoons minced fresh basil or 2 teaspoons dried

Pinch ground nutmeg

Pinch salt

Freshly ground white pepper, to taste

3/4 ounce freshly grated Parmesan cheese

Fresh tarragon sprigs, to garnish

1. In large pot of boiling water, cook spaghetti 8–10 minutes, until tender. Drain, discarding liquid; place into serving bowl. Keep warm.

2. Meanwhile, in large nonstick skillet, heat oil; add onions. Cook over medium-high heat, stirring frequently, 5 minutes, until softened. Add veal and garlic; cook, stirring to break up meat, 3–4 minutes, until no longer pink. Add tomatoes, parsley, minced tarragon, basil, nutmeg, salt and pepper; reduce heat to medium-low. Cook, stirring occasionally, 20–25 minutes, until sauce is thickened.

3. Top warm spaghetti with veal mixture; toss to combine. Sprinkle with cheese; serve garnished with tarragon sprigs.

Serving (2 cups) provides: 1 Fat, 1 1/2 Vegetables, 3 Proteins, 2 Breads.

Per serving: 416 Calories, 14 g Total Fat, 5 g Saturated Fat, 86 mg Cholesterol, 419 mg Sodium, 43 g Total Carbohydrate, 3 g Dietary Fiber, 29 g Protein, 180 mg Calcium.

BREAKFAST

Tangerine, 1 large
Fortified Cold Cereal, 3/4 ounce
Skim Milk, 1 cup
Coffee or Tea (optional)

LIGHT MEAL

Salad Niçoise (In medium bowl, combine 1 cup torn Romaine lettuce leaves, 1/2 cup cooked cut green beans, 4 ounces cooked potato, diced, 6 cherry tomatoes, halved, 2 ounces drained canned water-packed tuna, 1/2 hard-cooked egg white, chopped, 3 large or 5 small pitted black olives, sliced, 2 tablespoons red wine vinegar, 1 anchovy fillet, rinsed and chopped, 1/2 teaspoon olive oil and freshly ground black pepper, to taste.)
Raspberries, 3/4 cup
Iced Decaffeinated Coffee

MAIN MEAL

Spaghetti with Herbed Veal Sauce, 1 serving (see recipe)
Grilled Vegetables (Preheat grill according to manufacturer's directions. Grill 1/2 cup *each* thickly sliced zucchini, yellow squash, sliced green bell pepper, pared eggplant, red onion and fennel, turning as needed, until lightly browned and tender.)
Garlicky Artichoke Hearts (In small bowl, combine 1/2 cup cooked artichoke hearts, 1 tablespoon red wine vinegar, and 2 garlic cloves, minced; refrigerate at least 1 hour.)
Italian Bread, 1 slice (1 ounce), with 2 teaspoons reduced-calorie tub margarine
Diet Ginger Ale

SNACK

Aspartame-Sweetened Black Cherry Nonfat Yogurt, 1 cup

This menu provides: 2 Milks, 3 Fats, 2 Fruits, 12 1/2 Vegetables, 4 Proteins, 5 Breads, 20 Optional Calories.

Per serving: 27 g Fat, 22 g Fiber.

Spaghetti with Herbed Veal Sauce

RISOTTO WITH VEAL, MUSHROOMS AND SAFFRON

Makes 4 servings

1 tablespoon + 1 teaspoon olive oil
1 cup chopped onions
5 ounces lean ground veal
1 cup sliced shiitake mushrooms
2 cups sliced white mushrooms
7 ounces Arborio or other short-grain rice
3 1/2 cups hot low-sodium chicken broth
8 fluid ounces (1 cup) dry white wine
Pinch saffron threads, dissolved in 1/4 cup hot water
1/4 cup minced fresh flat-leaf parsley
1 tablespoon + 1 teaspoon freshly grated Parmesan cheese
Freshly ground black pepper, to taste

1. In medium saucepan, heat oil; add onions. Cook over medium-high heat, stirring frequently, 5 minutes, until softened. Add veal; cook, stirring to break up meat, 3–4 minutes, until no longer pink. Add shiitake and white mushrooms; cook, stirring frequently, 5 minutes, until mushrooms are tender.

2. Add rice to vegetable mixture; stir to combine. Cook, stirring constantly, 1 minute. Add 1/2 cup of the broth and the wine; cook, stirring constantly, until liquid is absorbed. Stir in dissolved saffron.

3. Continuing to stir, add remaining broth, 1/2 cup at a time; cook, stirring constantly after each addition, 18 minutes, until all liquid is absorbed, rice is tender and mixture is creamy. Remove from heat; stir in parsley, cheese and pepper.

Serving (1 cup) provides: 1 Fat, 2 Vegetables, 1 Protein, 1 3/4 Breads, 80 Optional Calories.

Per serving: 367 Calories, 10 g Total Fat, 3 g Saturated Fat, 30 mg Cholesterol, 169 mg Sodium, 47 g Total Carbohydrate, 2 g Dietary Fiber, 15 g Protein, 65 mg Calcium.

BREAKFAST

Apple-Cinnamon Pancake (Place 1 frozen pancake on microwavable plate; top with 1 small apple, cored and sliced. Dot evenly with 1 teaspoon reduced-calorie tub margarine; sprinkle with pinch cinnamon. Microwave on High [100% power] until apple is soft and pancake is heated through.)
Skim Milk, 1 cup
Coffee or Tea (optional)

LIGHT MEAL

Grilled Chicken Salad (In medium bowl, combine 1 cup torn spinach leaves, 1/2 medium tomato, sliced, 1/2 medium roasted red bell pepper, sliced, 1/2 cup cooked artichoke hearts, 3 ounces skinless boneless grilled chicken breast, sliced, 2 teaspoons red wine vinegar, 1 teaspoon olive oil and freshly ground black pepper, to taste.)
Flatbreads, 1 1/2 ounces
Reduced-Calorie Chocolate-Flavored Pudding (made with skim milk), 1/2 cup
Jasmine Tea

MAIN MEAL

Risotto with Veal, Mushrooms and Saffron, 1 serving (see recipe)
Carrot-Zucchini Salad (In small bowl, combine 1 cup shredded carrot, 1/2 cup shredded zucchini, 1 teaspoon *each* minced fresh cilantro and fresh lime juice, 1/2 teaspoon olive oil, 1/2 teaspoon ground cumin, 1/4 teaspoon cinnamon and freshly ground black pepper, to taste.)
Very Cherry Delight (In small bowl, combine 1/2 cup aspartame-sweetened cherry nonfat yogurt and 12 large cherries, pitted and coarsely chopped.)
Sparkling Mineral Water

SNACK

Pretzels, 3/4 ounce

This menu provides: 2 Milks, 3 Fats, 2 Fruits, 10 Vegetables, 4 Proteins, 5 3/4 Breads, 120 Optional Calories.

Per serving: 28 g Fat, 20 g Fiber.

7 2
SLICED VEAL WITH TUNA SAUCE (VITELLO TONNATO)

We've transformed this classic Italian dish into a low-fat entrée while retaining all the flavor of the original. To keep preparation at a minimum during the hectic mealtime hour, make the sauce earlier in the day and refrigerate it until needed.

Makes 4 servings

2 ounces drained canned water-packed tuna
1 tablespoon plain nonfat yogurt
2 teaspoons fresh lemon juice
¹/4 teaspoon salt
Pinch ground white pepper
1 tablespoon minced fresh flat-leaf parsley
9 ounces lean boneless loin of veal
1 tablespoon rinsed drained capers
Lemon wedges, to garnish

1. Preheat oven to 350° F.

2. In mini–food processor, combine tuna, yogurt, juice, salt and pepper; purée until smooth. Add parsley; process to combine.

3. Spray large cast-iron skillet with nonstick cooking spray; heat. Add veal; cook over high heat, turning as needed, until browned on all sides.

4. Transfer skillet to oven; bake 20 minutes, until veal is cooked through. Remove from oven; set aside to cool.

5. Transfer veal to cutting board; slice thinly. Divide veal evenly among 4 plates. Top each portion of veal with one-fourth of the tuna mixture; sprinkle evenly with capers. Serve garnished with lemon wedges.

Serving (1³/4 ounces veal, 1 tablespoon tuna mixture) provides: 2 Proteins, 2 Optional Calories.

Per serving: 97 Calories, 2 g Total Fat, 1 g Saturated Fat, 57 mg Cholesterol, 302 mg Sodium, 1 g Total Carbohydrate, 0 g Dietary Fiber, 17 g Protein, 22 mg Calcium.

Veal Chops with Sage and Wine

Makes 4 servings

3 tablespoons all-purpose flour
Four 5-ounce lean veal loin chops
1 tablespoon + 1 teaspoon olive oil
12 fresh sage leaves, minced
4 fluid ounces ($^1/_2$ cup) dry white wine
Pinch salt
Freshly ground black pepper, to taste
Fresh sage sprigs, to garnish

1. Place flour onto sheet of wax paper or paper plate; add veal chops, turning to coat evenly.

2. In large nonstick skillet, heat oil; add veal chops and minced sage leaves. Cook over medium-high heat, turning veal chops once, 6 minutes, until golden brown and cooked through. Transfer veal chops to serving platter; keep warm.

3. In same skillet, combine wine, salt and pepper; bring liquid to a boil; cook, stirring frequently, until liquid is thickened. Pour wine mixture over veal chops; serve garnished with sage sprigs.

Serving (1 veal chop, 1 tablespoon wine mixture) provides: 1 Fat, 3 Proteins, $^1/_4$ Bread, 25 Optional Calories.

Per serving: 213 Calories, 8 g Total Fat, 2 g Saturated Fat, 91 mg Cholesterol, 138 mg Sodium, 5 g Total Carbohydrate, 0 g Dietary Fiber, 24 g Protein, 26 mg Calcium.

BREAKFAST
Blackberries, $^3/_4$ cup
Frozen Pancakes, 2, heated, with 2 teaspoons *each* maple syrup and reduced-calorie tub margarine
Skim Milk, 1 cup
Coffee or Tea (optional)

LIGHT MEAL
Shrimp Cocktail (Line plate with 4 lettuce leaves; top with 2 ounces peeled and deveined cooked medium shrimp. Serve with 1 tablespoon cocktail sauce.)
Cocktail (Party-Style) Pumpernickel Bread, 3 slices (1 ounce)
Pickled Beet and Onion Salad (In medium bowl, combine 1 cup cooked sliced beets, $^1/_2$ cup sliced onion, 2 tablespoons cider vinegar, sugar substitute to equal 2 teaspoons sugar and freshly ground pepper, to taste; refrigerate, covered, at least 1 hour.)
Kiwi Fruit, 1 medium
Unsweetened Peach-Flavored Seltzer

MAIN MEAL
Veal Chops with Sage and Wine, 1 serving (see recipe)
Cooked Brown Rice, $^1/_2$ cup, mixed with $^1/_2$ cup cooked sliced mushrooms
Green Beans with Tomatoes (In small bowl, combine 1 cup *each* cooked whole green beans and chopped tomato, 1 tablespoon minced fresh flat-leaf parsley, 1 teaspoon *each* olive oil and red wine vinegar and freshly ground black pepper, to taste.)
Reduced-Calorie Vanilla-Flavored Pudding (made with skim milk), $^1/_2$ cup
Decaffeinated Coffee or Tea

SNACK
Graham Crackers, 3 ($2^1/_2$" squares), with 2 teaspoons reduced-calorie strawberry spread
Skim Milk, $^1/_2$ cup

This menu provides: 2 Milks, 3 Fats, 2 Fruits, 9 Vegetables, 4 Proteins, $5^1/_4$ Breads, 130 Optional Calories.

Per serving: 26 g Fat, 23 g Fiber.

VEAL CHOPS WITH MUSHROOM STUFFING

Veal chops are elegant and flavorful—the perfect dish to serve when someone special comes for dinner. This dish is so easy, you'll want to treat yourself like company and prepare it often.

Makes 4 servings

$^1/_2$ cup diced onion
1 cup sliced mushrooms
1 garlic clove, minced
$^1/_2$ teaspoon dried thyme leaves
2 tablespoons red wine vinegar
Four 3-ounce loin veal chops, sliced horizontally to form a pocket
$^1/_2$ teaspoon salt
$^1/_4$ teaspoon freshly ground black pepper
2 teaspoons olive oil
$^1/_2$ cup low-sodium beef broth

1. Preheat oven to 400° F.

2. Spray medium nonstick skillet with nonstick cooking spray; heat. Add onion; cook over medium-high heat, stirring frequently, 5 minutes, until softened. Add mushrooms, garlic and thyme; cook, stirring frequently, 5 minutes, until mushrooms are tender. Add 1 tablespoon of the vinegar; cook, stirring constantly, 2 minutes, until flavors are blended.

3. Sprinkle veal, inside and out, with salt and pepper. Stuff each veal pocket with one-fourth of the mushroom mixture; secure open edge with toothpick.

4. In large cast-iron skillet, heat oil; add stuffed veal. Cook over high heat, turning once, 2 minutes, until veal is browned on both sides.

5. Transfer skillet to oven; bake 15 minutes, until veal is cooked through. Transfer veal to serving platter. Remove and discard toothpicks; keep veal warm.

6. In same skillet, combine broth and remaining 1 tablespoon vinegar; cook over medium-high heat, scraping up browned bits from bottom of skillet, 3 minutes, until heated through and well combined. Pour broth mixture over warm veal.

Serving (1 stuffed veal chop, 1 tablespoon broth mixture) provides: $^1/_2$ Fat, $^3/_4$ Vegetable, 2 Proteins, 5 Optional Calories.

Per serving: 138 Calories, 5 g Total Fat, 1 g Saturated Fat, 68 mg Cholesterol, 361 mg Sodium, 3 g Total Carbohydrate, 1 g Dietary Fiber, 18 g Protein, 26 mg Calcium.

BREAKFAST
Blueberries, $^3/_4$ cup
Frozen Pancakes, 2, heated, with 2 teaspoons *each* reduced-calorie tub margarine and maple syrup
Skim Milk, 1 cup
Coffee or Tea (optional)

LIGHT MEAL
Sliced Egg Sandwich (Layer 1 hard-cooked egg, sliced, $^1/_4$ cup watercress leaves, 2 tomato slices and 2 teaspoons reduced-calorie mayonnaise between 2 slices reduced-calorie whole-wheat bread.)
Carrot and Celery Sticks, 1 cup *each*
Watermelon, 3 × 2" wedge
Coffee "Egg Cream" (In tall glass, combine 1 cup diet coffee soda and $^1/_2$ cup skim milk.)

MAIN MEAL
Veal Chops with Mushroom Stuffing, 1 serving (see recipe)
Roasted New Potatoes, 4 ounces
Steamed Asparagus, 6 spears, with 1 teaspoon *each* reduced-calorie tub margarine and fresh lemon juice
Arugula and Cucumber Salad, 2 cups, with 1 tablespoon fat-free ranch dressing
Wine Spritzer (In wineglass, combine $^1/_2$ cup *each* unsweetened seltzer and non-alcoholic white wine [4 fluid ounces].)

SNACK
Reduced-Calorie Granola Bar, 1 (1 ounce)
Skim Milk, $^1/_2$ cup

This menu provides: 2 Milks, 3 Fats, 2 Fruits, $10^3/_4$ Vegetables, 3 Proteins, 5 Breads, 125 Optional Calories.

Per serving: 28 g Fat, 23 g Fiber.

VEAL MEDALLIONS WITH DILL SAUCE

This light dill sauce is flavored with white wine for an elegant touch.

Makes 4 servings

Four 3-ounce lean boneless veal scallops (cut from leg)
2 teaspoons all-purpose flour
$^1/_4$ teaspoon salt
Pinch freshly ground black pepper
1 tablespoon + 1 teaspoon reduced-calorie tub margarine
2 fluid ounces ($^1/_4$ cup) dry white wine
1 tablespoon fresh lemon juice
1 tablespoon minced fresh dill, or $^1/_2$ teaspoon dried
Minced fresh flat-leaf parsley, to garnish

1. Place veal scallops between 2 sheets of wax paper; with meat mallet or bottom of heavy saucepan, pound veal to $^1/_8$" thickness. Remove and discard wax paper.

2. On sheet of wax paper or paper plate, combine flour, salt and pepper; add veal, turning to coat evenly.

3. In medium nonstick skillet, melt margarine; add veal. Cook over medium-high heat, turning once, 2 minutes, until veal is cooked through. Transfer veal to serving platter; keep warm.

4. In same skillet, combine wine and juice; cook, stirring quickly, 2 minutes, until slightly thickened. Add dill; cook, stirring constantly, 1 minute, until flavors are blended. Pour wine mixture over warm veal; garnish with parsley.

Serving (2 ounces veal, 1 tablespoon wine mixture) provides: $^1/_2$ Fat, 2 Proteins, 20 Optional Calories.

Per serving: 124 Calories, 3 g Total Fat, 1 g Saturated Fat, 66 mg Cholesterol, 227 mg Sodium, 2 g Total Carbohydrate, 0 g Dietary Fiber, 18 g Protein, 9 mg Calcium.

BREAKFAST
Orange Sections, $^1/_2$ cup
Shredded Wheat Cereal, $^3/_4$ ounce
Skim Milk, 1 cup
Coffee or Tea (optional)

LIGHT MEAL
Spicy Tuna Salad (In small bowl, combine 4 ounces drained canned water-packed tuna, $^1/_4$ cup *each* diced green bell pepper and celery, 1 tablespoon *each* reduced-calorie mayonnaise and fresh lemon juice and 1 teaspoon minced, deveined and seeded jalapeño pepper [wear gloves to prevent irritation].)
Cherry Tomatoes, 6
Crispbreads, $1^1/_2$ ounces
Aspartame-Sweetened Vanilla Nonfat Yogurt, 1 cup
Unsweetened Seltzer

MAIN MEAL
Veal Medallions with Dill Sauce, 1 serving (see recipe)
Boiled New Potatoes, 4 ounces
Dilled Carrots (In small bowl, combine 1 cup cooked sliced carrot, 1 tablespoon minced fresh dill and 2 teaspoons reduced-calorie tub margarine.)
Arugula and Endive Salad, 2 cups, with 1 tablespoon fat-free Italian dressing
Baked Apple (Preheat oven to 350° F. Pare 1 small apple halfway down from stem end; core and place into small baking dish. Sprinkle apple with 1 teaspoon granulated sugar and $^1/_4$ teaspoon cinnamon; add $^1/_4$" water to pan. Bake, covered, 30 minutes, until tender.)
Sparkling Mineral Water with Lime Wedge

SNACK
Bagel, 1 small (2 ounces), split and toasted, with 1 tablespoon nonfat cream cheese and 1 teaspoon grape jam

This menu provides: 2 Milks, 3 Fats, 2 Fruits, 8 Vegetables, 4 Proteins, 6 Breads, 70 Optional Calories.

Per serving: 15 g Fat, 23 g Fiber.

BREAKFAST

Cantaloupe, $^1/_4$ small, with lime wedge

Herb Omelet (In small bowl, beat 1 egg, $^1/_4$ cup skim milk and 1 teaspoon *each* minced fresh chives, fresh tarragon leaves and fresh flat-leaf parsley until frothy. Spray small nonstick skillet with nonstick cooking spray; heat. Pour egg mixture into skillet, tilting to cover bottom of pan. Cook over medium-high heat until underside is set, lifting edges with spatula to let uncooked egg flow underneath; fold in half.)

Reduced-Calorie Multi-Grain Bread, 2 slices, toasted, with 1 teaspoon *each* reduced-calorie tub margarine and honey

Skim Milk, 1 cup

Coffee or Tea (optional)

LIGHT MEAL

Asparagus Bisque (In blender, combine 2 cups cooked cut asparagus, 1 cup low-sodium chicken broth, $^1/_4$ cup skim milk and pinch ground white pepper; purée until smooth. Transfer to small saucepan; cook over low heat, stirring frequently, until warm.)

Open-Face Cream Cheese and Olive Sandwich (Spread 1 slice pumpernickel bread with 1 tablespoon nonfat cream cheese; top with 3 large or 5 small pimiento-stuffed green olives, sliced.)

Plums, 2 small

Unsweetened Citrus-Flavored Seltzer

MAIN MEAL

Veal Scaloppine with Tomatoes, Mushrooms and Peppers, 1 serving (see recipe)

Cooked Wide Noodles, $^1/_2$ cup

Steamed Sliced Zucchini, 1 cup

Garlic Bread (Spread 1-ounce slice Italian bread with $^1/_2$ teaspoon minced fresh garlic or the pulp of 1 roasted garlic clove; drizzle with $^1/_2$ teaspoon olive oil. Place onto nonstick baking sheet; broil until lightly browned.)

Spiced Vanilla Yogurt (In small bowl, combine $^1/_2$ cup aspartame-sweetened vanilla nonfat yogurt and $^1/_4$ teaspoon *each* cinnamon, ground ginger and ground nutmeg.)

Sparkling Mineral Water

SNACK

Plain Popcorn, hot-air popped, 3 cups, with 1 teaspoon reduced-calorie tub margarine, melted

This menu provides: 2 Milks, 3 Fats, 2 Fruits, $10^1/_2$ Vegetables, 3 Proteins, 5 Breads, 80 Optional Calories.

Per serving: 32 g Fat, 38 g Fiber.

VEAL SCALOPPINE WITH TOMATOES, MUSHROOMS AND PEPPERS

Makes 4 servings

1 tablespoon + 1 teaspoon olive oil
1 cup finely chopped onions
2 garlic cloves, thinly sliced
4 medium green bell peppers, seeded and cut into $^1/_2$" strips
Four 3-ounce lean boneless veal scallops (cut from leg)
2 cups canned whole Italian tomatoes (no salt added), drained and chopped
2 cups drained canned whole mushrooms
4 fluid ounces ($^1/_2$ cup) dry white wine
$^1/_4$ cup minced fresh flat-leaf parsley
1 bay leaf
1 teaspoon dried oregano leaves
Pinch salt
Freshly ground black pepper, to taste
Fresh flat-leaf parsley sprigs, to garnish

1. In large nonstick skillet, heat oil; add onions and garlic. Cook over medium-high heat, stirring frequently, 5 minutes, until onions are softened. Add bell peppers; cook, stirring frequently, 5 minutes, until bell peppers are softened. Remove vegetables; set aside.

2. To same skillet, add veal; cook, turning once, 5 minutes, until golden brown on both sides. Return vegetable mixture to skillet; stir to combine. Stir in tomatoes, mushrooms, wine, minced parsley, bay leaf, oregano, salt and black pepper; bring liquid to a boil. Reduce heat to low; simmer 20–25 minutes, until veal is very tender and vegetable mixture is thickened. Remove and discard bay leaf. Serve garnished with parsley.

Serving (1 veal scallop, $1^1/_2$ cups vegetable mixture) provides: 1 Fat, $4^1/_2$ Vegetables, 2 Proteins, 25 Optional Calories.

Per serving: 239 Calories, 7 g Total Fat, 1 g Saturated Fat, 66 mg Cholesterol, 601 mg Sodium, 20 g Total Carbohydrate, 3 g Dietary Fiber, 22 g Protein, 74 mg Calcium.

VEAL SCALOPPINE WITH MUSTARD SAUCE

Pounding the veal gently between sheets of wax paper helps to tenderize the meat.

Makes 4 servings

Four 3-ounce lean boneless veal scallops (cut from leg)
2 teaspoons all-purpose flour
$^1/_4$ teaspoon salt
Pinch freshly ground black pepper
1 tablespoon + 1 teaspoon reduced-calorie tub margarine
$^1/_2$ cup low-sodium chicken broth
$^1/_4$ cup evaporated skimmed milk
$^1/_2$ teaspoon dry mustard
$^1/_4$ teaspoon Dijon-style mustard
Minced fresh flat-leaf parsley, to garnish

1. Place veal scallops between 2 sheets of wax paper; with meat mallet or bottom of heavy saucepan, pound veal to $^1/_8$" thickness. Remove and discard wax paper.

2. On sheet of wax paper or paper plate, combine flour, salt and pepper; add veal, turning to coat evenly.

3. In medium nonstick skillet, melt margarine; add veal. Cook over medium-high heat, turning once, 2 minutes, until veal is cooked through. Transfer veal to serving platter; keep warm.

4. In same skillet, combine broth, milk and dry and Dijon-style mustards; cook, stirring constantly, 4 minutes, until slightly thickened. Pour broth mixture over warm veal; garnish with parsley.

Serving (2 ounces veal, 2 tablespoons broth mixture) provides: $^1/_2$ Fat, 2 Proteins, 20 Optional Calories.

Per serving: 129 Calories, 4 g Total Fat, 1 g Saturated Fat, 67 mg Cholesterol, 266 mg Sodium, 3 g Total Carbohydrate, 0 g Dietary Fiber, 20 g Protein, 54 mg Calcium.

BREAKFAST
Cherries, 12 large
Frozen Waffle, 1, heated, with 1 teaspoon *each* reduced-calorie tub margarine and maple syrup
Skim Milk, $^3/_4$ cup
Coffee or Tea (optional)

LIGHT MEAL
Spinach-Orange Salad (In medium bowl, combine 2 cups spinach leaves, $^1/_2$ cup shredded carrot, $^1/_4$ cup *each* fennel, jicama and mushroom slices and orange sections, $1^1/_2$ ounces reduced-fat Muenster cheese, julienned, and 1 tablespoon fat-free creamy Italian dressing.)
Breadsticks, 2 long
Strawberries, $^1/_2$ cup
Iced Tea

MAIN MEAL
Veal Scaloppine with Mustard Sauce, 1 serving (see recipe)
Cooked Couscous, $^1/_2$ cup, with 1 teaspoon *each* reduced-calorie tub margarine and minced fresh flat-leaf parsley
Steamed Snow Peas, 1 cup
Caesar Salad (In medium bowl, combine 2 cups torn Romaine lettuce leaves, $^1/_4$ cup packaged croutons and 1 tablespoon fat-free Caesar salad dressing.)
Roll, 1 ounce
Sugar-Free Chocolate Nonfat Frozen Yogurt, 4 fluid ounces
Sparkling Mineral Water with Mint Sprig

SNACK
Graham Crackers, 3 ($2^1/_2$" squares)
Skim Milk, 1 cup

This menu provides: 2 Milks, 3 Fats, 2 Fruits, $12^1/_2$ Vegetables, 4 Proteins, $5^1/_2$ Breads, 125 Optional Calories.

Per serving: 29 g Fat, 22 g Fiber.

BREAKFAST

Papaya, $^1/_2$ medium
Bagels with Smoked Salmon, 1 serving (see recipe)
Cucumber Slices, 1 cup
Skim Milk, 1 cup
Coffee or Tea (optional)

LIGHT MEAL

Turkey Sandwich (Layer 2 ounces skinless boneless
 roast turkey breast, sliced, $^1/_2$ medium tomato,
 sliced, $^1/_2$ cup arugula leaves, 2 teaspoons reduced-
 calorie mayonnaise and 1 teaspoon prepared mustard between 2 slices reduced-calorie rye bread.)
Carrot and Celery Sticks, 1 cup *each*
Apple, 1 small
Diet Cola

MAIN MEAL

Broiled Veal Chop, 2 ounces
Cooked Brown Rice, 1 cup
Steamed Cut Green and Wax Beans, 1 cup
Torn Romaine Lettuce Leaves, 2 cups, with 1 table-
 spoon blue cheese dressing
Lemon Cookie Yogurt (In small bowl, combine
 1 cup aspartame-sweetened lemon nonfat yogurt
 and 3 vanilla wafers, crushed.)
Sparkling Mineral Water

SNACK

Buttery Popcorn (Lightly spray 3 cups hot-air
 popped plain popcorn with nonstick cooking
 spray. Sprinkle popcorn with $^1/_4$ teaspoon butter-
 flavor granules; toss to coat evenly.)

This menu provides: 2 Milks, 3 Fats, 2 Fruits,
$13^1/_2$ Vegetables, $4^1/_2$ Proteins, $5^1/_2$ Breads,
50 Optional Calories.

Per serving: 27 g Fat, 24 g Fiber.

BAGELS WITH SMOKED SALMON

Makes 4 servings

$^1/_3$ cup + 2 teaspoons nonfat cream cheese
2 tablespoons minced scallions
$^3/_4$ teaspoon minced fresh dill
1 teaspoon skim milk
Four 1-ounce bagels, split
2 large plum tomatoes, thinly sliced
Four $^1/_2$-ounce slices smoked salmon (lox)
2 teaspoons finely diced red onion
2 teaspoons rinsed drained capers

1. In small bowl, combine cream cheese, scallions, dill and milk.

2. Spread one-fourth of the cheese mixture onto bottom half of each bagel. Top cheese mixture evenly with tomato slices; drape 1 smoked salmon slice over each portion of tomatoes. Top each portion of salmon with $^1/_2$ teaspoon *each* of the onion and capers, then 1 remaining bagel half.

Serving (1 sandwich) provides: $^1/_2$ Vegetable, $^1/_2$ Protein, 1 Bread, 25 Optional Calories.

Per serving: 121 Calories, 1 g Total Fat, 0 g Saturated Fat, 6 mg Cholesterol, 386 mg Sodium, 18 g Total Carbohydrate, 1 g Dietary Fiber, 9 g Protein, 89 mg Calcium.

FISH

79
SHRIMP NEWBURG IN PHYLLO CUPS

Makes 4 servings

4 ounces fresh or thawed frozen phyllo dough (about 6 sheets)*
2 tablespoons reduced-calorie stick margarine
2 tablespoons all-purpose flour
$^1/_4$ teaspoon salt
Pinch ground red pepper
1$^1/_2$ cups evaporated skimmed milk
$^1/_4$ cup egg substitute
20 medium shrimp, cooked, peeled and deveined
1 fluid ounce (2 tablespoons) dry sherry
Pinch freshly ground nutmeg

1. Preheat oven to 350° F. Spray four 6-ounce custard cups with nonstick cooking spray.

2. To prepare phyllo cups, stack phyllo sheets together. Fold sheets in half, then in half again, forming a 5" square. Slit open sides of phyllo square to separate into 24 individual squares.

3. Place 1 phyllo square onto work surface; spray lightly with nonstick cooking spray. Top with 5 more phyllo squares, each sprayed lightly with nonstick cooking spray, placing top 3 squares diagonally over bottom 3 squares. Repeat 3 more times, forming 4 phyllo stacks.

4. Gently press each phyllo stack into a prepared custard cup; place onto large baking sheet. Bake 8–10 minutes, until phyllo is lightly browned. Remove from oven; let stand 5 minutes. Carefully remove phyllo cups from custard cups; set onto wire rack to cool.

5. To prepare shrimp Newburg, in medium saucepan, melt margarine; stir in flour, salt and pepper. Add milk; cook over medium-high heat, stirring constantly, until mixture comes to a boil and is thickened.

6. In small bowl, with wire whisk, slowly stir half of the hot milk mixture into egg substitute. Stirring constantly with wire whisk, slowly pour egg mixture into remaining milk mixture; cook over medium-low heat, stirring constantly, until mixture comes just to a boil. Stir in shrimp, sherry and nutmeg; cook, stirring constantly, just until heated through.

7. Divide shrimp Newburg evenly among phyllo cups.

Serving (1 filled phyllo cup) provides: $^3/_4$ Milk, 1 Fat, 1$^1/_2$ Proteins, 1 Bread, 20 Optional Calories.

Per serving: 297 Calories, 7 g Total Fat, 1 g Saturated Fat, 112 mg Cholesterol, 581 mg Sodium, 30 g Total Carbohydrate, 0 g Dietary Fiber, 26 g Protein, 326 mg Calcium.

BRUNCH

Shrimp Newburg in Phyllo Cups, 1 serving (see recipe)

Steamed Asparagus, 6 spears, with Lemon "Butter" (In small cup or bowl, combine 1 teaspoon *each* reduced-calorie tub margarine, melted, and fresh lemon juice.)

Steamed Baby Carrots, 1 cup

Watercress and Radicchio Salad, 2 cups, with $^1/_2$ cup red bell pepper strips and 1 tablespoon fat-free honey-mustard dressing

Roll, 1 ounce, with 1 teaspoon reduced-calorie tub margarine

Sugar-Free Berry-Flavored Gelatin, $^1/_2$ cup, topped with $^1/_4$ cup aspartame-sweetened raspberry nonfat yogurt

Coffee or Tea (optional)

MAIN MEAL

Skinless Roast Chicken Breast, 3 ounces

Cooked Wide Noodles, 1 cup, with 2 teaspoons reduced-calorie tub margarine

Cooked Sliced Beets, 1 cup

Spinach-Vegetable Salad (In medium bowl, combine 2 cups torn spinach leaves, $^1/_2$ cup *each* sliced mushrooms and red onion, 1 tablespoon imitation bacon bits and 1 tablespoon fresh lemon juice.)

Peach Yogurt (In small bowl, combine $^3/_4$ cup plain nonfat yogurt and $^1/_2$ cup drained canned peach slices [no sugar added].)

Unsweetened Black Cherry–Flavored Seltzer

SNACK

Plain Popcorn, hot-air popped, 3 cups, with 2 tablespoons raisins

This menu provides: 2 Milks, 3 Fats, 2 Fruits, 16 Vegetables, 4$^1/_2$ Proteins, 5 Breads, 80 Optional Calories.

Per serving: 26 g Fat, 27 g Fiber.

Phyllo dough dries out quickly. To help keep the individual squares soft and pliable, keep them covered with plastic wrap until ready to use.

80

SCRAMBLED EGGS WITH SMOKED SALMON

Makes 2 servings

1 tablespoon stick margarine
1 ounce smoked salmon (lox), chopped
3 tablespoons diced red onion
2 eggs
3 egg whites
Freshly ground black pepper, to taste

1. In medium nonstick skillet, melt margarine; add salmon and onion. Cook over medium-high heat, stirring frequently, 2–3 minutes, until salmon is lightly browned.

2. In medium bowl, combine eggs and egg whites. Pour egg mixture over salmon mixture; cook, stirring constantly, until mixture is set. Serve with pepper.

Serving (half of mixture) provides: $1^1/_2$ Fats, $^1/_4$ Vegetable, 2 Proteins.

Per serving: 173 Calories, 11 g Total Fat, 3 g Saturated Fat, 216 mg Cholesterol, 325 mg Sodium, 3 g Total Carbohydrate, 0 g Dietary Fiber, 14 g Protein, 35 mg Calcium.

POTSTICKERS WITH GINGER SAUCE

Makes 4 servings

Potstickers:

5 ounces scrod fillet

3 tablespoons chopped drained canned water chestnuts

2 tablespoons minced scallion

1 1/2 teaspoons cornstarch

1 1/2 teaspoons rice wine vinegar

1 teaspoon minced pared fresh ginger root

1 teaspoon reduced-sodium soy sauce

1 garlic clove, minced

1/2 teaspoon oriental sesame oil

20 wonton skins (3" squares)

Dipping Sauce:

1/4 cup reduced-sodium soy sauce

1/4 cup rice wine vinegar

2 teaspoons minced scallion

2 teaspoons minced pared fresh ginger root

1/2 teaspoon oriental sesame oil

1. To prepare filling, in food processor, combine scrod, water chestnuts, scallion, cornstarch, vinegar, ginger, soy sauce, garlic and oil; with on-off motion, pulse processor 4–5 times, just until mixture forms a paste.

2. To prepare potstickers, place wonton skins onto work surface; spoon an equal amount of fish paste onto center of each skin. Lightly moisten edges of skin with water; fold skins diagonally over filling, forming triangles; press edges together to seal.

3. In large nonstick skillet, bring 1" water to a boil; add 10 potstickers in a single layer (water should cover potstickers). Reduce heat to medium-low; cook, covered, 5 minutes, until wrappers are cooked and filling is cooked through. With slotted spoon, transfer potstickers to plate; keep warm. Repeat with remaining potstickers, adding more water to skillet if necessary.

4. To prepare sauce, in small bowl, combine soy sauce, vinegar, scallion, ginger, oil and 2 tablespoons water; serve with potstickers for dipping.

Serving (5 potstickers, 2 generous tablespoons sauce) provides: 1/4 Fat, 1/2 Protein, 1 Bread, 10 Optional Calories.

Per serving: 165 Calories, 2 g Total Fat, 0 g Saturated Fat, 18 mg Cholesterol, 871 mg Sodium, 25 g Total Carbohydrate, 1 g Dietary Fiber, 11 g Protein, 30 mg Calcium.

BRUNCH

Potstickers with Ginger Sauce, 1 serving (see recipe)

Cooked Brown Rice, 1 cup

Stir-Fried Vegetables (In nonstick skillet or wok, heat 1 1/2 teaspoons oriental sesame oil; add 1 cup *each* cubed pared eggplant, bean sprouts and sliced radishes. Cook over medium-high heat, stirring constantly, until vegetables are tender; sprinkle with 2 teaspoons rice wine vinegar.)

Mandarin Orange Sections, 1/2 cup, with 1 teaspoon shredded coconut

Green Tea

MAIN MEAL

Grilled Turkey Burger, 2 ounces, with 1 slice nonfat process American cheese on 2-ounce hamburger roll with Russian dressing (In small cup or bowl, combine 2 1/2 teaspoons *each* reduced-calorie mayonnaise and ketchup.)

Oven "Fries" (Preheat oven to 450° F. Cut 5 ounces all-purpose potato into sticks; place onto nonstick baking sheet. Spray potato sticks lightly with nonstick cooking spray; sprinkle with 1/4 teaspoon *each* salt and paprika. Bake 8–10 minutes until potato sticks are crispy outside and tender inside.)

Tomato and Spanish Onion Slices, 1 cup, on 2 iceberg lettuce leaves

Reduced-Calorie Chocolate Dairy Shake, 1 serving

SNACK

Mixed Berry Yogurt (In small bowl, combine 3/4 cup plain nonfat yogurt and 1/4 cup *each* blueberries, blackberries and raspberries.)

This menu provides: 2 Milks, 3 Fats, 2 Fruits, 8 1/2 Vegetables, 3 Proteins, 6 Breads, 30 Optional Calories.

Per serving: 22 g Fat, 22 g Fiber.

Potstickers with Ginger Sauce

GRILLED SWORDFISH WITH BERRY SALSA

Fruity salsa complements flavorful swordfish in this beautiful brunch or dinner entrée. Remember to zest the orange before juicing it.

Makes 4 servings

¹/₄ cup strawberries, hulled and coarsely chopped
¹/₄ cup fresh orange juice
3 tablespoons blueberries
2 tablespoons minced fresh cilantro
1 tablespoon diced red onion
1 teaspoon chopped deveined seeded jalapeño pepper (wear gloves to prevent irritation)
¹/₄ teaspoon granulated sugar
Pinch salt
2 tablespoons reduced-calorie stick margarine, melted and cooled
¹/₂ teaspoon grated orange zest*
Four 5-ounce boneless swordfish steaks
4 cups mesclun or other salad greens

1. To prepare salsa, in small bowl, combine strawberries, 1 tablespoon of the juice, the blueberries, cilantro, onion, pepper, sugar and salt; let stand 1 hour.

2. To prepare marinade, in gallon-size sealable plastic bag, combine margarine, zest and remaining 3 tablespoons juice; add swordfish. Seal bag, squeezing out air; turn to coat fish. Refrigerate 1 hour, turning bag occasionally.

3. Preheat outdoor barbecue grill or indoor stove-top grill according to manufacturer's directions.

4. Drain the marinade into a small saucepan; bring to a rolling boil; boil for 1 minute, stirring constantly. Remove from heat. Grill swordfish over hot coals or on stove-top grill, turning once and brushing frequently with marinade, 6–8 minutes, until fish flakes easily when tested with fork.

5. Divide mesclun evenly among 4 plates. Top each portion of mesclun with 1 grilled swordfish steak; top each steak with one-fourth of the salsa.

Serving (1 swordfish steak, 1 cup mesclun, 2 tablespoons salsa) provides: 2 Vegetables, 2 Proteins, 55 Optional Calories.

Per serving: 222 Calories, 9 g Total Fat, 2 g Saturated Fat, 55 mg Cholesterol, 235 mg Sodium, 6 g Total Carbohydrate, 1 g Dietary Fiber, 29 g Protein, 50 mg Calcium.

82

BRUNCH

Low-Sodium Tomato Juice, 1 cup, with 1 teaspoon low-sodium Worcestershire sauce, pinch freshly ground black pepper and 1 celery stick
Grilled Swordfish with Berry Salsa, 1 serving (see recipe)
Cooked Long-Grain and Wild Rice, 1 cup
Steamed Asparagus, 9 spears
Roll, 1 ounce, with 2 teaspoons reduced-calorie tub margarine
Pudding Parfait (In stemmed glass, layer ¹/₂ cup *each* reduced-calorie chocolate-flavored and vanilla-flavored puddings [made with skim milk].)
Skim Milk, ¹/₂ cup
Coffee or Tea (optional)

MAIN MEAL

Grilled Lamb Chop, 2 ounces
Cooked Couscous, 1 cup, with 2 teaspoons reduced-calorie tub margarine
Steamed Broccoli Rabe, 1 cup, with 1 teaspoon olive oil and 1 garlic clove, minced
Torn Romaine Lettuce Leaves, 2 cups, with 1 tablespoon fat-free Caesar salad dressing
Cherries, 12 large
Sparkling Mineral Water with Lime Wedge

SNACK

Honeydew Balls, 1 cup, with 1 teaspoon shredded coconut
Decaffeinated Cappuccino, made with skim milk, 5 fluid ounces

This menu provides: 2 Milks, 3 Fats, 2 Fruits, 12 Vegetables, 4 Proteins, 5 Breads, 160 Optional Calories.

Per serving: 34 g Fat, 22 g Fiber.

The zest of the orange is the peel without any of the pith (white membrane). To remove zest from orange, use a zester or the fine side of a vegetable grater.

Grilled Swordfish with Berry Salsa

83

CRAB IN
CANTALOUPE BASKETS

Makes 4 servings

$^1/_3$ cup + 2 teaspoons plain nonfat yogurt
2 tablespoons reduced-calorie mayonnaise
1 tablespoon minced fresh flat-leaf parsley
1 tablespoon minced fresh tarragon leaves
1 tablespoon minced scallion
1 tablespoon white wine tarragon vinegar
2 small cantaloupes
8 ounces cooked crabmeat, flaked
$^1/_2$ cup coarsely chopped celery
2 cups watercress leaves

1. To prepare dressing, in mini–food processor or blender, combine yogurt, mayonnaise, parsley, tarragon, scallion and vinegar; purée until smooth. Set aside.

2. Cut cantaloupes in half crosswise; remove and discard seeds. Scoop out cantaloupe pulp, leaving shells intact; cut pulp into $^3/_4$" chunks.

3. In medium bowl, combine crabmeat, celery and cantaloupe chunks. Line cantaloupe shells with watercress; divide crabmeat mixture evenly among lined shells. Top each portion with one-fourth of the dressing.

Serving ($1^1/_2$ cups crab mixture, $^1/_2$ cup watercress, 2 tablespoons dressing) provides: $^3/_4$ Fat, 2 Fruits, $1^1/_4$ Vegetables, 1 Protein, 10 Optional Calories.

Per serving: 176 Calories, 4 g Total Fat, 1 g Saturated Fat, 60 mg Cholesterol, 256 mg Sodium, 22 g Total Carbohydrate, 3 g Dietary Fiber, 15 g Protein, 158 mg Calcium.

BRUNCH

Crab in Cantaloupe Baskets, 1 serving (see recipe)
Chilled Cooked Asparagus, 6 spears, with 1 lemon wedge
Carrot and Celery Sticks, 1 cup *each,* with Vegetable Dip (In small bowl, combine $^1/_2$ cup plain nonfat yogurt and 1 packet instant vegetable broth and seasoning mix.)
Flatbreads, $1^1/_2$ ounces
Sugar-Free Vanilla Nonfat Frozen Yogurt, 4 fluid ounces
Champagne Sparkler (In stemmed glass, combine $^1/_2$ cup sparkling mineral water and 2 fluid ounces [$^1/_4$ cup] champagne; add enough ice cubes to fill glass.)

MAIN MEAL

Baked Lean Ham, 2 ounces
Baked Sweet Potato, 3 ounces, with 1 teaspoon reduced-calorie tub margarine
Steamed Zucchini and Yellow Squash Slices, 1 cup
Sliced Cucumber and Tomato Salad, 2 cups, with Balsamic Vinaigrette (In small jar with tight-fitting lid or small bowl, combine 2 teaspoons balsamic vinegar, 1 teaspoon olive oil and pinch garlic powder; cover and shake well or, with wire whisk, blend until combined.)
Roll, 1 ounce, with $1^1/_2$ teaspoons reduced-calorie tub margarine
Aspartame-Sweetened Vanilla Nonfat Yogurt, $^3/_4$ cup
Unsweetened Cranberry Seltzer

SNACK

Graham Crackers, 3 ($2^1/_2$" squares)
Root Beer "Float" (In tall glass, combine 1 cup diet root beer and $^1/_3$ cup skim milk; add enough ice cubes to fill glass.)

This menu provides: 2 Milks, 3 Fats, 2 Fruits, $12^1/_4$ Vegetables, 3 Proteins, 5 Breads, 120 Optional Calories.

Per serving: 23 g Fat, 28 g Fiber.

CRAB AND ASPARAGUS STRATA

BRUNCH

Crab and Asparagus Strata, 1 serving (see recipe)

Steamed Baby Carrots, 1 cup, with 2 teaspoons reduced-calorie tub margarine

Watercress and Radicchio Salad, 2 cups, with 4 tomato wedges and 1 tablespoon French dressing

Flatbreads, 1¹/₂ ounces

Fresh Raspberry Coupe (In stemmed glass, layer ³/₄ cup raspberries and 1 cup aspartame-sweetened vanilla nonfat yogurt.)

Light Wine Spritzer (In wineglass, combine ¹/₂ cup *each* unsweetened seltzer and dry light white wine.)

MAIN MEAL

Broiled Flank Steak, 2 ounces

Baked Potato, 8 ounces, with 2 tablespoons nonfat sour cream and 1 tablespoon chives

Steamed Whole Green Beans, 1 cup

Pickled Beets (In medium bowl, combine 1 cup cooked sliced beets, ¹/₂ cup sliced onion, ¹/₄ cup cider vinegar, sugar substitute to equal 2 teaspoons sugar, pinch salt and freshly ground black pepper to taste; refrigerate, covered, at least 1 hour.)

Honeydew Melon, 2" wedge

Unsweetened Seltzer

SNACK

Graham Crackers, 3 (2¹/₂" squares)

Skim Milk, 1 cup

This menu provides: 2 Milks, 3 Fats, 2 Fruits, 12¹/₄ Vegetables, 3¹/₂ Proteins, 5¹/₂ Breads, 100 Optional Calories.

Per serving: 25 g Fat, 33 g Fiber.

For a brunch dish that looks like you were up at dawn fussing, prepare this lovely and elegant entrée the night before, then simply bake it in the morning.

Makes 6 servings

4 ounces French or Italian bread, cut into 1" cubes

3 ounces reduced-fat Swiss cheese, coarsely grated

12 asparagus spears, blanched and cut diagonally into 1" pieces

2 ounces drained canned crabmeat, flaked

1¹/₄ cups skim milk

1 cup egg substitute

1 tablespoon minced fresh tarragon leaves, or 1 teaspoon dried

1 teaspoon grated lemon zest*

¹/₄ teaspoon salt

¹/₄ teaspoon ground white pepper

1. Spray 11 × 7" baking dish with nonstick cooking spray; spread 2 cups of the bread cubes in prepared dish. Top bread evenly with cheese, then asparagus, crabmeat and remaining bread cubes.

2. In large bowl, with wire whisk, combine milk, egg substitute, tarragon, zest, salt and pepper; pour evenly over bread mixture. Refrigerate, covered, overnight.

3. Preheat oven to 325° F.

4. Bake strata, uncovered, 1 hour and 10 minutes, until lightly browned and knife inserted in center comes out clean.

Serving (one-sixth of strata) provides: ¹/₄ Vegetable, 1¹/₂ Proteins, ¹/₂ Bread, 30 Optional Calories.

Per serving: 148 Calories, 3 g Total Fat, 2 g Saturated Fat, 17 mg Cholesterol, 381 mg Sodium, 15 g Total Carbohydrate, 1 g Dietary Fiber, 14 g Protein, 110 mg Calcium.

The zest of the lemon is the peel without any of the pith (white membrane). To remove zest from lemon, use a zester or the fine side of a vegetable grater; wrap lemon in plastic wrap and refrigerate for use at another time.

85

CRAB IN
PHYLLO TRIANGLES

Makes 6 servings

2 tablespoons reduced-calorie stick margarine
2 teaspoons olive oil
$^1/_2$ cup minced scallions
One 10-ounce package frozen chopped spinach, cooked,
  drained and squeezed dry
6 ounces cooked crabmeat
$^1/_2$ cup nonfat cottage cheese
2 eggs, lightly beaten
$2^1/_4$ ounces feta cheese, crumbled
$^1/_4$ cup minced fresh flat-leaf parsley
$^1/_4$ cup minced fresh dill
1 tablespoon plain dried bread crumbs
$^1/_4$ teaspoon salt
Pinch freshly ground black pepper
6 ounces fresh or thawed frozen phyllo dough (about 9 sheets)*

1. Preheat oven to 375° F. Spray nonstick baking sheet with nonstick cooking spray.

2. In small saucepan, combine margarine and oil. Place over low heat; cook until margarine is melted and mixture is heated. Set aside; keep warm.

3. Transfer 1 tablespoon warm margarine mixture to medium nonstick skillet; heat. Add scallions; cook over medium-high heat, stirring frequently, 1 minute, until just softened.

4. Transfer scallion mixture to large bowl. With fork, stir in spinach, crabmeat, cottage cheese, eggs, feta cheese, parsley, dill, bread crumbs, salt and pepper.

5. Stack 3 phyllo sheets on work surface; brush evenly with one-sixth of the remaining margarine mixture. Cut stack in half lengthwise, making 2 strips. Spoon one-sixth of the spinach mixture onto one corner of each phyllo strip; fold flag-style, making 2 filled triangles. Repeat, making 4 more triangles.

6. Place triangles, seam-side down, onto prepared baking sheet; brush evenly with any remaining margarine mixture. Bake 35 minutes, until golden brown and heated through. Serve warm or at room temperature.

Serving (1 triangle) provides: 1 Fat, $^3/_4$ Vegetable, $1^1/_2$ Proteins, 1 Bread, 5 Optional Calories.

Per serving: 233 Calories, 10 g Total Fat, 3 g Saturated Fat, 110 mg Cholesterol, 606 mg Sodium, 20 g Total Carbohydrate, 1 g Dietary Fiber, 15 g Protein, 178 mg Calcium.

BRUNCH
Cantaloupe, $^1/_4$ small
Crab in Phyllo Triangles, 1 serving (see recipe)
Roasted New Potatoes, 4 ounces, with 1 teaspoon
  reduced-calorie tub margarine
Broiled Tomato (Cut 1 medium tomato in half crosswise; place, cut-side up, into broiler pan. Sprinkle
  tomato with $^1/_4$ teaspoon dried oregano leaves;
  broil until lightly browned and heated through.)
Torn Romaine Lettuce Leaves and Sliced Zucchini,
  2 cups, with Tarragon Basil Vinaigrette (In small
  jar with tight-fitting lid or small bowl, combine
  2 teaspoons tarragon vinegar, 1 teaspoon olive oil
  and pinch dried basil; cover and shake well or,
  with wire whisk, blend until combined.)
Aspartame-Sweetened Vanilla Nonfat Yogurt, 1 cup
Coffee or Tea (optional)

MAIN MEAL
Grilled Pork Chop, 2 ounces
Cooked Wide Noodles, 1 cup, with 1 teaspoon
  reduced-calorie tub margarine and $^1/_2$ teaspoon
  caraway seeds
Steamed Cabbage Wedge, 1 cup
Tossed Green Salad, 2 cups, with 1 tablespoon fat-
  free ranch dressing
Granny Smith Apple, 1 small
Sparkling Mineral Water with Lime Wedge

SNACK
Reduced-Fat Swiss Cheese, $^3/_4$ ounce
Fat-Free Crackers, 7
Skim Milk, 1 cup

This menu provides: 2 Milks, 3 Fats, 2 Fruits, $12^3/_4$ Vegetables, $4^1/_2$ Proteins, 5 Breads, 35 Optional Calories.

Per serving: 31 g Fat, 22 g Fiber.

*Phyllo dough dries out quickly. To help keep the individual sheets soft and pliable, keep them covered with plastic wrap until ready to use.

86
CRAB, PEAR AND
CHEESE STRUDEL

Makes 4 servings

2 small pears, pared, cored and chopped
8 ounces cooked crabmeat, flaked
3 ounces skim-milk mozzarella cheese, coarsely grated
2 ounces cooked lean Virginia ham, finely chopped
$^3/4$ cup drained canned water chestnuts, finely minced
$^1/2$ cup thinly sliced scallions
1 tablespoon fresh lemon juice
$^1/4$ teaspoon crushed red pepper flakes
4 ounces fresh or thawed frozen phyllo dough (about 6 sheets)*
1 tablespoon + 1 teaspoon canola oil
1 teaspoon plain dried bread crumbs

1. Preheat oven to 375° F. Spray 15 × 10" jelly-roll pan with nonstick cooking spray.

2. In large bowl, combine pears, crabmeat, cheese, ham, water chestnuts, scallions, juice and red pepper flakes.

3. Place 1 phyllo sheet onto 16" sheet of wax paper; brush evenly with $^1/2$ teaspoon of the oil. Top with another phyllo sheet; brush evenly with $^1/2$ teaspoon of the oil. Repeat with remaining phyllo sheets, brushing each with $^1/2$ teaspoon oil. Sprinkle top sheet evenly with bread crumbs.

4. Spoon pear mixture lengthwise along one side of phyllo stack, about 1" from edge of stack; fold the 1" of stack over pear mixture. Fold short edges of stack over pear mixture; roll jelly-roll fashion, using wax paper to help lift dough. Transfer roll to prepared pan; brush evenly with remaining 1 teaspoon oil. With sharp knife, lightly score top of roll. Bake 25–30 minutes, until lightly browned and heated through. Remove from oven; let stand 10 minutes. Cut into 4 equal portions.

Serving (one-fourth of strudel) provides: 1 Fat, $^1/2$ Fruit, $^1/4$ Vegetable, $2^1/2$ Proteins, $1^1/4$ Breads, 5 Optional Calories.

Per serving: 329 Calories, 12 g Total Fat, 3 g Saturated Fat, 77 mg Cholesterol, 575 mg Sodium, 33 g Total Carbohydrate, 3 g Dietary Fiber, 23 g Protein, 220 mg Calcium.

*Phyllo dough dries out quickly. To help keep the individual sheets soft and pliable, keep them covered with plastic wrap until ready to use.

LOBSTER AND ASPARAGUS CRÊPES

Makes 4 servings

Crêpes:
1/2 cup skim milk
1/3 cup + 2 teaspoons all-purpose flour
1 egg
1 egg white
2 teaspoons canola oil
1/4 teaspoon salt
1 tablespoon minced fresh chives

Filling:
24 thin asparagus spears
10 ounces cooked shelled lobster, cut into chunks

"Hollandaise" Sauce:
1/4 cup nonfat mayonnaise (10 calories per tablespoon)
1/4 cup hot water
1/4 teaspoon grated lemon zest*
2 tablespoons fresh lemon juice
Pinch ground red pepper

1. To prepare crêpes, in blender, combine milk, flour, egg, egg white, oil and salt; process until smooth. Transfer batter to 1-cup glass measure; stir in chives. Let stand 30 minutes.

2. Spray 6" nonstick skillet or crêpe pan with nonstick cooking spray; heat. Pour one-eighth of the batter (about 2 tablespoons) into skillet, tilting to cover bottom of pan. Cook over medium-high heat 30 seconds, until underside is lightly browned. Turn crêpe over; cook 5 seconds, until dry. Transfer crêpe to plate; cover with wax paper. Repeat, making 7 more crêpes, stirring batter before each use and stacking crêpes with wax paper between them to keep crêpes from sticking to each other.

3. Preheat oven to 350° F. Spray 11 × 7" baking dish with nonstick cooking spray.

4. To prepare filling, in large pot of boiling water, cook asparagus 3 minutes, until just tender. Drain, discarding liquid; rinse with cold water. Drain again; set aside.

5. Place 1 crêpe onto work surface; top with 3 cooked asparagus spears. Top asparagus with one-eighth of the lobster; roll crêpe to enclose. Place, seam-side down, into prepared baking dish. Repeat, making 7 more stuffed crêpes. Bake, covered, 15 minutes, until heated through.

6. To prepare sauce, in double boiler, with wire whisk, combine mayonnaise and water, blending until smooth; cook over simmering water, stirring constantly with wire whisk, 1–2 minutes, until heated. Remove from heat; stir in zest, juice and pepper. (Sauce should be thick but pourable; if too thick, stir in 1–2 tablespoons water, 1 teaspoon at a time, until desired consistency.)

7. Place 2 filled crêpes onto each of 4 plates; top each portion with one-fourth of the sauce.

BRUNCH

Papaya, 1/2 medium, with lime wedge
Lobster and Asparagus Crêpes, 1 serving (see recipe)
Steamed Baby Carrots, 1 cup, with 1 teaspoon reduced-calorie tub margarine
Bibb Lettuce and Endive Salad, 2 cups, with Raspberry Vinaigrette (In small jar with tight-fitting lid or small bowl, combine 1 tablespoon raspberry vinegar and 1 teaspoon olive oil; cover and shake well or, with wire whisk, blend until combined.)
Crispbreads, 1 1/2 ounces
Cherry Parfait (In stemmed glass, layer 1/2 cup reduced-calorie vanilla-flavored pudding [made with skim milk] and 12 large cherries, pitted and chopped.)
Cappuccino, made with skim milk, 5 fluid ounces

MAIN MEAL

Grilled Turkey and Vegetables (Preheat grill according to manufacturer's directions. Grill one 3-ounce boneless turkey cutlet and 1 cup *each* sliced eggplant and zucchini, turning as needed and basting with 1 tablespoon barbecue sauce, until turkey is cooked through and vegetables are lightly browned and tender.)
Cooked Polenta, 1/2 cup, with 1 teaspoon reduced-calorie tub margarine
Semolina Roll, 1 ounce, with 1 teaspoon reduced-calorie tub margarine
Aspartame-Sweetened Coffee Nonfat Yogurt, 1 cup
Iced Tea with Lemon Wedge

SNACK

Plain Popcorn, hot-air popped, 3 cups, with 1 teaspoon freshly grated Parmesan cheese
Diet Lemon-Lime Soda

This menu provides: 2 Milks, 3 Fats, 2 Fruits, 11 Vegetables, 3 1/2 Proteins, 5 1/2 Breads, 95 Optional Calories.

Per serving: 24 g Fat, 22 g Fiber.

Serving (2 filled crêpes, 2 tablespoons sauce) provides: 1/2 Fat, 1 Vegetable, 1 1/2 Proteins, 1/2 Bread, 25 Optional Calories.

Per serving: 212 Calories, 7 g Total Fat, 1 g Saturated Fat, 105 mg Cholesterol, 557 mg Sodium, 17 g Total Carbohydrate, 1 g Dietary Fiber, 22 g Protein, 110 mg Calcium.

*The zest of the lemon is the peel without any of the pith (white membrane). To remove zest from lemon, use a zester or the fine side of a vegetable grater.

88
CRUSTLESS TUNA QUICHE

Makes 6 servings

6 ounces drained canned water-packed white tuna, flaked
$3^3/_4$ ounces reduced-fat Swiss cheese, coarsely grated
1 cup cooked chopped kale, squeezed dry
$^1/_2$ cup diced red bell pepper
$^1/_2$ cup diced onion
2 tablespoons all-purpose flour
$^1/_2$ teaspoon salt
1 cup egg substitute
1 cup skim milk
$^1/_2$ teaspoon hot pepper sauce
2 large plum tomatoes, thinly sliced

1. Preheat oven to 350° F. Spray 9" round baking dish or pie plate with nonstick cooking spray.

2. In medium bowl, combine tuna, cheese, kale, bell pepper, onion, flour and salt; transfer to prepared dish, spreading evenly.

3. In same bowl, with wire whisk, combine egg substitute, milk and hot pepper sauce; pour over tuna mixture. Bake 30 minutes, until set around edges.

4. Arrange tomato slices around edge of tuna mixture; bake 10–15 minutes longer, until knife inserted in center comes out clean and tomatoes are slightly softened. Let stand 10 minutes; cut into 6 equal wedges.

Serving (1 wedge) provides: 1 Vegetable, 2 Proteins, 25 Optional Calories.

Per serving: 151 Calories, 4 g Total Fat, 2 g Saturated Fat, 22 mg Cholesterol, 462 mg Sodium, 9 g Total Carbohydrate, 2 g Dietary Fiber, 19 g Protein, 85 mg Calcium.

WESTERN SCROD AND HAM OMELET

Makes 2 servings

5 ounces scrod fillets
2 eggs
2 egg whites
$^1/_2$ teaspoon salt
1 ounce cooked smoked ham, finely chopped
2 tablespoons finely minced red onion
2 tablespoons finely minced green bell pepper
1 tablespoon minced fresh cilantro
1 tablespoon reduced-calorie stick margarine

1. Preheat broiler.

2. In medium nonstick skillet, bring 2 cups water to a boil. Reduce heat to low; add scrod. Poach scrod 5–7 minutes, until fish flakes easily when tested with fork. With slotted spoon, transfer scrod to paper towels to drain. Flake scrod; set aside.

3. In medium bowl, with fork, combine eggs, egg whites and salt; stir in ham, onion, bell pepper, cilantro and flaked scrod.

4. In large nonstick skillet with flameproof or removable handle, melt margarine; add egg mixture, tilting to cover bottom of pan. Cook over medium-high heat until underside is set, lifting edges with spatula to let uncooked egg flow underneath. Broil 1–2 minutes, until top is set; with spatula, fold omelet in half. Slide omelet onto serving platter; cut in half.

Serving (one-half omelet) provides: 1 Fat, $^1/_4$ Vegetable, $2^1/_2$ Proteins, 20 Optional Calories.

Per serving: 198 Calories, 9 g Total Fat, 2 g Saturated Fat, 250 mg Cholesterol, 975 mg Sodium, 2 g Total Carbohydrate, 0 g Dietary Fiber, 25 g Protein, 48 mg Calcium.

BRUNCH
Orange Sections, $^1/_2$ cup
Western Scrod and Ham Omelet, 1 serving (see recipe)
Stewed Rhubarb, $^1/_2$ cup
Torn Curly Endive, 2 cups, with $^1/_2$ cup *each* shredded zucchini and sliced mushrooms and 1 tablespoon balsamic vinegar
Crispbreads, $^3/_4$ ounce
Gingersnaps, 1 ounce
Cappuccino, made with skim milk, 5 fluid ounces

MAIN MEAL
Spaghetti with Meat Sauce (In medium nonstick skillet, cook 3 ounces extra-lean ground beef [10% or less fat] over medium-high heat, stirring to break up meat, 2–3 minutes, until no longer pink. Drain; return to skillet. Add $^1/_2$ cup tomato sauce [no salt added] and $^1/_4$ teaspoon *each* dried basil and oregano leaves; stir to combine. Pour meat mixture over 1 cup hot cooked spaghetti; sprinkle with 1 tablespoon freshly grated Parmesan cheese.)
Tossed Green Salad, 2 cups, with $^1/_2$ cup *each* red and green bell pepper strips and 1 tablespoon blue cheese dressing
Italian Bread, 1 ounce
Reduced-Calorie Butterscotch-Flavored Pudding (made with skim milk), $^1/_2$ cup
Diet Lemon-Lime Soda

SNACK
Plain Popcorn, hot-air popped, 3 cups
Double Strawberry Shake (In blender, combine 1 cup frozen strawberries, 1 cup cold water and 1 packet reduced-calorie strawberry dairy shake mix; purée until smooth and thick.)

This menu provides: 2 Milks, 3 Fats, 2 Fruits, $15^1/_4$ Vegetables, $4^1/_2$ Proteins, 6 Breads, 130 Optional Calories.

Per serving: 35 g Fat, 21 g Fiber.

90
SCRAMBLED EGGS WITH COD AND ROASTED RED PEPPER

Makes 4 servings

10 ounces cod fillet
4 eggs
4 egg whites
¹/₄ teaspoon salt
¹/₄ teaspoon freshly ground black pepper
2 teaspoons olive oil
1 garlic clove, minced
¹/₂ cup roasted red bell pepper, patted dry
¹/₄ teaspoon dried sage leaves, crumbled
Four 1-ounce slices country white bread (¹/₂" slices), toasted
1 tablespoon + 1 teaspoon anchovy paste

1. In medium nonstick skillet, bring 2 cups water to a boil. Reduce heat to low; add cod. Poach cod 5–7 minutes, until fish flakes easily when tested with fork. With slotted spoon, transfer cod to paper towels to drain. Flake cod; set aside.

2. In medium bowl, with wire whisk, combine eggs, egg whites, salt and black pepper.

3. In large nonstick skillet, heat oil; add garlic. Cook over medium-low heat, stirring frequently, until golden brown. Add egg mixture; cook, stirring gently, until mixture forms soft, creamy curds. With fork, stir in bell pepper, sage and flaked cod; cook, stirring occasionally, 1–2 minutes, until mixture is heated through.

4. Spread each toast slice with 1 teaspoon of the anchovy paste; place each on a plate. Top each toast slice with one-fourth of the egg mixture.

Serving (1 slice toast, ¹/₂ cup egg mixture) provides: ¹/₂ Fat, ¹/₄ Vegetable, 2¹/₄ Proteins, 1 Bread, 20 Optional Calories.

Per serving: 265 Calories, 9 g Total Fat, 2 g Saturated Fat, 247 mg Cholesterol, 700 mg Sodium, 17 g Total Carbohydrate, 1 g Dietary Fiber, 26 g Protein, 86 mg Calcium.

91

CLAM AND POTATO FRITTATA

Makes 4 servings

1 cup cut asparagus (2" pieces)
1 tablespoon + 1 teaspoon olive oil
1 medium tomato, seeded and minced
1/2 cup thinly sliced red onion
3 garlic cloves, minced
1 teaspoon minced fresh oregano leaves
8 ounces cooked red potatoes, cut into 1/2" pieces

4 ounces drained canned whole baby clams
1/4 teaspoon salt
1/4 teaspoon freshly ground black pepper
4 eggs
4 egg whites
1 1/2 ounces Asiago cheese, grated

1. In large pot of boiling water, cook asparagus 3 minutes, until just tender. Drain, discarding liquid; rinse with cold water. Drain again; set aside.

2. Preheat broiler.

3. In large nonstick skillet with flameproof or removable handle, heat 2 teaspoons of the oil; add half of the tomato, the onion, garlic and oregano. Cook over medium-high heat, stirring frequently, 5 minutes, until onion is softened. Add potatoes; cook, stirring occasionally, 4 minutes, until potatoes are lightly browned. Add drained asparagus; cook, stirring frequently, until heated through.

4. Transfer vegetable mixture to large bowl; wipe skillet clean. Add clams, salt and pepper to vegetable mixture; stir to combine.

5. In medium bowl, with wire whisk, combine eggs, egg whites and 1 ounce of the cheese. Add egg mixture to vegetable mixture; stir to combine.

6. In same skillet, heat remaining 2 teaspoons oil; add egg mixture, spreading to cover bottom of skillet. Cook over medium-low heat 5 minutes, until bottom is browned and edges are set.

7. Transfer skillet to broiler; broil 1-2 minutes, until top is lightly browned and mixture is set.

8. Cut frittata into 4 equal wedges; place 1 wedge on each of 4 plates. Top each wedge with an equal amount of remaining tomato and cheese.

Serving (1 wedge, 2 tablespoons tomato, 3/4 teaspoon cheese) provides: 1 Fat, 1 1/4 Vegetables, 2 1/4 Proteins, 1/2 Bread, 5 Optional Calories.

Per serving: 295 Calories, 13 g Total Fat, 5 g Saturated Fat, 239 mg Cholesterol, 416 mg Sodium, 19 g Total Carbohydrate, 2 g Dietary Fiber, 23 g Protein, 170 mg Calcium.

BRUNCH

Clam and Potato Frittata, 1 serving (see recipe)
Steamed Sliced Broccoli Rabe, 1 cup, with 1 teaspoon olive oil and 1 garlic clove, minced
Tossed Green Salad, 2 cups, with 1 ounce drained canned red kidney beans, 1/2 cup cucumber slices and 1 tablespoon fat-free Italian dressing
Roll, 1 ounce, with 1 teaspoon reduced-calorie tub margarine
Pineapple, 1/8 medium
Skim Milk, 1 cup
Coffee or Tea (optional)

MAIN MEAL

Roast Pork, 2 ounces
Roasted New Potatoes, 4 ounces
Steamed Cabbage Wedge, 1
Arugula and Bibb Lettuce Salad, 2 cups, with 1/4 cup packaged croutons and 1 tablespoon balsamic vinegar
Blueberries, 3/4 cup
Sparkling Mineral Water

SNACK

Whole-Wheat Pretzels, 1 1/2 ounces
Skim Milk, 1 cup

This menu provides: 2 Milks, 3 Fats, 2 Fruits, 13 1/4 Vegetables, 4 3/4 Proteins, 5 Breads, 10 Optional Calories.

Per serving: 32 g Fat, 21 g Fiber.

Clam and Potato Frittata

92

TROUT AMANDINE WITH POTATO GALETTES

Makes 4 servings

10 ounces red Bliss potatoes
2 teaspoons olive oil
Pinch salt
Pinch freshly ground black pepper
4 fluid ounces ($^1/_2$ cup) dry white wine
$^1/_4$ cup fresh lemon juice
4 lemon slices

2 fresh flat-leaf parsley sprigs
Four 5-ounce trout fillets
2 teaspoons reduced-calorie tub margarine
1 ounce slivered almonds, toasted*
1 tablespoon minced fresh flat-leaf parsley

1. Preheat oven to 375° F. Spray nonstick baking sheet with nonstick cooking spray.

2. To prepare galettes, with sharp knife, slice potatoes $^1/_8$" thick; transfer to medium bowl. Add oil, salt and pepper; toss gently.

3. On work surface, arrange potato slices evenly into four 5" circles, overlapping slices as necessary; press slices together.

4. Spray large nonstick skillet with nonstick cooking spray; heat. With wide metal spatula, transfer 2 potato circles to skillet; cook over medium-low heat 5 minutes, until centers of potato slices are translucent and edges are slightly curled and lightly browned. With same spatula, turn potato circles over; cook 5 minutes, until lightly browned on bottom. Transfer galettes to prepared baking sheet; repeat with remaining potato circles. Bake 10 minutes, until crispy.

5. Meanwhile, in clean large skillet, combine wine, juice, lemon slices and parsley sprigs; bring liquid to a boil. Add fish in a single layer; reduce heat to low. Simmer, covered, 4–6 minutes, until fish flakes easily when tested with fork.

6. With slotted spatula, transfer each fish fillet to plate; keep warm.

7. Remove and discard lemon slices and parsley sprigs from wine mixture; add margarine, swirling skillet until margarine is melted. Spoon one-fourth of the wine mixture over each warm fish fillet; sprinkle evenly with almonds and minced parsley. Serve each portion with 1 potato galette.

Serving (1 fish fillet, 1$^1/_2$ tablespoons wine mixture, 1 potato galette) provides: 1$^1/_4$ Fats, 2$^1/_4$ Proteins, $^1/_2$ Bread, 25 Optional Calories.

Per serving: 368 Calories, 17 g Total Fat, 2 g Saturated Fat, 82 mg Cholesterol, 132 mg Sodium, 17 g Total Carbohydrate, 2 g Dietary Fiber, 32 g Protein, 94 mg Calcium.

To toast almonds, in small nonstick skillet, cook almonds over low heat, stirring constantly, until golden brown; immediately transfer to heat-resistant plate to cool.

BRUNCH

Trout Amandine with Potato Galette, 1 serving (see recipe)
Steamed Asparagus, 6 spears
Steamed Whole Baby Carrots, 1 cup
Crispbreads, $^3/_4$ ounce, with 1$^1/_2$ teaspoons reduced-calorie tub margarine
Bibb Lettuce and Watercress Salad, 2 cups, with 1 ounce sliced avocado and 1 tablespoon fat-free Italian dressing
Blueberries, $^3/_4$ cup
Coffee or Tea (optional)

MAIN MEAL

Broiled Flank Steak, 2 ounces
Cooked Chopped Broccoli, 1 cup
Black Bean and Rice Salad (In small bowl, combine $^3/_4$ cup cooked brown rice, 1 ounce drained cooked black beans, $^1/_4$ cup salsa and $^1/_2$ teaspoon minced, deveined and seeded jalapeño pepper [wear gloves to prevent irritation].)
Cherry-Raisin Yogurt (In small bowl, combine 1 cup aspartame-sweetened cherry-vanilla nonfat yogurt and 2 tablespoons raisins.)
Sparkling Mineral Water

SNACK

Pretzel Sticks, 1$^1/_2$ ounces
Skim Milk, 1 cup

This menu provides: 2 Milks, 3 Fats, 2 Fruits, 10 Vegetables, 4$^3/_4$ Proteins, 5 Breads, 45 Optional Calories.

Per serving: 35 g Fat, 25 g Fiber.

93
LIME-GRILLED TROUT WITH MEXICAN CORN FRITTERS

Makes 4 servings

Two 12-ounce whole rainbow trout,
   cleaned, scaled and thoroughly
   washed*
$^1/_4$ cup fresh lime juice
1 tablespoon olive oil
$^1/_4$ teaspoon ground red pepper
2 egg whites
$^1/_4$ teaspoon salt

1 cup drained canned corn kernels
2 tablespoons minced scallions
1 tablespoon all-purpose flour
2 teaspoons chopped deveined
   seeded jalapeño pepper (wear
   gloves to prevent irritation)
$^1/_2$ teaspoon double-acting baking
   powder

1. Make 3 or 4 diagonal slashes on both sides of each fish.

2. To prepare marinade, in gallon-size sealable plastic bag, combine juice, oil and half of the ground red pepper; add fish. Seal bag, squeezing out air; turn to coat fish. Refrigerate at least 1 hour, turning bag occasionally.

3. In medium bowl, combine egg whites, salt and remaining ground red pepper; with electric mixer, beat until stiff peaks form. Fold in corn, scallions, flour, jalapeño pepper and baking powder.

4. Spray large nonstick skillet or griddle with nonstick cooking spray; heat. Drop half the egg white mixture by tablespoonfuls into skillet, making six 2" fritters. Cook 2–3 minutes, until edges of fritters are set; turn and cook 2–3 minutes longer. With spatula, remove fritters from skillet; keep warm. Repeat, making 6 more fritters.

5. Preheat outdoor barbecue grill or indoor stove-top grill according to manufacturer's directions.

6. Drain marinade into small saucepan; bring to a rolling boil; boil for 1 minute, stirring constantly. Remove from heat. Grill trout over hot coals or on stove-top grill, turning once and brushing with remaining marinade, 5–7 minutes, until fish flakes easily when tested with fork.

7. Remove skin and bones from fish; remove both fillets from each trout in a single piece. Serve each fillet with 3 fritters.

Serving (1 trout fillet, 3 fritters) provides: 1 Protein, $^1/_2$ Bread, 50 Optional Calories.

Per serving: 162 Calories, 5 g Total Fat, 1 g Saturated Fat, 40 mg Cholesterol, 386 mg Sodium, 13 g Total Carbohydrate, 1 g Dietary Fiber, 18 g Protein, 89 mg Calcium.

*A 12-ounce rainbow trout will yield about 4 ounces cooked fish.

Angel Hair with Smoked Salmon and Caviar

This elegant entrée is a perfect brunch dish when celebrating a special occasion or whenever you want a special treat!

Makes 4 servings

6 ounces angel hair pasta (capellini)
1 tablespoon + 1 teaspoon reduced-calorie tub margarine
$^1/_4$ cup sliced scallions
$^1/_4$ cup low-sodium chicken broth
2 tablespoons heavy cream
1 fluid ounce (2 tablespoons) vodka
3 ounces smoked salmon, cut into thin strips
1 ounce drained red lumpfish caviar

1. In large pot of boiling water, cook pasta 3 minutes, until tender. Drain, discarding liquid; place into serving bowl. Keep warm.

2. In small nonstick skillet, melt margarine; add scallions. Cook over medium-high heat, stirring constantly, 1 minute, until just softened. Reduce heat to low; add broth, cream and vodka. Cook, stirring constantly, just until heated through (do not boil).

3. Pour broth mixture over warm pasta; toss to combine. Add smoked salmon and caviar; toss again.

Serving (1 cup) provides: $^1/_2$ Fat, $^1/_4$ Vegetable, 1 Protein, 2 Breads, 45 Optional Calories.

Per serving: 262 Calories, 8 g Total Fat, 2 g Saturated Fat, 57 mg Cholesterol, 320 mg Sodium, 33 g Total Carbohydrate, 1 g Dietary Fiber, 12 g Protein, 20 mg Calcium.

BRUNCH

Orange Sparkler (In stemmed glass, combine $^1/_2$ cup sparkling mineral water and 2 tablespoons thawed frozen orange juice concentrate; add enough ice cubes to fill glass.)

Angel Hair with Smoked Salmon and Caviar, 1 serving (see recipe)

Steamed Asparagus, 6 spears, with Lemon "Butter" (In small cup or bowl, combine 1 teaspoon *each* reduced-calorie tub margarine, melted, and fresh lemon juice.)

Steamed Sliced Carrots, 1 cup

Watercress, Radicchio and Endive Salad, 2 cups, with 1 tablespoon fat-free Italian dressing

Roll, 1 ounce, with 1 teaspoon reduced-calorie tub margarine

Peach Melba (Scoop 4 fluid ounces sugar-free vanilla nonfat frozen yogurt into small bowl. Pare, pit and slice $^1/_2$ medium peach. Surround frozen yogurt with peach slices; top with $1^1/_2$ teaspoons raspberry spreadable fruit.)

Coffee or Tea (optional)

MAIN MEAL

Sirloin Steak, 2 ounces

Baked Potato, 8 ounces, with 3 tablespoons plain nonfat yogurt and 1 tablespoon minced scallion

Steamed Zucchini and Yellow Squash Slices, 1 cup

Tomato, 1 medium, sliced, with 1 teaspoon balsamic vinegar

Sugar-Free Cherry-Flavored Gelatin, $^1/_2$ cup, with 1 tablespoon thawed frozen light whipped topping (8 calories per tablespoon)

Decaffeinated Cappuccino, made with skim milk, 5 fluid ounces

SNACK

Peanut Butter–Vanilla Shake (In blender, combine 1 cup skim milk, 3 ice cubes, sugar substitute to equal 2 teaspoons sugar, $1^1/_2$ teaspoons smooth peanut butter and 1 teaspoon vanilla extract; purée until smooth.)

This menu provides: 2 Milks, 3 Fats, 2 Fruits, $11^1/_2$ Vegetables, 3 Proteins, 5 Breads, 120 Optional Calories.

Per serving: 25 g Fat, 22 g Fiber.

EASY SEAFOOD LASAGNA

Makes 4 servings

4 ounces curly or plain lasagna noodles (4 noodles)
1 1/2 cups coarsely shredded zucchini
1 cup coarsely shredded carrot
1/2 cup chopped onion
1/2 cup part-skim ricotta cheese
4 ounces drained canned shrimp, patted dry
4 ounces drained canned crabmeat, squeezed dry
1 tablespoon minced fresh basil
2 teaspoons fresh lime juice
1/4 teaspoon ground red pepper
1 tablespoon cornstarch
1/4 teaspoon salt
2 cups tomato sauce (no salt added)
1 1/2 ounces skim-milk mozzarella cheese, grated

1. Preheat oven to 375° F.

2. In large pot of boiling water, cook lasagna noodles 10–12 minutes, until tender. Drain, discarding liquid; rinse with cold water. Drain again. Cut each noodle in half lengthwise; keeping noodles flat and separate, cover with plastic wrap and set aside.

3. In large nonstick skillet, combine zucchini, carrot, onion and 1/3 cup water; bring liquid to a boil. Cook over medium-high heat, stirring constantly, until water is evaporated and vegetables are dry (do not brown).

4. Transfer cooked vegetables to large bowl. Add ricotta cheese, shrimp, crabmeat, basil, juice and pepper; with fork, mix well.

5. Place cooked noodles onto work surface; spread each with an equal amount of cheese mixture. Starting at narrow ends, loosely roll noodles jelly-roll fashion; place into 10 × 7" baking dish, cut-side down.

6. In medium saucepan, combine cornstarch and salt; add tomato sauce, stirring until cornstarch is dissolved. Cook over medium-low heat, stirring constantly, until mixture comes to a boil and is slightly thickened. Spoon sauce mixture over and around lasagna rolls; sprinkle rolls evenly with mozzarella cheese. Bake, covered, 45 minutes, until heated through. Remove from oven; let stand 10 minutes.

Serving (2 lasagna rolls, one-fourth of the sauce) provides: 3 1/2 Vegetables, 2 Proteins, 1 1/4 Breads, 15 Optional Calories.

Per serving: 312 Calories, 6 g Total Fat, 3 g Saturated Fat, 90 mg Cholesterol, 404 mg Sodium, 40 g Total Carbohydrate, 4 g Dietary Fiber, 25 g Protein, 229 mg Calcium.

BRUNCH

Grapefruit Sparkler (In stemmed glass, combine 1/2 cup sparkling mineral water and 2 tablespoons thawed frozen grapefruit juice concentrate; add enough ice cubes to fill glass.)
Easy Seafood Lasagna, 1 serving (see recipe)
Steamed Broccoli, 4 spears, with 1 lemon wedge
Arugula and Curly Endive Salad, 2 cups, with 1/2 cup cucumber slices and 1 tablespoon fat-free creamy Italian dressing
Breadsticks, 2 long
Strawberries, 1 cup, with 1 tablespoon thawed frozen light whipped topping (8 calories per tablespoon)
Cappuccino, made with skim milk, 5 fluid ounces

MAIN MEAL

Mustard-Broiled Chicken Breast (In cup or small bowl, combine 1 teaspoon Dijon-style mustard and 1 garlic clove, minced; spread onto 3-ounce skinless boneless chicken breast. Broil chicken until cooked through.)
Corn and Rice Medley (In small bowl, combine 1/2 cup *each* cooked corn kernels and long-grain brown rice, 1 tablespoon minced scallions and 2 teaspoons reduced-calorie tub margarine.)
Steamed Whole Green Beans, 1 cup
Sliced Tomato, 1 medium, on 2 iceberg lettuce leaves, with Basil Vinaigrette (In small jar with tight-fitting lid or small bowl, combine 1 tablespoon balsamic vinegar, 2 teaspoons olive oil and 1 teaspoon minced fresh basil; cover and shake well or, with wire whisk, blend until combined.)
Reduced-Calorie Butterscotch-Flavored Pudding (made with skim milk), 1/2 cup
Iced Tea with Mint Sprig

SNACK

Gingersnaps, 1 ounce
Skim Milk, 1 cup

This menu provides: 2 Milks, 3 Fats, 2 Fruits, 15 1/4 Vegetables, 4 Proteins, 5 1/4 Breads, 125 Optional Calories.

Per serving: 30 g Fat, 21 g Fiber.

96

SALMON SOUFFLÉ ROLL

Makes 6 servings

Soufflé:

2 cups skim milk

²/₃ cup minus 1 tablespoon
all-purpose flour

¹/₂ teaspoon salt

Pinch freshly ground black pepper

3 tablespoons reduced-calorie tub
margarine

2¹/₄ ounces freshly grated
Parmesan cheese

4 eggs, separated

Filling:

1 tablespoon + 1 teaspoon
reduced-calorie tub margarine

¹/₂ cup thinly sliced scallions

3 garlic cloves, minced

¹/₂ cup finely minced mushrooms

One 10-ounce package frozen
chopped spinach, cooked and
squeezed dry

2 tablespoons minced fresh basil

¹/₂ cup part-skim ricotta cheese

1 tablespoon Dijon-style mustard

Pinch ground nutmeg

6 ounces drained canned salmon,
flaked

Fresh basil leaves and lemon
wedges, to garnish

1. To prepare soufflé, in medium bowl, whisk milk, all but 2 teaspoons of the flour, the salt and pepper, blending until flour is dissolved.

2. In medium saucepan, melt 2 tablespoons + 2 teaspoons of the margarine; stir in milk mixture. Cook over low heat, stirring, 4–5 minutes, until mixture comes to a boil and thickens; stir in Parmesan cheese.

3. In medium bowl, with wire whisk, beat egg yolks just until smooth. Continuing to beat, add half of the milk mixture, then beat yolk mixture into remaining milk mixture. Let stand, stirring occasionally, 15 minutes.

4. Meanwhile, preheat oven to 375° F. Spray 15 × 10" jelly-roll pan with nonstick cooking spray.

5. Line prepared pan with wax paper, allowing paper to extend at short ends. Spread wax paper with remaining 1 teaspoon margarine; sprinkle evenly with remaining 2 teaspoons flour.

6. In small bowl, with electric mixer on high speed, beat egg whites until stiff peaks form. With wire whisk, gently fold beaten whites into cooled milk mixture, one-third at a time, until mixture is smooth; pour into prepared pan, spreading evenly. Bake 40 minutes, until golden brown.

7. Remove soufflé from oven; leave oven on. Place sheet of wax paper over soufflé; top with inverted 15 × 10" jelly-roll pan. Invert pans and soufflé together; lift off top pan. Let stand 1 minute. Using small sharp knife, carefully remove top sheet of wax paper.

8. To prepare filling, in clean medium saucepan, melt margarine; add scallions and garlic. Cook over medium-high heat, stirring frequently, 2 minutes, until softened. Add mushrooms; cook 5 minutes, until mushrooms are tender. Stir in spinach and basil; cook 2 minutes, until heated. Remove from heat; stir in ricotta cheese, mustard and nutmeg.

9. Spread soufflé evenly with filling, then salmon. Roll up soufflé from short end; transfer to jelly-roll pan, discarding wax paper. Bake, loosely covered, 10–15 minutes, until heated.

10. Cut roll into 6 equal portions; serve garnished with basil and lemon.

Serving (1 portion) provides: ¹/₄ Milk, 1 Fat, 1 Vegetable, 2¹/₂ Proteins, ¹/₂ Bread, 15 Optional Calories.

Per serving: 301 Calories, 15 g Total Fat, 5 g Saturated Fat, 171 mg Cholesterol, 813 mg Sodium, 19 g Total Carbohydrate, 2 g Dietary Fiber, 23 g Protein, 456 mg Calcium.

BRUNCH

Pineapple, ¹/₈ medium

Salmon Soufflé Roll, 1 serving (see recipe)

Steamed Sliced Carrots, 1 cup, with 1 tablespoon minced fresh flat-leaf parsley and 1 lemon wedge

Radicchio and Belgian Endive Salad, 2 cups, with 1 tablespoon fat-free Italian dressing

Roll, 1 ounce, with 1 teaspoon reduced-calorie tub margarine

Angel Food Cake, 2 ounces, with ¹/₂ cup strawberries, sliced

Skim Milk, 1 cup

Coffee or Tea (optional)

MAIN MEAL

Skinless Roast Chicken Breast, 2 ounces

Baked Sweet Potato, 6 ounces, with 1 teaspoon reduced-calorie tub margarine

Steamed Italian Green Beans, 1 cup

Shredded Green Cabbage and Carrot Salad, 1 cup, with 1 tablespoon fat-free ranch dressing

Plum, 1 small

Unsweetened Mandarin Orange–Flavored Seltzer

SNACK

Graham Crackers, 3 (2¹/₂" squares)

Peanut Butter–Chocolate Shake (In blender, combine ³/₄ cup skim milk, 3 ice cubes, 1 teaspoon *each* smooth peanut butter and chocolate syrup and sugar substitute to equal 2 teaspoons sugar; purée.

This menu provides: 2 Milks, 3 Fats, 2 Fruits, 11 Vegetables, 4³/₄ Proteins, 4³/₄ Breads, 130 Optional Calories.

Per serving: 32 g Fat, 24 g Fiber.

SHRIMP AND SCALLOP SHELLS

Makes 4 servings

BRUNCH

White Grape Sparkler (In stemmed glass, combine $^1/_2$ cup sparkling mineral water and 1 tablespoon + 1 teaspoon thawed frozen white grape juice concentrate; add enough ice cubes to fill glass.)

Shrimp and Scallop Shells, 1 serving (see recipe)

Cooked Green Peas, $^1/_2$ cup, with 1 tablespoon minced fresh mint and 1 teaspoon reduced-calorie tub margarine

Watercress and Endive Salad, 2 cups, with 1 tablespoon fat-free French dressing

Crispbreads, $^3/_4$ ounce

Raspberries, $^3/_4$ cup

Skim Milk, $^1/_2$ cup

Coffee or Tea (optional)

MAIN MEAL

Broiled Turkey Burger, 2 ounces, on 2-ounce hamburger roll with 2 teaspoons ketchup

Oven "Fries" (Preheat oven to 450° F. Cut 5 ounces all-purpose potato into sticks; place onto nonstick baking sheet. Spray potato sticks lightly with nonstick cooking spray; sprinkle with $^1/_4$ teaspoon each salt and paprika. Bake 8–10 minutes, until potato sticks are crispy outside and tender inside.)

Dill Pickle, 1 medium

Tossed Green Salad, 2 cups, with 6 cherry tomatoes, $^1/_2$ cup sliced cucumber and 1 tablespoon Thousand Island dressing

Reduced-Calorie Chocolate-Flavored Pudding (made with skim milk), $^1/_2$ cup

Diet Root Beer

SNACK

Vanilla "Egg Cream" (In tall glass, combine 1 cup diet cream soda and $^1/_2$ cup skim milk.)

This menu provides: 2 Milks, 3 Fats, 2 Fruits, 13 Vegetables, 4 Proteins, 5 Breads, 100 Optional Calories.

Per serving: 26 g Fat, 21 g Fiber.

---

1 tablespoon reduced-calorie stick margarine

2 cups thinly sliced mushrooms

2 tablespoons finely minced shallots

1 garlic clove, minced

1 cup evaporated skimmed milk

2 fluid ounces ($^1/_4$ cup) dry white wine

2 tablespoons all-purpose flour

Pinch salt

Pinch freshly ground black pepper

15 ounces deveined peeled medium shrimp

5 ounces bay scallops

1 tablespoon minced fresh flat-leaf parsley

1. In large nonstick skillet, melt margarine; add mushrooms, shallots and garlic. Cook over medium-high heat, stirring frequently, 5 minutes, until mushrooms are tender. Remove from skillet; set aside.

2. In medium bowl, with wire whisk, combine milk, wine, flour, salt and pepper, blending until flour is dissolved. Pour into same skillet; cook over medium-low heat, stirring constantly, 2 minutes, until thickened (do not boil). Add shrimp, scallops and cooked mushroom mixture; cook, stirring frequently, 3–4 minutes, until shrimp turn pink and scallops are opaque in center.

3. Divide shrimp mixture evenly among 4 scallop shells or small au gratin dishes; sprinkle evenly with parsley.

Serving ($^1/_2$ cup) provides: $^1/_2$ Milk, $^1/_2$ Fat, 1 Vegetable, 2 Proteins, 30 Optional Calories.

Per serving: 244 Calories, 4 g Total Fat, 1 g Saturated Fat, 176 mg Cholesterol, 358 mg Sodium, 15 g Total Carbohydrate, 1 g Dietary Fiber, 34 g Protein, 258 mg Calcium.

9 8

POTATO-TOPPED FISH PIE

Makes 4 servings

Potato Topping:

15 ounces russet or all-purpose
   potatoes, pared and cubed
$^1/_2$ cup skim milk
1 tablespoon reduced-calorie stick
   margarine
$^1/_4$ teaspoon salt
Pinch paprika

Filling:

1 cup diagonally sliced carrot
1 cup frozen Italian green beans

10 ounces scrod fillets
$^1/_4$ cup minced fresh flat-leaf
   parsley
1 tablespoon minced fresh dill
3 tablespoons all-purpose flour
$^1/_2$ teaspoon salt
Pinch freshly ground black pepper
$1^1/_2$ cups skim milk
2 tablespoons reduced-calorie stick
   margarine
1 cup sliced mushrooms

1. To prepare topping, place potatoes into medium saucepan; add water to cover. Bring liquid to a boil; reduce heat to low. Simmer 15–20 minutes, until potatoes are tender. Drain, discarding liquid. Return potatoes to saucepan; cook over low heat, stirring frequently, 1 minute, until dry.

2. With potato masher or fork, mash potatoes. Add milk, margarine, salt and paprika; beat until smooth and creamy. Set aside.

3. To prepare filling, in medium saucepan, cook carrot in boiling water to cover 8 minutes, until just tender. Add green beans; cook 3–5 minutes, until vegetables are tender. Drain, discarding liquid; transfer vegetables to large bowl.

4. Meanwhile, in medium nonstick skillet, bring 2 cups water to a boil. Reduce heat to low; add scrod. Poach scrod 5–7 minutes, until fish flakes easily when tested with fork. With slotted spoon, transfer scrod to paper towels to drain.

5. Flake scrod; add to bowl with vegetables. Add parsley and dill; toss to combine. Set aside.

6. Preheat oven to 375° F.

7. In medium bowl, combine flour, salt and pepper; with wire whisk, add milk, blending until flour is dissolved.

8. In clean medium saucepan, melt margarine; add mushrooms. Cook over low heat, stirring frequently, 2 minutes, until mushrooms are just softened. With wire whisk, blend in milk mixture; continuing to stir with wire whisk, cook 4–5 minutes, until mixture comes to a boil and thickens.

9. Pour milk mixture over fish mixture; stir to combine. Transfer mixture to $1^1/_2$-quart casserole; spoon potato mixture over fish mixture in a ring, pressing potato mixture to rim of casserole and leaving a 2" opening in center. Bake 25–30 minutes, until potato topping is lightly browned and filling is bubbling. Remove from oven; let stand 10 minutes.

BRUNCH

Orange Sections, $^1/_2$ cup
Potato-Topped Fish Pie, 1 serving (see recipe)
Arugula, Watercress and Romaine Lettuce Salad,
   2 cups, with $^1/_2$ cup tomato slices, $^1/_4$ cup pack-
   aged croutons and 1 tablespoon fat-free Thousand
   Island dressing
Italian Bread, 1 slice (1 ounce), with 1 teaspoon
   reduced-calorie tub margarine
Reduced-Calorie Chocolate-Flavored Pudding (made
   with skim milk), $^1/_2$ cup
Skim Milk, $^1/_2$ cup
Coffee or Tea (optional)

MAIN MEAL

Skinless Roast Turkey Breast, 3 ounces, with $^1/_4$ cup
   fat-free turkey gravy (15 calories per $^1/_4$ cup)
Cooked Long-Grain Brown Rice, 1 cup, with 1 tea-
   spoon reduced-calorie tub margarine
Steamed Broccoli Florets, 1 cup, with 1 lemon wedge
Torn Iceberg Lettuce, 2 cups, with $^1/_2$ cup *each* sliced
   cucumber and shredded carrot and 1 tablespoon
   fat-free Italian dressing
Kiwi Fruit, 1 medium
Sparkling Mineral Water

SNACK

Graham Crackers, 3 ($2^1/_2$" squares)
Skim Milk, $^1/_2$ cup

This menu provides: 2 Milks, 3 Fats, 2 Fruits,
$14^1/_2$ Vegetables, 4 Proteins, $5^1/_2$ Breads,
80 Optional Calories.

Per serving: 17 g Fat, 23 g Fiber.

Serving (1 cup filling, $^1/_2$ cup topping) provides:
$^1/_2$ Milk, $1^1/_2$ Fats, $1^1/_2$ Vegetables, 1 Protein,
1 Bread.

Per serving: 270 Calories, 5 g Total Fat,
1 g Saturated Fat, 33 mg Cholesterol,
633 mg Sodium, 35 g Total Carbohydrate,
4 g Dietary Fiber, 21 g Protein, 202 mg Calcium.

Serving (2 filled tortillas) provides: 1 Fat, 2¹/₂ Vegetables, 1¹/₂ Proteins, 2 Breads, 30 Optional Calories.

Per serving: 356 Calories, 11 g Total Fat, 2 g Saturated Fat, 91 mg Cholesterol, 985 mg Sodium, 36 g Total Carbohydrate, 2 g Dietary Fiber, 24 g Protein, 145 mg Calcium.

9 9
MOO SHU BASS

Makes 4 servings

3 tablespoons reduced-sodium soy sauce
1 fluid ounce (2 tablespoons) dry sherry
3 tablespoons hoisin sauce
13 ounces sea bass fillets, cut into ¹/₂" pieces
8 dried tree ear or shiitake mushrooms
Eight 6" flour tortillas
2 tablespoons low-sodium chicken broth
¹/₂ teaspoon granulated sugar
1 tablespoon + 1 teaspoon canola oil
1 egg, beaten
2 cups thinly sliced napa cabbage
1¹/₂ cups thinly sliced bok choy
1 cup slivered scallions
1 teaspoon grated pared fresh ginger root

1. Preheat oven to 350° F.

2. In medium bowl, combine 2 tablespoons of the soy sauce, 1 tablespoon of the sherry and 1 teaspoon of the hoisin sauce; add fish, turning to coat. Set aside.

3. Place mushrooms into small bowl; add boiling water to cover. Let stand 15 minutes, until softened. Drain, discarding liquid; squeeze mushrooms dry. Slice mushrooms; set aside.

4. Meanwhile, wrap tortillas in foil; bake 10 minutes, until heated through. Remove tortillas from oven; set aside.

5. In clean small bowl, combine broth, sugar, remaining 1 tablespoon soy sauce and remaining 1 tablespoon sherry; set aside.

6. In large nonstick skillet, heat 1 teaspoon of the oil; spread evenly to coat bottom of skillet. Add egg, tilting to cover bottom of pan. Cook over medium-high heat 1 minute, until dry on top. Transfer cooked egg to cutting board; cut into thin strips.

7. In same skillet, heat 1 teaspoon of the remaining oil; spread evenly to coat bottom of skillet. Add fish mixture; cook, stirring frequently, 2–3 minutes, until fish flakes easily when tested with fork. Remove fish mixture from skillet; wipe skillet clean. Set fish mixture aside.

8. In same skillet, heat remaining 2 teaspoons oil; add cabbage, bok choy, scallions, ginger and soaked mushrooms. Cook over medium-high heat, stirring frequently, 2–3 minutes, until vegetables are wilted. Add reserved soy sauce mixture, egg strips and fish mixture; cook, stirring frequently, 1 minute, until heated through.

9. To assemble, place tortillas onto work surface; spread 1 teaspoon of the remaining hoisin sauce along center of each tortilla. Divide fish mixture evenly among tortillas; fold one side of each tortilla over fish mixture, then fold in adjacent sides, leaving top open.

▷100
PANE BAGNA

Makes 4 servings

4 rinsed drained anchovy fillets, chopped
2 teaspoons rinsed drained capers
1½ teaspoons minced fresh oregano
1 tablespoon + 1 teaspoon olive oil
2 teaspoons balsamic vinegar
Two 4½-ounce French bread rolls (10 × 3½" each), halved horizontally
1 large garlic clove, halved and slightly crushed
16 large fresh basil leaves
2 medium tomatoes, thinly sliced
½ cup thinly sliced red onion
4 ounces drained canned water-packed white tuna, flaked

1. In small bowl, combine anchovies, capers and oregano, mashing with back of spoon until as smooth as possible. Add oil, vinegar and 1 tablespoon + 1 teaspoon water, stirring until smooth; set aside.

2. To assemble sandwiches, rub cut sides of rolls with garlic; discard remaining garlic. Drizzle bottom of each roll half with 1 tablespoon anchovy mixture; top each with 4 basil leaves. Top each portion of basil with half of the tomatoes and onion, then half of the tuna; drizzle each with half of the remaining anchovy mixture. Top each with 4 remaining basil leaves, then remaining roll half. Wrap sandwiches in foil; refrigerate 1 hour, until flavors are blended. Before serving, cut sandwiches crosswise into halves.

Serving (one-half sandwich) provides: 1 Fat, 1¼ Vegetables, ½ Protein, 2¼ Breads, 10 Optional Calories.

Per serving: 203 Calories, 7 g Total Fat, 1 g Saturated Fat, 14 mg Cholesterol, 499 mg Sodium, 23 g Total Carbohydrate, 2 g Dietary Fiber, 13 g Protein, 71 mg Calcium.

BREAKFAST
Apricots, 3 medium
Frozen Waffle, 1, heated, with 2 teaspoons maple syrup
Grilled Turkey Ham, 1 ounce
Skim Milk, 1 cup
Coffee or Tea (optional)

LIGHT MEAL
Pane Bagna, 1 serving (see recipe)
Cherry Tomatoes, 6
Cauliflower and Broccoli Florets, 1 cup *each*
Reduced-Calorie Vanilla-Flavored Pudding (made with skim milk), ½ cup
Unsweetened Seltzer with Lemon Wedge

MAIN MEAL
Grilled Skinless Chicken Breast, 2 ounces
Cooked Corn on the Cob, 1 small ear, with 2 teaspoons reduced-calorie tub margarine
Steamed Baby Carrots, 1 cup, with minced fresh dill
Spinach, Radicchio and Bibb Lettuce Salad, 2 cups, with 1 tablespoon fat-free Italian dressing
Fruit Salad, ½ cup
Diet Grape Soda

SNACK
Fig Bars, 2
Skim Milk, ½ cup

This menu provides: 2 Milks, 3 Fats, 2 Fruits, 12¼ Vegetables, 3½ Proteins, 4¾ Breads, 155 Optional Calories.

Per serving: 24 g Fat, 24 g Fiber.

Pane Bagna

101

TUNA BURGERS IN POCKETS

Makes 2 servings

¹/₂ cup minced red onion
¹/₄ cup chopped celery
1 tablespoon nonfat cream cheese
2 teaspoons minced fresh dill
1 teaspoon fresh lemon juice
4 ounces drained canned water-packed white tuna, flaked
¹/₄ cup plain dried bread crumbs
¹/₄ teaspoon freshly ground black pepper
¹/₄ cup plain nonfat yogurt
1 small (1-ounce) sourdough pita, heated and halved crosswise
4 iceberg lettuce leaves
1 large plum tomato, cut into 6 lengthwise slices

1. Spray medium nonstick skillet with nonstick cooking spray; heat. Add onion and celery; cook over medium heat, stirring frequently, 5 minutes, until vegetables are softened. Add cream cheese, 1 teaspoon of the dill and the juice; stir to combine. Add tuna, 3 tablespoons of the bread crumbs and the pepper; stir to combine. Remove from heat; form tuna mixture into two 3-inch patties.

2. Place remaining 1 tablespoon bread crumbs onto sheet of wax paper or paper plate; one at a time, press each patty into crumbs, turning to coat.

3. Spray clean medium nonstick skillet with nonstick cooking spray; heat. Add patties; cook over medium-high heat, covered, turning once, 6 minutes, until browned on both sides and heated through.

4. In small bowl, combine yogurt and remaining 1 teaspoon dill.

5. Fill each pita half with 2 lettuce leaves, then 1 tuna burger and half the tomato slices; top each burger with half of the yogurt mixture.

Serving (1 filled pita half) provides: 1³/₄ Vegetables, 1 Protein, 1 Bread, 40 Optional Calories.

Per serving: 224 Calories, 3 g Total Fat, 1 g Saturated Fat, 25 mg Cholesterol, 491 mg Sodium, 27 g Total Carbohydrate, 2 g Dietary Fiber, 22 g Protein, 154 mg Calcium.

BREAKFAST
Strawberries, 1 cup
Reduced-Calorie Granola Bar, 1 (1 ounce)
Skim Milk, 1 cup
Coffee or Tea (optional)

LIGHT MEAL
Tuna Burgers in Pockets, 1 serving (see recipe)
Dill Pickle, 1 medium
Creamy Chick-Pea Salad (In small bowl, combine 1 medium roasted red bell pepper, sliced, 2 ounces drained canned chick-peas, 6 large kalamata olives and 1 tablespoon fat-free ranch dressing.)
Sugar-Free Lime-Flavored Gelatin, ¹/₂ cup
Sparkling Mineral Water

MAIN MEAL
Steamed Artichoke, 1 medium, with Lemon Vinaigrette (In small jar with tight-fitting lid or small bowl, combine 1 tablespoon cider vinegar, 1 teaspoon olive oil and ¹/₂ teaspoon grated lemon zest; cover and shake well or, with wire whisk, blend until combined.)
Skinless Roast Turkey Breast, 2 ounces
Cooked Couscous, 1 cup, with 2 tablespoons minced fresh flat-leaf parsley
Steamed Baby Carrots, 1 cup
Roll, 1 ounce, with 2 teaspoons reduced-calorie tub margarine
Apple, 1 small
Unsweetened Citrus-Flavored Seltzer

SNACK
Reduced-Calorie Vanilla Dairy Shake, 1 serving

This menu provides: 2 Milks, 3 Fats, 2 Fruits, 8³/₄ Vegetables, 4 Proteins, 5 Breads, 90 Optional Calories.

Per serving: 28 g Fat, 27 g Fiber.

BREAKFAST
Orange Sections, $^1/_2$ cup
Poached Egg, 1
Whole-Wheat English Muffin, $^1/_2$ (1 ounce), toasted,
with 1 teaspoon reduced-calorie tub margarine
Skim Milk, 1 cup
Coffee or Tea (optional)

LIGHT MEAL
Curried Tuna and Grape Salad Sandwich, 1 serving
(see recipe)
Chilled Cooked Asparagus, 9 spears, with Raspberry
Vinaigrette (In small jar with tight-fitting lid or
small bowl, combine 1 tablespoon raspberry vine-
gar and 1 teaspoon olive oil; cover and shake well
or, with wire whisk, blend until combined.)
Carrot and Cucumber Sticks, 1 cup *each*
Reduced-Calorie Chocolate-Flavored Pudding (made
with skim milk), $^1/_2$ cup
Sparkling Mineral Water

MAIN MEAL
Broiled Skinless Chicken Breast, 2 ounces
Whipped Acorn Squash (In food processor, combine
1 cup hot cooked pared acorn squash, $1^1/_2$ tea-
spoons reduced-calorie tub margarine, 1 teaspoon
maple syrup and pinch cinnamon; purée until
smooth.)
Steamed Whole Green Beans, 1 cup
Watercress and Mushroom Salad, 2 cups, with
1 tablespoon fat-free Italian dressing
Sliced Strawberries, $^3/_4$ cup
Non-Alcoholic White Wine, 4 fluid ounces

SNACK
Oat-Bran Pretzels, $1^1/_2$ ounces
Vanilla "Egg Cream" (In tall glass, combine 1 cup
diet cream soda and $^1/_2$ cup skim milk.)

This menu provides: 2 Milks, 3 Fats, 2 Fruits,
$12^1/_2$ Vegetables, 4 Proteins, 5 Breads, 120 Optional
Calories.

Per serving: 27 g Fat, 30 g Fiber.

102
CURRIED TUNA AND
GRAPE SALAD SANDWICH

Makes 4 servings

8 ounces drained canned water-packed white tuna, flaked
$^1/_2$ cup coarsely chopped celery
$^1/_2$ cup diced yellow or red bell pepper
$^1/_4$ cup minced scallions
$^1/_4$ cup plain nonfat yogurt
2 tablespoons reduced-calorie mayonnaise
1 teaspoon mild or hot curry powder
20 small or 12 large seedless red grapes, halved
Four 2-ounce hard crusty rolls
$^1/_2$ cup packed well-washed spinach leaves

1. In medium bowl, combine tuna, celery, bell pepper, scallions, yogurt, mayonnaise and curry powder; stir in grapes.

2. With serrated knife, cut a thin slice off top of each roll; set roll tops aside. Remove and discard 1 ounce soft bread from center of each roll. Line inside of rolls with spinach, allowing ends of leaves to extend outside of rolls; top each portion of spinach with one-fourth of the tuna mixture, then one reserved roll top.

Serving (1 sandwich) provides: $^3/_4$ Fat, $^1/_4$ Fruit, 1 Vegetable, 1 Protein, 1 Bread, 10 Optional Calories.

Per serving: 215 Calories, 5 g Total Fat, 1 g Saturated Fat, 27 mg Cholesterol, 451 mg Sodium, 23 g Total Carbohydrate, 2 g Dietary Fiber, 20 g Protein, 82 mg Calcium.

103
Open-Face Grilled Swordfish Sandwich with Carrot Slaw

Makes 4 servings

$^3/_4$ cup julienned carrot
$^1/_4$ cup thinly sliced red onion
I tablespoon fresh lime juice
I teaspoon granulated sugar
$^1/_2$ teaspoon grated pared fresh ginger root
I tablespoon + I teaspoon olive oil
$^1/_2$ teaspoon salt
Pinch ground red pepper
Four 5-ounce boneless swordfish steaks
I cup radish sprouts
Four 2-ounce slices sourdough bread (each about $^3/_4$" thick), toasted
2 tablespoons + 2 teaspoons fat-free blue cheese dressing

1. In medium bowl, combine carrot, onion, juice, sugar and ginger; let stand 30 minutes.

2. Preheat outdoor barbecue grill or indoor stove-top grill according to manufacturer's directions.

3. In small cup or bowl, combine oil, salt and pepper; brush evenly over both sides of each swordfish steak.

4. Grill swordfish over hot coals or on stove-top grill, turning once, 6–8 minutes, until fish flakes easily when tested with fork.

5. Add sprouts to carrot mixture; toss to combine.

6. Spoon one-fourth of the carrot mixture onto each toast slice; top each portion with 1 swordfish steak and 2 teaspoons dressing.

Serving (1 sandwich) provides: 1 Fat, 1 Vegetable, 2 Proteins, 2 Breads, 15 Optional Calories.

Per serving: 400 Calories, 12 g Total Fat, 3 g Saturated Fat, 55 mg Cholesterol, 835 mg Sodium, 37 g Total Carbohydrate, 2 g Dietary Fiber, 34 g Protein, 64 mg Calcium.

BREAKFAST
Pink Grapefruit, $^1/_2$ medium
Toasted Oat Cereal, $1^1/_2$ ounces
Skim Milk, 1 cup
Coffee or Tea (optional)

LIGHT MEAL
Creamy Zucchini Soup (In food processor, combine $^1/_2$ cup *each* chopped zucchini and low-sodium chicken broth, 2 tablespoons evaporated skimmed milk and 1 tablespoon minced fresh dill; purée until smooth. Transfer mixture to small saucepan; heat.)
Open-Face Grilled Swordfish Sandwich with Carrot Slaw, 1 serving (see recipe)
Celery and Cucumber Sticks, 1 cup *each*
Blueberries, $^3/_4$ cup
Iced Tea with Mint Sprig

MAIN MEAL
Low-Sodium Tomato Juice, 1 cup
Grilled Skinless Chicken Breast, 2 ounces
Cooked Brown Rice, $^1/_2$ cup
Grilled Vegetables (Preheat grill according to manufacturer's directions. Grill $^1/_2$ cup *each* sliced zucchini, sliced yellow squash, sliced green bell pepper, sliced pared eggplant, sliced red onion and sliced fennel, turning as needed, until lightly browned and tender.)
Romaine and Watercress Salad, 2 cups, with 1 tablespoon Thousand Island dressing
Reduced-Calorie Chocolate-Flavored Pudding (made with skim milk), $^1/_2$ cup
Sparkling Mineral Water

SNACK
Plain Popcorn, hot-air popped, 3 cups
Cola "Float" (In tall glass, scoop 4 fluid ounces sugar-free vanilla nonfat frozen yogurt; add enough diet cola to fill glass.)

This menu provides: 2 Milks, 3 Fats, 2 Fruits, 18 Vegetables, 4 Proteins, 6 Breads, 115 Optional Calories.

Per serving: 28 g Fat, 21 g Fiber.

DANISH OPEN-FACE SARDINE SANDWICH

Makes 2 servings

BREAKFAST
Banana Smoothie (In blender, combine 1 cup skim milk, $^1/_2$ medium banana, sliced, 2 ice cubes and 2 teaspoons honey; purée until smooth.)
Baking Powder Biscuit, 1 (2" diameter), with 1 teaspoon strawberry jam
Coffee or Tea (optional)

LIGHT MEAL
Danish Open-Face Sardine Sandwich, 1 serving (see recipe)
Pickled Beets (In medium bowl, combine 1 cup cooked sliced beets, $^1/_2$ cup sliced onion, $^1/_4$ cup cider vinegar, sugar substitute to equal 2 teaspoons sugar, pinch salt and freshly ground black pepper, to taste; refrigerate, covered, at least 1 hour.)
Carrot Sticks, 1 cup
Aspartame-Sweetened Peach Nonfat Yogurt, 1 cup
Iced Herbal Tea

MAIN MEAL
Light Red Wine Spritzer (In wineglass, combine $^1/_2$ cup *each* unsweetened seltzer and dry light red wine.)
Broiled Lean Lamb Chop, 2 ounces
Cooked Rotelle Pasta, 1 cup, with $^1/_4$ cup chopped tomato, and 1 teaspoon *each* olive oil and minced fresh basil
Roll, 1 (1 ounce), with 1 teaspoon reduced-calorie tub margarine
Steamed Escarole, 1 cup
Cantaloupe, $^1/_4$ small

SNACK
Plain Popcorn, hot-air popped, 3 cups, with 1 teaspoon reduced-calorie tub margarine, melted
Diet Cola

This menu provides: 2 Milks, 3 Fats, 2 Fruits, 9 Vegetables, $3^1/_2$ Proteins, $5^3/_4$ Breads, 120 Optional Calories.

Per serving: 35 g Fat, 23 g Fiber.

3 tablespoons nonfat sour cream
2 tablespoons Dijon-style mustard
1 tablespoon minced fresh dill
$^1/_4$ teaspoon grated lemon zest*
Two 1-ounce slices Westphalian-style dark pumpernickel or limpa rye bread
$^1/_2$ medium tomato, thinly sliced
$^1/_4$ cup packed well-washed trimmed spinach leaves
$^1/_4$ cup thinly sliced radishes
$^1/_4$ cup thinly sliced red onion
$^1/_4$ cup thinly sliced cucumber
2 ounces drained canned water-packed skinless boneless sardines
1 hard-cooked egg, sliced
2 lemon wedges

1. In small bowl, combine sour cream, mustard, dill and zest.

2. To assemble sandwiches, spread each slice of bread with 1 tablespoon sour cream mixture; top each with half of the tomato, spinach, radishes, onion and cucumber. Arrange half of the sardines on top of vegetables; top each with half of the egg slices and half of the remaining sour cream mixture. Serve with lemon wedges.

Serving (1 sandwich) provides: $1^1/_2$ Vegetables, $1^1/_2$ Proteins, 1 Bread, 15 Optional Calories.

Per serving: 263 Calories, 12 g Total Fat, 3 g Saturated Fat, 146 mg Cholesterol, 639 mg Sodium, 22 g Total Carbohydrate, 3 g Dietary Fiber, 14 g Protein, 182 mg Calcium.

The zest of the lemon is the peel without any of the pith (white membrane). To remove zest from lemon, use a zester or the fine side of a vegetable grater; wrap lemon in plastic wrap and refrigerate for use at another time.

105
SALMON FOCACCIA MELT

Makes 4 servings

$^3/_4$ cup plain nonfat yogurt

2 tablespoons finely chopped onion

1 tablespoon minced fresh dill

$^1/_2$ teaspoon grated lemon zest*

5 ounces skinless boneless drained canned water-packed salmon, flaked

$^3/_4$ ounce part-skim mozzarella cheese, grated

Two 4-ounce focaccia shells

1. Preheat oven to 450° F.

2. In small bowl, combine yogurt, onion, dill and zest.

3. In separate small bowl, with fork, combine salmon, cheese and $^1/_2$ cup of the yogurt mixture; spread half of the salmon mixture onto each focaccia shell. Place shells onto nonstick baking sheet; bake 7 minutes, until golden brown and heated through. Cut focaccia shells into halves; serve with remaining yogurt mixture.

Serving ($^1/_2$ focaccia shell, 1 tablespoon remaining yogurt mixture) provides: $^1/_4$ Milk, $1^1/_2$ Proteins, 2 Breads.

Per serving: 253 Calories, 6 g Total Fat, 2 g Saturated Fat, 24 mg Cholesterol, 546 mg Sodium, 29 g Total Carbohydrate, 1 g Dietary Fiber, 18 g Protein, 268 mg Calcium.

The zest of the lemon is the peel without any of the pith (white membrane). To remove zest from lemon, use a zester or the fine side of a vegetable grater; wrap lemon in plastic wrap and refrigerate for use at another time.

BREAKFAST

Grapefruit Sections, $^1/_2$ cup

English Muffin, $^1/_2$ (1 ounce), toasted, with 1 tablespoon peanut butter and 2 teaspoons raspberry jam

Skim Milk, $^3/_4$ cup

Coffee or Tea (optional)

LIGHT MEAL

Salmon Focaccia Melt, 1 serving (see recipe)

Steamed Sliced Zucchini, 1 cup

Shredded Red and Green Cabbage, 1 cup, with 6 cherry tomatoes and 1 tablespoon fat-free ranch dressing

Pear, 1 small

Iced Tea with Mint Sprig

MAIN MEAL

Grilled Lean Pork Chop, 2 ounces

Baked Sweet Potato, 3 ounces, with 2 teaspoons reduced-calorie tub margarine

Stewed Okra and Tomatoes, 1 cup

Chicory and Red Leaf Lettuce Salad, 2 cups, with $^1/_2$ cup chilled cooked green lima beans and 1 teaspoon *each* olive oil and balsamic vinegar

Sugar-Free Mixed Fruit–Flavored Gelatin, $^1/_2$ cup

Unsweetened Lime-Flavored Seltzer

SNACK

Graham Crackers, 3 ($2^1/_2$" squares)

Hot Cocoa (In small saucepan, with wire whisk, combine 1 cup skim milk and 1 tablespoon unsweetened cocoa powder, blending until cocoa is dissolved. Cook over low heat, stirring constantly, until heated. Stir in sugar substitute to equal 4 teaspoons sugar and 1 teaspoon vanilla extract; pour into heated mug.)

This menu provides: 2 Milks, 3 Fats, 2 Fruits, 11 Vegetables, $4^1/_2$ Proteins, 6 Breads, 75 Optional Calories.

Per serving: 35 g Fat, 31 g Fiber.

106
ANCHOVY-TOMATO FLATS

The crust for these individual pizzas has a crispy, crackerlike texture.

Makes 4 servings

1 cup + 2 tablespoons all-purpose flour
2 tablespoons yellow cornmeal
$^1/_4$ teaspoon salt
2 teaspoons olive oil
$^1/_2$ cup chopped onion
4 large plum tomatoes, thinly sliced
3 ounces part-skim mozzarella cheese, coarsely grated
8 rinsed drained anchovy fillets
2 tablespoons minced fresh basil

1. Preheat oven to 425° F.

2. To prepare dough, in medium bowl or food processor, combine flour, cornmeal and salt. Gradually add $^1/_3$ cup + 2 teaspoons water (keep motor running if using food processor), stirring or processing just until mixture holds together. Wrap dough in plastic wrap; let stand 15 minutes.

3. Meanwhile, in small nonstick skillet, heat oil; add onion. Cook over medium-high heat, stirring frequently, 7 minutes, until lightly browned. Remove from heat; set aside.

4. Remove dough from plastic wrap; divide into 4 equal pieces. Working with 1 dough piece at a time and keeping remaining pieces wrapped, roll each dough piece into a 5" circle; place circles onto nonstick baking sheet. Bake 5 minutes, until firm and dry. Remove circles from oven; leave oven on. With large metal spatula, flatten any circles that puffed while baking.

5. Spread each circle with one-fourth of the onion mixture. Top each portion of onion mixture with one-fourth of the tomato slices; sprinkle evenly with cheese. Arrange 2 anchovy fillets in a crisscross pattern over each portion of cheese; sprinkle evenly with basil. Bake 10 minutes, until cheese is melted and tomatoes are tender.

Serving (1 anchovy-tomato flat) provides: $^1/_2$ Fat, $1^1/_4$ Vegetables, 1 Protein, $1^3/_4$ Breads, 15 Optional Calories.

Per serving: 254 Calories, 7 g Total Fat, 3 g Saturated Fat, 17 mg Cholesterol, 534 mg Sodium, 35 g Total Carbohydrate, 2 g Dietary Fiber, 12 g Protein, 181 mg Calcium.

CAJUN PIZZA

For a different but equally delicious pizza, try using part-skim mozzarella cheese in place of the feta.

Makes 8 servings

2^1/$_4$ cups all-purpose flour
^{1}/$_4$ cup yellow cornmeal
^{1}/$_4$ teaspoon salt
2 teaspoons olive oil
^{3}/$_4$ cup diced onions
^{1}/$_2$ cup diced green bell pepper
^{1}/$_2$ cup coarsely chopped celery
2 garlic cloves, minced
^{3}/$_4$ cup canned Spanish-style tomato sauce
1 small bay leaf
^{1}/$_2$ teaspoon dried oregano leaves
^{1}/$_4$ teaspoon dried thyme leaves
Pinch ground red pepper
32 medium shrimp (about 1 pound), peeled and deveined
3 ounces feta cheese, crumbled

1. Preheat oven to 475° F.

2. To prepare dough, in medium bowl, combine 2 cups of the flour, the cornmeal and salt; gradually stir in ^{3}/$_4$ cup water, stirring until mixture holds together.

3. Sprinkle work surface with remaining ^{1}/$_4$ cup flour; transfer dough to prepared surface. Knead dough 2 minutes; set aside, covered, 10 minutes.

4. Meanwhile, in medium nonstick skillet, heat oil; add onions, bell pepper, celery and garlic. Cook over medium-high heat, stirring frequently, 5 minutes, until vegetables are softened. Add tomato sauce, bay leaf, oregano, thyme, ground red pepper and ^{1}/$_4$ cup water; bring mixture to a boil. Reduce heat to low; simmer, stirring occasionally, 10 minutes, until mixture is thickened.

5. Roll dough into a 12" circle; transfer to 12" pizza pan, pressing to form a stand-up rim. Bake 12 minutes. Remove crust from oven; leave oven on.

6. Remove and discard bay leaf from tomato sauce mixture. Spread tomato sauce mixture over baked crust to within ^{1}/$_2$" of rim; top evenly with shrimp and cheese. Bake 5 minutes, until shrimp turn pink and cheese is melted. Cut into 8 equal wedges.

Serving (one-eighth of pizza) provides: ^{1}/$_4$ Fat, ^{3}/$_4$ Vegetable, 1^1/$_2$ Proteins, 1^3/$_4$ Breads.

Per serving: 260 Calories, 5 g Total Fat, 2 g Saturated Fat, 96 mg Cholesterol, 386 mg Sodium, 35 g Total Carbohydrate, 2 g Dietary Fiber, 18 g Protein, 103 mg Calcium.

BREAKFAST

Spiced Baked Apple (Preheat oven to 350° F. Pare 1 small apple halfway down from stem end; place into small baking dish. Sprinkle apple with 1 teaspoon granulated sugar and ^{1}/$_4$ teaspoon *each* ground allspice and ground nutmeg; add ^{1}/$_4$" water to pan. Bake, covered, 30 minutes, until tender. If desired, refrigerate, covered, overnight.)
Cinnamon-Raisin English Muffin, ^{1}/$_2$ (1 ounce), toasted, with ^{1}/$_3$ cup nonfat ricotta cheese
Skim Milk, 1 cup
Coffee or Tea (optional)

LIGHT MEAL

Cajun Pizza, 1 serving (see recipe)
Steamed Artichoke Hearts and Mushrooms, 1 cup, with 1 tablespoon fresh lemon juice, ^{3}/$_4$ teaspoon olive oil and ^{1}/$_4$ teaspoon dried oregano leaves
Red and Green Leaf Lettuce Salad, 2 cups, with 6 cherry tomatoes and 1 tablespoon fat-free Thousand Island dressing
Kiwi Fruit, 1 medium
Sparkling Mineral Water

MAIN MEAL

Broiled Turkey Burger, 2 ounces, on 2-ounce hamburger roll with ^{1}/$_4$ cup salsa
Confetti Corn (In small bowl, combine ^{1}/$_2$ cup *each* chilled cooked corn kernels and diced roasted red bell pepper, ^{1}/$_4$ cup sliced scallions, 1 ounce diced avocado, 1 tablespoon *each* red wine vinegar and minced fresh cilantro and 1 teaspoon olive oil.)
Carrot and Celery Sticks, 1 cup *each*
Frozen Lemon Pop (Pour ^{1}/$_2$ cup low-calorie lemonade-flavored drink into small paper cup; freeze until almost firm. Insert ice-cream-bar stick vertically into partially frozen drink; freeze until solid. Unmold.)
Iced Tea

SNACK

Pudding Parfait (In stemmed glass, layer ^{1}/$_2$ cup *each* reduced-calorie chocolate-flavored and vanilla-flavored puddings [made with skim milk].)

This menu provides: 2 Milks, 3 Fats, 2 Fruits, 14^1/$_4$ Vegetables, 4^1/$_2$ Proteins, 5^3/$_4$ Breads, 120 Optional Calories.

Per serving: 26 g Fat, 22 g Fiber.

Cajun Pizza

108

CAVATELLI WITH SHRIMP AND ARUGULA

Makes 4 servings

8 sun-dried tomato halves (not packed in oil)
6 ounces cavatelli pasta
1 tablespoon + 1 teaspoon olive oil
6 garlic cloves, minced
$^1/_4$ teaspoon crushed red pepper flakes
24 medium shrimp (about 11 ounces), peeled
  and deveined (tails left on)
4 cups packed arugula leaves
$^1/_2$ cup thinly sliced scallions
$^1/_4$ teaspoon salt

1. Place tomatoes into small bowl; add boiling water to cover. Let stand 30 minutes, until softened; drain, discarding liquid. Cut tomatoes into thin strips; set aside.

2. Meanwhile, in large pot of boiling water, cook cavatelli 8–10 minutes, until tender. Drain, reserving $^1/_4$ cup liquid; place cavatelli into serving bowl. Keep warm.

3. In large nonstick skillet, heat oil; add garlic and red pepper flakes. Cook over medium-high heat, stirring constantly, 1 minute. Add shrimp; cook, stirring frequently, 2–3 minutes, until shrimp turn pink. Add arugula, scallions and reserved tomatoes; cook, stirring frequently, 1 minute, until arugula is wilted.

4. Top warm cavatelli with shrimp mixture; toss to combine. Sprinkle with salt and reserved liquid; toss again.

Serving (1 cup cavatelli, $^1/_2$ cup vegetable mixture, 6 shrimp) provides: 1 Fat, $3^1/_4$ Vegetables, $1^1/_2$ Proteins, 2 Breads.

Per serving: 321 Calories, 7 g Total Fat, 1 g Saturated Fat, 129 mg Cholesterol, 295 mg Sodium, 39 g Total Carbohydrate, 4 g Dietary Fiber, 25 g Protein, 137 mg Calcium.

BREAKFAST
Mixed Berry Yogurt Crunch (In small bowl, combine $^3/_4$ cup plain nonfat yogurt, $^1/_4$ cup *each* blueberries, raspberries and blackberries and 1 ounce granola.)
Coffee or Tea (optional)

LIGHT MEAL
Cavatelli with Shrimp and Arugula, 1 serving (see recipe)
Torn Romaine Lettuce Leaves, 2 cups, with 6 cherry tomatoes and 1 tablespoon fat-free Thousand Island dressing
Breadsticks, 2 long
Sugar-Free Lemon-Flavored Gelatin, $^1/_2$ cup
Diet Cola with Lime Wedge

MAIN MEAL
Grilled Sirloin Steak, 3 ounces
Cooked Corn on the Cob, 1 small ear, with 2 teaspoons reduced-calorie tub margarine
Grilled Onions and Mushrooms (Preheat grill according to manufacturer's directions. Grill $^1/_2$ cup *each* sliced onion and mushrooms, turning as needed, until lightly browned and tender.)
Italian Spinach Salad (In medium bowl, combine 2 cups torn spinach leaves, $^1/_2$ cup *each* sliced mushrooms and sliced red onion, 2 teaspoons imitation bacon bits and $1^1/_2$ teaspoons Italian dressing.)
Honeydew Melon, 2" wedge
Unsweetened Seltzer

SNACK
Aspartame-Sweetened Vanilla Nonfat Yogurt, 1 cup

This menu provides: 2 Milks, 3 Fats, 2 Fruits, $16^1/_4$ Vegetables, $4^1/_2$ Proteins, 5 Breads, 110 Optional Calories.

Per serving: 32 g Fat, 24 g Fiber.

109
CHINESE SEAFOOD SOUP

*This mild-flavored seafood soup is chock-full of vegetables, noodles
and seafood—it's a meal in a bowl!*

Makes 4 servings

6 ounces thin noodles
4 cups low-sodium chicken broth
3 cups thinly sliced Chinese cabbage
2 tablespoons reduced-sodium soy sauce
2 tablespoons rice wine vinegar
3 garlic cloves, minced
12 medium clams
16 medium shrimp (about 8 ounces), peeled and deveined
$^1/_2$ cup thinly sliced scallions
1 teaspoon oriental sesame oil

1. In large pot of boiling water, cook noodles 5–6 minutes, until tender.
Drain; set aside. Keep warm.

2. In large saucepan, combine broth, cabbage, soy sauce, vinegar and garlic. Bring liquid to a boil; add clams. Reduce heat to low; simmer, covered,
3 minutes. Add shrimp; simmer, covered, 2 minutes, until clams open and
shrimp turn pink (discard any clams that don't open). Stir in scallions, oil
and cooked noodles.

Serving (2 cups) provides: $^1/_4$ Fat, 1$^3/_4$ Vegetables, 1$^1/_2$ Proteins, 2 Breads,
20 Optional Calories.

Per serving: 300 Calories, 7 g Total Fat, 2 g Saturated Fat, 136 mg Cholesterol,
531 mg Sodium, 38 g Total Carbohydrate, 2 g Dietary Fiber, 26 g Protein,
131 mg Calcium.

110
New England Clam Chowder

Makes 4 servings

10 ounces all-purpose potatoes, pared and cut into $^1/_2$" cubes
1 cup chopped onions
2 teaspoons reduced-calorie tub margarine
1 cup evaporated skimmed milk
1 cup skim milk
6 ounces drained canned minced clams
$^1/_2$ cup bottled clam juice
1 tablespoon minced fresh thyme leaves or 1 teaspoon dried
Pinch salt
Pinch ground white pepper

1. In large saucepan, combine potatoes, onions, margarine and 1 cup water; bring liquid to a boil. Reduce heat to low; simmer, covered, 13–15 minutes, until potatoes are tender.

2. With slotted spoon, transfer 1 cup potato mixture to food processor or blender; purée until smooth.

3. Return pureed mixture to saucepan; stir in evaporated skimmed and skim milks, clams, juice, thyme, salt and pepper. Cook over medium heat, stirring frequently, 10 minutes, until heated through (do not boil).

Serving ($1^1/_2$ cups) provides: $^3/_4$ Milk, $^1/_4$ Fat, $^1/_2$ Vegetable, $^3/_4$ Protein, $^1/_2$ Bread.

Per serving: 215 Calories, 2 g Total Fat, 0 g Saturated Fat, 32 mg Cholesterol, 273 mg Sodium, 29 g Total Carbohydrate, 2 g Dietary Fiber, 20 g Protein, 323 mg Calcium.

BREAKFAST
Banana, $^1/_2$ medium
Raisin French Toast (In small bowl, combine $^1/_4$ cup egg substitute, 2 tablespoons water, $^1/_2$ teaspoon vanilla extract and pinch cinnamon. In small nonstick skillet, melt $2^1/_2$ teaspoons reduced-calorie tub margarine. Dip 1 slice cinnamon-raisin bread into egg mixture; transfer to skillet. Cook, over medium heat, 3–4 minutes per side, turning once, until browned on both sides. Transfer to plate; repeat with 1 additional slice cinnamon-raisin bread and remaining egg mixture. Top with 1 teaspoon maple syrup.)
Grilled Canadian-Style Bacon, 1 ounce
Skim Milk, $^1/_2$ cup
Coffee or Tea (optional)

LIGHT MEAL
New England Clam Chowder, 1 serving (see recipe)
Oyster Crackers, 20
Steamed Whole Green Beans and Baby Carrots, 1 cup *each*
Caesar Salad (In medium bowl, combine 2 cups torn Romaine lettuce leaves, $^1/_4$ cup packaged croutons and 1 tablespoon fat-free Caesar salad dressing.)
Seedless Red Grapes, 20 small or 12 large
Sparkling Mineral Water

MAIN MEAL
Chilled Antipasto Salad (On plate, decoratively arrange 1 cup *each* carrot and celery sticks, $^1/_2$ cup *each* roasted red bell pepper strips, chilled cooked artichoke hearts and fennel strips and 2 ounces drained cooked chick-peas; sprinkle with $1^1/_2$ teaspoons Italian dressing.)
Roll, 1 ounce
Reduced-Calorie Chocolate-Flavored Pudding (made with skim milk), $^1/_2$ cup
Unsweetened Seltzer with Lemon Wedge

SNACK
Cola "Float" (In tall glass, scoop 4 fluid ounces sugar-free vanilla nonfat frozen yogurt; add enough diet cola to fill glass.)

This menu provides: 2 Milks, 3 Fats, 2 Fruits, $15^1/_2$ Vegetables, $3^3/_4$ Proteins, 6 Breads, 125 Optional Calories.

Per serving: 23 g Fat, 21 g Fiber.

111
MANHATTAN
CLAM CHOWDER

Makes 4 servings

2 teaspoons reduced-calorie tub margarine
$^{1}/_{2}$ cup chopped onion
$^{1}/_{4}$ cup chopped celery
$^{1}/_{4}$ cup chopped carrot
5 ounces all-purpose potato, pared and cut into $^{1}/_{2}$" cubes
1 cup canned whole tomatoes, coarsely chopped (no salt added)
$^{1}/_{2}$ cup bottled clam juice
$1^{1}/_{2}$ teaspoons minced fresh thyme leaves or $^{1}/_{2}$ teaspoon dried
$1^{1}/_{2}$ teaspoons minced fresh marjoram leaves or $^{1}/_{2}$ teaspoon dried
Pinch ground white or red pepper
6 ounces drained canned minced clams

1. In large saucepan, melt margarine; add onion, celery and carrot. Cook over medium-high heat, stirring frequently, 5 minutes, until vegetables are softened.

2. Add potato, tomatoes, juice, thyme, marjoram, pepper and 2 cups water to onion mixture; bring liquid to a boil. Reduce heat to low; simmer, covered, 20 minutes, until potato is tender. Stir in clams; cook, uncovered, stirring occasionally, 3 minutes, until mixture is heated through.

Serving (1 cup) provides: $^{1}/_{4}$ Fat, 1 Vegetable, $^{3}/_{4}$ Protein, $^{1}/_{4}$ Bread.

Per serving: 124 Calories, 2 g Total Fat, 0 g Saturated Fat, 28 mg Cholesterol, 238 mg Sodium, 14 g Total Carbohydrate, 2 g Dietary Fiber, 13 g Protein, 75 mg Calcium.

112
WARM MIXED SEAFOOD SALAD

Makes 4 servings

2 cups torn Boston or red leaf lettuce leaves (bite-size pieces)
1 cup torn radicchio leaves (bite-size pieces)
1 cup watercress leaves
2 tablespoons olive oil
8 ounces medium shrimp, peeled and deveined
5 ounces sea scallops, cut into halves, or bay scallops
5 ounces monkfish fillets, cut into 1" pieces
1 tablespoon finely minced shallot
2 tablespoons fresh lemon juice
Pinch salt
Pinch freshly ground black pepper

1. In large bowl, combine lettuce, radicchio and watercress; set aside.

2. In large nonstick skillet, heat $1^1/2$ teaspoons of the oil; add shrimp, scallops, monkfish and shallots. Cook over medium-high heat, stirring frequently, 2–3 minutes, until seafood is golden brown. Remove from heat; keep warm.

3. To prepare dressing, in small jar with tight-fitting lid or small bowl, combine juice, salt, pepper, remaining 1 tablespoon + $1^1/2$ teaspoons oil and 1 tablespoon water; cover and shake well or, with wire whisk, blend until combined. Pour half of the dressing over lettuce mixture; toss to combine.

4. Divide lettuce mixture evenly among 4 plates; top each portion with one-fourth of the warm seafood mixture. Drizzle each salad evenly with remaining dressing.

Serving (1 cup lettuce mixture, one-fourth of the seafood mixture, $1^1/2$ teaspoons remaining dressing) provides: $1^1/2$ Fats, 2 Vegetables, $1^3/4$ Proteins.

Per serving: 190 Calories, 9 g Total Fat, 1 g Saturated Fat, 107 mg Cholesterol, 188 mg Sodium, 4 g Total Carbohydrate, 0 g Dietary Fiber, 23 g Protein, 81 mg Calcium.

BREAKFAST
Kiwi Fruit, 1 medium
Herb Scramble (In small microwavable bowl, combine $1/2$ cup egg substitute, 1 teaspoon minced fresh flat-leaf parsley and $1/4$ teaspoon *each* dried oregano leaves and basil; microwave on Medium-High [70% power], $1^1/2$–2 minutes, stirring once or twice, until set.)
Reduced-Calorie Whole-Wheat Bread, 2 slices, toasted, with 2 teaspoons strawberry jam
Skim Milk, 1 cup
Coffee or Tea (optional)

LIGHT MEAL
Warm Mixed Seafood Salad, 1 serving (see recipe)
Cooked Corn on the Cob, 1 small ear, with 1 teaspoon reduced-calorie tub margarine
Flatbreads, $3/4$ ounce
Watermelon, 3 × 2" wedge
Unsweetened Seltzer

MAIN MEAL
Mozzarella-Vegetable Sandwich (Split open one 1-ounce roll. Onto bottom half of roll, layer $1^1/2$ ounces nonfat mozzarella cheese, sliced, $1/4$ cup alfalfa sprouts and 2 tomato slices. Drizzle with 1 teaspoon olive oil; top with remaining roll half.)
Cucumber and Carrot Sticks, 1 cup *each*
Frozen Punch on-a-Stick (Pour $1/2$ cup low-calorie fruit punch–flavored drink into small paper cup; freeze until almost firm. Insert ice-cream-bar stick vertically into partially frozen drink; freeze until solid. Unmold.)
Iced Herbal Tea

SNACK
Fig Bars, 2
Skim Milk, 1 cup

This menu provides: 2 Milks, 3 Fats, 2 Fruits, 7 Vegetables, $4^3/4$ Proteins, $4^1/2$ Breads, 105 Optional Calories.

Per serving: 25 g Fat, 24 g Fiber.

113
MEXICAN SEVICHE

*Try our version of seviche, the Mexican delicacy that uses lemon juice
rather than heat to "cook" the fish—in an edible bowl! Tostada shells
are tortillas shaped into a cup, then baked to hold their shape; two
shells should weigh about $^3/_4$ ounce.*

Makes 4 servings

8 ounces red snapper fillets, cut into $1^1/_4$" cubes
8 ounces sea scallops, halved
$^1/_4$ cup fresh lemon juice
$^1/_2$ teaspoon salt
2 medium tomatoes, seeded and diced
$^1/_4$ cup diced red onion
2 tablespoons minced fresh cilantro
1 tablespoon + 1 teaspoon olive oil
2 teaspoons minced deveined seeded jalapeño pepper
    (wear gloves to prevent irritation)
$1^1/_2$ teaspoons minced fresh marjoram leaves
4 blue corn tostada shells
2 cups shredded Romaine lettuce leaves

1. In gallon-size sealable plastic bag, combine snapper, scallops, juice and salt. Seal bag, squeezing out air; turn to coat fish. Refrigerate 3–4 hours, turning bag occasionally.

2. In large bowl, combine tomatoes, onion, cilantro, oil, pepper and marjoram; refrigerate, covered, stirring occasionally, until chilled.

3. Drain fish mixture and discard the marinade. Add fish mixture to tomato mixture; toss to combine.

4. Line each tostada shell with $^1/_2$ cup lettuce; top each portion of lettuce with one-fourth of the fish mixture.

Serving (1 cup seviche, $^1/_2$ cup lettuce) provides: 1 Fat, $2^1/_4$ Vegetables, 2 Proteins, $^1/_2$ Bread, 10 Optional Calories.

Per serving: 246 Calories, 9 g Total Fat, 1 g Saturated Fat, 40 mg Cholesterol, 512 mg Sodium, 18 g Total Carbohydrate, 3 g Dietary Fiber, 23 g Protein, 83 mg Calcium.

SOUTHWESTERN SHRIMP AND FRUIT SALAD

Makes 4 servings

2 medium pink grapefruits
1 tablespoon + 1 teaspoon olive oil
1 tablespoon fresh lime juice
1 tablespoon minced fresh mint leaves
1 teaspoon honey
1/4 teaspoon salt
Pinch ground red pepper
2 cups watercress leaves
24 cooked medium shrimp, peeled and deveined (tails left on)
2 medium kiwi fruits, pared and sliced
1 cup sliced pared jicama

1. Peel and section grapefruits over bowl to catch juices; set grapefruit sections aside.

2. To prepare dressing, in small jar with tight-fitting lid or small bowl, combine oil, lime juice, mint, honey, salt, pepper and reserved grapefruit juice; cover and shake well or, with wire whisk, blend until combined.

3. Line serving platter with watercress. Arrange shrimp, kiwi fruits, jicama and grapefruit sections on watercress; drizzle evenly with dressing.

Serving (one-fourth of salad) provides: 1 Fat, 1 1/2 Fruits, 1 1/2 Vegetables, 1 1/2 Proteins, 5 Optional Calories.

Per serving: 208 Calories, 6 g Total Fat, 1 g Saturated Fat, 166 mg Cholesterol, 337 mg Sodium, 20 g Total Carbohydrate, 3 g Dietary Fiber, 20 g Protein, 90 mg Calcium.

BREAKFAST
Strawberries, 1/2 cup
Shredded Wheat Cereal, 1 1/2 ounces
Skim Milk, 1 cup
Coffee or Tea (optional)

LIGHT MEAL
Southwestern Shrimp and Fruit Salad, 1 serving (see recipe)
Nonfat Tortilla Chips, 2 ounces, with Salsa-Cream Dip (In small bowl, top 1/2 cup salsa with 2 tablespoons nonfat sour cream.)
Sugar-Free Lime-Flavored Gelatin, 1/2 cup, with 1 tablespoon thawed frozen light whipped topping (8 calories per tablespoon)
Sparkling Mineral Water

MAIN MEAL
Sliced London Broil, 3 ounces
Mashed Potatoes (In small bowl, with electric mixer, combine 4 ounces hot cooked potato, peeled and cubed, 1 tablespoon *each* reduced-calorie tub margarine and low-sodium beef broth and ground white pepper, to taste.)
Steamed Asparagus, 6 spears
Steamed Zucchini and Yellow Squash Slices, 1 cup, with 1 teaspoon reduced-calorie tub margarine
Tossed Green Salad, 2 cups, with 1/2 cup *each* yellow and red bell pepper strips and 1 tablespoon fat-free creamy Italian dressing
Reduced-Calorie Vanilla-Flavored Pudding (made with skim milk), 1/2 cup
Diet Orange Soda

SNACK
Reduced-Calorie Granola Bar, 1 (1 ounce)
Skim Milk, 1/2 cup

This menu provides: 2 Milks, 3 Fats, 2 Fruits, 12 1/2 Vegetables, 4 1/2 Proteins, 6 Breads, 125 Optional Calories.

Per serving: 28 g Fat, 21 g Fiber.

115
SHRIMP SALAD IN A BOAT

Makes 2 servings

6 ounces cooked small shrimp, peeled and deveined
$^1/_4$ cup diced pared jicama
$^1/_4$ cup diced green bell pepper
$^1/_4$ cup diced onion
2 tablespoons + 2 teaspoons reduced-calorie mayonnaise
2 tablespoons minced fresh cilantro
2 teaspoons fresh lime juice
1 teaspoon chopped deveined seeded jalapeño pepper
   (wear gloves to prevent irritation)
Two 3-ounce hoagie rolls
2 Romaine lettuce leaves

1. In medium bowl, combine shrimp, jicama, bell pepper, onion, mayonnaise, cilantro, juice and jalapeño pepper.

2. With serrated knife, cut a thin slice off top of each roll; set roll tops aside. Remove and discard 1 ounce soft bread from center of each roll. Line inside of rolls with lettuce; top each portion of lettuce with half of the shrimp mixture, then one reserved roll top.

Serving (1 sandwich) provides: 2 Fats, 1 Vegetable, $1^1/_2$ Proteins, 2 Breads.

Per serving: 318 Calories, 9 g Total Fat, 2 g Saturated Fat, 136 mg Cholesterol, 568 mg Sodium, 35 g Total Carbohydrate, 3 g Dietary Fiber, 23 g Protein, 100 mg Calcium.

116
CRAB SALAD IN ARTICHOKE FLOWER

Makes 2 servings

2 whole medium artichokes
2 lemon slices
2 tablespoons minced celery
2 tablespoons plain nonfat yogurt
1 tablespoon + 1 teaspoon reduced-calorie mayonnaise
1 tablespoon minced fresh cilantro
2 teaspoons fresh lime juice
1 teaspoon minced deveined seeded jalapeño pepper
  (wear gloves to prevent irritation)
6 asparagus spears, cut into 2" pieces
6 ounces drained canned crabmeat, flaked
$^1/_2$ small mango, pared, pitted and diced

1. Cut off stem end of each artichoke flush with base so that artichokes stand upright; remove and discard tough outer leaves. With scissors, trim 1" from top of each artichoke.

2. Place artichokes and lemon slices into large saucepan; add water to cover. Bring liquid to a boil. Reduce heat; simmer 15 minutes, until artichokes are tender. With slotted spoon, remove artichokes from water; discard lemon slices. Place upside-down onto paper towels to drain. Refrigerate, covered, 2 hours, until chilled.

3. Meanwhile, in medium bowl, combine celery, yogurt, mayonnaise, cilantro, juice and pepper; stir in asparagus and crabmeat. Refrigerate, covered, until chilled.

4. Gently spread leaves of artichokes to resemble a flower; remove and discard chokes (fuzzy center portion of artichokes).

5. Add mango to crabmeat mixture; stir to combine. Spoon an equal amount of crabmeat mixture into each artichoke. Place 1 artichoke on each of 2 plates and serve.

Serving (1 artichoke, 1$^1/_4$ cups crabmeat mixture) provides: 1 Fat, $^1/_2$ Fruit, 1$^3/_4$ Vegetables, 1$^1/_2$ Proteins, 10 Optional Calories.

Per serving: 226 Calories, 4 g Total Fat, 1 g Saturated Fat, 79 mg Cholesterol, 477 mg Sodium, 27 g Total Carbohydrate, 8 g Dietary Fiber, 24 g Protein, 197 mg Calcium.

BREAKFAST
Strawberry Shake (In blender, combine 1 cup skim buttermilk, $^1/_2$ cup strawberries and 1 teaspoon *each* honey and vanilla; purée until smooth.)
Cinnamon-Raisin English Muffin, $^1/_2$ (1 ounce), toasted, with 2 teaspoons reduced-calorie tub margarine
Coffee or Tea (optional)

LIGHT MEAL
Crab Salad in Artichoke Flower, 1 serving (see recipe)
Tomato, 1 medium, sliced
Breadsticks, 2 long
Sugar-Free Mixed Fruit-Flavored Gelatin, $^1/_2$ cup, with 1 tablespoon thawed frozen light whipped topping (8 calories per tablespoon)
Sparkling Mineral Water

MAIN MEAL
Grilled Turkey Cutlet, 3 ounces
Cooked Long-Grain and Wild Rice, 1 cup
Steamed Whole Green Beans and Yellow Squash Sticks, 1 cup *each*
Tossed Green Salad, 2 cups, with 1 tablespoon fat-free Italian dressing
Roll, 1 ounce, with 2 teaspoons reduced-calorie tub margarine
Cherries, 12 large
Iced Decaffeinated Cappuccino, made with skim milk, 5 fluid ounces

SNACK
Reduced-Calorie Chocolate-Flavored Pudding (made with skim milk), $^1/_2$ cup

This menu provides: 2 Milks, 3 Fats, 2 Fruits, 11$^3/_4$ Vegetables, 4$^1/_2$ Proteins, 5 Breads, 95 Optional Calories.

Per serving: 22 g Fat, 20 g Fiber.

BREAKFAST

Orange Sections, $^1/_2$ cup
English Muffin, 1 (2 ounces), split and toasted, with
   2 teaspoons reduced-calorie tub margarine
Skim Milk, 1 cup
Coffee or Tea (optional)

LIGHT MEAL

Cottage Cheese Salad (In medium bowl, combine
   $^1/_2$ cup *each* nonfat cottage cheese, broccoli florets
   and shredded carrot and $^1/_4$ cup *each* sliced radishes
   and scallions.)
Whole Green Beans and Carrot Sticks, 1 cup *each*
Melba Rounds, 6
Aspartame-Sweetened Cherry-Vanilla Nonfat Yogurt,
   1 cup
Iced Tea with Lemon Wedge

MAIN MEAL

Catfish Fajitas, 1 serving (see recipe)
Spinach 'n' Bean Salad (In medium bowl, combine
   2 cups torn spinach leaves, $^1/_2$ cup *each* sliced
   mushrooms and red onion, 2 ounces drained
   cooked white beans, 1 tablespoon imitation
   bacon bits and 1 tablespoon ranch dressing.)
Pineapple, $^1/_8$ medium
Sparkling Mineral Water

SNACK

Buttery Popcorn (Lightly spray 3 cups hot-air
   popped plain popcorn with nonstick cooking
   spray. Sprinkle popcorn with $^1/_4$ teaspoon butter-
   flavor granules; toss to coat evenly.)

This menu provides: 2 Milks, 3 Fats, 2 Fruits,
15$^1/_2$ Vegetables, 4 Proteins, 6 Breads, 50 Optional
Calories.

Per serving: 34 g Fat, 32 g Fiber.

117
CATFISH FAJITAS

Makes 2 servings

2 teaspoons grated lemon zest*
$^1/_2$ teaspoon minced fresh thyme leaves
$^1/_4$ teaspoon salt
Pinch ground red pepper
Two 5-ounce catfish fillets
1 medium tomato, seeded and diced
$^1/_4$ cup diced green bell pepper
$^1/_4$ cup diced red onion
$^1/_4$ cup plain nonfat yogurt
1 teaspoon hot fruit sauce†
1 cup shredded Romaine lettuce leaves
Four 6" flour tortillas

1. In small bowl, combine zest, thyme, salt and ground red pepper; rub into both sides of each catfish fillet. Refrigerate, covered, at least 4 hours or overnight.

2. Meanwhile, in medium bowl, combine tomato, bell pepper, onion, yogurt and fruit sauce; refrigerate, covered, until chilled.

3. Preheat outdoor barbecue grill according to manufacturer's directions, or preheat broiler and spray rack in broiler pan with nonstick cooking spray.

4. Cut fish fillets in half lengthwise. Thread 2 fish strips onto each of 2 long metal skewers. Grill fish over hot coals or place onto prepared rack in broiler pan and broil 4" from heat, turning once, 6 minutes, until fish flakes easily when tested with fork. Remove fish strips from skewers.

5. To assemble fajitas, place $^1/_4$ cup lettuce onto center of each tortilla; top each portion of lettuce with 1 fish strip and one-fourth of the tomato mixture. Roll tortillas to enclose.

Serving (2 fajitas) provides: 2$^1/_2$ Vegetables, 2 Proteins, 2 Breads, 20 Optional Calories.

Per serving: 364 Calories, 13 g Total Fat, 3 g Saturated Fat, 47 mg Cholesterol, 557 mg Sodium, 32 g Total Carbohydrate, 3 g Dietary Fiber, 28 g Protein, 133 mg Calcium.

*The zest of the lemon is the peel without any of the pith (white membrane). To remove zest from lemon, use a zester or the fine side of a vegetable grater; wrap lemon in plastic wrap and refrigerate for use at another time.

†Hot fruit sauce, such as PickaPeppa sauce, is available in many supermarkets and gourmet stores; if you can't find it, substitute 1 tablespoon steak sauce and a pinch of ground red pepper.

MEXICAN SCALLOP FAJITAS

Makes 4 servings

2 teaspoons canola oil
2 teaspoons fresh lemon juice
1 garlic clove, minced
1/2 teaspoon ground cumin
1/4 teaspoon mild or hot chili powder
1/4 teaspoon ground red pepper
10 ounces sea scallops, halved
Four 6" flour tortillas
1 cup julienned carrot
1 cup thinly sliced red bell pepper
8 medium scallions, cut into 1" pieces
1 cup mild, medium or hot salsa
1/4 cup plain nonfat yogurt

1. Preheat oven to 350° F.

2. In medium bowl, combine oil, juice, garlic, cumin, chili powder and ground red pepper; add scallops, turning to coat. Set aside for 10 minutes, stirring occasionally.

3. Meanwhile, wrap tortillas in foil; bake 10 minutes, until heated through. Remove tortillas from oven; set aside.

4. Spray large nonstick skillet with nonstick cooking spray; heat. Add carrot and bell pepper; cook over medium-high heat, stirring frequently, 5 minutes, until softened. Add scallions and reserved scallop mixture; cook, stirring frequently, 3 minutes, until scallops are opaque in center. Remove from heat; set aside.

5. In small bowl, combine salsa and yogurt.

6. To assemble fajitas, spread 1 tablespoon salsa mixture along center of each warm tortilla; top each portion of salsa mixture with one-fourth of the scallop mixture. Roll tortillas to enclose; serve with remaining salsa mixture.

Serving (1 fajita, 1/4 cup remaining salsa mixture) provides: 1/2 Fat, 2 1/4 Vegetables, 1 Protein, 1 Bread, 10 Optional Calories.

Per serving: 202 Calories, 4 g Total Fat, 0 g Saturated Fat, 24 mg Cholesterol, 875 mg Sodium, 24 g Total Carbohydrate, 2 g Dietary Fiber, 15 g Protein, 94 mg Calcium.

BREAKFAST

Orange Sections, 1/2 cup
Reduced-Calorie Whole-Wheat Bread, 2 slices, toasted, with 2 teaspoons reduced-calorie tub margarine
Grilled Canadian-Style Bacon, 1 ounce
Skim Milk, 1 cup
Coffee or Tea (optional)

LIGHT MEAL

Turkey Club (Layer 2 ounces skinless boneless roast turkey breast, sliced, 1/2 cup radish sprouts, 4 tomato slices, 4 Boston lettuce leaves and 2 teaspoons reduced-calorie mayonnaise between 3 slices reduced-calorie rye bread.)
Zucchini and Yellow Squash Sticks, 1 cup *each*
Sugar-Free Vanilla Nonfat Frozen Yogurt, 4 fluid ounces
Diet Cherry Cola

MAIN MEAL

Mexican Scallop Fajitas, 1 serving (see recipe)
Cooked Long-Grain Brown Rice, 1 cup
Romaine, Red Onion and Jicama Salad, 2 cups, with 1/2 cup *each* sliced celery and carrot and 1 tablespoon fat-free ranch dressing
"Fried" Banana (In small nonstick skillet, melt 1 teaspoon reduced-calorie tub margarine; add 1/2 medium banana, sliced. Cook over medium-high heat, turning slices as needed, until lightly browned; sprinkle with 1 teaspoon packed light or dark brown sugar.)
Unsweetened Seltzer with Lime Wedge

SNACK

Plain Popcorn, hot-air popped, 1 1/2 cups
Vanilla Shake (In blender, combine 3/4 cup skim milk, 3 ice cubes, sugar substitute to equal 2 teaspoons sugar and 1 teaspoon vanilla extract; purée until smooth.)

This menu provides: 2 Milks, 3 Fats, 2 Fruits, 14 3/4 Vegetables, 4 Proteins, 6 Breads, 95 Optional Calories.

Per serving: 23 g Fat, 23 g Fiber.

119
POTATO-CRUSTED SCROD

Makes 4 servings

10 ounces all-purpose potatoes, pared and coarsely shredded
2 teaspoons olive oil
¹/₂ cup chopped onion
¹/₂ cup coarsely shredded carrot
1 tablespoon minced fresh dill
¹/₂ teaspoon salt
¹/₄ teaspoon freshly ground black pepper
Four 4-ounce scrod fillets
2 teaspoons Dijon-style mustard

1. Preheat oven to 400° F. Spray 11 × 7" baking dish with nonstick cooking spray.

2. Place potatoes into medium saucepan; add water to cover. Bring liquid to a boil; reduce heat to low. Simmer 10–12 minutes, until potatoes are tender. Drain, discarding liquid; set aside.

3. In medium nonstick skillet, heat oil; add onion and carrot. Cook over medium-high heat, stirring frequently, 5 minutes, until vegetables are softened. Add dill, salt, pepper and cooked potatoes; stir gently to combine. Remove from heat; set aside to cool slightly.

4. Spread each scrod fillet with ¹/₂ teaspoon mustard. Place fillets in a single layer into prepared baking dish; top each with one-fourth of the potato mixture, spreading evenly to coat and pressing down gently. Bake 15 minutes, until fish flakes easily when tested with fork.

Serving (1 scrod fillet) provides: ¹/₂ Fat, ¹/₂ Vegetable, 1¹/₂ Proteins, ¹/₂ Bread.

Per serving: 187 Calories, 3 g Total Fat, 0 g Saturated Fat, 49 mg Cholesterol, 405 mg Sodium, 16 g Total Carbohydrate, 2 g Dietary Fiber, 22 g Protein, 37 mg Calcium.

BREAKFAST
Orange Sections, ¹/₂ cup
Cooked Oatmeal, ¹/₂ cup, with 1 teaspoon *each* reduced-calorie tub margarine and firmly packed light or dark brown sugar
Skim Milk, 1 cup
Coffee or Tea (optional)

LIGHT MEAL
Grilled Turkey Burger, 2 ounces, on 1 large (2-ounce) pita, opened to form pocket, with ¹/₄ cup *each* shredded iceberg lettuce leaves and diced tomato and 1 tablespoon fat-free honey-mustard dressing
Zucchini-Corn Salad (In small bowl, combine 1 cup chopped zucchini, ¹/₂ cup *each* chilled cooked corn kernels and chopped scallions, ¹/₂ cup plain nonfat yogurt and ¹/₄ teaspoon dried oregano leaves.)
Frozen Fruit Pop (Pour ¹/₂ cup low-calorie fruit punch–flavored drink into small paper cup; freeze until almost firm. Insert ice-cream-bar stick vertically into partially frozen drink; freeze until solid. Unmold.)
Diet Cola with Lemon Wedge

MAIN MEAL
Potato-Crusted Scrod, 1 serving (see recipe)
Cooked Spaghetti Squash, 1 cup, with 2 teaspoons reduced-calorie tub margarine
Steamed Whole Green Beans and Carrot Sticks, 1 cup *each*
Garlic-Herb Bread (Spread 1-ounce slice Italian bread with ¹/₂ teaspoon minced fresh garlic or 1 roasted garlic clove and ¹/₂ teaspoon *each* minced fresh basil and oregano leaves; drizzle with 1 teaspoon olive oil. Place onto nonstick baking sheet; broil until lightly browned.)
Blueberries, ³/₄ cup, with 1 tablespoon thawed frozen light whipped topping (8 calories per tablespoon)
Iced Tea

SNACK
Root Beer "Float" (In tall glass, combine 1 cup diet root beer and ¹/₃ cup skim milk; add enough ice cubes to fill glass.)

This menu provides: 2 Milks, 3 Fats, 2 Fruits, 10¹/₂ Vegetables, 3¹/₂ Proteins, 5¹/₂ Breads, 50 Optional Calories.

Per serving: 21 g Fat, 21 g Fiber.

BREAKFAST

Pink Grapefruit, $^1/_2$ medium
English Muffin, $^1/_2$ (1 ounce), toasted, with 2 tea-
spoons reduced-calorie tub margarine
Aspartame-Sweetened Strawberry Nonfat Yogurt,
1 cup
Coffee or Tea (optional)

LIGHT MEAL

Chicken Salad (In small bowl, combine 2 ounces
skinless boneless cooked chicken breast, chopped,
$^1/_2$ cup chopped celery, 2 teaspoons reduced-
calorie mayonnaise and pinch freshly ground
black pepper.)
Crispbreads, $1^1/_2$ ounces
Tomato, 1 medium, sliced, with 1 tablespoon *each*
minced fresh basil and balsamic vinegar
Pear, 1 small
Sparkling Mineral Water

MAIN MEAL

Low-Sodium Mixed Vegetable Juice, 1 cup
Fish and Chips, 1 serving (see recipe), with 1 table-
spoon malt or cider vinegar or fresh lemon juice
Steamed Whole Green Beans, 1 cup
Tossed Green Salad, 2 cups, with $^1/_2$ cup *each* sliced
green bell pepper and radishes and 1 tablespoon
fat-free honey-mustard dressing
Reduced-Calorie Vanilla-Flavored Pudding (made
with skim milk), $^1/_2$ cup
Diet Ginger Ale

SNACK

Graham Crackers, 3 ($2^1/_2$" squares)
Skim Milk, $^1/_2$ cup

This menu provides: 2 Milks, 3 Fats, 2 Fruits,
13 Vegetables, $3^1/_2$ Proteins, $5^1/_2$ Breads,
60 Optional Calories.

Per serving: 22 g Fat, 26 g Fiber.

FISH AND CHIPS

*Serve this British specialty with malt vinegar or fresh lemon juice, to
be sprinkled on the fish and chips at the table. If sole is unavailable,
other delicate, white-fleshed fish can be used; try scrod or whiting.*

Makes 4 servings

Four 5-ounce baking potatoes
1 tablespoon + 1 teaspoon canola oil
$^3/_4$ teaspoon paprika
$^1/_3$ cup + 2 teaspoons fine plain dried bread crumbs
$^3/_4$ teaspoon salt
Pinch ground red pepper
Four 4-ounce sole fillets

1. Preheat oven to 450° F. Spray 15 × 10" jelly-roll pan with nonstick
cooking spray.

2. Cut potatoes into halves, then cut halves into 3 wedges each; place into
medium bowl. Sprinkle potatoes with 1 teaspoon of the oil and $^1/_4$ teaspoon of the paprika; toss to coat. Place coated potato wedges in a single
layer onto one side of prepared pan; bake 15 minutes, until just tender.
Remove potatoes from oven; leave oven on.

3. Meanwhile, in shallow bowl or pie plate, combine bread crumbs, salt,
pepper and remaining $^1/_2$ teaspoon paprika; with fork, stir in remaining
1 tablespoon oil, blending until crumbs are evenly moistened. One at a
time, press fillets into crumb mixture, turning to coat both sides (fillets
will not be completely coated); place coated fillets in a single layer onto
pan with potatoes. Bake 12 minutes, until fish flakes easily when tested
with fork and potatoes are browned and tender.

Serving (1 fish fillet, 6 potato wedges) provides: 1 Fat, $1^1/_2$ Proteins,
$1^1/_2$ Breads.

Per serving: 291 Calories, 7 g Total Fat, 1 g Saturated Fat, 54 mg Cholesterol,
60 mg Sodium, 31 g Total Carbohydrate, 3 g Dietary Fiber, 26 g Protein,
65 mg Calcium.

121
CRAB AND RICE CAKES

Looking for a way to get dinner on the table fast? Try preparing, coating and refrigerating these easy and delicious patties in advance, then cooking them just minutes before serving.

Makes 4 servings

4 ounces yogurt cheese*
$^1/_2$ medium tomato, seeded and cut into $^1/_4$" pieces
$^1/_4$ medium green bell pepper, cut into $^1/_4$" pieces
8 ounces drained canned crabmeat, flaked
1 cup cold cooked long-grain brown rice
3 tablespoons plain dried bread crumbs
2 tablespoons + 2 teaspoons reduced-calorie mayonnaise
2 tablespoons minced fresh flat-leaf parsley
1 tablespoon Creole-style or natural stone-ground mustard
1 tablespoon low-sodium Worcestershire sauce
$^1/_2$ teaspoon ground red pepper
1 egg white
2 tablespoons yellow cornmeal
1 tablespoon + 1 teaspoon reduced-calorie tub margarine
2 cups torn salad greens

1. In small bowl, combine yogurt cheese, tomato and bell pepper; refrigerate, covered, until chilled.

2. In large bowl, combine crabmeat, rice, bread crumbs, mayonnaise, parsley, mustard, Worcestershire sauce and ground red pepper; stir in egg white. Form mixture into eight $2^1/_4 \times ^1/_2$" patties.

3. Place cornmeal onto sheet of wax paper or paper plate; one at a time, press each patty into cornmeal, turning to coat.

4. In large nonstick skillet, melt margarine; add patties. Cook over medium-high heat, turning once, 5–6 minutes, until golden brown and crispy.

5. Divide salad greens evenly among 4 plates; top each portion with 2 crab cakes.

Serving (2 crab cakes, $^1/_2$ cup salad greens) provides: $^1/_4$ Milk, $1^1/_2$ Fats, $1^3/_4$ Vegetables, 1 Protein, 1 Bread, 5 Optional Calories.

Per serving: 225 Calories, 6 g Total Fat, 1 g Saturated Fat, 54 mg Cholesterol, 411 mg Sodium, 23 g Total Carbohydrate, 1 g Dietary Fiber, 18 g Protein, 162 mg Calcium.

To make yogurt cheese, spoon $^3/_4$ cup plain nonfat yogurt into coffee filter or cheesecloth-lined strainer; place over bowl. Refrigerate, covered, at least 5 hours or overnight. Discard liquid in bowl.

BREAKFAST
Mango, $^1/_2$ small
Frozen Pancakes, 2, heated, with 2 teaspoons *each* maple syrup and reduced-calorie tub margarine
Skim Milk, 1 cup
Coffee or Tea (optional)

LIGHT MEAL
Roast Beef Pita (Cut large [2-ounce] whole-wheat pita in half crosswise; open to form 2 pockets. Fill each pocket with 1 ounce cooked lean boneless roast beef, thinly sliced, 2 tomato slices, 1 Romaine lettuce leaf and 1 teaspoon prepared mustard.)
Carrot and Cucumber Sticks, 1 cup *each*
Granny Smith Apple, 1 small
Diet Celery Soda

MAIN MEAL
Crab and Rice Cakes, 1 serving (see recipe)
Steamed Whole Green Beans, 1 cup, with 1 teaspoon reduced-calorie tub margarine
Shredded Red and Green Cabbage, 1 cup, with 1 tablespoon fat-free Italian dressing
Reduced-Calorie Butterscotch-Flavored Pudding (made with skim milk), $^1/_2$ cup
Sparkling Mineral Water

SNACK
Plain Popcorn, hot-air popped, 3 cups
Double Chocolate "Float" (In tall glass, scoop 4 fluid ounces sugar-free chocolate nonfat frozen yogurt; add enough diet chocolate soda to fill glass.)

This menu provides: 2 Milks, 3 Fats, 2 Fruits, $11^1/_4$ Vegetables, 3 Proteins, 6 Breads, 130 Optional Calories.

Per serving: 24 g Fat, 22 g Fiber.

122
CODFISH CAKES WITH TOMATO-CORN SALSA

Makes 4 servings

2 medium tomatoes, seeded and diced
1 cup cooked corn kernels
1 tablespoon minced fresh cilantro
1 tablespoon fresh lime juice
2 teaspoons chopped deveined seeded jalapeño pepper (wear gloves to
    prevent irritation)
10 ounces all-purpose potatoes, pared and cut into $^1/_2$" pieces
10 ounces cod fillets, cut into 1" pieces
$^1/_2$ cup chopped onion
$^1/_2$ teaspoon salt
Pinch freshly ground black pepper
1 tablespoon + 1 teaspoon all-purpose flour
1 tablespoon + 1 teaspoon vegetable oil

1. To prepare salsa, in small bowl, combine tomatoes, corn, cilantro, juice and jalapeño pepper; refrigerate, covered, until chilled.

2. To prepare codfish cakes, place potatoes into medium saucepan; add water to cover. Bring liquid to a boil; reduce heat to low. Simmer 10–15 minutes, until potatoes are tender. Drain, discarding liquid; set aside.

3. In food processor, combine cod, onion, salt, pepper and cooked potatoes; purée until smooth. Transfer fish mixture to medium bowl; refrigerate, covered, 1 hour, until firm enough to hold its shape. Form mixture into eight $2^1/_2$" patties.

4. Place flour onto sheet of wax paper or paper plate; one at a time, press each patty into flour, turning to coat.

5. In large nonstick skillet, heat oil; add patties. Cook over medium-high heat, turning once, 6–8 minutes, until golden brown and cooked through. Serve codfish cakes with chilled salsa.

Serving (2 codfish cakes, $^1/_2$ cup salsa) provides: 1 Fat, $1^1/_2$ Vegetables, 1 Protein, 1 Bread, 10 Optional Calories.

Per serving: 234 Calories, 6 g Total Fat, 1 g Saturated Fat, 30 mg Cholesterol, 331 mg Sodium, 31 g Total Carbohydrate, 4 g Dietary Fiber, 17 g Protein, 28 mg Calcium.

123

SPICY CALAMARI AND SHRIMP BROCHETTES

Makes 4 servings

1 tablespoon + 1 teaspoon olive oil
1 teaspoon minced deveined seeded jalapeño pepper (wear gloves to prevent irritation)
1 tablespoon fresh lime juice
4 garlic cloves, minced
$^1/_4$ teaspoon crushed red pepper flakes
10 ounces cleaned calamari, cut into 1" circles
10 ounces medium shrimp, peeled and deveined (tails left on)
1 cup drained canned baby corn
1 cup snow peas, blanched

1. To prepare marinade, in gallon-size sealable plastic bag, combine oil, jalapeño pepper, juice, garlic and red pepper flakes; add calamari and shrimp. Seal bag, squeezing out air; turn to coat seafood. Refrigerate 1 hour, turning bag occasionally.

2. Preheat broiler. Spray rack in broiler pan with nonstick cooking spray.

3. Drain marinade into small saucepan; bring to a rolling boil; boil for 1 minute, stirring constantly. Remove from heat.

4. Alternating ingredients, onto each of 4 long metal skewers, thread one-fourth of the calamari, shrimp, corn and pea pods. Place skewers onto prepared rack; broil 4" from heat, turning once and brushing frequently with marinade, 4–5 minutes, until calamari is opaque and shrimp turn pink.

Serving (1 skewer) provides: $^1/_2$ Vegetable, 2 Proteins, $^1/_2$ Bread, 40 Optional Calories.

Per serving: 211 Calories, 7 g Total Fat, 1 g Saturated Fat, 273 mg Cholesterol, 144 mg Sodium, 8 g Total Carbohydrate, 2 g Dietary Fiber, 27 g Protein, 94 mg Calcium.

BREAKFAST
Tangerine, 1 large
Toasted Oat Cereal, $^3/_4$ ounce
Skim Milk, $^1/_2$ cup
Coffee or Tea (optional)

LIGHT MEAL
Turkey Ham Sandwich (Layer 2 ounces lean cooked turkey ham, sliced, 2 Romaine lettuce leaves, $^1/_4$ cup cucumber slices, 2 tomato slices, 2 red onion slices and 2 teaspoons prepared mustard between 2 slices reduced-calorie rye bread.)
Carrot and Celery Sticks, 1 cup *each*
Reduced-Calorie Vanilla-Flavored Pudding (made with skim milk), $^1/_2$ cup
Diet Orange Soda

MAIN MEAL
Spicy Calamari and Shrimp Brochettes, 1 serving (see recipe)
Cooked Long-Grain Brown Rice, 1 cup, with 2 tablespoons cooked minced shallots
Steamed Spinach, 1 cup, with 2 teaspoons reduced-calorie tub margarine
Watercress and Radicchio Salad, 2 cups, with 2 ounces drained cooked chick-peas and 1 tablespoon French dressing
Honeydew Melon, 2" wedge, with 1 lime wedge
Unsweetened Seltzer

SNACK
Aspartame-Sweetened Blueberry Nonfat Yogurt, 1 cup

This menu provides: 2 Milks, 3 Fats, 2 Fruits, 12$^1/_4$ Vegetables, 5 Proteins, 4$^1/_2$ Breads, 80 Optional Calories.

Per serving: 28 g Fat, 21 g Fiber.

124

RED SNAPPER, FENNEL AND ARTICHOKE KABOBS

Makes 4 servings

12 large kalamata olives, pitted and thinly sliced
$^1/_4$ cup minced fresh flat-leaf parsley
1 tablespoon + 1 teaspoon olive oil
1 tablespoon fresh lemon juice
$^1/_2$ teaspoon fennel seeds, crushed
15 ounces red snapper fillets, cut into $1^1/_2$" cubes
$^1/_4$ teaspoon salt
Pinch freshly ground black pepper
1 cup cooked large artichoke hearts, quartered

1. Preheat outdoor barbecue grill according to manufacturer's directions, or preheat broiler and spray rack in broiler pan with nonstick cooking spray.

2. In small bowl, combine olives, parsley, oil, juice and fennel seeds; set aside.

3. Sprinkle fish on all sides with salt and pepper; alternating ingredients, onto each of 4 long metal skewers, thread one-fourth of the fish and one-fourth of the artichoke hearts. Grill over hot coals or place onto prepared rack in broiler pan and broil 4" from heat 3–4 minutes, until fish flakes easily when tested with fork.

4. Place 1 kabob onto each of 4 plates; carefully remove skewers. Sprinkle evenly with olive mixture.

Serving (1 kabob, $1^1/_2$ tablespoons olive mixture) provides: $1^1/_2$ Fats, $^1/_2$ Vegetable, $1^1/_2$ Proteins.

Per serving: 217 Calories, 10 g Total Fat, 1 g Saturated Fat, 39 mg Cholesterol, 490 mg Sodium, 8 g Total Carbohydrate, 3 g Dietary Fiber, 24 g Protein, 55 mg Calcium.

125

GRILLED TUNA WITH BEAN-TOMATO SALSA

Makes 4 servings

8 ounces drained cooked white kidney (cannellini) beans
2 large plum tomatoes, seeded and diced
2 tablespoons minced fresh basil
2 teaspoons fresh lemon juice
2 teaspoons olive oil
2 garlic cloves, minced
Pinch crushed red pepper flakes
Four 5-ounce boneless tuna steaks
2 cups arugula leaves

1. To prepare salsa, in medium bowl, combine beans, tomatoes, basil and juice; refrigerate, covered, until chilled.

2. Meanwhile, in small cup or bowl, combine oil, garlic and red pepper flakes; rub into fish on all sides. Refrigerate, covered, 1 hour.

3. Preheat outdoor barbecue grill or indoor stove-top grill according to manufacturer's directions.

4. Grill tuna over hot coals or on stove-top grill, turning once, 6 minutes, until fish flakes easily when tested with fork.

5. Divide arugula evenly among 4 plates. Top each portion of arugula with 1 grilled tuna steak; top evenly with salsa.

Serving ($^1/_2$ cup arugula, 1 tuna steak, $^1/_2$ cup salsa) provides: $^1/_2$ Fat, $1^1/_2$ Vegetables, 3 Proteins.

Per serving: 308 Calories, 10 g Total Fat, 2 g Saturated Fat, 54 mg Cholesterol, 66 mg Sodium, 15 g Total Carbohydrate, 3 g Dietary Fiber, 39 g Protein, 52 mg Calcium.

BREAKFAST
Orange Sections, $^1/_2$ cup
Vanilla Yogurt Crunch (In small bowl, combine 1 cup aspartame-sweetened vanilla nonfat yogurt and 1 tablespoon wheat germ.)
Cinnamon-Raisin Bagel, $^1/_2$ small (1 ounce), toasted, with 1 teaspoon reduced-calorie tub margarine
Coffee or Tea (optional)

LIGHT MEAL
Teriyaki Turkey Cutlet (In quart-size sealable plastic bag, combine 3 ounces skinless boneless turkey breast and 1 tablespoon teriyaki sauce. Seal bag, squeezing out air; turn to coat turkey. Refrigerate at least 2 hours or overnight, turning bag occasionally. Preheat grill according to manufacturer's directions. Drain turkey, discarding liquid. Grill turkey 6 minutes, turning once, until cooked through.)
Cooked Wide Noodles, 1 cup, with 2 teaspoons *each* freshly grated Parmesan cheese and reduced-calorie tub margarine
Steamed Snow Peas, 1 cup
Sugar-Free Pineapple-Flavored Gelatin, $^1/_2$ cup
Iced Tea with Lemon Wedge

MAIN MEAL
Grilled Tuna with Bean-Tomato Salsa, 1 serving (see recipe)
Grilled Vegetables (Preheat grill according to manufacturer's directions. Grill $^1/_2$ cup *each* sliced zucchini, sliced yellow squash, sliced green bell pepper, sliced pared eggplant, sliced red onion and sliced fennel 6–8 minutes, turning as needed, until lightly browned and tender.)
Garlic-Herb Bread (Spread 1-ounce slice Italian bread with $^1/_2$ teaspoon minced fresh garlic or 1 roasted garlic clove and $^1/_2$ teaspoon *each* minced fresh basil and oregano leaves; drizzle with 1 teaspoon olive oil. Place onto nonstick baking sheet; broil until lightly browned.)
Watermelon, 3 × 2" wedge
Unsweetened Seltzer

SNACK
Pretzels, $1^1/_2$ ounces
Skim Milk, 1 cup

This menu provides: 2 Milks, 3 Fats, 2 Fruits, $9^1/_2$ Vegetables, 5 Proteins, 6 Breads, 80 Optional Calories.

Per serving: 30 g Fat, 22 g Fiber.

BREAKFAST

Broiled Grapefruit (Sprinkle $^1/_2$ medium grapefruit with 1 teaspoon firmly packed light or dark brown sugar; place onto nonstick baking sheet. Broil 2–3 minutes, until topping is bubbling.)

Herb Scramble (In small microwavable bowl, combine $^1/_2$ cup egg substitute, 1 teaspoon minced fresh flat-leaf parsley and $^1/_4$ teaspoon *each* dried oregano leaves and basil; microwave on Medium-High [70% power], 1–2 minutes, stirring once or twice, until set.)

Bagel, $^1/_2$ small (1 ounce), toasted, with 1 tablespoon nonfat cream cheese

Skim Milk, 1 cup

Coffee or Tea (optional)

LIGHT MEAL

Bulgur Salad (In medium bowl, combine 2 cups torn Romaine lettuce leaves, 1 cup chilled cooked bulgur wheat, 2 ounces drained cooked chick-peas, $^1/_2$ cup diced tomato, $^1/_4$ cup sliced scallions, and 1 tablespoon fat-free Caesar salad dressing.)

Crispbreads, $^3/_4$ ounce

Strawberries, $^1/_2$ cup

Unsweetened Seltzer with Lime Wedge

MAIN MEAL

Asian-Flavored Swordfish with Pineapple-Banana Salsa, 1 serving (see recipe)

Cooked Soba Noodles, 1 cup

Steamed Sugar Snap Peas, 1 cup

Chinese Cabbage and Bean Sprout Salad, 2 cups, with Ginger Vinaigrette (In small jar with tight-fitting lid or small bowl, combine 2 teaspoons rice wine vinegar, 1 teaspoon vegetable oil and $^1/_2$ teaspoon minced pared fresh ginger root; cover and shake well or, with wire whisk, blend until combined.)

Sugar-Free Lemon-Flavored Gelatin, $^1/_2$ cup

Green Tea

SNACK

Peanut Butter-Vanilla Shake (In blender, combine 1 cup skim milk, 3 ice cubes, sugar substitute to equal 2 teaspoons sugar, $1^1/_2$ teaspoons smooth peanut butter and 1 teaspoon vanilla extract; purée until smooth.)

This menu provides: 2 Milks, 3 Fats, 2 Fruits, $11^3/_4$ Vegetables, 5 Proteins, 6 Breads, 60 Optional Calories.

Per serving: 22 g Fat, 28 g Fiber.

126
ASIAN-FLAVORED SWORDFISH WITH PINEAPPLE-BANANA SALSA

Makes 4 servings

$^1/_2$ cup drained canned pineapple chunks (no sugar added), halved

$^1/_2$ medium banana, diced

2 tablespoons chopped red bell pepper

2 tablespoons minced scallions

1 tablespoon minced fresh cilantro

2 teaspoons minced deveined seeded jalapeño pepper (wear gloves to prevent irritation)

1 tablespoon fresh lime juice

2 teaspoons grated pared fresh ginger root

2 teaspoons canola oil

1 teaspoon anise seeds, crushed

Pinch granulated sugar

Four 5-ounce boneless swordfish steaks

1. To prepare salsa, in medium bowl, combine pineapple, banana, bell pepper, scallions, cilantro and jalapeño pepper; refrigerate, covered, until chilled.

2. To prepare fish, in small bowl, combine juice, ginger, oil, anise seeds and sugar; brush over both sides of fish. Refrigerate, covered, 30 minutes.

3. Preheat outdoor barbecue grill or indoor stove-top grill according to manufacturer's directions.

4. Grill swordfish over hot coals or on stove-top grill, turning once, 6–8 minutes, until fish flakes easily when tested with fork. Serve with salsa.

Serving (1 swordfish steak, $^1/_4$ cup salsa) provides: $^1/_2$ Fat, $^1/_2$ Fruit, $^1/_4$ Vegetable, 2 Proteins.

Per serving: 229 Calories, 8 g Total Fat, 2 g Saturated Fat, 55 mg Cholesterol, 129 mg Sodium, 10 g Total Carbohydrate, 1 g Dietary Fiber, 29 g Protein, 18 mg Calcium.

127
SPAGHETTI WITH CLAM SAUCE

Makes 4 servings

4 sun-dried tomato halves (not packed in oil)
6 ounces spaghetti
1 tablespoon + 1 teaspoon olive oil
$^1/_2$ cup diced onion
1 garlic clove, minced
$^1/_2$ cup bottled clam juice
$^1/_2$ cup clam-tomato juice
$^1/_4$ cup tomato paste (no salt added)
2 tablespoons minced fresh flat-leaf parsley
2 tablespoons minced fresh basil
6 ounces drained canned minced clams

1. Place tomatoes into small bowl; add boiling water to cover. Let stand 30 minutes, until softened; drain, discarding liquid. Finely chop tomatoes; set aside.

2. Meanwhile, in large pot of boiling water, cook spaghetti 8–10 minutes, until tender. Drain, discarding liquid; place into serving bowl. Keep warm.

3. In large nonstick skillet, heat oil; add onion and garlic. Cook over medium-high heat, stirring frequently, 5 minutes, until onion is softened. Stir in clam and clam-tomato juices, tomato paste, 1 tablespoon of the parsley, 1 tablespoon of the basil and the chopped tomatoes; bring liquid to a boil. Reduce heat to low; simmer, stirring occasionally, 3–5 minutes, until slightly thickened. Stir in clams; cook, stirring occasionally, 1 minute, until mixture is heated through.

4. Top warm spaghetti with clam mixture; toss to combine. Sprinkle with remaining 1 tablespoon parsley and 1 tablespoon basil; toss again.

Serving (1 cup spaghetti, $^1/_2$ cup clam mixture) provides: 1 Fat, $1^1/_2$ Vegetables, $^3/_4$ Protein, 2 Breads.

Per serving: 306 Calories, 6 g Total Fat, 1 g Saturated Fat, 28 mg Cholesterol, 221 mg Sodium, 44 g Total Carbohydrate, 3 g Dietary Fiber, 18 g Protein, 79 mg Calcium.

BREAKFAST
Honeydew Melon, 2" wedge
Western Scramble in a Pocket (In small nonstick skillet, heat 1 teaspoon reduced-calorie tub margarine; add 2 tablespoons *each* sliced mushrooms, minced red onion and chopped green bell pepper. Cook over medium-high heat, stirring frequently, 5 minutes, until vegetables are softened. Add $^1/_2$ cup egg substitute; cook, stirring constantly, until mixture is set. Split 1 small [1-ounce] pita halfway around edge; open to form pocket. Fill pita pocket with scrambled mixture.)
Skim Milk, $^3/_4$ cup
Coffee or Tea (optional)

LIGHT MEAL
Steamed Vegetable Platter (On plate, decoratively arrange $^1/_2$ cup *each* chilled steamed broccoli florets, cauliflower florets, zucchini slices, thinly sliced carrot and spaghetti squash. Drizzle vegetables with 2 teaspoons reduced-calorie tub margarine, melted; sprinkle with $^3/_4$ ounce freshly grated Parmesan cheese.)
Breadsticks, 2 long
Pear, 1 small
Unsweetened Cranberry-Flavored Seltzer

MAIN MEAL
Steamed Artichoke, 1 medium, with Lemon "Butter" (In small cup or bowl, combine 1 teaspoon *each* reduced-calorie tub margarine, melted, and fresh lemon juice.)
Spaghetti with Clam Sauce, 1 serving (see recipe)
Steamed Asparagus, 6 spears, with 1 teaspoon fresh lemon juice
Romaine and Watercress Salad, 2 cups, with 1 tablespoon fat-free Italian dressing
Italian Bread, 1 slice (1 ounce)
Sugar-Free Chocolate Nonfat Frozen Yogurt, 4 fluid ounces
Decaffeinated Cappuccino, made with skim milk, 5 fluid ounces

SNACK
Graham Crackers, 3 ($2^1/_2$" squares)
Skim Milk, $^1/_2$ cup

This menu provides: 2 Milks, 3 Fats, 2 Fruits, $13^1/_4$ Vegetables, $3^3/_4$ Proteins, 6 Breads, 55 Optional Calories.

Per serving: 29 g Fat, 25 g Fiber.

BREAKFAST

Seedless Green Grapes, 20 small or 12 large
Reduced-Fat Cheddar Cheese, $^3/_4$ ounce
Whole-Wheat English Muffin, $^1/_2$ (1 ounce), toasted, with 1 teaspoon orange marmalade
Skim Milk, $^1/_2$ cup
Coffee or Tea (optional)

LIGHT MEAL

Roast Veal, 2 ounces
Cooked Wide Noodles, 1 cup, with 1 teaspoon reduced-calorie tub margarine and $^1/_2$ teaspoon poppy seeds
Steamed Whole Green Beans, 1 cup
Spinach and Radish Salad, 2 cups, with 1 tablespoon fat-free French dressing
Plum, 1 small
Diet Lemon-Lime Soda

MAIN MEAL

Low-Sodium Tomato Juice, 1 cup
California-Style Pasta with Clams, 1 serving (see recipe)
Radicchio and Belgian Endive Salad, 2 cups, with Raspberry Vinaigrette (In small jar with tight-fitting lid or small bowl, combine 1 tablespoon raspberry vinegar and 1 teaspoon olive oil; cover and shake well or, with wire whisk, blend until combined.)
French Bread, 1 slice (1 ounce), with 1 teaspoon reduced-calorie tub margarine
Vanilla-Raisin Pudding (In small bowl, combine $^1/_2$ cup reduced-calorie vanilla-flavored pudding [made with skim milk] and 1 tablespoon raisins.)
Unsweetened Seltzer with Mint Sprig

SNACK

Reduced-Calorie Vanilla Dairy Shake, 1 serving

This menu provides: 2 Milks, 3 Fats, 2 Fruits, 14 Vegetables, 4 Proteins, 6 Breads, 85 Optional Calories.

Per serving: 29 g Fat, 22 g Fiber.

128 CALIFORNIA-STYLE PASTA WITH CLAMS

Makes 4 servings

5$^1/_4$ ounces spaghetti or fusilli pasta
1 tablespoon + 1 teaspoon olive oil
1 cup julienned zucchini
1 cup julienned carrot
1$^1/_2$ cups sliced mushrooms
8 medium scallions, cut into 1" pieces
$^1/_4$ cup minced fresh basil
24 medium clams
$^1/_2$ cup fresh or thawed frozen green peas

1. In large pot of boiling water, cook spaghetti 8–10 minutes, until tender. Drain, discarding liquid; set aside.

2. Meanwhile, in large nonstick skillet, heat oil; add zucchini and carrot. Cook over medium-high heat, stirring frequently, 5 minutes, until softened. Stir in mushrooms, scallions and 2 tablespoons of the basil; top with clams. Add $^1/_2$ cup water; bring liquid to a boil. Reduce heat to low; simmer, covered, 5–7 minutes, until clams open (discard any clams that do not open).

3. With slotted spoon, transfer clams to serving platter, arranging them around edge of platter.

4. Add peas and cooked spaghetti to vegetable mixture; cook, tossing constantly, until heated through. Transfer to center of platter with clams; sprinkle with remaining basil.

Serving (1 cup spaghetti mixture, 6 clams) provides: 1 Fat, 2 Vegetables, 1 Protein, 2 Breads.

Per serving: 266 Calories, 6 g Total Fat, 1 g Saturated Fat, 19 mg Cholesterol, 50 mg Sodium, 39 g Total Carbohydrate, 3 g Dietary Fiber, 15 g Protein, 85 mg Calcium.

129
CURRIED SHRIMP AND CLAMS

Makes 4 servings

4¹/₂ ounces orzo (rice-shaped pasta)
1 tablespoon + 1 teaspoon olive oil
1 cup coarsely chopped onions
1 small apple, pared, cored and diced
¹/₂ cup diced green bell pepper
2 garlic cloves, minced
1 tablespoon all-purpose flour
2 teaspoons mild or hot curry powder
¹/₂ teaspoon ground ginger
Pinch crushed red pepper flakes, or to taste
1 cup low-sodium chicken broth
1 tablespoon fresh lemon juice
2 tablespoons golden raisins
12 medium clams
12 large shrimp (about 6¹/₂ ounces), peeled and deveined (tails left on)

1. In large pot of boiling water, cook orzo 9 minutes, until tender. Drain, discarding liquid; place into serving bowl. Keep warm.

2. Meanwhile, in large nonstick skillet, heat oil; add onions, apple, bell pepper and garlic. Cook over medium-high heat, stirring frequently, 6–7 minutes, until mixture is lightly browned. Stir in flour, curry powder, ginger and red pepper flakes; cook, stirring constantly, 1 minute. Gradually stir in broth, juice and ¹/₂ cup water; bring liquid to a boil. Reduce heat to low; stir in raisins. Simmer, covered, stirring occasionally, 10 minutes, until slightly thickened.

3. Top curry mixture with clams; cook, covered, 3 minutes. Add shrimp; cook, covered, 2–4 minutes, until clams open and shrimp turn pink (discard any clams that do not open). Serve over warm orzo.

Serving (³/₄ cup orzo, ¹/₃ cup curry mixture, 3 clams, 3 shrimp) provides: 1 Fat, ¹/₂ Fruit, ³/₄ Vegetable, 1¹/₂ Proteins, 1¹/₂ Breads, 15 Optional Calories.

Per serving: 306 Calories, 7 g Total Fat, 1 g Saturated Fat, 96 mg Cholesterol, 134 mg Sodium, 40 g Total Carbohydrate, 3 g Dietary Fiber, 21 g Protein, 73 mg Calcium.

BREAKFAST
Cantaloupe, ¹/₄ small
Nonfat Cottage Cheese, ¹/₂ cup
Flatbreads, ³/₄ ounce
Skim Milk, 1 cup
Coffee or Tea (optional)

LIGHT MEAL
Chicken Salad (In small bowl, combine 2 ounces skinless boneless cooked chicken breast, chopped, ¹/₂ cup chopped celery, 2 teaspoons reduced-calorie mayonnaise and pinch freshly ground black pepper.)
Vegetable Platter (Line plate with 2 lettuce leaves; top with 4 tomato slices, ¹/₂ cup *each* green bell pepper strips and thinly sliced jicama and 1 ounce sliced avocado. Sprinkle with 2 teaspoons balsamic vinegar.)
Melba Slices, 4
Sugar-Free Strawberry-Flavored Gelatin, ¹/₂ cup, with 1 tablespoon thawed frozen light whipped topping (8 calories per tablespoon)
Iced Tea

MAIN MEAL
Curried Shrimp and Clams, 1 serving (see recipe)
Cooked Long-Grain Brown Rice, ¹/₂ cup
Steamed Broccoli and Cauliflower Florets, 1 cup *each*
Cucumber Slices, 1 cup, with ¹/₄ cup *each* chopped scallion and plain nonfat yogurt
Strawberries, ¹/₂ cup, sprinkled with 1 teaspoon shredded coconut
Unsweetened Seltzer

SNACK
Nonfat Tortilla Chips, 1 ounce, with Yogurt-Cilantro Dip (In small bowl, combine ¹/₂ cup plain nonfat yogurt, 1 tablespoon minced fresh cilantro and pinch garlic powder.)

This menu provides: 2 Milks, 3 Fats, 2 Fruits, 11³/₄ Vegetables, 4¹/₂ Proteins, 5¹/₂ Breads, 40 Optional Calories.

Per serving: 22 g Fat, 25 g Fiber.

FUSILLI WITH TOMATOES, ANCHOVIES AND CAPERS

Makes 4 servings

6 ounces fusilli pasta
2 teaspoons olive oil
$^1/2$ cup finely chopped onion
4 garlic cloves, minced
$1^1/2$ cups canned whole Italian tomatoes (no salt added), chopped
$1^1/2$ teaspoons minced fresh basil
$1^1/2$ teaspoons minced fresh oregano leaves
8 anchovy fillets, chopped
2 teaspoons rinsed drained capers
$1^1/2$ ounces feta cheese, crumbled

1. In large pot of boiling water, cook fusilli 10 minutes, until tender. Drain, discarding liquid; place into serving bowl. Keep warm.

2. Meanwhile, in medium saucepan, heat oil; add onion and garlic. Cook over medium-high heat, stirring frequently, 5 minutes, until onion is softened. Add tomatoes, basil and oregano; bring liquid to a boil. Reduce heat to low; simmer, stirring occasionally, 5–10 minutes, until slightly thickened. Stir in anchovies and capers.

3. Top warm fusilli with tomato mixture; toss to combine. Sprinkle with cheese; toss again.

Serving (1 cup pasta, $^1/3$ cup tomato mixture, one-fourth of the cheese) provides: $^1/2$ Fat, 1 Vegetable, $^1/2$ Protein, 2 Breads, 15 Optional Calories.

Per serving: 253 Calories, 6 g Total Fat, 2 g Saturated Fat, 14 mg Cholesterol, 600 mg Sodium, 39 g Total Carbohydrate, 2 g Dietary Fiber, 11 g Protein, 117 mg Calcium.

131
PENNE WITH SCALLOPS AND ASPARAGUS

Makes 4 servings

6 ounces penne pasta
$^1/_4$ cup nonfat mayonnaise (10 calories per tablespoon)
$^1/_4$ cup low-sodium chicken broth
1 tablespoon grated lemon zest*
1 tablespoon fresh lemon juice
1 tablespoon + 1 teaspoon canola oil
2 teaspoons grated pared fresh ginger root
2 garlic cloves, minced
12 asparagus spears, cut diagonally into 2" pieces
10 ounces sea scallops, halved
$^1/_4$ cup plain nonfat yogurt
2 tablespoons minced fresh cilantro

1. In large pot of boiling water, cook penne 13 minutes, until tender. Drain, discarding liquid; place into serving bowl. Keep warm.

2. In small bowl, combine mayonnaise, broth, zest and juice; set aside.

3. In large nonstick skillet, heat oil; add ginger and garlic. Cook over medium-high heat, stirring constantly, 30 seconds. Add asparagus; cook, stirring frequently, 2 minutes, until just tender. Add scallops; cook, stirring frequently, 3 minutes, until scallops are opaque in center.

4. Add yogurt and reserved mayonnaise mixture to scallop mixture; reduce heat to low. Cook, stirring constantly, until mixture is heated through (do not boil).

5. Top warm penne with scallop mixture; toss to coat. Serve sprinkled with cilantro.

Serving (1 cup pasta, $^1/_2$ cup scallop mixture) provides: 1 Fat, $^1/_2$ Vegetable, 1 Protein, 2 Breads, 20 Optional Calories.

Per serving: 294 Calories, 6 g Total Fat, 1 g Saturated Fat, 24 mg Cholesterol, 241 mg Sodium, 39 g Total Carbohydrate, 1 g Dietary Fiber, 20 g Protein, 69 mg Calcium.

*The zest of the lemon is the peel without any of the pith (white membrane). To remove zest from lemon, use a zester or the fine side of a vegetable grater.

BREAKFAST

Pink Grapefruit, $^1/_2$ medium
Herb Scramble (In small microwavable bowl, combine $^1/_2$ cup egg substitute, 1 teaspoon minced fresh flat-leaf parsley and $^1/_4$ teaspoon *each* dried oregano leaves and basil; microwave on Medium-High [70% power], $1^1/_2$–2 minutes, stirring once or twice, until set.)
Bagel, $^1/_2$ small (1 ounce), toasted, with 1 teaspoon reduced-calorie tub margarine
Skim Milk, 1 cup

LIGHT MEAL

Turkey Burger (In small bowl, combine 3 ounces skinless ground turkey breast, 3 tablespoons seasoned dried bread crumbs and 1 tablespoon ketchup; form into patty; broil, turning once, until cooked through. Split 1 small [1-ounce] pita halfway around edge; open to form pocket. Place broiled turkey burger into pita pocket.)
Dill Pickle, 1 medium
Celery and Carrot Sticks, 1 cup *each*
Sugar-Free Chocolate Nonfat Frozen Yogurt, 4 fluid ounces

MAIN MEAL

Penne with Scallops and Asparagus, 1 serving (see recipe)
Broiled Tomato (Cut 1 medium tomato in half crosswise; place, cut-side up, into broiler pan. Sprinkle tomato with $^1/_4$ teaspoon dried oregano leaves; broil until lightly browned and heated through.)
Tossed Green Salad, 2 cups, with $^1/_2$ cup shredded carrot and Tarragon-Basil Vinaigrette (In small jar with tight-fitting lid or small bowl, combine 2 teaspoons tarragon vinegar, 1 teaspoon olive oil and pinch dried basil; cover and shake well or, with wire whisk, blend until combined.)
Italian Bread, 1 slice (1 ounce), with 1 teaspoon reduced-calorie tub margarine
Raspberries, $^3/_4$ cup, with 1 tablespoon thawed frozen light whipped topping (8 calories per tablespoon)
Sparkling Mineral Water

SNACK

Chocolate "Egg Cream" (In tall glass, combine 1 cup diet chocolate soda and $^3/_4$ cup skim milk.)

This menu provides: 2 Milks, 3 Fats, 2 Fruits, $13^1/_2$ Vegetables, 5 Proteins, 6 Breads, 95 Optional Calories.

Per serving: 21 g Fat, 21 g Fiber.

132
ORANGE ROUGHY FLORENTINE WITH PASTA

Makes 4 servings

1 garlic clove, minced
1 teaspoon cornstarch
Pinch salt
Pinch ground red pepper
$^3/_4$ cup evaporated skimmed milk
15 ounces orange roughy fillets, cut into $^3/_4$" pieces
2 cups packed finely chopped well-washed trimmed spinach
1 tablespoon minced fresh basil
$^1/_2$ teaspoon grated orange zest*
4 cups cooked small pasta shells
$1^1/_2$ ounces freshly grated Romano cheese

1. Spray 2-quart microwavable casserole with nonstick cooking spray; add garlic. Microwave on High (100% power) 30 seconds. Add cornstarch, salt and pepper; with wire whisk, gradually add milk, blending until mixture is smooth. Microwave on High 3–$4^1/_2$ minutes, until mixture is thickened, stirring every $1^1/_2$ minutes.

2. Stir in fish, spinach and basil; with vented cover, microwave on High 4 minutes, stirring after 2 minutes. Let stand, covered, 1 minute, until fish flakes easily when tested with fork. Stir in zest.

3. Divide shells evenly among 4 shallow soup bowls. Top each portion of shells with one-fourth of the fish mixture; sprinkle evenly with cheese.

Serving ($^3/_4$ cup fish mixture, 1 cup shells, one-fourth of the cheese) provides: $^1/_4$ Milk, 1 Vegetable, 2 Proteins, 2 Breads, 15 Optional Calories.

Per serving: 390 Calories, 12 g Total Fat, 0 g Saturated Fat, 34 mg Cholesterol, 317 mg Sodium, 41 g Total Carbohydrate, 3 g Dietary Fiber, 29 g Protein, 309 mg Calcium.

The zest of the orange is the peel without any of the pith (white membrane). To remove zest from orange, use a zester or the fine side of a vegetable grater; wrap orange in plastic wrap and refrigerate for use at another time.

LINGUINE WITH FRESH TUNA SAUCE

Makes 4 servings

6 ounces linguine

2 teaspoons olive oil

10 ounces boneless tuna steaks, cut into 16 equal pieces

$^1/_4$ cup chopped onion

$^1/_4$ cup chopped carrot

2 garlic cloves, minced

1$^1/_2$ cups canned whole Italian tomatoes (no salt added), chopped

4 fluid ounces ($^1/_2$ cup) dry white wine

One 2 × $^1/_2$" strip lemon zest*

3 tablespoons minced fresh flat-leaf parsley

1 tablespoon grated lemon zest*

1. In large pot of boiling water, cook linguine 8–10 minutes, until tender. Drain, discarding liquid; place into serving bowl. Keep warm.

2. Meanwhile, in large nonstick skillet, heat 1 teaspoon of the oil; add tuna. Cook over medium-high heat, stirring frequently, 2 minutes, until fish is lightly browned and flakes easily when tested with fork. Remove fish from skillet; set aside.

3. In same skillet, heat remaining 1 teaspoon oil; add onion, carrot and half of the garlic. Cook over medium-high heat, stirring frequently, 5 minutes, until vegetables are softened. Add tomatoes, wine and zest strip; bring liquid to a boil. Reduce heat to low; simmer, stirring occasionally, 5–10 minutes, until slightly thickened. Remove and discard zest strip; stir in reserved fish.

4. In small bowl, combine parsley, grated zest and remaining garlic.

5. Top warm linguine with tuna mixture; toss to combine. Sprinkle with parsley mixture; toss again.

Serving (1 cup linguine, $^1/_2$ cup sauce, 1 tablespoon parsley mixture) provides: $^1/_2$ Fat, 1 Vegetable, 1 Protein, 2 Breads, 25 Optional Calories.

Per serving: 329 Calories, 7 g Total Fat, 1 g Saturated Fat, 27 mg Cholesterol, 183 mg Sodium, 38 g Total Carbohydrate, 2 g Dietary Fiber, 23 g Protein, 46 mg Calcium.

The zest of the lemon is the peel without any of the pith (white membrane). To remove zest from lemon in strips, use a zester or vegetable peeler; for grated zest, use zester or the fine side of a vegetable grater. Wrap lemon in plastic wrap and refrigerate for use at another time.

BREAKFAST

Fruited Ricotta Cheese (In small bowl, combine $^1/_2$ cup fruit salad and $^1/_3$ cup nonfat ricotta cheese.)

Pumpernickel Bagel, $^1/_2$ small (1 ounce), toasted, with 1 teaspoon reduced-calorie tub margarine

Skim Milk, 1 cup

Coffee or Tea (optional)

LIGHT MEAL

Avocado and Swiss Sandwich (Layer 1 ounce sliced avocado, $^3/_4$ ounce reduced-fat Swiss cheese, $^1/_4$ cup alfalfa sprouts, 2 tomato slices and 1 teaspoon Dijon-style mustard onto $^1/_2$ [1 ounce] toasted English muffin.)

Kidney Bean Salad (In small bowl, combine 2 ounces drained cooked red kidney beans, $^1/_4$ cup *each* diced onion and green bell pepper and 1 tablespoon fat-free Italian dressing.)

Carrot and Turnip Sticks, 1 cup *each*

Reduced-Calorie Butterscotch-Flavored Pudding (made with skim milk), $^1/_2$ cup

Iced Herbal Tea

MAIN MEAL

Linguine with Fresh Tuna Sauce, 1 serving (see recipe)

Steamed Spinach, 1 cup, with 1 garlic clove, minced

Tossed Green Salad, 2 cups, with $^1/_2$ cup sliced jicama, $^1/_4$ cup packaged croutons and 1 tablespoon fat-free ranch dressing

Roll, 1 ounce, with 1 teaspoon reduced-calorie tub margarine

Watermelon, 3 × 2" wedge

Sparkling Mineral Water

SNACK

Coffee "Egg Cream" (In tall glass, combine 1 cup diet coffee soda and $^1/_2$ cup skim milk.)

This menu provides: 2 Milks, 3 Fats, 2 Fruits, 14 Vegetables, 4 Proteins, 5$^1/_2$ Breads, 90 Optional Calories.

Per serving: 25 g Fat, 24 g Fiber.

134
BLACKENED CATFISH WITH TOMATO–GREEN PEPPER RELISH

Makes 4 servings

2 medium tomatoes, seeded and diced
$^1/_2$ cup diced green bell pepper
$^1/_2$ cup diced celery
2 tablespoons minced fresh flat-leaf parsley
1 tablespoon fresh lime juice
2 teaspoons paprika
1 teaspoon onion powder
1 teaspoon garlic powder
$^1/_2$ teaspoon dried thyme leaves
$^1/_2$ teaspoon dried oregano leaves
Pinch freshly ground black pepper
Pinch ground red pepper
Four 5-ounce catfish fillets
2 tablespoons reduced-calorie stick margarine, melted

1. To prepare relish, in small bowl, combine tomatoes, bell pepper, celery, parsley and juice; set aside.

2. To prepare fish, on sheet of wax paper or paper plate, combine paprika, onion powder, garlic powder, thyme, oregano and black and ground red peppers; add fish, turning to coat evenly.

3. Spray large nonstick skillet with nonstick cooking spray; heat. Add fish fillets; drizzle with half of the margarine. Cook over high heat 2–3 minutes, until fish is blackened on bottom; with wide metal spatula, turn fish over. Drizzle fish with remaining margarine; cook 2–3 minutes, until fish flakes easily when tested with fork. Serve fish topped with relish.

Serving (1 catfish fillet, $^1/_2$ cup relish) provides: 1 Fat, 1$^1/_2$ Vegetables, 2 Proteins.

Per serving: 238 Calories, 13 g Total Fat, 3 g Saturated Fat, 47 mg Cholesterol, 137 mg Sodium, 7 g Total Carbohydrate, 2 g Dietary Fiber, 23 g Protein, 26 mg Calcium.

135
FLOUNDER ROULADES À L'ORANGE

Makes 2 servings

1 tablespoon reduced-calorie stick margarine
$^1/_4$ cup finely minced shallots
1 teaspoon grated orange zest*
Pinch dried tarragon leaves
Two 5-ounce flounder fillets
$^1/_4$ teaspoon salt
Pinch freshly ground black pepper
$^1/_4$ cup fresh orange juice
2 fluid ounces ($^1/_4$ cup) dry white wine
1 teaspoon cornstarch, dissolved in 1 tablespoon cold water
1 tablespoon minced fresh flat-leaf parsley

1. Preheat oven to 375° F. Spray 8" round shallow baking dish with non-stick cooking spray.

2. To prepare roulades, in small skillet, melt margarine; add shallots. Cook over medium-high heat, stirring frequently, 2–3 minutes, until tender. Stir in zest and tarragon; remove from heat.

3. Cut fish fillets in half lengthwise; place onto work surface. Sprinkle fillets with salt and pepper; spread evenly with half of the shallot mixture. Starting at wide ends, roll fillets jelly-roll fashion; place into prepared baking dish, cut-side down.

4. Pour juice and wine over rolled fillets; sprinkle evenly with remaining shallot mixture. Bake 15 minutes, until fish flakes easily when tested with fork.

5. With slotted spoon, transfer roulades to serving platter, reserving cooking liquid; keep fish warm.

6. To prepare sauce, pour cooking liquid through sieve into small saucepan; discard solids. Stir dissolved cornstarch into cooking liquid; cook over medium-high heat, stirring constantly, 2 minutes, until thickened. Spoon liquid evenly over warm roulades; sprinkle with parsley.

Serving (2 roulades, 2 tablespoons sauce) provides: 1 Fat, $^1/_4$ Fruit, $^1/_4$ Vegetable, 2 Proteins, 30 Optional Calories.

Per serving: 212 Calories, 5 g Total Fat, 1 g Saturated Fat, 68 mg Cholesterol, 458 mg Sodium, 8 g Total Carbohydrate, 0 g Dietary Fiber, 28 g Protein, 47 mg Calcium.

*The zest of the orange is the peel without any of the pith (white membrane). To remove zest from orange, use a zester or the fine side of a vegetable grater.

BREAKFAST
Papaya, $^1/_2$ medium
Nonfat Cottage Cheese, $^1/_2$ cup
Reduced-Calorie Multi-Grain Bread, 2 slices, toasted, with 2 teaspoons reduced-calorie margarine
Skim Milk, $^1/_2$ cup
Coffee or Tea (optional)

LIGHT MEAL
Chilled Antipasto Salad (On plate, decoratively arrange $^1/_2$ cup *each* drained roasted red bell pepper strips, chilled cooked artichoke hearts and fennel strips and 2 ounces drained cooked chick-peas; sprinkle with $1^1/_2$ teaspoons Italian dressing.)
Breadsticks, 2 long
Strawberries, $^3/_4$ cup
Iced Espresso

MAIN MEAL
Flounder Roulades à l'Orange, 1 serving (see recipe)
Cooked Brown and Wild Rice, 1 cup
Steamed Asparagus, 6 spears, with 1 lemon wedge
Tossed Green Salad, 2 cups, with 1 tablespoon fat-free Italian dressing and 1 teaspoon freshly grated Parmesan cheese
Reduced-Calorie Vanilla-Flavored Pudding (made with skim milk), $^1/_2$ cup

SNACK
Plain Popcorn, hot-air popped, 3 cups
Reduced-Calorie Chocolate Fudge Dairy Shake, 1 serving

This menu provides: 2 Milks, 3 Fats, 2 Fruits, $8^1/_4$ Vegetables, 4 Proteins, 5 Breads, 85 Optional Calories.

Per serving: 22 g Fat, 28 g Fiber.

⌘ 1 3 6 ⌘
GRECIAN-STUFFED FLOUNDER

Makes 4 servings

1 cup cooked chopped spinach, drained and squeezed dry
1 1/2 ounces feta cheese, crumbled
1/2 teaspoon grated lemon zest*
2 tablespoons + 2 teaspoons fresh lemon juice
2 teaspoons minced fresh dill
Four 4-ounce flounder fillets
2 fluid ounces (1/4 cup) dry white wine
1 1/2 teaspoons cornstarch
2 tablespoons minced fresh flat-leaf parsley

1. Preheat oven to 375° F. Spray 8" square baking pan with nonstick cooking spray.

2. To prepare stuffing, in medium bowl, combine spinach, cheese, zest, 1 tablespoon + 1 teaspoon of the juice and the dill.

3. Place one-fourth of the stuffing onto center of each fish fillet; fold thin end of fillets over stuffing, then roll fillets to enclose. Place stuffed fillets, seam-side down, into prepared baking pan.

4. In small bowl, combine wine, remaining 1 tablespoon + 1 teaspoon juice and 1/4 cup water; pour over stuffed fillets. Bake, covered, 15 minutes, until fish flakes easily when tested with fork and stuffing is heated through. With slotted spatula, transfer stuffed fillets to serving platter, reserving liquid; keep fish warm.

5. To prepare sauce, transfer reserved liquid to small saucepan. Sprinkle liquid with cornstarch; with wire whisk, blend until cornstarch is dissolved. Cook over medium-high heat, stirring frequently, 1 minute, until mixture is slightly thickened; pour over warm stuffed fillets. Serve sprinkled with parsley.

Serving (1 stuffed fish fillet, 2 tablespoons sauce) provides: 1/2 Vegetable, 2 Proteins, 15 Optional Calories.

Per serving: 161 Calories, 4 g Total Fat, 2 g Saturated Fat, 64 mg Cholesterol, 244 mg Sodium, 4 g Total Carbohydrate, 1 g Dietary Fiber, 24 g Protein, 141 mg Calcium.

*The zest of the lemon is the peel without any of the pith (white membrane). To remove zest from lemon, use a zester or the fine side of a vegetable grater.

BREAKFAST
Mango, 1/2 small
English Muffin, 1/2 (1 ounce), toasted, with 1/3 cup nonfat ricotta cheese
Skim Milk, 1 cup
Coffee or Tea (optional)

LIGHT MEAL
Oriental Pasta Salad (In medium bowl, combine 1 cup cooked rotelle pasta, 1/2 cup *each* bean sprouts and sliced celery, 2 ounces drained cooked red kidney beans, 1 tablespoon rice wine vinegar and 1 teaspoon oriental sesame oil.)
Flatbreads, 3/4 ounce
Pineapple, 1/8 medium
Iced Tea with Lemon Wedge

MAIN MEAL
Grecian-Stuffed Flounder, 1 serving (see recipe)
Cooked Brown Rice, 1/2 cup
Broiled Tomato (Cut 1 medium tomato in half. Sprinkle cut sides of tomato with 1 teaspoon seasoned dried bread crumbs each; dot each with 1 teaspoon reduced-calorie tub margarine. Place onto nonstick baking sheet; broil until lightly browned.)
Chicory and Romaine Lettuce Salad, 2 cups, with 1/2 cup roasted red bell pepper strips, 6 large or 10 small Greek olives and 1 tablespoon fat-free Italian dressing
Sugar-Free Vanilla Nonfat Frozen Yogurt, 4 fluid ounces
Unsweetened Seltzer with Lime Wedge

SNACK
Vanilla Wafers, 3
Skim Milk, 3/4 cup

This menu provides: 2 Milks, 3 Fats, 2 Fruits, 9 1/2 Vegetables, 4 Proteins, 5 1/2 Breads, 115 Optional Calories.

Per serving: 30 g Fat, 20 g Fiber.

137

HALIBUT WITH TOMATO-LEMON-CAPER COULIS

Makes 4 servings

Four 5-ounce boneless halibut steaks
1 tablespoon + 1 teaspoon olive oil
$^1/_4$ teaspoon salt
$^1/_4$ teaspoon freshly ground black pepper
6 medium fresh garlic cloves, minced
8 large plum tomatoes, seeded and diced
1 large lemon, peeled and sectioned
2 tablespoons minced fresh basil
1 tablespoon rinsed drained capers
1 teaspoon balsamic vinegar
8 cups chopped trimmed washed broccoli rabe

1. Preheat oven to 400° F.

2. To prepare halibut, brush each halibut steak with $^3/_4$ teaspoon of the oil; sprinkle with salt and pepper. Arrange fish in shallow baking dish just large enough to hold fish in a single layer; bake 10–12 minutes, until fish flakes easily when tested with fork.

3. Meanwhile, to prepare coulis, in medium nonstick skillet, heat remaining 1 teaspoon oil; add two-thirds of the garlic. Cook over medium-high heat, stirring constantly, until tender. Add tomatoes, lemon, basil and capers; cook, stirring frequently, 3 minutes, until tomatoes are softened. Stir in vinegar. Remove from heat; keep warm.

4. Rinse broccoli rabe with cold water; do not dry. In large pot, combine wet broccoli rabe and remaining garlic; cook over medium-high heat, covered, 2–3 minutes, until broccoli rabe is wilted. Drain.

5. Divide broccoli rabe evenly among 4 plates; top each portion with 1 halibut steak and one-fourth of the warm coulis.

Serving ($^1/_2$ cup broccoli rabe, 1 halibut steak, $^1/_3$ cup coulis) provides: 1 Fat, 6 Vegetables, 2 Proteins.

Per serving: 267 Calories, 9 g Total Fat, 1 g Saturated Fat, 45 mg Cholesterol, 346 mg Sodium, 16 g Total Carbohydrate, 5 g Dietary Fiber, 35 g Protein, 208 mg Calcium.

MONKFISH FLORENTINE

Makes 4 servings

2 tablespoons all-purpose flour
$^1/_4$ teaspoon salt
$^1/_4$ teaspoon freshly ground black pepper
I pound 4 ounces monkfish fillets, cut into 2" pieces
I tablespoon + I teaspoon olive oil
I cup sliced shiitake mushrooms
2 tablespoons minced shallots
2 tablespoons balsamic vinegar
8 cups packed chopped trimmed washed spinach leaves
I lemon, cut into wedges

1. On sheet of wax paper or paper plate, combine flour, salt and pepper; add fish, turning to coat evenly.

2. In large nonstick skillet, heat 1 tablespoon of the oil; add fish. Cook over medium-high heat, stirring frequently, 6–8 minutes, until fish is browned and flakes easily when tested with fork. Remove fish from skillet; keep warm.

3. In same skillet, heat remaining 1 teaspoon oil; add mushrooms and shallots. Cook over medium-high heat, stirring frequently, 5 minutes, until vegetables are tender. Add vinegar; cook, stirring constantly, 30 seconds. Remove from heat; keep warm.

4. In large saucepan, heat 2 tablespoons water; add spinach. Cook over medium-high heat, stirring occasionally, until wilted. Drain, discarding liquid.

5. Divide spinach evenly among 4 plates; top each portion with one-fourth of the warm fish and one-fourth of the mushroom mixture. Serve with lemon wedges.

Serving (one-fourth of the spinach, fish and mushroom mixture) provides:
1 Fat, $4^1/_2$ Vegetables, 2 Proteins, 15 Optional Calories.

Per serving: 207 Calories, 7 g Total Fat, 1 g Saturated Fat, 35 mg Cholesterol, 274 mg Sodium, 13 g Total Carbohydrate, 4 g Dietary Fiber, 26 g Protein, 171 mg Calcium.

BREAKFAST

Cooked Oatmeal, $^1/_2$ cup, with 2 tablespoons golden raisins
Skim Milk, $^3/_4$ cup
Coffee or Tea (optional)

LIGHT MEAL

Turkey Sandwich (Layer 2 ounces skinless boneless roast turkey breast, sliced, $^1/_2$ medium tomato, sliced, $^1/_2$ cup arugula leaves, 2 teaspoons reduced-calorie mayonnaise and 1 teaspoon prepared mustard between 2 slices reduced-calorie rye bread.)
Red and Green Bell Pepper Strips, 1 cup *each*
Aspartame-Sweetened Coffee Nonfat Yogurt, 1 cup
Diet Cherry Cola

MAIN MEAL

Monkfish Florentine, 1 serving (see recipe)
Baked Potato, 8 ounces, with 3 tablespoons plain nonfat yogurt and 1 tablespoon minced fresh chives
Steamed Baby Carrots, 1 cup, with 2 teaspoons reduced-calorie tub margarine
Watercress and Sliced Tomato Salad, 2 cups, with 1 tablespoon fat-free Italian dressing
Orange, 1 small
Unsweetened Seltzer

SNACK

Cajun Popcorn (Lightly spray 3 cups hot-air popped plain popcorn with nonstick cooking spray. Sprinkle popcorn with $^1/_4$ teaspoon Cajun seasoning; toss to coat evenly.)
Diet Raspberry Ginger Ale

This menu provides: 2 Milks, 3 Fats, 2 Fruits, $16^1/_2$ Vegetables, 4 Proteins, 5 Breads, 20 Optional Calories.

Per serving: 25 g Fat, 27 g Fiber.

139

MONKFISH WITH HERBED TOMATOES

Makes 2 servings

2 teaspoons olive oil
1 teaspoon minced fresh tarragon leaves, or $^1/4$ teaspoon dried
1 garlic clove, minced
Pinch salt
Pinch ground white pepper
One 10-ounce monkfish fillet, halved lengthwise
12 cherry tomatoes, halved
$^3/4$ teaspoon cornstarch
Additional minced fresh tarragon leaves, to garnish

1. In 8–9" microwavable pie plate or 8" square microwavable baking dish, combine oil, tarragon, garlic, salt and pepper; microwave on High (100% power), covered with wax paper, 2 minutes, stirring once.

2. Add fish to oil mixture; turn to coat. Microwave on High, covered with wax paper, 4 minutes; turn fish over, rearranging fillets. Surround fish with tomatoes; turn to coat. Microwave on High, covered with wax paper, 2–3 minutes, until fish flakes easily when tested with fork and tomatoes are just softened.

3. Cut each fish fillet into 3 equal pieces. With slotted spatula, transfer to serving platter; top with cherry tomatoes. Set fish aside; keep warm. Reserve pan juices.

4. To prepare sauce, in small bowl, with wire whisk, combine cornstarch and 1 tablespoon water, blending until cornstarch is dissolved. Add dissolved cornstarch to reserved pan juices, stirring constantly with wire whisk until blended. Microwave on High, uncovered, 1–2 minutes, until mixture is thickened, stirring once. Spoon sauce over fish and tomatoes; serve garnished with additional minced tarragon.

Serving (3 pieces fish, $^1/2$ cup tomatoes, one-half of the sauce) provides: 1 Fat, 1 Vegetable, 2 Proteins, 5 Optional Calories.

Per serving: 167 Calories, 7 g Total Fat, 1 g Saturated Fat, 35 mg Cholesterol, 97 mg Sodium, 4 g Total Carbohydrate, 1 g Dietary Fiber, 21 g Protein, 20 mg Calcium.

Cold Poached Salmon with Minted Zucchini-Yogurt Dressing

Makes 4 servings

3/4 cup plain nonfat yogurt
1/4 cup nonfat sour cream
3 tablespoons minced fresh mint leaves
Pinch ground red pepper
1/2 cup julienned zucchini
4 fluid ounces (1/2 cup) dry white wine
1 small onion, halved
1/4 teaspoon grated lemon zest*
2 lemon slices
Four 3-ounce salmon steaks

1. To prepare dressing, in small bowl, combine yogurt, sour cream, mint, zest and pepper; stir in zucchini. Refrigerate, covered, until chilled.

2. Meanwhile, in large nonstick skillet, combine wine, onion, lemon slices and 2 cups water; bring liquid to a boil. Reduce heat to low; add salmon steaks. Poach salmon 3–4 minutes, until fish flakes easily when tested with fork.

3. With slotted spatula, transfer fish to serving platter; discard poaching liquid and solids. Refrigerate fish, covered, until chilled.

4. Top each chilled salmon steak with one-fourth of the dressing.

Serving (1 salmon steak, 1/4 cup + 1 tablespoon dressing) provides: 1/4 Milk, 1/4 Vegetable, 2 Proteins, 35 Optional Calories.

Per serving: 161 Calories, 5 g Total Fat, 1 g Saturated Fat, 48 mg Cholesterol, 80 mg Sodium, 5 g Total Carbohydrate, 0 g Dietary Fiber, 21 g Protein, 119 mg Calcium.

*The zest of the lemon is the peel without any of the pith (white membrane). To remove zest from lemon, use a zester or the fine side of a vegetable grater; wrap lemon in plastic wrap and refrigerate for use at another time.

BREAKFAST

Honeydew Melon, 2" wedge
Herb Scramble (In small microwavable bowl, combine 1/2 cup egg substitute, 1 teaspoon minced fresh flat-leaf parsley and 1/4 teaspoon *each* dried oregano leaves and basil; microwave on Medium-High [70% power], 1–1 1/2 minutes, stirring once or twice, until set.)
Reduced-Calorie Whole-Wheat Bread, 2 slices, toasted, with 2 teaspoons reduced-calorie tub margarine
Skim Milk, 3/4 cup
Coffee or Tea (optional)

LIGHT MEAL

Cheese-Stuffed Potato (Cut a lengthwise slit about 1" deep into 8-ounce baked potato, cutting to within 1/2" of each end; gently squeeze ends together until potato opens. Top potato pulp with 3/4 ounce reduced-fat cheddar cheese, grated, then 1/4 cup minced scallions; microwave on High [100% power], 1–1 1/2 minutes, until heated through.)
Zucchini Sticks, 1 cup
Cherry Tomatoes, 6
Aspartame-Sweetened Mixed Berry Nonfat Yogurt, 1 cup
Sparkling Mineral Water

MAIN MEAL

Cold Poached Salmon with Minted Zucchini-Yogurt Dressing, 1 serving (see recipe)
Steamed Asparagus, 6 spears
Boston Lettuce and Watercress Salad, 2 cups, with 1 tablespoon French dressing
Flatbreads, 3/4 ounce
Pineapple, 1/8 medium
Iced Tea

SNACK

Plain Popcorn, hot-air popped, 3 cups, with 1 teaspoon freshly grated Parmesan cheese
Diet Grape Ginger Ale

This menu provides: 2 Milks, 3 Fats, 2 Fruits, 8 3/4 Vegetables, 5 Proteins, 5 Breads, 45 Optional Calories.

Per serving: 24 g Fat, 26 g Fiber.

⟩141⟨
SALMON FILLETS WITH POTATO SAUCE

Makes 4 servings

$^1/4$ cup red wine vinegar

2 tablespoons firmly packed light or dark brown sugar

Four 3-ounce salmon fillets

$^3/4$ cup low-sodium chicken broth

1 garlic clove, minced

1$^1/2$ ounces instant potato flakes

1 tablespoon white wine vinegar

1 teaspoon olive oil

1 teaspoon minced fresh thyme leaves

Fresh thyme or chive sprigs, to garnish

1. In small saucepan, combine red wine vinegar and sugar; cook over low heat, stirring constantly, 1 minute, until sugar is dissolved. Pour vinegar mixture into 11 × 7" flameproof baking dish; add salmon, turning to coat. Let stand 20 minutes.

2. Preheat broiler.

3. To prepare sauce, in medium saucepan, combine broth and garlic; bring liquid to a boil. Remove from heat; stir in potato flakes, white wine vinegar and oil, stirring until mixture is smooth. Set aside.

4. Drain salmon, discarding liquid; return salmon to baking dish and sprinkle with minced thyme. Broil salmon 4" from heat 5 minutes, until fish flakes easily when tested with fork.

5. Divide potato sauce evenly among 4 plates; top each portion with 1 broiled salmon fillet. Serve garnished with thyme sprigs.

Serving (1 salmon fillet, 3 tablespoons potato sauce) provides: $^1/4$ Fat, 2 Proteins, 35 Optional Calories.

Per serving: 203 Calories, 7 g Total Fat, 1 g Saturated Fat, 47 mg Cholesterol, 73 mg Sodium, 17 g Total Carbohydrate, 0 g Dietary Fiber, 18 g Protein, 25 mg Calcium.

SALMON EN PAPILLOTE

Makes 4 servings

$^1/_4$ cup plain nonfat yogurt
1 tablespoon thawed frozen orange juice concentrate
1 teaspoon fresh lemon juice
1 tablespoon minced scallion
1 tablespoon minced fresh flat-leaf parsley
1$^1/_2$ teaspoons grated orange zest*
Four 3-ounce salmon fillets
$^1/_2$ cup julienned carrot
$^1/_2$ cup julienned snow peas

1. Preheat oven to 425° F.

2. In small bowl, combine yogurt, orange juice concentrate and lemon juice; set aside.

3. In separate small bowl, combine scallion, parsley and zest; set aside.

4. Place each salmon fillet onto a 15 × 12" sheet of foil. Top each fillet with 2 tablespoons of the carrot, 2 tablespoons of the snow peas and one-fourth of the scallion mixture; drizzle each portion with 1 tablespoon water. Enclose fish in foil, making 4 individual packets; crimp edges to seal.

5. Place packets onto baking sheet; bake 10–12 minutes, until fish flakes easily when tested with fork and vegetables are just tender.

6. Open foil packets carefully. Transfer each portion of fish and vegetables to a plate; top each with one-fourth of the yogurt mixture.

Serving (1 salmon fillet, 1 portion of vegetables, 1 tablespoon yogurt mixture) provides: $^1/_2$ Vegetable, 2 Proteins, 15 Optional Calories.

Per serving: 151 Calories, 5 g Total Fat, 1 g Saturated Fat, 47 mg Cholesterol, 54 mg Sodium, 6 g Total Carbohydrate, 1 g Dietary Fiber, 18 g Protein, 55 mg Calcium.

The zest of the orange is the peel without any of the pith (white membrane). To remove zest from orange, use a zester or the fine side of a vegetable grater; wrap orange in plastic wrap and refrigerate for use at another time.

BREAKFAST

Fresh Fig, 1 large
Pumpernickel Bagel, 1 small (2 ounces), with 2 teaspoons reduced-calorie tub margarine
Skim Milk, $^3/_4$ cup
Coffee or Tea (optional)

LIGHT MEAL

Egg Salad Sandwich (In small bowl, combine 1 hard-cooked egg, minced, $^1/_4$ cup *each* chopped celery and chopped red onion and 2 teaspoons reduced-calorie mayonnaise; spread between 2 slices reduced-calorie rye bread.)
Cucumber and Zucchini Sticks, 1 cup *each*
Sugar-Free Chocolate Nonfat Frozen Yogurt, 4 fluid ounces
Diet Grape Soda

MAIN MEAL

Salmon en Papillote, 1 serving (see recipe)
Baked Potato, 8 ounces, with 2 tablespoons nonfat sour cream and 1 teaspoon minced chives
Steamed Spinach, 1 cup, with 2 teaspoons *each* reduced-calorie tub margarine and fresh lemon juice
Torn Romaine and Bibb Lettuce Leaves, 2 cups, with 1 tablespoon fat-free French dressing
Raspberries, $^3/_4$ cup, with 1 tablespoon thawed frozen light whipped topping (8 calories per tablespoon)
Unsweetened Seltzer with Lemon Wedge

SNACK

Aspartame-Sweetened Black Cherry Nonfat Yogurt, 1 cup

This menu provides: 2 Milks, 3 Fats, 2 Fruits, 11$^1/_2$ Vegetables, 3 Proteins, 5 Breads, 115 Optional Calories.

Per serving: 27 g Fat, 22 g Fiber.

143
SCROD WITH HORSERADISH MERINGUE AND BEET RELISH

Makes 4 servings

2 cups cooked julienned beets
1 cup thinly sliced red onions
2 tablespoons rice wine vinegar
2 teaspoons granulated sugar
4 ounces yogurt cheese*
$^1/_3$ cup prepared white horseradish, drained and squeezed dry
1 teaspoon salt
4 egg whites
Four 5-ounce scrod fillets
1 tablespoon minced fresh dill

1. To prepare relish, in medium bowl, combine beets, onions, vinegar and 1 teaspoon of the sugar; refrigerate, covered, until chilled.

2. Preheat oven to 425° F. Spray 11 × 7" baking dish with nonstick cooking spray.

3. In small bowl, combine yogurt cheese, horseradish and salt; set aside.

4. In small bowl, with electric mixer, beat egg whites until soft peaks form. Add remaining 1 teaspoon sugar; beat until stiff but not dry. Fold in yogurt cheese mixture.

5. Place fish in a single layer into prepared baking dish; spread each with an equal amount of egg white mixture. Bake 8–10 minutes, until fish flakes easily when tested with fork. Sprinkle fish with dill; serve with relish.

Serving (1 scrod fillet, $^1/_2$ cup relish) provides: $^1/_4$ Milk, $1^1/_2$ Vegetables, $2^1/_4$ Proteins, 15 Optional Calories.

Per serving: 214 Calories, 1 g Total Fat, 0 g Saturated Fat, 61 mg Cholesterol, 767 mg Sodium, 16 g Total Carbohydrate, 3 g Dietary Fiber, 33 g Protein, 135 mg Calcium.

*To make yogurt cheese, spoon $^3/_4$ cup plain nonfat yogurt into coffee filter or cheesecloth-lined strainer; place over bowl. Refrigerate, covered, at least 5 hours or overnight. Discard liquid in bowl.

144
TANDOORI SCROD

Makes 4 servings

³/₄ cup plain nonfat yogurt
¹/₄ cup minced scallions
1 tablespoon garam masala*
1 tablespoon fresh lime juice
1¹/₂ teaspoons minced deveined seeded jalapeño pepper (wear gloves to prevent irritation)
1¹/₂ teaspoons grated pared fresh ginger root
¹/₂ teaspoon ground turmeric
Four 5-ounce scrod fillets
1 lime, cut into wedges

1. In blender or food processor, combine yogurt, scallions, garam masala, juice, pepper, ginger and turmeric; purée until smooth. Transfer to gallon-size sealable plastic bag; add scrod. Seal bag, squeezing out air; turn to coat fish. Refrigerate overnight, turning bag occasionally.

2. Preheat broiler. Spray rack in broiler pan with nonstick cooking spray.

3. Transfer fish mixture to shallow flameproof baking dish just large enough to hold fish in a single layer; broil 4" from heat 6–8 minutes, until fish flakes easily when tested with fork and yogurt mixture is bubbling. Serve with lime wedges.

Serving (1 scrod fillet, one-fourth of the yogurt mixture) provides: ¹/₄ Milk, ¹/₄ Vegetable, 2 Proteins

Per serving: 155 Calories, 1 g Total Fat, 0 g Saturated Fat, 62 mg Cholesterol, 111 mg Sodium, 7 g Total Carbohydrate, 1 g Dietary Fiber, 28 g Protein, 126 mg Calcium.

*Garam masala is available in most Asian groceries; if you can't find it, substitute 1 tablespoon mild or hot curry powder.

BREAKFAST
Blueberries, Raspberries and Blackberries, ¹/₄ cup *each*
Reduced-Calorie Whole-Wheat Bread, 2 ounces, toasted, with 2 teaspoons reduced-calorie tub margarine
Skim Milk, 1 cup
Coffee or Tea (optional)

LIGHT MEAL
Chicken Salad Sandwich (In small bowl, combine 2 ounces skinless boneless cooked chicken breast, chopped, ¹/₂ cup chopped celery, 2 teaspoons reduced-calorie mayonnaise and pinch freshly ground black pepper; spread between 2 slices reduced-calorie rye bread.)
Cucumber and Carrot Sticks, 1 cup *each*
Reduced-Calorie Chocolate-Flavored Pudding (made with skim milk), ¹/₂ cup
Diet Black Cherry Soda

MAIN MEAL
Tandoori Scrod, 1 serving (see recipe)
Cooked Basmati Rice, 1 cup
Steamed Broccoli, 4 spears, with 1 tablespoon fresh lemon juice
Cucumber Salad (In small bowl, combine ¹/₂ cup cucumber slices, 1 teaspoon *each* vegetable oil and rice wine vinegar and pinch ground white pepper.)
Baked Apple (Preheat oven to 350° F. Pare 1 small apple halfway down from stem end; place into small baking dish. Sprinkle apple with 1 teaspoon granulated sugar and ¹/₄ teaspoon cinnamon; add ¹/₄" water to pan. Bake, covered, 30 minutes, until tender.)
Sparkling Mineral Water

SNACK
Frozen Strawberry Parfait (In stemmed glass, layer 4 fluid ounces sugar-free strawberry nonfat frozen yogurt and 3 tablespoons graham cracker crumbs.)

This menu provides: 2 Milks, 3 Fats, 2 Fruits, 8¹/₄ Vegetables, 4 Proteins, 5 Breads, 105 Optional Calories.

Per serving: 22 g Fat, 23 g Fiber.

LIGHT MEAL
Roast Beef Sandwich (Layer 1 1/2 ounces cooked lean boneless roast beef, thinly sliced, 2 tomato slices and 2 iceberg lettuce leaves and 1 tablespoon fat-free Thousand Island dressing between 2 slices reduced-calorie rye bread.)
Celery and Carrot Sticks, 1 cup *each*
Sugar-Free Lemon-Flavored Gelatin, 1/2 cup, with 1 tablespoon thawed frozen light whipped topping (8 calories per tablespoon)
Iced Herbal Tea

MAIN MEAL
Mediterranean Shrimp, 1 serving (see recipe)
Cooked Orzo Pasta, 1/2 cup, with 1/2 cup cooked green peas
Steamed Broccoli Rabe, 1 cup
Romaine and Cucumber Salad, 2 cups, with 1/2 cup sliced red onion and 1 tablespoon Caesar salad dressing
Seedless Red Grapes, 20 small or 12 large
Unsweetened Raspberry-Flavored Seltzer

SNACK
Chocolate-Almond Shake (In blender, combine 2/3 cup cold water, 3 ice cubes, 1 packet reduced-calorie chocolate dairy shake mix and 1 teaspoon almond extract; purée until smooth and thick.)

This menu provides: 2 Milks, 3 Fats, 2 Fruits, 13 1/2 Vegetables, 3 Proteins, 5 Breads, 65 Optional Calories.

Per serving: 23 g Fat, 32 g Fiber.

145
MEDITERRANEAN SHRIMP

Makes 4 servings

1 tablespoon + 1 teaspoon olive oil
2 cups finely diced pared eggplant
1/2 cup diced red onion
1 garlic clove, minced
5 large plum tomatoes, seeded and finely diced
4 fluid ounces (1/2 cup) dry white wine
1 tablespoon minced fresh oregano leaves or marjoram leaves
10 ounces medium shrimp, peeled and deveined
1 1/2 ounces feta cheese, crumbled
2 tablespoons minced fresh flat-leaf parsley

1. In large nonstick skillet, heat oil; add eggplant. Cook over medium-high heat, stirring frequently, 5 minutes, until lightly browned. Add onion and garlic; cook, stirring frequently, 1 minute.

2. Add tomatoes, wine, oregano and 1/2 cup water to vegetable mixture; bring liquid to a boil. Reduce heat to low; simmer, stirring occasionally, 5 minutes, until most of the liquid is evaporated.

3. Add shrimp to vegetable mixture; cook, stirring frequently, 3 minutes, until shrimp turn pink. Serve sprinkled with cheese and parsley.

Serving (1 cup) provides: 1 Fat, 2 1/2 Vegetables, 1 1/2 Proteins, 25 Optional Calories.

Per serving: 198 Calories, 8 g Total Fat, 2 g Saturated Fat, 117 mg Cholesterol, 235 mg Sodium, 9 g Total Carbohydrate, 2 g Dietary Fiber, 17 g Protein, 124 mg Calcium.

146

LEMON SOLE WITH ORIENTAL FLAVORS

Any delicate, white-fleshed fish would be great in this recipe; if you'd like, try flounder or cod in place of the lemon sole.

Makes 2 servings

Two 5-ounce lemon sole fillets
$^1/_4$ cup thinly sliced scallions
1 tablespoon reduced-sodium soy sauce
1 tablespoon rice wine vinegar
1 teaspoon oriental sesame oil
1 teaspoon grated orange zest*
1 teaspoon grated pared fresh ginger root

1. In shallow 11 × 7" microwavable baking dish, arrange fish fillets in a single layer, tucking thin ends under; sprinkle with scallions.

2. In small bowl, combine soy sauce, vinegar, oil, zest and ginger; pour evenly over fish. With vented cover, microwave on High (100% power) 4 minutes; let stand 1 minute, until fish flakes easily when tested with fork.

Serving (1 sole fillet) provides: $^1/_2$ Fat, $^1/_4$ Vegetable, 2 Proteins.

Per serving: 161 Calories, 4 g Total Fat, 1 g Saturated Fat, 68 mg Cholesterol, 417 mg Sodium, 2 g Total Carbohydrate, 0 g Dietary Fiber, 27 g Protein, 38 mg Calcium.

The zest of the orange is the peel without any of the pith (white membrane). To remove zest from orange, use a zester or the fine side of a vegetable grater; wrap orange in plastic wrap and refrigerate for use at another time.

BREAKFAST
Orange Sections, $^1/_2$ cup
Scramble in a Pita (In small nonstick skillet, melt
  1 teaspoon reduced-calorie tub margarine; add
  2 tablespoons *each* chopped onion and green bell
  pepper. Cook over medium-high heat, stirring frequently, 5 minutes, until vegetables are softened.
  Add $^1/_4$ cup egg substitute; cook, stirring frequently, until mixture is just set. Cut small
  [1-ounce] whole-wheat pita in half crosswise;
  open to form 2 pockets. Fill each pocket with half
  of the scramble mixture.)
Skim Milk, 1 cup
Coffee or Tea (optional)

LIGHT MEAL
Chicken Sandwich (Layer 2 ounces skinless boneless
  cooked chicken breast, sliced, 2 tomato slices,
  $^1/_4$ cup shredded iceberg lettuce and 1 tablespoon
  fat-free Thousand Island dressing between 2 slices
  reduced-calorie rye bread.)
Carrot and Zucchini Sticks, 1 cup *each*
Apple, 1 small
Diet Black Cherry Soda

MAIN MEAL
Lemon Sole with Oriental Flavors, 1 serving (see
  recipe)
Cooked Brown Rice, 1 cup
Sesame Snow Peas (In small skillet, heat 1 teaspoon
  oriental sesame oil; add 1 cup snow peas. Cook
  over medium-high heat, stirring frequently,
  3 minutes, until just tender. Sprinkle with $^1/_4$ teaspoon sesame seeds; cook, stirring frequently,
  1 minute.)
Torn Romaine Lettuce and Bean Sprouts, 1 cup
  each, with Ginger Vinaigrette (In small jar with
  tight-fitting lid or small bowl, combine 2 teaspoons rice wine vinegar, 1 teaspoon vegetable oil
  and $^1/_2$ teaspoon minced pared fresh ginger root;
  cover and shake well or, with wire whisk, blend
  until combined.)
Lime Sherbet, $^1/_2$ cup
Jasmine Tea

SNACK
Graham Crackers, 3 ($2^1/_2$" squares)
Skim Milk, 1 cup

This menu provides: 2 Milks, 3 Fats, 2 Fruits,
$11^3/_4$ Vegetables, 5 Proteins, 5 Breads, 150 Optional
Calories.

Per serving: 29 g Fat, 22 g Fiber.

147
SOLE WITH PUMPKIN SEED BUTTER

Makes 4 servings

2 tablespoons all-purpose flour
Pinch ground red pepper
Four 3-ounce sole fillets
2 tablespoons whipped butter
2 teaspoons green pumpkin seeds
1 teaspoon fresh lime juice
2 tablespoons minced fresh cilantro

1. On sheet of wax paper or paper plate, combine flour and pepper; one at a time, place each sole fillet into flour mixture, turning to coat.

2. In large nonstick skillet, melt 1$^1/_2$ teaspoons of the butter; add 2 sole fillets. Cook over medium-high heat, turning once, 4 minutes, until golden brown on both sides and fish flakes easily when tested with fork. Transfer each cooked fillet to a plate; repeat with 1$^1/_2$ teaspoons of the remaining butter and remaining sole fillets.

3. In same skillet, heat remaining 1 tablespoon butter; add pumpkin seeds and juice. Cook, stirring constantly, 15 seconds; spoon evenly over fish. Sprinkle each portion evenly with cilantro.

Serving (1 sole fillet, 1 teaspoon pumpkin seed butter) provides: 1 Protein, 60 Optional Calories.

Per serving: 129 Calories, 5 g Total Fat, 3 g Saturated Fat, 51 mg Cholesterol, 108 mg Sodium, 3 g Total Carbohydrate, 0 g Dietary Fiber, 17 g Protein, 18 mg Calcium.

148
INDIAN-SCENTED SWORDFISH

Makes 2 servings

1 teaspoon minced pared fresh ginger root
1 garlic clove, minced
1/2 teaspoon mild or hot curry powder
1/4 teaspoon ground cumin
Pinch salt
Pinch ground turmeric
Two 6-ounce swordfish steaks
2 tablespoons plain nonfat yogurt
1 tablespoon minced fresh cilantro

1. In small bowl, combine ginger, garlic, curry powder, cumin, salt, turmeric and 1/4 teaspoon water, stirring to form a paste; rub into fish on all sides.

2. Place fish into 9" square or round microwavable baking dish, with thickest part of each steak facing edge of dish. With vented cover, microwave on High (100% power) 5 minutes, rotating dish one-quarter turn after 3 minutes.

3. With slotted spatula, transfer fish to serving platter; keep warm. Strain pan juices into small bowl; stir in yogurt and cilantro. Top fish with yogurt mixture.

Serving (1 swordfish steak, 2 tablespoons yogurt mixture) provides: 2 Proteins, 10 Optional Calories.

Per serving: 190 Calories, 6 g Total Fat, 2 g Saturated Fat, 57 mg Cholesterol, 208 mg Sodium, 2 g Total Carbohydrate, 0 g Dietary Fiber, 30 g Protein, 44 mg Calcium.

BREAKFAST
Cantaloupe, 1/4 small
English Muffin, 1 (2 ounces), split and toasted, with 1 tablespoon nonfat cream cheese
Skim Milk, 1/2 cup
Coffee or Tea (optional)

LIGHT MEAL
Turkey Sandwich (Layer 2 ounces skinless boneless roast turkey breast, sliced, 1/2 medium tomato, sliced, 1/2 cup arugula leaves, 2 teaspoons reduced-calorie mayonnaise and 1 teaspoon prepared mustard between 2 slices reduced-calorie rye bread.)
Red and Green Bell Pepper Strips, 1 cup *each*
Marinated Artichoke Hearts (In small bowl, combine 1/2 cup cooked artichoke hearts and 1 tablespoon fat-free Italian dressing; refrigerate, covered, at least 1 hour or overnight.)
Aspartame-Sweetened Strawberry Nonfat Yogurt, 1 cup
Iced Tea

MAIN MEAL
Indian-Scented Swordfish, 1 serving (see recipe)
Cooked Brown Rice, 1 cup
Steamed Broccoli and Cauliflower Florets, 1 cup *each*, with 2 teaspoons reduced-calorie tub margarine
Romaine and Red Leaf Lettuce Salad, 2 cups, with 1 teaspoon *each* olive oil and red wine vinegar
Whole-Wheat Pita, 1 small (1 ounce)
Kiwi Fruit, 1 medium
Unsweetened Seltzer

SNACK
Reduced-Calorie Vanilla-Flavored Pudding (made with skim milk), 1/2 cup

This menu provides: 2 Milks, 3 Fats, 2 Fruits, 15 Vegetables, 4 Proteins, 6 Breads, 70 Optional Calories.

Per serving: 26 g Fat, 24 g Fiber.

BREAKFAST

Tangerine, 1 large
Frozen Pancakes, 2, heated, with 2 teaspoons *each*
  maple syrup and reduced-calorie tub margarine
Grilled Canadian-Style Bacon, 1 ounce
Skim Milk, 1 cup
Coffee or Tea (optional)

LIGHT MEAL

Canned Vegetable Soup, 1 cup, with 20 oyster
  crackers
Tossed Green Salad, 2 cups, with $^1/_2$ cup *each* roasted
  red bell pepper strips and sliced celery, $1^1/_2$ ounces
  nonfat mozzarella cheese, diced, and 1 tablespoon
  fat-free Italian dressing
Italian Bread, 1 slice (1 ounce), with $1^1/_2$ teaspoons
  reduced-calorie tub margarine
Sugar-Free Strawberry Nonfat Frozen Yogurt, 4 fluid
  ounces
Unsweetened Seltzer

MAIN MEAL

Swordfish Provençal, 1 serving (see recipe)
Roasted Potato Slices, 4 ounces, with $^1/_4$ teaspoon
  each garlic powder and paprika
Steamed Escarole, 1 cup
Iceberg Lettuce Wedge, 1, with 1 tablespoon fat-free
  Thousand Island dressing
Orange Sections, $^1/_2$ cup, with 1 teaspoon shredded
  coconut
Iced Tea

SNACK

Plain Popcorn, hot-air popped, $1^1/_2$ cups
Vanilla Shake (In blender, combine $^3/_4$ cup skim
  milk, 3 ice cubes, sugar substitute to equal 2 teaspoons sugar and 1 teaspoon vanilla extract; purée
  until smooth.)

This menu provides: 2 Milks, 3 Fats, 2 Fruits,
11 Vegetables, 4 Proteins, 6 Breads, 130 Optional
Calories.

Per serving: 33 g Fat, 20 g Fiber.

ᗷ149
SWORDFISH PROVENÇAL

Makes 4 servings

1 tablespoon + 1 teaspoon olive oil
8 large garlic cloves, minced
Four 5-ounce boneless swordfish steaks
$^1/_2$ cup red onion wedges
$^1/_2$ teaspoon fennel seeds
$1^1/_2$ cups canned whole Italian tomatoes (no salt added), chopped
6 large or 10 small Greek olives, pitted and thinly sliced
2 tablespoons slivered fresh basil leaves

1. In small bowl, combine 1 tablespoon of the oil and one-half of the garlic; rub over one side of each swordfish steak. Refrigerate, covered, 1 hour.

2. Preheat broiler. Line broiler pan with foil.

3. In large nonstick skillet, heat remaining 1 teaspoon oil; add onion, fennel seeds and remaining garlic. Cook over low heat, stirring frequently, 7–8 minutes, until onion is softened. Stir in tomatoes; bring mixture to a boil. Reduce heat to low; simmer, stirring occasionally, 10 minutes, until slightly thickened.

4. Meanwhile, arrange swordfish steaks in prepared broiler pan, garlic-side up; broil 4" from heat, turning once, 6 minutes, until fish flakes easily when tested with fork.

5. Place 1 swordfish steak on each of 4 plates. Top each steak with one-fourth of the tomato mixture; sprinkle evenly with olives and basil.

Serving (1 swordfish steak, $^1/_4$ cup tomato mixture, one-fourth of the olives and basil) provides: $1^1/_4$ Fats, 1 Vegetable, 2 Proteins.

Per serving: 271 Calories, 13 g Total Fat, 2 g Saturated Fat, 55 mg Cholesterol, 511 mg Sodium, 8 g Total Carbohydrate, 1 g Dietary Fiber, 30 g Protein, 65 mg Calcium.

150

SWORDFISH WITH MUSTARD-DILL SAUCE

Makes 4 servings

Four 5-ounce boneless swordfish steaks
1 tablespoon + 1 teaspoon olive oil
1/3 cup + 2 teaspoons nonfat sour cream
2 tablespoons Dijon-style mustard
1 tablespoon minced fresh dill
Lemon wedges and fresh dill sprigs, to garnish

1. Preheat outdoor barbecue grill or indoor stove-top grill according to manufacturer's directions.

2. Brush each swordfish steak with 1 teaspoon of the oil; grill over hot coals or on stove-top grill, turning once, 6–8 minutes, until fish flakes easily when tested with fork.

3. Meanwhile, to prepare sauce, in small bowl, combine sour cream, mustard and minced dill.

4. Transfer swordfish to serving platter; top each steak with one-fourth of the sauce. Serve garnished with lemon wedges and dill sprigs.

Serving (1 swordfish steak, 2 tablespoons sauce) provides: 1 Fat, 2 Proteins, 15 Optional Calories.

Per serving: 234 Calories, 10 g Total Fat, 2 g Saturated Fat, 55 mg Cholesterol, 323 mg Sodium, 2 g Total Carbohydrate, 0 g Dietary Fiber, 30 g Protein, 37 mg Calcium.

BREAKFAST
Cooked Cream of Wheat Cereal, 1 cup, with 2 tablespoons dried cranberries
Skim Milk, 1 cup
Coffee or Tea (optional)

LIGHT MEAL
Baked Skinless Chicken Breast, 2 ounces
Romaine-Orange Salad (In medium bowl, combine 2 cups torn Romaine lettuce leaves, 1/2 cup *each* orange sections, sliced red onion and sliced jicama and 1 tablespoon fat-free Italian dressing.)
Roll, 1 ounce, with 1 teaspoon reduced-calorie tub margarine
Sugar-Free Vanilla Nonfat Frozen Yogurt, 4 fluid ounces
Iced Tea with Lemon Wedge

MAIN MEAL
Swordfish with Mustard-Dill Sauce, 1 serving (see recipe)
Baked Potato, 8 ounces, with 1 tablespoon reduced-calorie tub margarine
Cooked Julienned Beets, 1/2 cup
Red and Green Leaf Lettuce Salad, 2 cups, with 2 ounces drained cooked chick-peas, 1/2 cup shredded carrot and 1 tablespoon balsamic vinegar
Sugar-Free Raspberry-Flavored Gelatin, 1/2 cup, with 1 tablespoon thawed frozen light whipped topping (8 calories per tablespoon)
Sparkling Mineral Water

SNACK
Vanilla Wafers, 3
Skim Milk, 3/4 cup

This menu provides: 2 Milks, 3 Fats, 2 Fruits, 12 Vegetables, 5 Proteins, 5 1/2 Breads, 115 Optional Calories.

Per serving: 28 g Fat, 21 g Fiber.

RED TROUT WITH VEGETABLES EN PAPILLOTE

Makes 4 servings

1 cup julienned carrot
1 cup julienned snow peas
$^1/_2$ cup julienned scallions
Four 4-ounce red trout fillets
2 teaspoons minced fresh thyme leaves
1 teaspoon grated lemon zest*
1 garlic clove, minced
$^1/_4$ teaspoon salt
Pinch freshly ground black pepper
2 tablespoons fresh lemon juice
1 tablespoon + 1 teaspoon olive oil

1. Preheat oven to 425° F. Spray four 15 × 12" sheets of foil with non-stick cooking spray.

2. Place one-fourth of the carrot, snow peas and scallions onto center of each prepared sheet of foil; top each portion of vegetables with 1 trout fillet.

3. In cup or small bowl, combine thyme, zest, garlic, salt and pepper; sprinkle evenly over fish. Drizzle each portion with $1^1/_2$ teaspoons of the juice and 1 teaspoon of the oil. Enclose fish in foil, making 4 individual packets; crimp edges to seal.

4. Place packets onto baking sheet; bake 10–12 minutes, until fish flakes easily when tested with fork and vegetables are just tender.

5. Open foil packets carefully; transfer contents of each packet to a plate.

Serving (1 trout fillet, $^1/_2$ cup vegetables, liquid remaining in packet) provides: 1 Fat, $1^1/_4$ Vegetables, $1^1/_2$ Proteins.

Per serving: 249 Calories, 13 g Total Fat, 2 g Saturated Fat, 66 mg Cholesterol, 207 mg Sodium, 8 g Total Carbohydrate, 2 g Dietary Fiber, 25 g Protein, 88 mg Calcium.

The zest of the lemon is the peel without any of the pith (white membrane). To remove zest from lemon, use a zester or the fine side of a vegetable grater.

152
SWEET AND SOUR TROUT

Makes 4 servings

2 tablespoons cornstarch

2 tablespoons reduced-sodium soy sauce

2 tablespoons rice wine vinegar

2 tablespoons oriental fish sauce*

1 tablespoon + 1 teaspoon granulated sugar

2 tablespoons all-purpose flour

Four 4-ounce trout fillets

2 tablespoons canola oil

1/2 cup sliced scallions

3 garlic cloves, minced

1 tablespoon minced pared fresh ginger root

2 medium tomatoes, seeded and diced

1 cup julienned carrot

1 cup julienned pared daikon (Japanese white radish)*

1. In small bowl, combine cornstarch, soy sauce, vinegar, fish sauce, sugar and 1 cup water, stirring until cornstarch and sugar are dissolved; set aside.

2. Place flour onto sheet of wax paper or paper plate; one at a time, place each trout fillet into flour, turning to coat.

3. In large nonstick skillet, heat 1 tablespoon of the oil; add 2 coated fillets. Cook over medium-high heat, turning once, 5–6 minutes, until fish is golden brown and flakes easily when tested with fork. Set aside; keep warm. Repeat with remaining oil and fish fillets.

4. In same skillet, combine scallions, garlic and ginger; cook over medium-high heat, stirring frequently, 1 minute, until scallions are just softened. Add tomatoes, carrot and daikon; cook, stirring frequently, 2–3 minutes, until carrot is just tender. Stir in cornstarch mixture; reduce heat to medium and cook, stirring constantly, 2–3 minutes, until mixture is thickened. Spoon tomato mixture over warm trout fillets.

Serving (1 trout fillet, 1/2 cup tomato mixture) provides: 1 1/2 Fats, 2 1/4 Vegetables, 1 1/2 Proteins, 70 Optional Calories.

Per serving: 339 Calories, 16 g Total Fat, 2 g Saturated Fat, 66 mg Cholesterol, 681 mg Sodium, 22 g Total Carbohydrate, 2 g Dietary Fiber, 27 g Protein, 82 mg Calcium.

*Oriental fish sauce and daikon are available in most Asian groceries.

BREAKFAST

Honeydew Melon, 2" wedge

Frozen Waffle, 1, heated, with 2 teaspoons maple syrup

Grilled Canadian-Style Bacon, 1 ounce

Skim Milk, 1 cup

Coffee or Tea (optional)

LIGHT MEAL

Roast Beef Sandwich (Layer 1 1/2 ounces cooked lean boneless roast beef, thinly sliced, 2 tomato slices and 2 iceberg lettuce leaves and 1 tablespoon fat-free Thousand Island dressing between 2 slices reduced-calorie rye bread.)

Whole Radishes and Cucumber Sticks, 1 cup *each*

Apple, 1 small

Diet Cola

MAIN MEAL

Sweet and Sour Trout, 1 serving (see recipe)

Cooked Brown Rice, 1 cup

Steamed Broccoli, 4 spears, with 1 teaspoon reduced-calorie tub margarine

Red and Green Leaf Lettuce Salad, 2 cups, with 1/2 cup green bell pepper strips and 1 tablespoon fat-free Italian dressing

Sugar-Free Lemon-Flavored Gelatin, 1/2 cup, with 1 tablespoon thawed frozen light whipped topping (8 calories per tablespoon)

Unsweetened Seltzer with Lemon Wedge

SNACK

Graham Crackers, 3 (2 1/2" squares)

Skim Milk, 1 cup

This menu provides: 2 Milks, 3 Fats, 2 Fruits, 14 1/4 Vegetables, 4 Proteins, 5 Breads, 145 Optional Calories.

Per serving: 35 g Fat, 20 g Fiber.

BREAKFAST

Papaya, $^1/_2$ medium

Egg White Salad Muffin (In small bowl, combine 3 hard-cooked egg whites, chopped, $^1/_4$ cup finely chopped celery and 1 tablespoon reduced-calorie mayonnaise; scoop onto $^1/_2$ [1 ounce] toasted English muffin.)

Skim Milk, 1 cup

Coffee or Tea

LIGHT MEAL

Spinach, Bean and Chicken Salad (In medium bowl, combine 2 cups torn spinach leaves, 2 ounces drained cooked cannellini [white kidney] beans, 1 ounce skinless boneless cooked chicken breast, diced, $^1/_2$ cup plain nonfat yogurt and 1 tablespoon reduced-calorie mayonnaise.)

Carrot and Celery Sticks, 1 cup *each*

Breadsticks, 2 long

Plum, 1 small

Unsweetened Seltzer with Lime Wedge

MAIN MEAL

Wonton Soup (In small saucepan, combine 1 cup low-sodium chicken broth and 3 boiled wontons; heat.)

Sweet and Sour Shrimp, 1 serving (see recipe)

Steamed Long-Grain Brown Rice, 1 cup

Steamed Cauliflower Florets, 1 cup

Fortune Cookie, 1

Chinese Tea

SNACK

Root Beer "Float" (In tall glass, combine 1 cup diet root beer and $^1/_3$ cup skim milk; add enough ice cubes to fill glass.)

This menu provides: 2 Milks, 3 Fats, 2 Fruits, $9^3/_4$ Vegetables, $4^1/_2$ Proteins, 5 Breads, 90 Optional Calories.

Per serving: 19 g Fat, 23 g Fiber.

153
SWEET AND SOUR SHRIMP

Makes 4 servings

1 cup diagonally sliced carrots (thin slices)

1 cup julienned green bell pepper

$^3/_4$ cup drained canned sliced water chestnuts

8 medium scallions, cut into $^1/_2$" pieces

1 teaspoon grated pared fresh ginger root

1 cup canned pineapple chunks (no sugar added), drained (reserve $^1/_4$ cup juice)

12 large shrimp, peeled and deveined

2 tablespoons reduced-sodium soy sauce

1 tablespoon firmly packed light or dark brown sugar

1 tablespoon cornstarch

1 tablespoon cider vinegar

1. In 11 × 7" microwavable baking dish, combine carrots, bell pepper, water chestnuts, scallions, ginger and 2 tablespoons water. With vented cover, microwave on High (100% power) 2–2$^1/_2$ minutes, until vegetables are just softened.

2. Stir pineapple chunks into vegetable mixture; arrange shrimp in a single layer over vegetables. With vented cover, microwave on High 3$^1/_2$–4$^1/_2$ minutes, until shrimp turn pink (do not overcook or shrimp will become tough). Set aside; keep warm.

3. In small microwavable bowl, combine soy sauce, brown sugar, cornstarch, vinegar, reserved $^1/_4$ cup pineapple juice and $^1/_4$ cup water; stir until sugar and cornstarch are dissolved. Microwave on High 3$^1/_2$–4 minutes, until thickened, stirring once. Pour soy sauce mixture over shrimp mixture; stir to combine.

Serving (3 shrimp, $^3/_4$ cup vegetable mixture) provides: $^1/_2$ Fruit, 1$^1/_4$ Vegetables, 1 Protein, $^1/_4$ Bread, 20 Optional Calories.

Per serving: 164 Calories, 1 g Total Fat, 0 g Saturated Fat, 86 mg Cholesterol, 402 mg Sodium, 26 g Total Carbohydrate, 3 g Dietary Fiber, 13 g Protein, 63 mg Calcium.

154

SEA BASS WITH CHINESE FLAVORS

Makes 4 servings

One 1³/₄-pound whole sea bass, cleaned, scaled and thoroughly washed
  (head and tail removed, if desired)*
2 tablespoons slivered pared fresh ginger root
¹/₂ cup slivered scallions
1 tablespoon fermented black beans (black bean sauce), rinsed and
  lightly mashed†
2 tablespoons reduced-sodium soy sauce
1 fluid ounce (2 tablespoons) dry sherry
2 teaspoons oriental sesame oil
2 garlic cloves, minced

1. Make 3 diagonal slashes on both sides of fish. Insert half of the ginger
into slashes and body cavity of fish; place half of the scallions into body
cavity. Transfer fish to heatproof dish; spread evenly with black beans,
remaining ginger and remaining scallions.

2. To prepare sauce, in small bowl, combine soy sauce, sherry, oil and garlic; pour evenly over fish.

3. Fill large saucepan with 1" water; set steamer rack into saucepan. Place
dish with fish onto rack. Bring water to a boil; reduce heat to low. Steam
fish over simmering water, covered, 15 minutes, until fish flakes easily
when tested with fork.

Serving (4 ounces fish, 2 tablespoons sauce) provides: ¹/₂ Fat, ¹/₄ Vegetable,
2 Proteins, 15 Optional Calories.

Per serving: 184 Calories, 5 g Total Fat, 1 g Saturated Fat, 58 mg Cholesterol,
509 mg Sodium, 3 g Total Carbohydrate, 0 g Dietary Fiber, 27 g Protein,
32 mg Calcium.

*A 1³/₄-pound sea bass will yield about 1 pound cooked fish.

†Fermented black beans are available in most Asian groceries.

BREAKFAST
Peach, 1 medium, sliced
Bite-Size Shredded Wheat Cereal, 1¹/₂ ounces
Skim Milk, 1 cup
Coffee or Tea (optional)

LIGHT MEAL
Low-Sodium Mixed Vegetable Juice, 1 cup
Spinach-Cheese Salad (In medium bowl, combine
  2 cups torn spinach leaves, 2 ounces drained
  cooked chick-peas, ³/₄ ounce nonfat Swiss cheese,
  diced, ¹/₂ cup *each* sliced mushrooms and sliced
  red onion and 1 tablespoon blue cheese dressing.)
Whole-Wheat Roll, 1 ounce, with 1 teaspoon
  reduced-calorie tub margarine
Frozen Fruit Pop, 1 bar
Unsweetened Lemon-Lime–Flavored Seltzer

MAIN MEAL
Sea Bass with Chinese Flavors, 1 serving (see recipe)
Cooked Long-Grain Brown Rice, 1 cup
Cooked Whole Green Beans, 1 cup
Fresh Lichees, 10 medium
Jasmine Tea

SNACK
Aspartame-Sweetened Blueberry Nonfat Yogurt,
  1 cup

This menu provides: 2 Milks, 3 Fats, 2 Fruits,
10¹/₄ Vegetables, 3¹/₂ Proteins, 5 Breads,
60 Optional Calories.

Per serving: 21 g Fat, 20 g Fiber.

155
THAI-STYLE NOODLES WITH SEA BASS

Makes 4 servings

8 small dried Chinese mushrooms
3 ounces vermicelli
$^1/_2$ cup snow peas, halved
1 tablespoon + 1 teaspoon canola oil
$^1/_2$ cup sliced scallions
4 garlic cloves, crushed
10 ounces sea bass fillets, cut into $^3/_4$" strips
$^1/_2$ cup drained canned sliced bamboo shoots
3 tablespoons oriental fish sauce*
3 tablespoons balsamic vinegar

1. Place mushrooms into small bowl; add boiling water to cover. Let stand 15 minutes, until softened. Drain, discarding liquid; squeeze mushrooms dry. Remove and discard tough stems; slice mushrooms. Set aside.

2. In large pot of boiling water, cook vermicelli 8–10 minutes, until tender. Drain, discarding liquid; place into serving bowl. Keep warm.

3. In small saucepan of boiling water, cook snow peas 1 minute, until bright green and just tender. Drain, discarding liquid; rinse with cold water. Drain again; set aside.

4. In large nonstick skillet, heat oil; add scallions and garlic. Cook over medium-high heat, stirring frequently, 2 minutes, until softened. Add fish, bamboo shoots, fish sauce, vinegar, reserved mushrooms and reserved snow peas; cook, stirring frequently, 2 minutes, until fish flakes easily when tested with fork.

5. Spoon fish mixture over warm vermicelli; toss to combine.

Serving (one-fourth of mixture) provides: 1 Fat, 1 Vegetable, 1 Protein, 1 Bread, 35 Optional Calories.

Per serving: 243 Calories, 8 g Total Fat, 1 g Saturated Fat, 29 mg Cholesterol, 502 mg Sodium, 24 g Total Carbohydrate, 1 g Dietary Fiber, 19 g Protein, 36 mg Calcium.

Oriental fish sauce is available in most Asian groceries.

156
ORIENTAL OYSTERS

Makes 2 servings

$^1/_4$ cup julienned carrot
$^1/_4$ cup julienned snow peas
1 tablespoon minced pared fresh ginger root
1 tablespoon hoisin sauce
4 garlic cloves, crushed
1 tablespoon reduced-sodium soy sauce
$^1/_2$ fluid ounce (1 tablespoon) dry sherry
1 teaspoon canola oil
6 medium oysters, shucked
1 tablespoon sliced scallion
1 cup hot cooked brown rice

1. In small saucepan of boiling water, cook carrot and snow peas 1 minute, until colors are bright and vegetables are just tender. Drain, discarding liquid; rinse with cold water. Drain again; set aside.

2. In cup or small bowl, combine ginger, hoisin sauce and garlic; in separate cup or small bowl, combine soy sauce and sherry.

3. In medium nonstick skillet, heat oil; add ginger mixture. Cook over medium heat, stirring constantly, 15 seconds, just until mixture is heated (do not burn). In a single layer, add oysters, then soy sauce mixture; cook, without stirring, 1 minute, until oysters curl at edges. Add cooked vegetables; cook, stirring constantly, 1 minute, until mixture is well coated and heated through. Sprinkle with scallion; serve over rice.

Serving (1 cup) provides: $^1/_2$ Fat, $^1/_2$ Vegetable, $^1/_2$ Protein, 1 Bread, 20 Optional Calories.

Per serving: 210 Calories, 4 g Total Fat, 1 g Saturated Fat, 16 mg Cholesterol, 502 mg Sodium, 34 g Total Carbohydrate, 3 g Dietary Fiber, 6 g Protein, 50 mg Calcium.

BREAKFAST
Banana, $^1/_2$ medium
Toasted Oat Cereal, $^3/_4$ ounce
Skim Milk, 1 cup
Coffee or Tea (optional)

LIGHT MEAL
Grilled Ham and Cheese Sandwich (Spread 1 side of each of 2 slices reduced-calorie rye bread with 1 teaspoon reduced-calorie tub margarine; layer 1 ounce cooked ham, sliced, and 1 slice nonfat process American cheese between unspread sides of bread. In small nonstick skillet, cook sandwich over medium-high heat, 5 minutes, turning once, until sandwich is golden brown and heated through.)
Torn Spinach Leaves, 2 cups, with $^1/_2$ cup sliced radishes, 2 ounces drained cooked chick-peas and 1 tablespoon fat-free Italian dressing
Aspartame-Sweetened Coffee Nonfat Yogurt, 1 cup
Diet Ginger Ale

MAIN MEAL
Boiled Wontons, 3, with 2 teaspoons reduced-sodium soy sauce
Oriental Oysters, 1 serving (see recipe)
Steamed Broccoli, 4 spears, with 1 lemon wedge
Steamed Baby Carrots, 1 cup
Tangerine, 1 large
Herbal Tea

SNACK
Rice Cakes, 2, with 1$^1/_2$ teaspoons *each* peanut butter and strawberry jam

This menu provides: 2 Milks, 3 Fats, 2 Fruits, 9$^1/_2$ Vegetables, 3$^1/_2$ Proteins, 4$^3/_4$ Breads, 50 Optional Calories.

Per serving: 21 g Fat, 21 g Fiber.

This menu provides: 2 Milks, 3 Fats, 2 Fruits,
13$^3/_4$ Vegetables, 3 Proteins, 6 Breads, 60 Optional
Calories.

Per serving: 22 g Fat, 23 g Fiber.

157
RISOTTO WITH SCALLOPS AND ASPARAGUS

*There's no need to stand over a hot stove while making this risotto; it's
easily prepared in the microwave oven!*

Makes 4 servings

2 teaspoons olive oil
$^1/_2$ cup finely diced red onion
8 ounces Arborio or other short-grain rice
1$^1/_4$ cups low-sodium chicken broth
12 thin asparagus spears, cut diagonally into 1" pieces
10 ounces bay scallops
1$^1/_2$ ounces Asiago cheese, finely grated
$^1/_2$ teaspoon grated lemon zest*
1 tablespoon fresh lemon juice
$^1/_4$ teaspoon salt
Freshly ground black pepper, to taste

1. In 2-quart microwavable casserole, microwave oil on High (100%
power) 30 seconds, until hot. Stir in onion; microwave on High 2 minutes. Stir in rice; microwave on High 2 minutes.

2. Add broth and 2 cups water to rice mixture; stir to combine.
Microwave on High 14 minutes, stirring after 7 minutes, until most of the
liquid is absorbed.

3. Stir asparagus into rice mixture; microwave on High 5 minutes. Stir in
scallops; microwave on High 2 minutes, until scallops are opaque in center, rice is tender and all of the liquid is absorbed.

4. Stir cheese, zest, juice, salt and pepper into rice mixture; stir until
cheese is melted.

Serving (1$^1/_4$ cups) provides: $^1/_2$ Fat, $^3/_4$ Vegetable, 1$^1/_2$ Proteins, 2 Breads,
5 Optional Calories.

Per serving: 358 Calories, 7 g Total Fat, 3 g Saturated Fat, 31 mg Cholesterol,
411 mg Sodium, 51 g Total Carbohydrate, 2 g Dietary Fiber, 21 g Protein,
132 mg Calcium.

**The zest of the lemon is the peel without any of the pith (white membrane). To
remove zest from lemon, use a zester or the fine side of a vegetable grater.*

158
PAELLA

Makes 4 servings

8 sun-dried tomato halves (not packed in oil)
1 tablespoon + 1 teaspoon olive oil
1 cup coarsely chopped onions
1 cup coarsely chopped green bell pepper
4 garlic cloves, crushed
6 ounces regular long-grain rice
3 cups low-sodium chicken broth
$^1/_4$ teaspoon crushed saffron threads
$^1/_4$ teaspoon salt
Pinch ground red pepper
10 ounces medium shrimp, peeled and deveined
5 ounces turbot or catfish fillets, cut into $1^1/_2 \times 1$" pieces
12 medium clams
1 cup fresh or thawed frozen green peas
1 cup cooked artichoke hearts, halved
1 ounce cooked sweet or hot Italian pork sausage, thinly sliced

1. Place tomatoes into small bowl; add boiling water to cover. Let stand 20 minutes, until softened; drain, discarding liquid. Chop tomatoes; set aside.

2. In large pot or Dutch oven, heat oil; add onions, bell pepper and garlic. Cook over medium-high heat, stirring frequently, 5 minutes, until onion is softened. Add rice; cook, stirring constantly, 2 minutes.

3. Stir broth, saffron, salt and ground red pepper into onion mixture; bring liquid to a boil. Reduce heat to low; simmer, covered, 10 minutes, until most of the liquid is absorbed. Stir in shrimp, turbot, clams, peas, artichoke hearts, sausage and chopped tomatoes; cook, covered, 10 minutes, until shrimp turn pink, turbot flakes easily when tested with fork and clams open. Discard any unopened clams.

Serving (2 cups) provides: 1 Fat, $2^1/_4$ Vegetables, $2^1/_4$ Proteins, 2 Breads, 15 Optional Calories.

Per serving: 489 Calories, 15 g Total Fat, 3 g Saturated Fat, 139 mg Cholesterol, 469 mg Sodium, 55 g Total Carbohydrate, 6 g Dietary Fiber, 35 g Protein, 117 mg Calcium.

BREAKFAST
Hot Maple Oatmeal (In small bowl, combine $^1/_2$ cup hot cooked oatmeal, 2 tablespoons raisins and 1 teaspoon maple syrup.)
Skim Milk, $^1/_2$ cup
Coffee or Tea (optional)

LIGHT MEAL
Grilled Swiss Cheese Sandwich (Toast 2 slices reduced-calorie rye bread; top each with 1 slice nonfat process Swiss cheese. Place onto nonstick baking sheet; broil 1–2 minutes, until heated.)
Carrot and Celery Sticks, 1 cup *each*, with Vegetable Dip (In small bowl, combine $^1/_2$ cup plain nonfat yogurt and 1 packet instant vegetable broth and seasoning mix.)
Peach, 1 medium
Diet Lemonade, 1 cup

MAIN MEAL
Low-Sodium Mixed Vegetable Juice, 1 cup
Paella, 1 serving (see recipe)
Tossed Green Salad, 2 cups, with 1 tablespoon Thousand Island dressing
Reduced-Calorie Vanilla-Flavored Pudding (made with skim milk), $^1/_2$ cup
Decaffeinated Espresso with Lemon Twist

SNACK
Plain Popcorn, hot-air popped, 3 cups
Root Beer "Float" (In tall glass, combine 1 cup diet root beer and $^1/_3$ cup skim milk; add enough ice cubes to fill glass.)

This menu provides: 2 Milks, 3 Fats, 2 Fruits, $12^1/_4$ Vegetables, $3^1/_4$ Proteins, 5 Breads, 85 Optional Calories.

Per serving: 26 g Fat, 21 g Fiber.

159

Mozzarella in Carozza

Makes 4 servings

3 ounces skim-milk mozzarella cheese, coarsely grated
6 rinsed drained anchovy fillets, chopped
2 tablespoons minced fresh flat-leaf parsley
2 teaspoons olive oil
2 teaspoons fresh lemon juice
1 garlic clove, minced
8 ounces Italian bread, cut diagonally into 8 equal slices
1 egg
$^1/_4$ cup skim milk

1. In small bowl, with fork, combine cheese, anchovies, parsley, oil, juice and garlic.

2. To assemble sandwiches, spread each of 4 bread slices with one-fourth of the cheese mixture; top each with 1 remaining bread slice.

3. In shallow bowl or pie plate, with fork, combine egg and milk, beating until well blended. Add sandwiches, turning as needed, until egg mixture is absorbed.

4. Spray large nonstick skillet with nonstick cooking spray; heat. Add sandwiches; cook over medium-low heat, 3 minutes, until browned on bottom. Turn sandwiches over; cook, covered, 3 minutes, until cheese is melted and sandwiches are browned.

Serving (1 sandwich) provides: $^1/_2$ Fat, $1^1/_4$ Proteins, 2 Breads, 15 Optional Calories.

Per serving: 268 Calories, 10 g Total Fat, 3 g Saturated Fat, 69 mg Cholesterol, 675 mg Sodium, 30 g Total Carbohydrate, 2 g Dietary Fiber, 14 g Protein, 224 mg Calcium.

BREAKFAST
Blueberries, $^3/_4$ cup
Frozen Pancakes, 2, heated, with 2 teaspoons *each* maple syrup and reduced-calorie tub margarine
Skim Milk, $^3/_4$ cup
Coffee or Tea (optional)

LIGHT MEAL
Spinach and Cheddar-Stuffed Potato (Cut a lengthwise slit about 1" deep into 8-ounce baked potato, cutting to within $^1/_2$" of each end; gently squeeze ends together until potato opens. Top potato pulp with 1 teaspoon reduced-calorie tub margarine, then $^1/_2$ cup cooked chopped spinach and $^3/_4$ ounce reduced-fat cheddar cheese, grated; microwave on High [100% power], $1^1/_2$–2 minutes until heated through.)
Chilled Cooked Julienned Beets, $^1/_2$ cup
Carrot and Celery Sticks, 1 cup *each*
Sugar-Free Chocolate Nonfat Frozen Yogurt, 4 fluid ounces
Iced Decaffeinated Cappuccino, made with skim milk, 5 fluid ounces

MAIN MEAL
Low-Sodium Mixed Vegetable Juice, 1 cup
Mozzarella in Carozza, 1 serving (see recipe)
Chilled Antipasto Salad (On plate, decoratively arrange $^1/_2$ cup *each* drained roasted red bell pepper strips, chilled cooked artichoke hearts and fennel strips and 2 ounces drained cooked chickpeas; sprinkle with $1^1/_2$ teaspoons Italian dressing.)
Honeydew Melon, 2" wedge, with lime wedge
Sparkling Mineral Water with Lemon Wedge

SNACK
Coffee Shake (In blender, combine $^1/_2$ cup skim milk, 2 ice cubes, sugar substitute to equal 1 teaspoon sugar and 1 teaspoon instant decaffeinated coffee powder; purée until smooth.)

This menu provides: 2 Milks, 3 Fats, 2 Fruits, 11 Vegetables, $3^1/_4$ Proteins, 6 Breads, 95 Optional Calories.

Per serving: 30 g Fat, 24 g Fiber.

LIGHT MEAL
Broiled Lamb Chop, 2 ounces
Cooked Green Peas, $^1/_2$ cup, with 1 tablespoon
  minced fresh mint and 1 teaspoon reduced-calorie
  tub margarine
Steamed Sliced Carrots, 1 cup
Red Leaf Lettuce and Watercress Salad, 2 cups, with
  2 ounces drained cooked chick-peas, $^1/_2$ cup *each*
  sliced mushrooms and green bell peppers and
  1 tablespoon fat-free ranch dressing
Roll, 1 ounce, with 1 teaspoon reduced-calorie tub
  margarine
Sugar-Free Strawberry Nonfat Frozen Yogurt, 4 fluid
  ounces
Sparkling Mineral Water

MAIN MEAL
Thai Hot and Sour Soup, 1 serving (see recipe)
Torn Romaine Lettuce and Cucumber Slices, 2 cups,
  with $^1/_4$ cup sliced scallions and Ginger
  Vinaigrette (In small jar with tight-fitting lid or
  small bowl, combine 2 teaspoons rice wine vinegar, 1 teaspoon vegetable oil and $^1/_2$ teaspoon
  minced pared fresh ginger root; cover and shake
  well or, with wire whisk, blend until combined.)
Apple, 1 small
Iced Tea with Lemon Wedge

SNACK
Graham Crackers, 3 ($2^1/_2$" squares)
Peanut Butter-Chocolate Shake (In blender, combine
  $^3/_4$ cup skim milk, 3 ice cubes, 1 teaspoon *each*
  smooth peanut butter and chocolate syrup and
  sugar substitute to equal 2 teaspoons sugar; purée
  until smooth.)

This menu provides: 2 Milks, 3 Fats, 2 Fruits,
$13^3/_4$ Vegetables, 5 Proteins, 5 Breads, 110 Optional
Calories.

Per serving: 32 g Fat, 20 g Fiber.

160
THAI HOT AND SOUR SOUP

Makes 4 servings

4 ounces regular long-grain rice
5 cups low-sodium chicken broth
Two 1$^1/_2$" Thai red or green chiles, seeded, deveined and finely minced
  (wear gloves to prevent irritation)
3 tablespoons rice wine vinegar
1 tablespoon fresh lime juice
Pinch granulated sugar
2 cups julienned pared daikon (Japanese white radish)*
1 pound 4 ounces sea bass fillets, cut into $^3/_4$" strips
3 tablespoons minced fresh cilantro

1. In medium saucepan, bring 1$^1/_2$ cups water to a boil; add rice. Reduce heat to low; simmer, covered, 17 minutes, until rice is tender and all liquid is absorbed. Remove from heat; keep warm.

2. Meanwhile, in small bowl, combine 2 tablespoons of the broth, the chiles, vinegar, juice and sugar; set aside.

3. In large saucepan, bring remaining broth to a boil; reduce heat to low. Add daikon; simmer 5 minutes, until daikon is tender. Add fish and the chile mixture; simmer 3–5 minutes, until fish flakes easily when tested with fork. Stir in cilantro.

4. Scoop one-fourth of the warm rice into $^1/_2$-cup dry measure, pressing down gently until rice holds together; unmold into shallow soup bowl. Repeat with remaining rice. Divide broth mixture evenly over rice.

Serving (2 cups broth mixture, $^1/_2$ cup rice) provides: 1$^1/_4$ Vegetables, 2 Proteins, 1 Bread, 25 Optional Calories.

Per serving: 285 Calories, 6 g Total Fat, 2 g Saturated Fat, 58 mg Cholesterol, 251 mg Sodium, 28 g Total Carbohydrate, 0 g Dietary Fiber, 33 g Protein, 57 mg Calcium.

*Daikon is available in most Asian groceries.

MUSSELS IN TOMATO BROTH

Makes 4 servings

2 tablespoons minced fresh flat-leaf parsley
1 teaspoon grated lemon zest*
1 tablespoon + 1 teaspoon olive oil
$^1/_2$ cup chopped onion
4 garlic cloves, minced
3 large plum tomatoes, blanched peeled, seeded and coarsely chopped
8 fluid ounces (1 cup) dry white wine
36 medium mussels, scrubbed and debearded

1. In small cup or bowl, combine parsley and zest; set aside.

2. In large pot or Dutch oven, heat oil; add onion and garlic. Cook over medium-high heat, stirring frequently, 7 minutes, until onion is lightly browned. Add tomatoes; cook, stirring frequently, 1 minute. Add wine and half of the parsley mixture; bring liquid to a boil. Add mussels. Reduce heat to low; simmer, covered, 3–4 minutes, until mussels open.

3. Place 9 mussels into each of 4 soup bowls; add one-fourth of the cooking liquid to each portion of mussels. Serve sprinkled with remaining parsley mixture.

Serving (9 mussels, $^3/_4$ cup liquid) provides: 1 Fat, 1 Vegetable, $1^1/_2$ Proteins, 50 Optional Calories.

Per serving: 174 Calories, 7 g Total Fat, 1 g Saturated Fat, 24 mg Cholesterol, 252 mg Sodium, 8 g Total Carbohydrate, 1 g Dietary Fiber, 11 g Protein, 42 mg Calcium.

The zest of the lemon is the peel without any of the pith (white membrane). To remove zest from lemon, use a zester or the fine side of a vegetable grater; wrap lemon in plastic wrap and refrigerate for use at another time.

BREAKFAST
Cantaloupe, $^1/_4$ small
Bite-Size Shredded Wheat Cereal, $1^1/_2$ ounces
Skim Milk, 1 cup
Coffee or Tea (optional)

LIGHT MEAL
Pastrami Sandwich (Layer 1 ounce turkey pastrami, sliced, 2 tomato slices, 2 iceberg lettuce leaves, $^1/_4$ cup alfalfa sprouts and 1 teaspoon prepared spicy brown mustard between 2 slices reduced-calorie rye bread.)
Dill Pickle, 1 medium
Shredded Green and Red Cabbage, 1 cup, with $1^1/_2$ teaspoons coleslaw dressing
Frozen Fruit Pop, 1 bar
Diet Cream Soda

MAIN MEAL
Steamed Artichoke, 1 medium, with Lemon "Butter" (In small cup or bowl, combine 1 teaspoon *each* reduced-calorie tub margarine, melted, and fresh lemon juice.)
Mussels in Tomato Broth, 1 serving (see recipe)
Steamed Sliced Broccoli Rabe, 1 cup
Tossed Green Salad, 2 cups, with 1 tablespoon fat-free creamy Italian dressing
Italian Bread, 1 slice (1 ounce), with 1 teaspoon reduced-calorie tub margarine
Strawberries, 1 cup
Decaffeinated Espresso

SNACK
Reduced-Fat Cheddar Cheese, $^3/_4$ ounce
Fat-Free Crackers, 7
Skim Milk, 1 cup

This menu provides: 2 Milks, 3 Fats, 2 Fruits, $13^1/_2$ Vegetables, $3^1/_2$ Proteins, 5 Breads, 115 Optional Calories.

Per serving: 25 g Fat, 26 g Fiber.

Mussels in Tomato Broth

162
OYSTER BISQUE

Makes 4 servings

 $^1/_2$ cup julienned carrot
 $^1/_2$ cup julienned celery
2 teaspoons canola oil
1 cup finely chopped onions
 $1^1/_2$ ounces regular long-grain rice
 $1^1/_2$ cups low-sodium chicken broth
 $^1/_2$ cup skim milk
Pinch ground red pepper
6 ounces drained canned oysters (reserve $^1/_2$ cup liquid)
Pinch salt
Minced fresh flat-leaf parsley, to garnish

1. In small saucepan of boiling water, cook carrot and celery 1–2 minutes, until barely tender. Drain, discarding liquid; pat dry and set aside.

2. In medium saucepan, heat oil; add onions. Cook over medium-high heat, stirring frequently, 5 minutes, until softened. Add rice; cook, stirring constantly, 2 minutes. Add 1 cup of the broth and 1 cup water; bring liquid to a boil. Reduce heat to low; simmer, covered, 15 minutes, until rice is tender. Remove from heat; set aside until slightly cooled.

3. Transfer rice mixture to food processor; purée until smooth. Return mixture to saucepan; add milk, pepper, remaining $^1/_2$ cup broth and $^1/_2$ cup water. Cook over medium heat, stirring constantly, until heated through (do not boil). Stir in oysters, reserved liquid and salt; cook, stirring constantly, 2 minutes, just until heated.

4. Divide oyster mixture evenly among 4 soup bowls; add one-fourth of the cooked vegetables to each portion. Serve sprinkled with parsley.

Serving (1 cup) provides: $^1/_2$ Fat, 1 Vegetable, $^3/_4$ Protein, $^1/_4$ Bread, 30 Optional Calories.

Per serving: 151 Calories, 5 g Total Fat, 1 g Saturated Fat, 40 mg Cholesterol, 191 mg Sodium, 19 g Total Carbohydrate, 1 g Dietary Fiber, 9 g Protein, 97 mg Calcium.

BREAKFAST
Blueberry Yogurt (In small bowl, combine $^3/_4$ cup *each* plain nonfat yogurt and blueberries.)
Herb Scramble (In small microwavable bowl, combine $^1/_2$ cup egg substitute, 1 teaspoon minced fresh flat-leaf parsley and $^1/_4$ teaspoon *each* dried oregano leaves and basil; microwave on Medium-High [70% power], $1^1/_2$ –2 minutes, stirring once or twice, until set.)
English Muffin, $^1/_2$ (1 ounce), toasted, with 2 teaspoons reduced-calorie tub margarine
Coffee or tea (optional)

LIGHT MEAL
Cheese Pizza, thin crust, 1 slice ($^1/_{12}$ th of 14–16" pie)
Carrot and Zucchini Sticks, 1 cup *each*
Torn Iceberg Lettuce Leaves, 2 cups, with $^1/_2$ cup chilled cooked artichoke hearts and 2 ounces drained cooked chick-peas and $1^1/_2$ teaspoons Italian dressing
Apple, 1 small
Diet Lemon Soda

MAIN MEAL
Oyster Bisque, 1 serving (see recipe)
Stuffed Baked Potato (Cut a lengthwise slit about 1" deep into 8-ounce baked potato, cutting to within $^1/_2$ " of each end; gently squeeze ends together until potato opens. Top potato pulp with $^1/_2$ cup cooked chopped broccoli and 1 tablespoon freshly grated Parmesan cheese; microwave on High [100% power] until heated through.)
Steamed Brussels Sprouts, 1 cup, sprinkled with 1 tablespoon fresh lemon juice
Sugar-Free Pineapple-Flavored Gelatin, $^1/_2$ cup, with 1 tablespoon thawed frozen light whipped topping (8 calories per tablespoon)
Sparkling Mineral Water

SNACK
Aspartame-Sweetened Strawberry-Banana Nonfat Yogurt, 1 cup

This menu provides: 2 Milks, 3 Fats, 2 Fruits, $13^1/_2$ Vegetables, $4^3/_4$ Proteins, $4^3/_4$ Breads, 80 Optional Calories.

Per serving: 25 g Fat, 29 g Fiber.

BREAKFAST

Frozen French Toast, 1 slice, heated, with 2 teaspoons maple syrup

Strawberry-Vanilla Yogurt (In small bowl, combine 1 cup *each* strawberries, sliced, and aspartame-sweetened vanilla nonfat yogurt.)

Coffee or Tea (optional)

LIGHT MEAL

Virginia Ham Platter (Roll 2 ounces cooked Virginia ham slices into cylinders. Line plate with 4 iceberg lettuce leaves; decoratively arrange ham rolls and 1 cup *each* cucumber and tomato slices on lettuce. Serve with 2 teaspoons horseradish mustard.)

Flatbreads, ³/₄ ounce

Sugar-Free Vanilla Nonfat Frozen Yogurt, 4 fluid ounces

Diet Cherry Cola

MAIN MEAL

Mexican Shrimp and Corn Chowder, 1 serving (see recipe)

Torn Romaine Lettuce Leaves, 2 cups, with ¹/₂ cup *each* jicama and red onion slices, 1 ounce sliced avocado and 1 tablespoon fat-free creamy Italian dressing

Roll, 1 ounce, with 2 teaspoons reduced-calorie tub margarine

Honeydew Melon, 2" wedge

Diet Root Beer

SNACK

Plain Popcorn, hot-air popped, 3 cups, with 2 teaspoons reduced-calorie tub margarine, melted

---

This menu provides: 2 Milks, 3 Fats, 2 Fruits, 11¹/₂ Vegetables, 4¹/₄ Proteins, 5 Breads, 110 Optional Calories.

Per serving: 28 g Fat, 23 g Fiber.

163

MEXICAN SHRIMP AND CORN CHOWDER

Queso fresco, a fresh Mexican cheese, is wonderful in this hearty soup; if unavailable, try goat or farmer's cheese.

Makes 4 servings

8 ounces deveined peeled medium shrimp (tails left on), reserve shells

¹/₂ cup chopped onion

1 garlic clove, halved

2 cups thawed frozen corn kernels

1¹/₂ cups evaporated skimmed milk

¹/₂ cup roasted red bell pepper, diced

¹/₄ cup diced deveined seeded poblano chile (wear gloves to prevent irritation)

1 tablespoon cornstarch

2 tablespoons minced fresh cilantro

¹/₄ teaspoon salt

1¹/₂ ounces queso fresco, crumbled

1. To prepare shrimp stock, rinse shrimp shells well under cold running water. In medium saucepan, combine shrimp shells, onion, garlic and 1¹/₂ cups water; bring liquid to a boil. Reduce heat to low; simmer, covered, 15 minutes.

2. Transfer shell mixture to food processor; purée 30 seconds, until shells are crushed.

3. Place fine sieve over 2- or 4-cup liquid measure; strain shell mixture through sieve, discarding solids. Liquid should measure 1 cup; if necessary, return liquid to saucepan and cook until reduced in volume to 1 cup.

4. In clean food processor, purée 1 cup of the corn.

5. In large saucepan, combine milk, bell pepper, chile, shrimp stock and pureed and whole-kernel corn; bring just to a simmer (do not boil). Cook, stirring frequently, 10 minutes, until flavors are blended.

6. Dissolve cornstarch in 2 tablespoons cold water; stir into milk mixture; cook, stirring constantly, until slightly thickened. Add shrimp; cook, stirring frequently, 2 minutes, until shrimp turn pink. Stir in cilantro and salt.

7. Divide shrimp mixture evenly among 4 bowls; top each portion with an equal amount of cheese.

Serving (1¹/₄ cups) provides: ³/₄ Milk, ¹/₂ Vegetable, 1¹/₄ Proteins, 1 Bread, 10 Optional Calories.

Per serving: 260 Calories, 4 g Total Fat, 2 g Saturated Fat, 98 mg Cholesterol, 444 mg Sodium, 33 g Total Carbohydrate, 2 g Dietary Fiber, 23 g Protein, 371 mg Calcium.

HERBED LEEK AND POTATO SOUP WITH RED SNAPPER

This hearty soup thickens upon standing; before reheating, add water, a few spoonfuls at a time, until the soup reaches the desired thickness.

Makes 4 servings

2 teaspoons olive oil
1 cup thinly sliced leeks (white portion only)
1 cup thinly sliced fennel
4 cups boiling water
10 ounces all-purpose potatoes, pared and cut into $^1/_2$" pieces
1 tablespoon minced fresh thyme leaves or 1 teaspoon dried
$^1/_2$ teaspoon salt
$^1/_4$ teaspoon ground white pepper
10 ounces red snapper fillets, cut into $1^1/_2 \times 1$" pieces
2 tablespoons minced fresh flat-leaf parsley
$^1/_4$ teaspoon hot pepper sauce

1. In large nonstick saucepan, heat oil; add leeks and fennel. Cook over medium-high heat, stirring frequently, 5 minutes, until vegetables are softened.

2. Add water, potatoes, thyme, salt and pepper to vegetable mixture; bring liquid to a boil. Reduce heat to low; simmer 15 minutes, until potatoes are just tender.

3. Add fish to potato mixture; stir to combine. Simmer 3 minutes, until fish flakes easily when tested with fork. Stir in parsley and hot pepper sauce.

Serving ($1^1/_2$ cups) provides: $^1/_2$ Fat, 1 Vegetable, 1 Protein, $^1/_2$ Bread.

Per serving: 169 Calories, 3 g Total Fat, 1 g Saturated Fat, 26 mg Cholesterol, 364 mg Sodium, 18 g Total Carbohydrate, 2 g Dietary Fiber, 17 g Protein, 68 mg Calcium.

BREAKFAST
Raspberries, Blueberries and Blackberries, $^1/_4$ cup *each*
Hard-Cooked Egg, 1
Cooked Whole Hominy, $^1/_2$ cup, with 1 teaspoon reduced-calorie tub margarine
Skim Milk, 1 cup
Coffee or Tea (optional)

LIGHT MEAL
BBQ Roast Beef Sandwich (Layer 2 ounces cooked lean boneless roast beef, thinly sliced, 2 tomato slices and 1 tablespoon barbecue sauce between 2 slices pumpernickel bread.)
Watercress and Sliced Radish Salad, 2 cups, with Dijon Vinaigrette (In small jar with tight-fitting lid or small bowl, combine 2 teaspoons rice wine vinegar, 1 teaspoon vegetable oil and $^1/_2$ teaspoon Dijon-style mustard; cover and shake well or, with wire whisk, blend until combined.)
Cucumber Salad (In small bowl, combine $^1/_2$ cup cucumber slices, 1 teaspoon *each* vegetable oil and rice wine vinegar and pinch ground white pepper.)
Sugar-Free Strawberry Nonfat Frozen Yogurt, 4 fluid ounces
Unsweetened Seltzer

MAIN MEAL
Herbed Leek and Potato Soup with Red Snapper, 1 serving (see recipe)
Cooked Broccoli, 4 spears, with 1 tablespoon fresh lemon juice
Tossed Green Salad, 2 cups, with 1 tablespoon fat-free Italian dressing
Flatbreads, $^3/_4$ ounce
Baked Apple (Preheat oven to 350° F. Pare 1 small apple halfway down from stem end; place into small baking dish. Sprinkle apple with 1 teaspoon granulated sugar and $^1/_4$ teaspoon cinnamon; add $^1/_4$" water to pan. Bake, covered, 30 minutes, until tender.)
Iced Herbal Tea with Mint Sprig

SNACK
Whole-Wheat Pretzels, $^3/_4$ ounce
Skim Milk, $^3/_4$ cup

This menu provides: 2 Milks, 3 Fats, 2 Fruits, $12^1/_2$ Vegetables, 4 Proteins, $5^1/_2$ Breads, 90 Optional Calories.

Per serving: 30 g Fat, 25 g Fiber.

BREAKFAST

Papaya, $^1/_2$ medium
Aspartame-Sweetened Vanilla Nonfat Yogurt, 1 cup
English Muffin, $^1/_2$ (1 ounce), toasted, with 2 teaspoons reduced-calorie tub margarine
Coffee or Tea (optional)

LIGHT MEAL

Turkey Pita (Split 1 large [2-ounce] pita halfway around edge; open to form pocket. Fill pita pocket with 2 ounces skinless boneless roast turkey breast, sliced, $^1/_2$ cup *each* spinach leaves and cucumber slices, 2 tomato slices and 2 teaspoons *each* reduced-calorie mayonnaise and prepared mustard.)
Carrot and Celery Sticks, 1 cup *each*
Seedless Red Grapes, 20 small or 12 large
Reduced-Calorie Chocolate Dairy Shake, 1 serving

MAIN MEAL

Groundnut Stew, 1 serving (see recipe)
Tossed Green Salad, 2 cups, with 1 tablespoon fatfree blue cheese dressing
Breadsticks, 2 long
Sugar-Free Raspberry-Flavored Gelatin, $^1/_2$ cup, with 1 tablespoon thawed frozen light whipped topping (8 calories per tablespoon)
Sparkling Mineral Water

SNACK

Buttery Popcorn (Lightly spray 3 cups hot-air popped plain popcorn with nonstick cooking spray. Sprinkle popcorn with $^1/_4$ teaspoon butterflavor granules; toss to coat evenly.)
Diet Cola

This menu provides: 2 Milks, 3 Fats, 2 Fruits, 12 Vegetables, 4 Proteins, $5^1/_2$ Breads, 40 Optional Calories.

Per serving: 31 g Fat, 24 g Fiber.

165

GROUNDNUT STEW

Try this unusual combination of flavors when you want something new and exciting. Since it thickens upon standing, before reheating add water, a few spoonfuls at a time, until the soup reaches the desired thickness.

Makes 4 servings

1 cup sliced onions
1 cup sliced red bell pepper
2 teaspoons finely chopped deveined seeded jalapeño pepper
  (wear gloves to prevent irritation)
2 garlic cloves, minced
2 cups low-sodium chicken broth
8 ounces sweet potatoes, pared and cut into $^3/_4$" pieces
$^1/_2$ teaspoon salt
$^1/_4$ teaspoon ground red pepper
$^1/_2$ cup boiling water
$^1/_4$ cup smooth peanut butter
10 ounces orange roughy fillets, cut into $1^1/_2 \times 1$" pieces
1 cup frozen sliced okra

1. In large saucepan, combine onions, bell pepper, jalapeño pepper, garlic and 2 tablespoons water; cook over low heat, covered, 2 minutes, until vegetables are softened and liquid is evaporated.

2. Add broth, sweet potatoes, salt and ground red pepper to vegetable mixture; bring liquid to a boil. Reduce heat to low; simmer, covered, 15 minutes, until sweet potato is just tender.

3. Meanwhile, in small bowl, combine boiling water and peanut butter, stirring until mixture is smooth.

4. Stir peanut butter mixture into sweet potato mixture, then stir in fish and okra; bring liquid to a boil. Reduce heat to low; simmer, covered, 10–12 minutes, until fish flakes easily when tested with fork.

Serving ($1^1/_4$ cups) provides: 1 Fat, $1^1/_2$ Vegetables, 2 Proteins, $^1/_2$ Bread, 10 Optional Calories.

Per serving: 297 Calories, 15 g Total Fat, 2 g Saturated Fat, 14 mg Cholesterol, 462 mg Sodium, 26 g Total Carbohydrate, 5 g Dietary Fiber, 19 g Protein, 83 mg Calcium.

166
FISH STEW AVGOLEMONO

*Red snapper fillets may be used in place of the halibut
in this hearty stew.*

Makes 4 servings

3 tablespoons all-purpose flour
$^1/_4$ teaspoon freshly ground black pepper
15 ounces boneless halibut steaks, cut into 1$^1/_2$" pieces
1 tablespoon + 1 teaspoon olive oil
1 cup slivered onions
4 garlic cloves, minced
10 ounces all-purpose potatoes, pared and cut into 1" pieces
2 cups sliced carrots ($^1/_2$" slices)
1 cup bottled clam juice
$^1/_4$ cup egg substitute
$^1/_4$ cup fresh lemon juice
Minced fresh dill, to garnish

1. On sheet of wax paper or paper plate, combine flour and pepper; add fish, turning to coat evenly. Set aside.

2. In large saucepan, heat 1 tablespoon of the oil; add fish. Cook over medium-high heat, turning as needed, 2–3 minutes, until fish is browned on all sides. Remove fish from saucepan; set aside.

3. In same saucepan, heat remaining 1 teaspoon oil; add onions and garlic. Cook over medium-high heat, stirring frequently, 5 minutes, until onions are softened. Add potatoes, carrots, juice and 2 cups water; bring liquid to a boil. Reduce heat to low; simmer, covered, 15 minutes, until potatoes are just tender.

4. Add browned fish to potato mixture; simmer, covered, 5 minutes, until fish flakes easily when tested with fork. With slotted spoon, remove solids from saucepan; set aside.

5. In medium bowl, with wire whisk, combine egg substitute and lemon juice; continuing to stir with whisk, slowly add $^1/_4$ cup clam juice mixture. Stirring constantly with wire whisk, slowly pour egg mixture into remaining clam juice mixture; cook over medium-low heat, stirring constantly, 4–5 minutes, until slightly thickened (do not boil).

6. Return solids to saucepan; cook, stirring occasionally, just until heated through. Serve garnished with dill.

Serving (1$^1/_2$ cups) provides: 1 Fat, 1$^1/_2$ Vegetables, 1$^3/_4$ Proteins, $^3/_4$ Bread, 5 Optional Calories.

Per serving: 292 Calories, 7 g Total Fat, 1 g Saturated Fat, 35 mg Cholesterol, 238 mg Sodium, 29 g Total Carbohydrate, 4 g Dietary Fiber, 28 g Protein, 100 mg Calcium.

BREAKFAST
Pineapple Yogurt (In small bowl, combine 1 cup aspartame-sweetened vanilla nonfat yogurt and $^1/_2$ cup drained canned pineapple chunks [no sugar added].)
Mini Bagel, 1 (1 ounce), split and toasted, with 1 teaspoon *each* peanut butter and apricot jam
Coffee or Tea (optional)

LIGHT MEAL
Egg Salad Sandwich (In small bowl, combine 1 hard-cooked egg, chopped, $^1/_4$ cup *each* chopped celery and minced red onion and 2 teaspoons reduced-calorie mayonnaise; spread between 2 slices reduced-calorie rye bread.)
Whole Radishes and Zucchini Sticks, 1 cup *each*
Plain Popcorn, hot-air popped, 3 cups
Unsweetened Lime-Flavored Seltzer

MAIN MEAL
Fish Stew Avgolemono, 1 serving (see recipe)
Torn Romaine Lettuce Leaves, 2 cups, with $^1/_2$ cup *each* sliced cucumber and red onion and 1 tablespoon fat-free Italian dressing
Pita, 1 small (1 ounce)
Orange, 1 small
Decaffeinated Coffee or Tea

SNACK
Reduced-Fat Cheddar Cheese, $^3/_4$ ounce
Fat-Free Crackers, 7
Skim Milk, 1 cup

This menu provides: 2 Milks, 3 Fats, 2 Fruits, 12$^1/_2$ Vegetables, 3$^3/_4$ Proteins, 5$^3/_4$ Breads, 25 Optional Calories.

Per serving: 27 g Fat, 21 g Fiber.

BREAKFAST

Cooked Oatmeal, $^1/_2$ cup, with 2 tablespoons raisins and 1 teaspoon firmly packed light or dark brown sugar
Skim Milk, 1 cup
Coffee or Tea (optional)

LIGHT MEAL

Smoked Turkey Pita (Cut small [1-ounce] whole-wheat pita in half crosswise; open to form 2 pockets. Fill each pocket with 1 ounce cooked skinless boneless smoked turkey breast, thinly sliced, 2 tomato slices, 1 Romaine lettuce leaf and 1 teaspoon reduced-calorie mayonnaise.)
Red Bell Pepper Strips and Zucchini Sticks, 1 cup *each*
Sugar-Free Vanilla Nonfat Frozen Yogurt, 4 fluid ounces
Diet Grape Ginger Ale

MAIN MEAL

Caldo Gallego with Sea Bass, 1 serving (see recipe)
Torn Iceberg and Romaine Lettuce Leaves, 2 cups, with $^1/_2$ cup *each* sliced mushrooms and cucumber and 1 tablespoon fat-free creamy Italian dressing
Semolina Roll, 1 ounce, with 1 teaspoon reduced-calorie tub margarine
Pear, 1 small
Sparkling Mineral Water with Lime Wedge

SNACK

Plain Popcorn, hot-air popped, 3 cups, with 2 teaspoons reduced-calorie tub margarine, melted
Skim Milk, $^3/_4$ cup

This menu provides: 2 Milks, 3 Fats, 2 Fruits, 13 Vegetables, $3^1/_4$ Proteins, $5^1/_4$ Breads, 90 Optional Calories.

Per serving: 23 g Fat, 21 g Fiber.

167
CALDO GALLEGO WITH SEA BASS

Makes 4 servings

2 teaspoons olive oil
$^1/_2$ cup chopped onion
4 garlic cloves, crushed
5 ounces all-purpose potato, pared and cut into $^1/_4$" pieces
1 cup canned whole tomatoes (no salt added), coarsely chopped
$^1/_2$ cup diced carrot ($^1/_4$" pieces)
2 packets low-sodium instant chicken broth and seasoning mix
$^1/_2$ teaspoon dried oregano leaves
1 small bay leaf
10 ounces sea bass fillets, cut into 1" strips
1 cup cooked chopped kale
2 ounces drained cooked chick-peas

1. In large saucepan, heat oil; add onion and garlic. Cook over medium-high heat, stirring frequently, 5 minutes, until onion is softened. Stir in potato, tomatoes, carrot, broth mix, oregano, bay leaf and 4 cups water; bring liquid to a boil. Reduce heat to low; simmer 30 minutes, until potato is very tender.

2. Add fish, kale and chick-peas to potato mixture; cook, stirring occasionally, 5 minutes, until fish flakes easily when tested with fork. Remove and discard bay leaf.

Serving ($1^3/_4$ cups) provides: $^1/_2$ Fat, $1^1/_2$ Vegetables, $1^1/_4$ Proteins, $^1/_4$ Bread, 5 Optional Calories.

Per serving: 187 Calories, 4 g Total Fat, 0 g Saturated Fat, 29 mg Cholesterol, 165 mg Sodium, 20 g Total Carbohydrate, 4 g Dietary Fiber, 17 g Protein, 73 mg Calcium.

168
GRILLED TUNA AND VEGETABLE SALAD

This recipe is great with swordfish, too!

Makes 4 servings

Twelve $1/4$" eggplant slices
$1/4$ teaspoon salt
2 tablespoons rice wine vinegar
1 tablespoon + 1 teaspoon oriental sesame oil
2 teaspoons sesame seeds
2 garlic cloves, minced
$1/4$ teaspoon ground red pepper
2 medium zucchini, cut into thin lengthwise slices
2 medium yellow bell peppers, seeded and quartered
Four 5-ounce boneless tuna steaks

1. Place eggplant slices in a single layer onto paper towels; sprinkle evenly with salt. Let stand 15 minutes; pat dry.

2. In small bowl, combine vinegar, oil, sesame seeds, garlic and ground red pepper; brush over one side of zucchini slices, bell pepper wedges, tuna steaks and dried eggplant slices.

3. Preheat outdoor barbecue grill or indoor stove-top grill according to manufacturer's directions.

4. Grill vegetables over hot coals or on stove-top grill, turning as needed, until tender. Remove vegetables from grill; keep warm.

5. Grill tuna, turning once, 6 minutes, until fish flakes easily when tested with fork. Serve tuna with grilled vegetables.

Serving (1 tuna steak, one-fourth of the vegetables) provides: 1 Fat, $2^3/4$ Vegetables, 2 Proteins, 10 Optional Calories.

Per serving: 289 Calories, 12 g Total Fat, 3 g Saturated Fat, 54 mg Cholesterol, 195 mg Sodium, 8 g Total Carbohydrate, 2 g Dietary Fiber, 35 g Protein, 46 mg Calcium.

BREAKFAST
Kiwi Fruit, 1 medium
Shredded Wheat Cereal, $3/4$ ounce
Skim Milk, 1 cup
Coffee or Tea (optional)

LIGHT MEAL
Ham and Cheese Sandwich (Layer 1 ounce cooked Virginia Ham, sliced, 1 slice nonfat process Swiss cheese, $1/2$ cup drained chopped roasted red bell pepper, $1/4$ cup radish sprouts and 1 teaspoon Dijon-style mustard between 2 slices reduced-calorie multi-grain bread.)
Carrot and Celery Sticks, 1 cup *each*
Vanilla Wafers, 3
Skim Milk, 1 cup

MAIN MEAL
Low-Sodium Mixed Vegetable Juice, 1 cup
Grilled Tuna and Vegetable Salad, 1 serving (see recipe)
Steamed New Potatoes, 4 ounces, with 2 teaspoons *each* minced fresh flat-leaf parsley and reduced-calorie tub margarine
Flatbreads, $3/4$ ounce
Apricots, 3 medium
Unsweetened Citrus-Flavored Seltzer

SNACK
Mini Bagel, 1 (1 ounce), split and toasted, with 1 teaspoon *each* peanut butter and apricot jam

This menu provides: 2 Milks, 3 Fats, 2 Fruits, $10^1/4$ Vegetables, $3^1/2$ Proteins, $5^1/2$ Breads, 50 Optional Calories.

Per serving: 27 g Fat, 27 g Fiber.

169
WARM TUNA-SPINACH SALAD WITH ASIAN FLAVORS

Makes 4 servings

8 cups packed chopped trimmed well-washed spinach leaves
1 cup sliced mushrooms
$^3/_4$ cup drained canned water chestnuts
$^1/_4$ cup sliced scallions
15 ounces boneless tuna steaks
2 teaspoons vegetable oil
$^1/_4$ cup rice wine vinegar
2 tablespoons reduced-sodium soy sauce
2 teaspoons oriental sesame oil
1 teaspoon granulated sugar
1 slice pared fresh ginger root

1. In large bowl, combine spinach, mushrooms, water chestnuts and scallions; set aside.

2. Brush tuna on both sides with 1 teaspoon of the vegetable oil.

3. Heat large nonstick skillet; add tuna. Cook over medium-high heat, turning once, 1–2 minutes, until fish flakes easily when tested with fork. Transfer tuna to cutting board; cut into $^1/_2$" strips. Set aside; keep warm.

4. To prepare dressing, in same skillet, combine vinegar, soy sauce, sesame oil, sugar, ginger, remaining 1 teaspoon vegetable oil and $^1/_3$ cup water; bring liquid to a boil. Remove and discard ginger. Pour dressing over spinach mixture; toss until spinach is wilted.

5. Divide spinach mixture evenly among 4 plates; top each with one-fourth of the warm tuna.

Serving (2 cups spinach mixture, 3 ounces tuna) provides: 1 Fat, $4^3/_4$ Vegetables, $1^1/_2$ Proteins, $^1/_4$ Bread, 5 Optional Calories.

Per serving: 258 Calories, 10 g Total Fat, 2 g Saturated Fat, 40 mg Cholesterol, 458 mg Sodium, 13 g Total Carbohydrate, 5 g Dietary Fiber, 30 g Protein, 146 mg Calcium.

170

Swordfish, Asparagus and Endive Salad

Makes 4 servings

2 tablespoons olive oil
2 teaspoons grated lemon zest*
2 tablespoons fresh lemon juice
1 tablespoon minced fresh tarragon leaves
1 tablespoon finely minced chives
12 asparagus spears
Four 5-ounce boneless swordfish steaks
1 1/2 cups watercress leaves
1 medium Belgian endive, leaves separated

1. To prepare dressing, in small jar with tight-fitting lid or small bowl, combine oil, zest, juice, tarragon, chives and 2 tablespoons water; cover and shake well or, with wire whisk, blend until combined. Set aside.

2. In large pot of boiling water, cook asparagus 3 minutes, until just tender. Drain, discarding liquid; set aside.

3. Preheat outdoor barbecue grill or indoor stove-top grill according to manufacturer's directions.

4. Grill swordfish over hot coals or on stove-top grill, turning once, 6 minutes, until fish flakes easily when tested with fork.

5. Divide watercress, endive, cooked asparagus and grilled swordfish evenly among 4 plates; drizzle evenly with dressing.

Serving (1 swordfish steak, one-fourth of the vegetables, 1 tablespoon dressing) provides: 1 1/2 Fats, 1 3/4 Vegetables, 2 Proteins.

Per serving: 254 Calories, 13 g Total Fat, 3 g Saturated Fat, 57 mg Cholesterol, 139 mg Sodium, 4 g Total Carbohydrate, 1 g Dietary Fiber, 31 g Protein, 37 mg Calcium.

The zest of the lemon is the peel without any of the pith (white membrane). To remove zest from lemon, use a zester or the fine side of a vegetable grater.

BREAKFAST
Papaya, 1/2 medium
Frozen Waffle, 1, heated, with 2 teaspoons maple syrup and 1 teaspoon reduced-calorie tub margarine
Skim Milk, 1 cup
Coffee or Tea (optional)

LIGHT MEAL
Grilled Cheese and Tomato Sandwich (Toast 2 slices reduced-calorie rye bread; top each with 1/2 medium tomato, sliced, and 1 slice nonfat process American cheese. Place onto nonstick baking sheet; broil 1–2 minutes, until heated.)
Shredded Green and Red Cabbage, 1 cup, with 1 tablespoon fat-free peppercorn ranch dressing
Cucumber Sticks and Whole Radishes, 1 cup *each*
Reduced-Calorie Chocolate-Flavored Pudding (made with skim milk), 1/2 cup
Diet Black Cherry Soda

MAIN MEAL
Swordfish, Asparagus and Endive Salad, 1 serving (see recipe)
Steamed New Potatoes, 4 ounces, with 1 tablespoon minced fresh parsley
Steamed Baby Carrots, 1 cup
Flatbreads, 3/4 ounce
Raspberries, 3/4 cup
Unsweetened Lime-Flavored Seltzer

SNACK
Reduced-Fat Cheddar Cheese, 3/4 ounce
Fat-Free Crackers, 7
Skim Milk, 1/2 cup

This menu provides: 2 Milks, 3 Fats, 2 Fruits, 11 3/4 Vegetables, 4 Proteins, 5 Breads, 90 Optional Calories.

Per serving: 27 g Fat, 27 g Fiber.

BREAKFAST

Banana, $^1/_2$ medium, sliced
Crispy Rice Cereal, $^3/_4$ ounce
Skim Milk, 1 cup
Coffee or Tea (optional)

LIGHT MEAL

Tomato Soup, canned, 1 cup, with 20 oyster crackers
Cheese and Veggie Sandwich (Layer $^1/_4$ cup *each*
alfalfa sprouts, spinach leaves and drained roasted
red bell pepper strips, 1 slice nonfat process Swiss
cheese and 1 tablespoon fat-free Thousand Island
dressing between 2 slices reduced-calorie whole-
wheat bread.)
Carrot and Cucumber Sticks, 1 cup *each*
Aspartame-Sweetened Raspberry Nonfat Yogurt,
1 cup
Sparkling Mineral Water

MAIN MEAL

Steamed Artichoke, 1 medium, with Lemon
Vinaigrette (In small jar with tight-fitting lid or
small bowl, combine 1 tablespoon cider vinegar,
1 teaspoon olive oil and $^1/_2$ teaspoon grated lemon
zest; cover and shake well or, with wire whisk,
blend until combined.)
Greek Shrimp Salad, 1 serving (see recipe)
Roll, 1 ounce
Sugar-Free Orange-Flavored Gelatin, $^1/_2$ cup, with
1 tablespoon thawed frozen light whipped topping (8 calories per tablespoon)
Iced Tea with Mint Sprig

SNACK

Peanut Butter–Raisin Crackers (Spread 3 graham
crackers [$2^1/_2$" squares] with 1 tablespoon peanut
butter; sprinkle with 2 tablespoons raisins.)

This menu provides: 2 Milks, 3 Fats, 2 Fruits,
$9^1/_2$ Vegetables, $3^1/_2$ Proteins, 5 Breads, 85 Optional
Calories.

Per serving: 33 g Fat, 24 g Fiber.

GREEK SHRIMP SALAD

Makes 4 servings

15 ounces medium shrimp, peeled and deveined
1 lemon slice
2 tablespoons fresh lemon juice
1 tablespoon olive oil
1 tablespoon minced fresh oregano leaves, or $^1/_2$ teaspoon dried
2 teaspoons minced fresh mint leaves
1 garlic clove, minced
$1^1/_2$ cups torn chicory leaves
$1^1/_2$ cups torn Romaine lettuce leaves
2 large plum tomatoes, cut into thin wedges
2 tablespoons minced scallions
6 large kalamata olives, pitted and thinly sliced
$1^1/_2$ ounces feta cheese, crumbled

1. In large saucepan, bring 1 quart water to a boil; add shrimp and lemon slice. Bring liquid to a boil; reduce heat to low. Simmer 1–2 minutes, until shrimp turn pink. Drain, discarding liquid and lemon slice; set aside.

2. To prepare dressing, in small jar with tight-fitting lid or small bowl, combine juice, oil, oregano, mint, garlic and 1 tablespoon water; cover and shake well or, with wire whisk, blend until combined.

3. Pour 2 tablespoons of the dressing over cooked shrimp; toss to combine. Refrigerate, covered, until chilled.

4. To prepare salad, in large bowl, combine chicory, Romaine lettuce, tomatoes, scallions, olives and chilled shrimp. Pour remaining dressing over salad; toss to coat. Serve sprinkled with cheese.

Serving ($1^1/_2$ cups) provides: 1 Fat, 1 Vegetable, 2 Proteins.

Per serving: 221 Calories, 11 g Total Fat, 3 g Saturated Fat, 171 mg Cholesterol, 439 mg Sodium, 9 g Total Carbohydrate, 2 g Dietary Fiber, 25 g Protein, 193 mg Calcium.

172
LOBSTER NIÇOISE

Makes 4 servings

1 pound 4 ounces small new potatoes
2 cups whole green beans
4 cups thinly sliced Romaine lettuce leaves
12 ounces cooked shelled lobster, cut into chunks
24 cherry tomatoes, halved
$1/4$ cup balsamic vinegar
2 tablespoons fresh lemon juice
1 tablespoon + 1 teaspoon olive oil
1 tablespoon minced fresh tarragon leaves
$1/4$ teaspoon salt
$1/4$ teaspoon freshly ground black pepper

1. Place potatoes into large saucepan; add water to cover. Bring liquid to a boil; reduce heat to low. Simmer 12–15 minutes, until potatoes are tender. With slotted spoon, remove potatoes from saucepan. Rinse with cold water; drain. Refrigerate, covered, until chilled.

2. Meanwhile, in same pot of boiling water, cook green beans 3 minutes, until bright green and just tender. Drain, discarding liquid. Rinse with cold water; drain again. Refrigerate, covered, until chilled.

3. To assemble salad, line serving platter with lettuce leaves. Cut potatoes into halves; arrange potatoes, green beans, lobster and tomatoes on lettuce.

4. To prepare dressing, in small jar with tight-fitting lid or small bowl, combine vinegar, juice, oil, tarragon, salt and pepper; cover and shake well or, with wire whisk, blend until combined. Pour dressing over salad.

Serving (one-fourth of salad, 2 tablespoons dressing) provides: 1 Fat, 4 Vegetables, $1^1/2$ Proteins, 1 Bread.

Per serving: 281 Calories, 6 g Total Fat, 1 g Saturated Fat, 61 mg Cholesterol, 483 mg Sodium, 36 g Total Carbohydrate, 5 g Dietary Fiber, 23 g Protein, 101 mg Calcium.

BREAKFAST
Kiwi Fruit, 1 medium
Raisin Bran Cereal, $3/4$ ounce
Skim Milk, $1/2$ cup
Coffee or Tea (optional)

LIGHT MEAL
Smoked Chicken Sandwich (Layer 2 ounces skinless boneless smoked chicken breast, sliced, 2 iceberg lettuce leaves, $1/4$ cup radish sprouts and 2 teaspoons reduced-calorie mayonnaise between 2 slices reduced-calorie multi-grain bread.)
Cucumber Salad (In small bowl, combine $1/2$ cup cucumber slices, 1 teaspoon *each* vegetable oil and rice wine vinegar and pinch ground white pepper.)
Celery and Carrot Sticks, 1 cup *each*
Aspartame-Sweetened Black Cherry Nonfat Yogurt, 1 cup
Iced Tea

MAIN MEAL
Lobster Niçoise, 1 serving (see recipe)
Flatbreads, $1^1/2$ ounces
Reduced-Calorie Butterscotch-Flavored Pudding (made with skim milk), $1/2$ cup
Sparkling Mineral Water with Mint Sprig

SNACK
Papaya, $1/2$ medium

This menu provides: 2 Milks, 3 Fats, 2 Fruits, 10 Vegetables, $3^1/2$ Proteins, 5 Breads, 40 Optional Calories.

Per serving: 21 g Fat, 30 g Fiber.

ORIENTAL SEAFOOD-PASTA SALAD

For even more Asian flavor, try using your favorite oriental noodle in place of the angel hair pasta in this salad.

Makes 4 servings

2 tablespoons reduced-sodium soy sauce
2 teaspoons oriental sesame oil
1 teaspoon granulated sugar
1 teaspoon grated pared fresh ginger root
1 teaspoon rice wine vinegar
$^1/_2$ cup snow peas
$^1/_2$ cup thinly sliced red bell pepper
$^1/_2$ cup cut asparagus (2" pieces)
$^1/_2$ cup julienned carrot
6 ounces angel hair pasta (capellini)
8 ounces cooked medium or large shrimp, peeled and deveined
$^1/_2$ cup drained canned baby corn, halved lengthwise

1. In small bowl, combine soy sauce, oil, sugar, ginger and vinegar, stirring until sugar is dissolved; set aside.

2. In large pot of boiling water, cook snow peas, bell pepper and asparagus 1–2 minutes, until colors are bright and vegetables are just tender. With slotted spoon, transfer vegetables to bowl of ice water; set aside.

3. In same pot of boiling water, cook carrot 1 minute, until bright orange and just tender; with slotted spoon, transfer to same bowl of ice water; set aside.

4. In same pot of boiling water, cook pasta 3 minutes, until tender. Drain, discarding liquid; rinse with cold water. Drain again; transfer to large bowl.

5. Add soy sauce mixture to pasta; toss to combine. Drain vegetables, patting dry with paper towels; add vegetables, shrimp and corn to pasta mixture; toss again.

Serving (1 cup) provides: $^1/_2$ Fat, 1 Vegetable, 1 Protein, $2^1/_4$ Breads, 5 Optional Calories.

Per serving: 268 Calories, 4 g Total Fat, 1 g Saturated Fat, 111 mg Cholesterol, 439 mg Sodium, 38 g Total Carbohydrate, 3 g Dietary Fiber, 19 g Protein, 54 mg Calcium.

BREAKFAST
Banana, $^1/_2$ medium, sliced
Fortified Cold Cereal, $^3/_4$ ounce
Skim Milk, $^1/_2$ cup
Coffee or Tea (optional)

LIGHT MEAL
Grilled Cheese and Tomato Sandwich (Split and toast one 2-ounce English muffin. Top one muffin half with $^3/_4$ ounce reduced-fat cheddar cheese; top the other muffin half with $^1/_2$ medium tomato, sliced. Place onto nonstick baking sheet; broil until heated through. Place cheese-topped muffin half onto tomato slices, cheese-side down.)
Carrot and Celery Sticks, 1 cup *each*
Reduced-Calorie Butterscotch-Flavored Pudding (made with skim milk), $^1/_2$ cup
Diet Black Cherry Soda

MAIN MEAL
Oriental Seafood-Pasta Salad, 1 serving (see recipe)
Stir-Fried Vegetables (In nonstick skillet or wok, heat $1^1/_2$ teaspoons oriental sesame oil; add 1 cup *each* cubed pared eggplant, bean sprouts and sliced radishes. Cook over medium-high heat, stirring constantly, 2–3 minutes, until vegetables are tender; sprinkle with 2 teaspoons rice wine vinegar.)
Pineapple, $^1/_8$ medium
Chinese Tea

SNACK
Rice Cake, 1, with 1 tablespoon peanut butter
Reduced-Calorie Vanilla Dairy Shake, 1 serving

This menu provides: 2 Milks, 3 Fats, 2 Fruits, 12 Vegetables, 3 Proteins, $5^3/_4$ Breads, 45 Optional Calories.

Per serving: 27 g Fat, 21 g Fiber.

CUBAN COD, RICE AND BEAN SALAD

Serve this salad chilled or at room temperature.

Makes 4 servings

4 ounces long-grain rice
10 ounces cod fillets
2 tablespoons canola oil
2 tablespoons sherry wine vinegar
1/2 teaspoon ground cumin
1/4 teaspoon salt
1/4 teaspoon ground red pepper
8 ounces drained cooked black beans
1/2 cup diced red onion
1/2 cup diced green bell pepper
2 cups arugula leaves
2 small navel oranges, peeled and cut into 6 slices each

1. In medium saucepan, bring 1 1/2 cups water to a boil; add rice. Reduce heat to low; simmer, covered, 15–20 minutes, until rice is tender and all liquid is absorbed. Remove from heat; set aside to cool.

2. Meanwhile, in large nonstick skillet, bring 3 cups water to a boil. Reduce heat to low; add cod fillets. Poach cod 8–9 minutes, until fish flakes easily when tested with fork.

3. With slotted spatula, transfer cod to paper towels to drain.

4. To prepare dressing, in small jar with tight-fitting lid or small bowl, combine oil, vinegar, cumin, salt and ground red pepper; cover and shake well or, with wire whisk, blend until combined.

5. In large bowl, combine beans, onion, bell pepper and cooled rice. Pour dressing over bean mixture; toss lightly to combine. If desired, refrigerate, covered, until chilled.

6. Divide arugula evenly among 4 plates; top each portion with one-fourth of the bean mixture. Flake cod; top each portion of bean mixture with one-fourth of the cod. Place 3 orange slices onto each plate alongside salad.

Serving (1/2 cup arugula, 1 cup bean mixture, 2 ounces cod, 3 orange slices) provides: 1 1/2 Fats, 1/2 Fruit, 1 1/2 Vegetables, 2 Proteins, 1 Bread.

Per serving: 339 Calories, 8 g Total Fat, 1 g Saturated Fat, 30 mg Cholesterol, 186 mg Sodium, 46 g Total Carbohydrate, 4 g Dietary Fiber, 21 g Protein, 88 mg Calcium.

PANZANELLA

Makes 4 servings

4 ounces Italian bread, thickly sliced
1 garlic clove, halved
2 cups chopped plum tomatoes
6 ounces skim-milk mozzarella cheese, diced
2 tablespoons minced fresh flat-leaf parsley
1 tablespoon rinsed drained capers
2 tablespoons balsamic vinegar
1 tablespoon + 1 teaspoon olive oil
2 anchovy fillets, mashed
$^1/_4$ teaspoon salt
$^1/_4$ teaspoon freshly ground black pepper

1. Preheat oven to 400° F.

2. Rub bread on all sides with cut side of garlic; cut bread into cubes. Place bread cubes onto nonstick baking sheet; bake 7 minutes, until crispy.

3. In large bowl, combine tomatoes, cheese, parsley, capers and baked bread cubes. In small jar with tight-fitting lid or small bowl, combine vinegar, oil, anchovies, salt and pepper; cover and shake well or, with wire whisk, blend until combined. Pour over tomato mixture; toss to combine.

Serving ($1^1/_3$ cups) provides: 1 Fat, 1 Vegetable, 1 Protein, 1 Bread, 5 Optional Calories.

Per serving: 203 Calories, 6 g Total Fat, 1 g Saturated Fat, 9 mg Cholesterol, 799 mg Sodium, 21 g Total Carbohydrate, 2 g Dietary Fiber, 16 g Protein, 262 mg Calcium.

BREAKFAST

Honeydew Melon, 2" wedge
Cheddar Omelet (Spray small nonstick skillet with nonstick cooking spray; heat. Pour $^1/_4$ cup egg substitute into skillet, tilting to cover bottom of pan. Cook over medium-high heat until underside is set, lifting edges with spatula to let uncooked egg flow underneath. Sprinkle $^3/_4$ ounce reduced-fat cheddar cheese, grated, evenly over one side of omelet; with spatula, fold other side over cheese to enclose.)
Reduced-Calorie Whole-Wheat Bread, 2 slices, toasted, with 2 teaspoons reduced-calorie tub margarine
Skim Milk, 1 cup
Coffee or Tea (optional)

LIGHT MEAL

Nonfat Cottage Cheese, $^1/_2$ cup, with 6 dried apricot halves, diced
Crispbreads, $1^1/_2$ ounces
Iced Tea with Mint Leaves

MAIN MEAL

Panzanella, 1 serving (see recipe)
Chick-Peas with Roasted Red Pepper (In small bowl, combine 1 medium drained roasted red bell pepper, sliced, 2 ounces drained canned chick-peas and $1^1/_2$ teaspoons Italian dressing.)
Roll, 1 ounce
Reduced-Calorie Chocolate-Flavored Pudding (made with skim milk), $^1/_2$ cup
Sparkling Mineral Water

SNACK

Vanilla "Egg Cream" (In tall glass, combine 1 cup diet cream soda and $^1/_2$ cup skim milk.)

This menu provides: 2 Milks, 3 Fats, 2 Fruits, 3 Vegetables, 5 Proteins, 5 Breads, 45 Optional Calories.

Per serving: 25 g Fat, 22 g Fiber.

176
SARDINE SALAD PLATTER

Makes 2 servings

2 tablespoons minced fresh mint leaves
2 tablespoons fresh lemon juice
1 tablespoon + 1 teaspoon olive oil
Pinch salt
1 cup arugula leaves
6 Belgian endive leaves
6 radicchio leaves
6 cucumber ribbons*
2 ounces drained canned water-packed skinless boneless sardines
1 hard-cooked egg, halved
2 teaspoons finely diced red onion

1. To prepare dressing, in small jar with tight-fitting lid or small bowl, combine mint, juice, oil, salt and 2 tablespoons water; cover and shake well or, with wire whisk, blend until combined.

2. Arrange $^1/_2$ cup arugula, 3 endive and radicchio leaves, 3 cucumber ribbons, 1 ounce sardines and 1 egg half on each of 2 plates; sprinkle each with 1 teaspoon onion and half of the dressing.

Serving (1 salad) provides: 2 Fats, 1$^3/_4$ Vegetables, 1$^1/_2$ Proteins.

Per serving: 229 Calories, 20 g Total Fat, 4 g Saturated Fat, 146 mg Cholesterol, 130 mg Sodium, 4 g Total Carbohydrate, 1 g Dietary Fiber, 10 g Protein, 127 mg Calcium.

To make cucumber ribbons, pare 1 medium cucumber. Run vegetable peeler lengthwise down one side of cucumber; continue on same side of cucumber until seeds are visible. Turn cucumber; repeat. Discard seeds.

Chicken Club Sandwiches

To streamline your time, toast the bread in the oven (why wait for the toaster?) while you slice the sandwich ingredients.

Makes 4 servings

12 slices reduced-calorie whole-wheat bread
1 tablespoon + 1 teaspoon Dijon-style mustard
2 teaspoons imitation bacon bits
1 medium tomato, thinly sliced
4 Romaine lettuce leaves
12 ounces skinless boneless cooked chicken breasts, sliced
4 ounces pared avocado, thinly sliced
$^{1}/_{2}$ cup alfalfa sprouts

1. Preheat oven to 400° F.

2. Place bread slices directly onto oven rack; bake, turning once, 3–4 minutes, until lightly toasted on both sides.

3. Spread 4 toast slices with 1 teaspoon mustard each.

4. To assemble sandwiches, place mustard-spread toast slices, spread-side up, onto work surface; sprinkle each with one-fourth of the bacon bits. Top each with one-fourth of the tomato slices, 1 lettuce leaf, another toast slice, one-fourth of the chicken, avocado and alfalfa sprouts and 1 remaining toast slice. Cut each sandwich diagonally into 4 triangles; secure triangles with toothpicks.

Serving (4 triangles) provides: 1 Fat, 1 Vegetable, 3 Proteins, 1$^{1}/_{2}$ Breads, 5 Optional Calories.

Per serving: 341 Calories, 9 g Total Fat, 2 g Saturated Fat, 72 mg Cholesterol, 518 mg Sodium, 35 g Total Carbohydrate, 9 g Dietary Fiber, 35 g Protein, 81 mg Calcium.

BREAKFAST
Orange Sections, $^{1}/_{2}$ cup
Bagel, $^{1}/_{2}$ small (1 ounce), toasted, with 1 tablespoon nonfat cream cheese
Aspartame-Sweetened Vanilla Nonfat Yogurt, 1 cup
Coffee or Tea (optional)

LIGHT MEAL
Chicken Club Sandwiches, 1 serving (see recipe)
Carrot and Cucumber Sticks, 1 cup *each*, with Yogurt-Cilantro Dip (In small bowl, combine $^{1}/_{2}$ cup plain nonfat yogurt, 1 tablespoon minced fresh cilantro and pinch garlic powder.)
Strawberries, 1 cup
Iced Tea with Mint Sprig

MAIN MEAL
Tuna Salad Pita (In small bowl, combine 4 ounces drained canned water-packed tuna, $^{1}/_{4}$ cup *each* chopped onion and celery, 2 teaspoons reduced-calorie mayonnaise and $^{1}/_{4}$ teaspoon lemon-pepper seasoning. Cut large (2-ounce) whole-wheat pita in half, crosswise; open to form 2 pockets. Fill each pocket with half of the tuna mixture; top each portion of tuna with $^{1}/_{4}$ cup alfalfa sprouts.)
Celery Sticks and Broccoli Florets, 1 cup *each*
Sugar-Free Cherry-Flavored Gelatin, $^{1}/_{2}$ cup
Diet Lemon-Lime Soda

SNACK
Plain Popcorn, hot-air popped, 3 cups, with 2 teaspoons reduced-calorie margarine, melted
Root Beer "Float" (In tall glass, combine 1 cup diet root beer and $^{1}/_{3}$ cup skim milk; add enough ice cubes to fill glass.)

This menu provides: 2 Milks, 3 Fats, 2 Fruits, 11 Vegetables, 5 Proteins, 5$^{1}/_{2}$ Breads, 30 Optional Calories.

Per serving: 21 g Fat, 36 g Fiber.

POULTRY

This menu provides: 2 Milks, 3 Fats, 2 Fruits,
$14^3/_4$ Vegetables, 5 Proteins, 6 Breads, 100 Optional
Calories.

Per serving: 27 g Fat, 25 g Fiber.

Serving (1 sandwich, 4 tomato wedges) provides:
1 Fat, $2^1/_4$ Vegetables, 2 Proteins, 2 Breads,
25 Optional Calories.

Per serving: 329 Calories, 7 g Total Fat,
1 g Saturated Fat, 41 mg Cholesterol,
812 mg Sodium, 37 g Total Carbohydrate,
3 g Dietary Fiber, 23 g Protein,
76 mg Calcium.

178
WARM POACHED CHICKEN ON BAGUETTE WITH MINT SALSA

Makes 4 servings

One 8-ounce baguette (long, crusty
    bread roll), about 12 × 2"
2 tablespoons minced shallots
1 medium minced deveined seeded
    jalapeño pepper (wear gloves to
    prevent irritation)
2 garlic cloves, minced
$^3/_4$ teaspoon salt
$^1/_4$ teaspoon freshly ground black
    pepper
4 large ripe plum tomatoes, seeded
    and coarsely chopped
$^1/_4$ cup minced fresh mint leaves
1 tablespoon + 1 teaspoon olive oil
1 tablespoon white wine vinegar
8 fluid ounces (1 cup) dry light
    white wine
5 whole black peppercorns
2 bay leaves
10 ounces skinless boneless chicken
    breasts
12 Bibb or Boston lettuce leaves
2 large ripe plum tomatoes, each
    cut lengthwise in 8 wedges

1. Preheat oven to 350° F. Adjust oven rack to divide oven in half.

2. With serrated knife, split baguette almost through horizontally; cut vertically into 4 equal pieces. Keeping baguette together, wrap tightly in foil; bake in center of oven 15 minutes, until heated through. Remove from oven; keep warm.

3. To prepare salsa, in medium bowl, combine shallots, jalapeño pepper, garlic, $^1/_4$ teaspoon of the salt and the black pepper. Add chopped tomatoes, mint, oil and vinegar; toss to combine. Let stand 15 minutes, until flavors are blended.

4. Meanwhile, in large skillet, combine wine, peppercorns, bay leaves, remaining $^1/_2$ teaspoon salt and 2 cups water; bring liquid to a boil. Add chicken; return liquid to a boil. Reduce heat to low; poach chicken, covered, 10 minutes, until cooked through. With slotted spoon, remove chicken from liquid; discard liquid, peppercorns and bay leaves. Let chicken stand 5 minutes.

5. Slice warm chicken into $^1/_4$" slices.

6. To assemble sandwiches, place 1 baguette quarter onto each of 4 plates. Line cut side of each baguette quarter with 3 lettuce leaves; top each portion of lettuce with 2 ounces of the sliced chicken and one-fourth of the salsa. Serve with tomato wedges.

CHICKEN TACO SANDWICHES

There are so many contrasting tastes and textures in these sandwiches—spicy chicken, cool tomatoes, crisp lettuce—that you won't miss the beef.

Makes 4 servings

10 ounces skinless boneless chicken breasts
2 garlic cloves, minced
$^3/_4$ teaspoon dried oregano leaves
$^3/_4$ teaspoon ground cumin
Four 2-ounce French or kaiser rolls, split
$^1/_4$ cup medium or hot salsa
2 cups shredded iceberg lettuce leaves
2 cups diced tomatoes
$1^1/_2$ ounces reduced-fat cheddar cheese, grated
$^1/_4$ cup nonfat sour cream

1. In medium saucepan, combine chicken, garlic, oregano, cumin and 1 cup water; bring liquid to a boil. Reduce heat to low; simmer, covered, turning chicken occasionally, 10–12 minutes, until chicken is cooked through and juices run clear when pierced with fork. With slotted spoon, remove chicken from saucepan; reserve cooking liquid. Set chicken aside to cool.

2. With fork, shred cooled chicken.

3. Cook reserved cooking liquid over high heat 1–2 minutes, until reduced in volume to about $^1/_4$ cup. Add shredded chicken; stir to coat. Remove from heat.

4. To assemble sandwiches, place 1 roll bottom onto each of 4 plates. Spread each with 1 tablespoon salsa; top each with one-fourth of the chicken mixture, lettuce, tomatoes and cheese, 1 tablespoon sour cream and 1 roll top.

Serving (1 sandwich) provides: $2^1/_4$ Vegetables, $2^1/_2$ Proteins, 2 Breads, 10 Optional Calories.

Per serving: 307 Calories, 5 g Total Fat, 2 g Saturated Fat, 49 mg Cholesterol, 655 mg Sodium, 37 g Total Carbohydrate, 3 g Dietary Fiber, 27 g Protein, 197 mg Calcium.

BREAKFAST
Raspberries, $^3/_4$ cup
Shredded Wheat Cereal, $^3/_4$ ounce
Skim Milk, $^1/_2$ cup
Coffee or Tea (optional)

LIGHT MEAL
Chicken Taco Sandwiches, 1 serving (see recipe)
Cooked Brown Rice, 1 cup
Cooked Sliced Zucchini and Yellow Squash, 1 cup *each*, with 1 teaspoon reduced-calorie tub margarine
Chicory and Shredded Carrot Salad, 2 cups, with 1 tablespoon fat-free ranch dressing
Reduced-Calorie Chocolate-Flavored Pudding (made with skim milk), $^1/_2$ cup
Iced Tea

MAIN MEAL
Spinach–Chick-Pea Salad (In medium bowl, combine 2 cups torn spinach leaves, 4 ounces drained cooked chick-peas, 6 cherry tomatoes, halved, $^1/_4$ cup diced red onion and 1 tablespoon Italian dressing.)
Whole-Wheat Roll, 1 ounce, with 1 teaspoon reduced-calorie tub margarine
Seedless Green Grapes, 20 small or 12 large
Sparkling Mineral Water

SNACK
Aspartame-Sweetened Lemon Nonfat Yogurt, 1 cup

This menu provides: 2 Milks, 3 Fats, 2 Fruits, $15^3/_4$ Vegetables, $4^1/_2$ Proteins, 6 Breads, 70 Optional Calories.

Per serving: 26 g Fat, 38 g Fiber.

180
CAJUN CHICKEN SANDWICH

Makes 4 servings

Four 2-ounce soft rolls, split
$^{1}/_{2}$ teaspoon ground cumin
$^{1}/_{2}$ teaspoon garlic powder
$^{1}/_{2}$ teaspoon salt
$^{1}/_{2}$ teaspoon freshly ground black pepper
$^{1}/_{2}$ teaspoon dried thyme leaves
$^{1}/_{4}$ teaspoon paprika
Pinch ground red pepper
10 ounces skinless boneless chicken breasts
2 tablespoons + 2 teaspoons reduced-calorie mayonnaise
2 medium tomatoes, sliced
$^{1}/_{2}$ cup thinly sliced red onion

1. Preheat oven to 350° F. Adjust oven rack to divide oven in half.

2. Wrap rolls in foil; bake in center of oven 8–10 minutes, until heated through. Remove from oven; keep warm.

3. Meanwhile, in cup or small bowl, combine cumin, garlic powder, salt, black pepper, thyme, paprika and ground red pepper.

4. Place chicken breasts, skinned-side down, between 2 sheets of wax paper; with meat mallet or bottom of heavy saucepan, pound chicken until $^{1}/_{2}$" thick. Remove and discard wax paper. Sprinkle chicken on both sides with all but $^{1}/_{4}$ teaspoon of the cumin mixture; spray lightly with nonstick cooking spray.

5. Spray large nonstick skillet with nonstick cooking spray; heat. Add chicken; cook over medium-high heat, turning once, 6 minutes, until cooked through and juices run clear when pierced with fork. Transfer chicken to cutting board; let stand 5 minutes.

6. Thinly slice chicken; set aside.

7. Add mayonnaise to reserved $^{1}/_{4}$ teaspoon cumin mixture; stir to combine.

8. To assemble sandwiches, place 1 roll onto each of four plates. Spread split sides of rolls evenly with mayonnaise mixture. Place one-fourth of the chicken onto bottom half of each roll; top with one-fourth of the tomato and onion slices, then top half of roll.

Serving (1 sandwich) provides: 1 Fat, $1^{1}/_{4}$ Vegetables, 2 Proteins, 2 Breads.

Per serving: 305 Calories, 8 g Total Fat, 2 g Saturated Fat, 45 mg Cholesterol, 679 mg Sodium, 35 g Total Carbohydrate, 2 g Dietary Fiber, 22 g Protein, 94 mg Calcium.

181

CHICKEN FAJITAS WITH FRESH TOMATILLO SALSA

Makes 4 servings

6 medium tomatillos, husked*
1 medium quartered deveined seeded jalapeño pepper (wear gloves to prevent irritation)
1 small garlic clove, peeled
2 large plum tomatoes, quartered
1/2 medium red onion, halved
1/4 cup packed whole fresh cilantro leaves
1/2 teaspoon salt

1/2 teaspoon freshly ground black pepper
1/4 teaspoon ground cumin
10 ounces skinless boneless chicken breasts
Four 6" flour tortillas
1 1/2 cups shredded iceberg lettuce leaves
8 cherry tomatoes, halved

1. Adjust oven rack to divide oven in half. Preheat oven to 350° F.

2. Place tomatillos into medium saucepan; add water to cover. Bring liquid to a boil; reduce heat to low. Cook, covered, 8 minutes, until tomatillos are tender; drain, discarding liquid.

3. In food processor, combine jalapeño pepper and garlic; pulse until minced. Add plum tomatoes, onion, cilantro and cooked tomatillos; pulse 3–4 times, until coarsely chopped (do not purée). Set aside.

4. In small cup or bowl, combine salt, black pepper and cumin; rub onto both sides of chicken.

5. Spray large nonstick skillet with nonstick cooking spray; heat. Add chicken; cook over medium-high heat, turning once, 8 minutes, until browned on all sides and juices run clear when chicken is pierced with fork. Remove from heat; let stand 5 minutes.

6. Transfer chicken to cutting board; cut into thin strips.

7. Meanwhile, wrap tortillas in foil; bake in center of oven 8–10 minutes, until heated through.

8. To assemble fajitas, place warm tortillas in a single layer onto work surface; top each with one-fourth of lettuce. Arrange one-fourth of the chicken strips along center of each tortilla; top each portion of chicken with 1/4 cup reserved tomatillo mixture. Fold sides of tortillas over filling to enclose; place, seam-side down, onto serving platter. Spoon remaining tomatillo mixture crosswise along center of fajitas; surround with cherry tomato halves.

Serving (1 fajita) provides: 2 3/4 Vegetables, 2 Proteins, 1 Bread.

Per serving: 196 Calories, 3 g Total Fat, 0 g Saturated Fat, 42 mg Cholesterol, 423 mg Sodium, 21 g Total Carbohydrate, 2 g Dietary Fiber, 21 g Protein, 70 mg Calcium.

BREAKFAST
Orange Sections, 1/2 cup
Whole-Wheat Bagel, 1 small (2 ounces), split and toasted, with 1 tablespoon nonfat cream cheese
Skim Milk, 1/2 cup
Coffee or Tea (optional)

LIGHT MEAL
Chicken Fajitas with Fresh Tomatillo Salsa, 1 serving (see recipe)
Cucumber and Carrot Sticks, 1 cup *each*
Nonfat Tortilla Chips, 2 ounces, with Salsa-Cream Dip (In small bowl, top 1/2 cup salsa with 2 tablespoons nonfat sour cream.)
Reduced-Calorie Vanilla-Flavored Pudding (made with skim milk), 1/2 cup
Unsweetened Seltzer

MAIN MEAL
Grilled Red Snapper, 4 ounces
Baked Potato, 4 ounces, with 1 teaspoon reduced-calorie tub margarine
Steamed Spinach, 1 cup, with 1 teaspoon reduced-calorie tub margarine
Tossed Green Salad, 2 cups, with 2 ounces drained cooked pinto beans and 1 tablespoon Italian dressing
Aspartame-Sweetened Cherry-Vanilla Nonfat Yogurt, 1 cup
Sparkling Mineral Water with Lime Wedge

SNACK
Mango, 1/2 small

This menu provides: 2 Milks, 3 Fats, 2 Fruits, 14 3/4 Vegetables, 5 Proteins, 6 Breads, 75 Optional Calories.

Per serving: 22 g Fat, 24 g Fiber.

*If desired, 6 canned whole tomatillos may be substituted for the fresh; omit step 2 in method.

LIGHT MEAL

Chicken Enchiladas, 1 serving (see recipe)
Cooked Long-Grain Rice, ^{1}/$_2$ cup, with 1 tablespoon
   minced fresh cilantro and 1^1/$_2$ teaspoons reduced-
   calorie tub margarine
Tossed Green Salad, 2 cups, with ^{1}/$_2$ cup drained
   roasted red bell pepper strips, 6 large pitted black
   olives, and 1 tablespoon fat-free ranch dressing
Reduced-Calorie Vanilla-Flavored Pudding (made
   with skim milk), ^{1}/$_2$ cup, with 1 tablespoon
   thawed frozen light whipped topping (8 calories
   per tablespoon)
Non-Alcoholic Beer, 12 fluid ounces

MAIN MEAL

Open-Face Tuna Salad Sandwich (In small bowl,
   combine 4 ounces drained canned water-packed
   tuna, flaked, ^{1}/$_2$ cup chopped celery, 2 teaspoons
   reduced-calorie mayonnaise and pinch freshly
   ground black pepper. Toast 2 slices reduced-
   calorie whole-wheat bread; top each toast slice
   with half of the tuna mixture.)
Zucchini and Yellow Squash Sticks, 1 cup *each*
Pear, 1 small
Unsweetened Seltzer with Lemon Wedge

SNACK

Aspartame-Sweetened Raspberry Nonfat Yogurt,
   1 cup, with ^{3}/$_4$ ounce crunchy cereal nuggets

This menu provides: 2 Milks, 3 Fats, 2 Fruits,
12^1/$_2$ Vegetables, 4 Proteins, 6 Breads, 120 Optional
Calories.

Per serving: 22 g Fat, 25 g Fiber.

182
CHICKEN ENCHILADAS

These simple enchiladas are tasty and filling.

Makes 4 servings

1^1/$_2$ cups canned whole tomatoes
   (no salt added), drained
^{1}/$_2$ cup chopped onion
3 garlic cloves, minced
1^1/$_2$ teaspoons mild or hot chili
   powder
^{1}/$_2$ teaspoon ground cumin
^{1}/$_2$ teaspoon dried oregano leaves
^{1}/$_4$ teaspoon salt
Pinch ground red pepper

Pinch cinnamon
1 teaspoon vegetable or olive oil
1 cup diced red bell pepper
1 cup diced green bell pepper
1 cup diced onions
Eight 6" corn tortillas
4 ounces skinless boneless cooked
   chicken breast, shredded
3 ounces reduced-fat Monterey
   Jack cheese, grated

1. Preheat the oven to 375° F.

2. To prepare sauce, in food processor or blender, combine tomatoes, chopped onion, garlic, chili powder, cumin, oregano, salt, ground red pepper and cinnamon; purée until smooth.

3. Transfer tomato mixture to medium saucepan; bring mixture to a boil. Reduce heat to low; simmer, stirring occasionally, 20 minutes, until thickened.

4. Meanwhile, in large nonstick skillet, heat oil; add red and green bell peppers and diced onions. Cook over medium-high heat, stirring frequently, 5 minutes, until vegetables are softened.

5. Spread ^{1}/$_4$ cup tomato mixture into bottom of 13 × 9" baking pan; set pan and remaining sauce aside.

6. To assemble enchiladas, place tortillas onto work surface; spoon an equal amount of bell pepper mixture along center of each tortilla. Top bell pepper mixture evenly with chicken, then all but 2 tablespoons of the cheese. Fold sides of tortillas over filling to enclose; place, seam-side down and 2" apart, into prepared baking pan. Top tortillas evenly with remaining sauce; sprinkle evenly with reserved 2 tablespoons cheese. Bake 25–30 minutes, until heated through and bubbling.

Serving (2 enchiladas) provides: ^{1}/$_4$ Fat, 2^1/$_2$ Vegetables, 2 Proteins, 2 Breads.

Per serving: 290 Calories, 8 g Total Fat, 3 g Saturated Fat, 39 mg Cholesterol, 561 mg Sodium, 37 g Total Carbohydrate, 5 g Dietary Fiber, 21 g Protein, 332 mg Calcium.

183
CHICKEN CHILAQUILES

Chilaquiles, often known as Mexican soul food, are a national dish in Mexico—and a popular way to use up yesterday's tortillas. They are also perfect for leftover chicken.

Makes 4 servings

1 cup thinly sliced onions, separated into rings
Six 6" corn tortillas, cut into $^1/_2$" strips
8 ounces skinless boneless cooked chicken breasts, shredded
2 medium tomatoes, diced
1 cup medium or hot salsa
$^3/_4$ cup low-sodium chicken broth
3 ounces reduced-fat cheddar cheese, grated

1. Preheat oven to 350° F. Spray 13 × 9" baking pan with nonstick cooking spray.

2. Spray medium nonstick skillet with nonstick cooking spray; heat. Add onions; cook over medium-high heat, stirring frequently, 2–3 minutes, until softened.

3. Place half the tortilla strips into prepared baking pan, covering bottom of pan and overlapping strips as necessary. Top tortillas with half the chicken, half the tomatoes, half the cooked onions and half the salsa; repeat layers. Pour broth over mixture; bake, covered, 25 minutes. Sprinkle evenly with cheese; bake, uncovered, 10 minutes, until cheese is melted and mixture is bubbling.

Serving (one quarter of mixture) provides: $2^1/_2$ Vegetables, 3 Proteins, $1^1/_2$ Breads, 5 Optional Calories.

Per serving: 296 Calories, 8 g Total Fat, 4 g Saturated Fat, 6 mg Cholesterol, 937 mg Sodium, 31 g Total Carbohydrate, 4 g Dietary Fiber, 28 g Protein, 276 mg Calcium.

BREAKFAST
Grapefruit, $^1/_2$ medium
Reduced-Calorie Whole-Wheat Bread, 2 slices, toasted, with 2 teaspoons reduced-calorie tub margarine
Skim Milk, 1 cup
Coffee or Tea (optional)

LIGHT MEAL
Low-Sodium Mixed Vegetable Juice, 1 cup
Chicken Chilaquiles, 1 serving (see recipe)
Celery and Carrot Sticks, 1 cup *each*
Apple, 1 small
Iced Decaffeinated Coffee

MAIN MEAL
Broiled Rainbow Trout, 3 ounces, with 1 lemon wedge
Baked Acorn Squash, 7 ounces, drizzled with 1 teaspoon maple syrup
Steamed Spinach, 1 cup, with 2 teaspoons reduced-calorie tub margarine
Tossed Green Salad, 2 cups, with 1 ounce *each* drained cooked red kidney beans and diced avocado and 1 tablespoon fat-free Italian dressing
Sugar-Free Strawberry-Flavored Gelatin, $^1/_2$ cup, with 1 tablespoon thawed frozen light whipped topping (8 calories per tablespoon)
Sparkling Mineral Water

SNACK
Raisin Bran Cereal, $1^1/_2$ ounces
Skim Milk, 1 cup

This menu provides: 2 Milks, 3 Fats, 2 Fruits, 15 Vegetables, 5 Proteins, $5^1/_2$ Breads, 45 Optional Calories.

Per serving: 29 g Fat, 30 g Fiber.

7. To assemble shortcakes, place 1 crêpe onto
each of 4 plates; top each with $^1/_2$ cup of the
chicken mixture. Repeat layers 2 more times.

**Serving (3 crêpes, 1$^1/_2$ cups chicken mixture) pro-
vides:** 1$^1/_2$ Fats, 3$^1/_2$ Vegetables, 2 Proteins,
1$^1/_2$ Breads, 45 Optional Calories.

Per serving: 353 Calories, 11 g Total Fat,
2 g Saturated Fat, 139 mg Cholesterol,
979 mg Sodium, 36 g Total Carbohydrate,
5 g Dietary Fiber, 25 g Protein, 141 mg Calcium.

184

CHINESE CHICKEN CRÊPE SHORTCAKE

Makes 4 servings

$^1/_2$ cup all-purpose flour
$^1/_4$ teaspoon salt
2 eggs
$^1/_2$ cup skim milk
1 tablespoon reduced-calorie tub margarine, melted
1 tablespoon minced scallion
$^1/_4$ cup reduced-sodium soy sauce
2 fluid ounces ($^1/_4$ cup) mirin (Japanese cooking wine)
1 tablespoon cornstarch
2 teaspoons grated lemon zest
1 tablespoon + 1$^1/_2$ teaspoons oriental sesame oil

8 ounces skinless boneless chicken breasts, cut diagonally into 4 × $^1/_4$" strips
4 garlic cloves, minced
1 tablespoon grated pared fresh ginger root
2 cups sliced white mushrooms
2 cups julienned red bell peppers
2 cups cut asparagus
2 cups drained pickled baby corn
1 cup diagonally sliced lemon grass or scallions

1. To make crêpes, in medium bowl, combine flour and salt. In small bowl, with wire whisk, lightly beat eggs; stir milk, margarine and 1 table-spoon cold water into eggs. Add egg mixture to flour mixture, 2 table-spoons at a time, beating with wire whisk after each addition, until batter is smooth; stir in minced scallions. Let stand 10 minutes.

2. Spray 6" nonstick crêpe pan or skillet with nonstick cooking spray; heat. Pour 2 tablespoons batter into pan, tilting to cover bottom of pan. Cook 30 seconds, until underside is set, lifting edges with spatula to let uncooked batter flow underneath. Turn and cook other side 15–20 sec-onds, until lightly browned. Slide crêpe onto wax paper. Repeat with remaining batter, making 12 crêpes, stacking each crêpe between sheets of wax paper.

3. To make sauce, in small bowl, with wire whisk, combine soy sauce, mirin, cornstarch and zest, blending until cornstarch is dissolved; set aside.

4. To prepare chicken, in wok or large nonstick skillet, heat 2 teaspoons of the oil; add chicken and garlic. Cook over medium-high heat, stirring frequently, 1–2 minutes, until chicken is no longer pink. With slotted spoon, remove chicken mixture from skillet; set aside.

5. In same wok, heat remaining 2$^1/_2$ teaspoons oil; add ginger. Cook over medium-high heat, stirring constantly, 1 minute. Add mushrooms and bell peppers; cook, stirring frequently, 5 minutes, until vegetables are ten-der. Add asparagus and corn; cook, stirring frequently, 2 minutes, until asparagus is just tender. Add lemon grass; cook, stirring constantly, 1 minute, until just softened.

6. Add prepared sauce and cooked chicken to vegetable mixture; cook, stirring constantly, 2 minutes, until chicken is cooked through and sauce is thickened.

185
CHICKEN CRÊPES WITH FRESH PEACH SAUCE

Makes 4 servings

3/4 cup all-purpose flour
1 tablespoon + 2 teaspoons granu-
    lated sugar
1/4 teaspoon salt
2 eggs
2 cups skim milk
1 tablespoon reduced-calorie tub
    margarine, melted
2/3 cup peach nectar

3 tablespoons reduced-calorie tub
    margarine
1 tablespoon (1/2 fluid ounce)
    orange liqueur
6 ounces skinless boneless cooked
    chicken breasts, cut into 4 × 1"
    pieces
3 medium peaches, pared, pitted
    and each cut into 16 wedges

1. To make crêpes, in medium bowl, combine 1/2 cup of the flour, 1 table-spoon of the sugar and the salt. In small bowl, with wire whisk, lightly beat eggs. With wire whisk, stir 1/2 cup of the milk and the melted margarine into eggs. Add egg mixture to flour mixture, 2 tablespoons at a time, beat-ing after each addition, until batter is smooth; let stand 10 minutes.

2. Meanwhile, to prepare sauce, in separate medium bowl, with wire whisk, combine the remaining 11/2 cups milk, 1/2 cup of the nectar and the remaining 2 teaspoons sugar, blending until sugar is dissolved; set aside.

3. In medium saucepan, melt margarine; with wire whisk, blend in the remaining 1/4 cup flour. Continuing to blend, cook over medium-high heat 3 minutes, until mixture is bubbling. Gradually add milk mixture, beating constantly with wire whisk; cook, stirring constantly, 3 minutes, until mixture is thickened. Remove from heat; stir in liqueur.

4. Transfer 2/3 cup milk mixture to small bowl; stir in remaining nectar.

5. Add chicken to remaining milk mixture; cook over medium-high heat, stirring frequently, 2 minutes, until mixture is heated through. Remove from heat; keep warm.

6. Spray 6" nonstick crêpe pan or skillet with nonstick cooking spray; heat. Pour 2 tablespoons batter into pan, tilting to cover bottom of pan. Cook 30 seconds, until underside is set, lifting edges with spatula to let uncooked batter flow underneath. Turn and cook other side 15–20 sec-onds, until lightly browned. Slide crêpe onto wax paper. Repeat, making 12 crêpes, stacking each crêpe between sheets of wax paper.

7. To assemble crêpes, place 1 crêpe onto work surface; spoon 2 table-spoons chicken mixture along center of crêpe. Top chicken mixture with 3 peach wedges. Fold sides of crêpe over filling to enclose; place, seam-side down, onto serving platter. Repeat, making 11 more filled crêpes; top with reserved milk mixture and remaining 12 peach wedges.

This menu provides: 2 Milks, 3 Fats, 2 Fruits, 11 Vegetables, 5 Proteins, 51/2 Breads, 120 Optional Calories.

Per serving: 32 g Fat, 20 g Fiber.

Serving (3 filled crêpes, 1/2 cup sauce + 3 peach wedges) provides: 1/2 Milk, 11/2 Fats, 11/4 Fruits, 2 Proteins, 1 Bread, 30 Optional Calories.

Per serving: 391 Calories, 12 g Total Fat, 2 g Saturated Fat, 145 mg Cholesterol, 365 mg Sodium, 47 g Total Carbohydrate, 2 g Dietary Fiber, 24 g Protein, 181 mg Calcium.

186
CHICKEN, ROASTED PEPPERS AND ORZO

Roasted peppers add a wonderful flavor to this Greek-inspired entrée.

Makes 4 servings

1 medium green bell pepper, halved and seeded
1 medium red bell pepper, halved and seeded
6 ounces orzo (rice-shaped pasta)
8 ounces skinless boneless chicken breasts
2 tablespoons minced fresh flat-leaf parsley
1 tablespoon minced fresh mint leaves
1 tablespoon fresh lemon juice
2 teaspoons olive or vegetable oil
$^1/_2$ teaspoon salt
$^1/_4$ teaspoon freshly ground black pepper, or to taste
$1^1/_2$ ounces feta cheese, finely crumbled

1. Preheat oven to 400° F.

2. Place green and red bell peppers, cut-side down, onto 15 × 10" jelly-roll pan; roast 25–30 minutes, until skins are blistered and charred.

3. Meanwhile, in large pot of boiling water, cook orzo 9 minutes, until tender. Drain, discarding liquid; place into serving bowl.

4. Transfer bell peppers to paper bag; let stand 5 minutes.

5. Peel bell peppers; dice, reserving 1 thin strip from each pepper half to garnish. Add diced pepper to bowl with orzo; set aside.

6. In large skillet, bring 3 cups water to a boil. Add chicken; return liquid to a boil. Reduce heat to low; poach chicken, covered, 10 minutes, until cooked through. With slotted spoon, remove chicken from liquid; discard liquid. Set chicken aside to cool.

7. Cut cooled chicken into bite-size pieces; add to bowl with orzo and peppers.

8. In small jar with tight-fitting lid or small bowl, combine parsley, mint, juice, oil, salt and pepper; cover and shake well or, with wire whisk, blend until combined. Pour parsley mixture over orzo mixture; toss to coat. Add cheese; toss again. Garnish with reserved bell pepper strips.

Serving ($1^1/_2$ cups) provides: $^1/_2$ Fat, 1 Vegetable, 2 Proteins, 2 Breads.

Per serving: 283 Calories, 6 g Total Fat, 2 g Saturated Fat, 42 mg Cholesterol, 434 mg Sodium, 36 g Total Carbohydrate, 2 g Dietary Fiber, 21 g Protein, 76 mg Calcium.

187
CHICKEN-BROCCOLI RISOTTO

The high starch content of short-grain Arborio rice, combined with the gradual addition of liquid, produces a creamy, delicate dish with separate, firm grains of rice.

Makes 4 servings

2 cups small broccoli florets
2 cups low-sodium chicken broth
1 tablespoon + 1 teaspoon reduced-calorie tub margarine
10 ounces skinless boneless chicken breasts, cut into bite-size pieces
¹/₄ teaspoon salt
1 cup finely chopped onions
¹/₄ teaspoon freshly ground black pepper
6 ounces Arborio or other short-grain rice
4 fluid ounces (¹/₂ cup) dry white wine
2 tablespoons freshly grated Parmesan cheese
¹/₄ teaspoon grated lemon zest*

1. Fill large saucepan with 1" water; set steamer rack into saucepan. Place broccoli onto rack. Bring water to a boil; reduce heat to low. Steam broccoli over simmering water, covered, 4–5 minutes, until just tender.

2. In small saucepan, combine broth and 1 cup water; bring liquid to a boil. Reduce heat to low; let simmer while preparing chicken.

3. In large saucepan, melt 2 teaspoons of the margarine; add chicken and salt. Cook over medium-high heat, stirring frequently, 4 minutes, until chicken is cooked through. With slotted spoon, remove chicken from saucepan; set aside.

4. In same saucepan, melt remaining 2 teaspoons margarine; add onions and pepper. Cook over medium-high heat, stirring frequently, 5 minutes, until onions are softened. Add rice; cook, stirring constantly, 1 minute. Add wine; cook, stirring constantly, until most of the liquid is absorbed.

5. Add ¹/₂ cup hot broth mixture to rice mixture; cook, stirring constantly, until liquid is absorbed. Continuing to stir, add all but ¹/₄ cup of the remaining broth mixture, ¹/₂ cup at a time; cook, stirring constantly after each addition, 18 minutes, until all liquid is absorbed, rice is tender and mixture is creamy.

6. Stir cheese, zest, steamed broccoli, cooked chicken and remaining ¹/₄ cup broth mixture into rice mixture; cook, stirring frequently, 2 minutes, until heated through.

BREAKFAST
Mango, ¹/₂ small
Reduced-Calorie Whole-Wheat Bread, 2 slices, toasted, with 2 teaspoons reduced-calorie tub margarine
Skim Milk, 1 cup
Coffee or Tea (optional)

LIGHT MEAL
Chicken-Broccoli Risotto, 1 serving (see recipe)
Steamed Sliced Carrots, 1 cup, with 1 teaspoon reduced-calorie tub margarine
Sugar-Free Strawberry-Flavored Gelatin, ¹/₂ cup, with 1 tablespoon thawed frozen light whipped topping (8 calories per tablespoon)
Sparkling Mineral Water

MAIN MEAL
Baked Ham, 2 ounces
Cooked Barley, 1 cup
Steamed Swiss Chard, 1 cup
Tossed Green Salad, 2 cups, with ¹/₂ cup *each* red and green bell pepper strips, 2 ounces drained cooked chick-peas, 6 large pitted black olives and 1 tablespoon fat-free Italian dressing
Pineapple, ¹/₈ medium
Unsweetened Citrus-Flavored Seltzer

SNACK
Plain Popcorn, hot-air popped, 3 cups
Skim Milk, 1 cup

This menu provides: 2 Milks, 3 Fats, 2 Fruits, 11¹/₂ Vegetables, 5 Proteins, 5¹/₂ Breads, 75 Optional Calories.

Per serving: 25 g Fat, 36 g Fiber.

Serving (1 cup) provides: ¹/₂ Fat, 1¹/₂ Vegetables, 2 Proteins, 1¹/₂ Breads, 50 Optional Calories.

Per serving: 326 Calories, 5 g Total Fat, 1 g Saturated Fat, 43 mg Cholesterol, 337 mg Sodium, 42 g Total Carbohydrate, 3 g Dietary Fiber, 24 g Protein, 92 mg Calcium.

The zest of the lemon is the peel without any of the pith (white membrane). To remove zest from lemon, use a zester or the fine side of a vegetable grater; wrap lemon in plastic wrap and refrigerate for use at another time.

188
CHICKEN HASH

This is a quick and hearty meal-in-a-skillet.

Makes 4 servings

1 pound 4 ounces red potatoes, cut into $^1/_2$" cubes
2 teaspoons vegetable oil
10 ounces skinless boneless chicken breasts, cut into $^1/_2$" cubes
2 cups chopped onions
2 cups coarsely chopped red bell pepper
1 medium minced deveined seeded jalapeño pepper
   (wear gloves to prevent irritation)
3 garlic cloves, minced
$^1/_2$ teaspoon salt
1 cup thawed frozen corn kernels
$^1/_2$ cup low-sodium chicken broth
$^1/_4$ cup minced fresh cilantro

1. Place potatoes into medium saucepan; add water to cover. Bring liquid to a boil; reduce heat to low. Simmer 5 minutes, until potatoes are partially cooked. Drain, discarding liquid; set aside.

2. In large nonstick skillet, heat oil; add chicken, onions, bell and jalapeño peppers, garlic and salt. Cook over medium-high heat, stirring frequently, 2–3 minutes, until chicken turns white and vegetables are softened.

3. Add corn and reserved potatoes to chicken mixture; cook, stirring frequently, 5 minutes, until potatoes are browned and crispy. Stir in broth; bring liquid just to a boil. Remove from heat; sprinkle with cilantro.

Serving ($1^1/_2$ cups) provides: $^1/_2$ Fat, $2^1/_4$ Vegetables, 2 Proteins, $1^1/_2$ Breads, 5 Optional Calories.

Per serving: 298 Calories, 4 g Total Fat, 1 g Saturated Fat, 41 mg Cholesterol, 355 mg Sodium, 44 g Total Carbohydrate, 6 g Dietary Fiber, 22 g Protein, 39 mg Calcium.

1 8 9
CHICKEN-CORN CAKES

Juicy chicken stirred into pancake batter makes a hearty meal in minutes. Try these topped with maple syrup for a sweet, homey entrée.

Makes 4 servings

$^3/_4$ cup all-purpose flour
$^1/_4$ cup yellow cornmeal
1 teaspoon granulated sugar
$^1/_2$ teaspoon double-acting baking powder
$^1/_2$ teaspoon salt
$^1/_4$ teaspoon baking soda
1 egg
$1^1/_2$ cups low-fat buttermilk (1.5% milk fat)
1 tablespoon + 1 teaspoon vegetable oil
$^1/_4$ teaspoon hot red pepper sauce
7 ounces skinless boneless cooked chicken breasts, finely chopped
1 cup thawed frozen corn kernels
$^1/_3$ cup thinly sliced scallions

1. In large bowl, combine flour, cornmeal, sugar, baking powder, salt and baking soda. In medium bowl, with wire whisk, lightly beat egg. With wire whisk, stir buttermilk, 1 tablespoon of the oil and the hot red pepper sauce into egg. Add wet ingredients to dry; stir just until blended. Add chicken, corn and scallions; stir just to combine (do not overmix).

2. In large nonstick skillet or griddle, heat remaining 1 teaspoon oil; spread evenly to coat bottom of skillet. Pour batter by $^1/_4$-cup measures into skillet, making 4 pancakes. Cook over medium-high heat 2–3 minutes, until bubbles appear on surface; turn and cook 2 minutes, until golden brown. With spatula, remove cakes to plate; keep warm. Repeat with remaining batter, making 4 more cakes.

Serving (2 cakes) provides: $^1/_4$ Milk, 1 Fat, $^1/_4$ Vegetable, 2 Proteins, 2 Breads, 15 Optional Calories.

Per serving: 343 Calories, 10 g Total Fat, 2 g Saturated Fat, 101 mg Cholesterol, 527 mg Sodium, 38 g Total Carbohydrate, 2 g Dietary Fiber, 25 g Protein, 172 mg Calcium.

BREAKFAST
Orange, 1 small
Open-Face Egg Sandwich (Spray small nonstick skillet with nonstick cooking spray; heat. Add $^1/_4$ cup egg substitute, $^1/_4$ cup diced drained roasted red bell pepper and pinch each salt, freshly ground black pepper and garlic powder. Cook over medium-high heat, stirring frequently, until mixture is set. Spoon onto 1 slice reduced-calorie whole-wheat bread, toasted; top with 2 tomato slices.)
Skim Milk, $^3/_4$ cup
Coffee or Tea (optional)

LIGHT MEAL
Chicken-Corn Cakes, 1 serving (see recipe), with 2 teaspoons maple syrup
Steamed Artichoke, 1 whole medium, with Lemon "Butter" (In small cup or bowl, combine 1 teaspoon *each* reduced-calorie tub margarine, melted, and fresh lemon juice.)
Red and Green Bell Pepper Strips, 1 cup *each*
Whole-Wheat Roll, 1 ounce, with 1 teaspoon reduced-calorie tub margarine
Aspartame-Sweetened Blueberry Nonfat Yogurt, 1 cup
Iced Herbal Tea

MAIN MEAL
Broiled Perch, 2 ounces
Cooked Lentils, 2 ounces
Steamed Green Peas and Diced Carrots, $^1/_2$ cup *each*
Steamed Beet Greens, 1 cup
Shredded Red and Green Cabbage, 1 cup, with $1^1/_2$ teaspoons coleslaw dressing
Pear, 1 small
Sparkling Mineral Water with Lemon Wedge

SNACK
Plain Popcorn, hot-air popped, 3 cups
Diet Root Beer

This menu provides: 2 Milks, 3 Fats, 2 Fruits, $11^1/_4$ Vegetables, 5 Proteins, $5^1/_2$ Breads, 45 Optional Calories.

Per serving: 24 g Fat, 38 g Fiber.

LIGHT MEAL
Chicken and Spinach Phyllo Pie, 1 serving (see
    recipe)
Carrot and Celery Sticks, 1 cup *each*
Cucumber Salad (In small bowl, combine 1/2 cup
    cucumber slices, 1 teaspoon *each* vegetable oil
    and rice wine vinegar and pinch ground white
    pepper.)
Cantaloupe, 1/4 small
Iced Herbal Tea

MAIN MEAL
Lentil Soup, canned, 1 cup, with 20 oyster crackers
    and 1 teaspoon freshly grated Parmesan cheese
Torn Romaine and Iceberg Lettuce Leaves, 2 cups,
    with 1/2 cup *each* sliced radishes and green bell
    pepper and 1 tablespoon fat-free Thousand Island
    dressing
Whole-Wheat Roll, 1 ounce, with 2 teaspoons
    reduced-calorie tub margarine
Sugar-Free Raspberry-Flavored Gelatin, 1/2 cup
Decaffeinated Cappuccino, made with skim milk,
    5 fluid ounces

SNACK
Oat-Bran Pretzels, 1 1/2 ounces
Skim Milk, 1/2 cup

This menu provides: 2 Milks, 3 Fats, 2 Fruits,
12 3/4 Vegetables, 4 1/4 Proteins, 5 1/2 Breads,
95 Optional Calories.

Per serving: 32 g Fat, 31 g Fiber.

Serving (1 rectangle) provides: 1 Fat, 1 3/4 Vegetables, 2 1/4 Proteins, 1/2 Bread, 30 Optional Calories.

Per serving: 257 Calories, 12 g Total Fat,
5 g Saturated Fat, 50 mg Cholesterol, 594 mg
Sodium, 18 g Total Carbohydrate, 2 g Dietary Fiber,
20 g Protein, 252 mg Calcium.

*Phyllo dough dries out quickly. To help keep the indi-
vidual sheets soft and pliable, keep them covered with
plastic wrap until ready to use.*

190
CHICKEN AND SPINACH PHYLLO PIE

Phyllo, which means "leaf" in Greek, is the name for tissue-thin layers of pastry dough; the dough can be purchased fresh or frozen in the supermarket.

Makes 6 servings

1 tablespoon olive oil
1 cup finely chopped onions
2 garlic cloves, minced
10 ounces skinless boneless chicken
    breasts, cut into bite-size pieces
1/2 teaspoon salt
1/2 teaspoon freshly ground black
    pepper
Two 10-ounce packages thawed
    frozen chopped spinach, drained
    and squeezed dry

1/2 cup part-skim ricotta cheese
3 ounces feta cheese, finely crum-
    bled
2 tablespoons minced fresh mint
    leaves
2 tablespoons light cream
4 ounces fresh or thawed frozen
    phyllo dough (about 6 sheets)*
2 tablespoons reduced-calorie tub
    margarine, melted

1. Preheat oven to 350° F. Spray 9" square baking dish with nonstick cooking spray.

2. In large nonstick skillet, heat oil; add onions and garlic. Cook over medium-high heat, stirring frequently, 5 minutes, until onions are soft-ened. Add chicken, salt and pepper; cook, stirring frequently, 4 minutes, until chicken is no longer pink. With slotted spoon, transfer chicken mix-ture to medium bowl; set aside.

3. In same skillet, cook spinach over medium-high heat, stirring fre-quently, 3 minutes, until all liquid has evaporated. Transfer spinach to bowl with chicken mixture; toss to combine. Let stand until cool.

4. Stir ricotta and feta cheeses, mint and cream into cooled chicken mixture.

5. Spray both sides of each phyllo sheet with nonstick cooking spray; fold each sheet in half. Fit 2 folded phyllo sheets into prepared dish, folding sheet if necessary so that it covers bottom of dish; brush evenly with 1 1/2 teaspoons margarine.

6. Top phyllo sheets with one-third of the spinach mixture; top with 1 folded phyllo sheet. Brush evenly with 1 1/2 teaspoons margarine. Repeat 2 more times, ending with remaining folded phyllo sheet and brushing evenly with remaining 1 1/2 teaspoons margarine. Bake 20 minutes, until lightly browned. Cut into six 4 1/2 × 3" rectangles.

191
No-Crust Chicken-Asparagus Quiche

Quiche becomes super light and easy by simply omitting the crust; it's chock-full of fresh asparagus, savory cheddar cheese and chicken.

Makes 6 servings

2 cups cut asparagus (1" pieces)
2 tablespoons all-purpose flour
1/2 teaspoon salt
1/4 teaspoon freshly ground black pepper
Pinch ground red pepper, or to taste
8 ounces skinless boneless chicken breasts, cut into 1/2" pieces

2 teaspoons vegetable oil
1/2 cup finely chopped red bell pepper
1/2 cup chopped onion
1 cup skim milk
3 eggs
4 1/2 ounces reduced-fat cheddar cheese, grated

1. Preheat oven to 350° F. Spray 8" pie plate with nonstick cooking spray.

2. In large pot of boiling water, cook asparagus 3 minutes, until just tender. Drain, discarding liquid; rinse with cold water. Drain again; set aside 6 asparagus tips to garnish.

3. On sheet of wax paper or paper plate, combine flour, salt and black and ground red peppers; add chicken, turning to coat evenly.

4. In large nonstick skillet, heat 1 teaspoon of the oil; add chicken, reserving any remaining flour mixture. Cook over medium-high heat, stirring constantly, 4–5 minutes, until chicken is no longer pink. Remove chicken from skillet; set aside.

5. In same skillet, heat remaining 1 teaspoon oil; add bell pepper, onion and reserved flour mixture. Cook over medium-high heat, stirring constantly, 5 minutes, until vegetables are softened. Remove vegetable mixture from skillet; set aside.

6. In medium bowl, with wire whisk, combine milk and eggs, blending until mixture is frothy; stir in cheese, asparagus, chicken and vegetable mixture. Pour mixture into prepared pie plate; bake 40 minutes, until knife inserted in center comes out clean.

7. Arrange reserved asparagus tips like spokes of a wheel onto center of quiche; let stand 5 minutes. Cut into 6 equal wedges.

Serving (1 wedge) provides: 1/4 Fat, 1 Vegetable, 2 1/2 Proteins, 30 Optional Calories.

Per serving: 195 Calories, 9 g Total Fat, 4 g Saturated Fat, 144 mg Cholesterol, 426 mg Sodium, 8 g Total Carbohydrate, 1 g Dietary Fiber, 22 g Protein, 269 mg Calcium.

BREAKFAST
Banana, 1/2 medium, sliced
Bran Flakes Cereal, 1 1/2 ounces
Skim Milk, 1 cup
Coffee or Tea (optional)

LIGHT MEAL
No-Crust Chicken-Asparagus Quiche, 1 serving (see recipe)
Chilled Cooked Whole Green Beans, 1 cup
Arugula and Romaine Lettuce Salad, 2 cups, with 6 cherry tomatoes, 2 ounces drained cooked chick-peas and 1 tablespoon fat-free Thousand Island dressing
Semolina Roll, 1 ounce, with 1 teaspoon reduced-calorie tub margarine
Orange, 1 small
Iced Tea

MAIN MEAL
Broiled Red Snapper, 4 ounces
Pasta Primavera (In medium skillet, heat 1 teaspoon olive oil; add 1/2 cup *each* sliced onion, mushrooms and red bell pepper and 1 garlic clove, minced. Cook over medium-high heat, stirring frequently, 5 minutes, until vegetables are tender. Add 1 cup cooked rotelle pasta, 1/2 cup tomato sauce [no salt added] and 5 small pitted black olives; cook, stirring frequently, until mixture is heated through. Serve sprinkled with 1 teaspoon freshly grated Parmesan cheese.)
Italian Bread, 1 slice (1 ounce), with 1 1/2 teaspoons reduced-calorie tub margarine
Sugar-Free Cherry-Flavored Gelatin, 1/2 cup, with 1 tablespoon thawed frozen light whipped topping (8 calories per tablespoon)
Sparkling Mineral Water

SNACK
Aspartame-Sweetened Vanilla Nonfat Yogurt, 1 cup

This menu provides: 2 Milks, 3 Fats, 2 Fruits, 13 Vegetables, 5 1/2 Proteins, 6 Breads, 80 Optional Calories.

Per serving: 31 g Fat, 20 g Fiber.

192
BUFFALO CHICKEN FINGERS

This version of Buffalo wings reins in the fat and calories, but it still packs the great flavor of its namesake!

Makes 6 servings

1$^{1}/_{2}$ cups plain nonfat yogurt
3 ounces nonfat blue cheese, crumbled
1 tablespoon Neufchâtel cheese
$^{1}/_{2}$ fluid ounce (1 tablespoon) dry sherry
1 teaspoon Worcestershire sauce
$^{1}/_{4}$ teaspoon celery seeds
$^{1}/_{2}$ cup tarragon vinegar
2 tablespoons vegetable oil
2 garlic cloves, minced
$^{1}/_{4}$ teaspoon ground red pepper
$^{1}/_{4}$ teaspoon salt
13 ounces skinless boneless chicken breasts, cut into
 twenty-four 4 × 1" "fingers"

1. Preheat outdoor barbecue grill according to manufacturer's directions, or preheat broiler and spray rack in broiler pan with nonstick cooking spray.

2. To prepare sauce, in small bowl, combine yogurt, blue and Neufchâtel cheeses, sherry, Worcestershire sauce and celery seeds; refrigerate, covered, until chilled.

3. To prepare chicken, in small bowl, with wire whisk, combine vinegar, oil, garlic, pepper and salt; brush both sides of chicken "fingers" with some of the vinegar mixture.

4. Grill chicken over hot coals or place onto prepared rack in broiler pan and broil 4" from heat, turning once and basting with remaining vinegar mixture, 3 minutes, until chicken is browned and juices run clear when pierced with fork. Serve with sauce for dipping.

Serving (4 chicken "fingers", $^{1}/_{3}$ cup sauce) provides: $^{1}/_{4}$ Milk, 2 Proteins, 55 Optional Calories.

Per serving: 206 Calories, 10 g Total Fat, 4 g Saturated Fat, 49 mg Cholesterol, 390 mg Sodium, 7 g Total Carbohydrate, 0 g Dietary Fiber, 21 g Protein, 206 mg Calcium.

COLD SESAME NOODLES

Noodle shops are popping up all over, and there's good reason!
Popular dishes such as this make an ideal meal.

Makes 4 servings

6 ounces spaghettini
$^1/_2$ cup diagonally julienned scallions
3 tablespoons reduced-sodium soy sauce
2 tablespoons minced fresh cilantro
2 tablespoons firmly packed light or dark brown sugar
2 tablespoons balsamic vinegar
1 tablespoon + 1 teaspoon oriental sesame oil
2 teaspoons minced pared fresh ginger root
2 garlic cloves, minced
Pinch ground red pepper
8 ounces skinless boneless cooked chicken breasts, shredded
1 medium cucumber, seeded and diagonally julienned
1 medium carrot, diagonally julienned
$^1/_2$ cup diagonally julienned pared daikon (Japanese white radish) or red
   radishes
2 teaspoons sesame seeds, toasted*

1. In large pot of boiling water, cook spaghettini 8–10 minutes, until tender. Drain, discarding liquid; rinse under cold running water until cool. Drain 5 minutes; transfer to large shallow serving bowl. Add scallions; toss to combine. Set aside.

2. Meanwhile, to prepare dressing, in small jar with tight-fitting lid or small bowl, combine soy sauce, cilantro, brown sugar, vinegar, oil, ginger, garlic and pepper; cover and shake well or, with wire whisk, blend until combined. Pour half of the dressing over spaghettini mixture; toss to combine.

3. In medium bowl, combine chicken, cucumber, carrot and daikon; mound in center of spaghettini mixture. Drizzle evenly with remaining dressing; sprinkle with sesame seeds.

Serving (1 cup spaghettini mixture, 1 cup chicken mixture) provides: 1 Fat, $1^1/_2$ Vegetables, 2 Proteins, 2 Breads, 30 Optional Calories.

Per serving: 357 Calories, 8 g Total Fat, 1 g Saturated Fat, 48 mg Cholesterol, 512 mg Sodium, 46 g Total Carbohydrate, 2 g Dietary Fiber, 25 g Protein, 65 mg Calcium.

*To toast sesame seeds, in small nonstick skillet, cook seeds over low heat, stirring constantly, until golden brown; immediately transfer to heat-resistant plate to cool.

BREAKFAST
Kiwi Fruit, 1 medium
Reduced-Calorie Rye Bread, 2 slices, toasted, with
   2 teaspoons reduced-calorie tub margarine
Skim Milk, 1 cup
Coffee or Tea (optional)

LIGHT MEAL
Cold Sesame Noodles, 1 serving (see recipe)
Steamed Snow Peas, 1 cup
Steamed Spinach, 1 cup
Tangerine, 1 large
Chinese Tea

MAIN MEAL
Black Bean Soup (In small saucepan, combine
   $1^1/_2$ cups low-sodium chicken broth, $^1/_2$ cup *each*
   diced celery and carrot, 2 ounces drained cooked
   black beans and 1 ounce diced cooked ham; bring
   liquid to a boil. Reduce heat to low; simmer
   10 minutes, until vegetables are tender.)
Carrot and Celery Sticks, 1 cup *each*
Tossed Green Salad, 2 cups, with 6 cherry tomatoes
   and 1 tablespoon fat-free Italian dressing
Roll, 1 ounce, with 2 teaspoons reduced-calorie tub
   margarine
Reduced-Calorie Chocolate-Flavored Pudding (made
   with skim milk), $^1/_2$ cup
Sparkling Mineral Water

SNACK
Nonfat Cottage Cheese, $^1/_2$ cup
Fat-Free Crackers, 7
Skim Milk, $^1/_2$ cup

This menu provides: 2 Milks, 3 Fats, 2 Fruits, $16^1/_2$ Vegetables, 5 Proteins, 5 Breads, 105 Optional Calories.

Per serving: 29 g Fat, 30 g Fiber.

194
MAUI CHICKEN SALAD

Makes 4 servings

$^1/_3$ cup fresh lime juice
2 tablespoons rice wine vinegar
3 tablespoons minced fresh mint leaves
$^1/_2$ teaspoon granulated sugar
$^1/_4$ teaspoon freshly ground black pepper
Pinch salt
2 tablespoons macadamia nut or walnut oil
10 ounces skinless boneless chicken breasts
$^1/_4$ medium pineapple, pared, cored and cut into 1" chunks
2 medium kiwi fruits, pared, halved and sliced
1 cup strawberries, sliced
$^1/_2$ small mango, pared, pitted and cut into $^1/_2$" chunks
2 tablespoons shredded coconut, toasted*
Fresh mint sprigs, to garnish

1. To prepare dressing, in blender or food processor, combine juice, vinegar, minced mint, sugar, pepper and salt; process until well blended. With motor running, slowly pour oil through feed tube; process 1 minute, until slightly thickened.

2. To prepare salad, in large skillet, bring 3 cups water to a boil. Add chicken; return liquid to a boil. Reduce heat to low; poach chicken, covered, 10 minutes, until cooked through. With slotted spoon, remove chicken from liquid; discard liquid. Set chicken aside to cool.

3. Cut cooled chicken into bite-size pieces; place into medium bowl. Add 2 tablespoons dressing; toss to combine.

4. In large bowl, combine pineapple, kiwi fruits, strawberries, mango and remaining dressing; transfer to large serving platter. Top fruit mixture with chicken mixture; sprinkle with coconut. Serve garnished with mint sprigs.

Serving ($1^1/_2$ cups) provides: $1^1/_2$ Fats, $1^1/_2$ Fruits, 2 Proteins, 10 Optional Calories.

Per serving: 235 Calories, 9 g Total Fat, 2 g Saturated Fat, 41 mg Cholesterol, 89 mg Sodium, 23 g Total Carbohydrate, 4 g Dietary Fiber, 18 g Protein, 35 mg Calcium.

*To toast coconut, preheat oven to 350° F. Spread coconut onto nonstick baking sheet; bake 5 minutes, until golden brown. Remove from oven; let cool.

CHICKEN, TOMATO AND MOZZARELLA SALAD

This salad of plump tomatoes, shreds of chicken, slivers of fresh basil and fresh-from-the-farm greens makes a perfect summer meal.

Makes 4 servings

2 large garlic cloves

^{1}/4 cup tomato sauce (no salt added)

3 tablespoons red wine vinegar

^{1}/2 teaspoon freshly ground black pepper

^{1}/4 teaspoon salt

1 tablespoon + 1 teaspoon olive oil

8 large radicchio leaves, torn into bite-size pieces

4 large chicory leaves, torn into bite-size pieces

4 large Romaine lettuce leaves, torn into bite-size pieces

1 medium cucumber, pared, seeded and diced

2 medium tomatoes, thinly sliced

8 ounces skinless boneless cooked chicken breasts, julienned

3 ounces nonfat mozzarella cheese, julienned

^{1}/2 cup slivered red onion

6 large basil leaves, slivered

2 tablespoons minced fresh flat-leaf parsley

1. To prepare dressing, in blender or food processor, with motor running, drop garlic through feed tube; process 30 seconds, until minced. Add tomato sauce, vinegar, pepper, salt and 3 tablespoons water; purée 30 seconds, until smooth. With motor running, slowly pour oil through feed tube; process 1 minute, until slightly thickened.

2. To prepare salad, in large bowl, combine radicchio, chicory, Romaine lettuce and cucumber. Add 1 tablespoon dressing; toss to coat.

3. Transfer lettuce mixture to large round serving platter; top with tomatoes, chicken, cheese and onion, arranged in clusters.

4. Stir basil and parsley into remaining dressing; drizzle evenly over salad.

Serving (2 cups) provides: 1 Fat, 3 Vegetables, 2^1/2 Proteins.

Per serving: 210 Calories, 7 g Total Fat, 1 g Saturated Fat, 52 mg Cholesterol, 377 mg Sodium, 11 g Total Carbohydrate, 2 g Dietary Fiber, 26 g Protein, 186 mg Calcium.

BREAKFAST

Blackberries, ^{3}/4 cup

Nonfat Cottage Cheese, ^{1}/2 cup

English Muffin, ^{1}/2 (1 ounce), toasted, with 1 teaspoon reduced-calorie tub margarine

Skim Milk, 1 cup

Coffee or Tea (optional)

LIGHT MEAL

Vegetable Soup, canned, 1 cup

Chicken, Tomato and Mozzarella Salad, 1 serving (see recipe)

Roll, 1 ounce, with 1 teaspoon reduced-calorie tub margarine

Sugar-Free Chocolate Nonfat Frozen Yogurt, 4 fluid ounces

Sparkling Mineral Water

MAIN MEAL

Baked Halibut, 3 ounces, with 1 teaspoon reduced-calorie tub margarine and pinch *each* garlic powder and paprika

Baked Potato, 8 ounces, with 3 tablespoons plain nonfat yogurt and 1 tablespoon minced fresh chives

Steamed Asparagus, 6 spears, with Lemon "Butter" (In small cup or bowl, combine 1 teaspoon *each* reduced-calorie tub margarine, melted, and fresh lemon juice.)

Steamed Red Bell Pepper Strips, 1 cup

Tossed Green Salad, 2 cups, with ^{1}/2 cup sliced cucumber and 1 tablespoon fat-free Italian dressing

Peach, 1 medium

Diet Lemonade, 1 cup

SNACK

Plain Popcorn, hot-air popped, 3 cups

Vanilla "Egg Cream" (In tall glass, combine 1 cup diet cream soda and ^{1}/2 cup skim milk.)

This menu provides: 2 Milks, 3 Fats, 2 Fruits, 12 Vegetables, 5 Proteins, 5^1/2 Breads, 80 Optional Calories.

Per serving: 25 g Fat, 28 g Fiber.

This menu provides: 2 Milks, 3 Fats, 2 Fruits, 15 Vegetables, 4 Proteins, $5^1/2$ Breads, 70 Optional Calories.

Per serving: 24 g Fat, 28 g Fiber.

196
BARBECUED CHICKEN SALAD

Makes 4 servings

2 teaspoons mild or hot chili powder
2 teaspoons onion powder
1 teaspoon garlic powder
1 teaspoon paprika
10 ounces skinless boneless chicken breasts
8 cups torn Romaine lettuce leaves
2 medium tomatoes, each sliced into 8 wedges
1 cup cooked corn kernels
2 thin red onion slices, separated into rings
2 tablespoons fat-free ranch dressing

1. Preheat oven to 350° F.

2. To prepare barbecue rub, in small bowl, combine chili, onion and garlic powders and paprika; rub evenly over both sides of chicken breasts.

3. Place chicken onto large sheet of foil; wrap chicken in foil, crimping edges to seal. Place foil packet onto baking sheet; bake 8 minutes. Carefully open foil packet; bake 4 minutes, until chicken is cooked through and juices run clear when pierced with fork. Set aside to cool.

4. Meanwhile, place lettuce into large bowl; top with tomatoes, corn and onion.

5. With fork, shred cooled chicken; add to lettuce mixture. Drizzle evenly with dressing.

Serving ($2^1/2$ cups) provides: 5 Vegetables, 2 Proteins, $^1/2$ Bread, 10 Optional Calories.

Per serving: 183 Calories, 2 g Total Fat, 0 g Saturated Fat, 41 mg Cholesterol, 160 mg Sodium, 22 g Total Carbohydrate, 5 g Dietary Fiber, 21 g Protein, 63 mg Calcium.

197
OPEN-FACE SMOKED BLT&T

Makes 4 servings

We've taken the ever-popular BLT and updated it with turkey bacon and smoked turkey to create this BLT&T—bacon, lettuce, tomato and turkey sandwich.

3 tablespoons + 1 teaspoon light sour cream
2 tablespoons + 2 teaspoons reduced-calorie mayonnaise
10 small black olives, pitted and chopped
$^3/_4$ teaspoon freshly ground black pepper
6 ounces skinless boneless smoked turkey breast, thinly sliced
8 slices reduced-calorie multi-grain bread
12 medium loose-leaf lettuce leaves
4 medium beefsteak tomatoes, sliced
2 medium red onions, thinly sliced
4 slices crisp-cooked lean turkey bacon (30 calories per slice)

1. Preheat oven to 350° F. Adjust oven rack to divide oven in half.

2. In small bowl, combine sour cream, mayonnaise, olives and pepper; refrigerate, covered, until chilled.

3. Stack turkey slices; wrap in sheet of foil, crimping edges to seal. Stack bread slices; wrap in sheet of foil, crimping edges to seal. Place foil packets onto baking sheet; bake in center of oven 5–8 minutes, until turkey and bread are warmed.

4. To assemble sandwiches, spread one side of each warm bread slice with 1 tablespoon of the sour cream mixture; place 2 bread slices, spread-side up, onto each of 4 plates. Arrange 3 lettuce leaves, one-fourth of the tomato and onion slices, $1^1/_2$ ounces warm turkey and 1 crisp bacon slice across both slices of bread; top each with one-fourth of the remaining sour cream mixture.

Serving (1 sandwich) provides: $1^1/_4$ Fats, $3^1/_4$ Vegetables, $1^1/_2$ Proteins, 1 Bread, 45 Optional Calories.

Per serving: 274 Calories, 11 g Total Fat, 2 g Saturated Fat, 35 mg Cholesterol, 963 mg Sodium, 32 g Total Carbohydrate, 8 g Dietary Fiber, 17 g Protein, 80 mg Calcium.

BREAKFAST
Grapefruit, $^1/_2$ medium
Cheddar Scramble (Spray small nonstick skillet with nonstick cooking spray; heat. Add $^1/_4$ cup egg substitute; cook, stirring frequently, until mixture is just set. Sprinkle with $^3/_4$ ounce reduced-fat cheddar cheese, grated; cook, stirring frequently, until cheese is melted.)
Reduced-Calorie Whole-Wheat Bread, 2 slices, toasted, with 2 teaspoons reduced-calorie tub margarine
Skim Milk, $^1/_2$ cup
Coffee or Tea (optional)

LIGHT MEAL
Tomato Soup, canned, 1 cup, with 2 ounces drained cooked red kidney beans
Open-Face Smoked BLT&T, 1 serving (see recipe)
Carrot and Cucumber Sticks, 1 cup *each*
Seedless Green Grapes, 6 large
Iced Tea

MAIN MEAL
Spaghetti with Fresh Tomato Sauce (In small saucepan, combine 1 cup chopped tomatoes, $^1/_2$ cup chopped onion, 2 garlic cloves, minced, and $^1/_4$ teaspoon dried Italian seasoning; cook over medium-low heat, stirring occasionally, 10 minutes, until onion is tender and flavors are blended. Serve over 1 cup cooked whole-wheat spaghetti.)
Marinated Artichoke Hearts (In small bowl, combine $^1/_2$ cup cooked artichoke hearts and 1 tablespoon fat-free Italian dressing; refrigerate, covered, at least 1 hour or overnight.)
Spinach-Vegetable Salad (In medium bowl, combine 2 cups torn spinach leaves, $^1/_2$ cup *each* sliced mushrooms and red onion, 1 tablespoon imitation bacon bits and 1 tablespoon fresh lemon juice.)
Italian Bread, 1 slice (1 ounce), with $1^1/_2$ teaspoons reduced-calorie tub margarine
Aspartame-Sweetened Raspberry Nonfat Yogurt, 1 cup, with 1 tablespoon raisins
Sparkling Mineral Water

SNACK
Graham Crackers, 3 ($2^1/_2$" squares)
Skim Milk, $^1/_2$ cup

This menu provides: 2 Milks, 3 Fats, 2 Fruits, $19^1/_4$ Vegetables, $4^1/_2$ Proteins, 6 Breads, 125 Optional Calories.

Per serving: 34 g Fat, 41 g Fiber.

Open-Face Smoked BLT&T

198

GRILLED TURKEY SANDWICHES CUBANO

Makes 4 servings

Four 2-ounce hard rolls or four 2-ounce slices French bread, split lengthwise

2 teaspoons prepared mustard

$1^1/2$ ounces lean smoked turkey breast cold cuts (up to 2 grams fat per serving)

$1^1/2$ ounces reduced-fat Swiss cheese, very thinly sliced

$^1/2$ medium dill pickle, thinly sliced lengthwise

2 teaspoons olive oil

1. To assemble sandwiches, place bottom halves of rolls onto work surface; spread each with $^1/2$ teaspoon mustard. Top each with one-fourth of the turkey, cheese and pickle, then 1 roll top.

2. With pastry brush, lightly brush outside of each sandwich with oil.

3. Heat medium nonstick skillet; add 2 sandwiches. Cook over medium-high heat, pressing sandwiches down with bottom of separate heavy skillet or other heavy heat-resistant object, 1–$1^1/2$ minutes, until lightly toasted on bottom. Turn sandwiches over; cook until lightly toasted and flattened. Transfer each sandwich to plate; repeat with remaining sandwiches.

Serving (1 sandwich) provides: $^1/2$ Fat, $^1/4$ Vegetable, $^3/4$ Protein, 2 Breads.

Per serving: 232 Calories, 7 g Total Fat, 2 g Saturated Fat, 10 mg Cholesterol, 569 mg Sodium, 31 g Total Carbohydrate, 1 g Dietary Fiber, 11 g Protein, 57 mg Calcium.

BREAKFAST

Banana, $^1/2$ medium, sliced

Bran Flakes Cereal, $^3/4$ ounce

Reduced-Calorie Whole-Wheat Bread, 2 slices, toasted, with 1 teaspoon each reduced-calorie tub margarine and apple butter

Skim Milk, $^1/2$ cup

Coffee or Tea (optional)

LIGHT MEAL

Grilled Turkey Sandwiches Cubano, 1 serving (see recipe)

Red Bell Pepper Strips and Broccoli Florets, 1 cup each

Cherry Tomatoes, 6

Pear, 1 small

Diet Grape Soda

MAIN MEAL

Baked Chicken Breast, 3 ounces

Cooked Whole-Wheat Spaghetti, 1 cup, with 1 cup cooked diced eggplant and $^1/2$ cup tomato sauce (no salt added)

Torn Romaine Lettuce Leaves, 2 cups, with $^1/2$ cup each shredded red cabbage and sliced celery, 2 ounces drained cooked red kidney beans and 1 tablespoon Italian dressing

Reduced-Calorie Chocolate-Flavored Pudding (made with skim milk), $^1/2$ cup

Sparkling Mineral Water with Lemon Wedge

SNACK

Aspartame-Sweetened Black Cherry Nonfat Yogurt, 1 cup

This menu provides: 2 Milks, 3 Fats, 2 Fruits, $15^1/4$ Vegetables, $4^3/4$ Proteins, 6 Breads, 50 Optional Calories.

Per serving: 24 g Fat, 32 g Fiber.

199
TURKEY GAZPACHO SALAD

*The refreshing soup gazpacho inspired this salad—the addition of
turkey transforms it into a sparkling light meal.*

8 ounces skinless boneless cooked turkey breast, cut into bite-size pieces
2 cups coarsely chopped plum tomatoes
$1^1/_2$ cups coarsely chopped green bell peppers
1 cup thawed frozen corn kernels
1 cup coarsely chopped celery
1 cup diced seeded cucumber
$^1/_2$ cup finely chopped red onion
$^1/_4$ cup red wine vinegar
1 tablespoon + 1 teaspoon olive oil
1 teaspoon Dijon-style mustard
$^1/_2$ teaspoon freshly ground black pepper
$^1/_2$ teaspoon granulated sugar
$^1/_2$ teaspoon dried tarragon leaves
$^1/_4$ teaspoon salt
1 cup medium or hot salsa
$2^1/_2$ cups packed torn curly-leaf lettuce leaves (bite-size pieces)
$1^1/_2$ cups packaged croutons

1. In large shallow serving bowl, combine turkey, tomatoes, bell peppers,
corn, celery, cucumber and onion; set aside.

2. In small jar with tight-fitting lid or small bowl, combine vinegar, oil,
mustard, black pepper, sugar, tarragon and salt; cover and shake well or,
with wire whisk, blend until combined. Pour vinegar mixture over turkey
mixture; toss to coat. Add salsa; toss again.

3. Arrange lettuce around edge of salad. Serve immediately or refrigerate,
covered, until chilled. Sprinkle with croutons just before serving.

Serving (2 cups) provides: $1^3/_4$ Fats, $5^1/_4$ Vegetables, 2 Proteins, $1^1/_4$ Breads.

Per serving: 279 Calories, 7 g Total Fat, 1 g Saturated Fat, 47 mg Cholesterol,
960 mg Sodium, 34 g Total Carbohydrate, 5 g Dietary Fiber, 22 g Protein,
86 mg Calcium.

200
TURKEY À LA KING

Makes 4 servings

1 cup low-sodium chicken broth
8 whole black peppercorns
10 ounces skinless boneless turkey
  breast
$^1/_4$ cup reduced-calorie stick
  margarine
2 cups thinly sliced mushrooms
1 cup coarsely chopped green bell
  pepper
$^1/_2$ cup thinly sliced scallions
$^1/_3$ cup + 2 teaspoons all-purpose
  flour
2 cups skim milk

$^1/_2$ cup drained canned pimientos,
  cut into strips
$^1/_2$ fluid ounce (1 tablespoon) dry
  sherry
$^1/_2$ teaspoon salt
$^1/_2$ teaspoon ground white pepper
$^1/_4$ cup minced fresh flat-leaf
  parsley
Four crust-trimmed 1-ounce slices
  multi-grain bread, toasted and
  cut into 4 triangles each
$^1/_4$ teaspoon paprika

1. In large skillet, combine $^1/_2$ cup of the broth, the peppercorns and 1 cup water; bring liquid to a boil. Add turkey; return liquid to a boil. Reduce heat to low; poach turkey, covered, 7 minutes, until cooked through. With slotted spoon, transfer turkey to cutting board; discard liquid and peppercorns. Let turkey cool; cut into bite-size pieces. Set aside.

2. In large nonstick skillet, melt 1 tablespoon of the margarine; add mushrooms. Cook over medium-high heat, stirring frequently, 5 minutes, until tender. With slotted spoon, remove mushrooms from skillet; set aside.

3. In same skillet, combine bell pepper and scallions; cook, stirring frequently, 5 minutes, until bell pepper is tender. With slotted spoon, remove bell pepper mixture from skillet; set aside.

4. In same skillet, melt remaining 3 tablespoons margarine; sprinkle with flour. Cook over medium-high heat, stirring constantly, 3 minutes, until mixture is bubbling. With wire whisk, gradually add milk and remaining $^1/_2$ cup broth; continuing to stir, cook 5 minutes, until mixture is thickened. Add pimientos, sherry, salt, white pepper, cooked turkey, mushrooms and bell pepper mixture; cook, stirring frequently, 3 minutes, until mixture is heated through. Remove from heat; stir in parsley.

5. Place 4 toast triangles onto each of 4 plates; top each with one-fourth of the turkey mixture. Sprinkle evenly with paprika.

Serving (1 cup turkey mixture, 4 toast triangles) provides: $^1/_2$ Milk, 2 Fats, 2 Vegetables, 2 Proteins, $1^1/_2$ Breads, 10 Optional Calories.

Per serving: 319 Calories, 8 g Total Fat, 2 g Saturated Fat, 46 mg Cholesterol, 670 mg Sodium, 34 g Total Carbohydrate, 4 g Dietary Fiber, 28 g Protein, 212 mg Calcium.

BREAKFAST
Blackberries, $^3/_4$ cup
Toasted Oat Cereal, $^3/_4$ ounce
Skim Milk, 1 cup
Coffee or Tea (optional)

LIGHT MEAL
Turkey à la King, 1 serving (see recipe)
Steamed Sliced Carrots, 1 cup
Torn Spinach Leaves, 2 cups, with $^1/_2$ cup sliced cucumber and 1 tablespoon fat-free Italian dressing
Orange, 1 small
Iced Herbal Tea

MAIN MEAL
Broiled Extra-Lean Hamburger, 2 ounces, on 2-ounce hamburger roll with 2 Romaine lettuce leaves, 2 tomato slices and 2 teaspoons ketchup
Coleslaw, $^1/_4$ cup
Celery Sticks, 1 cup
Frozen Raspberry Pop (Pour $^1/_2$ cup low-calorie raspberry-flavored drink into small paper cup; freeze until almost firm. Insert ice-cream-bar stick vertically into partially frozen drink; freeze until solid. Unmold.)
Diet Black Cherry Soda

SNACK
Reduced-Calorie Chocolate-Flavored Pudding (made with skim milk), $^1/_2$ cup, with 3 tablespoons graham cracker crumbs

This menu provides: 2 Milks, 3 Fats, 2 Fruits, $12^1/_2$ Vegetables, 4 Proteins, $5^1/_2$ Breads, 70 Optional Calories.

Per serving: 25 g Fat, 24 g Fiber.

LIGHT MEAL
Turkey Sausage Pizza, 1 serving (see recipe)
Carrot and Celery Sticks, 1 cup *each*
Caesar Salad (In medium bowl, combine 2 cups torn
Romaine lettuce leaves, $^1/_4$ cup packaged croutons
and 1 tablespoon fat-free Caesar salad dressing.)
Sugar-Free Strawberry Nonfat Frozen Yogurt, 4 fluid
ounces
Iced Tea with Mint Sprig

MAIN MEAL
Baked Ziti (Preheat oven to 350° F. In medium
bowl, combine $^1/_2$ cup part-skim ricotta cheese,
2 tablespoons tomato sauce [no salt added] and
$^1/_4$ teaspoon *each* garlic powder, dried oregano
leaves and basil. Add $^3/_4$ cup cooked ziti macaroni;
stir to combine. Transfer to small shallow baking
dish; top with $^1/_4$ cup tomato sauce [no salt
added] and $^3/_4$ ounce skim-milk mozzarella
cheese, grated. Bake 15–20 minutes, until cheese
is melted and mixture is bubbling.)
Steamed Red and Green Bell Pepper Strips, 1 cup
each
Romaine and Bibb Lettuce Salad, 2 cups, with 1 cup
cucumber slices, 1 ounce drained cooked red kidney beans and 1 tablespoon Italian dressing.
Italian Bread, 1 slice (1 ounce), with 1 teaspoon
reduced-calorie tub margarine
Sugar-Free Lime-Flavored Gelatin, $^1/_2$ cup
Sparkling Mineral Water

SNACK
Banana Shake (In blender, combine $^3/_4$ cup skim
milk, $^1/_2$ medium banana, sliced, 3 ice cubes and
sugar substitute to equal 2 teaspoons sugar; purée
until smooth.)

This menu provides: 2 Milks, 3 Fats, 2 Fruits,
$20^1/_4$ Vegetables, 5 Proteins, 6 Breads, 85 Optional
Calories.

Per serving: 35 g Fat, 22 g Fiber.

201
TURKEY SAUSAGE PIZZA

*Turkey sausage has become a supermarket staple throughout the
country; try it in place of pork sausage in this classic pizza.*

Makes 4 servings

1 teaspoon all-purpose flour
8 ounces refrigerated, frozen or ready-made pizza dough
$^1/_4$ cup tomato sauce (no salt added)
$^3/_4$ cup sliced red bell pepper
$^1/_4$ cup thinly sliced red onion
4 ounces cooked turkey sausage, crumbled
$1^1/_2$ ounces skim-milk mozzarella cheese, grated
2 tablespoons minced fresh basil leaves
$^1/_4$ teaspoon freshly ground black pepper, or to taste

1. Preheat oven to 450° F.

2. Sprinkle flour onto work surface. Place dough onto floured surface;
turn to coat. With rolling pin or fingers, stretch dough into 10–12" circle;
transfer to nonstick baking sheet.

3. Spread tomato sauce onto dough. Arrange bell pepper and onion over
sauce; sprinkle vegetables with sausage, cheese, basil and black pepper.
Bake 20 minutes, until crust is browned and crisp.

Serving (one-quarter pizza) provides: $^3/_4$ Vegetable, $1^1/_2$ Proteins, 2 Breads,
5 Optional Calories.

Per serving: 256 Calories, 8 g Total Fat, 3 g Saturated Fat, 25 mg Cholesterol,
598 mg Sodium, 32 g Total Carbohydrate, 2 g Dietary Fiber, 14 g Protein,
94 mg Calcium.

202
SLOPPY JOES

A meal in a sandwich, this spicy dinner is as simple as it is scrumptious. To keep the fat at bay, be sure to use chicken ground from skinless breasts.

Makes 4 servings

Four 2-ounce hamburger rolls, split
2 teaspoons olive oil
2 cups chopped red bell peppers
1 cup chopped red onions
3 garlic cloves, minced
$^1/_4$ teaspoon freshly ground black pepper
15 ounces ground skinless chicken breasts
$^1/_2$ teaspoon salt
$^1/_2$ cup tomato sauce (no salt added)
$^1/_4$ cup bottled chili sauce
1 tablespoon Worcestershire sauce
$^1/_4$ teaspoon hot red pepper sauce, or to taste
1 tablespoon red wine vinegar

1. Preheat oven to 300° F.

2. Wrap hamburger rolls in foil; bake 15 minutes, until warm.

3. Meanwhile, in large nonstick skillet, heat oil; add bell peppers, onions, garlic and black pepper. Cook over medium-high heat, stirring frequently, 3 minutes, until vegetables are softened.

4. Add chicken and salt; cook, stirring to break up meat, 4–5 minutes, until chicken is no longer pink. Stir in tomato, chili, Worcestershire and hot red pepper sauces; bring liquid just to a boil. Reduce heat to low; simmer, stirring frequently, 5 minutes, until mixture is thickened. Stir in vinegar.

5. Place bottom half of each roll onto each of 4 plates; top with one-fourth of the chicken mixture, then 1 remaining roll half.

Serving ($^3/_4$ cup chicken mixture, 1 hamburger roll) provides: $^1/_2$ Fat, 2 Vegetables, 3 Proteins, 2 Breads, 20 Optional Calories.

Per serving: 365 Calories, 7 g Total Fat, 1 g Saturated Fat, 62 mg Cholesterol, 950 mg Sodium, 44 g Total Carbohydrate, 3 g Dietary Fiber, 32 g Protein, 117 mg Calcium.

BREAKFAST
Cantaloupe, $^1/_4$ small
Reduced-Calorie Whole-Wheat Bread, 2 slices, toasted, with 2 teaspoons apricot jam
Skim Milk, $^1/_2$ cup
Coffee or Tea (optional)

LIGHT MEAL
Spinach and Bean Salad (In medium bowl, combine 2 cups torn spinach leaves, $^1/_2$ cup *each* sliced mushrooms and red onion, 2 ounces drained cooked white beans, 1 tablespoon imitation bacon bits and 1 tablespoon ranch dressing.)
Breadsticks, 2 long
Fruit Salad, $^1/_2$ cup
Sparkling Mineral Water

MAIN MEAL
Sloppy Joes, 1 serving (see recipe)
Baked Beans, without meat, canned, $^1/_2$ cup
Caesar Salad (In medium bowl, combine 2 cups torn Romaine lettuce leaves, $^1/_4$ cup packaged croutons and 1 tablespoon fat-free Caesar salad dressing.)
Aspartame-Sweetened Vanilla Nonfat Yogurt, 1 cup
Sparkling Mineral Water with Lime Wedge

SNACK
Graham Crackers, 3 ($2^1/_2$" squares)
Decaffeinated Cappuccino, made with skim milk, 5 fluid ounces

---

This menu provides: 2 Milks, 3 Fats, 2 Fruits, $12^1/_2$ Vegetables, 5 Proteins, $5^1/_2$ Breads, 140 Optional Calories.

Per serving: 24 g Fat, 31 g Fiber.

BREAKFAST
Orange, 1 small
Shredded Wheat Cereal, $^3/4$ ounce
Skim Milk, 1 cup
Coffee or Tea (optional)

LIGHT MEAL
Cheddar Toss (In medium bowl, combine 2 cups
  tossed green salad, 2 ounces drained cooked red
  kidney beans, $^1/4$ cup diced red onion, $^3/4$ ounce
  reduced-fat cheddar cheese, cubed, and 1 tablespoon Italian dressing.)
Celery and Carrot Sticks, 1 cup *each*
Melba Slices, 4
Sugar-Free Berry-Flavored Gelatin, $^1/2$ cup, with
  1 tablespoon thawed frozen light whipped topping (8 calories per tablespoon)
Diet Cola with Lemon Wedge

MAIN MEAL
Chicken Souvlaki, 1 serving (see recipe)
Cooked Barley, 1 cup, with $^1/2$ cup cooked sliced
  mushrooms
Steamed Spinach, 1 cup
Steamed Sliced Yellow Squash, 1 cup
Honeydew Melon, 2" wedge
Sparkling Mineral Water

SNACK
Whole-Wheat English Muffin, $^1/2$ (1 ounce), toasted,
  with 1 teaspoon *each* peanut butter and grape jam
Skim Milk, $^3/4$ cup

This menu provides: 2 Milks, 3 Fats, 2 Fruits,
14 Vegetables, 4 Proteins, 6 Breads, 65 Optional
Calories.

Per serving: 22 g Fat, 35 g Fiber.

CHICKEN SOUVLAKI

This popular dish of meat marinated in olive oil, lemon juice and
herbs, then skewered and grilled, comes from Greece.

Makes 4 servings

1 tablespoon + 1 teaspoon fresh lemon juice
2 teaspoons olive oil
3 garlic cloves, minced
1 teaspoon dried oregano leaves
$^1/2$ teaspoon ground cumin
$^1/2$ teaspoon freshly ground black pepper
$^1/4$ teaspoon salt
10 ounces skinless boneless chicken breasts, cut into sixteen 5 × $^3/4$" strips
1 cup plain nonfat yogurt
$^1/2$ medium cucumber, pared, seeded and shredded
$^1/2$ cup grated radishes
2 tablespoons minced fresh mint leaves
1 tablespoon minced fresh dill
4 small (1-ounce) pitas, quartered

1. Soak sixteen 10" bamboo skewers in water 30 minutes.

2. Preheat outdoor barbecue grill according to manufacturer's directions,
or preheat broiler and spray rack in broiler pan with nonstick cooking
spray.

3. To prepare marinade, in gallon-size sealable plastic bag, combine juice,
oil, garlic, oregano, cumin, pepper and salt; add chicken. Seal bag, squeezing out air; turn to coat chicken. Refrigerate 15 minutes, turning bag
occasionally.

4. Meanwhile, in small bowl, combine yogurt, cucumber, radishes, mint
and dill; set aside.

5. Drain and discard marinade. Thread an equal amount of chicken onto
each prepared skewer, inserting skewer into each chicken strip 2–3 times.
Grill chicken over hot coals or place onto prepared rack in broiler pan and
broil 4" from heat 4–5 minutes, turning frequently, until chicken is
cooked through. Serve with pita quarters and yogurt mixture for dipping.

Serving (4 skewers, $^1/4$ cup yogurt mixture, 4 pita quarters) provides: $^1/4$ Milk,
$^1/2$ Vegetable, 2 Proteins, 1 Bread, 30 Optional Calories.

Per serving: 206 Calories, 3 g Total Fat, 1 g Saturated Fat, 42 mg Cholesterol,
315 mg Sodium, 22 g Total Carbohydrate, 8 g Dietary Fiber, 22 g Protein,
162 mg Calcium.

204
CHICKEN PO' BOYS

In New Orleans, these sandwiches are filled with a variety of foods. Our Po' Boy is stuffed with Cajun chicken, Monterey Jack cheese and plump red tomatoes.

Makes 4 servings

One 8-ounce baguette, about 12 × 2"
3 tablespoons + 1 teaspoon nonfat sour cream
2 tablespoons + 2 teaspoons reduced-calorie mayonnaise
1 tablespoon hickory-flavored barbecue sauce
2 teaspoons hot green (jalapeño) pepper sauce
8 ounces skinless boneless chicken breasts
1 teaspoon Cajun or Creole seasoning, or to taste*
2 teaspoons vegetable oil
1 garlic clove, minced
4 cups shredded iceberg lettuce leaves
3 ounces reduced-fat Monterey Jack cheese, sliced
2 medium beefsteak tomatoes, thinly sliced

1. Preheat oven to 350° F. Adjust oven rack to divide oven in half.

2. With serrated knife, split baguette horizontally almost through roll. Wrap baguette tightly in foil; bake in center of oven 15 minutes, until heated through. Remove from oven; keep warm.

3. Meanwhile, in cup or small bowl, combine sour cream, mayonnaise and barbecue and pepper sauces; set aside.

4. Place chicken between 2 sheets of wax paper; with meat mallet or bottom of heavy saucepan, pound chicken to ¹/₂" thickness. Remove and discard wax paper; cut chicken into 3" pieces. Sprinkle chicken pieces on both sides with Cajun seasoning.

5. In large nonstick skillet, heat oil; add garlic. Cook over medium-high heat, stirring constantly, 1 minute, until softened. Add chicken; cook, turning as needed, 5–6 minutes, until chicken is cooked through.

6. To assemble sandwiches, place warm baguette onto work surface. Spread bottom half with sour cream mixture; top evenly with lettuce, then cooked chicken, cheese and tomatoes. With serrated knife, cut baguette crosswise into 4 equal pieces.

Serving (one-fourth filled baguette) provides: 1¹/₂ Fats, 3 Vegetables, 2¹/₂ Proteins, 2 Breads, 15 Optional Calories.

Per serving: 367 Calories, 12 g Total Fat, 4 g Saturated Fat, 51 mg Cholesterol, 930 mg Sodium, 38 g Total Carbohydrate, 3 g Dietary Fiber, 27 g Protein, 296 mg Calcium.

*Cajun and Creole seasonings are available in the spice section of most supermarkets.

BREAKFAST
Apple, 1 small
Parmesan Scramble (Spray small nonstick skillet with nonstick cooking spray; heat. Add ¹/₄ cup egg substitute; cook, stirring frequently, until mixture is just set. Sprinkle with 1 teaspoon freshly grated Parmesan cheese; cook, stirring frequently, until cheese is melted.)
Reduced-Calorie Whole-Wheat Bread, 2 slices, toasted, with 1 teaspoon *each* reduced-calorie tub margarine and apple butter
Skim Milk, ¹/₂ cup
Coffee or Tea (optional)

LIGHT MEAL
Macaroni Salad (In medium bowl, combine 1 cup cooked elbow macaroni, ¹/₄ cup diced celery, 2 sun-dried tomato halves [not packed in oil], diced, 2 teaspoons reduced-calorie mayonnaise and 1 teaspoon *each* fresh lemon juice and red wine vinegar.)
Steamed Broccoli Florets, 1 cup
Reduced-Calorie Butterscotch-Flavored Pudding (made with skim milk), ¹/₂ cup
Iced Herbal Tea

MAIN MEAL
Chicken Po' Boys, 1 serving (see recipe)
Baked Beans, without meat, canned, ¹/₂ cup
Tossed Green Salad, 2 cups, with ¹/₂ cup *each* shredded carrot and sliced cucumber and 1 tablespoon fat-free Italian dressing
Watermelon, 3 × 2" wedge
Unsweetened Mandarin Orange–Flavored Seltzer

SNACK
Reduced-Calorie Chocolate Dairy Shake, 1 serving

This menu provides: 2 Milks, 3 Fats, 2 Fruits, 13 Vegetables, 4¹/₂ Proteins, 5 Breads, 120 Optional Calories.

Per serving: 23 g Fat, 36 g Fiber.

205
CHICKEN AND CHEESE ENCHILADAS

Enchiladas, the Mexican version of rolled-up sandwiches, can be found on menus for morning, noon and evening meals.

Makes 4 servings

$^3/_4$ cup nonfat sour cream
$^1/_2$ cup thinly sliced scallions
$^1/_4$ cup minced fresh cilantro
$^1/_2$ teaspoon ground cumin
10 ounces skinless boneless chicken breasts, cut into strips
$^1/_2$ teaspoon salt
2 teaspoons vegetable oil
2 garlic cloves, minced
Four 6" flour tortillas
3 ounces reduced-fat cheddar cheese, grated
$^1/_2$ cup mild or medium salsa
$^1/_2$ cup chopped tomato
Fresh cilantro sprigs, to garnish

1. Preheat oven to 350° F. Spray 13 × 9" baking pan with nonstick cooking spray.

2. In small bowl, combine sour cream, scallions, minced cilantro and cumin; set aside.

3. Sprinkle chicken on all sides with salt. Heat oil in large nonstick skillet; add chicken and garlic. Cook over medium-high heat, stirring frequently, 4 minutes, until chicken is cooked through.

4. To assemble enchiladas, place tortillas in a single layer onto work surface. Arrange one-fourth of the chicken mixture along center of each tortilla; top each portion of chicken with an equal amount of reserved sour cream mixture. Fold sides of tortillas over filling to enclose; place, seam-side down, into prepared baking pan. Sprinkle evenly with cheese; bake, tightly covered, 25 minutes, until filling is hot and bubbling and cheese is melted.

5. Spoon salsa crosswise along center of enchiladas; sprinkle salsa with tomato. Serve garnished with cilantro sprigs.

Serving (1 enchilada) provides: $^1/_2$ Fat, 1 Vegetable, 3 Proteins, 1 Bread, 30 Optional Calories.

Per serving: 277 Calories, 9 g Total Fat, 3 g Saturated Fat, 56 mg Cholesterol, 935 mg Sodium, 19 g Total Carbohydrate, 1 g Dietary Fiber, 29 g Protein, 295 mg Calcium.

206
Chicken Chili

Chipotle peppers in adobo sauce is a wonderfully versatile product, available in Hispanic grocery stores; purée it in a blender or food processor and store it in the fridge. Add a spoonful or two to sauces, chili or dressings; its smoky heat is instantly addictive.

Makes 4 servings

4 ounces regular long-grain rice
2 teaspoons corn oil
1 1/2 cups chopped onions
1 cup chopped red bell pepper
1 cup chopped yellow bell pepper
1/2 cup chopped green bell pepper
13 ounces skinless boneless chicken breasts, cut into 1" chunks
1 medium minced deveined seeded jalapeño pepper (wear gloves to prevent irritation)
1 tablespoon mild or hot chili powder
1/2 teaspoon cumin seed
1 1/2 cups low-sodium chicken broth
2 tablespoons yellow cornmeal, mixed with 2 tablespoons water
1 teaspoon pureed canned chipotle peppers in adobo sauce, or to taste
2 tablespoons minced fresh cilantro

1. In medium saucepan, bring 1 1/2 cups water to a boil; add rice. Reduce heat to low; simmer, covered, 17 minutes, until rice is tender and all liquid is absorbed. Remove from heat; keep warm.

2. In large nonstick skillet, heat oil; add onions and red, yellow and green bell peppers. Cook over medium heat, stirring frequently, 5 minutes, until vegetables are softened. Add chicken, jalapeño pepper, chili powder and cumin seed; cook, stirring occasionally, 5 minutes, until chicken is cooked through.

3. Add broth, cornmeal mixture and chipotle peppers; bring liquid to a boil. Reduce heat to low; simmer, stirring occasionally, 15 minutes, until mixture is thickened and flavors are blended. Serve over warm rice; sprinkle with cilantro.

Serving (1 1/4 cups chili, 1/2 cup rice) provides: 1/2 Fat, 2 1/4 Vegetables, 2 1/2 Proteins, 1 1/4 Breads, 10 Optional Calories.

Per serving: 299 Calories, 5 g Total Fat, 1 g Saturated Fat, 53 mg Cholesterol, 138 mg Sodium, 37 g Total Carbohydrate, 3 g Dietary Fiber, 26 g Protein, 52 mg Calcium.

BREAKFAST
Grapefruit, 1/2 medium
Reduced-Calorie Multi-Grain Bread, 2 slices, toasted, with 2 teaspoons reduced-calorie tub margarine
Skim Milk, 1 cup
Coffee or Tea (optional)

LIGHT MEAL
Tuna Salad Sandwich (In small bowl, combine 4 ounces drained canned water-packed tuna, flaked, 1/2 cup chopped celery, 2 teaspoons reduced-calorie mayonnaise and pinch freshly ground black pepper; spread between 2 slices reduced-calorie rye bread.)
Whole Mushrooms, 1 cup
Cherry Tomatoes, 6
Pear, 1 small
Iced Herbal Tea

MAIN MEAL
Chicken Chili, 1 serving (see recipe)
Nonfat Tortilla Chips, 1 ounce
Chopped Iceberg Lettuce and Diced Tomatoes, 1/2 cup *each*
Cooked Whole Wax Beans, 1 cup, with 1 teaspoon reduced-calorie tub margarine
Sugar-Free Chocolate Nonfat Frozen Yogurt, 4 fluid ounces
Unsweetened Seltzer with Lime Wedge

SNACK
Plain Popcorn, hot-air popped, 3 cups
Skim Milk, 3/4 cup

This menu provides: 2 Milks, 3 Fats, 2 Fruits, 10 1/4 Vegetables, 4 1/2 Proteins, 5 1/4 Breads, 60 Optional Calories.

Per serving: 22 g Fat, 24 g Fiber.

207
CHICKEN-CORN-CHILI BAKE

*The Chili-Mac, once popular in school lunchrooms, has been updated.
This version uses chicken instead of beef, plus plenty of corn, beans
and cheese.*

Makes 4 servings

$4^1/_2$ ounces elbow macaroni
7 ounces ground skinless chicken breasts
1 cup chopped onions
1 cup chopped green bell pepper
2 tablespoons mild or hot chili powder
2 garlic cloves, minced
$^3/_4$ teaspoon ground cumin
$^1/_2$ teaspoon dried oregano leaves
$^1/_4$ teaspoon salt
$^1/_4$ teaspoon granulated sugar
$^1/_4$ teaspoon ground red pepper
2 cups canned Mexican-style stewed tomatoes, chopped
1 cup thawed frozen corn kernels
4 ounces drained cooked red kidney beans
$3^3/_4$ ounces reduced-fat Monterey Jack cheese, grated

1. Preheat oven to 375° F. Spray shallow 2-quart casserole or au gratin
dish with nonstick cooking spray.

2. In large pot of boiling water, cook macaroni 8–10 minutes, until tender. Drain, discarding liquid. Set aside; keep warm.

3. Meanwhile, spray large nonstick skillet with nonstick cooking spray;
heat. Add chicken, onions and $^3/_4$ cup of the bell pepper; cook, stirring to
break up meat, 4–5 minutes, until no longer pink. Add chili powder,
garlic, cumin, oregano, salt, sugar and ground red pepper; cook, stirring
constantly, 1 minute, until flavors are blended.

4. Add tomatoes, corn and beans to chicken mixture; bring mixture to a
boil. Stir in cooked macaroni; remove from heat.

5. Stir all but $^1/_4$ cup of the cheese into macaroni mixture; transfer to
prepared casserole. Sprinkle evenly with remaining cheese; bake 25 minutes, until mixture is bubbling. Sprinkle with remaining $^1/_4$ cup bell
pepper.

Serving (2 cups) provides: 2 Vegetables, 3 Proteins, 2 Breads.

Per serving: 391 Calories, 7 g Total Fat, 4 g Saturated Fat, 48 mg Cholesterol,
999 mg Sodium, 53 g Total Carbohydrate, 5 g Dietary Fiber, 30 g Protein,
287 mg Calcium.

208
PIZZA RUSTICA

Makes 4 servings

1½ cups marinara sauce

2 tablespoons tomato paste (no salt added)

One ¼-ounce packet active dry yeast

⅔ cup lukewarm water (105–115° F)

1 teaspoon granulated sugar

2 cups minus 2 tablespoons all-purpose flour

¼ teaspoon salt

1 tablespoon + 2½ teaspoons olive oil

2 cups thinly sliced mushrooms

4 garlic cloves, minced

10 ounces ground skinless chicken breasts

1 cup coarsely chopped red onions

1 tablespoon minced fresh oregano

¼ teaspoon crushed red pepper flakes

1 medium red bell pepper, seeded and cut into thin strips

½ medium green bell pepper, seeded and cut into thin strips

½ medium yellow bell pepper, seeded and cut into thin strips

3 ounces peppered goat cheese, crumbled

¼ cup slivered fresh basil

1. Preheat oven to 450° F. Spray 14" pizza pan with nonstick cooking spray.

2. To prepare sauce, in medium bowl, combine marinara sauce and tomato paste, stirring until paste is dissolved; set aside.

3. To prepare dough, in small bowl, sprinkle yeast over water; stir in sugar. Let stand 5 minutes, until mixture is foamy.

4. In large bowl, combine 1¾ cups of the flour and the salt. Make a well in center of flour mixture; pour yeast mixture and 1 tablespoon of the oil into well. With wooden spoon, stir yeast mixture, slowly incorporating flour mixture, until mixture forms a soft dough.

5. Sprinkle work surface with remaining 2 tablespoons flour. Transfer dough to floured surface; knead 3 minutes, until dough is smooth and elastic. Transfer to prepared pizza pan, flattening dough with fingers to fit pan and pressing to form a stand-up rim; set aside.

6. To prepare topping, in large nonstick skillet, heat 1 teaspoon of the remaining oil; add mushrooms and half of the garlic. Cook over medium-high heat, stirring frequently, 5 minutes, until mushrooms are tender. With slotted spoon, remove mushroom mixture from skillet; set aside.

7. In same skillet, combine chicken, onions, oregano, pepper flakes and remaining garlic; cook, stirring to break up meat, 4–5 minutes, until no longer pink. Remove from heat.

8. Spread dough with sauce; top evenly with chicken mixture, mushroom mixture, red, green and yellow bell peppers, cheese and basil. Sprinkle evenly with remaining 1½ teaspoons oil; bake 20 minutes, until crust is crispy and cheese is melted. Cut into 8 wedges.

Serving (2 wedges) provides: 2½ Fats, 4 Vegetables, 3 Proteins, 2½ Breads, 5 Optional Calories.

Per serving: 530 Calories, 16 g Total Fat, 5 g Saturated Fat, 56 mg Cholesterol, 950 mg Sodium, 68 g Total Carbohydrate, 4 g Dietary Fiber, 31 g Protein, 165 mg Calcium.

Pizza Rustica

209
CHICKEN-STUFFED PEPPERS

Makes 4 servings

4 ounces regular long-grain rice
4 medium green, red or yellow bell peppers
2 teaspoons olive oil
1 cup minced red onions
4 garlic cloves, minced
10 ounces ground skinless chicken breasts
$^1/_2$ teaspoon salt

$^1/_2$ teaspoon freshly ground black pepper
1 cup crushed tomatoes (no salt added)
$^1/_2$ cup slivered fresh basil
1 cup tomato sauce (no salt added)
2 medium tomatoes, cut into wedges

1. Preheat oven to 350° F. Spray 8" round baking dish with nonstick cooking spray.

2. In medium saucepan, bring $1^1/_2$ cups water to a boil; add rice. Reduce heat to low; simmer, covered, 17 minutes, until rice is tender and all liquid is absorbed. Remove from heat; set aside.

3. Meanwhile, with paring knife, cut off stem ends of bell peppers. Remove and discard seeds; reserve peppers and stem ends.

4. In large pot of boiling water, cook peppers and stem ends 5 minutes, until softened; with slotted spoon, transfer peppers and stem ends to paper towels; place cut-side down to drain.

5. In large nonstick skillet, heat oil; add onions and garlic. Cook over medium-high heat, stirring frequently, 5 minutes, until onions are softened. Add chicken, salt and black pepper; cook, stirring to break up meat, 4–5 minutes, until no longer pink. Add crushed tomatoes, $^1/_4$ cup of the basil and the cooked rice; cook, stirring constantly, 3 minutes, until mixture comes to a boil.

6. Spoon one-fourth of the chicken mixture into each drained bell pepper; top each with a stem end. Stand peppers upright in prepared baking dish; bake 30 minutes.

7. Meanwhile, in cup or small bowl, combine tomato sauce and remaining $^1/_4$ cup basil.

8. Spoon tomato sauce mixture over baked peppers; bake 10 minutes longer, until peppers are very tender and filling and sauce are heated through.

9. Transfer stuffed peppers and sauce to serving platter; surround with tomato wedges.

BREAKFAST
Blackberries, $^3/_4$ cup
Reduced-Calorie Multi-Grain Bread, 2 slices, toasted, with 2 slices nonfat process American cheese and 2 teaspoons reduced-calorie tub margarine
Skim Milk, 1 cup
Coffee or Tea (optional)

LIGHT MEAL
Egg Drop Soup, 1 cup
Shrimp Spring Roll, 1
Steamed Bok Choy and Sliced Mushrooms, 1 cup, with 1 tablespoon reduced-sodium soy sauce
Sugar-Free Pineapple-Flavored Gelatin, $^1/_2$ cup
Chinese Tea

MAIN MEAL
Chicken-Stuffed Peppers, 1 serving (see recipe)
Marinated Artichoke Hearts (In small bowl, combine $^1/_2$ cup cooked artichoke hearts and 1 tablespoon fat-free Italian dressing; refrigerate, covered, at least 1 hour or overnight.)
Cooked Collard Greens, 1 cup, with 1 teaspoon balsamic vinegar
Roll, 1 ounce, with 1 teaspoon reduced-calorie tub margarine
Kiwi Fruit, 1 medium, pared and sliced, with $^3/_4$ cup plain nonfat yogurt
Sparkling Mineral Water

SNACK
Plain Popcorn, hot-air popped, 3 cups
Diet Cola

This menu provides: 2 Milks, 3 Fats, 2 Fruits, $10^1/_4$ Vegetables, $3^3/_4$ Proteins, 5 Breads, 40 Optional Calories.

Per serving: 25 g Fat, 33 g Fiber.

Serving (1 stuffed pepper, $^1/_4$ cup sauce, $^1/_2$ cup tomato wedges) provides: $^1/_2$ Fat, 5 Vegetables, 2 Proteins, 1 Bread.

Per serving: 303 Calories, 4 g Total Fat, 1 g Saturated Fat, 41 mg Cholesterol, 445 mg Sodium, 45 g Total Carbohydrate, 5 g Dietary Fiber, 22 g Protein, 111 mg Calcium.

BREAKFAST
Blackberries, $^3/_4$ cup
Reduced-Calorie Multi-Grain Bread, 2 slices,
    toasted, with $2^1/_2$ teaspoons reduced-calorie tub
    margarine
Skim Milk, $^1/_2$ cup
Coffee or Tea (optional)

LIGHT MEAL
Cheese Pizza, thin crust, 1 slice
Tossed Green Salad, 2 cups, with $^1/_2$ cup roasted red
    bell pepper strips and 1 tablespoon fat-free Italian
    dressing
Pear, 1 small
Iced Herbal Tea

MAIN MEAL
Mexican Chicken Spaghettini, 1 serving (see recipe)
Steamed Cauliflower and Broccoli Florets, 1 cup
    each
Torn Romaine and Red Leaf Lettuce Leaves, 2 cups,
    with $^1/_2$ cup *each* red and yellow bell pepper
    strips, 5 small black olives and 1 tablespoon fat-
    free peppercorn ranch dressing
Reduced-Calorie Chocolate-Flavored Pudding (made
    with skim milk), $^1/_2$ cup
Diet Root Beer

SNACK
Graham Crackers, 3 ($2^1/_2$" squares)
Skim Milk, 1 cup

This menu provides: 2 Milks, 3 Fats, 2 Fruits,
$16^1/_2$ Vegetables, 4 Proteins, $5^1/_2$ Breads,
65 Optional Calories.

Per serving: 24 g Fat, 32 g Fiber.

210
MEXICAN CHICKEN SPAGHETTINI

We've tossed spaghettini with a fresh tomato salsa, then topped it with chicken for a spaghetti dinner with a different twist.

Makes 4 servings

6 ounces spaghettini or spaghetti
$1^1/_2$ cups coarsely chopped tomatoes
$^1/_2$ cup chopped scallions
2 tablespoons minced fresh cilantro
1 tablespoon fresh lime juice
1 tablespoon vegetable oil
2 teaspoons minced deveined seeded jalapeño pepper (wear gloves to
    prevent irritation)
$^3/_4$ teaspoon salt
2 teaspoons mild or hot chili powder
$^3/_4$ teaspoon ground cumin
Pinch ground red pepper, or to taste
15 ounces skinless boneless chicken breasts, cut into 1" pieces
Fresh cilantro sprigs, to garnish

1. In large pot of boiling water, cook spaghettini 8–10 minutes, until tender. Drain, discarding liquid; place into serving bowl. Keep warm.

2. Meanwhile, in medium bowl, combine tomatoes, scallions, minced cilantro, juice, 2 teaspoons of the vegetable oil, the jalapeño pepper and $^1/_4$ teaspoon of the salt; set aside.

3. On sheet of wax paper or paper plate, combine chili powder, cumin, ground red pepper and remaining $^1/_2$ teaspoon salt; add chicken, turning to coat evenly.

4. In large nonstick skillet, heat remaining 1 teaspoon oil; add chicken. Cook over medium-high heat, stirring constantly, 4 minutes, until chicken is browned on all sides and cooked through.

5. Pour tomato mixture over warm spaghettini; toss to combine. Top with cooked chicken; serve garnished with cilantro sprigs.

Serving (3 ounces chicken, $1^1/_4$ cups spaghettini mixture) provides: $^3/_4$ Fat, 1 Vegetable, 3 Proteins, 2 Breads.

Per serving: 330 Calories, 6 g Total Fat, 1 g Saturated Fat, 62 mg Cholesterol, 505 mg Sodium, 37 g Total Carbohydrate, 3 g Dietary Fiber, 31 g Protein, 42 mg Calcium.

211

CHICKEN LINGUINE WITH ROASTED RED PEPPER PESTO

Roasted peppers help create a flavorful pesto in this new twist on a favorite pasta dish.

Makes 4 servings

4 medium red bell peppers
4 garlic cloves, peeled
$^{1}/_{4}$ cup packed fresh flat-leaf
  parsley
8 fresh large basil leaves
1 tablespoon + 1 teaspoon olive oil
$^{3}/_{4}$ teaspoon freshly ground black
  pepper

$^{1}/_{2}$ teaspoon salt
6 ounces linguine
10 ounces skinless boneless chicken
  breasts, cut into thin strips
1 tablespoon fresh lemon juice

1. Preheat broiler. Line baking sheet or pie pan with foil.

2. Place whole peppers onto prepared baking sheet. Broil peppers 2" from heat, turning frequently with tongs, until skin is charred on all sides.* Transfer peppers to paper bag; close and let cool. Peel and seed peppers over bowl to catch juices; cut into 2" chunks.

3. Fit food processor with steel blade; with motor running, drop garlic through feed tube. Add parsley, basil and roasted red peppers through feed tube; process, stopping processor and using rubber spatula to scrape sides of bowl as necessary, until finely chopped. With motor running, slowly add oil, $^{1}/_{4}$ teaspoon of the pepper and $^{1}/_{4}$ teaspoon of the salt through feed tube, processing until just combined (do not purée).

4. In large pot of boiling water, cook linguine 10 minutes, until tender. Drain, discarding liquid; place into serving bowl. Keep warm.

5. Meanwhile, sprinkle chicken evenly with remaining $^{1}/_{2}$ teaspoon pepper and remaining $^{1}/_{4}$ teaspoon salt. Spray large nonstick skillet with nonstick cooking spray; heat. Add chicken; cook over medium-high heat, stirring frequently, 4 minutes, until cooked through.

6. Spoon chicken over warm linguine; drizzle evenly with juice. Top chicken with reserved bell pepper mixture; toss to combine. Serve warm or at room temperature.

Serving (1$^{1}/_{2}$ cups) provides: 1 Fat, 2 Vegetables, 2 Proteins, 2 Breads.

Per serving: 329 Calories, 8 g Total Fat, 1 g Saturated Fat, 48 mg Cholesterol, 324 mg Sodium, 40 g Total Carbohydrate, 3 g Dietary Fiber, 24 g Protein, 65 mg Calcium.

BREAKFAST
Orange Sections, $^{1}/_{2}$ cup
Poached Egg, 1
Reduced-Calorie Multi-Grain Bread, 2 slices,
  toasted, with 2 teaspoons reduced-calorie tub
  margarine
Skim Milk, $^{1}/_{2}$ cup
Coffee or Tea (optional)

LIGHT MEAL
Scalloped Potatoes and Ham (Preheat oven to
  350° F. In small baking dish, layer 2 ounces lean
  cooked ham and 4 ounces cooked all-purpose
  potato, peeled and thinly sliced; top with $^{1}/_{2}$ cup
  skim milk and pinch *each* salt and freshly ground
  black pepper. Bake 15–20 minutes until mixture
  is heated through.)
Steamed Baby Carrots, 1 cup
Reduced-Calorie Chocolate-Flavored Pudding (made
  with skim milk), $^{1}/_{2}$ cup
Unsweetened Seltzer

MAIN MEAL
Chicken Linguine with Roasted Red Pepper Pesto,
  1 serving (see recipe)
Steamed Collard Greens, 1 cup
Steamed Whole Wax Beans, 1 cup
Arugula and Radicchio Salad, 2 cups, with $^{1}/_{2}$ cup
  sliced celery and 1 tablespoon fat-free Thousand
  Island dressing
Garlic-Herb Bread (Spread 1-ounce slice Italian
  bread with $^{1}/_{2}$ teaspoon minced fresh garlic or
  1 roasted garlic clove and $^{1}/_{2}$ teaspoon *each*
  minced fresh basil and oregano leaves; drizzle with
  1 teaspoon olive oil. Place onto nonstick baking
  sheet; broil until lightly browned.)
Pear, 1 small
Decaffeinated Cappuccino, made with skim milk,
  5 fluid ounces

SNACK
Plain Popcorn, hot-air popped, 3 cups
Diet Grape Soda

This menu provides: 2 Milks, 3 Fats, 2 Fruits,
13 Vegetables, 5 Proteins, 6 Breads, 60 Optional
Calories.

Per serving: 31 g Fat, 32 g Fiber.

*If desired, peppers may be roasted over an open
flame, holding peppers with tongs and turning frequently, for 10 minutes, until charred on all sides.

LIGHT MEAL
Chick-Pea Salad (In small bowl, combine 2 ounces drained cooked chick-peas, $^1/_2$ cup *each* cooked sliced carrot and green bell pepper strips and 1 tablespoon fat-free Italian dressing.)
Cooked Turnip Greens, 1 cup
Whole-Wheat Roll, 1 ounce, with 2 teaspoons reduced-calorie tub margarine
Carambola (Star Fruit), 1 medium
Iced Herbal Tea

MAIN MEAL
Minestrone Soup, canned, 1 cup
Chicken Thighs Pizzaiolo on Pappardelle, 1 serving (see recipe)
Cooked Artichoke Hearts, 1 cup
Tossed Green Salad, 2 cups, with $^1/_2$ cup sliced cucumber and 1 teaspoon *each* olive oil and balsamic vinegar
Vanilla Wafers, 3
Decaffeinated Cappuccino, made with skim milk, 5 fluid ounces

SNACK
Graham Crackers, 3 ($2^1/_2$" squares)
Skim Milk, $^1/_2$ cup

This menu provides: 2 Milks, 3 Fats, 2 Fruits, $13^3/_4$ Vegetables, 5 Proteins, $5^1/_2$ Breads, 75 Optional Calories.

Per serving: 32 g Fat, 29 g Fiber.

212
CHICKEN THIGHS PIZZAIOLO ON PAPPARDELLE

In Italian, pizzaiolo refers to a fresh tomato sauce flavored with herbs and garlic. When layered over chicken thighs and topped with cheese, you have a super dinner dish. Serve it over pappardelle, very wide egg noodles—for an especially pretty dish, look for ones with pinked edges. If pappardelle is unavailable, try tagliatelle or fettuccine.

Makes 4 servings

1 teaspoon olive oil
1 cup thinly sliced mushrooms
2 garlic cloves, minced
10 ounces skinless boneless chicken thighs
$^1/_2$ teaspoon freshly ground black pepper
1 cup marinara sauce
3 ounces skim-milk mozzarella cheese, grated
6 ounces pappardelle pasta
$^1/_4$ cup minced fresh basil, or 1 tablespoon dried

1. Preheat oven to 375° F. Spray 12" au gratin dish or 11 × 7" baking dish with nonstick cooking spray.

2. In medium nonstick skillet, heat oil; add mushrooms and garlic. Cook over medium-high heat, stirring frequently, 5 minutes, until mushrooms are browned and tender. Remove from heat; set aside.

3. Place chicken into prepared dish; sprinkle evenly with pepper. Pour marinara sauce over chicken. Top with mushroom mixture; sprinkle evenly with cheese. Bake 20–25 minutes, until chicken is cooked through and juices run clear when pierced with fork.

4. Meanwhile, in large pot of boiling water, cook pappardelle 10–12 minutes, until tender. Drain, discarding liquid; place into serving bowl.

5. Top pappardelle with chicken mixture; sprinkle with basil.

Serving (one-fourth of chicken mixture, 1 cup pappardelle) provides: 1 Fat, $1^1/_4$ Vegetables, 3 Proteins, 2 Breads.

Per serving: 360 Calories, 10 g Total Fat, 3 g Saturated Fat, 71 mg Cholesterol, 558 mg Sodium, 41 g Total Carbohydrate, 1 g Dietary Fiber, 26 g Protein, 192 mg Calcium.

Chicken Stir-Fry with Poppy Seed Noodles

This healthful and delicious meal can be whipped up in a flash.

Makes 4 servings

6 ounces thin egg noodles

1 tablespoon poppy seeds

1 tablespoon + 1 teaspoon vegetable oil

15 ounces skinless boneless chicken breasts, cut into bite-size pieces

1/2 teaspoon salt

1/2 teaspoon freshly ground black pepper

1 cup chopped onions

1 medium red bell pepper, seeded and cut into thin strips

4 garlic cloves, minced

2 fluid ounces (1/4 cup) dry white wine

2 cups cubed butternut or acorn squash

1/2 cup low-sodium chicken broth

2 teaspoons minced fresh sage leaves, or 1/2 teaspoon dried

2 teaspoons minced fresh thyme leaves, or 1/2 teaspoon dried

1. In large pot of boiling water, cook noodles 5–6 minutes, until tender. Drain, discarding liquid; transfer to medium bowl. Add poppy seeds and 1 teaspoon of the oil; toss to combine. Cover with plastic wrap; keep warm.

2. Sprinkle chicken on all sides with salt and pepper.

3. In wok or large nonstick skillet, heat remaining 1 tablespoon oil; add chicken. Cook over medium-high heat, stirring frequently, 4 minutes, until lightly browned and cooked through. With slotted spoon, remove chicken from wok; set aside.

4. In same wok, combine onions, bell pepper and garlic; cook, stirring frequently, 5 minutes, until vegetables are softened. Add wine; bring liquid to a boil. Reduce heat to low; simmer, stirring occasionally, 5 minutes.

5. Add squash, broth, sage and thyme to vegetable mixture; bring liquid to a boil. Reduce heat to low; simmer 5 minutes, until squash is tender.

6. Add cooked chicken to vegetable mixture; cook, stirring frequently, 2 minutes, until heated through.

7. Transfer warm noodle mixture to serving platter; top with chicken mixture.

Serving (2 cups) provides: 1 Fat, 1 Vegetable, 3 Proteins, 2 1/2 Breads, 25 Optional Calories.

Per serving: 403 Calories, 9 g Total Fat, 2 g Saturated Fat, 102 mg Cholesterol, 372 mg Sodium, 46 g Total Carbohydrate, 4 g Dietary Fiber, 33 g Protein, 117 mg Calcium.

BREAKFAST

Strawberries, 1 cup

Reduced-Calorie Multi-Grain Bread, 2 slices, toasted, with 2 teaspoons reduced-calorie tub margarine

Skim Milk, 3/4 cup

Coffee or Tea (optional)

LIGHT MEAL

Lentil-Rice Salad (In medium bowl, combine 2 cups torn Romaine lettuce leaves, 4 ounces drained cooked lentils, 1/2 cup cooked brown rice, 1/4 cup *each* diced onion, diced red bell pepper and diced tomato and 1 tablespoon fat-free Italian dressing.)

Vanilla Sugar-Free Nonfat Frozen Yogurt, 4 fluid ounces

Iced Tea

MAIN MEAL

Chicken Stir-Fry with Poppy Seed Noodles, 1 serving (see recipe)

Steamed Broccoli, 4 spears, with 1 teaspoon fresh lemon juice

Steamed Baby Carrots, 1 cup

Cabbage Slaw (In medium bowl, combine 1/2 cup shredded red cabbage, 2 teaspoons *each* reduced-calorie mayonnaise and red wine vinegar, 1 teaspoon caraway seeds and pinch granulated sugar.)

Aspartame-Sweetened Vanilla Nonfat Yogurt, 1 cup, with 2 tablespoons raisins

Sparkling Mineral Water

SNACK

Plain Popcorn, hot-air popped, 3 cups

Unsweetened Black Cherry–Flavored Seltzer

This menu provides: 2 Milks, 3 Fats, 2 Fruits, 11 1/2 Vegetables, 5 Proteins, 5 1/2 Breads, 100 Optional Calories.

Per serving: 22 g Fat, 34 g Fiber.

214
SWEET AND SPICY
CHICKEN WITH ORZO

*Orzo, a rice-shaped macaroni, makes a perfect accompaniment for
this sweet ginger-spiced chicken.*

Makes 4 servings

6 ounces orzo (rice-shaped pasta)
2 tablespoons minced fresh flat-leaf parsley
1 tablespoon + 1 teaspoon olive oil
$^1/_2$ cup finely chopped onion
6 medium garlic cloves, minced
$^1/_2$ teaspoon cinnamon
$^1/_2$ teaspoon salt
$^1/_4$ teaspoon ground ginger
$^1/_4$ teaspoon ground red pepper
$1^3/_4$ cups tomato sauce (no salt added)
1 tablespoon honey
15 ounces skinless boneless chicken breasts, cut into thin strips

1. In large pot of boiling water, cook orzo 9 minutes, until tender. Drain, discarding liquid; place into serving bowl. Add parsley and 2 teaspoons of the oil; toss to combine. Keep warm.

2. Meanwhile, in medium saucepan, heat remaining 2 teaspoons oil; add onion, garlic, cinnamon, salt, ginger and pepper. Cook over medium-high heat, stirring frequently, 5 minutes, until onion is softened. Add tomato sauce and honey; cook, stirring frequently, 3 minutes, until bubbling. Remove from heat; keep warm.

3. Spray large nonstick skillet with nonstick cooking spray; heat. Add chicken; cook over high heat, stirring constantly, 4 minutes, until chicken is cooked through. Spoon chicken over orzo mixture; top with tomato sauce mixture.

Serving (3 ounces chicken, one-fourth of the orzo, $^1/_2$ cup sauce mixture) provides: 1 Fat, 2 Vegetables, 3 Proteins, 2 Breads, 15 Optional Calories.

Per serving: 401 Calories, 9 g Total Fat, 2 g Saturated Fat, 72 mg Cholesterol, 359 mg Sodium, 47 g Total Carbohydrate, 3 g Dietary Fiber, 34 g Protein, 52 mg Calcium.

215
Moroccan Chicken on Saffron Rice

Chicken teams up with leeks, dried apricots and fresh oranges to create a dish with Moroccan flair. Served with saffron-tinted rice, this dish truly has a native touch.

Makes 4 servings

6 ounces long-grain rice
Pinch saffron threads
2 teaspoons olive oil
Four 4-ounce skinless boneless chicken breasts
2 cups thinly sliced well-washed leeks
12 dried apricot halves, thinly sliced
1 teaspoon ground cumin
$^1/_4$ teaspoon cinnamon
$^1/_4$ teaspoon crushed red pepper flakes
2 cups coarsely chopped tomatoes
1 cup low-sodium chicken broth
1 cup orange sections

1. In medium saucepan, bring 2 cups water to a boil; stir in rice and saffron. Reduce heat to low; cook, covered, 20 minutes, until all water is absorbed and rice is tender. Remove from heat; keep warm.

2. Meanwhile, in large nonstick skillet, heat oil; add chicken. Cook over medium-high heat, turning once, 8 minutes, until browned on all sides and juices run clear when chicken is pierced with fork. Remove chicken from skillet; set aside.

3. In same skillet, combine leeks, apricots, cumin, cinnamon and red pepper flakes; cook, stirring frequently, 5 minutes, until leeks are softened. Add tomatoes and broth; bring liquid to a boil. Reduce heat to low; simmer, covered, 3 minutes, until mixture is heated through.

4. Return chicken to skillet; stir in orange sections. Cook, turning chicken occasionally, 3 minutes, until chicken is heated through.

5. Spoon warm rice mixture onto serving platter. Top rice mixture with cooked chicken breasts; surround chicken with vegetable mixture.

Serving (1 chicken breast, $^3/_4$ cup rice, $^3/_4$ cup vegetable mixture) provides: $^1/_2$ Fat, 1 Fruit, 2 Vegetables, 3 Proteins, $1^1/_2$ Breads, 5 Optional Calories.

Per serving: 406 Calories, 5 g Total Fat, 1 g Saturated Fat, 66 mg Cholesterol, 125 mg Sodium, 58 g Total Carbohydrate, 4 g Dietary Fiber, 32 g Protein, 93 mg Calcium.

BREAKFAST
Mango, $^1/_2$ small
Hard-Cooked Egg, 1
Bagel, $^1/_2$ small (1 ounce), with 1 teaspoon reduced-calorie tub margarine
Skim Milk, $^3/_4$ cup
Coffee or Tea (optional)

LIGHT MEAL
Tomato-Artichoke Salad (In medium bowl, combine 2 cups torn Romaine lettuce leaves, 1 cup cooked artichoke hearts, quartered, 1 large plum tomato, sliced, $^3/_4$ ounce reduced-fat Swiss cheese, diced, and 1 tablespoon Italian dressing.)
Aspartame-Sweetened Lemon Nonfat Yogurt, 1 cup
Breadsticks, 2 long
Diet Cola

MAIN MEAL
Moroccan Chicken on Saffron Rice, 1 serving (see recipe)
Steamed Spinach, 1 cup
Steamed Sliced Carrots, 1 cup
Watercress and Romaine Lettuce Salad, 2 cups, with 1 tablespoon fat-free ranch dressing
Sugar-Free Vanilla Nonfat Frozen Yogurt, 4 fluid ounces
Sparkling Mineral Water

SNACK
Whole-Wheat Pretzel Sticks, $1^1/_2$ ounces

This menu provides: 2 Milks, 3 Fats, 2 Fruits, 17 Vegetables, 5 Proteins, $5^1/_2$ Breads, 75 Optional Calories.

Per serving: 29 g Fat, 29 g Fiber.

Moroccan Chicken on Saffron Rice

216

CURRIED CHICKEN THIGHS WITH PARSLEYED BASMATI RICE

Makes 4 servings

6 ounces basmati or long-grain rice
$^1/_4$ cup minced flat-leaf parsley
1 pound 8 ounces skinless chicken thighs
$^3/_4$ teaspoon salt
2 teaspoons vegetable oil
1 cup chopped onions
1 tablespoon mild or hot curry powder

$^1/_2$ teaspoon ground ginger
$^1/_2$ teaspoon granulated sugar
Pinch crushed red pepper flakes, or to taste
1 cup low-sodium chicken broth
$^3/_4$ cup plain nonfat yogurt
2 teaspoons cornstarch
1 cup fresh or thawed frozen green peas

1. In medium saucepan, bring 2 cups water to a boil; stir in rice. Reduce heat to low; cook, covered, 20 minutes, until all water is absorbed and rice is tender. Remove from heat; stir in parsley. Set aside; keep warm.

2. Meanwhile, sprinkle chicken on all sides with $^1/_2$ teaspoon of the salt. In large nonstick skillet, heat 1 teaspoon of the oil; add chicken thighs. Cook over medium-high heat, turning once, 4 minutes, until chicken is browned on all sides. Remove from skillet; set aside.

3. In same skillet, heat remaining 1 teaspoon oil; add onions. cook, stirring frequently, 3 minutes, until softened. Stir in curry powder, ginger, sugar, red pepper flakes and remaining $^1/_4$ teaspoon salt; cook, stirring constantly, 1 minute.

4. Return chicken to skillet; turn to coat. Add broth; bring liquid to a boil. Reduce heat to low; simmer, covered, 20 minutes, until chicken is cooked through.

5. In small bowl, with wire whisk, combine yogurt and cornstarch, blending until cornstarch is dissolved. Add yogurt mixture and peas to chicken mixture; stir to combine. Cook, stirring frequently, just until heated through (do not boil).

6. Spoon warm rice mixture onto serving platter; top with chicken mixture.

Serving (3 ounces chicken, one-fourth of the curry sauce, $^3/_4$ cup rice) provides: $^1/_4$ Milk, $^1/_2$ Fat, $^1/_2$ Vegetable, 3 Proteins, 2 Breads, 10 Optional Calories.

Per serving: 389 Calories, 9 g Total Fat, 2 g Saturated Fat, 95 mg Cholesterol, 595 mg Sodium, 49 g Total Carbohydrate, 3 g Dietary Fiber, 33 g Protein, 133 mg Calcium.

BREAKFAST
Raisins, 2 tablespoons
Cooked Oatmeal, $^1/_2$ cup, with 2 teaspoons reduced-calorie tub margarine
Aspartame-Sweetened Strawberry-Banana Nonfat Yogurt, 1 cup
Coffee or Tea (optional)

LIGHT MEAL
Cooked Whole-Wheat Spaghetti, 1 cup, with $^1/_4$ cup tomato sauce (no salt added) and 1 teaspoon freshly grated Parmesan cheese
Cooked Artichoke Hearts, $^1/_2$ cup, with 1 tablespoon balsamic vinegar
Torn Romaine Lettuce Leaves, 2 cups, with $^1/_2$ cup sliced cucumber, 2 ounces drained cooked red kidney beans and 1 tablespoon fat-free Caesar salad dressing
Reduced-Calorie Chocolate-Flavored Pudding (made with skim milk), $^1/_2$ cup
Sparkling Mineral Water

MAIN MEAL
Curried Chicken Thighs with Parsleyed Basmati Rice, 1 serving (see recipe)
Steamed Baby Carrots, 1 cup, with $1^1/_2$ teaspoons reduced-calorie tub margarine
Steamed Whole Green Beans, 1 cup
Chapati, 1 piece (5" diameter)
Kiwi Fruit, 1 medium
Sparkling Mineral Water with Lime Wedge

SNACK
Sugar-Free Strawberry Nonfat Frozen Yogurt, 4 fluid ounces

This menu provides: 2 Milks, 3 Fats, 2 Fruits, $11^1/_2$ Vegetables, 4 Proteins, 6 Breads, 130 Optional Calories.

Per serving: 25 g Fat, 29 g Fiber.

*To toast sesame seeds, in small nonstick skillet, cook
seeds over low heat, stirring constantly, until golden
brown; immediately transfer to heat-resistant plate to
cool.*

SESAME CHICKEN WITH SNOW PEAS

*Stir-fries are a healthful way of eating. Here, ginger and sesame seeds
add zest to mild chicken and snow peas.*

Makes 4 servings

6 ounces regular long-grain rice
1 tablespoon vegetable oil
15 ounces skinless boneless chicken
breasts, cut diagonally into
4 × $^1/_4$" strips
$^1/_4$ teaspoon salt
2 medium carrots, julienned
2 cups snow peas, stem ends and
strings removed
1 cup julienned scallions
$1^1/_2$ teaspoons grated pared fresh
ginger root
$^1/_4$ teaspoon crushed red pepper
flakes
$^1/_2$ cup low-sodium chicken broth
2 tablespoons reduced-sodium soy
sauce
1 fluid ounce (2 tablespoons) dry
sherry
2 teaspoons cornstarch
1 teaspoon oriental sesame oil
1 tablespoon sesame seeds,
toasted*

1. In medium saucepan, bring 2 cups water to a boil; stir in rice. Reduce
heat to low; cook, covered, 20 minutes, until all water is absorbed and rice
is tender. Remove from heat; keep warm.

2. In large nonstick skillet, heat 1 teaspoon of the vegetable oil; add
chicken and salt. Cook over medium-high heat, stirring constantly, 2–3
minutes, until chicken turns white. With slotted spoon, remove chicken
from skillet; set aside.

3. In same skillet, heat remaining 2 teaspoons oil. Add carrots; cook, stirring constantly, 1 minute. Add snow peas, scallions, ginger and pepper
flakes; cook, stirring constantly, 3 minutes, until vegetables are softened.
Return chicken to skillet; stir to combine.

4. In small bowl, with wire whisk, combine broth, soy sauce, sherry,
cornstarch and sesame oil, blending until cornstarch is dissolved. Stir
broth mixture into chicken mixture; cook, stirring constantly, until liquid
comes to a boil and is slightly thickened.

5. Line serving platter with warm rice. Mound chicken mixture in center
of rice-lined platter; sprinkle with sesame seeds.

Serving ($1^1/_2$ cups chicken mixture, $^3/_4$ cup rice) provides: 1 Fat,
$2^1/_2$ Vegetables, 3 Proteins, $1^1/_2$ Breads, 25 Optional Calories.

Per serving: 408 Calories, 8 g Total Fat, 1 g Saturated Fat, 62 mg Cholesterol,
546 mg Sodium, 50 g Total Carbohydrate, 5 g Dietary Fiber, 32 g Protein,
113 mg Calcium.

FIVE-SPICE CHICKEN ON CHINESE NOODLE JULIENNE

Makes 4 servings

3 ounces spaghettini

Four 4-ounce chicken legs, skinned

2 teaspoons reduced-sodium soy sauce

$^3/_4$ teaspoon salt

$^1/_2$ teaspoon Chinese five-spice powder*

$^1/_2$ teaspoon firmly packed light or dark brown sugar

1 tablespoon + 1 teaspoon oriental sesame oil

1 medium red bell pepper, seeded and julienned

1 medium zucchini, julienned

1 tablespoon finely chopped pared fresh ginger root

2 garlic cloves, minced

8 medium scallions, thinly sliced

$^1/_2$ cup shredded Savoy cabbage

2 teaspoons sesame seeds, toasted†

1. Preheat outdoor barbecue grill according to manufacturer's directions, or preheat broiler and spray rack in broiler pan with nonstick cooking spray.

2. In large pot of boiling water, cook spaghettini 8–10 minutes, until tender. Drain, discarding liquid; set aside.

3. Brush chicken on all sides with soy sauce. In small cup or bowl, combine $^1/_4$ teaspoon of the salt, the five-spice powder and brown sugar; sprinkle chicken evenly with salt mixture. Grill chicken over hot coals or place onto prepared rack in broiler pan and broil 4" from heat, turning frequently, 8–10 minutes, until cooked through and juices run clear when chicken is pierced with fork. Set aside; keep warm.

4. In large nonstick skillet, heat oil; add bell pepper, zucchini, ginger, garlic and remaining $^1/_2$ teaspoon salt; cook over medium-high heat, stirring frequently, 5 minutes, until vegetables are softened. Stir in scallions and cabbage; cook, stirring constantly, 4 minutes, until cabbage is wilted.

5. Add cooked spaghettini to vegetable mixture; cook, tossing constantly, 3–4 minutes, until heated through. Transfer spaghettini mixture to serving platter; top with chicken legs. Serve sprinkled with toasted sesame seeds.

Serving (1 chicken leg, 1$^1/_2$ cups spaghettini mixture) provides: 1 Fat, 1$^1/_2$ Vegetables, 2 Proteins, 1 Bread, 10 Optional Calories.

Per serving: 263 Calories, 11 g Total Fat, 2 g Saturated Fat, 53 mg Cholesterol, 573 mg Sodium, 22 g Total Carbohydrate, 2 g Dietary Fiber, 20 g Protein, 54 mg Calcium.

BREAKFAST

Pear, 1 small

Reduced-Calorie Whole-Wheat Bread, 2 slices, toasted, with 2 teaspoons reduced-calorie tub margarine, $^1/_2$ teaspoon granulated sugar and $^1/_4$ teaspoon cinnamon

Skim Milk, 1 cup

Coffee or Tea (optional)

LIGHT MEAL

Grilled Fat-Free Frankfurter, 2 ounces, on 2-ounce frankfurter roll, with $^1/_4$ cup drained sauerkraut

Celery and Carrot Sticks, 1 cup *each*

Watermelon, 3 × 2" wedge

Diet Lemonade, 1 cup

MAIN MEAL

Five-Spice Chicken on Chinese Noodle Julienne, 1 serving (see recipe)

Steamed Whole Green Beans, 1 cup

Torn Bibb Lettuce, 2 cups, with $^1/_2$ cup straw mushrooms and 1 teaspoon *each* vegetable oil and rice wine vinegar

Sugar-Free Pineapple-Flavored Gelatin, $^1/_2$ cup

Green Tea

SNACK

Fig Bars, 2

Skim Milk, 1 cup

This menu provides: 2 Milks, 3 Fats, 2 Fruits, 13 Vegetables, 4 Proteins, 4$^1/_2$ Breads, 100 Optional Calories.

Per serving: 29 g Fat, 24 g Fiber.

---

*Five-spice powder is available in most supermarkets and Asian groceries.

†To toast sesame seeds, in small nonstick skillet, cook seeds over low heat, stirring constantly, until golden brown; immediately transfer to heat-resistant plate to cool.

CHICKEN SZECHUAN ON GREEN RICE

Makes 4 servings

8 ounces long-grain rice

$^1/_4$ teaspoon salt

1 cup minced scallions

$^1/_2$ cup minced trimmed washed spinach leaves

$^1/_4$ cup minced fresh flat-leaf parsley

1 fluid ounce (2 tablespoons) dry sherry

2 tablespoons reduced-sodium soy sauce

1 tablespoon firmly packed light or dark brown sugar

1 tablespoon grated orange zest*

2 teaspoons oriental sesame oil

2 teaspoons vegetable oil

15 ounces skinless boneless chicken breasts, cut diagonally into 4 × $^1/_4$" strips

4 garlic cloves, minced

$1^1/_2$ teaspoons grated pared fresh ginger root

$^1/_4$ teaspoon crushed red pepper flakes

2 cups sliced bok choy (1" pieces)

$^1/_2$ medium red bell pepper, seeded and cut into 1" pieces

$^1/_2$ medium green bell pepper, seeded and cut into 1" pieces

1. In medium saucepan, bring $2^2/_3$ cups water to a boil; add rice. Reduce heat to low; simmer, covered, 20 minutes, until rice is tender and all liquid is absorbed. Stir in the salt, $^1/_2$ cup of the scallions, the spinach and parsley; keep warm.

2. In small bowl, with wire whisk, combine sherry, soy sauce, brown sugar and zest, blending until sugar is dissolved; set aside.

3. In wok or large nonstick skillet, heat sesame and vegetable oils; add chicken. Cook over medium-high heat, stirring frequently, 1–2 minutes, until chicken is cooked through. With slotted spoon, remove chicken from wok; set aside.

4. In same wok, combine garlic, ginger and red pepper flakes; cook, stirring constantly, 1 minute, until garlic is softened. Add bok choy and red and green bell peppers; cook, stirring frequently, 4–5 minutes, until vegetables are just tender.

5. Stir remaining $^1/_2$ cup scallions, reserved sherry mixture and cooked chicken into vegetable mixture; cook, stirring constantly, 2 minutes, until vegetables and chicken are well coated and mixture is heated through.

6. Line serving platter with warm rice mixture; top with chicken mixture.

BREAKFAST
Blueberries, $^3/_4$ cup
Bran Flakes Cereal, $^3/_4$ ounce
Skim Milk, $^1/_2$ cup
Coffee or Tea (optional)

LIGHT MEAL
Cooked Whole-Wheat Spaghetti, 1 cup, with $^1/_4$ cup tomato sauce (no salt added) and 1 teaspoon freshly grated Parmesan cheese
Tossed Green Salad, 2 cups, with $^1/_2$ cup shredded red cabbage, 2 ounces drained cooked red kidney beans and 1 tablespoon Italian dressing
Peach, 1 medium
Cappuccino, made with skim milk, 5 fluid ounces

MAIN MEAL
Low-Sodium Chicken Broth, 1 cup, with $^1/_2$ cup cooked thin noodles
Chicken Szechuan on Green Rice, 1 serving (see recipe)
Steamed Sliced Carrots, 1 cup
Steamed Broccoli Florets, 1 cup
Sugar-Free Orange-Flavored Gelatin, $^1/_2$ cup
Chinese Tea

SNACK
Reduced-Calorie Strawberry Dairy Shake, 1 serving

This menu provides: 2 Milks, 3 Fats, 2 Fruits, $12^1/_4$ Vegetables, 4 Proteins, 6 Breads, 60 Optional Calories.

Per serving: 21 g Fat, 28 g Fiber.

Serving (1 cup chicken mixture, 1 cup rice mixture) provides: 1 Fat, $2^1/_4$ Vegetables, 3 Proteins, 2 Breads, 20 Optional Calories.

Per serving: 458 Calories, 6 g Total Fat, 1 g Saturated Fat, 62 mg Cholesterol, 544 mg Sodium, 55 g Total Carbohydrate, 2 g Dietary Fiber, 31 g Protein, 111 mg Calcium.

The zest of the orange is the peel without any of the pith (white membrane). To remove zest from orange, use a zester or the fine side of a vegetable grater; wrap orange in plastic wrap and refrigerate for use at another time.

220
Chicken "Fried" Rice

We've turned fried rice from a fat trap to a low-fat treat—enjoy it whenever you please!

Makes 4 servings

8 ounces regular long-grain rice

1 tablespoon + 1 teaspoon oriental sesame oil

12 ounces skinless boneless chicken breasts, cut into $^1/_2$" pieces

1 cup finely chopped onions

$1^1/_2$ teaspoons minced pared fresh ginger root

2 garlic cloves, minced

Pinch crushed red pepper flakes

1 medium zucchini, cut into $^1/_2$" pieces

1 cup coarsely chopped red bell pepper

1 cup snow peas, stem ends and strings removed, cut into 1" pieces

9 asparagus spears, cut into $^1/_2$" pieces

1 egg, beaten

3 tablespoons reduced-sodium soy sauce

1. In medium saucepan, bring $2^1/_2$ cups water to a boil; stir in rice. Reduce heat to low; cook, covered, 20 minutes, until all water is absorbed and rice is tender. Remove from heat; set aside.

2. In large nonstick skillet, heat 1 tablespoon of the oil; add chicken, onions, ginger, garlic and red pepper flakes. Cook over medium-high heat, stirring frequently, 2–3 minutes, until chicken turns white. Add zucchini, bell pepper, snow peas and asparagus; cook, stirring frequently, 3–4 minutes, until chicken is cooked through and vegetables are softened.

3. With wooden spoon, push chicken mixture to sides of skillet, leaving center of skillet empty. Add egg to center of skillet; cook, stirring egg constantly, 2 minutes, until set. Stir chicken mixture and reserved rice into scrambled egg, then stir in soy sauce and remaining 1 teaspoon oil; cook, stirring constantly, 5 minutes, until heated through and flavors are blended.

Serving (2 cups) provides: 1 Fat, $2^1/_2$ Vegetables, $2^1/_2$ Proteins, 2 Breads.

Per serving: 419 Calories, 8 g Total Fat, 1 g Saturated Fat, 102 mg Cholesterol, 529 mg Sodium, 57 g Total Carbohydrate, 3 g Dietary Fiber, 29 g Protein, 76 mg Calcium.

BREAKFAST

Grapefruit, $^1/_2$ medium

Open-Face Egg Sandwich (Spray small nonstick skillet with nonstick cooking spray; heat. Add $^1/_4$ cup egg substitute, $^1/_4$ cup diced roasted red bell pepper and pinch *each* salt, freshly ground black pepper and garlic powder. Cook over medium-high heat, stirring frequently, until mixture is set. Spoon onto 1 slice reduced-calorie whole-wheat bread, toasted; top with 2 tomato slices.)

Skim Milk, 1 cup

Coffee or Tea (optional)

LIGHT MEAL

Tomato Melt (Spread each of 2 slices reduced-calorie whole-wheat bread with 1 teaspoon reduced-calorie mayonnaise each; top each with 2 thick tomato slices and $^3/_4$ ounce nonfat mozzarella cheese, grated. Broil until cheese is melted.)

Carrot and Celery Sticks, 1 cup *each*

Aspartame-Sweetened Strawberry-Banana Nonfat Yogurt, 1 cup

Diet Black Cherry Soda

MAIN MEAL

Chicken "Fried" Rice, 1 serving (see recipe)

Steamed Broccoli, 4 spears

Tossed Green Salad, 2 cups, with $^1/_2$ cup *each* bean sprouts and drained canned sliced bamboo shoots and Ginger Vinaigrette (In small jar with tight-fitting lid or small bowl, combine 2 teaspoons rice wine vinegar, 1 teaspoon vegetable oil and $^1/_2$ teaspoon minced pared fresh ginger root; cover and shake well or, with wire whisk, blend until combined.)

Tangerine, 1 large

Chinese Tea

SNACK

Whole-Wheat Bagel, 1 small (2 ounces), split and toasted, with 2 teaspoons apple butter

This menu provides: 2 Milks, 3 Fats, 2 Fruits, $17^1/_2$ Vegetables, $4^1/_2$ Proteins, $5^1/_2$ Breads, 20 Optional Calories.

Per serving: 21 g Fat, 28 g Fiber.

221
THAI CHICKEN WITH PEANUT SAUCE

*This spicy-sweet twist on the popular Indonesian satay is delicious
served over brown rice.*

Makes 4 servings

¹/₄ cup drained canned mandarin
    orange sections (no sugar added)
¹/₄ cup + 1 teaspoon reduced-
    sodium soy sauce
1 tablespoon fresh orange juice
1 teaspoon minced fresh flat-leaf
    parsley
1 teaspoon oriental sesame oil
¹/₄ teaspoon ground ginger
2 pinches freshly ground black
    pepper
7 ounces skinless boneless chicken
    breasts, cut into 8 strips
3 tablespoons creamy peanut
    butter

2 tablespoons dark corn syrup
1 tablespoon minced pared fresh
    ginger root
¹/₂ fluid ounce (1 tablespoon) dry
    sherry
1 tablespoon distilled white vinegar
1 teaspoon sesame seeds, lightly
    toasted*
1 small garlic clove, minced
Pinch ground red pepper
Fresh cilantro sprigs and minced
    fresh cilantro, to garnish

1. To prepare marinade, in blender or mini food processor, combine
orange sections, ¹/₄ cup of the soy sauce, juice, parsley, oil, ground ginger
and one pinch of the black pepper. Transfer marinade to gallon-size sealable plastic bag; add chicken. Seal bag, squeezing out air; turn to coat
chicken. Refrigerate 4–6 hours or overnight, turning bag occasionally.

2. Soak eight 8" bamboo skewers in water 30 minutes.

3. Preheat outdoor barbecue grill according to manufacturer's directions,
or preheat broiler and spray rack in broiler pan with nonstick cooking
spray.

4. To prepare peanut sauce, in small microwavable bowl, combine
peanut butter, corn syrup, ginger root, sherry, vinegar, sesame seeds, the
remaining soy sauce, garlic and the red and remaining pinch of black peppers; set aside.

5. Drain and discard marinade. Thread 1 chicken piece on each prepared
skewer; grill chicken over hot coals or place onto prepared rack in broiler
pan and broil 4" from heat, turning as needed, 3–4 minutes, until golden
brown.

6. Microwave sauce on Medium (50% power) 10–15 seconds, until
slightly warm (do not overcook or sauce will separate). Serve chicken with
sauce, garnished with cilantro.

222
VIETNAMESE CHICKEN KABOBS

These chunks of chicken and fresh vegetables marinate, Vietnamese-style, in a mixture of ginger, honey and soy sauce; then, keeping with traditions of the country, they're skewered, quickly cooked and served with a peanut dipping sauce.

Makes 4 servings

2 tablespoons reduced-sodium soy sauce
1 tablespoon + 1 teaspoon honey
6 garlic cloves, minced
2 teaspoons minced pared fresh ginger root
14 ounces skinless boneless chicken breasts, cut into 1¼" cubes
¼ cup hoisin sauce
1 ounce finely chopped unsalted dry-roasted peanuts
Pinch crushed red pepper flakes
16 cherry tomatoes
12 medium whole mushrooms
1 medium zucchini, halved lengthwise, then cut into ½" slices

1. Preheat outdoor barbecue grill according to manufacturer's directions, or preheat broiler and spray rack in broiler pan with nonstick cooking spray.

2. To prepare marinade, in gallon-size sealable plastic bag, combine 1 tablespoon of the soy sauce, the honey, garlic and ginger; add chicken. Seal bag, squeezing out air; turn to coat chicken. Refrigerate 30 minutes, turning bag occasionally.

3. Meanwhile, to prepare dipping sauce, in small bowl, combine hoisin sauce, peanuts, pepper flakes, the remaining 1 tablespoon soy sauce and 2 tablespoons water; set aside.

4. Drain and discard marinade. Alternating ingredients, onto each of 8 long metal skewers, thread one-fourth of the tomatoes, mushrooms, zucchini and chicken; grill over hot coals or place onto prepared rack in broiler pan and broil 4" from heat, turning as needed, 8 minutes, until chicken is golden brown and cooked through and vegetables are tender. Serve with dipping sauce.

Serving (2 skewers, 2 tablespoons sauce) provides: ½ Fat, 1½ Vegetables, 3 Proteins, 50 Optional Calories.

Per serving: 253 Calories, 5 g Total Fat, 1 g Saturated Fat, 58 mg Cholesterol, 687 mg Sodium, 24 g Total Carbohydrate, 2 g Dietary Fiber, 27 g Protein, 35 mg Calcium.

BREAKFAST
Grapefruit, ½ medium
Bagel, ½ small (1 ounce), toasted, with 1 teaspoon apricot jam
Skim Milk, 1 cup
Coffee or Tea (optional)

LIGHT MEAL
Shrimp Pita (In medium bowl, combine 4 ounces peeled deveined cooked shrimp, chopped, ¼ cup chopped celery, 2 teaspoons reduced-calorie mayonnaise and 1 teaspoon fresh lemon juice. Cut large [2-ounce] pita in half crosswise; open to form 2 pockets. Fill each pocket with half of the shrimp mixture.)
Cucumber Slices, 1 cup
Cherry Tomatoes, 6
Aspartame-Sweetened Black Cherry Nonfat Yogurt, 1 cup
Iced Tea

MAIN MEAL
Vietnamese Chicken Kabobs, 1 serving (see recipe)
Cooked Long-Grain Rice, 1 cup
Steamed Snow Peas, 1 cup, with 1 teaspoon reduced-calorie tub margarine
Torn Romaine Lettuce Leaves, 2 cups, with ½ cup shredded carrot and Ginger Vinaigrette (In small jar with tight-fitting lid or small bowl, combine 2 teaspoons rice wine vinegar, 1 teaspoon vegetable oil and ½ teaspoon minced pared fresh ginger root; cover and shake well or, with wire whisk, blend until combined.)
Plum, 1 large
Jasmine Tea

SNACK
Plain Popcorn, hot-air popped, 3 cups

This menu provides: 2 Milks, 3 Fats, 2 Fruits, 12 Vegetables, 5 Proteins, 6 Breads, 65 Optional Calories.

Per serving: 21 g Fat, 21 g Fiber.

Vietnamese Chicken Kabobs

223
GRILLED DRUMSTICKS TANDOORI

In Indian cuisine, tandoori describes food that is first marinated in a spicy yogurt mixture, then roasted in a tandoor, or clay oven. We've made these drumsticks easier by giving you the option of grilling or broiling them.

Makes 4 servings

1¹/₂ cups plain nonfat yogurt
4 garlic cloves, minced
¹/₂ teaspoon ground cardamom
¹/₂ teaspoon ground coriander
¹/₂ teaspoon ground ginger
¹/₂ teaspoon salt
¹/₄ teaspoon ground cumin
¹/₂ teaspoon granulated sugar
Pinch ground red pepper, or to taste
Four 5-ounce chicken legs, skinned
2 tablespoons minced fresh cilantro

1. To prepare marinade, in small bowl, combine yogurt, garlic, cardamom, coriander, ginger, salt, cumin, sugar and pepper.

2. Transfer half the yogurt mixture to gallon-size sealable plastic bag; add chicken. Seal bag, squeezing out air; turn to coat chicken. Refrigerate at least 2 hours or overnight, turning bag occasionally.

3. Meanwhile, stir cilantro into remaining yogurt mixture; refrigerate, covered, until chilled.

4. Remove chicken from refrigerator; let stand 30 minutes.

5. Meanwhile, preheat outdoor barbecue grill according to manufacturer's directions, or preheat broiler and spray rack in broiler pan with non-stick cooking spray.

6. Remove chicken from bag; discard marinade. Grill chicken over hot coals or place onto prepared rack in broiler pan and broil 4" from heat, turning frequently, 10–12 minutes, until cooked through and juices run clear when chicken is pierced with fork. Serve with reserved yogurt mixture for dipping.

Serving (1 chicken leg, 3 tablespoons yogurt dip) provides: ¹/₄ Milk, 2¹/₂ Proteins, 25 Optional Calories.

Per serving: 192 Calories, 6 g Total Fat, 2 g Saturated Fat, 68 mg Cholesterol, 404 mg Sodium, 8 g Total Carbohydrate, 0 g Dietary Fiber, 24 g Protein, 188 mg Calcium.

BREAKFAST
Apple, 1 small
Reduced-Calorie Whole-Wheat Bread, 2 slices, toasted, with 2 teaspoons reduced-calorie tub margarine and 1 teaspoon honey
Skim Milk, ³/₄ cup
Coffee or Tea (optional)

LIGHT MEAL
Hamburger on Bun, fast-food, 1 small
Side Salad, fast-food, 1, with 1 tablespoon fat-free Italian dressing
Diet Cola

MAIN MEAL
Grilled Drumsticks Tandoori, 1 serving (see recipe)
Vegetable Couscous (In small nonstick skillet, heat 1¹/₂ teaspoons olive oil; add ¹/₂ cup *each* chopped onion and red bell pepper and 1 garlic clove, minced. Cook over medium-high heat, stirring frequently, 5 minutes, until vegetables are tender. Add 1 cup cooked couscous; cook, stirring frequently, until heated through.)
Steamed Asparagus, 6 spears, with Lemon "Butter" (In small cup or bowl, combine 1 teaspoon *each* reduced-calorie tub margarine, melted, and fresh lemon juice.)
Romaine and Iceberg Lettuce Salad, 2 cups, with ¹/₂ cup *each* sliced cucumber and shredded carrot and 1 tablespoon fat-free creamy Italian dressing
Aspartame-Sweetened Lemon Nonfat Yogurt, 1 cup
Iced Tea

SNACK
Cherries, 12 large

This menu provides: 2 Milks, 3 Fats, 2 Fruits, 10 Vegetables, 3³/₄ Proteins, 5 Breads, 85 Optional Calories.

Per serving: 34 g Fat, 20 g Fiber.

224
MEXICAN-STYLE ROAST CHICKEN

Poblano chiles—large, dark green chile peppers—give a mild yet distinctive flavor to this pleasant roasted chicken.

Makes 8 servings

3 medium poblano chiles, seeded, deveined and cut into chunks
2 medium onions, halved lengthwise
$^1/_2$ cup packed fresh cilantro
$^1/_4$ cup fresh lime juice
$^1/_2$ teaspoon salt
$^1/_2$ teaspoon freshly ground black pepper
One 4-pound 8-ounce roasting chicken

1. Preheat oven to 350° F.

2. In food processor, combine chiles, 3 of the onion halves, the cilantro, juice, $^1/_4$ teaspoon of the salt and $^1/_4$ teaspoon of the pepper; process until finely chopped (do not purée).

3. Gently loosen skin from breast and leg portions of chicken; stuff chile mixture evenly under skin.

4. Sprinkle large cavity of chicken with remaining $^1/_4$ teaspoon salt and $^1/_4$ teaspoon pepper, then add remaining onion half; truss chicken. Place chicken, breast-side up, onto rack in large roasting pan; roast 2–2$^1/_4$ hours, until chicken is cooked through and juices run clear when pierced with fork or meat thermometer inserted into thickest portion of thigh registers 180° F. Remove from oven; let stand 10 minutes.

5. Remove and discard skin from chicken and onion half from cavity; scrape off and discard chile mixture. Carve chicken.

Serving (3 ounces chicken) provides: 3 Proteins.

Per serving: 173 Calories, 6 g Total Fat, 2 g Saturated Fat, 76 mg Cholesterol, 211 mg Sodium, 3 g Total Carbohydrate, 0 g Dietary Fiber, 25 g Protein, 21 mg Calcium.

225

PEPPERED CHICKEN ITALIENNE

A whole bulb of garlic roasts inside this tempting chicken, giving it an Italian touch.

Makes 8 servings

One 4-pound 8-ounce roasting chicken
1 cup packed fresh basil leaves
$^1/_2$ teaspoon salt
1 whole large garlic bulb, outer skin removed
1 teaspoon freshly ground black pepper
1 teaspoon paprika
2 cups sliced mushrooms
2 cups thinly sliced red onions
4 medium red bell peppers, seeded and thinly sliced
1 medium yellow bell pepper, seeded and thinly sliced

1. Preheat oven to 350° F.

2. Gently loosen skin from breast portion of chicken; reserving 6 basil leaves, stuff remaining leaves evenly under skin.

3. Sprinkle chicken cavities with salt, then place garlic bulb into large cavity; truss chicken.

4. Sprinkle chicken evenly with black pepper and paprika. Place chicken, breast-side up, onto rack in large roasting pan; roast 2–2$^1/_4$ hours, until chicken is cooked through and juices run clear when pierced with fork or meat thermometer inserted into thickest portion of thigh registers 180° F. Remove from oven; let stand 10 minutes.

5. Meanwhile, spray large nonstick skillet with nonstick cooking spray; heat. Add mushrooms; cook over medium-high heat, stirring frequently, 5 minutes, until mushrooms are tender. Remove mushrooms from skillet; set aside.

6. In same skillet, combine onions and red and yellow bell peppers; cook, stirring frequently, 5 minutes, until vegetables are softened. Remove vegetables from skillet; set aside with mushrooms.

7. Remove and discard skin from chicken and garlic from cavity; scrape off and discard cooked basil. Carve chicken; serve with vegetable mixture. Garnish with reserved basil leaves.

Serving (3 ounces chicken, 1$^1/_2$ cups vegetable mixture) provides:
2$^1/_4$ Vegetables, 3 Proteins.

Per serving: 211 Calories, 7 g Total Fat, 2 g Saturated Fat, 76 mg Cholesterol, 218 mg Sodium, 11 g Total Carbohydrate, 2 g Dietary Fiber, 27 g Protein, 107 mg Calcium.

BREAKFAST
Banana, $^1/_2$ medium
Open-Face Egg Sandwich (Spray small nonstick skillet with nonstick cooking spray; heat. Add $^1/_4$ cup egg substitute, $^1/_4$ cup diced drained roasted red bell pepper and pinch *each* salt, freshly ground black pepper and garlic powder. Cook over medium-high heat, stirring frequently, until mixture is set. Spoon onto 1 slice reduced-calorie whole-wheat bread, toasted; top with 2 tomato slices.)
Skim Milk, 1 cup

LIGHT MEAL
Vegetable Soup, canned, 1 cup
Grilled Cheese and Tomato Sandwich (Split and toast one 2-ounce English muffin. Top one muffin half with $^3/_4$ ounce reduced-fat cheddar cheese; top the other muffin half with $^1/_2$ medium tomato, sliced. Place onto nonstick baking sheet; broil until heated through. Place cheese-topped muffin half onto tomato slices, cheese-side down.)
Carrot and Celery Sticks, 1 cup *each*
Reduced-Calorie Vanilla-Flavored Pudding (made with skim milk), $^1/_2$ cup
Diet Black Cherry Soda

MAIN MEAL
Peppered Chicken Italienne, 1 serving (see recipe)
Cooked Brown Rice, 1 cup, with 2 tablespoons minced fresh flat-leaf parsley and 2 teaspoons reduced-calorie tub margarine
Steamed Brussels Sprouts, 1 cup, with Lemon "Butter" (In small cup or bowl, combine 1 teaspoon *each* reduced-calorie tub margarine, melted, and fresh lemon juice.)
Romaine and Escarole Salad, 2 cups, with 6 cherry tomatoes, $^1/_2$ cup cucumber slices and 1 tablespoon fat-free ranch dressing
Plum, 1 large
Decaffeinated Cappuccino, made with skim milk, 5 fluid ounces

SNACK
Rice Cakes, 2, with 1$^1/_2$ teaspoons *each* peanut butter and grape jam

This menu provides: 2 Milks, 3 Fats, 2 Fruits, 17$^1/_4$ Vegetables, 5 Proteins, 6 Breads, 105 Optional Calories.

Per serving: 31 g Fat, 32 g Fiber.

Peppered Chicken Italienne

226

LEMON-THYME ROAST CHICKEN

Makes 8 servings

One 4-pound 8-ounce roasting chicken
1 teaspoon freshly ground black pepper
$^1/_2$ teaspoon salt
2 large lemons
6 garlic cloves, peeled
Six 4" fresh thyme sprigs or 2 teaspoons dried thyme leaves
Additional fresh thyme sprigs, to garnish

1. Preheat oven to 350° F.

2. Sprinkle chicken cavities with $^1/_2$ teaspoon of the pepper and $^1/_4$ teaspoon of the salt.

3. On work surface, roll lemons, pressing down slightly with heel of your hand, until softened. With skewer or toothpick, pierce each lemon 15 times about 1" deep. Place pierced lemons, 5 garlic cloves and thyme into large cavity of chicken; place remaining garlic clove into small cavity. Truss chicken.

4. Sprinkle chicken evenly with remaining $^1/_2$ teaspoon pepper and $^1/_4$ teaspoon salt. Place chicken, breast-side up, onto rack in large roasting pan; roast 2–2$^1/_4$ hours, until chicken is cooked through and juices run clear when pierced with fork or meat thermometer inserted into thickest portion of thigh registers 180° F. Remove from oven; let stand 10 minutes.

5. Remove and discard skin from chicken and lemons, garlic and thyme from cavities; carve chicken. Serve garnished with additional thyme sprigs.

Serving (3 ounces chicken) provides: 3 Proteins.

Per serving: 165 Calories, 6 g Total Fat, 2 g Saturated Fat, 76 mg Cholesterol, 210 mg Sodium, 1 g Total Carbohydrate, 0 g Dietary Fiber, 25 g Protein, 23 mg Calcium.

BREAKFAST
Nectarine, 1 small
Cornflakes, $^3/_4$ ounce
Skim Milk, $^3/_4$ cup
Coffee or Tea (optional)

LIGHT MEAL
Ratatouille Gratinée (In medium saucepan, heat 1 teaspoon vegetable oil; add $^1/_2$ cup *each* cubed onion, green bell pepper, zucchini and eggplant and 2 garlic cloves, minced. Cook over medium-high heat, stirring frequently, 5 minutes, until vegetables are softened. Add 1 cup crushed tomatoes [no salt added] and $^1/_2$ teaspoon *each* dried oregano and basil leaves. Bring mixture to a boil; reduce heat to low. Cook, stirring frequently, until vegetables are very tender and flavors are blended. Transfer to small flameproof crock. Sprinkle with $^3/_4$ ounce reduced-fat cheddar cheese; broil until cheese is melted.)
Torn Romaine and Bibb Lettuce Leaves, 2 cups, with 1 tablespoon fat-free Italian dressing
Roll, 1 ounce, with 1 teaspoon reduced-calorie tub margarine
Sugar-Free Vanilla Nonfat Frozen Yogurt, 4 fluid ounces
Iced Herbal Tea

MAIN MEAL
Lemon-Thyme Roast Chicken, 1 serving (see recipe)
Baked Potato, 8 ounces, with 2 teaspoons reduced-calorie tub margarine
Steamed Baby Carrots, 1 cup
Steamed Zucchini and Yellow Squash Slices, 1 cup, with 1 teaspoon reduced-calorie tub margarine
Blackberries, $^3/_4$ cup, with 1 tablespoon thawed frozen light whipped topping (8 calories per tablespoon)
Sparkling Mineral Water with Mint Sprig

SNACK
Reduced-Calorie Strawberry Dairy Shake, 1 serving

This menu provides: 2 Milks, 3 Fats, 2 Fruits, 14 Vegetables, 4 Proteins, 4 Breads, 65 Optional Calories.

Per serving: 29 g Fat, 26 g Fiber.

This menu provides: 2 Milks, 3 Fats, 2 Fruits, 14 Vegetables, $4^1/_2$ Proteins, 5 Breads, 65 Optional Calories.

Per serving: 27 g Fat, 22 g Fiber.

To make scallion brushes, trim off root end of scallions and all but 4" of the green tops. Place scallions onto cutting board; insert point of sharp knife lengthwise at the spot where white and green portions of the scallions meet. Gently slice through green portions. Repeat slicing several times, cutting green portions into thin strips. Place scallions into bowl of ice water; let stand until green portions curl.

227
SALSA-STUFFED CHICKEN

Supermarkets and ethnic groceries are stocked with an array of salsas these days. To stuff these chicken breasts, choose a chunky one.

Makes 4 servings

8 ounces long-grain rice
$^1/_2$ teaspoon salt
$^1/_2$ teaspoon freshly ground black pepper
1 cup finely chopped scallions
Four 3-ounce skinless boneless chicken breasts
$1^1/_2$ ounces reduced-fat Monterey Jack cheese, finely grated
$^1/_2$ cup mild, medium or hot chunky salsa
4 scallion brushes, to garnish*

1. Spray four 6" bowls with nonstick cooking spray.

2. In medium saucepan, bring $2^2/_3$ cups water to a boil; add rice, $^1/_4$ teaspoon of the salt and $^1/_4$ teaspoon of the pepper. Reduce heat to low; simmer, covered, 20 minutes, until rice is tender and all liquid is absorbed. Stir in $^1/_2$ cup of the chopped scallions; divide rice among prepared bowls. Set aside; keep warm.

3. Place chicken breasts, skinned-side down, between 2 sheets of wax paper; with meat mallet or bottom of heavy saucepan, pound chicken until very thin. Remove and discard wax paper.

4. Place chicken breasts, skinned-side down, onto work surface; sprinkle each with 2 tablespoons of the remaining scallions. Sprinkle each portion of scallions with one-fourth of the cheese; top each with 2 tablespoons salsa. Starting at narrow ends, roll chicken jelly-roll fashion; secure with toothpicks. Lightly spray each roll with nonstick cooking spray; sprinkle with remaining $^1/_4$ teaspoon salt and pepper.

5. Spray large nonstick skillet with nonstick cooking spray; heat. Add chicken rolls; cook, turning as needed, 5–6 minutes, until chicken is lightly browned and cooked through. Transfer chicken rolls to cutting board; let stand 5 minutes.

6. Slice chicken rolls $^1/_2$" thick.

7. Unmold rice onto 4 plates. Arrange one-fourth of the chicken slices around each portion of rice; garnish each with a scallion brush.

Serving (1 sliced chicken roll, 1 cup rice) provides: 1 Vegetable, $2^1/_2$ Proteins, 2 Breads.

Per serving: 368 Calories, 6 g Total Fat, 2 g Saturated Fat, 61 mg Cholesterol, 713 mg Sodium, 49 g Total Carbohydrate, 1 g Dietary Fiber, 27 g Protein, 125 mg Calcium.

PESTO-STUFFED CHICKEN BREASTS WITH FRESH TOMATO COULIS

Makes 4 servings

4 large plum tomatoes, seeded and
  chopped
1 tablespoon + 1 teaspoon olive oil
2 teaspoons balsamic vinegar
1/2 teaspoon salt
1/2 teaspoon freshly ground black
  pepper

6 ounces long-grain rice
1 large garlic clove, peeled
1 cup packed fresh flat-leaf parsley
1/2 teaspoon grated lemon zest*
Four 4-ounce skinless boneless
  chicken breasts

1. Preheat oven to 450° F. Spray baking sheet with nonstick cooking spray.

2. In small bowl, combine tomatoes, 2 teaspoons of the oil, the vinegar, 1/4 teaspoon salt and 1/4 teaspoon pepper; refrigerate, covered, until chilled.

3. In medium saucepan, bring 2 cups water to a boil; stir in rice. Reduce heat to low; cook, covered, 20 minutes, until all water is absorbed and rice is tender. Remove from heat; keep warm.

4. Meanwhile, fit food processor with steel blade; with motor running, drop garlic through feed tube. Add parsley, processing until finely chopped, stopping processor and using rubber spatula to scrape sides of bowl as necessary. With motor running, add lemon zest, remaining 2 teaspoons oil, remaining 1/4 teaspoon salt and remaining 1/4 teaspoon pepper through feed tube, processing until just combined (do not purée).

5. Place chicken breasts, skinned-side down, between 2 sheets of wax paper; with meat mallet or bottom of heavy saucepan, pound chicken to 1/4" thickness. Remove and discard top sheet of wax paper; spread chicken evenly with parsley mixture. Beginning at one short end, roll chicken breasts jelly-roll fashion to enclose filling; remove and discard paper.

6. Place chicken, seam-side down, onto prepared baking sheet; bake 10–12 minutes, until chicken is cooked through. Remove chicken from oven; let stand 5 minutes. Carefully cut chicken breasts crosswise.

7. Spoon tomato mixture onto round serving platter; arrange chicken slices in a circular pattern on tomato mixture. Surround chicken with warm rice; serve warm or at room temperature.

Serving (1 stuffed chicken breast, 1/2 cup tomato mixture, 3/4 cup rice) provides: 1 Fat, 1 Vegetable, 3 Proteins, 1 1/2 Breads.

Per serving: 360 Calories, 8 g Total Fat, 2 g Saturated Fat, 72 mg Cholesterol, 355 mg Sodium, 39 g Total Carbohydrate, 2 g Dietary Fiber, 31 g Protein, 71 mg Calcium.

BREAKFAST
Spiced Baked Apple (Preheat oven to 350° F. Pare 1 small apple halfway down from stem end; place into small baking dish. Sprinkle apple with 1 teaspoon granulated sugar and 1/4 teaspoon *each* ground allspice and freshly ground nutmeg; add 1/4" water to pan. Bake, covered, 30 minutes, until tender. If desired, refrigerate, overnight.)
English Muffin, 1/2 (1 ounce), toasted, with 1 teaspoon reduced-calorie tub margarine
Skim Milk, 3/4 cup

LIGHT MEAL
Cucumber Soup (In small bowl, combine 3/4 cup plain nonfat yogurt, 1/2 cup seeded and diced cucumber and pinch garlic powder; add cold water, 1 tablespoon at a time, until desired consistency.)
Tuna-Vegetable Salad in a Pita (In small bowl, combine 2 ounces drained canned water-packed white tuna, 1/4 cup *each* chopped celery and red onion and 2 teaspoons reduced-calorie mayonnaise. Split 1 small [1-ounce] whole-wheat pita halfway around edge; open to form pocket. Fill pocket with tuna mixture.)
Cherry Tomatoes, 6
Whole Mushrooms, 1 cup
Peach, 1 medium

MAIN MEAL
Pesto-Stuffed Chicken Breasts with Fresh Tomato Coulis, 1 serving (see recipe)
Steamed Diced Carrots and Green Peas, 1/2 cup *each*, with 1 teaspoon reduced-calorie tub margarine
Tossed Green Salad, 2 cups, with 1 tablespoon fat-free Italian dressing
Sugar-Free Vanilla Nonfat Frozen Yogurt, 4 fluid ounces
Sparkling Mineral Water

SNACK
Oat-Bran Pretzels, 3/4 ounce
Diet Grape Soda

This menu provides: 2 Milks, 3 Fats, 2 Fruits, 11 Vegetables, 4 Proteins, 5 1/2 Breads, 70 Optional Calories.

Per serving: 21 g Fat, 20 g Fiber.

*The zest of the lemon is the peel without any of the pith (white membrane). To remove zest from lemon, use a zester or the fine side of a vegetable grater; wrap lemon in plastic wrap and refrigerate for use at another time.

229
BLACKENED CHICKEN BREASTS WITH CAJUN CORN RELISH

*In Cajun country, a black iron skillet is a staple in most kitchens.
Since it holds heat very well, it's ideal for blackening meats, such as
these hot and spicy chicken breasts. If you don't have an iron skillet,
use a flat, heavy skillet instead.*

Makes 4 servings

1 teaspoon ground cumin
2 cups thawed frozen corn kernels
12 cherry tomatoes, quartered
$^1/_2$ cup shredded pared jicama
$^1/_2$ cup thinly sliced scallions
2 tablespoons fresh lime juice
$^1/_4$ teaspoon salt
Four 4-ounce skinless boneless chicken breasts
1 teaspoon Cajun seasoning

1. In small nonstick skillet, toast cumin over medium heat, stirring constantly, 2 minutes, until fragrant; transfer to large shallow bowl.

2. Add corn, tomatoes, jicama, scallions, juice and salt to toasted cumin;
toss to combine. Set aside.

3. Sprinkle chicken on all sides with Cajun seasoning. Spray large iron
skillet with nonstick cooking spray; heat. Add chicken; cook over medium-
high heat, turning once, 8 minutes, until browned on all sides and juices
run clear when chicken is pierced with fork.

4. Arrange cooked chicken breasts on top of corn mixture.

Serving (1 chicken breast, $^3/_4$ cup corn mixture) provides: 1 Vegetable,
3 Proteins, 1 Bread.

Per serving: 232 Calories, 4 g Total Fat, 1 g Saturated Fat, 72 mg Cholesterol,
427 mg Sodium, 20 g Total Carbohydrate, 3 g Dietary Fiber, 30 g Protein,
33 mg Calcium.

230
CHICKEN COUSCOUS

Makes 4 servings

1 tablespoon + 1 teaspoon olive oil	4 ounces couscous
2 garlic cloves, minced	1 tablespoon minced fresh mint
1 medium red bell pepper, seeded and chopped	leaves
	1 teaspoon grated orange zest*
1 medium yellow bell pepper, seeded and chopped	Four 4-ounce skinless boneless chicken breasts
3/4 teaspoon ground cumin	1/2 cup red bell pepper strips
1/2 teaspoon salt	1/2 cup yellow bell pepper strips
1/2 teaspoon freshly ground black pepper	

1. Preheat oven to 375° F. Spray nonstick baking sheet with nonstick cooking spray.

2. In large nonstick skillet, heat oil; add garlic. Cook over medium-high heat, stirring constantly, 1 minute, until fragrant. Add chopped red and yellow bell peppers; cook, stirring frequently, 5 minutes, until peppers are softened.

3. Add cumin, 1/4 teaspoon salt, 1/4 teaspoon black pepper and 1 cup water to vegetable mixture; stir to combine. Bring liquid to a boil; stir in couscous, mint and zest. Remove from heat; let stand, covered, 5 minutes, until couscous is tender and all liquid is absorbed. Fluff couscous mixture with fork. Set aside; keep warm.

4. Place chicken breasts, skinned-side down, between 2 sheets of wax paper; with meat mallet or bottom of heavy saucepan, pound chicken to 1/4" thickness. Remove and discard top sheet of wax paper.

5. Spoon 2 tablespoons couscous mixture along center of each chicken breast; keep remaining couscous mixture warm. Beginning at one short end, roll chicken breasts jelly-roll fashion to enclose filling; remove and discard bottom sheet of wax paper.

6. Place chicken, seam-side down, onto prepared baking sheet; sprinkle evenly with remaining 1/4 teaspoon salt and 1/4 teaspoon pepper. Bake 15 minutes, until chicken is cooked through. Remove from oven; let stand 5 minutes. Carefully cut chicken breasts crosswise into thin slices.

7. Spoon remaining warm couscous mixture onto round serving platter; arrange chicken slices in a circular pattern on couscous mixture. Surround with red and yellow bell pepper strips.

Serving (1 stuffed chicken breast, 1/3 cup additional couscous mixture, one-fourth of the bell pepper strips) provides: 1 Fat, 1 1/2 Vegetables, 3 Proteins, 1 Bread.

Per serving: 313 Calories, 8 g Total Fat, 1 g Saturated Fat, 72 mg Cholesterol, 342 mg Sodium, 27 g Total Carbohydrate, 2 g Dietary Fiber, 31 g Protein, 36 mg Calcium.

BREAKFAST
Raspberries, 3/4 cup
English Muffin, 1/2 (1 ounce), toasted, with 1 table-
spoon nonfat cream cheese
Skim Milk, 1 cup
Coffee or Tea (optional)

LIGHT MEAL
Vegetable Soup, canned, 1 cup
Carrot-Raisin Salad (In small bowl, combine 1 cup
shredded carrot, 2 tablespoons raisins and 1 tea-
spoon *each* granulated sugar, reduced-calorie may-
onnaise and fresh lemon juice.)
Saltines, 3, with 2 teaspoons reduced-calorie tub
margarine
Sugar-Free Cherry-Flavored Gelatin, 1/2 cup
Diet Ginger Ale

MAIN MEAL
Chicken Couscous, 1 serving (see recipe)
Steamed Spinach, 1 cup
Steamed Sliced Green Beans and Mushrooms,
1/2 cup *each*
Caesar Salad (In medium bowl, combine 2 cups torn
Romaine lettuce leaves, 1/4 cup packaged croutons
and 1 tablespoon fat-free Caesar salad dressing.)
Breadsticks, 2 long
Aspartame-Sweetened Cherry Vanilla Nonfat Yogurt,
1 cup
Sparkling Mineral Water with Lime Wedge

SNACK
Buttery Popcorn (Lightly spray 3 cups hot-air
popped plain popcorn with nonstick cooking
spray. Sprinkle popcorn with 1/4 teaspoon butter-
flavor granules; toss to coat evenly.)

This menu provides: 2 Milks, 3 Fats, 2 Fruits,
12 1/2 Vegetables, 3 Proteins, 5 1/2 Breads,
80 Optional Calories.

Per serving: 26 g Fat, 26 g Fiber.

*The zest of the orange is the peel without any of the
pith (white membrane). To remove zest from orange,
use a zester or the fine side of a vegetable grater;
wrap orange in plastic wrap and refrigerate for use at
another time.*

CHICKEN—WHEAT BERRY SAUTÉ

BREAKFAST
Banana, $^1/_2$ medium, sliced
Fortified Cold Cereal, $1^1/_2$ ounces
Skim Milk, $^1/_2$ cup
Coffee or Tea (optional)

LIGHT MEAL
Greek Salad (In medium bowl, combine 2 cups torn
   Romaine lettuce leaves, 1 large plum tomato,
   diced, $^1/_2$ cup cooked cut green beans, $^3/_4$ ounce
   feta cheese, crumbled, 3 large Greek olives and
   fresh lemon juice to taste.)
Whole-Wheat Pita, 1 small (1 ounce)
Seedless Green Grapes, 15 small or 9 large
Unsweetened Seltzer with Mint Sprig

MAIN MEAL
Chicken—Wheat Berry Sauté, 1 serving (see recipe)
Spinach-Onion Salad (In medium bowl, combine
   2 cups torn spinach leaves, $^1/_4$ cup sliced red
   onion, 2 teaspoons balsamic vinegar and 1 teaspoon *each* olive oil and imitation bacon bits.)
Roll, 1 ounce, with $1^1/_2$ teaspoons reduced-calorie
   tub margarine
Reduced-Calorie Vanilla-Flavored Pudding (made
   with skim milk), $^1/_2$ cup
Sparkling Mineral Water with Lime Wedge

SNACK
Graham Crackers, 3 ($2^1/_2$" squares)
Skim Milk, 1 cup

This menu provides: 2 Milks, 3 Fats, 2 Fruits,
$11^1/_4$ Vegetables, 4 Proteins, 6 Breads, 50 Optional
Calories.

Per serving: 34 g Fat, 21 g Fiber.

If you have never tried wheat berries, this recipe will hook you! Try it with cooked beef or lamb for a delicious change of pace.

Makes 4 servings

1 teaspoon olive oil
1 cup thinly sliced scallions
$^1/_2$ cup diced carrot
1 garlic clove, minced
2 cups cooked wheat berries
$^1/_2$ cup fresh orange juice
11 ounces skinless boneless cooked chicken breasts, diced
1 ounce slivered almonds
2 tablespoons minced fresh flat-leaf parsley
$^1/_2$ teaspoon minced fresh thyme leaves
$^1/_2$ teaspoon freshly ground black pepper
$^1/_4$ teaspoon salt

1. In large nonstick skillet, heat oil; add scallions. Cook over medium-high heat, stirring frequently, 4 minutes, until softened. Add carrot and garlic; cook, stirring frequently, 5 minutes, until carrot is softened.

2. Add wheat berries and juice to vegetable mixture; bring liquid to a boil. Reduce heat to low; simmer, stirring occasionally, 5 minutes, until liquid is absorbed. Add chicken, almonds, parsley, thyme, pepper and salt; cook, stirring frequently, 3–5 minutes, until mixture is heated through and flavors are blended.

Serving (1 cup) provides: $^3/_4$ Fat, $^1/_4$ Fruit, $^3/_4$ Vegetable, 3 Proteins, 1 Bread.

Per serving: 283 Calories, 8 g Total Fat, 1 g Saturated Fat, 66 mg Cholesterol, 204 mg Sodium, 24 g Total Carbohydrate, 5 g Dietary Fiber, 29 g Protein, 71 mg Calcium.

232
CHICKEN MAQUECHOUX

Maquechoux means "mock cabbage" and, as the name implies, this dish has no cabbage at all! It's actually a famous Cajun skillet dish of fresh corn, tomatoes and, of course, hot pepper, which we've transformed into an entrée by adding chicken.

Makes 4 servings

2 teaspoons olive oil
10 ounces skinless boneless chicken breasts, cut into thin strips
$^1/_2$ cup finely chopped onion
2 cups coarsely chopped green bell peppers
2 cups thawed frozen corn kernels
$^1/_2$ cup coarsely chopped celery
1 teaspoon minced fresh thyme leaves, or $^1/_4$ teaspoon dried
$^1/_2$ teaspoon salt
$^1/_2$ teaspoon freshly ground black pepper
$^1/_4$ teaspoon ground red pepper
2 cups coarsely chopped tomatoes

1. In large nonstick skillet, heat oil; add chicken and onion. Cook over medium-high heat, stirring frequently, 3 minutes, until onion is softened.

2. Add bell peppers, corn, celery, thyme, salt and black and red peppers to chicken mixture; cook, stirring frequently, 4 minutes, until chicken is cooked through.

3. Add tomatoes to chicken mixture; cook, stirring frequently, 2 minutes, until mixture is heated through.

Serving ($1^1/_2$ cups) provides: $^1/_2$ Fat, $2^1/_2$ Vegetables, 2 Proteins, 1 Bread.

Per serving: 208 Calories, 4 g Total Fat, 1 g Saturated Fat, 41 mg Cholesterol, 354 mg Sodium, 25 g Total Carbohydrate, 5 g Dietary Fiber, 20 g Protein, 33 mg Calcium.

BREAKFAST
Raspberries, $^3/_4$ cup
Wheat Flakes Cereal, $1^1/_2$ ounces
Skim Milk, $^1/_2$ cup
Coffee or Tea (optional)

LIGHT MEAL
Tuna-Stuffed Tomato (In small bowl, combine 4 ounces drained canned water-packed tuna, $^1/_4$ cup chopped celery and 2 teaspoons reduced-calorie mayonnaise. Cut 1 medium tomato in half; scoop out seeds and pulp, leaving firm shell. Stuff tuna mixture into tomato halves.)
Steamed Snow Peas, 1 cup
Steamed Sliced Carrots, 1 cup
Reduced-Calorie Vanilla-Flavored Pudding (made with skim milk), $^1/_2$ cup
Iced Tea with Lemon Wedge

MAIN MEAL
Chicken Maquechoux, 1 serving (see recipe)
Cooked Brown Rice, 1 cup, with 2 teaspoons reduced-calorie tub margarine
Collard Greens, 2 cups, sauteed in 1 teaspoon reduced-calorie tub margarine
Tossed Green Salad, 2 cups, with 1 tablespoon fat-free French dressing
Strawberry Smoothie (In blender, combine 1 cup skim milk, 1 cup strawberries, sliced, 2 ice cubes and 1 teaspoon strawberry jam; purée until smooth.)
Sparkling Mineral Water

SNACK
English Muffin, $^1/_2$ (1 ounce), toasted, with 1 teaspoon apricot jam

This menu provides: 2 Milks, 3 Fats, 2 Fruits, $15^1/_2$ Vegetables, 4 Proteins, 6 Breads, 90 Optional Calories.

Per serving: 19 g Fat, 33 g Fiber.

BREAKFAST
Strawberries, $^1/_2$ cup
Bran Flakes Cereal, $^3/_4$ ounce
Skim Milk, 1 cup
Coffee or Tea (optional)

LIGHT MEAL
Two-Bean Salad (In medium bowl, combine
    2 ounces drained cooked chick-peas, $^1/_2$ cup *each*
    cooked cut green beans, diced yellow bell pepper
    and diced tomato, 1 teaspoon *each* olive oil and
    red wine vinegar and pinch dried oregano leaves.)
Carrot Sticks, 1 cup
Crispbreads, $1^1/_2$ ounces
Plum, 1 small
Iced Tea with Lemon Wedge

MAIN MEAL
Chicken à l'Orange with Wild Rice Stuffing, 1 serv-
    ing (see recipe)
Steamed Broccoli and Cauliflower Florets, 1 cup
    each
Watercress and Belgian Endive Salad, 2 cups, with
    $^1/_2$ cup sliced radishes and 1 tablespoon fat-free
    French dressing
Whole-Wheat Roll, 1 ounce, with 1 teaspoon
    reduced-calorie tub margarine
Sugar-Free Cherry-Flavored Gelatin, $^1/_2$ cup
Sparkling Mineral Water with Mint Sprig

SNACK
Mini Rice Cakes, 3, with 1 tablespoon peanut butter
Skim Milk, 1 cup

This menu provides: 2 Milks, 3 Fats, 2 Fruits,
$14^1/_2$ Vegetables, 5 Proteins, $5^1/_2$ Breads,
115 Optional Calories.

Per serving: 26 g Fat, 36 g Fiber.

233
CHICKEN À L'ORANGE WITH WILD RICE STUFFING

Here's an ideal dish to serve to company. You can stuff the chicken breasts early in the day, then refrigerate them until baking time.

Makes 4 servings

2 cups prepared long-grain and wild rice mix, any variety
1 cup thinly sliced scallions
Four 4-ounce skinless boneless chicken breasts, each slit
    horizontally to form a pocket
$^1/_2$ cup fresh orange juice
4 fluid ounces ($^1/_2$ cup) dry white wine
1 teaspoon cornstarch
$^1/_2$ teaspoon salt
$^1/_2$ teaspoon freshly ground black pepper
$^1/_4$ teaspoon minced fresh rosemary leaves or pinch dried
1 teaspoon paprika
$1^1/_2$ cups orange sections
Fresh rosemary sprigs, to garnish

1. Preheat oven to 350° F. Spray 13 × 9" baking pan with nonstick cook-ing spray.

2. In medium bowl, combine rice and scallions; spoon an equal amount of rice mixture into each chicken breast pocket, reserving any remaining rice mixture.

3. Place stuffed breasts, seam-side down, into prepared baking dish; spoon any additional rice mixture around stuffed breasts. Set aside.

4. In small saucepan, with wire whisk, combine juice, wine, cornstarch, salt, pepper and rosemary, blending until cornstarch is dissolved. Place over high heat; bring to a boil. Cook, stirring constantly, 2 minutes, until slightly thickened.

5. Pour juice mixture over chicken; sprinkle evenly with paprika. Bake, covered, 20 minutes. Remove cover; bake 5 minutes, until chicken is browned and cooked through. Top with orange sections; serve garnished with rosemary.

Serving (1 stuffed chicken breast, one-fourth of the sauce, additional rice mixture and orange sections) provides: $^1/_2$ Fat, 1 Fruit, $^1/_2$ Vegetable, 3 Proteins, 1 Bread, 85 Optional Calories.

Per serving: 289 Calories, 4 g Total Fat, 1 g Saturated Fat, 55 mg Cholesterol, 673 mg Sodium, 36 g Total Carbohydrate, 3 g Dietary Fiber, 24 g Protein, 75 mg Calcium.

234

CHICKEN WITH GINGERED PEAR-AND-APPLE SAUCE

For this sauce, buy the ripest, juiciest pears you can find. Look for Bartletts or Anjous, with their yellowish green color and blush of red, during the fall and winter; in the spring, try Bosc pears, easily recognized by their russet skin and slender neck.

Makes 4 servings

12 ounces skinless boneless cooked chicken breasts, sliced
2 teaspoons vegetable oil
$^1/_4$ cup finely chopped shallots
2 teaspoons grated pared fresh ginger root
Pinch ground allspice
Pinch salt
Pinch freshly ground black pepper
2 large or 4 small pears, pared, cored and cut into $^1/_2$" pieces
1 small red Delicious apple, cored and cut into $^1/_2$" pieces
$^1/_2$ cup apple juice
2 fluid ounces ($^1/_4$ cup) dry white wine
$^1/_4$ teaspoon grated lemon zest*
Lemon slices, to garnish

1. Preheat oven to 350° F. Adjust oven rack to divide oven in half.

2. Wrap chicken in foil; bake in center of oven 8 minutes, until warmed.

3. Meanwhile, in medium nonstick skillet, heat oil; add shallots, ginger, allspice, salt and pepper. Cook over medium-high heat, stirring frequently, 3 minutes, until shallots are softened.

4. Add pears, apple, juice, wine and zest to shallot mixture; cook, stirring gently, 5 minutes, until fruits are softened.

5. Arrange warm chicken in circular pattern on large round serving platter; spoon fruit mixture into center. Serve garnished with lemon slices.

Serving (3 ounces chicken, $^3/_4$ cup fruit mixture) provides: $^1/_2$ Fat, $1^1/_2$ Fruits, $^1/_4$ Vegetable, 3 Proteins, 15 Optional Calories.

Per serving: 301 Calories, 6 g Total Fat, 1 g Saturated Fat, 72 mg Cholesterol, 99 mg Sodium, 33 g Total Carbohydrate, 5 g Dietary Fiber, 27 g Protein, 40 mg Calcium.

The zest of the lemon is the peel without any of the pith (white membrane). To remove zest from lemon, use a zester or the fine side of a vegetable grater; wrap lemon in plastic wrap and refrigerate for use at another time.

BREAKFAST
Strawberries, $^1/_2$ cup
Cooked Oatmeal, 1 cup, with 2 teaspoons reduced-calorie tub margarine and 1 teaspoon honey
Skim Milk, $^3/_4$ cup
Coffee or Tea (optional)

LIGHT MEAL
Peanut Butter and Jelly Sandwich (Spread 1 tablespoon peanut butter and 1 teaspoon grape jelly between 2 slices reduced-calorie whole-wheat bread.)
Carrot and Celery Sticks, 1 cup *each*
Oat-Bran Pretzels, $^3/_4$ ounce
Skim Milk, 1 cup

MAIN MEAL
Chicken with Gingered Pear-and-Apple Sauce, 1 serving (see recipe)
Cooked Brown Rice, 1 cup
Steamed Baby Carrots, 1 cup, with 1 teaspoon reduced-calorie tub margarine
Watercress and Belgian Endive Salad, 2 cups, with $^1/_2$ cup *each* red and green bell pepper strips and 1 tablespoon fat-free Italian dressing
Sugar-Free Chocolate Nonfat Frozen Yogurt, 4 fluid ounces
Sparkling Mineral Water with Lime Wedge

SNACK
Frozen Orange Pop (Pour $^1/_2$ cup low-calorie orange-flavored drink into small paper cup; freeze until almost firm. Insert ice-cream-bar stick vertically into partially frozen drink; freeze until solid. Unmold.)

This menu provides: 2 Milks, 3 Fats, 2 Fruits, $12^1/_4$ Vegetables, 4 Proteins, 6 Breads, 110 Optional Calories.

Per serving: 28 g Fat, 30 g Fiber.

This menu provides: 2 Milks, 3 Fats, 2 Fruits,
$13^1/_2$ Vegetables, 5 Proteins, 5 Breads, 110 Optional
Calories.

Per serving: 20 g Fat, 32 g Fiber.

235
POACHED CHICKEN IN WINE WITH TARRAGON-PEPPER CRÈME

*Poaching chicken in wine and broth not only adds flavor, it also keeps
chicken moist.*

Makes 4 servings

$^1/_2$ cup nonfat sour cream
1 tablespoon + 1 teaspoon reduced-calorie mayonnaise
1 tablespoon minced fresh tarragon leaves
$^1/_2$ teaspoon freshly ground green or black pepper
1 cup low-sodium chicken broth
2 fluid ounces ($^1/_4$ cup) dry white wine
8 whole green or black peppercorns
Four 4" fresh tarragon sprigs
15 ounces skinless boneless chicken breasts
Additional fresh tarragon sprigs, to garnish

1. In small serving bowl, combine sour cream, mayonnaise, minced tarragon and ground pepper; refrigerate, covered, until chilled.

2. Meanwhile, in large skillet, combine broth, wine, peppercorns and 4 tarragon sprigs; bring to a boil. Add chicken; return liquid to a boil. Reduce heat to low; poach chicken, covered, 10 minutes, until cooked through. With slotted spoon, remove chicken from liquid; discard liquid. Let chicken stand 10 minutes.

3. Transfer chicken to cutting board; slice thinly. Arrange chicken on serving platter in circular pattern. Place bowl with sour cream mixture onto center of platter; garnish with additional tarragon sprigs.

Serving (3 ounces chicken, 2 tablespoons sour cream mixture) provides:
$^1/_2$ Fat, 3 Proteins, 40 Optional Calories.

Per serving: 180 Calories, 5 g Total Fat, 1 g Saturated Fat, 74 mg Cholesterol, 118 mg Sodium, 3 g Total Carbohydrate, 0 g Dietary Fiber, 29 g Protein, 59 mg Calcium.

236
CHICKEN WITH APPLE BRANDY

In this skillet dish, apple brandy not only adds flavor, but it gives the finished dish a lovely golden glaze.

Makes 4 servings

$^1/_2$ teaspoon salt
$^1/_2$ teaspoon freshly ground black pepper
$^1/_4$ teaspoon cinnamon
$^1/_4$ teaspoon ground ginger
Four 4-ounce skinless boneless chicken breasts
1 tablespoon + 1 teaspoon vegetable oil
1 cup thinly sliced onions
4 small yellow Delicious apples, pared, cored and thinly sliced
1 cup apple cider or apple juice
1 fluid ounce (2 tablespoons) apple brandy

1. In small cup or bowl, combine salt, pepper, cinnamon and ginger; rub into chicken.

2. In large nonstick skillet, heat oil; add chicken. Cook over medium-high heat, turning once, 4 minutes, until browned on all sides. Remove chicken from skillet; set aside.

3. In same skillet, cook onions, stirring constantly, 5 minutes, until softened. Stir in apples; cook, turning apple slices occasionally, 3 minutes, until apples are golden brown and tender.

4. Add cider to apple mixture; bring liquid just to a boil. Return chicken to skillet; cook, turning chicken as needed, 4 minutes, until chicken is cooked through and juices run clear when pierced with fork. With slotted spoon, transfer chicken to serving platter; keep warm.

5. Stir brandy into apple mixture; cook 3 minutes, until mixture is bubbling and apples and onions are glazed. With slotted spoon, arrange apples and onions around chicken; drizzle evenly with remaining juices in skillet.

Serving (3 ounces chicken, $^3/_4$ cup apple-onion mixture) provides: 1 Fat, $1^1/_2$ Fruits, $^1/_2$ Vegetable, 3 Proteins, 20 Optional Calories.

Per serving: 286 Calories, 6 g Total Fat, 1 g Saturated Fat, 66 mg Cholesterol, 350 mg Sodium, 28 g Total Carbohydrate, 3 g Dietary Fiber, 27 g Protein, 33 mg Calcium.

BREAKFAST
Mango, $^1/_4$ small
Raisin Bran Cereal, $^3/_4$ ounce
Skim Milk, 1 cup
Coffee or Tea (optional)

LIGHT MEAL
Broiled Flounder, 2 ounces, with 1 lemon wedge
Mashed Cooked Acorn Squash, 1 cup, with 1 teaspoon reduced-calorie tub margarine and pinch cinnamon
Steamed Sliced Carrots, 1 cup
Whole-Wheat Roll, 1 ounce, with 1 teaspoon reduced-calorie tub margarine
Reduced-Calorie Butterscotch-Flavored Pudding (made with skim milk), $^1/_2$ cup
Diet Cherry Cola

MAIN MEAL
Chicken with Apple Brandy, 1 serving (see recipe)
Cooked Barley, 1 cup, with $^1/_2$ cup cooked sliced mushrooms
Cooked Sliced Beets, 1 cup
Steamed Asparagus Tips, 1 cup
Chicory and Watercress Salad, 2 cups, with $^1/_2$ cup *each* sliced cucumber and celery and Dijon Vinaigrette (In small jar with tight-fitting lid or small bowl, combine 2 teaspoons red wine vinegar, 1 teaspoon vegetable oil and $^1/_2$ teaspoon Dijon-style mustard; cover and shake well or, with wire whisk, blend until combined.)
Gingersnaps, $^1/_2$ ounce
Sparkling Mineral Water

SNACK
Vanilla "Egg Cream" (In tall glass, combine 1 cup diet cream soda and $^1/_2$ cup skim milk.)

This menu provides: 2 Milks, 3 Fats, 2 Fruits, $13^1/_2$ Vegetables, 4 Proteins, $5^1/_2$ Breads, 80 Optional Calories.

Per serving: 23 g Fat, 43 g Fiber.

BRANDIED CHICKEN WITH PEACHES AND PLUMS

*Brandy turns chicken and fresh fruit into an elegant meal that's
perfect for guests.*

Makes 4 servings

$^1/_3$ cup + 2 teaspoons all-purpose flour
$^1/_2$ teaspoon salt
$^1/_2$ teaspoon freshly ground black pepper
$^1/_4$ teaspoon ground nutmeg
Four 4-ounce skinless boneless chicken breasts
1 tablespoon + 1 teaspoon olive oil
1 cup slivered scallions
2 garlic cloves, minced
4 fluid ounces ($^1/_2$ cup) peach brandy
$^1/_3$ cup low-sodium chicken broth
$^1/_2$ teaspoon granulated sugar
2 large plums, pared, pitted and thinly sliced
2 medium peaches, pared, pitted and thinly sliced

1. On sheet of wax paper or paper plate, combine flour, salt, pepper and
nutmeg; add chicken, turning to coat evenly.

2. In large nonstick skillet, heat 2 teaspoons of the oil; add $^3/_4$ cup of the
scallions and the garlic. Cook over medium-high heat, stirring frequently,
5 minutes, until scallions are tender. With slotted spoon, remove scallion
mixture from skillet; set aside.

3. In same skillet, heat remaining 2 teaspoons oil; add coated chicken.
Cook over medium-high heat, turning once, 3–4 minutes, until chicken
is browned on both sides. Add brandy, broth, sugar and cooked scallion
mixture; stir to combine. Bring liquid to a boil; top chicken mixture with
plums. Reduce heat to low; simmer, covered, 5 minutes, until chicken is
cooked through and juices run clear when pierced with fork.

4. Add peaches and 3 tablespoons of the remaining scallions to chicken
mixture; cook, stirring occasionally, until heated through.

5. Transfer chicken breasts to serving platter; top with fruit mixture.
Serve sprinkled with remaining 1 tablespoon scallions.

Serving (1 chicken breast, $^1/_2$ cup fruit mixture) provides: 1 Fat, 1 Fruit,
$^1/_2$ Vegetable, 3 Proteins, $^1/_2$ Bread, 85 Optional Calories.

Per serving: 362 Calories, 7 g Total Fat, 1 g Saturated Fat, 66 mg Cholesterol,
361 mg Sodium, 35 g Total Carbohydrate, 3 g Dietary Fiber, 29 g Protein,
45 mg Calcium.

238

TEXAS BARBECUED CHICKEN

Down Texas way, the barbecue sauce is always made from a tomato base. Often, a little sweetness and vinegar are added—plus, of course, a lot of hot spice!

Makes 4 servings

2 teaspoons vegetable oil
1 cup finely chopped onions
1 cup canned whole tomatoes (no salt added), coarsely chopped
1/4 cup ketchup
2 tablespoons cider vinegar
2 tablespoons honey
1/4 teaspoon ground cumin
1/4 teaspoon dried oregano leaves
1/4 teaspoon salt
1/4 teaspoon freshly ground black pepper
1/4 teaspoon hot red pepper sauce, or to taste
Four 4-ounce skinless boneless chicken breasts

1. Preheat outdoor barbecue grill according to manufacturer's directions, or preheat broiler and spray rack in broiler pan with nonstick cooking spray.

2. To prepare sauce, in medium saucepan, heat oil; add onions. Cook over medium-high heat, stirring frequently, 5 minutes, until onions are softened. Stir in tomatoes, ketchup, vinegar, honey, cumin, oregano, salt, pepper and hot red pepper sauce; stirring constantly, bring mixture to a boil. Reduce heat to low; simmer, stirring frequently, 20 minutes, until sauce is thickened and color has deepened. Remove from heat; set aside.

3. Place chicken breasts, skinned-side down, between 2 sheets of wax paper; with meat mallet or bottom of heavy saucepan, pound chicken until 1/4" thick. Remove and discard wax paper. Grill chicken over hot coals or place onto prepared rack in broiler pan and broil 4" from heat, turning once and basting with half of the sauce, 6 minutes, until chicken is cooked through. Serve with remaining sauce.

Serving (3 ounces chicken, 2 tablespoons sauce) provides: 1/4 Fat, 1 Vegetable, 3 Proteins, 45 Optional Calories.

Per serving: 224 Calories, 4 g Total Fat, 1 g Saturated Fat, 66 mg Cholesterol, 497 mg Sodium, 19 g Total Carbohydrate, 1 g Dietary Fiber, 27 g Protein, 48 mg Calcium.

BREAKFAST
Banana, 1/2 medium, sliced
Bran Flakes Cereal, 3/4 ounce
Skim Milk, 1/2 cup
Coffee or Tea (optional)

LIGHT MEAL
Turkey-Broccoli Pita (Cut large [2-ounce] whole-wheat pita in half crosswise; open to form 2 pockets. Fill each pocket with 1 ounce skinless boneless cooked turkey breast, sliced, 1/2 cup broccoli florets and 1 teaspoon reduced-calorie mayonnaise.)
Carrot and Celery Sticks, 1 cup *each*
Aspartame-Sweetened Lemon Nonfat Yogurt, 1 cup
Unsweetened Mandarin Orange–Flavored Seltzer

MAIN MEAL
Texas Barbecued Chicken, 1 serving (see recipe)
Cooked Corn on the Cob, 1 small ear, with 1 1/2 teaspoons reduced-calorie tub margarine
Grilled Vegetables (Preheat outdoor barbecue grill or indoor stove-top grill according to manufacturer's directions. Grill 1/2 cup *each* sliced zucchini, sliced yellow squash, sliced green bell pepper, sliced pared eggplant, sliced red onion and sliced fennel over hot coals or stove top, turning as needed, until lightly browned and tender.)
Torn Iceberg Lettuce Leaves, 2 cups, with 6 cherry tomatoes and 1 tablespoon fat-free ranch dressing
Watermelon, 3 × 2" wedge
Diet Lemonade, 1 cup

SNACK
English Muffin, 1/2 (1 ounce), toasted, with 1 teaspoon *each* peanut butter and grape jam
Skim Milk, 1/2 cup

This menu provides: 2 Milks, 3 Fats, 2 Fruits, 18 Vegetables, 5 Proteins, 5 Breads, 85 Optional Calories.

Per serving: 16 g Fat, 27 g Fiber.

<table>
<tr><td>

BREAKFAST
Apple, 1 small
English Muffin, $^1/_2$ (1 ounce), toasted, with 1 teaspoon grape jam
Skim Milk, 1 cup
Coffee or Tea (optional)

LIGHT MEAL
Tuna Salad Sandwich (In small bowl, combine 4 ounces drained canned water-packed tuna, flaked, $^1/_2$ cup chopped celery, 2 teaspoons reduced-calorie mayonnaise and pinch freshly ground black pepper; spread between 2 slices reduced-calorie rye bread.)
Jicama and Carrot Sticks, 1 cup *each*
Graham Crackers, 3 (2$^1/_2$" squares)
Reduced-Calorie Chocolate Dairy Shake, 1 serving

MAIN MEAL
Carolina Barbecued Chicken, 1 serving (see recipe)
Cooked Corn on the Cob, 1 small ear, with 2 teaspoons reduced-calorie tub margarine
Steamed Asparagus, 6 spears, with 2 teaspoons reduced-calorie tub margarine and 1 teaspoon freshly grated Parmesan Cheese
Tossed Green Salad, 2 cups, with 1 large plum tomato, sliced, $^1/_2$ cup bean sprouts and 1 tablespoon fat-free Thousand Island dressing
Watermelon, 3 × 2" wedge
Diet Root Beer

SNACK
Plain Popcorn, hot-air popped, 3 cups

This menu provides: 2 Milks, 3 Fats, 2 Fruits, 13 Vegetables, 5 Proteins, 5 Breads, 80 Optional Calories.

Per serving: 27 g Fat, 27 g Fiber.

</td><td>

239
CAROLINA BARBECUED CHICKEN

In the Carolinas, folks mix the barbecue sauce with vinegar, plenty of spices and a dash of sugar—but no tomato. We've re-created this sauce, which gives a great taste to chicken.

Makes 4 servings

1 cup finely chopped onions
1 cup finely chopped green bell pepper
1 cup cider vinegar
3 tablespoons firmly packed light or dark brown sugar
2 teaspoons fresh lemon juice
$^1/_2$ teaspoon salt
$^1/_2$ teaspoon dry mustard
$^1/_4$ teaspoon crushed red pepper flakes, or to taste
$^1/_4$ teaspoon freshly ground black pepper, or to taste
One 2-pound 4-ounce chicken, skinned and cut into 8 equal pieces

1. Preheat outdoor barbecue grill according to manufacturer's directions, or preheat broiler and spray rack in broiler pan with nonstick cooking spray.

2. In small saucepan, combine onions, bell pepper, vinegar, brown sugar, juice, salt, dry mustard, pepper flakes and black pepper; stirring constantly, bring liquid to a boil. Reduce heat to low; simmer, stirring occasionally, 20 minutes, until flavors are blended.

3. Grill chicken over hot coals or place onto prepared rack in broiler pan and broil 4" from heat, turning as needed and basting with some of the onion mixture, 20 minutes, until browned and juices run clear when pierced with fork.

4. Transfer chicken to serving platter; top with remaining onion mixture.

Serving (3 ounces chicken, one-fourth of the onion mixture) provides:
1 Vegetable, 3 Proteins, 35 Optional Calories.

Per serving: 233 Calories, 6 g Total Fat, 2 g Saturated Fat, 76 mg Cholesterol, 353 mg Sodium, 19 g Total Carbohydrate, 1 g Dietary Fiber, 25 g Protein, 39 mg Calcium.

</td></tr>
</table>

240
Down-South Chicken and Dumplings

Makes 4 servings

One 2-pound 4-ounce chicken, skinned and cut into 8 equal pieces
$^3/_4$ teaspoon freshly ground black pepper
$^1/_2$ teaspoon salt
1 tablespoon + 1 teaspoon olive oil
2 cups carrot chunks
1 cup chopped onions
1 cup coarsely chopped celery
2$^1/_4$ cups all-purpose flour
5 cups low-sodium chicken broth
1 cup whole milk

1 tablespoon minced fresh thyme leaves, or 1 teaspoon dried
2 bay leaves
1 teaspoon double-acting baking powder
$^1/_4$ teaspoon baking soda
2 tablespoons + 2 teaspoons reduced-calorie tub margarine
$^3/_4$ cup skim buttermilk
$^1/_4$ cup minced fresh flat-leaf parsley
1 teaspoon fresh lemon juice

1. To prepare chicken, sprinkle chicken on all sides with pepper and $^1/_4$ teaspoon of the salt.

2. In large pot or Dutch oven, heat oil; add chicken. Cook over medium-high heat, turning as necessary, 5 minutes, until chicken is browned on all sides. Remove chicken from pot; set aside.

3. In same pot, combine carrots, onions and celery; cook, stirring frequently, 5 minutes, until onions are softened. Sprinkle vegetable mixture with $^1/_4$ cup of the flour; cook, stirring constantly, until vegetables are well coated.

4. With wire whisk, stir broth, milk and thyme into vegetable mixture, blending until flour is dissolved. Add bay leaves and browned chicken; bring liquid to a boil. Reduce heat to low; simmer, covered, stirring occasionally, 20 minutes, until chicken is cooked through and juices run clear when pierced with fork. Remove and discard bay leaves.

5. Meanwhile, to prepare dumplings, in medium bowl, combine 1$^3/_4$ cups of the remaining flour, the baking powder, remaining $^1/_4$ teaspoon salt and baking soda. With pastry blender or 2 knives, cut margarine into flour mixture until mixture resembles coarse crumbs. Stir in buttermilk, 1 tablespoon at a time, until mixture forms soft dough.

6. Sprinkle work surface with remaining $^1/_4$ cup flour. Transfer dough to prepared work surface; roll into 8" square, about 1" thick. Cut dough into sixteen 2" squares.

7. Carefully drop dough squares into chicken mixture; simmer, covered, 8 minutes, until dumplings are cooked through.

8. Stir parsley and juice into stew.

BREAKFAST
Orange Sections, $^1/_2$ cup
Bagel, $^1/_2$ small (1 ounce), toasted, with 1 tablespoon nonfat cream cheese
Skim Milk, 1 cup
Coffee or Tea (optional)

LIGHT MEAL
Ham and Cheese Sandwich (Layer 1 ounce cooked lean boiled ham, 1 slice nonfat process Swiss cheese, 2 Romaine lettuce leaves, 2 tomato slices and 1 teaspoon prepared mustard between 2 slices reduced-calorie multi-grain bread.)
Celery and Carrot Sticks, 1 cup *each*
Reduced-Calorie Chocolate-Flavored Pudding (made with skim milk), $^1/_2$ cup
Diet Black Cherry Soda

MAIN MEAL
Down-South Chicken and Dumplings, 1 serving (see recipe)
Steamed Sugar Snap Peas, 1 cup, with 2 teaspoons reduced-calorie tub margarine
Tossed Green Salad, 2 cups, with $^1/_2$ cup sliced radishes and 1 tablespoon fat-free Italian dressing
Strawberries, 1 cup
Unsweetened Seltzer

SNACK
Sugar-Free Cherry-Flavored Gelatin, $^1/_2$ cup, topped with $^1/_4$ cup aspartame-sweetened cherry-vanilla nonfat yogurt

This menu provides: 2 Milks, 3 Fats, 2 Fruits, 14 Vegetables, 4$^1/_2$ Proteins, 5 Breads, 125 Optional Calories.

Per serving: 31 g Fat, 30 g Fiber.

Serving (2 cups stew, 4 dumplings) provides:
$^1/_4$ Milk, 2 Fats, 2 Vegetables, 3 Proteins, 3 Breads, 55 Optional Calories.

Per serving: 625 Calories, 21 g Total Fat, 5 g Saturated Fat, 85 mg Cholesterol, 890 mg Sodium, 73 g Total Carbohydrate, 5 g Dietary Fiber, 41 g Protein, 295 mg Calcium.

Down-South Chicken and Dumplings

241
SOUTHERN "FRIED" BUTTERMILK CHICKEN

Here's "fried" chicken that tastes just like it does in the deep south. However, because it's dipped in skim buttermilk instead of whole milk or cream and baked instead of deep-fat fried, it's also guilt free!

Makes 4 servings

2 cups skim buttermilk
³/₄ cup all-purpose flour
³/₄ cup plain dried bread crumbs
2 tablespoons minced fresh thyme leaves, or 2 teaspoons dried
1 teaspoon salt
1 teaspoon freshly ground black pepper
1 pound 8 ounces chicken parts, skinned

1. Preheat oven to 400° F. Spray nonstick baking sheet with nonstick cooking spray.

2. Place buttermilk into shallow bowl. Place flour onto sheet of wax paper or paper plate; on separate sheet of wax paper or paper plate, combine bread crumbs, thyme, salt and pepper.

3. One at a time, coat each chicken part with flour, then dip into buttermilk, turning to coat; coat in bread crumb mixture. Place chicken parts onto prepared baking sheet 1–2" apart; spray lightly with nonstick cooking spray. Bake 40 minutes, until chicken is golden brown, cooked through and juices run clear when chicken is pierced with a fork.

Serving (3 ounces chicken) provides: ¹/₂ Milk, 3 Proteins, 2 Breads.

Per serving: 375 Calories, 8 g Total Fat, 2 g Saturated Fat, 78 mg Cholesterol, 944 mg Sodium, 40 g Total Carbohydrate, 2 g Dietary Fiber, 34 g Protein, 232 mg Calcium.

BREAKFAST
Raisins, 2 tablespoons
Shredded Wheat Cereal, ³/₄ ounce
Skim Milk, 1 cup
Coffee or Tea (optional)

LIGHT MEAL
Baked Swordfish, 2 ounces
Steamed Sliced Yellow Squash, 1 cup
Italian Spinach Salad (In medium bowl, combine 2 cups torn spinach leaves, ¹/₂ cup *each* sliced mushrooms and sliced red onion, 2 teaspoons imitation bacon bits and 1¹/₂ teaspoons Italian dressing.)
Sugar-Free Strawberry Nonfat Frozen Yogurt, 4 fluid ounces
Sparkling Mineral Water with Mint Sprig

MAIN MEAL
Southern-"Fried" Buttermilk Chicken, 1 serving (see recipe)
Baked Potato, 8 ounces, with 2 tablespoons nonfat sour cream
Steamed Collard Greens, 1 cup, with 2 teaspoons reduced-calorie tub margarine
Pear, 1 small
Iced Tea

SNACK
Plain Popcorn, hot-air popped, 3 cups, with 2 teaspoons reduced-calorie margarine, melted
Chocolate-Mint Cooler (In tall glass, combine 1 cup diet chocolate soda, ¹/₄ cup skim milk and ¹/₄ teaspoon peppermint extract; add enough ice cubes to fill glass.)

This menu provides: 2 Milks, 3 Fats, 2 Fruits, 10 Vegetables, 5 Proteins, 6 Breads, 90 Optional Calories.

Per serving: 27 g Fat, 27 g Fiber.

$^1/_4$" thick. With 2" decorative cookie cutter, cut
out 18 portions of dough, rerolling scraps of
dough as necessary. Arrange dough pieces on
top of chicken mixture; brush dough with
remaining half of the egg. Bake 30 minutes,
until chicken mixture is bubbling and crust is
golden brown.

Serving (1$^1/_2$ cups) provides: $^1/_2$ Milk, 1$^1/_2$ Fats,
2 Vegetables, 3 Proteins, 2$^1/_2$ Breads.

Per serving: 500 Calories, 14 g Total Fat, 3 g Saturated Fat, 106 mg Cholesterol, 833 mg Sodium,
593 g Total Carbohydrate, 5 g Dietary Fiber,
36 g Protein, 244 mg Calcium.

**Reserve remaining liquid to use in recipes calling for
low-sodium chicken broth.*

242
CHICKEN POT PIE

Makes 6 servings

Crust:
1 cup + 2 tablespoons all-purpose
  flour
3 tablespoons reduced-calorie tub
  margarine
$^1/_2$ teaspoon salt
$^1/_2$ teaspoon ground white pepper
$^1/_4$ cup ice water
1 egg, beaten

Filling:
One 2-pound 13-ounce chicken, cut
  into 8 equal pieces
4 garlic cloves, minced
2 bay leaves
$^1/_2$ teaspoon salt
2 cups carrot chunks

2 cups sliced celery
2 cups pearl onions, peeled and
  halved
3 tablespoons reduced-calorie tub
  margarine
$^1/_2$ cup + 1 tablespoon all-purpose
  flour
3 cups skim milk
1$^1/_2$ cups thawed frozen corn kernels
1$^1/_2$ cups thawed frozen tiny green
  peas
2 ounces lean boneless cooked ham,
  diced
1 tablespoon minced fresh thyme
  leaves, or 1 teaspoon dried
$^1/_4$ teaspoon freshly ground black
  pepper

1. To prepare crust, in food processor, combine 1 cup of the flour, the
margarine, salt and white pepper; process 1 minute, until mixture is
crumbly. Add water and half of the egg; process 1 minute, until mixture
forms a dough. Remove dough from food processor; form into ball. Wrap
dough ball in plastic wrap; refrigerate until chilled.

2. To prepare filling, in large pot with heatproof handles or Dutch oven,
combine chicken, garlic, bay leaves and salt; add water to cover. Bring
liquid to a boil. Reduce heat to low; simmer, covered, 30 minutes, until
chicken is cooked through and juices run clear when pierced with fork.

3. With slotted spoon, transfer chicken to cutting board; let cool; reserve
liquid, discarding bay leaves. Transfer liquid to large container; refrigerate,
covered, until fat congeals on top. Remove and discard congealed fat.
Remove and discard skin and bones from cooled chicken; cut into bite-size
pieces. Set aside.

4. Spray same pot with nonstick cooking spray; heat. Add carrots, celery
and onions; cook over medium-high heat, stirring frequently, 5 minutes,
until vegetables are softened. Remove vegetables from pot; set aside.

5. In same pot, melt margarine; add flour. Cook over medium-high heat,
stirring constantly, 3 minutes, until mixture is bubbling. With wire whisk,
gradually stir in milk and 1$^1/_2$ cups of the reserved liquid;* continuing to stir,
cook 3 minutes, until mixture is slightly thickened. Remove from heat; stir
in corn, peas, ham, thyme, pepper, cooked chicken and cooked vegetables.

6. Preheat oven to 350° F.

7. To complete crust, sprinkle work surface with remaining 2 tablespoons
flour. Transfer dough to prepared work surface; roll into 10" circle,

243

Chicken Stew Provençal

Plenty of garden vegetables team up with chicken to make this old-fashioned stew with delicious homemade flavor.

Makes 4 servings

One 2-pound 4-ounce chicken, cut into 8 equal pieces
3¹/₂ cups low-sodium chicken broth
2 bay leaves
¹/₂ teaspoon salt
1 tablespoon + 1 teaspoon olive oil
4 garlic cloves, minced
2 cups sliced mushrooms
2 cups carrot chunks
2 cups pearl onions, peeled and halved
¹/₃ cup + 2 teaspoons all-purpose flour
10 ounces small red potatoes, quartered
4 large plum tomatoes, seeded and diced
1 cup thawed frozen corn kernels
6 fluid ounces (³/₄ cup) dry light white wine
¹/₄ cup minced fresh flat-leaf parsley
1 teaspoon minced fresh dill
¹/₂ teaspoon freshly ground black pepper
1 teaspoon fresh lemon juice

1. In large pot or Dutch oven, combine chicken, broth, bay leaves and salt; bring liquid to a boil. Reduce heat to low; simmer, covered, 30 minutes, until chicken is cooked through and juices run clear when pierced with fork.

2. With slotted spoon, transfer chicken to cutting board; let cool; reserve liquid, discarding bay leaves.

3. Transfer liquid to 1-quart container; refrigerate, covered, until fat congeals on top. Remove and discard congealed fat.

4. Remove and discard skin and bones from cooled chicken; cut into bite-size pieces. Set aside.

5. In same pot, heat oil; add garlic. Cook over medium-high heat, stirring constantly, 1 minute, until softened. Add mushrooms, carrots and onions; cook, stirring frequently, 5 minutes, until carrots are just tender.

6. Sprinkle vegetable mixture with flour; stir until flour is dissolved. Add potatoes and reserved broth; bring liquid to a boil. Reduce heat to low; simmer, covered, 10 minutes, until potatoes are tender. Stir in tomatoes, corn, wine, parsley, dill and pepper; simmer, covered, 5 minutes, until liquid is slightly thickened. Remove from heat; stir in juice.

BREAKFAST
Raspberry Yogurt (In small bowl, combine ³/₄ cup *each* raspberries and plain nonfat yogurt.)
English Muffin, ¹/₂ (1 ounce), toasted, with 1 teaspoon peanut butter
Coffee or Tea (optional)

LIGHT MEAL
Tuna Salad Sandwich (In small bowl, combine 4 ounces drained canned water-packed tuna, flaked, ¹/₂ cup chopped celery, 2 teaspoons reduced-calorie mayonnaise and pinch freshly ground black pepper; spread between 2 slices reduced-calorie rye bread.)
Red and Green Bell Pepper Strips, 1 cup *each*
Sugar-Free Chocolate Nonfat Frozen Yogurt, 4 fluid ounces
Iced Tea

MAIN MEAL
Chicken Stew Provençal, 1 serving (see recipe)
Cooked Brown Rice, 1 cup
Chicory and Romaine Lettuce Salad, 2 cups, with ¹/₂ cup *each* sliced celery and jicama and 1 tablespoon fat-free Italian dressing
Honeydew Melon, 2" wedge
Sparkling Mineral Water

SNACK
Vanilla Milk "Shake" (In blender, combine ³/₄ cup skim milk, 3 ice cubes, sugar substitute to equal 2 teaspoons sugar and 1 teaspoon vanilla extract; purée until smooth.)

This menu provides: 2 Milks, 3 Fats, 2 Fruits, 15 Vegetables, 5 Proteins, 5¹/₂ Breads, 90 Optional Calories.

Per serving: 26 g Fat, 25 g Fiber.

Serving (2¹/₄ cups) provides: 1 Fat, 4 Vegetables, 3 Proteins, 1¹/₂ Breads, 35 Optional Calories.

Per serving: 465 Calories, 14 g Total Fat, 3 g Saturated Fat, 76 mg Cholesterol, 490 mg Sodium, 52 g Total Carbohydrate, 6 g Dietary Fiber, 34 g Protein, 102 mg Calcium.

Coq au Vin

Makes 6 servings

BREAKFAST

Pear, 1 small
Cinnamon-Raisin Bread, 1 slice, toasted, with 1 tea-
spoon reduced-calorie tub margarine
Skim Milk, ³/₄ cup
Coffee or Tea (optional)

LIGHT MEAL

Tuna Salad Pita (In small bowl, combine 4 ounces
drained canned water-packed tuna, ¹/₄ cup *each*
chopped onion and celery, 2 teaspoons reduced-
calorie mayonnaise and ¹/₄ teaspoon lemon pepper
seasoning. Cut large [2-ounce] whole-wheat pita
in half crosswise; open to form 2 pockets. Fill
each pocket with half of the tuna mixture; top
each portion of tuna with ¹/₄ cup alfalfa sprouts.)
Cucumber and Carrot Sticks, 1 cup *each*
Reduced-Calorie Chocolate Dairy Shake, 1 serving

MAIN MEAL

Steamed Artichoke, 1 whole medium, with Lemon
"Butter" (In small cup or bowl, combine 1 tea-
spoon each reduced-calorie tub margarine, melt-
ed, and fresh lemon juice.)
Coq au Vin, 1 serving (see recipe)
Cooked Barley, ¹/₂ cup
Steamed Brussels Sprouts, 1 cup, with 2 teaspoons
reduced-calorie tub margarine
Blackberries, ³/₄ cup, with 1 tablespoon thawed
frozen light whipped topping (8 calories per
tablespoon)
Sparkling Mineral Water

SNACK

Cola "Float" (In tall glass, scoop 4 fluid ounces
sugar-free vanilla nonfat frozen yogurt; add
enough diet cola to fill glass.)

This menu provides: 2 Milks, 3 Fats, 2 Fruits,
12¹/₂ Vegetables, 5 Proteins, 5¹/₂ Breads,
100 Optional Calories.

Per serving: 27 g Fat, 40 g Fiber.

Serving (1²/₃ cups) provides: 3¹/₂ Vegetables,
3 Proteins, 1¹/₂ Breads, 40 Optional Calories.

Per serving: 451 Calories, 9 g Total Fat,
2 g Saturated Fat, 81 mg Cholesterol,
536 mg Sodium, 54 g Total Carbohydrate,
7 g Dietary Fiber, 33 g Protein, 65 mg Calcium.

1 cup coarsely chopped onions
3 tablespoons all-purpose flour
³/₄ teaspoon salt
¹/₂ teaspoon freshly ground black
pepper
One 3-pound 6-ounce chicken,
skinned and cut into 8 equal
pieces
8 fluid ounces (1 cup) dry light red
wine
2 cups low-sodium chicken broth
¹/₃ cup + 2 teaspoons tomato
paste (no salt added)
1 tablespoon minced fresh thyme
leaves, or 1 teaspoon dried

¹/₂ teaspoon dried tarragon leaves
2 pounds 8 ounces small red potatoes, quartered
4 cups sliced mushrooms
4 medium carrots, cut into
1" pieces
2 teaspoons cornstarch, dissolved in
2 tablespoons cold water
¹/₄ cup minced fresh flat-leaf
parsley
2 tablespoons red wine vinegar
3 slices crisp-cooked lean turkey
bacon (30 calories per slice),
crumbled

1. Preheat oven to 375° F.

2. Spray large pot with heatproof handles or Dutch oven with nonstick
cooking spray; add onions. Cook over medium-high heat, stirring frequently, 5 minutes, until onions are softened. Remove onions from pot;
set aside.

3. On sheet of wax paper or paper plate, combine flour, ¹/₂ teaspoon of
the salt and the pepper; add chicken, turning to coat evenly.

4. Spray same pot with nonstick cooking spray; heat. Add chicken; cook
over medium-high heat, turning as needed, 6–7 minutes, until chicken is
browned on all sides. Remove chicken from pot; set aside.

5. In same pot, bring wine to a boil, scraping up any browned bits from
bottom of pot; cook 2 minutes. With wire whisk, stir in broth, tomato
paste, thyme, tarragon and remaining ¹/₄ teaspoon salt, blending until
paste is dissolved. Add potatoes, mushrooms, carrots, cooked onions and
browned chicken; bring liquid to a boil.

6. Transfer pot to oven; bake, covered, occasionally stirring gently, 25–30
minutes, until chicken is cooked through and juices run clear when
pierced with fork.

7. Remove chicken mixture from oven. With slotted spoon, transfer
chicken and vegetables to deep serving platter; keep warm.

8. Bring broth mixture to a boil; cook 5 minutes. With wire whisk, stir
in dissolved cornstarch; continuing to stir, cook 2 minutes, until mixture
is slightly thickened. Stir in parsley and vinegar. Pour broth mixture over
chicken and vegetables; sprinkle with crumbled bacon.

245
SPRING CHICKEN SOUP

Soup is not just for wintry months! This light and fresh-tasting chicken soup, with a hint of mint and lemon, makes an ideal springtime entrée.

Makes 4 servings

One 2-pound 4-ounce chicken, cut into 8 equal pieces
4 medium carrots
6 ounces parsnips
6 large garlic cloves, crushed
2 bay leaves
$^1/_2$ teaspoon salt
1 cup low-sodium chicken broth
1 cup thawed frozen tiny green peas
2 tablespoons minced fresh mint leaves
1 tablespoon grated lemon zest*
2 tablespoons fresh lemon juice
$^1/_2$ teaspoon freshly ground black pepper

1. In large pot or Dutch oven, combine chicken, carrots, parsnips, garlic, bay leaves, salt and 3 quarts water; bring liquid to a boil. Reduce heat to low; simmer 1 hour, until chicken is cooked through and juices run clear when pierced with fork.

2. With slotted spoon, transfer chicken, carrots and parsnips to cutting board; let cool.

3. Meanwhile, simmer liquid 30 minutes; remove and discard garlic and bay leaves.

4. Transfer liquid to 3-quart container; refrigerate, covered, until fat congeals on top. Remove and discard congealed fat.

5. Remove and discard skin and bones from cooled chicken; cut into bite-size pieces. Slice carrots and parsnips.

6. In same pot, combine broth, peas, mint, zest, juice, pepper, cooked chicken, sliced carrots and parsnips and reserved liquid; bring liquid to a boil. Reduce heat to low; simmer 5 minutes, until peas are cooked through and mixture is heated.

Serving (3 cups) provides: 2 Vegetables, 3 Proteins, 1 Bread, 5 Optional Calories.

Per serving: 288 Calories, 7 g Total Fat, 2 g Saturated Fat, 76 mg Cholesterol, 480 mg Sodium, 27 g Total Carbohydrate, 7 g Dietary Fiber, 30 g Protein, 89 mg Calcium.

The zest of the lemon is the peel without any of the pith (white membrane). To remove zest from lemon, use a zester or the fine side of a vegetable grater.

BREAKFAST
Blueberries, $^3/_4$ cup
Bran Flakes Cereal, $^3/_4$ ounce
Skim Milk, 1 cup
Coffee or Tea (optional)

LIGHT MEAL
Turkey Sandwich (Layer 2 ounces skinless boneless roast turkey breast, sliced, $^1/_2$ medium tomato, sliced, $^1/_2$ cup arugula leaves, 2 teaspoons reduced-calorie mayonnaise and 1 teaspoon mustard between 2 slices reduced-calorie rye bread.)
Cucumber Sticks and Broccoli Florets, 1 cup *each*
Sugar-Free Chocolate Nonfat Frozen Yogurt, 4 fluid ounces
Diet Cola

MAIN MEAL
Spring Chicken Soup, 1 serving (see recipe)
Tossed Green Salad, 2 cups, with $^1/_2$ cup red bell pepper strips, 6 large pitted black olives, $^1/_4$ cup packaged croutons and 1 tablespoon fat-free blue cheese dressing
French Bread, 1 slice (1 ounce), with 1 teaspoon reduced-calorie tub margarine
Kiwi Fruit, 1 medium
Sparkling Mineral Water

SNACK
Graham Crackers, 3 ($2^1/_2$" squares)
Skim Milk, $^3/_4$ cup

This menu provides: 2 Milks, 3 Fats, 2 Fruits, 13 Vegetables, 5 Proteins, $5^1/_2$ Breads, 75 Optional Calories.

Per serving: 24 g Fat, 25 g Fiber.

246
MACARONI AND CHICKEN SALAD

When you want macaroni salad, try this healthful combination of pasta and vegetables in a mustard-spiced yogurt dressing; you'll never crave the heavy old-fashioned version again!

Makes 4 servings

3 ounces elbow macaroni
$^3/4$ cup plain nonfat yogurt
2 tablespoons reduced-calorie mayonnaise
1 tablespoon Dijon-style mustard
1 teaspoon celery seeds
$^1/4$ teaspoon salt
$^1/4$ teaspoon freshly ground black pepper
8 ounces skinless boneless cooked chicken breasts, cut into $^1/2$" cubes
2 large plum tomatoes, diced
1 cup minced red onions
$^1/2$ cup shredded carrot
$^1/2$ cup chopped celery

1. In large pot of boiling water, cook macaroni 9–10 minutes, until tender. Drain, discarding liquid; rinse. Drain again; set aside.

2. In large bowl, with wire whisk, combine yogurt, mayonnaise, mustard, celery seeds, salt and pepper, blending to mix well. Add chicken, tomatoes, onions, carrot, celery and reserved macaroni; toss to combine. Serve immediately or refrigerate, covered, until chilled.

Serving (1$^1/2$ cups) provides: $^1/4$ Milk, $^3/4$ Fat, 1$^1/2$ Vegetables, 2 Proteins, 1 Bread.

Per serving: 253 Calories, 5 g Total Fat, 1 g Saturated Fat, 52 mg Cholesterol, 367 mg Sodium, 28 g Total Carbohydrate, 2 g Dietary Fiber, 24 g Protein, 130 mg Calcium.

247
CHICKEN AND POTATO SALAD

Make potato salad in a fresh new way with a mustard-vinegar dressing instead of a heavy, fat-laden one. To turn it into a main dish, we've added chunks of chicken.

Makes 4 servings

10 ounces small red potatoes, quartered
³/₄ teaspoon salt
10 ounces skinless boneless chicken breasts, cut into 1" pieces
1 medium red bell pepper, seeded and coarsely chopped
1 medium yellow bell pepper, seeded and coarsely chopped
8 medium scallions, thinly sliced
2 tablespoons minced fresh flat-leaf parsley
1 tablespoon minced fresh thyme leaves, or 1 teaspoon dried
1 tablespoon grated lemon zest*
¹/₃ cup red wine vinegar
1 tablespoon + 1 teaspoon olive oil
1 tablespoon coarse-grain Dijon-style mustard
¹/₂ teaspoon freshly ground black pepper
8 Bibb or Boston lettuce leaves

1. In medium saucepan, combine potatoes and ¹/₂ teaspoon of the salt; add water to cover. Bring liquid to a boil. Reduce heat to low; simmer 10–15 minutes, until potatoes are tender. Drain, discarding liquid; rinse with cold water. Drain again. Transfer potatoes to large bowl; set aside.

2. In large skillet, bring 2 cups water to a boil. Add chicken; return liquid to a boil. Reduce heat to low; poach chicken 6 minutes, until cooked through.

3. With slotted spoon, transfer chicken to bowl with potatoes. Add red and yellow bell peppers, scallions, parsley, thyme and zest to potato mixture; toss to combine.

4. In small jar with tight-fitting lid or small bowl, combine vinegar, oil, mustard, pepper and remaining ¹/₄ teaspoon salt; cover and shake well or, with wire whisk, blend until combined. Pour vinegar mixture over potato mixture; toss gently to coat. Refrigerate, covered, at least 2 hours or overnight.

5. Just before serving, arrange lettuce leaves around edges of potato mixture.

Serving (1 cup) provides: 1 Fat, 1¹/₂ Vegetables, 2 Proteins, ¹/₂ Bread.

Per serving: 219 Calories, 7 g Total Fat, 1 g Saturated Fat, 48 mg Cholesterol, 416 mg Sodium, 18 g Total Carbohydrate, 2 g Dietary Fiber, 20 g Protein, 42 mg Calcium.

BREAKFAST
Pear, 1 small
Bagel, ¹/₂ small (1 ounce), toasted, with 1 teaspoon *each* reduced-calorie tub margarine and strawberry jam
Skim Milk, 1 cup
Coffee or Tea (optional)

LIGHT MEAL
Split-Pea Soup, canned, 1 cup, with 20 oyster crackers
Carrot and Celery Sticks, 1 cup *each*
Roll, 1 ounce, with 1 teaspoon reduced-calorie tub margarine
Seedless Green Grapes, 20 small or 12 large
Iced Tea with Lemon Wedge

MAIN MEAL
Chicken and Potato Salad, 1 serving (see recipe)
Sliced Zucchini, 1 cup, and 6 cherry tomatoes, halved, and 1 garlic clove, minced, sauteed in 1 teaspoon olive oil
Torn Romaine and Red Leaf Lettuce Leaves, 2 cups, with ¹/₂ cup sliced red onion, 2 ounces drained cooked pinto beans and 1 tablespoon fat-free Italian dressing
Aspartame-Sweetened Blueberry Nonfat Yogurt, 1 cup
Unsweetened Seltzer

SNACK
Oat-Bran Pretzels, 1¹/₂ ounces

This menu provides: 2 Milks, 3 Fats, 2 Fruits, 13¹/₂ Vegetables, 5 Proteins, 5¹/₂ Breads, 50 Optional Calories.

Per serving: 25 g Fat, 33 g Fiber.

The zest of the lemon is the peel without any of the pith (white membrane). To remove zest from lemon, use a zester or the fine side of a vegetable grater; wrap lemon in plastic wrap and refrigerate for use at another time.

248
TEX-MEX CHICKEN, CORN AND BLACK BEAN SALAD

*Combine Southwestern favorites — corn, black beans, salsa, chicken
and fresh vegetables — and you have a robust main-dish salad
everyone will love.*

Makes 4 servings

8 ounces skinless boneless cooked chicken breasts, cut into thin strips
8 ounces drained cooked black beans
2 cups thawed frozen corn kernels
2 cups coarsely chopped tomatoes
1 cup thinly sliced red onions
1 cup medium or hot salsa
$^1/_3$ cup red wine vinegar
2 tablespoons minced fresh cilantro
8 curly lettuce leaves
1 ounce nonfat tortilla chips, broken

1. In large bowl, combine chicken, beans, corn, tomatoes, onions, salsa,
vinegar and cilantro; refrigerate, covered, at least 2 hours or overnight.

2. Line serving platter with lettuce leaves. Top lettuce with chicken mixture; sprinkle with tortilla chips.

Serving ($1^1/_2$ cups) provides: 3 Vegetables, 3 Proteins, $1^1/_4$ Breads.

Per serving: 321 Calories, 4 g Total Fat, 1 g Saturated Fat, 48 mg Cholesterol,
707 mg Sodium, 46 g Total Carbohydrate, 6 g Dietary Fiber, 27 g Protein,
67 mg Calcium.

249
GRILLED CHICKEN CAESAR SALAD

A newfound favorite: the ever-popular Caesar salad, teamed up with chicken. Grill the chicken on the barbecue to add even more flavor.

Makes 4 servings

^{1}/$_4$ cup fresh lemon juice
3 garlic cloves, minced
15 ounces skinless boneless chicken breasts
^{1}/$_3$ cup nonfat sour cream
^{1}/$_4$ cup reduced-calorie mayonnaise
3 tablespoons freshly grated Parmesan cheese
2 tablespoons minced fresh flat-leaf parsley
1 tablespoon skim milk
^{3}/$_4$ teaspoon salt
^{1}/$_2$ teaspoon freshly ground black pepper
^{1}/$_2$ teaspoon Worcestershire sauce
^{1}/$_4$ teaspoon anchovy paste
8 cups torn Romaine lettuce leaves
5 large plum tomatoes, cut into thin wedges
^{1}/$_2$ cup sliced red onion, separated into rings

1. To prepare marinade, in gallon-size sealable plastic bag, combine 3 tablespoons of the juice and half the garlic; add chicken. Seal bag, squeezing out air; turn to coat chicken. Refrigerate 30 minutes, turning bag occasionally.

2. Preheat outdoor barbecue grill according to manufacturer's directions, or preheat broiler and spray rack in broiler pan with nonstick cooking spray.

3. To prepare salad dressing, in small bowl, combine sour cream, mayonnaise, 1 tablespoon of the cheese, the parsley, milk, salt, pepper, Worcestershire sauce, anchovy paste and remaining garlic; with wire whisk, add remaining juice, blending until well combined. Set aside.

4. Drain and discard marinade. Grill chicken over hot coals or place onto prepared rack in broiler pan and broil 4" from heat, turning once, 5–6 minutes, until chicken is golden brown, cooked through and juices run clear when pierced with fork.

5. Meanwhile, in large bowl, combine lettuce, tomatoes and onion.

6. Slice chicken breasts. Pour dressing over salad; toss to coat. Arrange chicken slices on salad; sprinkle with remaining 2 tablespoons cheese.

BREAKFAST
Banana, ^{1}/$_2$ medium, sliced
Fortified Cold Cereal, ^{3}/$_4$ ounce
Skim Milk, ^{3}/$_4$ cup
Coffee or Tea (optional)

LIGHT MEAL
Beans and Franks (In small saucepan, combine ^{1}/$_2$ cup canned baked beans [without meat] and 1 ounce fat-free frankfurter, sliced; heat.)
Carrot and Celery Sticks, 1 cup *each*
Whole-Wheat Roll, 1 ounce, with 1 teaspoon reduced-calorie tub margarine
Aspartame-Sweetened Strawberry Nonfat Yogurt, 1 cup
Iced Tea

MAIN MEAL
Creamy Broccoli Soup (In food processor, combine ^{1}/$_2$ cup *each* chopped broccoli and low-sodium chicken broth, 2 tablespoons evaporated skimmed milk and 1 tablespoon minced fresh dill; purée until smooth. Transfer mixture to small saucepan; heat.)
Grilled Chicken Caesar Salad, 1 serving (see recipe)
Italian Bread, 1 slice (1 ounce), with 1 teaspoon reduced-calorie tub margarine
Peach, 1 medium
Sparkling Mineral Water

SNACK
Plain Popcorn, hot-air popped, 3 cups, with 1 teaspoon reduced-calorie margarine, melted

This menu provides: 2 Milks, 3 Fats, 2 Fruits, 11 Vegetables, 5 Proteins, 4 Breads, 90 Optional Calories.

Per serving: 20 g Fat, 31 g Fiber.

Serving (3 cups) provides: 1^1/$_2$ Fats, 5^1/$_2$ Vegetables, 3 Proteins, 40 Optional Calories.

Per serving: 236 Calories, 7 g Total Fat, 2 g Saturated Fat, 70 mg Cholesterol, 686 mg Sodium, 12 g Total Carbohydrate, 3 g Dietary Fiber, 31 g Protein, 153 mg Calcium.

Grilled Chicken Caesar Salad

250
THAI CHICKEN SALAD

Thai cuisine is known for its spiciness — and this one lives up to that reputation. If you'd like it even hotter, just add more pepper flakes.

Makes 4 servings

10 ounces skinless boneless chicken breasts
$^1/_2$ teaspoon salt
2 medium carrots, julienned
2 medium cucumbers, seeded and julienned
2 medium celery stalks, julienned
1 medium red bell pepper, seeded and julienned
$^1/_2$ cup thinly sliced radishes
$^1/_4$ cup minced red onion
Pinch crushed red pepper flakes
$^1/_4$ cup fresh lime juice
$^1/_4$ cup rice wine vinegar
2 tablespoons vegetable oil
$^1/_4$ cup minced fresh cilantro
$^1/_2$ ounce dry-roasted shelled peanuts, coarsely chopped

1. Place chicken breasts, skinned-side down, between 2 sheets of wax paper; with meat mallet or bottom of heavy saucepan, pound chicken until slightly flattened. Remove and discard wax paper; sprinkle chicken on both sides with salt.

2. Spray large nonstick skillet with nonstick cooking spray; heat. Add chicken; cook over medium-high heat, turning once, 5 minutes, until chicken is cooked through. Remove from skillet; let cool.

3. Meanwhile, in large bowl, combine carrots, cucumbers, celery, bell pepper and radishes.

4. In small jar with tight-fitting lid or small bowl, combine onion, pepper flakes, juice, vinegar and oil; cover and shake well or, with wire whisk, blend until combined. Pour onion mixture over vegetable mixture; toss to coat.

5. Shred cooled chicken. Line serving platter with vegetable mixture; top with chicken. Serve sprinkled with cilantro and peanuts.

Serving (2 ounces chicken, 1 cup vegetable mixture) provides: $1^3/_4$ Fats, $3^1/_4$ Vegetables, 2 Proteins, 10 Optional Calories.

Per serving: 227 Calories, 11 g Total Fat, 2 g Saturated Fat, 48 mg Cholesterol, 381 mg Sodium, 13 g Total Carbohydrate, 4 g Dietary Fiber, 20 g Protein, 50 mg Calcium.

BREAKFAST
Orange Sections, $^1/_2$ cup
Bagel, 1 small (2 ounces), with $2^1/_2$ teaspoons reduced-calorie tub margarine
Skim Milk, 1 cup
Coffee or Tea (optional)

LIGHT MEAL
Roast Beef Sandwich (Layer $1^1/_2$ ounces cooked lean boneless roast beef, thinly sliced, 2 tomato slices and 2 iceberg lettuce leaves and 1 tablespoon fat-free Thousand Island dressing between 2 slices reduced-calorie rye bread.)
Celery and Carrot Sticks, 1 cup *each*
Strawberries, 1 cup
Iced Herbal Tea

MAIN MEAL
Thai Chicken Salad, 1 serving (see recipe)
Zucchini Sticks and Whole Mushrooms, 1 cup *each*
Whole-Wheat Pita, 1 large (2 ounces)
Aspartame-Sweetened Strawberry-Banana Nonfat Yogurt, 1 cup
Unsweetened Seltzer with Lime Slice

SNACK
Sugar-Free Raspberry-Flavored Gelatin, $^1/_2$ cup, with 1 tablespoon thawed frozen light whipped topping (8 calories per tablespoon)

This menu provides: 2 Milks, 3 Fats, 2 Fruits, $12^1/_4$ Vegetables, $3^1/_2$ Proteins, 5 Breads, 50 Optional Calories.

Per serving: 25 g Fat, 23 g Fiber.

*To toast almonds, in small nonstick skillet, cook almonds over low heat, stirring constantly, until golden brown; immediately transfer to heat-resistant plate to cool.

251
CURRIED CHICKEN WITH MANGO-CREAM CHUTNEY

Poached chicken breasts make this curried salad especially succulent. But what's the secret ingredient in the dressing? It's mango chutney, which adds sweetness and spice.

Makes 4 servings

15 ounces skinless boneless chicken breasts
1 teaspoon mild or hot curry powder
1/4 cup reduced-calorie mayonnaise
3 tablespoons mango chutney
2 tablespoons fresh lemon juice
1/2 teaspoon salt
1/4 teaspoon freshly ground black pepper
1/4 cup nonfat sour cream
1 tablespoon minced fresh flat-leaf parsley
2 small red Delicious apples, cored and cut into 1/2" chunks
1/2 cup thinly sliced celery
1/2 ounce slivered almonds, toasted*

1. In large skillet, bring 3 cups water to a boil. Add chicken; return liquid to a boil. Reduce heat to low; poach chicken, covered, 10 minutes, until cooked through. With slotted spoon, remove chicken from liquid; discard liquid. Let chicken stand 10 minutes.

2. Meanwhile, in small nonstick skillet, cook curry powder over medium heat, stirring constantly, 1 minute, until fragrant. Remove from heat; set aside.

3. In blender or food processor, combine mayonnaise, chutney, juice, salt and pepper; purée until smooth. Transfer mayonnaise mixture to large bowl; stir in sour cream, parsley and reserved curry powder.

4. Transfer poached chicken to cutting board; cut into bite-size pieces. Add chicken, apples and celery to mayonnaise mixture; toss to coat. Serve immediately, sprinkled evenly with almonds; or refrigerate, covered, until chilled and sprinkle evenly with almonds just before serving.

Serving (1 1/2 cups) provides: 1 3/4 Fats, 1/2 Fruit, 1/4 Vegetable, 3 Proteins, 40 Optional Calories.

Per serving: 263 Calories, 7 g Total Fat, 2 g Saturated Fat, 67 mg Cholesterol, 580 mg Sodium, 21 g Total Carbohydrate, 2 g Dietary Fiber, 27 g Protein, 56 mg Calcium.

COBB SALAD

In the 1930s, so the story goes, Robert Cobb, the owner of Hollywood's famous Brown Derby restaurant, prepared a salad using the ingredients he had on hand for a late supper guest. Cobb salad was born!

Makes 4 servings

$^1/_3$ cup + 2 teaspoons nonfat sour cream
$^1/_4$ cup plain nonfat yogurt
2 tablespoons minced shallots
2 tablespoons cider vinegar
1 teaspoon Dijon-style mustard
$^1/_4$ teaspoon salt
$^1/_4$ teaspoon freshly ground black pepper
4 cups torn Romaine lettuce leaves
4 cups torn iceberg lettuce leaves
2 cups watercress leaves
7 ounces skinless boneless cooked chicken breasts, sliced
4 large plum tomatoes, coarsely chopped
1 medium yellow bell pepper, seeded and coarsely chopped
1 medium red bell pepper, seeded and coarsely chopped
1 cup shredded carrot
4 ounces pared avocado, sliced
3 ounces blue cheese, crumbled
3 slices crisp-cooked lean turkey bacon (30 calories per slice), crumbled
1 egg, hard-cooked and sieved

1. To prepare dressing, in small jar with tight-fitting lid or small bowl, combine sour cream, yogurt, shallots, vinegar, mustard, salt, black pepper and 2 tablespoons water; cover and shake well or, with wire whisk, blend until combined.

2. To prepare salad, in large bowl, combine Romaine and iceberg lettuces, watercress and 2 tablespoons of the dressing, tossing until well coated.

3. Transfer lettuce mixture to large round serving platter; top with chicken, tomatoes, yellow and red bell peppers, carrot, avocado and cheese. Drizzle with remaining dressing; sprinkle evenly with bacon and egg.

Serving ($2^1/_4$ cups) provides: 1 Fat, $7^1/_2$ Vegetables, 3 Proteins, 45 Optional Calories.

Per serving: 330 Calories, 16 g Total Fat, 6 g Saturated Fat, 119 mg Cholesterol, 717 mg Sodium, 18 g Total Carbohydrate, 5 g Dietary Fiber, 29 g Protein, 282 mg Calcium.

BREAKFAST
Fresh Fig, 1 large
Reduced-Calorie Whole-Wheat Bread, 2 slices, toasted, with $1^1/_2$ teaspoons *each* reduced-calorie tub margarine and orange marmalade
Skim Milk, 1 cup
Coffee or Tea (optional)

LIGHT MEAL
Hummus, $^1/_4$ cup spread on 1 small (1 ounce) whole-wheat pita
Cucumber Sticks and Red Bell Pepper Strips, 1 cup *each*
Cherry Tomatoes, 6
Aspartame-Sweetened Blueberry Nonfat Yogurt, 1 cup
Iced Tea with Lemon Wedge

MAIN MEAL
Vegetable-Rice Soup (In small saucepan, combine 1 cup low-sodium chicken broth, $^1/_2$ cup cooked brown rice, $^1/_4$ cup *each* diced celery, red onion and carrot and 1 ounce drained cooked pinto beans; cook over medium-high heat until vegetables are tender and mixture is heated through.)
Cobb Salad, 1 serving (see recipe)
Semolina Roll, 1 ounce, with 1 teaspoon reduced-calorie tub margarine
Sugar-Free Lime-Flavored Gelatin, $^1/_2$ cup, with 1 tablespoon thawed frozen light whipped topping (8 calories per tablespoon)
Sparkling Mineral Water

SNACK
Plain Popcorn, hot-air popped, 3 cups, with 2 tablespoons raisins

This menu provides: 2 Milks, 3 Fats, 2 Fruits, 14 Vegetables, $4^3/_4$ Proteins, 5 Breads, 105 Optional Calories.

Per serving: 36 g Fat, 29 g Fiber.

Cobb Salad

253
GRILLED HENS WITH PINEAPPLE-HONEY SALSA

Cornish game hens go Hawaiian with this fresh pineapple-honey salsa. The extra salsa becomes a luscious basting sauce for the hens.

Makes 4 servings

$^1/_2$ medium pineapple, pared and cored
2 tablespoons chopped scallions
2 tablespoons reduced-sodium soy sauce
2 tablespoons honey
$^1/_4$ teaspoon freshly ground black pepper
Two 1-pound Cornish game hens, skinned and halved*

1. Preheat outdoor barbecue grill according to manufacturer's directions, or preheat broiler and spray rack in broiler pan with nonstick cooking spray.

2. Cut four $^3/_4$" crosswise slices from pineapple; set aside.

3. To prepare salsa, chop remaining pineapple; transfer to medium saucepan. Add scallions, soy sauce, honey and pepper to chopped pineapple; bring mixture to a boil. Reduce heat to low; simmer, stirring frequently, 3 minutes, until flavors are blended. Remove from heat; keep warm.

4. Transfer half of the salsa to blender or food processor; purée until smooth.

5. Grill hens over hot coals or place onto prepared rack in broiler pan and broil 4" from heat, turning once and basting with some of the pureed salsa, 20 minutes, until browned and glazed and juices run clear when pierced with fork.

6. During last 5 minutes of cooking time, grill pineapple slices, turning once and basting with remaining pureed salsa, until golden brown and glazed.

7. Arrange hens on serving platter; top with reserved salsa and 1 grilled pineapple slice.

Serving (one-half hen, 2 tablespoons salsa, 1 pineapple slice) provides:
1 Fruit, 3 Proteins, 90 Optional Calories.

Per serving: 287 Calories, 7 g Total Fat, 2 g Saturated Fat, 76 mg Cholesterol, 376 mg Sodium, 32 g Total Carbohydrate, 2 g Dietary Fiber, 26 g Protein, 30 mg Calcium.

A 1-pound Cornish game hen will yield about 6 ounces cooked poultry.

BREAKFAST
Strawberries, 1 cup
Reduced-Calorie Whole-Wheat Bread, 2 slices, toasted, with 2 teaspoons reduced-calorie tub margarine
Skim Milk, 1 cup
Coffee or Tea (optional)

LIGHT MEAL
Tuna-Pasta Salad (In medium bowl, combine $^1/_2$ cup cooked shell macaroni, 2 ounces drained canned water-packed white tuna, 6 cherry tomatoes, halved, $^1/_4$ cup diced red onion and 1 tablespoon fat-free Italian dressing.)
Cucumber and Carrot Sticks, 1 cup *each*
Reduced-Calorie Butterscotch-Flavored Pudding (made with skim milk), $^1/_2$ cup
Unsweetened Cranberry-Flavored Seltzer

MAIN MEAL
Grilled Hens with Pineapple-Honey Salsa, 1 serving (see recipe)
Baked Potato, 8 ounces, with 3 tablespoons plain nonfat yogurt and 1 tablespoon minced fresh chives
Steamed Whole Green Beans, 1 cup, with 2 teaspoons reduced-calorie tub margarine
Arugula and Watercress Salad, 2 cups, with 1 tablespoon fat-free Italian dressing
Sugar-Free Strawberry-Banana–Flavored Gelatin, $^1/_2$ cup, topped with $^1/_4$ cup aspartame-sweetened cherry-vanilla nonfat yogurt
Sparkling Mineral Water with Lime Wedge

SNACK
Whole-Wheat Bagel, $^1/_2$ small (1 ounce), toasted, with 1 teaspoon peanut butter

This menu provides: 2 Milks, 3 Fats, 2 Fruits, $11^1/_2$ Vegetables, 4 Proteins, 5 Breads, 150 Optional Calories.

Per serving: 24 g Fat, 28 g Fiber.

This menu provides: 2 Milks, 3 Fats, 2 Fruits,
11 Vegetables, 5 Proteins, 4$^1/_2$ Breads, 110 Optional
Calories.

Per serving: 26 g Fat, 21 g Fiber.

254
PLUM-GLAZED HENS

*Plum sauce, sometimes called duck sauce, can be found in the Asian-
foods section of most supermarkets or in Asian groceries. It's a sweet
and sour blend of plums and apricots, plus seasonings such as ginger.*

Makes 4 servings

2 tablespoons vegetable oil
1 tablespoon grated lemon zest*
4 garlic cloves, minced
$^1/_4$ teaspoon crushed red pepper flakes
Two 1-pound Cornish game hens, skinned and halved†
$^3/_4$ cup bottled plum (duck) sauce
Lemon wedges, to garnish

1. In gallon-size sealable plastic bag, combine oil, zest, garlic and pepper
flakes; add hen halves. Seal bag, squeezing out air; turn to coat hens.
Refrigerate, covered, 30 minutes. Drain hens and discard marinade.

2. Preheat outdoor barbecue grill according to manufacturer's directions,
or spray rack in broiler pan with nonstick cooking spray and preheat
broiler.

3. In small saucepan, cook plum sauce over medium-high heat, stirring
frequently, until sauce comes just to a boil. Remove sauce from heat.

4. Brush hens on both sides with some of the warm plum sauce; grill over
hot coals or place onto prepared rack in broiler pan and broil 4" from heat,
turning once and basting with some of the remaining plum sauce, 20 minutes, until browned, glazed and juices run clear when pierced with fork.

5. Transfer hens to serving platter; spread evenly with remaining plum
sauce. Serve garnished with lemon wedges.

Serving (one-half hen) provides: 1$^1/_2$ Fats, 3 Proteins, 30 Optional Calories.

Per serving: 288 Calories, 13 g Total Fat, 3 g Saturated Fat, 76 mg Cholesterol,
306 mg Sodium, 17 g Total Carbohydrate, 0 g Dietary Fiber, 26 g Protein,
148 mg Calcium.

**The zest of the lemon is the peel without any of the pith (white membrane). To
remove zest from lemon, use a zester or the fine side of a vegetable grater; wrap
lemon in plastic wrap and refrigerate for use at another time.*

†A 1-pound Cornish game hen will yield about 6 ounces cooked poultry.

255

FAST-FOOD—STYLE TURKEY BURGERS

You won't believe your taste buds when you sink your teeth into one of these special burgers — the flavor is just like it came from the drive-through!

Makes 4 servings

2 tablespoons + 2 teaspoons reduced-calorie mayonnaise
2 tablespoons + 2 teaspoons ketchup
2 teaspoons white wine vinegar
13 ounces ground skinless turkey breast, formed into 4 thin patties
4 slices nonfat process American cheese
Four 2-ounce hamburger rolls, split and warmed
1 medium tomato, cut into 4 slices
$^1/_2$ cup thinly sliced onion
$^1/_4$ cup dill pickle slices
1 cup shredded iceberg lettuce

1. In small bowl, combine mayonnaise, ketchup and vinegar; set aside.

2. In large nonstick skillet, cook turkey patties over medium-high heat, turning once, 8 minutes, until cooked through. Top each burger with 1 cheese slice; cook, covered, 30 seconds, until cheese is melted.

3. Place one burger onto bottom half of each roll; top each with one-fourth of the tomato, onion and pickle slices, then $^1/_4$ cup lettuce. Spread top half of each roll with one-fourth of the reserved mayonnaise mixture; place over lettuce to enclose.

Serving (1 burger) provides: 1 Fat, $1^1/_2$ Vegetables, 3 Proteins, 2 Breads, 10 Optional Calories.

Per serving: 354 Calories, 6 g Total Fat, 2 g Saturated Fat, 60 mg Cholesterol, 976 mg Sodium, 38 g Total Carbohydrate, 2 g Dietary Fiber, 33 g Protein, 209 mg Calcium.

BREAKFAST
Orange and Grapefruit Sections, $^1/_2$ cup
White Omelet Sandwich (In small bowl, beat 3 egg whites and pinch *each* salt and ground white pepper until frothy. In small nonstick skillet, melt 2 teaspoons reduced-calorie tub margarine; add egg white mixture. Cook, covered, until mixture is firm. Place omelet between 2 slices reduced-calorie whole-wheat toast.)
Skim Milk, $^3/_4$ cup
Coffee or Tea (optional)

LIGHT MEAL
Low-Sodium Chicken Broth, 1 cup
Shrimp with Chinese Vegetables in Oyster Sauce (In medium nonstick skillet, heat 1 teaspoon vegetable oil; add 3 ounces peeled and deveined shrimp; cook over medium-high heat, stirring frequently, until no longer pink. Add $^1/_2$ cup *each* sliced bok choy, bamboo shoots, carrot and onion; cook, stirring frequently, until vegetables are softened. Stir in 2 teaspoons oyster sauce.)
Cooked Brown Rice, $^1/_2$ cup
Pineapple, $^1/_8$ medium
Chinese Tea

MAIN MEAL
Fast-Food—Style Turkey Burgers, 1 serving (see recipe)
Baked Potato Sticks (Preheat oven to 450° F. Spray nonstick baking sheet with nonstick cooking spray. Pare one 5-ounce all-purpose potato; cut into sticks. Arrange potato sticks in a single layer on prepared baking sheet; sprinkle with pinch salt. Bake until potato sticks are crispy.)
Tossed Green Salad, 2 cups, with 6 cherry tomatoes and 1 tablespoon fat-free Thousand Island dressing
Sugar-Free Vanilla Nonfat Frozen Yogurt, 4 fluid ounces
Reduced-Calorie Chocolate Dairy Shake, 1 serving

SNACK
Buttery Popcorn (Lightly spray 3 cups hot-air popped plain popcorn with nonstick cooking spray. Sprinkle popcorn with $^1/_4$ teaspoon butter-flavor granules; toss to coat evenly.)
Diet Cola

This menu provides: 2 Milks, 3 Fats, 2 Fruits, $10^1/_2$ Vegetables, 5 Proteins, 6 Breads, 120 Optional Calories.

Per serving: 27 g Fat, 26 g Fiber.

BREAKFAST

Fresh Fig, 1 large
Reduced-Calorie Rye Bread, 2 slices, toasted, with
   2 teaspoons reduced-calorie tub margarine
Skim Milk, 1 cup
Coffee or Tea (optional)

LIGHT MEAL

Cheese Pizza, thin crust, 1 slice (^{1}/12 of 14–16" pie)
Carrot and Celery Sticks, 1 cup *each*
Tossed Green Salad, 2 cups, with ^{1}/2 cup *each*
   cucumber and radish slices and 1 tablespoon fat-
   free Italian dressing
Apple, 1 small, sliced, with 1 tablespoon peanut
   butter
Diet Lemon-Lime Soda

MAIN MEAL

Vegetable Soup, canned, 1 cup
Barbecued Burgers with Corn and Tomato Salsa,
   1 serving (see recipe)
Spinach-Caesar Salad (In medium bowl, combine
   2 cups torn spinach leaves, ^{1}/2 cup *each* sliced
   mushrooms and red onion, ^{1}/4 cup packaged
   croutons and 1 tablespoon fat-free Caesar salad
   dressing.)
Aspartame-Sweetened Vanilla Nonfat Yogurt, 1 cup
Iced Tea

SNACK

Sugar-Free Lime-Flavored Gelatin, ^{1}/2 cup, with
   1 tablespoon thawed frozen light whipped topping (8 calories per tablespoon)

This menu provides: 2 Milks, 3 Fats, 2 Fruits,
18^3/4 Vegetables, 5 Proteins, 5^1/4 Breads,
105 Optional Calories.

Per serving: 19 g Fat, 29 g Fiber.

Serving (1 burger with ^{1}/2 cup salsa) provides:
1^1/4 Vegetables, 3 Proteins, 1^3/4 Breads, 40 Optional
Calories.

Per serving: 306 Calories, 3 g Total Fat,
0 g Saturated Fat, 66 mg Cholesterol,
994 mg Sodium, 37 g Total Carbohydrate,
7 g Dietary Fiber, 34 g Protein, 99 mg Calcium.

256
BARBECUED BURGERS WITH CORN AND TOMATO SALSA

*Barbecued burgers, hot off the grill, become even better when made
with ground turkey breast. A corn and fresh tomato salsa adds both
color and extra flavor.*

Makes 4 servings

1^1/2 cups thawed frozen corn kernels
1 cup chopped tomato
1 cup finely chopped onions
1 tablespoon minced fresh cilantro
1 tablespoon fresh lime juice
^{3}/4 teaspoon salt
^{1}/2 cup finely chopped red bell pepper
2 garlic cloves, minced
^{3}/4 teaspoon ground cumin
^{1}/2 teaspoon freshly ground black pepper
15 ounces ground skinless turkey breast
^{1}/2 cup bottled chili sauce
Four 1-ounce reduced-calorie hamburger rolls, split
Fresh cilantro sprigs, to garnish

1. Preheat outdoor barbecue grill according to manufacturer's directions,
or preheat broiler and spray rack in broiler pan with nonstick cooking
spray.

2. In small bowl, combine corn, tomato, ^{1}/3 cup of the onions, the
minced cilantro, juice and ^{1}/4 teaspoon of the salt; refrigerate, covered,
until chilled.

3. Spray small nonstick skillet with nonstick cooking spray; heat. Add bell
pepper, garlic, cumin, black pepper, remaining ^{2}/3 cup onions and remaining ^{1}/2 teaspoon salt; cook over medium-high heat, stirring frequently,
3 minutes, until bell pepper is softened.

4. Transfer bell pepper mixture to medium bowl. Add turkey and chili
sauce; mix well. Shape into 4 equal patties.

5. Grill patties over hot coals or place onto prepared rack in broiler pan
and broil 4" from heat, turning once, 8–10 minutes, until golden brown
and cooked through.

6. During last few minutes of cooking, place rolls onto grill, split-side
down, or onto broiler rack, split-side up; cook 2–3 minutes, until toasted;
transfer to platter. Top bottom half of each roll with 1 burger; top each
with one-fourth of the corn mixture and 1 remaining roll half. Serve garnished with cilantro sprigs.

257
TURKEY DINNER IN A SANDWICH

After the turkey dinner, plan to use the leftover turkey in this sandwich. It's open-face to save on the bread and leave more room for the stuffing!

Makes 4 servings

4 slices reduced-calorie whole-wheat bread
1 tablespoon + 1 teaspoon reduced-calorie mayonnaise
1 cup prepared herb bread stuffing mix
4 curly lettuce leaves
8 ounces skinless boneless roast turkey breast, thinly sliced
$^1/_4$ cup cranberry sauce
2 small red Delicious apples, cored and thinly sliced
$^1/_2$ cup shredded carrot

1. Lightly toast bread; spread each toast slice with 1 teaspoon mayonnaise.

2. To assemble sandwiches, place toast, mayonnaise-side up, onto work surface; top each with $^1/_4$ cup stuffing, 1 lettuce leaf, 2 ounces turkey, 1 tablespoon cranberry sauce, one-fourth of the apple slices and 2 tablespoons carrot. Cut sandwiches diagonally into halves.

Serving (1 open-face sandwich) provides: $1^1/_4$ Fats, $^1/_2$ Fruit, $^3/_4$ Vegetable, 2 Proteins, 1 Bread, 40 Optional Calories.

Per serving: 299 Calories, 7 g Total Fat, 1 g Saturated Fat, 49 mg Cholesterol, 483 mg Sodium, 40 g Total Carbohydrate, 6 g Dietary Fiber, 22 g Protein, 58 mg Calcium.

BREAKFAST
Banana, $^3/_4$ medium, sliced
Bran Flakes Cereal, $^3/_4$ ounce
Skim Milk, 1 cup
Coffee or Tea (optional)

LIGHT MEAL
Tuna Salad Platter (In small bowl, combine 4 ounces skinless drained canned water-packed tuna, $^1/_2$ cup chopped celery, 2 teaspoons reduced-calorie mayonnaise and pinch freshly ground black pepper; serve on 4 Romaine lettuce leaves, surrounded by 1 cup *each* cucumber and carrot slices.)
Aspartame-Sweetened Blueberry Nonfat Yogurt, 1 cup
Iced Herbal Tea

MAIN MEAL
Turkey Dinner in a Sandwich, 1 serving (see recipe)
Baked Sweet Potato, 6 ounces, with $1^1/_2$ teaspoons reduced-calorie tub margarine
Steamed Broccoli and Cauliflower Florets, 1 cup
Torn Romaine Lettuce Leaves, 2 cups, with $^1/_2$ cup sliced mushrooms and 1 tablespoon fat-free Caesar salad dressing
Sugar-Free Raspberry-Flavored Gelatin, $^1/_2$ cup, with 1 tablespoon thawed frozen light whipped topping (8 calories per tablespoon)
Unsweetened Black Cherry–Flavored Seltzer

SNACK
Nonfat Process American Cheese, $1^1/_2$ ounces
Fat-Free Crackers, 7

This menu provides: 2 Milks, 3 Fats, 2 Fruits, $13^3/_4$ Vegetables, 5 Proteins, 5 Breads, 80 Optional Calories.

Per serving: 18 g Fat, 27 g Fiber.

BREAKFAST

Pineapple, $^1/_8$ medium
Bagel, $^1/_2$ small (1 ounce), with 2 teaspoons reduced-calorie tub margarine
Skim Milk, 1 cup
Coffee or Tea (optional)

LIGHT MEAL

Nonfat Cottage Cheese, $^1/_2$ cup, on 2 slices reduced-calorie whole-wheat bread, toasted, sprinkled with pinch cinnamon
Zucchini and Yellow Squash Sticks, 1 cup *each*
Sugar-Free Strawberry-Flavored Gelatin, $^1/_2$ cup
Diet Cola

MAIN MEAL

Turkey Divan, 1 serving (see recipe)
Cooked Farfalle Pasta, 1 cup, with 2 teaspoons reduced-calorie tub margarine and 1 teaspoon freshly grated Parmesan cheese
Cooked Sliced Beets, 1 cup
Watercress and Arugula Salad, 2 cups, with $^1/_2$ cup sliced radishes and 1 tablespoon fat-free Italian dressing
Pear, 1 small
Sparkling Mineral Water with Lime Wedge

SNACK

Reduced-Calorie Chocolate-Flavored Pudding (made with skim milk), $^1/_2$ cup

This menu provides: 2 Milks, 3 Fats, 2 Fruits, 12$^1/_2$ Vegetables, 4 Proteins, 5$^1/_2$ Breads, 75 Optional Calories.

Per serving: 30 g Fat, 26 g Fiber.

258
TURKEY DIVAN

Originally, in this dish, the freshly roasted slices of turkey and fresh broccoli were smothered in a rich cheese sauce, then served on a flaky buttery pastry. In our delicious version the sauce is made with skim milk and it's served on toast.

Makes 4 servings

Five crust-trimmed 1-ounce slices white bread, toasted and cut into 4 triangles each
12 broccoli spears
2 tablespoons + 2 teaspoons reduced-calorie tub margarine
$^1/_4$ cup all-purpose flour
$^1/_2$ teaspoon salt
$^1/_4$ teaspoon ground white pepper
2 cups skim milk
4$^1/_2$ ounces Brie cheese, cut into small pieces
6 ounces skinless boneless cooked turkey breast, thinly sliced
$^1/_4$ teaspoon paprika

1. Preheat broiler. Spray 4 shallow 6" round flameproof au gratin dishes with nonstick cooking spray.

2. Arrange 4 toast triangles with points facing outward in each prepared dish; reserve remaining 4 triangles.

3. Fill large saucepan with 1" water; set steamer rack into saucepan. Place broccoli onto rack. Bring water to a boil; reduce heat to low. Steam broccoli over simmering water, covered, 4–5 minutes, until just tender.

4. Place 3 steamed broccoli spears into each prepared dish; keep warm.

5. In large nonstick skillet, melt margarine; sprinkle with flour, salt and pepper. Cook over medium-high heat, stirring constantly, 3 minutes, until mixture is bubbling. With wire whisk, gradually add milk; continuing to stir, cook 5 minutes, until mixture is thickened. Stir in cheese; cook, stirring constantly, until cheese is melted.

6. Top each portion of broccoli with 1$^1/_2$ ounces of the turkey; pour one-fourth of the cheese mixture over turkey. Sprinkle evenly with paprika. Broil 4" from heat 1–2 minutes, until cheese mixture is bubbling; remove from broiler. Top each portion with 1 remaining toast triangle.

Serving (1 portion) provides: $^1/_2$ Milk, 1 Fat, 1$^1/_2$ Vegetables, 3 Proteins, 1$^1/_2$ Breads, 10 Optional Calories.

Per serving: 395 Calories, 16 g Total Fat, 1 g Saturated Fat, 70 mg Cholesterol, 840 mg Sodium, 34 g Total Carbohydrate, 3 g Dietary Fiber, 30 g Protein, 297 mg Calcium.

259
TURKEY PITAS

Makes 4 servings

4 small (1-ounce) whole-wheat pitas, cut crosswise into halves
³/₄ cup plain nonfat yogurt
1 medium cucumber, pared, cut in half lengthwise, seeded and thinly sliced
2 medium celery stalks, thinly sliced on the diagonal
¹/₂ cup thinly sliced red onion
1 medium minced deveined seeded jalapeño pepper (wear gloves to prevent irritation)
2 garlic cloves, minced
1 teaspoon mild or hot curry powder
¹/₂ teaspoon ground cumin
¹/₂ teaspoon salt
¹/₂ teaspoon freshly ground black pepper
8 ounces skinless boneless cooked turkey breast, cut into bite-size pieces
1 medium cucumber, seeded and julienned

1. Preheat oven to 350° F. Adjust oven rack to divide oven in half.

2. Wrap pita halves in foil; bake in center of oven 15 minutes, until warm.

3. Meanwhile, in small bowl, combine yogurt, cucumber slices, celery, onion, jalapeño pepper, garlic, curry powder, cumin, salt and black pepper.

4. Fill each pita half with 1 ounce turkey, then an equal amount of yogurt mixture; serve with julienned cucumber.

Serving (2 stuffed pita halves, one-fourth of the julienned cucumber) provides: ¹/₄ Milk, 1³/₄ Vegetables, 2 Proteins, 1 Bread.

Per serving: 200 Calories, 1 g Total Fat, 0 g Saturated Fat, 48 mg Cholesterol, 504 mg Sodium, 24 g Total Carbohydrate, 3 g Dietary Fiber, 23 g Protein, 126 mg Calcium.

BREAKFAST
Fresh Fig, 1 large
Cooked Oatmeal, 1 cup, with 2 teaspoons reduced-calorie tub margarine
Skim Milk, ³/₄ cup
Coffee or Tea (optional)

LIGHT MEAL
Broiled Fillet of Sole, 4 ounces
Cooked Long-Grain and Wild Rice, ¹/₂ cup *each*, with 2 teaspoons reduced-calorie tub margarine
Steamed Broccoli, 4 spears, with 1 lemon wedge
Torn Iceberg and Romaine Lettuce Leaves, 2 cups, with 6 cherry tomatoes, ¹/₂ cup sliced scallions and 1 tablespoon fat-free Thousand Island dressing
Roll, 1 ounce, with 2 teaspoons reduced-calorie tub margarine
Reduced-Calorie Chocolate-Flavored Pudding (made with skim milk), ¹/₂ cup
Decaffeinated Cappuccino, made with skim milk, 5 fluid ounces

MAIN MEAL
Turkey Pitas, 1 serving (see recipe)
Carrot Sticks and Whole Green Beans, 1 cup *each*
Apple, 1 small
Unsweetened Seltzer

SNACK
Frozen Fruit Pop, 1 bar

This menu provides: 2 Milks, 3 Fats, 2 Fruits, 13³/₄ Vegetables, 4 Proteins, 6 Breads, 105 Optional Calories.

Per serving: 23 g Fat, 20 g Fiber.

260
TURKEY TOSTADAS

*Tostadas, open-face Mexican sandwiches, layer ingredients onto crispy
corn tortillas. These feature tender cuts of turkey, fresh vegetables and
nonfat cheese and sour cream.*

Makes 4 servings

½ teaspoon freshly ground black pepper
¼ teaspoon salt
¼ teaspoon ground cumin
9 ounces skinless boneless turkey breast
Four ¾-ounce tostada shells
½ cup refried beans
½ cup shredded iceberg lettuce
2 tablespoons cider vinegar
2 tablespoons minced fresh cilantro
2 teaspoons vegetable oil
4 ounces pared avocado, diced
½ cup minced scallions
¼ cup nonfat sour cream
½ cup chunky salsa
1 medium tomato, diced
1½ ounces nonfat process American cheese, grated

1. Preheat oven to 350° F. Adjust oven rack to divide oven in half.

2. In cup or small bowl, combine pepper, salt and cumin; rub into turkey
on all sides.

3. Spray large nonstick skillet with nonstick cooking spray; heat. Add
turkey; cook over medium heat, turning once, 8 minutes, until browned,
cooked through and juices run clear when pierced with fork. Transfer
turkey to cutting board; let stand 5 minutes. Thinly slice turkey; set aside.

4. Stack tostada shells; wrap in sheet of foil, crimping edges to seal. Place
foil packet onto baking sheet; bake 8–10 minutes, until shells are warmed.

5. Meanwhile, in small saucepan, combine beans and 1 tablespoon water;
cook over medium heat, stirring constantly, 4–5 minutes, until mixture is
bubbling. Remove from heat; set aside.

6. In medium bowl, combine lettuce, vinegar, cilantro and oil; set aside.

7. In small bowl, combine avocado and scallions; set aside.

8. To assemble tostadas, place 1 warm tostada shell onto each of 4 plates;
spread each with one-fourth of the warm bean mixture. Top each portion
of beans with one-fourth of the turkey, then 1 tablespoon sour cream, one-
fourth of the lettuce mixture, salsa, avocado mixture, tomato and cheese.

261

TURKEY SPANISH RICE

We've flavored rice with Spanish vegetables and spices, then added turkey to turn it into a satisfying main dish.

Makes 4 servings

2 cups coarsely chopped green bell peppers
1 cup finely chopped onions
3 garlic cloves, minced
2 cups stewed tomatoes (no salt added)
6 ounces long-grain rice
$^1/_2$ teaspoon dried oregano leaves
10 ounces skinless boneless turkey breast, cut into 1" pieces
12 large pimiento-stuffed green olives, sliced
2 slices crisp-cooked bacon, crumbled

1. Spray large nonstick skillet with nonstick cooking spray; heat. Add bell peppers, onions and garlic; cook over medium-high heat, stirring frequently, 5 minutes, until vegetables are softened. Stir in tomatoes, rice, oregano and 2 cups water; bring liquid to a boil, stirring occasionally to break up tomatoes. Reduce heat to low; simmer, covered, 10 minutes.

2. Stir turkey, olives and bacon into tomato mixture; simmer, covered, 10 minutes, until turkey is cooked through, rice is tender and all liquid is absorbed.

Serving (1$^1/_2$ cups) provides: $^1/_2$ Fat, 2$^1/_2$ Vegetables, 2 Proteins, 1$^1/_2$ Breads, 20 Optional Calories.

Per serving: 336 Calories, 5 g Total Fat, 1 g Saturated Fat, 47 mg Cholesterol, 754 mg Sodium, 50 g Total Carbohydrate, 5 g Dietary Fiber, 24 g Protein, 90 mg Calcium.

BREAKFAST
Papaya, $^1/_2$ medium
Cooked Oatmeal, $^1/_2$ cup, with $^1/_2$ teaspoon firmly packed light or dark brown sugar
Reduced-Calorie Rye Bread, 2 slices, toasted, with 2 teaspoons reduced-calorie tub margarine
Skim Milk, 1 cup
Coffee or Tea (optional)

LIGHT MEAL
Roast Beef Sandwich (Layer 1$^1/_2$ ounces cooked lean boneless roast beef, thinly sliced, 2 tomato slices and 2 iceberg lettuce leaves and 1 tablespoon fat-free Thousand Island dressing between 2 slices reduced-calorie rye bread.)
Celery and Carrot Sticks, 1 cup *each*
Frozen Fruit Pop, 1 bar
Iced Tea with Mint Sprig

MAIN MEAL
Turkey Spanish Rice, 1 serving (see recipe)
Steamed Diced Eggplant, 1 cup, with 1$^1/_2$ teaspoons olive oil and pinch garlic powder
Steamed Whole Green Beans, 1 cup
Torn Red Leaf and Romaine Lettuce Leaves, 2 cups, with $^1/_2$ cup cucumber slices, 2 ounces drained cooked red kidney beans and 1 tablespoon fat-free Italian dressing
Sugar-Free Pineapple-Flavored Gelatin, $^1/_2$ cup, with 1 tablespoon thawed frozen light whipped topping (8 calories per tablespoon)
Unsweetened Lime-Flavored Seltzer

SNACK
Plain Popcorn, hot-air popped, 3 cups, with 2 tablespoons raisins
Skim Milk, 1 cup

This menu provides: 2 Milks, 3 Fats, 2 Fruits, 16$^1/_2$ Vegetables, 4$^1/_2$ Proteins, 5$^1/_2$ Breads, 115 Optional Calories.

Per serving: 27 g Fat, 26 g Fiber.

Serving (1 cup turkey mixture, $^3/_4$ cup rice) provides: $^3/_4$ Fat, $3^1/_2$ Vegetables, 3 Proteins, $1^1/_2$ Breads,
20 Optional Calories.

Per serving: 390 Calories, 5 g Total Fat,
1 g Saturated Fat, 66 mg Cholesterol,
535 mg Sodium, 50 g Total Carbohydrate,
5 g Dietary Fiber, 35 g Protein, 96 mg Calcium.

262
TURKEY TERIYAKI

*This Japanese-inspired stir-fry starts by marinating the turkey in a
soy sauce mixture, which adds extra flavor to this easy meal.*

Makes 4 servings

3 tablespoons reduced-sodium soy sauce
1 fluid ounce (2 tablespoons) dry sherry
1 tablespoon cornstarch
1 tablespoon minced pared fresh ginger root
4 garlic cloves, minced
1 teaspoon firmly packed light or dark brown sugar
$^1/_4$ teaspoon crushed red pepper flakes
15 ounces skinless boneless turkey breast, cut diagonally into 4 × $^1/_4$" strips
1 tablespoon vegetable oil
6 ounces regular long-grain rice
1 cup diagonally julienned scallions
2 cups sliced shiitake mushroom caps
1 medium red bell pepper, seeded and cut into thin strips
3 cups small broccoli florets

1. To prepare marinade, in gallon-size sealable plastic bag, combine soy sauce, sherry, cornstarch, 2 teaspoons of the ginger, the garlic, brown sugar and pepper flakes; add turkey. Seal bag, squeezing out air; turn to coat turkey. Refrigerate 15 minutes, turning bag occasionally.

2. Meanwhile, in large saucepan, heat 1 teaspoon of the oil; add rice, scallions and remaining 1 teaspoon ginger. Cook over medium-high heat, stirring constantly, 1 minute, until rice is opaque. Add 2 cups water; bring liquid to a boil. Reduce heat to low; simmer, covered, 20 minutes, until liquid is absorbed and rice is tender. Remove from heat; keep warm.

3. Meanwhile, drain turkey, reserving marinade.

4. In large nonstick skillet, heat remaining 2 teaspoons oil; add turkey. Cook over medium-high heat, stirring constantly, 3 minutes, until turkey is cooked through. With slotted spoon, remove turkey from skillet; set aside.

5. In same skillet, combine mushrooms and bell pepper; cook over medium-high heat, stirring constantly, 5 minutes, until vegetables are tender. Stir in broccoli; cook, stirring constantly, 3 minutes, until broccoli is just tender.

6. Add cooked turkey and reserved marinade to vegetable mixture; bring liquid to a boil. Cook, stirring constantly, 2 minutes, until liquid thickens slightly.

7. Spoon warm rice into a ring onto round serving platter; fill with turkey mixture.

263
PEKING-STYLE TURKEY

Hoisin sauce, frequently called Peking sauce, is a thick, reddish brown spicy sauce made from soy beans, chile peppers, garlic and plenty of spice. It's popular in Chinese-inspired stir-fries such as this one.

Makes 4 servings

14 ounces skinless boneless turkey breast, cut into 4 equal pieces
1/2 teaspoon salt
2 tablespoons hoisin sauce
2 teaspoons vegetable oil
1 tablespoon grated pared fresh ginger root
2 garlic cloves, minced
Pinch crushed red pepper flakes, or to taste
2 cups julienned bok choy
1 cup diagonally julienned yellow squash
1 cup diagonally julienned carrot
1/2 cup diagonally julienned scallions
1/2 cup diagonally julienned snow peas
1 ounce finely chopped unsalted dry-roasted cashews, toasted*

1. Place turkey between 2 sheets of wax paper; with meat mallet or bottom of heavy saucepan, pound turkey until 1/2" thick. Remove and discard wax paper; sprinkle turkey on both sides with salt.

2. Spray wok or large nonstick skillet with nonstick cooking spray; heat. Add turkey; cook over medium-high heat, turning turkey pieces once, 5 minutes, until browned on both sides and cooked through. Transfer turkey to serving platter; brush evenly with hoisin sauce. Set aside; keep warm.

3. In same wok, heat oil; add ginger, garlic and pepper flakes. Cook, stirring constantly, 1 minute, until garlic is softened. Add bok choy, squash, carrot and 2 tablespoons water; cook, stirring frequently, 5 minutes, until vegetables are tender. Stir in scallions and snow peas; cook, stirring frequently, 1 minute, until scallions and snow peas are wilted.

4. Spoon vegetable mixture around warm turkey; sprinkle evenly with cashews.

Serving (2³/4 ounces, 1 cup vegetable mixture) provides: 1 Fat, 2¹/2 Vegetables, 3 Proteins, 15 Optional Calories.

Per serving: 233 Calories, 7 g Total Fat, 1 g Saturated Fat, 62 mg Cholesterol, 517 mg Sodium, 15 g Total Carbohydrate, 2 g Dietary Fiber, 27 g Protein, 85 mg Calcium.

To toast cashews, in small nonstick skillet, cook cashews over low heat, stirring constantly, until golden brown; immediately transfer to heat-resistant plate to cool.

BREAKFAST
Orange Sections, 1/2 cup
Shredded Wheat Cereal, 3/4 ounce
Skim Milk, 1/2 cup
Coffee or Tea (optional)

LIGHT MEAL
Tuna Salad Pita (In small bowl, combine 4 ounces drained canned water-packed tuna, 1/4 cup *each* chopped onion and celery, 2 teaspoons reduced-calorie mayonnaise and 1/4 teaspoon lemon-pepper seasoning. Cut large [2-ounce] whole-wheat pita in half crosswise; open to form 2 pockets. Fill each pocket with half of the tuna mixture; top each portion of tuna with 1/4 cup alfalfa sprouts.)
Cucumber and Carrot Sticks, 1 cup *each*
Aspartame-Sweetened Mixed Berry Nonfat Yogurt, 1 cup
Iced Tea with Lemon Wedge

MAIN MEAL
Peking-Style Turkey, 1 serving (see recipe)
Cooked Brown Rice, 1 cup
Cooked Sliced Zucchini, 1 cup, with 2 teaspoons reduced-calorie tub margarine
Tossed Green Salad, 2 cups, with 1/2 cup *each* sliced celery and radishes and 1 tablespoon fat-free Italian dressing
Pineapple, 1/8 medium
Herbal Tea

SNACK
Vanilla "Egg Cream" (In tall glass, combine 1 cup diet cream soda and 1/2 cup skim milk.)

This menu provides: 2 Milks, 3 Fats, 2 Fruits, 16¹/2 Vegetables, 5 Proteins, 5 Breads, 20 Optional Calories.

Per serving: 20 g Fat, 32 g Fiber.

TURKEY CHOW MEIN

Makes 4 servings

BREAKFAST

Raisins, 2 tablespoons
Bran Flakes Cereal, $^3/_4$ ounce
Skim Milk, 1 cup
Coffee or Tea (optional)

LIGHT MEAL

Open-Face Tuna Melt (In small bowl, combine
   3 ounces drained water-packed tuna, $^1/_2$ cup finely chopped celery and 2 teaspoons reduced-calorie
   mayonnaise; spread onto 1 slice multi-grain toast.
   Top tuna with 1 slice nonfat process American
   cheese. Place onto nonstick baking sheet; broil
   1 minute, until cheese is melted.)
Cucumber Spears, 1 cup
Cherry Tomatoes, 6
Sugar-Free Lime-Flavored Gelatin, $^1/_2$ cup, with
   1 tablespoon thawed frozen light whipped topping (8 calories per tablespoon)
Diet Ginger Ale

MAIN MEAL

Low-Sodium Chicken Broth, 1 cup
Turkey Chow Mein, 1 serving (see recipe)
Cooked Brown Rice, $^1/_2$ cup
Steamed Sliced Carrots, 1 cup
Orange Sections, $^1/_2$ cup
Chinese Tea

SNACK

Plain Popcorn, hot-air popped, 3 cups
Reduced-Calorie Vanilla Dairy Shake, 1 serving

This menu provides: 2 Milks, 3 Fats, 2 Fruits,
10$^1/_2$ Vegetables, 5 Proteins, 5$^1/_2$ Breads,
90 Optional Calories.

Per serving: 21 g Fat, 24 g Fiber.

4 fluid ounces ($^1/_2$ cup) mirin (Japanese cooking wine)
$^1/_4$ cup reduced-sodium soy sauce
3 tablespoons cornstarch
15 ounces skinless boneless turkey tenderloins, cut into thin strips
2 teaspoons oriental sesame oil
1 tablespoon grated pared fresh ginger root
4 garlic cloves, minced
$^1/_4$ teaspoon crushed red pepper flakes, or to taste
2 medium red bell peppers, seeded and cut into thin strips
2 cups sliced mushrooms
1 cup diagonally sliced celery (thin slices)
2 cups julienned bok choy
16 medium scallions, julienned
1 cup bean sprouts
1$^1/_2$ cups drained canned sliced water chestnuts
2 cups packaged chow mein noodles

1. In small bowl, with wire whisk, combine mirin, 3 tablespoons of the soy sauce and the cornstarch, blending until cornstarch is dissolved; set aside.

2. In small bowl, combine turkey and remaining 1 tablespoon soy sauce.

3. In wok or large nonstick skillet, heat 1 teaspoon of the oil; add turkey mixture. Cook over medium-high heat, stirring frequently, 1–2 minutes, just until turkey is no longer pink. With slotted spoon remove turkey from wok; set aside.

4. In same wok, heat remaining 1 teaspoon oil; add ginger, garlic and pepper flakes. Cook over medium-high heat, stirring constantly, 1 minute, until garlic is softened. Add bell peppers, mushrooms and celery; cook, stirring frequently, 5 minutes, until vegetables are tender. Add bok choy, scallions, bean sprouts and 2 tablespoons water; cook, stirring frequently, 2 minutes, until boy choy is just tender.

5. Return turkey to wok; stir to combine. Add water chestnuts and reserved wine mixture; cook, stirring frequently, until mixture comes to a boil, thickens and turkey is cooked through.

6. Transfer turkey mixture to serving platter; top with chow mein noodles.

Serving (2 cups turkey mixture, $^1/_2$ cup noodles) provides: 2 Fats, 4$^1/_2$ Vegetables, 3 Proteins, 1$^1/_2$ Breads, 50 Optional Calories.

Per serving: 396 Calories, 10 g Total Fat, 2 g Saturated Fat, 66 mg Cholesterol, 858 mg Sodium, 40 g Total Carbohydrate, 6 g Dietary Fiber, 34 g Protein, 105 mg Calcium.

TURKEY-SPAGHETTI BAKE

Here's a great do-ahead spaghetti dish that can be assembled in the afternoon and baked right before dinner. If serving it for company, just double the recipe and bake it in a shallow 13 × 9" casserole or au gratin dish.

Makes 4 servings

6 ounces spaghetti
1 tablespoon + 1 teaspoon olive oil
1 cup chopped green bell pepper
$^1/_2$ cup chopped onion
4 garlic cloves, minced
10 ounces ground skinless turkey breast
$^1/_2$ teaspoon salt
$^1/_2$ teaspoon freshly ground black pepper
2 cups tomato sauce (no salt added)
$^1/_4$ cup slivered fresh basil
$^1/_4$ cup minced fresh flat-leaf parsley
3 ounces skim-milk mozzarella cheese, grated
$^1/_2$ medium tomato, thinly sliced
Fresh basil sprigs, to garnish

1. Preheat oven to 375° F. Spray shallow 2-quart flameproof casserole or au gratin dish with nonstick cooking spray.

2. In large pot of boiling water, cook spaghetti 8–10 minutes, until tender. Drain, discarding liquid; set aside.

3. In large nonstick skillet, heat oil; add bell pepper, onion and garlic. Cook over medium-high heat, stirring frequently, 5 minutes, until vegetables are softened.

4. Add turkey, salt and pepper to vegetable mixture; cook, stirring to break up meat, 4–5 minutes, until no longer pink. Stir in tomato sauce; bring mixture to a boil. Reduce heat to low; simmer, stirring frequently, 5 minutes. Remove from heat; stir in slivered basil and parsley.

5. Transfer half of the cooked spaghetti to prepared casserole, spreading evenly; top with half of the turkey mixture. Repeat layers; sprinkle evenly with cheese. Bake, covered, 25 minutes, until hot and bubbling. Remove from oven; reset oven to broil.

6. Broil spaghetti mixture 4" from heat 1–2 minutes, until golden brown. Top with tomato slices; garnish with basil sprigs.

Serving ($^1/_2$ cups) provides: 1 Fat, 3 Vegetables, 3 Proteins, 2 Breads.

Per serving: 399 Calories, 10 g Total Fat, 3 g Saturated Fat, 56 mg Cholesterol, 440 mg Sodium, 47 g Total Carbohydrate, 4 g Dietary Fiber, 31 g Protein, 196 mg Calcium.

BREAKFAST

Orange Sections, $^1/_2$ cup
Raisin Bran Cereal, $^3/_4$ ounce
Skim Milk, $^3/_4$ cup
Coffee or Tea (optional)

LIGHT MEAL

Cheese 'n' Broccoli Stuffed Potato (Cut one 4-ounce baked potato in half lengthwise; place, cut-side up, into small microwavable baking dish. Top potato with $^1/_2$ cup cooked chopped broccoli and $^3/_4$ ounce reduced-fat cheddar cheese; microwave at High [100% power] until cheese is melted and potato is heated through, $1^1/_2$–2 minutes.)
Steamed Sugar Snap Peas, 1 cup
Tossed Green Salad, 2 cups, with 1 tablespoon fat-free Thousand Island dressing
Sugar-Free Strawberry Nonfat Frozen Yogurt, 4 fluid ounces
Diet Cola

MAIN MEAL

Turkey-Spaghetti Bake, 1 serving (see recipe)
Cooked Chopped Broccoli, 1 cup, with 2 teaspoons reduced-calorie tub margarine and 1 teaspoon sesame seeds, toasted
Iceberg Lettuce Wedge, 1, with $1^1/_2$ teaspoons Italian dressing
Breadsticks, 2 long
Cantaloupe, $^1/_4$ small, with 1 lemon wedge
Sparkling Mineral Water

SNACK

Reduced-Calorie Chocolate Dairy Shake, 1 serving

This menu provides: 2 Milks, 3 Fats, 2 Fruits, 13 Vegetables, 4 Proteins, 5 Breads, 85 Optional Calories.

Per serving: 24 g Fat, 28 g Fiber.

TURKEY TETRAZZINI

As the legend goes, this dish, first made with chicken, was named for the opera singer Luisa Tetrazzini. Here, we've made it with turkey, but created a sherry-Parmesan sauce that's right in tune with the original dish.

Makes 4 servings

5¹/₄ ounces spaghetti
1 tablespoon + 1 teaspoon reduced-calorie tub margarine
3 cups thinly sliced mushrooms
¹/₂ cup chopped onion
1 teaspoon minced fresh thyme leaves, or ¹/₄ teaspoon dried
¹/₂ teaspoon salt
¹/₂ teaspoon freshly ground black pepper
3 tablespoons all-purpose flour
2 cups skim milk
1 cup low-sodium chicken broth
2 fluid ounces (¹/₄ cup) dry white wine
12 ounces skinless boneless cooked turkey breast, cut into bite-size pieces
2 tablespoons freshly grated Parmesan cheese
2 tablespoons minced fresh flat-leaf parsley

1. Preheat oven to 375° F. Spray shallow 2-quart casserole or au gratin dish with nonstick cooking spray.

2. In large pot of boiling water, cook spaghetti 8–10 minutes, until tender. Drain, discarding liquid; set aside.

3. Meanwhile, in large nonstick skillet, heat margarine; add mushrooms, onion, thyme, salt and pepper. Cook over medium-high heat, stirring frequently, 6–7 minutes, until mushrooms are golden brown.

4. Stir flour into mushroom mixture; cook, stirring constantly, 1 minute. Continuing to stir, gradually add milk; stir in broth and wine. Bring liquid to a boil. Reduce heat to low; simmer, stirring constantly, 1 minute, until slightly thickened. Add turkey, 1 tablespoon of the cheese and the cooked spaghetti; toss to combine.

5. Transfer spaghetti mixture to prepared casserole; sprinkle with parsley and remaining cheese. Bake 20 minutes, until golden brown and bubbling.

Serving (2 cups) provides: ¹/₂ Milk, ¹/₂ Fat, 1³/₄ Vegetables, 3 Proteins, 2 Breads, 35 Optional Calories.

Per serving: 385 Calories, 5 g Total Fat, 1 g Saturated Fat, 75 mg Cholesterol, 500 mg Sodium, 43 g Total Carbohydrate, 2 g Dietary Fiber, 38 g Protein, 222 mg Calcium.

BREAKFAST
Fresh Fig, 1 large
Wheat Flakes Cereal, ³/₄ ounce
Skim Milk, 1 cup
Coffee or Tea (optional)

LIGHT MEAL
Broiled Flounder, 4 ounces, with 1¹/₂ teaspoons tartar sauce
Cooked Brown Rice, ¹/₂ cup
Steamed Asparagus, 6 spears, with 1 teaspoon reduced-calorie tub margarine
Sugar-Free Raspberry-Flavored Gelatin, ¹/₂ cup, with 1 tablespoon thawed frozen light whipped topping (8 calories per tablespoon)
Unsweetened Seltzer

MAIN MEAL
Turkey Tetrazzini, 1 serving (see recipe)
Cooked Spinach, 1 cup
Cooked Baby Carrots, 1 cup
Tossed Green Salad, 2 cups, with ¹/₂ cup alfalfa sprouts and 1 tablespoon fat-free creamy Italian dressing
Garlic-Herb Bread (Spread 1-ounce slice Italian bread with ¹/₂ teaspoon minced fresh garlic or 1 roasted garlic clove and ¹/₂ teaspoon *each* minced fresh basil and oregano leaves; drizzle with 1 teaspoon olive oil. Place onto nonstick baking sheet; broil until lightly browned.)
Strawberries, 1 cup
Decaffeinated Cappuccino, made with skim milk, 5 fluid ounces

SNACK
Oat-Bran Pretzels, ³/₄ ounce

This menu provides: 2 Milks, 3 Fats, 2 Fruits, 11³/₄ Vegetables, 5 Proteins, 6 Breads, 75 Optional Calories.

Per serving: 24 g Fat, 24 g Fiber.

FARFALLE WITH TURKEY, ARUGULA AND PLUM TOMATOES

Festive farfalle pasta, shaped like bow-ties, pairs with cooked chicken and fresh plum tomatoes—plus a secret ingredient: arugula. This aromatic, piquant salad green adds a peppery touch to this elegant dish.

Makes 4 servings

4 cups coarsely chopped arugula
7 large plum tomatoes, blanched, peeled, seeded and coarsely chopped
8 ounces skinless boneless cooked turkey breast, cut into 1" pieces
$^1/_3$ cup red wine vinegar
$^1/_4$ cup minced shallots
1 tablespoon + 1 teaspoon olive oil
2 garlic cloves, minced
1 teaspoon freshly ground black pepper
$^1/_2$ teaspoon salt
6 ounces farfalle pasta (bow-tie–shaped macaroni)

1. In large bowl, combine arugula, tomatoes, turkey, vinegar, shallots, oil, garlic, pepper and salt; let stand, covered, 1 hour.

2. Meanwhile, in large pot of boiling water, cook farfalle 10–12 minutes, until tender. Drain, discarding liquid.

3. Add cooked farfalle to turkey mixture; toss to combine. Serve warm or at room temperature.

Serving ($2^1/_2$ cups) provides: 1 Fat, 4 Vegetables, 2 Proteins, 2 Breads.

Per serving: 310 Calories, 6 g Total Fat, 1 g Saturated Fat, 48 mg Cholesterol, 341 mg Sodium, 40 g Total Carbohydrate, 3 g Dietary Fiber, 24 g Protein, 70 mg Calcium.

BREAKFAST
Strawberries, 1 cup
Cornflakes, $^3/_4$ ounce
Skim Milk, 1 cup
Coffee or Tea (optional)

LIGHT MEAL
Vegetable-Bean Couscous (In small nonstick skillet, heat 1 teaspoon olive oil; add $^1/_2$ cup *each* chopped onion and chopped broccoli and 1 garlic clove, minced. Cook over medium-high heat, stirring frequently, 5 minutes, until vegetables are softened. Add $^1/_2$ cup cooked couscous and 2 ounces drained cooked chick-peas; stir to combine; cook 3–4 minutes, until couscous and chick-peas are heated through.)
Steamed Whole Green Beans and Carrot Sticks, 1 cup *each*
Banana Yogurt (In small bowl, combine $^3/_4$ cup plain nonfat yogurt, $^1/_2$ medium banana, sliced, and sugar substitute to equal 2 teaspoons sugar.)
Unsweetened Cranberry-Flavored Seltzer

MAIN MEAL
Farfalle with Turkey, Arugula and Plum Tomatoes, 1 serving (see recipe)
Tossed Green Salad, 2 cups, with 1 tablespoon fat-free blue cheese dressing
Roll, 1 ounce
Angel Food Cake, 2 ounces
Iced Tea

SNACK
Mini Rice Cakes, 3, with 1 tablespoon peanut butter

This menu provides: 2 Milks, 3 Fats, 2 Fruits, 14 Vegetables, $4^1/_4$ Proteins, $5^3/_4$ Breads, 95 Optional Calories.

Per serving: 24 g Fat, 24 g Fiber.

Farfalle with Turkey, Arugula and Plum Tomatoes

268
TURKEY-FUSILLI PRIMAVERA

Fusilli, a curly pasta, is perfect to team up with this stir-fry of turkey and plenty of fresh vegetables.

Makes 4 servings

2 cups small broccoli florets
6 ounces fusilli pasta
Pinch crushed red pepper flakes
6 large plum tomatoes, seeded and chopped
$^1/_4$ cup balsamic vinegar
$^1/_2$ teaspoon salt
$^1/_2$ teaspoon freshly ground black pepper
$^1/_4$ teaspoon granulated sugar
1 tablespoon + 1 teaspoon olive oil
2 cups sliced shiitake mushroom caps
2 cups red bell pepper strips
1 cup julienned zucchini
1 cup slivered red onions
4 garlic cloves, minced
12 ounces skinless boneless cooked turkey breast, cut into bite-size pieces
1 cup loosely packed slivered fresh basil
$^1/_4$ cup freshly grated Parmesan cheese

1. In large pot of boiling water, cook broccoli 3 minutes, until bright green and just tender. With slotted spoon, remove broccoli from water; set aside.

2. In same pot of boiling water, cook fusilli 8–10 minutes, until tender. Drain, discarding liquid; transfer to medium bowl. Add pepper flakes; toss to combine. Set aside; keep warm.

3. Meanwhile, in large bowl, combine tomatoes, vinegar, $^1/_4$ teaspoon of the salt, the black pepper and sugar; set aside.

4. In large nonstick skillet, heat 1 teaspoon of the oil; add mushrooms. Cook over medium-high heat, stirring frequently, 5 minutes, until mushrooms are tender. Stir mushroom mixture into tomato mixture; set aside.

5. In same skillet, heat remaining 1 tablespoon oil; add bell pepper, zucchini, onions, garlic and remaining $^1/_4$ teaspoon salt; cook, stirring frequently, 5 minutes, until vegetables are softened.

6. Add turkey, cooked broccoli and reserved tomato mixture to vegetable mixture; cook, stirring frequently, 2–3 minutes, until heated through.

7. Spoon turkey mixture over warm fusilli mixture; toss to combine. Sprinkle with basil and cheese; toss again.

BREAKFAST
Raisins, 2 tablespoons
Cornflakes, $^3/_4$ ounce
Skim Milk, 1 cup
Coffee or Tea (optional)

LIGHT MEAL
Grilled Fat-Free Frankfurter, 2 ounces, on 2-ounce
    frankfurter roll, with 1 teaspoon *each* pickle relish
    and prepared mustard
Coleslaw, $^1/_4$ cup
Celery and Carrot Sticks, 1 cup *each*
Nectarine, 1 small
Diet Cola

MAIN MEAL
Turkey-Fusilli Primavera, 1 serving (see recipe)
Arugula and Curly Endive Salad, 2 cups, with
    $^1/_2$ cup *each* sliced jicama and shredded carrot and
    1 tablespoon fat-free creamy Italian dressing
Garlic-Herb Bread (Spread 1-ounce slice Italian
    bread with $^1/_2$ teaspoon minced fresh garlic or
    1 roasted garlic clove and $^1/_2$ teaspoon *each*
    minced fresh basil and oregano leaves; drizzle with
    1 teaspoon olive oil. Place onto nonstick baking
    sheet; broil until lightly browned.)
Aspartame-Sweetened Raspberry Nonfat Yogurt,
    1 cup
Sparkling Mineral Water with Lime Wedge

SNACK
Frozen Fruit Pop, 1 bar

This menu provides: 2 Milks, 3 Fats, 2 Fruits, 16 Vegetables, 5 Proteins, 6 Breads, 100 Optional Calories.

Per serving: 20 g Fat, 22 g Fiber.

Serving (2 cups) provides: 1 Fat, $5^1/_2$ Vegetables, 3 Proteins, 2 Breads, 30 Optional Calories.

Per serving: 437 Calories, 8 g Total Fat, 2 g Saturated Fat, 75 mg Cholesterol, 447 mg Sodium, 54 g Total Carbohydrate, 6 g Dietary Fiber, 39 g Protein, 275 mg Calcium.

269
SOUTHWESTERN TURKEY ROAST

Makes 12 servings

1 tablespoon minced fresh flat-leaf parsley
1 tablespoon minced fresh oregano leaves, or 1 teaspoon dried
1 tablespoon fresh lime juice
2 teaspoons vegetable oil
3 garlic cloves, minced
1$^1/_4$ teaspoons salt
1 teaspoon mild or hot chili powder
$^3/_4$ teaspoon ground cumin
$^1/_2$ teaspoon freshly ground black pepper
One 3-pound 6-ounce turkey breast
Cherry tomatoes and celery stalks, to garnish (optional)

1. Preheat oven to 350° F.

2. In small cup or bowl, combine parsley, oregano, juice, oil, garlic, salt, chili powder, cumin and pepper.

3. Gently loosen skin from turkey; rub turkey with herb mixture. Place turkey, skin-side up, onto rack in large roasting pan; roast 1$^1/_2$–1$^3/_4$ hours, until turkey is cooked through and juices run clear when pierced with fork or meat thermometer registers 165° F. Remove from oven; let stand 10 minutes.

4. Transfer turkey to cutting board. Remove and discard turkey skin; thinly slice turkey. Arrange turkey slices on serving platter; garnish with cherry tomatoes and celery stalks, if desired.

Serving (3 ounces) provides: 3 Proteins, 5 Optional Calories.

Per serving: 125 Calories, 1 g Total Fat, 0 g Saturated Fat, 71 mg Cholesterol, 275 mg Sodium, 1 g Total Carbohydrate, 0 g Dietary Fiber, 26 g Protein, 18 mg Calcium.

270
APRICOT-GLAZED TURKEY-IN-A-BAG

Roasting a turkey inside a cooking bag is a foolproof way to keep it moist and juicy. Here, an apricot glaze adds a marvelous fruity taste.

Makes about 16 servings

One 12-pound turkey
³/4 teaspoon salt
³/4 teaspoon freshly ground black pepper
1 bunch fresh flat-leaf parsley
1 celery stalk with leaves, quartered
Four 5" fresh marjoram sprigs
Four 5" fresh thyme sprigs
One 5" fresh rosemary sprig
1 tablespoon all-purpose flour
2 tablespoons cornstarch
2 tablespoons reduced-sodium soy sauce
¹/2 teaspoon ground ginger
²/3 cup apricot preserves
3 tablespoons honey
2 garlic cloves, minced

1. Preheat oven to 325° F.

2. Sprinkle body and neck cavities of turkey with salt and pepper. Stuff neck cavity with one-fourth of the parsley; stuff body cavity with celery, marjoram, thyme, rosemary and remaining parsley. Truss turkey.

3. Place flour into 20 × 14" oven cooking bag; shake to coat inside of bag. Place turkey into bag; tie bag closed with nylon tie or kitchen string. Place bag into large roasting pan; with scissors or sharp knife, make six ¹/2" slits in top of bag. Roast turkey 2 hours.

4. Meanwhile, to prepare glaze, in medium saucepan, combine cornstarch, soy sauce and ginger, stirring until cornstarch is dissolved. Add preserves, honey and garlic; cook over medium-high heat, stirring constantly, 5 minutes, until mixture comes to a boil. Cook, continuing to stir, 1 minute.

5. Remove turkey from oven; leave oven on. Carefully cut bag open; with scissors or sharp knife, carefully remove and discard turkey skin. Brush turkey evenly with glaze; roast, uncovered, 30 minutes, until meat thermometer registers 180° F and turkey juices run clear when pierced with fork. Let stand 10 minutes; slice into 3-ounce portions.

Serving (3 ounces) provides: 3 Proteins, 45 Optional Calories.

Per serving: 198 Calories, 4 g Total Fat, 1 g Saturated Fat, 65 mg Cholesterol, 251 mg Sodium, 14 g Total Carbohydrate, 1 g Dietary Fiber, 25 g Protein, 37 mg Calcium.

BREAKFAST
Blackberries, ³/4 cup
Shredded Wheat Cereal, 1¹/2 ounces
Skim Milk, 1 cup
Coffee or Tea (optional)

LIGHT MEAL
Cottage Cheese-Fruit Salad (Line plate with 4 iceberg lettuce leaves. Top lettuce with ¹/2 cup nonfat cottage cheese; surround with ¹/2 cup fruit salad.)
Carrot and Celery Sticks, 1 cup *each*
Crispbreads, ³/4 ounce, with 1 teaspoon reduced-calorie tub margarine
Sugar-Free Pineapple-Flavored Gelatin, ¹/2 cup
Iced Tea

MAIN MEAL
Steamed Artichoke, 1 medium, with Lemon "Butter" (In small cup or bowl, combine 1 teaspoon *each* reduced-calorie tub margarine, melted, and fresh lemon juice.)
Apricot-Glazed Turkey-in-a-Bag, 1 serving (see recipe)
Cooked Barley, 1 cup
Steamed Broccoli, 4 spears
Tossed Green Salad, 2 cups, with 6 cherry tomatoes and 1 tablespoon creamy Italian dressing
Reduced-Calorie Chocolate-Flavored Pudding (made with skim milk), ¹/2 cup
Sparkling Mineral Water

SNACK
Vanilla "Egg Cream" (In tall glass, combine 1 cup diet cream soda and ¹/2 cup skim milk.)

This menu provides: 2 Milks, 3 Fats, 2 Fruits, 13 Vegetables, 4 Proteins, 5 Breads, 95 Optional Calories.

Per serving: 18 g Fat, 40 g Fiber.

271

STUFFED TURKEY BREAST WITH WILD MUSHROOMS AND LEEKS

This gourmet mushroom-leek stuffing turns a turkey breast into an easy and elegant company dish.

Makes 10 servings

1 tablespoon + 2 teaspoons olive oil
4 cups thinly sliced well-washed leeks
$^1/_2$ cup chopped onion
4 garlic cloves, minced
2 cups whole cremini or white mushrooms, woody ends trimmed
2 teaspoons minced fresh thyme leaves, or $^1/_2$ teaspoon dried
1 teaspoon salt
1 teaspoon freshly ground black pepper
5 slices firm white bread, cut into $^1/_2$" cubes
1 bunch fresh flat-leaf parsley, finely chopped
$^3/_4$ cup low-sodium chicken broth
One 2-pound 6-ounce skinless boneless turkey breast

1. Preheat oven to 350° F.

2. In large nonstick skillet, heat 2 teaspoons of the oil; add $3^3/_4$ cups of the leeks, the onion and garlic. Cook over medium-high heat, stirring frequently, 4 minutes, until leeks are just tender. With slotted spoon, transfer leek mixture to large bowl; set aside.

3. In same skillet, heat remaining 1 tablespoon oil; add mushrooms, thyme, $^1/_2$ teaspoon of the salt and $^1/_2$ teaspoon of the pepper. Cook over medium-high heat, stirring frequently, until mushrooms are browned and tender. With slotted spoon, transfer mushroom mixture to bowl with leek mixture. Add bread, parsley and broth to vegetable mixture; toss to combine and evenly moisten.

4. Place turkey, skinned-side down, onto work surface; spread turkey with vegetable mixture to within 1" of edges. Roll turkey to enclose filling; secure with kitchen string. Place stuffed turkey, seam-side down, onto rack in roasting pan; sprinkle evenly with remaining $^1/_2$ teaspoon salt and remaining $^1/_2$ teaspoon pepper. Roast stuffed turkey $1^1/_4$–$1^1/_2$ hours, until turkey is cooked through and juices run clear when pierced with fork, basting occasionally with pan juices.

5. Remove turkey from oven; let stand 10 minutes. Cut stuffed turkey into 10 equal slices; arrange slices on serving platter. Top with any remaining pan juices; sprinkle with remaining $^1/_4$ cup leeks.

272
GRILLED BUTTERFLIED TURKEY BREAST WITH JAMAICAN BARBECUE SAUCE

Makes 12 servings

$^1/_2$ cup finely chopped onion
$^1/_2$ cup finely chopped scallions
1 teaspoon salt
1 teaspoon freshly ground black pepper
$^3/_4$ teaspoon dried thyme leaves
1 small mango, pared, pitted and chopped
2 tablespoons minced fresh cilantro

1 tablespoon firmly packed light or dark brown sugar
2 teaspoons hot green (jalapeño) pepper sauce
$^1/_2$ teaspoon ground allspice
$^1/_4$ teaspoon cinnamon
2 teaspoons vegetable oil
One 2-pound 13-ounce skinless boneless turkey breast, butterflied
Fresh cilantro sprigs, to garnish

1. Preheat barbecue grill according to manufacturer's directions, or preheat broiler and spray rack in broiler pan with nonstick cooking spray.

2. To prepare sauce, spray medium saucepan with nonstick cooking spray; heat. Add onion, scallions, $^1/_2$ teaspoon of the salt, $^1/_2$ teaspoon of the pepper and $^1/_4$ teaspoon of the thyme; cook over medium-high heat, stirring frequently, 5 minutes, until vegetables are softened. Stir in mango, minced cilantro, brown sugar, hot sauce, allspice and cinnamon. Reduce heat to low; cook, stirring occasionally, 5 minutes, until flavors are blended. Set aside; keep warm.

3. To prepare turkey, in small cup or bowl, combine oil, remaining $^1/_2$ teaspoon salt, remaining $^1/_2$ teaspoon pepper and remaining $^1/_2$ teaspoon thyme; rub into turkey breast. Grill turkey over hot coals or place onto prepared rack in broiler pan and broil 4" from heat, turning once and basting occasionally with onion mixture, 20–22 minutes, until turkey is golden brown and cooked through and juices run clear when pierced with fork. Remove from heat; let stand 10 minutes.

4. Transfer turkey to cutting board; slice thinly. Arrange turkey slices on serving platter in circular pattern. Serve turkey with warm sauce; garnish with cilantro sprigs.

Serving (3 ounces turkey, 2 generous tablespoons sauce) provides: 3 Proteins, 20 Optional Calories.

Per serving: 131 Calories, 1 g Total Fat, 0 g Saturated Fat, 71 mg Cholesterol, 193 mg Sodium, 2 g Total Carbohydrate, 0 g Dietary Fiber, 26 g Protein, 17 mg Calcium.

BREAKFAST
Apple, 1 small
Raisin Bran Cereal, $^3/_4$ ounce
Skim Milk, 1 cup
Coffee or Tea (optional)

LIGHT MEAL
Ham and Cheese Sandwich (Layer 1 ounce lean boiled ham, 1 slice nonfat process Swiss cheese, 2 Romaine lettuce leaves, 2 tomato slices and 1 teaspoon prepared mustard between 2 slices reduced-calorie multi-grain bread.)
Italian Spinach Salad (In medium bowl, combine 2 cups torn spinach leaves, $^1/_2$ cup *each* sliced mushrooms and sliced red onion, 2 teaspoons imitation bacon bits and $1^1/_2$ teaspoons Italian dressing.)
Reduced-Calorie Chocolate-Flavored Pudding (made with skim milk), $^1/_2$ cup
Unsweetened Raspberry-Flavored Seltzer

MAIN MEAL
Grilled Butterflied Turkey Breast with Jamaican Barbecue Sauce, 1 serving (see recipe)
Grilled Potato-Vegetable Medley (Preheat outdoor barbecue grill according to manufacturer's directions, or preheat broiler and spray rack in broiler pan with nonstick cooking spray. Wrap 10 ounces cubed all-purpose potatoes, $^1/_2$ cup *each* sliced onion and carrot, 2 teaspoons reduced-calorie tub margarine and pinch *each* salt and freshly ground black pepper in sheet of foil; grill or broil 4" from heat, turning occasionally, 30–40 minutes, until potatoes are tender.)
Cooked Broccoli, 4 spears, with 2 teaspoons reduced-calorie tub margarine
Honeydew Melon, 2" wedge
Iced Tea

SNACK
Graham Crackers, 3 ($2^1/_2$" squares)
Vanilla "Egg Cream" (In tall glass, combine 1 cup diet cream soda and $^1/_2$ cup skim milk.)

This menu provides: 2 Milks, 3 Fats, 2 Fruits, 11 Vegetables, $4^1/_2$ Proteins, 5 Breads, 80 Optional Calories.

Per serving: 22 g Fat, 28 g Fiber.

BREAKFAST

Peach, 1 medium

Cooked Cream of Wheat Cereal, 1 cup

Skim Milk, 1 cup

Coffee or Tea (optional)

LIGHT MEAL

Split-Pea Soup, canned, 1 cup

Tossed Green Salad, 2 cups, with $^1/2$ cup sliced radishes and 1 tablespoon fat-free Italian dressing

Whole-Wheat Roll, 1 ounce, with 2 teaspoons reduced-calorie tub margarine

Sugar-Free Grape-Flavored Gelatin, $^1/2$ cup

Diet Cola

MAIN MEAL

Chinese-Lacquered Turkey Breast, 1 serving (see recipe)

Baked Potato, 8 ounces, with 2 teaspoons reduced-calorie tub margarine

Pureed Cooked Carrots, 1 cup, with 2 teaspoons reduced-calorie tub margarine and 1 teaspoon firmly packed light or dark brown sugar

Spinach Salad (In medium bowl, combine 2 cups torn spinach leaves, 2 teaspoons balsamic vinegar and 1 teaspoon imitation bacon bits.)

Whole Strawberries, $^3/4$ cup

Unsweetened Seltzer

SNACK

Aspartame-Sweetened Blueberry Nonfat Yogurt, 1 cup

This menu provides: 2 Milks, 3 Fats, 2 Fruits, 11 Vegetables, $4^1/2$ Proteins, 5 Breads, 100 Optional Calories.

Per serving: 17 g Fat, 33 g Fiber.

273
CHINESE-LACQUERED TURKEY BREAST

A deliciously sweet and zesty glaze gives a Chinese touch to this roast turkey breast.

Makes 12 servings

$^1/4$ cup reduced-sodium soy sauce

$^1/4$ cup honey

2 tablespoons firmly packed light or dark brown sugar

1 tablespoon grated orange zest*

3 garlic cloves, minced

One 2-pound 6-ounce boneless turkey breast

$1^1/2$ cups orange sections

1. To prepare marinade, in gallon-size sealable plastic bag, combine soy sauce, honey, brown sugar, zest and garlic; add turkey. Seal bag, squeezing out air; turn to coat turkey. Refrigerate at least 2 hours or overnight, turning bag occasionally.

2. Preheat oven to 350° F.

3. Drain marinade into small saucepan; bring to a rolling boil; boil for 1 minute. Remove from heat.

4. Place turkey breast, skin-side up, onto rack in large roasting pan; brush with some of the marinade. Roast, basting frequently with remaining marinade, 1 hour, until browned and glazed. Cover loosely with foil; roast 15–30 minutes longer, until turkey is cooked through and juices run clear when turkey is pierced with fork or meat thermometer registers 160° F. Remove from oven; let stand 10 minutes.

5. Transfer turkey to cutting board. Remove and discard turkey skin; thinly slice turkey. Arrange turkey slices on serving platter; surround with orange sections.

Serving ($2^1/2$ ounces turkey, 2 tablespoons orange sections) provides: $^1/4$ Fruit, $2^1/2$ Proteins, 30 Optional Calories.

Per serving: 141 Calories, 1 g Total Fat, 0 g Saturated Fat, 59 mg Cholesterol, 238 mg Sodium, 12 g Total Carbohydrate, 1 g Dietary Fiber, 22 g Protein, 23 mg Calcium.

*The zest of the orange is the peel without any of the pith (white membrane). To remove zest from orange, use a zester or the fine side of a vegetable grater.

274
TURKEY-ASPARAGUS STRATA

This tasty dish combines strips of turkey, fresh asparagus, shredded cheese and bread into a prepare-ahead, never-fail layered soufflé.

Makes 4 servings

2 teaspoons reduced-calorie tub margarine
8 ounces skinless boneless turkey tenderloin, cut into thin strips
2 garlic cloves, minced
1 medium onion, cut into thin strips
1 cup thinly sliced asparagus
Seven crust-trimmed 1-ounce slices white bread, cut into 4 triangles each
2 cups skim milk
3 eggs
3 tablespoons all-purpose flour
1 teaspoon Dijon-style mustard
$3/4$ teaspoon salt
$1/4$ teaspoon freshly ground black pepper
$3/4$ ounce reduced-fat cheddar cheese, grated

1. Preheat oven to 350° F. Spray 8" square baking dish with nonstick cooking spray.

2. In large nonstick skillet, melt margarine; add turkey and garlic. Cook over medium-high heat, stirring frequently, until turkey is cooked through. With slotted spoon, transfer turkey mixture to medium bowl.

3. In same skillet, cook onion over medium-high heat, stirring frequently, 5 minutes, until softened. Transfer cooked onion to bowl with turkey; toss to combine.

4. In medium saucepan of boiling water, cook asparagus 3 minutes, until just tender. Drain, discarding liquid; rinse under cold running water until cool. Drain again. Transfer to bowl with turkey and onion; toss to combine.

5. In prepared baking dish, layer 10 bread triangles and half of the turkey mixture; repeat layers. Top edge of turkey mixture with remaining 8 bread triangles, overlapping slightly.

6. In clean medium bowl, with electric mixer, combine milk, eggs, flour, mustard, salt and pepper; pour over turkey and bread layers. Bake 40 minutes, until mixture is set. Sprinkle evenly with cheese; bake 5 minutes, until cheese is melted and lightly browned.

BREAKFAST
Blackberries, $3/4$ cup
Aspartame-Sweetened Vanilla Nonfat Yogurt, 1 cup, with 3 tablespoons wheat germ
Coffee or Tea (optional)

LIGHT MEAL
Broiled Red Snapper, 3 ounces
Cooked Bulgur Wheat, 1 cup
Steamed Spinach, 1 cup, with 1 tablespoon reduced-calorie tub margarine
Steamed Whole Green Beans, 1 cup
Radicchio and Chicory Salad, 2 cups, with 6 cherry tomatoes and 1 tablespoon fat-free ranch dressing
Plum, 1 small
Sparkling Mineral Water

MAIN MEAL
Turkey-Asparagus Strata, 1 serving (see recipe)
Tomato Soup, canned, 1 cup
Carrot and Cucumber Sticks, 1 cup *each*
Crispbreads, $3/4$ ounce, with $2^1/2$ teaspoons reduced-calorie tub margarine
Strawberry Parfait (In stemmed glass, layer $1/2$ cup each reduced-calorie vanilla-flavored pudding [made with skim milk] and strawberries, sliced.)
Iced Tea

SNACK
Sugar-Free Raspberry-Flavored Gelatin, $1/2$ cup

This menu provides: 2 Milks, 3 Fats, 2 Fruits, $15^3/4$ Vegetables, 4 Proteins, 6 Breads, 115 Optional Calories.

Per serving: 29 g Fat, 40 g Fiber.

Serving (one-fourth of strata) provides: $1/2$ Milk, $1/4$ Fat, $3/4$ Vegetable, $2^1/2$ Proteins, 2 Breads.

Per serving: 360 Calories, 8 g Total Fat, 3 g Saturated Fat, 201 mg Cholesterol, 909 mg Sodium, 39 g Total Carbohydrate, 2 g Dietary Fiber, 30 g Protein, 295 mg Calcium.

BREAKFAST

Blueberries, $^3/_4$ cup
Frozen Waffle, 1, heated, with 2 teaspoons maple
   syrup
Skim Milk, $^1/_2$ cup
Coffee or Tea (optional)

LIGHT MEAL

Tuna Salad Sandwich (In small bowl, combine
   4 ounces drained canned water-packed tuna,
   flaked, $^1/_2$ cup chopped celery, 2 teaspoons
   reduced-calorie mayonnaise and pinch freshly
   ground black pepper; spread between 2 slices
   reduced-calorie rye bread.)
Cucumber and Carrot Sticks, 1 cup *each*
Aspartame-Sweetened Peach Nonfat Yogurt, 1 cup
Diet Cherry Cola

MAIN MEAL

Turkey Meatloaf, 1 serving (see recipe)
Steamed New Potatoes, 4 ounces, with 2 teaspoons
   each reduced-calorie tub margarine and minced
   fresh flat-leaf parsley
Steamed Spinach, 1 cup
Tossed Green Salad, 2 cups, with $^1/_2$ cup chilled
   cooked artichoke hearts and 1 tablespoon fat-free
   Italian dressing
Baked Apple (Preheat oven to 350° F. Pare 1 small
   apple halfway down from stem end; core and
   place into small baking dish. Sprinkle apple with
   1 teaspoon granulated sugar and $^1/_4$ teaspoon cinnamon; add $^1/_4$" water to pan. Bake, covered,
   30 minutes, until tender.)
Sparkling Mineral Water

SNACK

Vanilla Wafers, 3
Skim Milk, $^1/_2$ cup

This menu provides: 2 Milks, 3 Fats, 2 Fruits,
15 Vegetables, 5 Proteins, $4^1/_2$ Breads, 80 Optional
Calories.

Per serving: 19 g Fat, 27 g Fiber.

275
TURKEY MEATLOAF

*This meatloaf is much lighter than the typical ones made with beef.
Preparing it in the food processor makes it extra easy, too.*

Makes 4 servings

1 large garlic clove, peeled
2 cups whole mushrooms, woody stems trimmed
$^1/_2$ medium zucchini, cut into chunks
$^1/_2$ medium onion, halved
15 ounces ground skinless turkey breast
4 ounces Italian bread, torn into small pieces
1 cup tomato sauce (no salt added)
1 egg white
$^1/_2$ teaspoon salt
$^1/_2$ teaspoon freshly ground black pepper
$^1/_4$ teaspoon dried thyme leaves
8 curly loose-leafed lettuce leaves

1. Preheat oven to 375° F. Spray $8^1/_2 \times 4$" loaf pan with nonstick cooking spray.

2. In food processor, with motor running, drop garlic through feed tube; process until finely chopped. One at a time, drop mushrooms, zucchini and onion through feed tube, processing until finely chopped and scraping down sides of bowl as necessary (do not purée).

3. Transfer chopped vegetable mixture to large bowl; add turkey, bread, $^1/_2$ cup of the tomato sauce, the egg white, salt, pepper and thyme; mix well.

4. Transfer turkey mixture to prepared pan, spreading evenly; top with remaining $^1/_2$ cup tomato sauce. Bake 45–50 minutes, until cooked through. Remove from oven; let stand 5 minutes.

5. Line serving platter with lettuce leaves. Remove meatloaf from pan; transfer to prepared platter.

Serving (one-fourth of meatloaf) provides: 3 Vegetables, 3 Proteins, 1 Bread, 5 Optional Calories.

Per serving: 241 Calories, 2 g Total Fat, 0 g Saturated Fat, 66 mg Cholesterol, 521 mg Sodium, 23 g Total Carbohydrate, 3 g Dietary Fiber, 32 g Protein, 56 mg Calcium.

276
TURKEY PIE

Makes 6 servings

Filling:

4 cups low-sodium chicken broth

2 garlic cloves, minced

$^3/_4$ teaspoon freshly ground black pepper

$^1/_2$ teaspoon salt

One 1-pound 6-ounce skinless boneless turkey breast

2 cups baby carrots

1 cup thawed frozen green peas

2 cups peeled pearl onions

3 tablespoons reduced-calorie tub margarine

$^1/_2$ cup chopped onion

$^1/_2$ cup + 1 tablespoon all-purpose flour

$2^1/_4$ cups skim milk

$^1/_3$ cup minced fresh parsley

1 tablespoon minced fresh thyme leaves, or 1 teaspoon dried

1 teaspoon fresh lemon juice

Dumplings:

2 cups minus 2 tablespoons all-purpose flour

1 tablespoon + 1 teaspoon double-acting baking powder

2 teaspoons minced fresh rosemary leaves, or $^3/_4$ teaspoon dried

$^1/_4$ teaspoon salt

$^1/_4$ cup + 1 tablespoon reduced-calorie tub margarine

$^3/_4$ cup skim milk

1 egg, beaten

1. In large pot with heatproof handles or Dutch oven, combine broth, garlic, $^1/_4$ teaspoon of the pepper and $^1/_4$ teaspoon of the salt; bring liquid to a boil. Add turkey. Reduce heat to low; simmer 7–10 minutes, until turkey is cooked through and juices run clear when pierced with fork. Transfer turkey to cutting board; cool. Cut into bite-size pieces; set aside.

2. Add carrots and peas to broth; cook over medium-high heat 3 minutes, until tender. With slotted spoon, remove vegetables from broth; set aside.

3. Add pearl onions to broth; cook 3 minutes, until tender. With slotted spoon, remove onions from broth; set aside. Transfer broth to 1-quart bowl; set aside. Skim off any fat that rises to the surface.

4. In same pot, melt margarine; add chopped onion. Cook over medium-high heat, stirring frequently, 5 minutes, until softened. Sprinkle onion mixture with flour; cook, stirring constantly, 5 minutes, until mixture is bubbling. Gradually whisk in milk and reserved broth; continuing to stir, cook 3 minutes, until mixture is slightly thickened. Remove from heat; stir in parsley, thyme, juice, turkey, vegetables, remaining $^1/_2$ teaspoon pepper and remaining $^1/_4$ teaspoon salt. Set aside; keep warm.

5. In medium bowl, combine flour, baking powder, rosemary and salt. With pastry blender or 2 knives, cut margarine into flour mixture until mixture resembles coarse crumbs; make a well in center of flour mixture. In small bowl, combine milk and egg; pour into well. With wooden spoon, stir milk mixture, slowly incorporating flour mixture, until mixture forms a soft dough.

6. Return turkey mixture to heat; bring to a boil. Reduce heat to low; drop flour mixture by 2 heaping tablespoonfuls onto turkey mixture,

forming 12 dumplings. Simmer, covered, 15 minutes, until dumplings are cooked through.

7. Meanwhile, preheat broiler.

8. Remove cover from pot; broil 4" from heat 1–2 minutes, until dumplings are golden brown.

Serving ($1^1/_2$ cups turkey mixture, 2 dumplings) provides: $^1/_2$ Milk, 2 Fats, $1^1/_2$ Vegetables, 3 Proteins, $2^1/_2$ Breads, 15 Optional Calories.

Per serving: 507 Calories, 12 g Total Fat, 3 g Saturated Fat, 102 mg Cholesterol, 983 mg Sodium, 62 g Total Carbohydrate, 4 g Dietary Fiber, 41 g Protein, 421 mg Calcium.

BREAKFAST
Orange and Grapefruit Sections, $^1/_2$ cup
Reduced-Calorie Whole-Wheat Bread, 2 slices, toasted, with 2 slices nonfat process Swiss cheese
Skim Milk, 1 cup

LIGHT MEAL
Tuna-Pasta Salad (In medium bowl, combine $^1/_2$ cup cooked macaroni shells, 2 ounces drained canned water-packed white tuna, 6 cherry tomatoes, halved, $^1/_4$ cup diced red onion and 1 tablespoon fat-free Italian dressing.)
Cucumber Sticks and Whole Mushrooms, 1 cup *each*
Sugar-Free Lime-Flavored Gelatin, $^1/_2$ cup

MAIN MEAL
Turkey Pie, 1 serving (see recipe)
Steamed Broccoli, 4 spears, with 1 teaspoon reduced-calorie tub margarine
Torn Red and Green Leaf Lettuce Leaves, 2 cups, with $^1/_2$ cup sliced jicama and 1 tablespoon balsamic vinegar
Whole-Wheat Roll, 1 ounce, with 1 teaspoon reduced-calorie tub margarine
Reduced-Calorie Butterscotch-Flavored Pudding (made with skim milk), $^1/_2$ cup

SNACK
Frozen Seedless Green Grapes, 20 small or 12 large

This menu provides: 2 Milks, 3 Fats, 2 Fruits, 14 Vegetables, 5 Proteins, $5^1/_2$ Breads, 70 Optional Calories.

Per serving: 23 g Fat, 24 g Fiber.

**Serving (1 1/4 cups turkey mixture, 3/4 cup rice)
provides:** 1 Fat, 3 Vegetables, 3 Proteins, 1 3/4 Breads,
30 Optional Calories.

Per serving: 436 Calories, 6 g Total Fat,
1 g Saturated Fat, 66 mg Cholesterol,
440 mg Sodium, 58 g Total Carbohydrate,
4 g Dietary Fiber, 33 g Protein, 126 mg Calcium.

277
TURKEY MARENGO

Makes 4 servings

1 tablespoon olive oil
2 cups peeled small pearl onions
2 cups thinly sliced mushrooms
2 garlic cloves, minced
3 tablespoons all-purpose flour
2 teaspoons minced fresh thyme leaves, or 1/2 teaspoon dried
1/2 teaspoon salt
1/2 teaspoon freshly ground black pepper
15 ounces skinless boneless turkey breast, cut into 1" pieces
4 fluid ounces (1/2 cup) dry white wine
2 cups stewed tomatoes (no salt added), chopped
1/2 cup low-sodium chicken broth
10 small pitted black olives, thinly sliced
6 ounces long-grain rice
1/4 cup minced fresh flat-leaf parsley

1. Preheat oven to 375° F.

2. In large nonstick skillet, heat 2 teaspoons of the oil; add onions. Cook over medium-high heat, stirring frequently, 7 minutes, until onions are browned. With slotted spoon, transfer onions to shallow 1 1/2-quart casserole; set aside.

3. In same skillet, cook mushrooms and garlic, stirring frequently, 7 minutes, until mushrooms are golden brown; transfer to casserole with onions.

4. On sheet of wax paper or paper plate, combine flour, thyme, 1/4 teaspoon of the salt and the pepper; add turkey, turning to coat evenly.

5. In same skillet, heat remaining 1 teaspoon oil; add turkey, reserving any extra flour mixture. Cook over medium-high heat, stirring frequently, until turkey is browned on all sides; transfer to casserole with onions and mushrooms.

6. In same skillet, bring wine to a boil, scraping up any browned bits from bottom of pan. Stir in tomatoes, broth, olives, remaining 1/4 teaspoon salt and reserved flour mixture; cook, stirring frequently, 3 minutes, until mixture comes to a boil. Transfer to casserole with turkey and vegetables; stir to combine. Bake 30–35 minutes, until turkey is cooked through and mixture is bubbling.

7. Meanwhile, in medium saucepan, bring 2 cups water to a boil; add rice. Reduce heat to low; simmer, covered, 20 minutes, until rice is tender and all liquid is absorbed.

8. Line serving platter with rice. Top rice with turkey mixture; sprinkle with parsley.

278
POTATO AND TURKEY LYONNAISE

In the center of France lies Lyons—a city that's known for its excellent food. One popular dish from that region is Pommes de Terre Lyonnaise, *potatoes that have been sautéed with onions. Our version with turkey makes a tasty main meal.*

Makes 4 servings

1 pound 14 ounces boiling potatoes, pared and thinly sliced
$^3/_4$ teaspoon salt
2 tablespoons + 2 teaspoons reduced-calorie tub margarine
10 ounces skinless boneless turkey breast, cut into thin strips
2 cups slivered onions
2 teaspoons minced fresh rosemary leaves, or 1 teaspoon dried
$^1/_2$ teaspoon freshly ground black pepper
$^1/_4$ teaspoon granulated sugar
Fresh rosemary sprigs, to garnish

1. Place potatoes and $^1/_4$ teaspoon of the salt into large pot; add water to cover. Bring liquid to a boil; reduce heat to low. Simmer 5 minutes, until potatoes are just tender. Drain, discarding liquid; set potatoes aside.

2. In large nonstick skillet, melt 2 teaspoons of the margarine; add turkey and remaining $^1/_2$ teaspoon salt. Cook over medium-high heat, stirring constantly, 4 minutes, until turkey is no longer pink. With slotted spoon, remove turkey from skillet; set aside.

3. In same skillet, melt remaining 2 tablespoons margarine; add onions, minced rosemary, pepper and sugar. Cook over medium-high heat, stirring frequently, 5 minutes, until onions are softened. Add cooked potatoes; cook, stirring gently, 5 minutes, until potatoes are browned and very tender.

4. Return turkey to skillet; cook, stirring frequently, 2 minutes, until heated through. Serve garnished with rosemary sprigs.

Serving (2 cups) provides: 1 Fat, 1 Vegetable, 2 Proteins, $1^1/_2$ Breads.

Per serving: 313 Calories, 5 g Total Fat, 1 g Saturated Fat, 44 mg Cholesterol, 463 mg Sodium, 46 g Total Carbohydrate, 5 g Dietary Fiber, 23 g Protein, 45 mg Calcium.

BREAKFAST
Grapefruit, $^1/_2$ medium
Vegetable Scramble (Spray small nonstick skillet with nonstick cooking spray; heat. Add $^1/_4$ cup *each* chopped onion and red bell pepper; cook over medium-high heat, stirring frequently, 5 minutes, until vegetables are softened. Add $^1/_4$ cup egg substitute; cook, stirring frequently, until set.)
Reduced-Calorie Whole-Wheat Bread, 2 slices, toasted, with 2 teaspoons reduced-calorie tub margarine
Skim Milk, $^1/_2$ cup
Coffee or Tea (optional)

LIGHT MEAL
Chilled Cooked Shrimp, 4 ounces, with 2 tablespoons cocktail sauce and 1 lemon wedge
Macaroni-Vegetable Salad (In medium bowl, combine 1 cup chilled cooked whole-wheat macaroni shells, $^1/_2$ cup *each* diced red roasted bell pepper and cucumber, $^1/_4$ cup sliced scallions and 1 tablespoon fat-free Italian dressing.)
Broccoli and Cauliflower Florets, 1 cup *each*
Breadsticks, 2 long
Aspartame-Sweetened Lemon Nonfat Yogurt, 1 cup
Unsweetened Cranberry-Flavored Seltzer

MAIN MEAL
Potato and Turkey Lyonnaise, 1 serving (see recipe)
Steamed Asparagus, 6 spears
Steamed Baby Carrots, 1 cup
Italian Spinach Salad (In medium bowl, combine 2 cups torn spinach leaves, $^1/_2$ cup *each* sliced mushrooms and sliced red onion, 2 teaspoons imitation bacon bits and $1^1/_2$ teaspoons Italian dressing.)
Peach, 1 medium
Sparkling Mineral Water with Mint Sprig

SNACK
Vanilla Wafers, 3
Skim Milk, $^1/_2$ cup

This menu provides: 2 Milks, 3 Fats, 2 Fruits, $17^1/_2$ Vegetables, 5 Proteins, 6 Breads, 90 Optional Calories.

Per serving: 23 g Fat, 38 g Fiber.

This menu provides: 2 Milks, 3 Fats, 2 Fruits, 11 3/4 Vegetables, 5 Proteins, 5 Breads, 100 Optional Calories.

Per serving: 20 g Fat, 30 g Fiber.

*The zest of the lemon is the peel without any of the pith (white membrane). To remove zest from lemon, use a zester or the fine side of a vegetable grater; wrap lemon in plastic wrap and refrigerate for use at another time.

279

TURKEY SCALOPPINE WITH MUSHROOMS AND TOMATOES

In Italian, scaloppine *refers to a thin, tender slice of meat, often veal, which is usually coated with flour and quickly sauteed in a white wine sauce. Although we've substituted turkey for the veal, we've not compromised on the flavor.*

Makes 4 servings

2 tablespoons all-purpose flour
3/4 teaspoon salt
1/2 teaspoon freshly ground black pepper
15 ounces skinless boneless turkey breast, diagonally sliced into 3" pieces
1 tablespoon olive oil
2 cups sliced mushrooms
4 garlic cloves, minced
2 large plum tomatoes, thinly sliced
1/2 cup low-sodium chicken broth
2 fluid ounces (1/4 cup) dry white wine
1/2 teaspoon grated lemon zest*
2 tablespoons minced fresh flat-leaf parsley
1 large plum tomato, cut into 4 wedges

1. On sheet of wax paper or paper plate, combine flour, 1/2 teaspoon of the salt and the pepper; add turkey, turning to coat evenly.

2. In large nonstick skillet, heat 1 teaspoon of the oil; add mushrooms, garlic and remaining 1/4 teaspoon salt. Cook over medium-high heat, stirring frequently, 5 minutes, until mushrooms are tender. With slotted spoon, remove mushroom mixture from skillet; set aside.

3. In same skillet, heat 1 teaspoon of the remaining oil; add half of the turkey. Cook over medium-high heat, turning once, 4 minutes, until turkey is browned. Remove turkey from skillet; repeat, using remaining oil and turkey.

4. In same skillet, combine tomato slices, broth, wine, zest, cooked mushrooms and browned turkey; bring liquid to a boil. Cook, stirring constantly, 1–2 minutes, until turkey is cooked through and flavors are blended.

5. Transfer turkey mixture to serving platter; sprinkle with parsley. Serve with tomato wedges.

Serving (1 cup) provides: 3/4 Fat, 1 3/4 Vegetables, 3 Proteins, 30 Optional Calories.

Per serving: 198 Calories, 5 g Total Fat, 1 g Saturated Fat, 66 mg Cholesterol, 485 mg Sodium, 8 g Total Carbohydrate, 1 g Dietary Fiber, 28 g Protein, 30 mg Calcium.

280
TURKEY SAUSAGE, MUSHROOM AND PINEAPPLE KABOBS

Makes 4 servings

$^1/_3$ cup pineapple juice

1 tablespoon reduced-sodium soy sauce

2 teaspoons vegetable oil

Twelve 1-ounce cooked lean turkey breakfast sausages

16 medium mushroom caps

$^1/_2$ cup drained canned pineapple chunks (no sugar added)

8 medium scallions

1. Preheat outdoor barbecue grill according to manufacturer's directions, or preheat broiler and spray rack in broiler pan with nonstick cooking spray.

2. To prepare basting sauce, in small bowl, with wire whisk, combine juice, soy sauce and oil; set aside.

3. To prepare kabobs, cut sausages horizontally into halves. Alternating ingredients, onto each of 8 long metal skewers, thread sausage halves, mushroom caps and pineapple chunks. Brush evenly with one-third of the basting sauce; set remaining sauce aside.

4. Grill kabobs over hot coals or place onto prepared rack in broiler pan and broil 4" from heat, turning once and basting with remaining sauce, 6 minutes, until lightly browned. Serve with scallions.

Serving (2 kabobs, 2 scallions) provides: $^1/_4$ Fruit, $1^1/_4$ Vegetables, 3 Proteins, 35 Optional Calories.

Per serving: 217 Calories, 11 g Total Fat, 3 g Saturated Fat, 68 mg Cholesterol, 829 mg Sodium, 11 g Total Carbohydrate, 1 g Dietary Fiber, 15 g Protein, 80 mg Calcium.

BREAKFAST
Cantaloupe Chunks, $^3/_4$ cup
Cooked Cream of Wheat, $^1/_2$ cup
Reduced-Calorie Whole-Wheat Bread, 2 slices, toasted, with 2 teaspoons reduced-calorie tub margarine
Skim Milk, 1 cup
Coffee or Tea (optional)

LIGHT MEAL
Nonfat Cottage Cheese, $^1/_2$ cup, on 2 slices cinnamon-raisin bread, toasted
Zucchini Sticks, 1 cup
Cherry Tomatoes, 6
Orange, 1 small
Unsweetened Seltzer

MAIN MEAL
Turkey Sausage, Mushroom and Pineapple Kabobs, 1 serving (see recipe), on 1 cup tomato slices
Cooked Barley, $^1/_2$ cup, with $^1/_2$ cup cooked chopped onion
Shredded Iceberg Lettuce and Green Cabbage, 2 cups, with $^1/_2$ cup shredded carrot, 2 ounces drained cooked chick-peas and 1 tablespoon French dressing
Aspartame-Sweetened Raspberry Nonfat Yogurt, 1 cup
Iced Tea

SNACK
Pretzels, $^3/_4$ ounce
Diet Ginger Ale

This menu provides: 2 Milks, 3 Fats, 2 Fruits, $12^1/_4$ Vegetables, 5 Proteins, 6 Breads, 35 Optional Calories.

Per serving: 24 g Fat, 27 g Fiber.

281

GRILLED TURKEY CUTLETS WITH FRESH TOMATO SALSA

Turkey breast cutlets, individual portions of skinless boneless turkey breast, grill in minutes on the barbecue. Fresh tomato salsa makes the perfect serve-along.

Makes 4 servings

5 large plum tomatoes
¹/₂ cup finely chopped red onion
¹/₃ cup balsamic vinegar
2 tablespoons minced fresh basil, or 2 teaspoons dried
2 teaspoons olive or vegetable oil
1 teaspoon Dijon-style mustard
³/₄ teaspoon salt
¹/₂ teaspoon freshly ground black pepper
¹/₂ teaspoon granulated sugar
Four 4-ounce skinless boneless turkey breast cutlets
Fresh basil sprigs, to garnish

1. Preheat outdoor barbecue grill according to manufacturer's directions, or preheat broiler and spray rack in broiler pan with nonstick cooking spray.

2. In medium bowl, combine tomatoes and onion.

3. In small bowl, with wire whisk, combine vinegar, minced basil, oil, mustard, salt, pepper and sugar, blending until sugar is dissolved. Pour half the vinegar mixture over tomato mixture; toss to coat. Refrigerate tomato mixture, covered, tossing occasionally, until chilled.

4. Brush turkey evenly with some of the remaining vinegar mixture. Grill turkey over hot coals or place onto prepared rack in broiler pan and broil 4" from heat, turning once and brushing with remaining vinegar mixture, 4 minutes, until turkey is golden brown and cooked through and juices run clear when pierced with fork.

5. Arrange turkey on round serving platter in circular pattern; spoon tomato mixture into center of platter. Serve garnished with basil sprigs.

Serving (3 ounces turkey, ¹/₂ cup tomato mixture) provides: ¹/₄ Fat, 1¹/₂ Vegetables, 3 Proteins, 10 Optional Calories.

Per serving: 168 Calories, 3 g Total Fat, 1 g Saturated Fat, 66 mg Cholesterol, 503 mg Sodium, 7 g Total Carbohydrate, 1 g Dietary Fiber, 27 g Protein, 39 mg Calcium.

282
REST-OF-THE-TURKEY SOUP

Makes 4 servings

Broth:

One large turkey carcass, broken
  into 6–8 pieces
4$^1/_2$ cups low-sodium chicken broth
3 medium carrots, cut into
  1" pieces
2 medium celery stalks, cut into
  1" pieces
2 medium leeks, well washed and
  thinly sliced
1 large plum tomato, coarsely
  chopped
6 large garlic cloves, crushed
3 fresh thyme sprigs, or $^1/_2$ teaspoon dried thyme leaves
3 fresh flat-leaf parsley sprigs
2 bay leaves

Soup:

3 ounces Arborio or other short-
  grain rice
1 tablespoon + 1 teaspoon olive oil
2 cups thinly sliced shiitake mushrooms
2 cups diagonally sliced carrots
4 garlic cloves, minced
2 cups coarsely chopped Swiss
  chard, escarole or spinach leaves
$^1/_2$ cup thawed frozen corn kernels
12 ounces skinless boneless cooked
  turkey breast, cut into bite-size
  pieces
$^1/_4$ cup minced fresh flat-leaf
  parsley
$^1/_2$ teaspoon freshly ground black
  pepper
$^1/_4$ teaspoon salt

1. To prepare broth, in large pot, combine turkey carcass, broth, carrots, celery, leeks, tomato, garlic, thyme, parsley, bay leaves and 4$^1/_2$ cups water; bring liquid to a boil. Reduce heat to low; simmer 1$^1/_2$–2 hours, until liquid is reduced in volume by about one-third.

2. Line colander with cheesecloth; place over large bowl. Pour broth through cheesecloth, pressing with back of wooden spoon to extract as much liquid as possible. Reserve liquid; discard solids.

3. Refrigerate liquid, covered, until fat congeals on top. Remove and discard congealed fat.

4. To prepare soup, in same pot, combine rice and 6 cups of the reserved broth.* Bring liquid to a boil; reduce heat to low. Simmer, covered, 20 minutes, until rice is tender. Remove from heat; keep warm.

5. Meanwhile, in large nonstick skillet, heat oil; add mushrooms, carrots and garlic. Cook over medium-high heat, stirring frequently, 5 minutes, until vegetables are tender. Add Swiss chard and corn; cook, stirring constantly, 3 minutes, until chard is wilted.

6. Add turkey, parsley, pepper, salt and vegetable mixture to rice mixture; cook until heated through.

Serving (2 cups) provides: 1 Fat, 3 Vegetables,
3 Proteins, 1 Bread, 30 Optional Calories.

Per serving: 334 Calories, 9 g Total Fat,
2 g Saturated Fat, 71 mg Cholesterol,
381 mg Sodium, 36 g Total Carbohydrate,
4 g Dietary Fiber, 34 g Protein, 89 mg Calcium.

*Reserve remaining liquid to use in recipes calling for
low-sodium chicken or turkey broth.*

283

WARM SPINACH AND SMOKED TURKEY SALAD

*Here's a delicious way to "eat your spinach"! Traditional recipes are
loaded with oil; use orange juice to replace some of the oil and you'll
cut back the fat—but not the flavor!*

Makes 4 servings

8 cups packed spinach leaves, rinsed well, dried and
    torn into bite-size pieces
8 ounces skinless boneless smoked turkey breast, cut into
    bite-size pieces
2 cups thinly sliced mushrooms
$^1/_3$ cup orange juice
2 tablespoons fresh lemon juice
2 tablespoons cider vinegar
$^1/_4$ teaspoon salt
$^1/_4$ teaspoon freshly ground black pepper
$^1/_4$ teaspoon granulated sugar
2 teaspoons olive or vegetable oil
2 cups thinly sliced red onions, separated into rings
1$^1/_2$ ounces feta cheese, finely crumbled
2 tablespoons imitation bacon bits

1. In large bowl, combine spinach, turkey and mushrooms; set aside.

2. In small bowl, with wire whisk, combine orange and lemon juices,
vinegar, salt, pepper and sugar, blending until sugar is dissolved; set aside.

3. In small saucepan, heat oil; add onions. Cook over medium-high heat,
stirring frequently, 5 minutes, until softened. Stir in juice mixture; cook,
stirring constantly, until heated through.

4. Pour juice mixture over spinach mixture; toss to coat. Sprinkle evenly
with cheese and bacon bits; serve immediately.

Serving (2 cups) provides: $^1/_2$ Fat, 6 Vegetables, 2 Proteins, 25 Optional
Calories.

Per serving: 208 Calories, 7 g Total Fat, 3 g Saturated Fat, 29 mg Cholesterol,
931 mg Sodium, 20 g Total Carbohydrate, 6 g Dietary Fiber, 19 g Protein,
252 mg Calcium.

284

TURKEY-FRUIT SALAD WITH POPPY SEED DRESSING

For a salad that will suit your taste, use your favorite fresh fruits in season. To help keep the fat content down, we've pureed some of the fruit into the dressing.

Makes 4 servings

1 medium peach, pared, pitted and quartered
$^1/_3$ cup white grape juice
$^1/_3$ cup cider vinegar
2 tablespoons granulated sugar
2 tablespoons chopped red onion
1 tablespoon poppy seeds
$^3/_4$ teaspoon dry mustard
1 tablespoon + 1 teaspoon vegetable oil
12 ounces skinless boneless cooked turkey breast, cut into bite-size pieces
1 medium peach, pared, pitted and thinly sliced
12 large cherries, halved and pitted
1 cup cantaloupe chunks
1 cup watermelon chunks
1 medium kiwi fruit, pared and thinly sliced
1 small orange, peeled and sectioned
Fresh mint sprigs, to garnish

1. To prepare dressing, in food processor, combine peach quarters, juice, vinegar, sugar, onion, poppy seeds and mustard; purée until smooth. With motor running, slowly pour oil through feed tube; process 1 minute, until slightly thickened.

2. To prepare salad, arrange turkey, peach slices, cherries, cantaloupe, watermelon, kiwi fruit and orange on round serving platter; drizzle evenly with dressing. Serve garnished with mint.

Serving ($2^1/_4$ cups) provides: 1 Fat, 2 Fruits, 3 Proteins, 35 Optional Calories.

Per serving: 308 Calories, 7 g Total Fat, 1 g Saturated Fat, 71 mg Cholesterol, 53 mg Sodium, 36 g Total Carbohydrate, 3 g Dietary Fiber, 28 g Protein, 79 mg Calcium.

BREAKFAST
Puffed Rice Cereal, $^3/_4$ ounce
Skim Milk, $^3/_4$ cup
Reduced-Calorie Multi-Grain Bread, 2 slices, with 2 teaspoons reduced-calorie tub margarine
Coffee or Tea (optional)

LIGHT MEAL
Turkey Ham Sandwich (Layer 2 ounces lean cooked turkey ham, sliced, 2 Romaine lettuce leaves, $^1/_4$ cup cucumber slices, 2 tomato slices, 2 red onion slices and 2 teaspoons prepared mustard between 2 slices reduced-calorie rye bread.)
Carrot and Celery Sticks, 1 cup *each*
Sugar-Free Vanilla Nonfat Frozen Yogurt, 4 fluid ounces
Iced Tea

MAIN MEAL
Turkey-Fruit Salad with Poppy Seed Dressing, 1 serving (see recipe)
Chilled Steamed Whole Green Beans and Carrot Sticks, 1 cup *each*
Roll, 1 ounce, with 2 teaspoons reduced-calorie tub margarine
Aspartame-Sweetened Strawberry Nonfat Yogurt, 1 cup
Sparkling Mineral Water

SNACK
Buttery Popcorn (Lightly spray 3 cups hot-air popped plain popcorn with nonstick cooking spray. Sprinkle popcorn with $^1/_4$ teaspoon butter-flavor granules; toss to coat evenly.)

This menu provides: 2 Milks, 3 Fats, 2 Fruits, $9^1/_2$ Vegetables, 5 Proteins, 5 Breads, 85 Optional Calories.

Per serving: 28 g Fat, 25 g Fiber.

BREAKFAST
Banana, $^1/_2$ medium, sliced
Bite-Size Shredded Wheat Cereal, $^3/_4$ ounce
Skim Milk, 1 cup
Coffee or Tea (optional)

LIGHT MEAL
Broiled Flounder, 4 ounces, with lemon wedge
Baked Potato, 6 ounces, with 2 teaspoons reduced-calorie tub margarine
Steamed Sliced Carrots, 1 cup
Torn Iceberg and Red Leaf Lettuce Leaves, 2 cups, with $^1/_2$ cup sliced radishes and 1 tablespoon fat-free Italian dressing
Sugar-Free Chocolate Nonfat Frozen Yogurt, 4 fluid ounces
Sparkling Mineral Water

MAIN MEAL
Smoked Turkey Club Salad, 1 serving (see recipe)
Cooked Mashed Acorn Squash, 1 cup, with 1 teaspoon *each* reduced-calorie tub margarine and firmly packed light or dark brown sugar
Steamed Broccoli Florets, 1 cup, with 1 teaspoon reduced-calorie tub margarine
Crispbreads, $^3/_4$ ounce
Raspberries, $^3/_4$ cup
Iced Herbal Tea

SNACK
Oat-Bran Pretzels, $^3/_4$ ounce
Skim Milk, $^3/_4$ cup

This menu provides: 2 Milks, 3 Fats, 2 Fruits, $16^3/_4$ Vegetables, 5 Proteins, 6 Breads, 105 Optional Calories.

Per serving: 23 g Fat, 37 g Fiber.

285
SMOKED TURKEY CLUB SALAD

We've transformed the club sandwich into a main-dish salad with strips of smoked turkey and Jarlsberg cheese, wedges of ripe plum tomatoes and Romaine lettuce leaves. For a finishing touch, we've topped it with crumbled turkey bacon and some croutons, then drizzled it with a creamy scallion dressing.

Makes 4 servings

Dressing:
1 cup coarsely chopped roasted red bell peppers
10 cilantro leaves
8 medium scallions, quartered
$^1/_4$ cup nonfat sour cream
2 tablespoons rice wine vinegar
1 tablespoon + 1 teaspoon reduced-calorie mayonnaise
$^1/_4$ teaspoon granulated sugar

Salad:
8 cups torn Romaine lettuce leaves
2 cups shredded red cabbage
8 ounces skinless boneless smoked turkey breast, julienned
6 large plum tomatoes, cut lengthwise into 6 wedges each
1 medium cucumber, cut into 2 × $^1/_2$" strips
3 ounces light Jarlsberg cheese, julienned
1 cup packaged croutons
3 slices crisp-cooked lean turkey bacon (30 calories per slice), crumbled

1. To prepare dressing, in food processor, combine bell peppers, cilantro, scallions, sour cream, vinegar, mayonnaise and sugar; purée until smooth. Transfer dressing to bowl; refrigerate, covered, until chilled.

2. To prepare salad, in large bowl, combine lettuce, cabbage and $^1/_3$ cup of the dressing; toss to coat thoroughly.

3. Transfer lettuce mixture to large oval serving platter; top with turkey, tomatoes, cucumber and cheese, decoratively arranged in diagonal strips. Top evenly with croutons, then remaining dressing; sprinkle evenly with bacon.

Serving ($2^1/_2$ cups) provides: 1 Fat, $7^3/_4$ Vegetables, 3 Proteins, $^1/_2$ Bread, 35 Optional Calories.

Per serving: 267 Calories, 9 g Total Fat, 4 g Saturated Fat, 44 mg Cholesterol, 862 mg Sodium, 21 g Total Carbohydrate, 5 g Dietary Fiber, 25 g Protein, 108 mg Calcium.

286
Smoked Turkey Waldorf Salad

When the Waldorf salad was created in 1896, walnuts were not an ingredient. Today, they're a "must." Add smoked turkey, and you have a main-dish salad.

Makes 4 servings

4 small red Delicious apples, cored, quartered and thinly sliced lengthwise
$^1/_3$ cup + 2 teaspoons fresh lemon juice
$^1/_2$ cup nonfat sour cream
3 tablespoons half-and-half
2 tablespoons + 2 teaspoons reduced-calorie mayonnaise
$^1/_2$ teaspoon freshly ground black pepper
9 ounces skinless boneless smoked turkey breast, cut into $^1/_2$" cubes
1 cup coarsely chopped celery
4 cups torn curly leaf lettuce (bite-size pieces)
1 ounce shelled walnuts, finely chopped and toasted*

1. In medium bowl, combine apples and $^1/_4$ cup of the juice, tossing to coat. Drain, discarding liquid; set aside.

2. In large bowl, with wire whisk, combine sour cream, half-and-half, mayonnaise, pepper and remaining 2 tablespoons juice. Add turkey, celery and apples; toss to coat.

3. Line serving platter with lettuce. Mound turkey mixture in center of lettuce-lined platter; sprinkle evenly with walnuts.

Serving (2 cups) provides: $1^1/_2$ Fats, 1 Fruit, $2^1/_2$ Vegetables, $2^1/_2$ Proteins, 35 Optional Calories.

Per serving: 265 Calories, 11 g Total Fat, 3 g Saturated Fat, 34 mg Cholesterol, 709 mg Sodium, 26 g Total Carbohydrate, 4 g Dietary Fiber, 18 g Protein, 120 mg Calcium.

*To toast walnuts, in a small nonstick skillet, cook walnuts over low heat, stirring constantly, until golden brown; immediately transfer to heat-resistant plate to cool.

BREAKFAST
Mango, $^1/_4$ small
Raisin Bran Cereal, $1^1/_2$ ounces
Skim Milk, 1 cup
Coffee or Tea (optional)

LIGHT MEAL
Broiled Sole, 4 ounces, with lemon wedge
Baked Sweet Potato, 3 ounces, with 1 teaspoon *each* reduced-calorie tub margarine and maple syrup
Steamed Whole Green Beans, 1 cup
Tossed Green Salad, 2 cups, with 1 tablespoon fat-free French dressing
Reduced-Calorie Vanilla-Flavored Pudding (made with skim milk), $^1/_2$ cup
Diet Ginger Ale

MAIN MEAL
Smoked Turkey Waldorf Salad, 1 serving (see recipe)
Chilled Cooked Asparagus, 6 spears
French Bread, 1 slice (1 ounce), with 2 teaspoons reduced-calorie tub margarine
Strawberries, $^1/_2$ cup
Iced Tea

SNACK
Graham Crackers, 3 ($2^1/_2$" squares)
Skim Milk, $^1/_2$ cup

This menu provides: 2 Milks, 3 Fats, 2 Fruits, $9^1/_2$ Vegetables, $4^1/_2$ Proteins, 5 Breads, 110 Optional Calories.

Per serving: 25 g Fat, 20 g Fiber.

SUCCOTASH WITH CHEESE

*Usually a side dish, we've dressed up this hearty vegetable mélange
and made it a meatless entrée.*

Makes 4 servings

1 tablespoon + 1 teaspoon stick margarine
$^1/_2$ cup minced onion
2 garlic cloves, minced
2 cups thawed frozen baby green lima beans
$^1/_2$ teaspoon dried marjoram leaves
$^1/_2$ teaspoon salt
$1^1/_2$ cups stewed tomatoes (no salt added), chopped
2 cups thawed frozen corn kernels
3 ounces reduced-fat cheddar cheese, grated
2 tablespoons minced fresh flat-leaf parsley

1. In large saucepan, melt margarine; add onion and garlic. Cook over medium-high heat, stirring frequently, 5 minutes, until onion is softened.

2. Add lima beans, marjoram, salt and $^1/_4$ cup water to onion mixture; bring liquid to a boil. Reduce to low; simmer, covered, 10 minutes, until lima beans are softened. Stir in tomatoes; cook, uncovered, stirring frequently, 7 minutes, until mixture is slightly thickened. Stir in corn, cheese and parsley; cook, stirring constantly, until cheese is melted and mixture is heated through.

Serving (1 cup) provides: 1 Fat, 1 Vegetable, 1 Protein, 2 Breads.

Per serving: 310 Calories, 9 g Total Fat, 3 g Saturated Fat, 15 mg Cholesterol, 546 mg Sodium, 46 g Total Carbohydrate, 8 g Dietary Fiber, 17 g Protein, 265 mg Calcium.

MEATLESS

ZUCCHINI HASH WITH YOGURT SAUCE

Makes 4 servings

1 1/2 cups plain nonfat yogurt

1/2 cup minced fresh mint leaves

1/4 cup minced scallions

2 cups shredded zucchini

5 ounces all-purpose potato, pared and shredded

3 ounces feta cheese, crumbled

1/2 cup shredded carrot

1/2 cup grated onion

3 tablespoons all-purpose flour

1 egg white

1/2 teaspoon salt

1/2 teaspoon dried oregano leaves

1 tablespoon + 1 teaspoon olive oil

1. In small bowl, combine yogurt, 1/3 cup of the mint and the scallions; refrigerate, covered, until chilled.

2. Meanwhile, in large bowl, combine zucchini, potato, cheese, carrot, onion, flour, egg white, salt, oregano and remaining mint.

3. In large nonstick skillet, heat oil; spread evenly to coat bottom of skillet. Add zucchini mixture, pressing with back of wooden spoon to form a large pancake. Cook over medium-low heat 15 minutes, until bottom of pancake is crusty; with spatula, turn pancake over. Cook 10 minutes longer, until golden brown.

4. Divide zucchini pancake evenly among 4 plates; serve each portion with an equal amount of yogurt mixture.

Serving (3/4 cup zucchini mixture, 6 tablespoons yogurt mixture) provides:
1/2 Milk, 1 Fat, 1 3/4 Vegetables, 1 Protein, 1/2 Bread, 5 Optional Calories.

Per serving: 223 Calories, 9 g Total Fat, 4 g Saturated Fat, 21 mg Cholesterol, 600 mg Sodium, 24 g Total Carbohydrate, 2 g Dietary Fiber, 11 g Protein, 309 mg Calcium.

BREAKFAST

Orange, 1 small

Fat-Free Muffin, 2 ounces, with 2 teaspoons reduced-calorie tub margarine

Skim Milk, 1/2 cup

Coffee or Tea (optional)

LIGHT MEAL

Zucchini Hash with Yogurt Sauce, 1 serving (see recipe)

Celery and Carrot Sticks, 1 cup *each*

Italian Bread, 1 slice (1 ounce)

Cantaloupe Balls, 3/4 cup

Iced Tea

MAIN MEAL

Bean and Cheese Quesadillas with Chunky Salsa (Preheat oven to 350° F. Top each of two 6" flour tortillas with 3/4 ounce reduced-fat cheddar cheese, grated, and 1 ounce drained cooked pinto beans; place onto nonstick baking sheet. Bake until cheese is melted. Serve with Chunky Salsa, 1/2 cup.)

Steamed Broccoli, 4 spears, with 2 teaspoons reduced-calorie tub margarine

Fruit Ice, 1/2 cup

Decaffeinated Coffee or Tea

SNACK

Reduced-Calorie Strawberry Dairy Shake, 1 serving

This menu provides: 2 Milks, 3 Fats, 2 Fruits, 9 3/4 Vegetables, 4 Proteins, 4 1/2 Breads, 175 Optional Calories.

Per serving: 32 g Fat, 20 g Fiber.

289
THAI CURRIED VEGETABLES

Makes 4 servings

3 tablespoons shredded coconut
$^1/_4$ cup boiling water
2 teaspoons peanut oil
1 cup diced onions
2 garlic cloves, minced
2 cups pared acorn squash chunks (2" chunks)
3 ounces lentils
1 teaspoon mild or hot curry powder
$^1/_2$ teaspoon cinnamon
Pinch ground nutmeg

$1^1/_2$ cups stewed tomatoes (no salt added), chopped
1 tablespoon Thai or Vietnamese fish sauce*
1 teaspoon firmly packed light or dark brown sugar
$^1/_4$ teaspoon salt
1 cup drained canned baby corn
$^1/_4$ cup minced fresh cilantro
$^1/_4$ cup minced fresh basil
$^1/_4$ cup minced fresh mint leaves
2 tablespoons fresh lime juice

1. In small bowl, combine coconut and boiling water; set aside.

2. In large nonstick skillet, heat oil; add onions and garlic. Cook over medium-high heat, stirring frequently, 5 minutes, until onions are softened. Add squash, lentils, curry powder, cinnamon and nutmeg; stir to combine.

3. Add tomatoes, fish sauce, brown sugar, salt and $1^1/_4$ cups water to lentil mixture; bring liquid to a boil. Reduce heat to low; simmer, covered, 40 minutes, until lentils are softened.

4. Place fine sieve over small bowl; pour reserved coconut mixture through sieve, pushing with back of wooden spoon to extract as much liquid as possible. Reserve liquid; discard solids.

5. Stir coconut liquid into lentil mixture; add corn, cilantro, basil, mint and juice. Cook, stirring frequently, 5 minutes, until mixture is heated through and flavors are blended.

Serving ($1^1/_4$ cups) provides: $^1/_2$ Fat, $1^1/_4$ Vegetables, 1 Protein, 1 Bread, 25 Optional Calories.

Per serving: 210 Calories, 5 g Total Fat, 2 g Saturated Fat, 0 mg Cholesterol, 323 mg Sodium, 36 g Total Carbohydrate, 9 g Dietary Fiber, 10 g Protein, 224 mg Calcium.

Thai or Vietnamese fish sauce is available in most Asian groceries.

290
STUFFED ONIONS

Makes 4 servings

Four 10-ounce whole onions
1 tablespoon + 1 teaspoon olive oil
3 garlic cloves, minced
2 ounces long-grain rice
$^1/_2$ teaspoon salt
$^1/_2$ teaspoon dried oregano leaves
$^1/_2$ teaspoon grated lemon zest*
$^1/_4$ teaspoon freshly ground black pepper
2 cups chopped tomatoes
3 ounces freshly grated Parmesan cheese

1. Preheat oven to 400° F.

2. Cut a thin slice from stem end of each onion so it stands upright. With paring knife, cut out a wide, cone-shaped wedge from the top of each onion, leaving $^1/_4$" shell; chop wedges.

3. In large pot of boiling water, cook onion shells 8 minutes, until softened; with slotted spoon, transfer shells to paper towels, cut-side down, to drain.

4. In medium saucepan, heat 2 teaspoons of the oil; add $1^1/_2$ cups of the chopped onions and the garlic. Cook over medium-high heat, stirring frequently, 7 minutes, until onions are golden brown. Add rice; stir to coat. Stir in salt, oregano, zest, pepper and $1^1/_4$ cups water. Bring liquid to a boil. Reduce heat to low; simmer, covered, 20 minutes, until rice is tender and all liquid is absorbed.

5. Meanwhile, in large nonstick skillet, heat remaining 2 teaspoons oil; add remaining chopped onions. Cook over medium-high heat, stirring frequently, 5 minutes, until softened. Add tomatoes; bring sauce mixture just to a boil.

6. Stand onion shells upright in 9" square baking dish. Stir Parmesan cheese into rice mixture; spoon one-fourth of the mixture into each onion shell. Spoon sauce around stuffed onions; bake, covered, 15 minutes, until heated through. Uncover; bake 5 minutes longer, until rice mixture is golden brown.

Serving (1 stuffed onion, $^1/_2$ cup sauce) provides: 1 Fat, $4^1/_4$ Vegetables, 1 Protein, $^1/_2$ Bread.

Per serving: 319 Calories, 12 g Total Fat, 5 g Saturated Fat, 17 mg Cholesterol, 687 mg Sodium, 42 g Total Carbohydrate, 6 g Dietary Fiber, 14 g Protein, 367 mg Calcium.

The zest of the lemon is the peel without any of the pith (white membrane). To remove zest from lemon, use a zester or the fine side of a vegetable grater; wrap lemon in plastic wrap and refrigerate for use at another time.

BREAKFAST
Cooked Cream of Wheat, $^1/_2$ cup, with 2 tablespoons dried cranberries and 1 teaspoon sunflower seeds
Skim Milk, $^3/_4$ cup
Coffee or Tea (optional)

LIGHT MEAL
Stuffed Onions, 1 serving (see recipe)
Cauliflower and Sun-Dried Tomato Salad (In small bowl, soak 2 sun-dried tomato halves [not packed in oil] in warm water until softened. Drain; discard liquid. Chop tomatoes; return to bowl. Add 1 cup cauliflower florets, $^1/_2$ cup diced carrot and 1 teaspoon *each* olive oil and fresh lemon juice; toss to combine.)
Crispbreads, $^3/_4$ ounce
Unsweetened Mandarin Orange–Flavored Seltzer

MAIN MEAL
Pasta Chick-Pea Salad (In medium bowl, combine 1 cup cooked rotelle pasta, $^1/_2$ cup *each* broccoli florets, red bell pepper strips and sliced mushrooms, 2 ounces drained cooked chick-peas, $1^1/_2$ ounces nonfat mozzarella cheese, diced, 10 small pitted black olives and 2 tablespoons fat-free Italian dressing.)
Italian Bread, 1 slice (1 ounce)
Strawberry Sundae 'n' Crème (Scoop 4 fluid ounces strawberry frozen yogurt into small bowl; top with 1 teaspoon chocolate syrup, then 1 tablespoon thawed frozen light whipped topping [8 calories per tablespoon].)
Decaffeinated Cappuccino, made with skim milk, 5 fluid ounces

SNACK
Baked Apple (Preheat oven to 350° F. Pare 1 small apple halfway down from stem end; core and place into small baking dish. Sprinkle apple with 1 teaspoon granulated sugar and $^1/_4$ teaspoon cinnamon; add $^1/_4$" water to pan. Bake, covered, 30 minutes, until softened.)
Skim Milk, $^1/_2$ cup

This menu provides: 2 Milks, 3 Fats, 2 Fruits, $11^1/_4$ Vegetables, 3 Proteins, $5^1/_2$ Breads, 115 Optional Calories.

Per serving: 27 g Fat, 28 g Fiber.

291
KASHA AND ONIONS WITH BOW-TIE NOODLES

Makes 4 servings

$4^1/_2$ ounces bow-tie noodles
2 teaspoons olive oil
1 cup chopped onions
2 garlic cloves, minced
2 cups thickly sliced white mushrooms
2 cups thickly sliced shiitake mushrooms
$1^1/_2$ cups shredded carrots
$^3/_4$ teaspoon salt
$^1/_2$ teaspoon ground dried sage leaves
$^1/_4$ teaspoon freshly ground black pepper
4 ounces kasha (buckwheat groats)
1 egg
$2^1/_4$ ounces reduced-fat cheddar cheese, grated
$^1/_2$ cup minced fresh flat-leaf parsley

1. In large pot of boiling water, cook noodles 5–6 minutes, until tender. Drain, discarding liquid; set aside.

2. Meanwhile, in large nonstick skillet, heat oil; add onions and garlic. Cook over medium-high heat, stirring frequently, 7 minutes, until onions are golden brown. Add white and shiitake mushrooms; cook, stirring frequently, 5 minutes, until mushrooms are softened. Stir in carrots, salt, sage and pepper; cook, stirring frequently, 3 minutes, until carrots are just softened.

3. In small bowl, combine kasha and egg, stirring until kasha is well coated.

4. Spray small nonstick skillet with nonstick cooking spray; heat. Add kasha mixture; cook over medium-high heat, stirring constantly, 4 minutes, until mixture is dry.

5. Stir kasha mixture into vegetable mixture. Add $1^1/_2$ cups water; bring liquid to a boil. Reduce heat to low; simmer, covered, 15 minutes, until liquid is absorbed and kasha is tender. Add cheese, parsley and cooked noodles; cook, tossing constantly, until cheese is melted and mixture is heated through.

Serving ($1^1/_2$ cups) provides: $^1/_2$ Fat, $3^1/_4$ Vegetables, 1 Protein, $2^1/_2$ Breads.

Per serving: 361 Calories, 9 g Total Fat, 3 g Saturated Fat, 95 mg Cholesterol, 583 mg Sodium, 56 g Total Carbohydrate, 8 g Dietary Fiber, 17 g Protein, 201 mg Calcium.

PENNE WITH EGGPLANT AND TOMATOES

Makes 4 servings

6 ounces penne pasta
2 teaspoons olive oil
$^1/_2$ cup chopped onion
3 garlic cloves, minced
3 cups diced eggplant
$1^1/_2$ cups canned crushed tomatoes (no salt added)
2 teaspoons red wine vinegar
$^1/_2$ teaspoon dried rosemary leaves, crumbled
$^1/_2$ teaspoon salt
$^1/_2$ teaspoon granulated sugar
$^1/_4$ teaspoon crushed red pepper flakes
3 ounces freshly grated Parmesan cheese

1. In large pot of boiling water, cook penne 8–10 minutes, until tender. Drain, discarding liquid; set aside.

2. Meanwhile, in large nonstick skillet, heat oil; add onion and garlic. Cook over medium-high heat, stirring frequently, 5 minutes, until onion is softened. Add eggplant; toss to coat. Add $^1/_2$ cup water; bring liquid to a boil. Reduce heat to low; simmer, covered, 7 minutes, until eggplant is softened.

3. Stir tomatoes, vinegar, rosemary, salt, sugar and red pepper flakes into eggplant mixture; bring mixture to a boil. Reduce heat to low; simmer, uncovered, stirring occasionally, 5 minutes, until slightly thickened.

4. Add cheese to tomato mixture; stir to combine. Add cooked penne; cook, stirring frequently, until heated through.

Serving ($1^1/_2$ cups) provides: $^1/_2$ Fat, $2^1/_2$ Vegetables, 1 Protein, 2 Breads.

Per serving: 323 Calories, 10 g Total Fat, 4 g Saturated Fat, 17 mg Cholesterol, 823 mg Sodium, 43 g Total Carbohydrate, 3 g Dietary Fiber, 16 g Protein, 358 mg Calcium.

BREAKFAST

Yogurt and Melon (In small bowl, combine $^1/_2$ cup *each* cantaloupe and honeydew melon balls. Top melon with $^3/_4$ cup plain nonfat yogurt; drizzle with 1 teaspoon honey.)
English Muffin, $^1/_2$ (1 ounce), toasted, with 1 teaspoon reduced-calorie tub margarine
Coffee or Tea (optional)

LIGHT MEAL

Penne with Eggplant and Tomatoes, 1 serving (see recipe)
Romaine and Bibb Lettuce Salad, 2 cups, with 1 tablespoon fat-free Italian dressing
Sugar-Free Grape-Flavored Gelatin, $^1/_2$ cup, with 1 tablespoon thawed frozen light whipped topping (8 calories per tablespoon)
Iced Tea

MAIN MEAL

Red Bean Enchiladas (Preheat oven to 350° F. Spray small baking dish with nonstick cooking spray. Place two 6" corn tortillas on work surface; arrange 1 ounce drained cooked red beans, $^3/_4$ ounce reduced-fat Monterey Jack cheese, grated, and 2 tablespoons sliced scallions along center of each tortilla. Fold sides of tortillas over filling to enclose; place, seam-side down, into prepared baking dish. Spread tortillas evenly with $^1/_2$ cup salsa; bake 10–15 minutes, until bubbling and lightly browned.)
Cooked Brown Rice, $^1/_2$ cup, with 2 tablespoons drained canned chopped mild or hot green chiles and 2 teaspoons reduced-calorie tub margarine
Shredded Lettuce and Sliced Mushrooms Salad, 2 cups, with Sesame Vinaigrette (In small jar with tight-fitting lid or small bowl, combine 2 teaspoons red wine vinegar, 1 teaspoon vegetable oil and $^1/_2$ teaspoon sesame seeds, toasted; cover and shake well or, with wire whisk, blend until combined.)
Whole Strawberries, 1 cup
Non-Alcoholic Beer, 12 fluid ounces

SNACK

Reduced-Calorie Vanilla Dairy Shake, 1 serving

This menu provides: 2 Milks, 3 Fats, 2 Fruits, $13^1/_4$ Vegetables, 4 Proteins, 6 Breads, 100 Optional Calories.

Per serving: 35 g Fat, 20 g Fiber.

293
PENNE IN CREAMY GARLIC-CHEESE SAUCE

Makes 4 servings

8 garlic cloves, peeled
3 cups small broccoli florets
6 ounces penne pasta
2 cups evaporated skimmed milk
1 tablespoon + 1 teaspoon all-purpose flour
$1^1/_2$ ounces reduced-fat cheddar cheese, grated
$1^1/_2$ ounces freshly grated Parmesan cheese
$^1/_2$ teaspoon freshly ground black pepper
$^1/_4$ teaspoon salt

1. In large pot of boiling water, cook garlic 3 minutes, until softened. With slotted spoon, remove garlic from water. Mince garlic; set aside.

2. In same pot of boiling water, cook broccoli 3 minutes, until bright green and just softened. With slotted spoon, remove broccoli from water; set aside.

3. In same pot of boiling water, cook penne 8–10 minutes, until tender. Drain, discarding liquid; set aside.

4. Meanwhile, in large nonstick skillet, with wire whisk, combine milk and flour, blending until flour is dissolved. Cook over medium heat, stir-ring constantly with wire whisk, 4 minutes, until mixture is bubbling and thickened; stir in minced garlic.

5. Reduce heat to low. Add cheddar and Parmesan cheeses, pepper and salt to milk mixture; cook, stirring constantly, until cheeses are melted. Stir in cooked broccoli and penne; cook, stirring frequently, just until heated through.

Serving ($1^1/_2$ cups) provides: 1 Milk, $1^1/_2$ Vegetables, 1 Protein, 2 Breads, 10 Optional Calories.

Per serving: 384 Calories, 6 g Total Fat, 4 g Saturated Fat, 21 mg Cholesterol, 590 mg Sodium, 56 g Total Carbohydrate, 5 g Dietary Fiber, 27 g Protein, 673 mg Calcium.

294
FUSILLI WITH SUN-DRIED TOMATOES, RAISINS AND BROCCOLI RABE

Makes 4 servings

12 sun-dried tomato halves (not packed in oil)
$^1/_2$ cup golden raisins
$1^1/_2$ cups boiling water
$5^1/_2$ cups sliced broccoli rabe
6 ounces fusilli pasta
2 teaspoons olive oil
$^1/_2$ cup coarsely chopped onion
3 garlic cloves, minced
$^1/_2$ teaspoon salt
$^1/_4$ teaspoon freshly ground black pepper
$^1/_4$ teaspoon hot red pepper sauce
2 tablespoons + 2 teaspoons pignolia nuts (pine nuts)
$2^1/_4$ ounces freshly grated Parmesan cheese

1. Place tomatoes and raisins into small bowl; add the boiling water. Let stand 30 minutes, until softened; drain, reserving liquid. Coarsely chop tomatoes; set aside.

2. Meanwhile, in large pot of boiling water, cook broccoli rabe 3 minutes, until just softened. With slotted spoon, remove broccoli rabe from water; set aside.

3. In same pot of boiling water, cook fusilli 8–10 minutes, until tender. Drain, discarding liquid; set aside.

4. In large nonstick skillet, heat oil; add onion and garlic. Cook over medium-high heat, stirring frequently, 5 minutes, until onion is softened. Add salt, pepper, pepper sauce, cooked broccoli rabe, drained tomatoes and raisins and reserved soaking liquid; cook, stirring frequently, until flavors are blended. Add cooked fusilli; toss to combine. Add pignolia nuts and cheese; toss again.

Serving ($1^1/_2$ cups) provides: 1 Fat, 1 Fruit, $4^1/_2$ Vegetables, 1 Protein, 2 Breads.

Per serving: 398 Calories, 11 g Total Fat, 4 g Saturated Fat, 13 mg Cholesterol, 642 mg Sodium, 60 g Total Carbohydrate, 7 g Dietary Fiber, 19 g Protein, 325 mg Calcium.

BREAKFAST

Banana Yogurt (In small bowl, combine $^3/_4$ cup plain nonfat yogurt, $^1/_2$ medium banana, sliced and sugar substitute to equal 2 teaspoons sugar.)
Reduced-Calorie Sourdough Bread, 2 slices, toasted, with 2 teaspoons strawberry jam
Coffee or Tea (optional)

LIGHT MEAL

Fusilli with Sun-Dried Tomatoes, Raisins and Broccoli Rabe, 1 serving (see recipe)
Tossed Green Salad, 2 cups, with $^1/_2$ cup *each* red and green bell pepper strips and 1 tablespoon fat-free ranch dressing
Italian Bread, 1 slice (1 ounce), with 1 teaspoon reduced-calorie tub margarine
Unsweetened Berry-Flavored Seltzer

MAIN MEAL

Spinach-Cheese Omelet (Spray small nonstick skillet with nonstick cooking spray; heat. Add $^1/_4$ cup chopped onion and 1 garlic clove, minced; cook over medium-high heat, stirring frequently, 5 minutes, until onion is softened. Pour $^1/_2$ cup egg substitute into skillet, tilting to cover bottom of pan. Cook over medium-high heat until underside is set, lifting edges with spatula to let uncooked egg flow underneath. Top one side of omelet with $^1/_2$ cup cooked chopped spinach; sprinkle spinach with $^3/_4$ ounce reduced-fat Monterey Jack cheese, grated. With spatula, fold other side of omelet over cheese to enclose.)
Broccoli Florets and Whole Mushrooms, 1 cup *each*
Cucumber Slices and Alfalfa Sprout Salad, 2 cups, with Raspberry Vinaigrette (In small jar with tight-fitting lid or small bowl, combine 1 tablespoon raspberry vinegar and 1 teaspoon olive oil; cover and shake well or, with wire whisk, blend until combined.)
Roll, 1 ounce, with 1 teaspoon reduced-calorie tub margarine
Pudding Parfait (In stemmed glass, layer $^1/_2$ cup *each* reduced-calorie chocolate-flavored and vanilla-flavored pudding [made with skim milk].)
Decaffeinated Coffee or Tea

SNACK

Graham Crackers, 3 ($2^1/_2$" squares)

This menu provides: 2 Milks, 3 Fats, 2 Fruits, 20 Vegetables, 4 Proteins, 6 Breads, 130 Optional Calories.

Per serving: 34 g Fat, 30 g Fiber.

295
LINGUINE WITH ZUCCHINI, TOMATOES AND MINT

Makes 4 servings

6 ounces linguine

2 teaspoons olive oil

¹/₂ cup chopped onion

3 garlic cloves, minced

3 medium zucchini, quartered lengthwise, then thinly sliced

1¹/₂ cups canned crushed tomatoes

1 tablespoon balsamic vinegar

¹/₂ teaspoon salt

¹/₄ teaspoon granulated sugar

¹/₂ cup minced fresh mint leaves

3 ounces freshly grated Parmesan cheese

1. In large pot of boiling water, cook linguine 8–10 minutes, until tender. Drain, discarding liquid; set aside.

2. Meanwhile, in large nonstick skillet, heat oil; add onion and garlic. Cook over medium-high heat, stirring frequently, 5 minutes, until onion is softened. Add zucchini; cook, stirring frequently, 5 minutes, until softened.

3. Add tomatoes, vinegar, salt and sugar to vegetable mixture; cook, stirring frequently, 5 minutes, until mixture is slightly thickened. Stir in mint; cook, stirring frequently, 1 minute. Add cooked linguine; cook, tossing constantly, until heated through.

4. Divide linguine mixture among 4 plates; top each portion with one-fourth of the cheese.

Serving (1¹/₂ cups) provides: ¹/₂ Fat, 2¹/₂ Vegetables, 1 Protein, 2 Breads.

Per serving: 324 Calories, 10 g Total Fat, 5 g Saturated Fat, 17 mg Cholesterol, 824 mg Sodium, 43 g Total Carbohydrate, 3 g Dietary Fiber, 17 g Protein, 356 mg Calcium.

ASIAN NOODLES IN SATAY SAUCE

Traditionally made with udon noodles, this tasty dish works just as well with fettuccine, which is more readily available.

Makes 4 servings

6 ounces fettuccine

1¼ cups thinly sliced carrots

1¼ cups broccoli florets

1 cup thinly sliced mushrooms

1 cup halved snow peas

½ cup minced scallions

1 tablespoon minced pared fresh ginger root

3 garlic cloves, minced

¼ cup smooth or crunchy peanut butter

3 tablespoons reduced-sodium soy sauce

¼ cup fresh lime juice

1 tablespoon honey

1 cup diced red bell pepper

1. In large pot of boiling water, cook fettuccine 8–10 minutes, until tender. Drain, discarding liquid; set aside.

2. Meanwhile, in medium nonstick skillet, bring ¼ cup water to a boil. Add carrots, broccoli and mushrooms; return liquid to a boil. Reduce heat to low; simmer, covered, 4 minutes, until vegetables are just softened. Add snow peas, scallions, ginger and garlic; cook, uncovered, 2 minutes, until snow peas are softened.

3. In small bowl, combine peanut butter, soy sauce, juice, honey and ¼ cup water; stir into vegetable mixture. Add bell pepper and cooked noodles; toss to coat.

Serving (1½ cups) provides: 1 Fat, 3 Vegetables, 1 Protein, 2 Breads, 15 Optional Calories.

Per serving: 346 Calories, 10 g Total Fat, 2 g Saturated Fat, 40 mg Cholesterol, 562 mg Sodium, 52 g Total Carbohydrate, 6 g Dietary Fiber, 15 g Protein, 81 mg Calcium.

BREAKFAST

Apple, 1 small

Grilled Cheese Muffin (Toast ½ [1 ounce] English muffin; top with ¾ ounce reduced-fat cheddar cheese, 2 tomato slices and 1 teaspoon imitation bacon bits. Place onto nonstick baking sheet; broil until cheese is melted and tomato is heated through.)

Skim Milk, 1 cup

Coffee or Tea (optional)

LIGHT MEAL

Asian Noodles in Satay Sauce, 1 serving (see recipe)

Belgian Endive Leaves, 1 cup, with 1 teaspoon *each* olive oil and fresh lemon juice

Pineapple, ⅛ medium

Iced Tea

MAIN MEAL

Grilled Vegetables au Gratin (Preheat oven to 350° F; preheat grill according to manufacturer's directions. Grill ½ cup *each* broccoli florets, cauliflower florets, sliced yellow squash and tomato slices, turning as needed, until lightly browned and softened. Transfer vegetables to 8" square baking pan; sprinkle with ¾ ounce freshly grated Parmesan cheese. Bake 10 minutes, until cheese is melted.)

Tossed Green Salad, 2 cups, with 1 tablespoon fat-free Italian dressing

Garlic-Herb Bread (Spread 1-ounce slice Italian bread with ½ teaspoon minced fresh garlic or 1 roasted garlic clove and ½ teaspoon *each* minced fresh basil and oregano leaves; drizzle with 1 teaspoon olive oil. Place onto nonstick baking sheet; broil until lightly browned.)

Aspartame-Sweetened Strawberry-Banana Nonfat Yogurt, 1 cup

Decaffeinated Coffee or Tea

SNACK

Nonfat Cottage Cheese, ½ cup

Fat-Free Crackers, 7

This menu provides: 2 Milks, 3 Fats, 2 Fruits, 13½ Vegetables, 4 Proteins, 5 Breads, 30 Optional Calories.

Per serving: 34 g Fat, 22 g Fiber.

297
SOBA NOODLE SALAD

Makes 4 servings

2 cups thickly sliced shiitake mushrooms
I cup sliced fennel bulb
I cup cubed pared eggplant (I" pieces)
3 tablespoons balsamic vinegar
I tablespoon + I teaspoon olive oil
I tablespoon firmly packed light or dark brown sugar
$^1/_2$ teaspoon salt
6 ounces soba noodles (Japanese buckwheat noodles)*
8 ounces drained cooked red beans (preferably adzuki)
I cup diced red bell pepper

1. Preheat oven to 450° F.

2. In large bowl, combine mushrooms, fennel and eggplant. In small jar with tight-fitting lid or small bowl, combine vinegar, oil, brown sugar and salt; cover and shake well or, with wire whisk, blend until combined. Pour over vegetable mixture; toss to combine.

3. Spoon vegetable mixture onto large sheet of foil; fold foil to enclose vegetable mixture, crimping edges to seal. Place foil packet onto baking sheet; bake 25 minutes, until vegetables are softened.

4. In large pot of boiling water, cook noodles about 5 minutes, until ten- der. Drain, discarding liquid; place into serving bowl. Keep warm.

5. Carefully open foil packet. Transfer vegetable mixture to bowl with noodles; toss to combine. Add beans and bell pepper; toss again.

Serving ($1^3/_4$ cups) provides: 1 Fat, $2^1/_2$ Vegetables, 1 Protein, 2 Breads, 10 Optional Calories.

Per serving: 294 Calories, 5 g Total Fat, 1 g Saturated Fat, 0 mg Cholesterol, 643 mg Sodium, 54 g Total Carbohydrate, 3 g Dietary Fiber, 13 g Protein, 60 mg Calcium.

*Soba noodles are available in most Asian groceries.

298
RICE PILAF

Makes 4 servings

2 teaspoons olive oil
1 cup sliced scallions
3 garlic cloves, minced
1 cup diced red bell pepper
1 cup sliced shiitake mushrooms
4 ounces long-grain rice
$^1/_2$ teaspoon salt
$^1/_2$ teaspoon freshly ground black pepper
1 cup fresh or frozen green peas, thawed
3 ounces reduced-fat white cheddar cheese, grated

1. In large saucepan, heat oil; add scallions and garlic. Cook over medium-high heat, stirring frequently, 4 minutes, until scallions are softened. Stir in bell pepper and mushrooms; cook, stirring frequently, 5 minutes, until softened.

2. Add rice to vegetable mixture; stir to coat. Add salt, black pepper and $1^1/_2$ cups water; bring liquid to a boil. Reduce heat to low; simmer, covered, 20 minutes, until rice is tender and all liquid is absorbed.

3. Stir peas and cheese into rice mixture; cook, stirring frequently, 3 minutes, until peas are heated through and cheese is melted.

Serving ($1^1/_4$ cups) provides: $^1/_2$ Fat, $1^1/_2$ Vegetables, 1 Protein, $1^1/_2$ Breads.

Per serving: 238 Calories, 6 g Total Fat, 3 g Saturated Fat, 15 mg Cholesterol, 447 mg Sodium, 33 g Total Carbohydrate, 3 g Dietary Fiber, 12 g Protein, 233 mg Calcium.

BREAKFAST
Banana, $^1/_2$ medium
Mini Bagel, 1 (1 ounce), split and toasted, with 2 teaspoons peanut butter and 1 teaspoon grape jam
Skim Milk, 1 cup
Coffee or Tea (optional)

LIGHT MEAL
Rice Pilaf, 1 serving (see recipe)
Carrot and Celery Sticks, 1 cup *each*
Tossed Green Salad, 2 cups, with 1 tablespoon fat-free Thousand Island dressing
Roll, 1 ounce, with 1 teaspoon reduced-calorie tub margarine
Reduced-Calorie Chocolate-Flavored Pudding (made with skim milk), $^1/_2$ cup
Iced Tea

MAIN MEAL
Parmesan Omelet (Spray small nonstick skillet with nonstick cooking spray; heat. Add $^1/_4$ cup *each* chopped onion and green bell pepper; cook over medium-high heat, stirring frequently, 5 minutes, until vegetables are softened. Pour $^1/_2$ cup egg substitute into skillet, tilting to cover bottom of pan. Cook over medium-high heat until underside is set, lifting edges with spatula to let uncooked egg flow underneath. Sprinkle $^3/_4$ ounce freshly grated Parmesan cheese evenly over one side of omelet; with spatula, fold other side over cheese to enclose.)
Tomato Salad (In medium bowl, combine 1 medium tomato, diced, $^1/_4$ cup sliced red onion, 3 tablespoons minced fresh flat-leaf parsley and 1 tablespoon fat-free Italian dressing.)
Breadsticks, 2 long
Pineapple, $^1/_8$ medium
Decaffeinated Coffee or Tea

SNACK
Graham Crackers, 3 ($2^1/_2$" squares)
Vanilla "Egg Cream" (In tall glass, combine 1 cup diet cream soda and $^1/_2$ cup skim milk.)

This menu provides: 2 Milks, 3 Fats, 2 Fruits, 13 Vegetables, 4 Proteins, $5^1/_2$ Breads, 80 Optional Calories.

Per serving: 31 g Fat, 20 g Fiber.

BREAKFAST

Fresh Fig, 1 large
Breakfast Scramble (In small nonstick skillet, melt 1 teaspoon reduced-calorie tub margarine; add $^1/_4$ cup *each* chopped onion and green bell pepper. Cook over medium-high heat, stirring frequently, 5 minutes, until vegetables are softened. Add $^1/_4$ cup egg substitute; cook, stirring frequently, until set.)
English Muffin, $^1/_2$ (1 ounce), toasted, with 1 teaspoon reduced-calorie tub margarine
Skim Milk, 1 cup
Coffee or Tea (optional)

LIGHT MEAL

Brown Rice and Vegetable Pilaf, 1 serving (see recipe)
Chilled Blanched Asparagus, 6 spears, and 1 cup carrot sticks with Vegetable Dip (In small bowl, combine $^1/_2$ cup plain nonfat yogurt and 1 packet instant vegetable broth and seasoning mix.)
Unsweetened Peach-Flavored Seltzer

MAIN MEAL

Tofu-Vegetable Kabobs (Spray rack in broiler pan with nonstick cooking spray. Alternating ingredients, onto 2 long metal skewers, thread 4 ounces cubed firm tofu and 1 cup *each* cubed pared eggplant and pearl onions; brush with 2 tablespoons fat-free Italian dressing. Place skewers onto prepared rack; broil 4" inches from heat, turning as needed, until lightly browned.)
Corn Bread, 2" square
Cooked Green and Wax Beans, 1 cup, with 1 teaspoon reduced-calorie tub margarine
Tossed Green Salad, 2 cups, with $^1/_4$ cup packaged croutons and 1 tablespoon fat-free Thousand Island dressing
Broiled Grapefruit (Sprinkle $^1/_2$ medium grapefruit with 1 teaspoon firmly packed light or dark brown sugar; place onto nonstick baking sheet. Broil 2–3 minutes, until topping is bubbling.)
Iced Herbal Tea

SNACK

Graham Crackers, 3 ($2^1/_2$" squares)
Root Beer "Float" (In tall glass, combine 1 cup diet root beer and $^1/_3$ cup skim milk; add enough ice cubes to fill glass.)

This menu provides: 2 Milks, 3 Fats, 2 Fruits, $16^3/_4$ Vegetables, 4 Proteins, $5^1/_4$ Breads, 95 Optional Calories.

Per serving: 29 g Fat, 27 g Fiber.

299
BROWN RICE AND VEGETABLE PILAF

Makes 4 servings

$^1/_2$ ounce shelled pecans, coarsely chopped
2 teaspoons olive oil
1 cup chopped onions
4 garlic cloves, minced
1 cup diced red bell pepper
1 cup diced green bell pepper
$^1/_2$ cup thinly sliced carrot
2 cups thickly sliced mushrooms
8 ounces brown rice
$^3/_4$ teaspoon dried rosemary leaves, crumbled
$^3/_4$ teaspoon salt
$^3/_4$ teaspoon freshly ground black pepper
3 ounces reduced-fat white cheddar cheese, grated

1. Preheat oven or toaster over to 350° F.

2. In small baking pan, toast pecans 5 minutes, until fragrant and lightly browned; set aside.

3. In large saucepan or Dutch oven, heat oil; add onions and garlic. Cook over medium-high heat, stirring frequently, 5 minutes, until onions are softened. Add red and green bell peppers and carrot; cook, stirring frequently, 5 minutes, until peppers are softened. Add mushrooms; cook, stirring frequently, 5 minutes, until mushrooms are softened.

4. Add rice to vegetable mixture; stir to coat. Add rosemary, salt, black pepper and $2^1/_2$ cups water; bring liquid to a boil. Reduce heat to low; simmer, covered, 50 minutes, until rice is tender.

5. Add cheese and toasted pecans to hot rice mixture; stir until cheese is melted.

Serving ($1^1/_2$ cups) provides: 1 Fat, $2^3/_4$ Vegetables, 1 Protein, 2 Breads.

Per serving: 363 Calories, 10 g Total Fat, 4 g Saturated Fat, 15 mg Cholesterol, 590 mg Sodium, 55 g Total Carbohydrate, 5 g Dietary Fiber, 14 g Protein, 232 mg Calcium.

300
ASPARAGUS RISOTTO

Makes 4 servings

1 teaspoon olive oil
³/₄ cup thinly sliced scallions
2 cups thickly sliced mushrooms
5 ounces Arborio or other short-grain rice
2 fluid ounces (¹/₄ cup) dry sherry
¹/₂ teaspoon salt
1¹/₄ cups cut asparagus (1" pieces)
¹/₂ cup fresh or thawed frozen green peas
3 ounces freshly grated Parmesan cheese
¹/₂ teaspoon freshly ground black pepper

1. In large saucepan, heat oil; add scallions. Cook over medium-high heat, stirring frequently, 4 minutes, until softened. Add mushrooms; cook, stirring frequently, 5 minutes, until softened. Add rice; stir to coat. Stir in sherry; cook, stirring frequently, 4 minutes, until sherry is absorbed.

2. Add ¹/₂ cup water and the salt to rice mixture; cook, stirring constantly, until liquid is absorbed. Continuing to stir, add 1¹/₂ cups water, ¹/₂ cup at a time; cook, stirring constantly after each addition, 18–20 minutes, until all liquid is absorbed, rice is tender and mixture is creamy.

3. Stir asparagus and peas into rice mixture; cook, stirring occasionally, 4 minutes, until asparagus is softened. Stir in cheese and pepper.

Serving (1¹/₄ cups) provides: ¹/₄ Fat, 2 Vegetables, 1 Protein, 1¹/₂ Breads, 15 Optional Calories.

Per serving: 293 Calories, 8 g Total Fat, 4 g Saturated Fat, 17 mg Cholesterol, 677 mg Sodium, 37 g Total Carbohydrate, 2 g Dietary Fiber, 15 g Protein, 327 mg Calcium.

BREAKFAST
Strawberry Smoothie (In blender, combine 1 cup skim milk, ³/₄ cup sliced strawberries, 2 ice cubes and 1 teaspoon strawberry jam; purée until smooth.)
Reduced-Calorie Multi-Grain Bread, 2 slices, toasted, with 2 teaspoons reduced-calorie tub margarine
Coffee or Tea (optional)

LIGHT MEAL
Asparagus Risotto, 1 serving (see recipe)
Iceberg Lettuce Wedge, with 1 tablespoon fat-free creamy Italian dressing
Reduced-Calorie Vanilla-Flavored Pudding (made with skim milk), ¹/₂ cup
Unsweetened Seltzer

MAIN MEAL
Skewered Tofu and Vegetables (Spray rack in broiler pan with nonstick cooking spray. Alternating ingredients, onto 2 long metal skewers, thread 4 ounces cubed firm tofu, 1 cup red bell pepper squares and 1 cup pearl onions; brush with 2 tablespoons reduced-sodium soy sauce. Place skewers onto prepared rack; broil 4" from heat, turning as needed, until lightly browned.)
Cooked Linguine, 1 cup, with ¹/₄ cup marinara sauce
Sliced Cucumber and Shredded Carrot Salad, 2 cups, with 1 teaspoon *each* olive oil and balsamic vinegar
Mango, ¹/₂ small
Decaffeinated Coffee or Tea

SNACK
Reduced-Calorie Granola Bar, 1 (1 ounce)
Skim Milk, ¹/₂ cup

This menu provides: 2 Milks, 3 Fats, 2 Fruits, 11³/₄ Vegetables, 3 Proteins, 5¹/₂ Breads, 110 Optional Calories.

Per serving: 35 g Fat, 23 g Fiber.

BREAKFAST

Fortified Cold Cereal, $^3/4$ ounce, with 2 tablespoons raisins
Skim Milk, 1 cup
Coffee or Tea (optional)

LIGHT MEAL

Vegetable "Fried" Rice, 1 serving (see recipe)
Torn Romaine and Bibb Lettuce Leaves, 2 cups, with $^1/2$ cup sliced celery, $^1/4$ cup packaged croutons and 1 tablespoon fat-free honey-mustard dressing
Tangerine, 1 large
Diet Ginger Ale

MAIN MEAL

Cheese Pizza, thin crust, 1 slice ($^1/12$ of a 14"–16" pie)
Red and Green Bell Pepper Rings, 1 cup *each*
Tomato-Basil Salad (Arrange 1 cup tomato slices and 1 tablespoon minced fresh basil on salad plate; drizzle with 1 tablespoon fat-free Italian dressing.)
Sugar-Free Cherry-Flavored Gelatin, $^1/2$ cup, with 1 tablespoon thawed frozen light whipped topping (8 calories per tablespoon)
Decaffeinated Cappuccino, made with skim milk, 5 fluid ounces

SNACK

Graham Crackers, 3 ($2^1/2$" squares), with 1 tablespoon *each* peanut butter and apricot jam
Vanilla "Egg Cream" (In tall glass, combine 1 cup diet cream soda and $^1/2$ cup skim milk.)

This menu provides: 2 Milks, 3 Fats, 2 Fruits, $13^1/4$ Vegetables, 3 Proteins, $5^1/2$ Breads, 90 Optional Calories.

Per serving: 30 g Fat, 21 g Fiber.

301
VEGETABLE "FRIED" RICE

Here's a great way to use up leftover cooked rice. Next time you make rice, cook up some extra and save it for this recipe. No leftovers? No problem! Just follow the directions here for making it.

Makes 4 servings

6 ounces long-grain rice
3 eggs
$^1/2$ cup sliced scallions
$^1/2$ cup minced fresh cilantro
2 tablespoons reduced-sodium soy sauce
$^1/4$ teaspoon granulated sugar
2 teaspoons oriental sesame oil
1 cup julienned well-washed leeks
1 cup thinly sliced carrot
1 cup diced red bell pepper
2 tablespoons minced pared fresh ginger root
5 garlic cloves, minced
1 ounce unsalted dry-roasted peanuts, coarsely chopped
2 tablespoons rice wine or cider vinegar
$^1/2$ teaspoon salt

1. In medium saucepan, bring 2 cups water to a boil; add rice. Reduce heat to low; simmer, covered, 20 minutes, until rice is tender and all liquid is absorbed. Remove from heat; set aside.

2. In small bowl, with wire whisk, combine eggs, 2 tablespoons of the scallions, 2 tablespoons of the cilantro, 1 tablespoon of the soy sauce, the sugar and 2 tablespoons water, blending until sugar is dissolved.

3. Spray small nonstick skillet with nonstick cooking spray; heat. Add egg mixture, tilting to cover bottom of pan. Cook over medium-high heat until underside is set, lifting edges with spatula to let uncooked egg flow underneath. Remove egg mixture from skillet; let cool.

4. Cut cool egg mixture into $^1/2$" strips; set aside.

5. In large nonstick skillet, heat oil; add leeks, carrot and bell pepper. Cook over medium-high heat, stirring frequently, 5 minutes, until vegetables are softened. Add ginger and garlic; cook, stirring constantly, 1 minute. Add rice; cook, stirring constantly, 5 minutes, until mixture is heated through. Stir in peanuts, vinegar, salt, egg strips and remaining scallions, cilantro and soy sauce; cook, stirring frequently, 2 minutes, until liquid is evaporated and flavors are blended.

Serving ($1^1/4$ cups) provides: 1 Fat, $1^3/4$ Vegetables, 1 Protein, $1^1/2$ Breads.

Per serving: 328 Calories, 10 g Total Fat, 2 g Saturated Fat, 159 mg Cholesterol, 642 mg Sodium, 48 g Total Carbohydrate, 3 g Dietary Fiber, 11 g Protein, 81 mg Calcium.

302
GREEK RICE SALAD

Makes 4 servings

6 ounces long-grain rice
1 tablespoon olive oil
1 tablespoon fresh lemon juice
$^1/_2$ teaspoon dried oregano leaves
$^1/_4$ teaspoon ground red pepper
2 medium tomatoes, chopped
6 large Greek olives, pitted and quartered
$1^1/_2$ ounces feta cheese, crumbled
2 tablespoons minced fresh flat-leaf parsley

1. In medium saucepan, bring 2 cups water to a boil; add rice. Reduce heat to low; simmer, covered, 20 minutes, until rice is tender and all liquid is absorbed. Transfer to serving bowl.

2. Meanwhile, prepare marinade. In quart-size sealable plastic bag, combine oil, juice, oregano and pepper; add tomatoes and olives. Seal bag, squeezing out air; turn to coat tomatoes and olives. Let stand until rice is cooked, turning bag occasionally.

3. Drain marinade into hot rice; toss to combine. Let stand until room temperature.

4. Add cheese, parsley and marinated tomatoes and olives to cooled rice mixture; toss gently to combine.

Serving ($1^1/_2$ cups) provides: 1 Fat, 1 Vegetable, $^1/_2$ Protein, $1^1/_2$ Breads.

Per serving: 256 Calories, 9 g Total Fat, 2 g Saturated Fat, 9 mg Cholesterol, 362 mg Sodium, 39 g Total Carbohydrate, 2 g Dietary Fiber, 5 g Protein, 80 mg Calcium.

BREAKFAST
Bran Flakes Cereal, $1^1/_2$ ounces, with 2 dried dates, chopped
Skim Milk, $^1/_2$ cup
Coffee or Tea (optional)

LIGHT MEAL
Greek Rice Salad, 1 serving (see recipe)
Steamed Cauliflower and Broccoli Florets, 1 cup *each,* with $^1/_4$ teaspoon butter-flavor granules
Sugar-Free Lemon-Flavored Gelatin, $^1/_2$ cup
Unsweetened Mandarin Orange–Flavored Seltzer

MAIN MEAL
Sweet-and-Sour Tofu (In medium nonstick skillet, heat 1 teaspoon peanut oil; add 1 cup *each* chopped onion, green bell pepper and celery. Cook over medium-high heat, stirring frequently, until vegetables are softened. Add 4 ounces firm tofu, crumbled, and $^1/_2$ cup drained canned pineapple chunks [no sugar added], 1 tablespoon rice wine vinegar and 1 teaspoon *each* honey and reduced-sodium soy sauce; cook, stirring frequently, until heated through. Serve over $^1/_2$ cup cooked whole-wheat spaghetti.)
Aspartame-Sweetened Nonfat Peach Yogurt, 1 cup
Herbal Tea

SNACK
Crispbreads, $^3/_4$ ounce, with 1 tablespoon peanut butter
Skim Milk, $^1/_2$ cup

This menu provides: 2 Milks, 3 Fats, 2 Fruits, 11 Vegetables, $3^1/_2$ Proteins, $5^1/_2$ Breads, 30 Optional Calories.

Per serving: 34 g Fat, 24 g Fiber.

BREAKFAST

Grapefruit, $^1/_2$ medium
Bagel, 1 small (2 ounces), split and toasted, with
   2 teaspoons reduced-calorie tub margarine
Skim Milk, $^3/_4$ cup
Coffee or Tea (optional)

LIGHT MEAL

Onion Soup (In small saucepan, combine 1 cup low-
   sodium vegetable broth and $^1/_2$ cup chopped
   onion; cook until onion is softened. Sprinkle with
   1 teaspoon freshly grated Parmesan cheese; serve
   with 20 oyster crackers.)
Spicy Potato Salad, 1 serving (see recipe)
Carrot Sticks and Broccoli Florets, 1 cup *each*
Unsweetened Black Cherry–Flavored Seltzer

MAIN MEAL

Bean 'n' Cheese Burrito (Preheat oven to 350° F.
   Mash 2 ounces drained cooked red beans; spread
   along center of one 6" flour tortilla. Sprinkle
   beans with $^3/_4$ ounce reduced-fat cheddar cheese,
   grated, and 2 tablespoons chopped scallions; fold
   sides of tortilla over filling to enclose. Wrap burrito in foil; bake 10 minutes, until heated through
   and cheese is melted.)
Tossed Green Salad, 2 cups, with $^1/_2$ cup *each*
   cucumber and radish slices and 1 teaspoon *each*
   olive oil and balsamic vinegar
Sugar-Free Nonfat Vanilla Frozen Yogurt, 4 fluid
   ounces
Iced Tea with Lemon Wedge

SNACK

Cherry Parfait (In stemmed glass, layer $^1/_2$ cup
   reduced-calorie vanilla-flavored pudding [made
   with skim milk] and 12 large cherries, pitted and
   chopped.)

This menu provides: 2 Milks, 3 Fats, 2 Fruits,
12$^1/_2$ Vegetables, 3 Proteins, 5$^1/_2$ Breads,
135 Optional Calories.

Per serving: 28 g Fat, 23 g Fiber.

303
SPICY POTATO SALAD

Makes 4 servings

1 pound 14 ounces new potatoes
3 tablespoons white wine vinegar
1 tablespoon olive oil
$^3/_4$ teaspoon salt
$^1/_2$ teaspoon freshly ground black pepper
$^1/_4$ teaspoon hot red pepper sauce
$^1/_2$ cup minced red onion
1$^1/_2$ cups plain nonfat yogurt
2 tablespoons mango chutney
2 teaspoons reduced-calorie mayonnaise
1 cup diced celery
1 cup diced red bell pepper
4 hard-cooked eggs, diced
2 tablespoons minced fresh chives

1. Place potatoes into medium saucepan; add water to cover. Bring liquid to a boil. Reduce heat to low; simmer 20 minutes, until potatoes are just softened. Drain, discarding liquid; set aside until cool enough to handle.

2. Meanwhile, in large bowl, combine vinegar, oil, salt, black pepper and hot pepper sauce.

3. Cut cooked potatoes into $^1/_2$" pieces. Add potatoes to vinegar mixture; toss to combine. Add onion; toss again. Set potato mixture aside to cool; refrigerate, covered, 30 minutes, until chilled.

4. In separate large bowl, with wire whisk, combine yogurt, chutney and mayonnaise; stir in celery, bell pepper, hard-cooked eggs and chives. Add potato mixture; toss well.

Serving (2 cups) provides: $^1/_2$ Milk, 1 Fat, 1$^1/_4$ Vegetables, 1 Protein, 1$^1/_2$ Breads, 15 Optional Calories.

Per serving: 376 Calories, 10 g Total Fat, 2 g Saturated Fat, 215 mg Cholesterol, 622 mg Sodium, 56 g Total Carbohydrate, 5 g Dietary Fiber, 16 g Protein, 222 mg Calcium.

304
POTATO PANCAKES WITH APPLE-CHEESE DRESSING

Makes 4 servings

2 small McIntosh apples, cored and diced
1 1/2 cups minced scallions
1 1/3 cups low-fat (1%) cottage cheese
1/2 cup minced fresh dill
2 tablespoons light sour cream
1 pound 14 ounces Idaho potatoes, pared and shredded
1 egg white
1 tablespoon all-purpose flour
3/4 teaspoon salt
1/4 teaspoon double-acting baking powder
1 tablespoon + 1 teaspoon olive oil

1. Preheat oven to 350° F. Spray nonstick baking sheet with nonstick cooking spray.

2. To prepare dressing, in small bowl, combine apples, 1/2 cup of the scallions, the cheese, dill and sour cream; refrigerate, covered, until chilled.

3. To prepare pancakes, in large bowl, combine potatoes, egg white, flour, salt, baking powder and remaining 1 cup scallions.

4. In large nonstick skillet or griddle, heat 2 teaspoons of the oil; spread evenly to coat bottom of skillet. Divide potato mixture into 8 equal mounds, about 1/2 cup each; spoon 4 mounds into skillet, flattening with back of spoon to form pancakes. Cook over medium-high heat, turning once, 8 minutes, until golden brown on both sides; transfer to prepared baking sheet. Repeat with remaining oil and mounds. Bake 10 minutes, until cooked through and lightly crisp. Serve with dressing.

Serving (2 pancakes, 3/4 cup dressing) provides: 1 Fat, 1/2 Fruit, 3/4 Vegetable, 1 Protein, 1 1/2 Breads, 25 Optional Calories.

Per serving: 334 Calories, 7 g Total Fat, 2 g Saturated Fat, 6 mg Cholesterol, 783 mg Sodium, 54 g Total Carbohydrate, 5 g Dietary Fiber, 16 g Protein, 139 mg Calcium.

BREAKFAST
Nonfat Cottage Cheese, 1/2 cup, topped with 1/2 cup orange sections
Cooked Cream of Wheat Cereal, 1/2 cup
Skim Milk, 1/2 cup
Coffee or Tea (optional)

LIGHT MEAL
Potato Pancakes with Apple-Cheese Dressing, 1 serving (see recipe)
Cucumber Salad (In small bowl, combine 1/2 cup cucumber slices, 1 teaspoon *each* vegetable oil and rice wine vinegar and pinch ground white pepper.)
Grilled Zucchini (Preheat grill according to manufacturer's directions. Grill 1 cup sliced zucchini, turning as needed, until lightly browned and softened.)
Reduced-Calorie Chocolate-Flavored Pudding (made with skim milk), 1/2 cup
Unsweetened Seltzer

MAIN MEAL
Spaghetti with Tomato Sauce and Cheese (In small saucepan, combine 1/2 cup tomato sauce [no salt added] and 1/4 teaspoon *each* dried basil and oregano; stir to combine. Pour sauce mixture over 1 cup hot cooked spaghetti; sprinkle with 3/4 ounce freshly grated Parmesan cheese.)
Cooked Sliced Carrots, 1 cup
Caesar Salad (In medium bowl, combine 2 cups torn Romaine lettuce leaves, 1/4 cup packaged croutons and 1 tablespoon fat-free Caesar salad dressing.)
Garlic Bread (Spread 1-ounce slice Italian bread with 1/2 teaspoon minced fresh garlic or 1 roasted garlic clove; drizzle with 1/2 teaspoon olive oil. Place onto nonstick baking sheet; broil until lightly browned.)
Cinnamon-Peach Yogurt (In small bowl, combine 1 cup aspartame-sweetened vanilla nonfat yogurt, 1/4 cup drained canned peach slices [no sugar added] and 1/4 teaspoon cinnamon.)
Decaffeinated Espresso

SNACK
Sugar-Free Strawberry-Flavored Gelatin, 1/2 cup, with 1 tablespoon thawed frozen light whipped topping (8 calories per tablespoon)

This menu provides: 2 Milks, 3 Fats, 2 Fruits, 11 3/4 Vegetables, 3 Proteins, 6 Breads, 105 Optional Calories.

Per serving: 20 g Fat, 20 g Fiber.

Potato Pancakes with Apple-Cheese Dressing

305

ROOT VEGETABLE STEW WITH CHICK-PEAS

Makes 4 servings

2 teaspoons olive oil

1 cup diced well-washed leeks

5 ounces all-purpose potato, pared and cut into $1/2$" pieces

4 ounces sweet potato, pared and cut into $1/2$" pieces

1 cup carrot chunks (1" pieces)

1 cup parsnip chunks (1" pieces)

1 cup diced turnips ($1/2$" pieces)

$1/2$ teaspoon granulated sugar

$1/2$ teaspoon ground dried sage

$1/2$ teaspoon salt

$1/4$ teaspoon freshly ground black pepper

1 cup apple cider

$1/4$ cup tomato paste (no salt added)

2 tablespoons cider vinegar

8 ounces drained cooked chick-peas

$1/2$ cup minced fresh flat-leaf parsley

1. In large nonstick skillet, heat oil; add leeks. Cook over medium-high heat, stirring frequently, 5 minutes, until softened. Add all-purpose and sweet potatoes, carrot, parsnip and turnips; stir to coat. Sprinkle with sugar, sage, salt and pepper; stir to combine.

2. Add cider, tomato paste and vinegar to vegetable mixture; bring liquid to a boil. Reduce heat to low; simmer, covered, 20 minutes, until potatoes are softened.

3. Stir chick-peas into potato mixture; return liquid to a boil. Reduce heat to low; simmer, covered, until vegetables are softened and mixture is heated through. Stir in parsley.

Serving (1$1/2$ cups) provides: $1/2$ Fat, $1/2$ Fruit, 2 Vegetables, 1 Protein, 1 Bread.

Per serving: 282 Calories, 4 g Total Fat, 1 g Saturated Fat, 0 mg Cholesterol, 339 mg Sodium, 55 g Total Carbohydrate, 8 g Dietary Fiber, 8 g Protein, 105 mg Calcium.

BREAKFAST

Pita with Pear and Cheese (Pare, core and slice 1 small pear. Cut large [2-ounce] whole-wheat pita in half crosswise; open to form 2 pockets. Fill each pocket with half of the pear slices and $1/4$ cup nonfat cottage cheese.)

Skim Milk, 1 cup

Coffee or Tea (optional)

LIGHT MEAL

Root Vegetable Stew with Chick-Peas, 1 serving (see recipe)

Cooked Long-Grain Rice, $1/2$ cup, with 1 teaspoon reduced-calorie tub margarine

Cucumber and Tomato Slices, 1 cup *each,* with 1 tablespoon fat-free Italian dressing

Diet Orange Soda

MAIN MEAL

Zucchini Parmigiana (Preheat oven to 350° F. Spray nonstick baking sheet with nonstick cooking spray. Cut 2 medium zucchini lengthwise into halves. Dip zucchini halves into $1/2$ egg white, then into 3 tablespoons seasoned dried bread crumbs, turning to coat evenly. Place onto pre-pared baking sheet; bake 15–20 minutes, until zucchini is softened and coating is crispy. Leave oven on. Transfer zucchini to small baking dish. Top with $1/4$ cup tomato sauce [no salt added], $3/4$ ounce skim-milk mozzarella cheese, grated, and 1 teaspoon freshly grated Parmesan cheese; bake 10 minutes, until cheese is melted and mixture is heated through.)

Cooked Broccoli, 4 spears, with 2 teaspoons reduced-calorie tub margarine

Garlic-Herb Bread (Spread 1-ounce slice Italian bread with $1/2$ teaspoon minced fresh garlic or 1 roasted garlic clove and $1/2$ teaspoon *each* minced fresh basil and oregano leaves; drizzle with 1 teaspoon olive oil. Place onto nonstick baking sheet; broil until lightly browned.)

Aspartame-Sweetened Strawberry-Banana Nonfat Yogurt, 1 cup

Sparkling Mineral Water with Lemon Wedge

SNACK

Strawberries, $1/2$ cup, with 1 tablespoon thawed frozen light whipped topping (8 calories per tablespoon)

This menu provides: 2 Milks, 3 Fats, 2 Fruits, 13 Vegetables, 3 Proteins, 6 Breads, 35 Optional Calories.

Per serving: 25 g Fat, 31 g Fiber.

306
WHITE BEAN SOUP WITH SPINACH

Makes 4 servings

1 tablespoon + 1 teaspoon olive oil
3 garlic cloves, minced
$^1/_2$ teaspoon dried rosemary leaves
$^1/_4$ teaspoon crushed red pepper flakes
8 ounces drained cooked white beans
$^1/_2$ cup evaporated skimmed milk
2 tablespoons tomato paste (no salt added)
$^1/_2$ teaspoon salt
$^1/_4$ teaspoon freshly ground black pepper
$^1/_2$ cup finely diced carrot
2 cups shredded well-washed trimmed spinach leaves
$^1/_2$ cup drained roasted red bell peppers, cut into strips

1. In large saucepan, heat oil; add garlic, rosemary and red pepper flakes. Cook over low heat, stirring occasionally, 4 minutes, until garlic is softened.

2. Stir beans, milk, tomato paste, salt, black pepper and 2 cups water into garlic mixture; bring liquid to a boil. Reduce heat to low; simmer, stirring occasionally, 3 minutes, until mixture is heated through and flavors are blended.

3. Transfer bean mixture to blender or food processor; purée until smooth.

4. Return bean mixture to saucepan; bring to a boil. Add carrot; cook, stirring occasionally, 4 minutes, until carrot is softened. Stir in spinach and roasted peppers; cook, stirring occasionally, 3 minutes, until spinach is softened and mixture is heated through.

Serving (1 cup) provides: $^1/_4$ Milk, 1 Fat, 1$^3/_4$ Vegetables, 1 Protein.

Per serving: 173 Calories, 5 g Total Fat, 1 g Saturated Fat, 1 mg Cholesterol, 382 mg Sodium, 24 g Total Carbohydrate, 4 g Dietary Fiber, 9 g Protein, 186 mg Calcium.

307
MUSHROOM-BARLEY SOUP

Makes 4 servings

$^1/_2$ ounce dried porcini or shiitake mushrooms
$^1/_2$ cup warm water
2 teaspoons vegetable oil
1 cup chopped onions
3 garlic cloves, minced
1 medium carrot, halved lengthwise, then thinly sliced
1 cup diced red bell pepper
2 cups thinly sliced fresh shiitake mushrooms
1 cup thinly sliced white mushrooms
1 cup low-sodium mixed vegetable juice
8 ounces drained cooked white beans
3 ounces pearl barley
$^3/_4$ teaspoon dried rosemary leaves, crumbled
$^1/_2$ teaspoon salt
$^1/_2$ teaspoon freshly ground black pepper

1. In medium bowl, combine dried mushrooms and water; let stand 20 minutes. With slotted spoon, remove soaked mushrooms from liquid. Rinse and chop mushrooms; set aside. Reserve liquid.

2. Line sieve with medium coffee filter; place over small bowl. Pour mushroom liquid through filter. Reserve liquid; discard coffee filter containing any particles of dirt and sand.

3. In large saucepan or Dutch oven, heat oil; add onions and garlic. Cook over medium-high heat, stirring frequently, 5 minutes, until onions are softened. Stir in carrot and bell pepper; cook, stirring frequently, 5 minutes, until carrot and pepper are softened.

4. Stir in fresh shiitake and white mushrooms; cook, covered, 5 minutes, until mushrooms are softened. Stir in juice, beans, barley, rosemary, salt, black pepper, reserved mushroom liquid, soaked dried mushrooms and $3^1/_2$ cups water; bring liquid to a boil. Reduce heat to low; simmer, covered, 45 minutes, until barley is tender.

Serving ($1^3/_4$ cups) provides: $^1/_2$ Fat, $3^1/_2$ Vegetables, 1 Protein, 1 Bread.

Per serving: 249 Calories, 3 g Total Fat, 0 g Saturated Fat, 0 mg Cholesterol, 338 mg Sodium, 46 g Total Carbohydrate, 9 g Dietary Fiber, 11 g Protein, 97 mg Calcium.

BREAKFAST
Grapefruit, $^1/_2$ medium
Grilled Cheese Toast (Toast 1 slice reduced-calorie whole-wheat bread; top with $^3/_4$ ounce reduced-fat cheddar cheese, 2 tomato slices and 1 teaspoon imitation bacon bits. Place onto nonstick baking sheet; broil until cheese is melted and tomato is heated through.)
Skim Milk, 1 cup
Coffee or Tea (optional)

LIGHT MEAL
Mushroom-Barley Soup, 1 serving (see recipe)
Fat-Free Crackers, 7
Zucchini and Carrots Sticks, 1 cup *each*
Reduced-Calorie Butterscotch-Flavored Pudding (made with skim milk), $^1/_2$ cup
Unsweetened Lime-Flavored Seltzer

MAIN MEAL
Linguine with Red Clam Sauce (In small saucepan, combine $^1/_2$ cup marinara sauce and 2 ounces drained canned minced clams; cook over low heat, stirring frequently, until heated through. Pour over 1 cup hot cooked linguine; sprinkle with 1 teaspoon freshly grated Parmesan cheese.)
Tossed Green Salad, 2 cups, $^1/_2$ cup sliced red bell pepper and with 1 tablespoon fat-free Italian dressing
Garlic-Herb Bread (Spread 1-ounce slice Italian bread with $^1/_2$ teaspoon minced fresh garlic or 1 roasted garlic clove and $^1/_2$ teaspoon *each* minced fresh basil and oregano leaves; drizzle with 1 teaspoon olive oil. Place onto nonstick baking sheet; broil until lightly browned.)
Plums, 2 small
Diet Cola with Lemon Wedge

SNACK
Angel Food Cake, 2 ounces
Vanilla "Egg Cream" (In tall glass, combine 1 cup diet cream soda and $^1/_2$ cup skim milk.)

This menu provides: 2 Milks, 3 Fats, 2 Fruits, $14^1/_2$ Vegetables, $3^1/_4$ Proteins, $5^3/_4$ Breads, 140 Optional Calories.

Per serving: 23 g Fat, 26 g Fiber.

CABBAGE SOUP

Makes 4 servings

BREAKFAST
Blackberries, $^3/_4$ cup
English Muffin, $^1/_2$ (1 ounce), toasted, topped with
   1 poached egg
Skim Milk, $^3/_4$ cup
Coffee or Tea (optional)

LIGHT MEAL
Cabbage Soup, 1 serving (see recipe)
Cucumber Salad (In small bowl, combine $^1/_2$ cup
   cucumber slices, 1 teaspoon *each* vegetable oil
   and rice wine vinegar and pinch ground white
   pepper.)
Carrot and Celery Sticks, 1 cup *each*
Breadsticks, 2 short
Aspartame-Sweetened Strawberry Nonfat Yogurt,
   1 cup
Iced Tea

MAIN MEAL
Mexican Pizza (Preheat oven to 350° F. Top each of
   two 6" flour tortillas with $^1/_4$ cup salsa, 1 ounce
   drained cooked black beans, mashed, $^3/_4$ ounce
   reduced-fat Monterey Jack cheese, grated, and
   2 tablespoons drained canned chopped mild green
   chiles; place onto nonstick baking sheet. Bake
   until cheese is melted.)
Torn Iceberg and Red Leaf Lettuce Leaves, 2 cups,
   with 1 teaspoon *each* olive oil and red wine
   vinegar
Sugar-Free Nonfat Strawberry Frozen Yogurt, 4 fluid
   ounces
Sparkling Mineral Water with Lime Wedge

SNACK
Trail Mix (In small bowl, combine $1^1/_2$ ounces pretzel sticks, 2 tablespoons raisins and 1 teaspoon
   sunflower seeds.)

This menu provides: 2 Milks, 3 Fats, 2 Fruits,
15 Vegetables, 5 Proteins, 6 Breads, 75 Optional
Calories.

Per serving: 31 g Fat, 23 g Fiber.

2 ounces long-grain rice
1 tablespoon + 1 teaspoon olive oil
2 garlic cloves, slivered
1 cup thinly sliced carrot
$^1/_2$ cup diced green bell pepper
4 cups thinly sliced cabbage
1 teaspoon firmly packed light or dark brown sugar
$1^1/_2$ cups crushed tomatoes (no salt added)
8 ounces drained cooked red beans
$^3/_4$ teaspoon salt
2 tablespoons minced fresh dill
1 tablespoon balsamic or red wine vinegar
2 tablespoons nonfat sour cream

1. In small saucepan, bring $^3/_4$ cup water to a boil; add rice. Reduce heat to low; simmer, covered, 12–15 minutes, until rice is tender and all liquid is absorbed. Remove from heat; set aside.

2. In large saucepan or Dutch oven, heat oil; add garlic. Cook over medium-high heat, stirring constantly, 1 minute, until fragrant. Stir in carrot and bell pepper; cook, stirring frequently, 5 minutes, until peppers are softened. Add cabbage and sugar; cook, stirring frequently, 4 minutes, until cabbage is softened.

3. Add tomatoes, beans, salt and $2^1/_2$ cups water to vegetable mixture; bring liquid to a boil. Stir in cooked rice; return liquid to a boil. Reduce heat to low; simmer, stirring occasionally, 5 minutes, until mixture is heated through and flavors are blended. Stir in dill and vinegar.

4. Divide cabbage mixture among 4 soup bowls; top each portion with $1^1/_2$ teaspoons sour cream.

Serving ($1^3/_4$ cups) provides: 1 Fat, $3^1/_2$ Vegetables, 1 Protein, $^1/_2$ Bread, 10 Optional Calories.

Per serving: 226 Calories, 5 g Total Fat, 1 g Saturated Fat, 0 mg Cholesterol, 589 mg Sodium, 38 g Total Carbohydrate, 6 g Dietary Fiber, 9 g Protein, 107 mg Calcium.

HOT AND SPICY TOFU

Makes 4 servings

1 tablespoon + 1 teaspoon oriental sesame oil
1 tablespoon minced pared fresh ginger root
3 garlic cloves, minced
1 cup cut green beans (1" pieces)
$^1/_2$ cup julienned carrot
$^1/_2$ cup julienned red bell pepper
3 tablespoons chili sauce
1 tablespoon reduced-sodium soy sauce
$^1/_4$ teaspoon crushed red pepper flakes
8 ounces firm tofu, cut into 1" pieces

1. In large nonstick skillet, heat 1 tablespoon of the oil; add ginger and garlic. Cook over medium-high heat, stirring constantly, 1 minute, until softened. Add green beans, carrot and bell pepper; cook, stirring frequently, 5 minutes, until vegetables are softened.

2. In small bowl, combine chili sauce, soy sauce, red pepper flakes, remaining 1 teaspoon oil and $^1/_4$ cup water; stir into vegetable mixture. Stir in tofu; bring liquid to a boil. Reduce heat to low; simmer, stirring constantly, 1 minute, until mixture is heated through.

Serving (1 cup) provides: 1 Fat, 1 Vegetable, 1 Protein, 15 Optional Calories.

Per serving: 160 Calories, 10 g Total Fat, 1 g Saturated Fat, 0 mg Cholesterol, 336 mg Sodium, 11 g Total Carbohydrate, 1 g Dietary Fiber, 10 g Protein, 139 mg Calcium.

BREAKFAST
Banana, $^1/_2$ medium, sliced
Cornflakes, $^3/_4$ ounce
Skim Milk, $^3/_4$ cup
Coffee or Tea (optional)

LIGHT MEAL
Hot and Spicy Tofu, 1 serving (see recipe)
Cooked Brown Rice, 1 cup
Red and Green Bell Pepper Strips, 1 cup *each*
Cucumber Salad (In small bowl, combine $^1/_2$ cup cucumber slices, 1 teaspoon *each* vegetable oil and rice wine vinegar and pinch ground white pepper.)
Sugar-Free Nonfat Chocolate Frozen Yogurt, 4 fluid ounces
Iced Herbal Tea

MAIN MEAL
Cheese-Topped Grilled Vegetables (Preheat oven to 350° F; preheat grill according to manufacturer's directions. Grill $^1/_2$ cup *each* sliced red onion, red bell pepper, zucchini, mushrooms and carrot, turning as needed, until lightly browned and softened. Transfer vegetables to 8" square baking pan; top with 1$^1/_2$ ounces skim-milk mozzarella cheese, grated. Bake 10 minutes, until cheese is melted.)
Italian Bread, 2 slices (2 ounces), with 2 teaspoons reduced-calorie tub margarine
Broiled Peach (Cut 1 medium peach in half lengthwise; remove and discard pit. Place peach halves, cut-side up, onto nonstick baking sheet; sprinkle evenly with 1 teaspoon firmly packed light or dark brown sugar and pinch cinnamon. Broil 2–3 minutes, until topping is bubbling.)
Unsweetened Black Cherry–Flavored Seltzer

SNACK
Graham Crackers, 2 (2$^1/_2$" squares)
Double Chocolate Shake (In blender, combine $^2/_3$ cup cold water, 3 ice cubes, 1 packet reduced-calorie chocolate-flavored dairy shake mix and 1 teaspoon chocolate extract; purée until smooth and thick.)

This menu provides: 2 Milks, 3 Fats, 2 Fruits, 11 Vegetables, 3 Proteins, 6 Breads, 80 Optional Calories.

Per serving: 33 g Fat, 20 g Fiber.

GREEK PIZZA

This pizza brings together the zesty flavors of Greece and the crunchy goodness of all-American pizza.

Makes 4 servings

1 teaspoon all-purpose flour
8 ounces refrigerated, frozen or ready-made pizza crust dough
1 cup sliced tomato
$^1/_2$ cup sliced green bell pepper
$^1/_4$ cup thinly sliced red onion
3 ounces feta cheese, crumbled
6 large Greek olives, pitted and quartered
1 teaspoon dried oregano
$^1/_4$ teaspoon freshly ground black pepper, or to taste

1. Preheat oven to 450° F.

2. Sprinkle flour onto work surface. Place dough onto floured surface; turn to coat. With rolling pin or fingers, stretch dough into 10–12" circle; transfer to nonstick baking sheet.

3. Arrange tomato, bell pepper and onion on dough; sprinkle evenly with cheese, olives, oregano and black pepper. Bake 20 minutes, until crust is browned and crisp. Cut into 4 wedges.

Serving (1 wedge) provides: $^1/_4$ Fat, 1 Vegetable, 1 Protein, 2 Breads, 5 Optional Calories.

Per serving: 253 Calories, 9 g Total Fat, 4 g Saturated Fat, 19 mg Cholesterol, 788 mg Sodium, 32 g Total Carbohydrate, 2 g Dietary Fiber, 8 g Protein, 123 mg Calcium.

BREAKFAST

Cantaloupe, $^1/_4$ small
Breakfast Scramble (In small nonstick skillet, melt 1 teaspoon reduced-calorie tub margarine; add $^1/_4$ cup *each* chopped onion and green bell pepper. Cook over medium-high heat, stirring frequently, 5 minutes, until vegetables are softened. Add $^1/_4$ cup egg substitute; cook until set.)
Reduced-Calorie Whole-Wheat Bread, 2 slices, toasted, with $2^1/_2$ teaspoons reduced-calorie tub margarine
Skim Milk, 1 cup

LIGHT MEAL

Greek Pizza, 1 serving (see recipe)
Tossed Green Salad, 2 cups, with 1 tablespoon fat-free Italian dressing
Aspartame-Sweetened Lemon Nonfat Yogurt, 1 cup

MAIN MEAL

Rice-and-Beans Primavera (Spray medium nonstick skillet with nonstick cooking spray; heat. Add $^1/_4$ cup *each* sliced yellow squash, asparagus, scallions, and diced red onion; cook over medium-high heat, stirring, 5 minutes, until vegetables are softened. Stir in $^1/_2$ cup cooked brown rice, 2 ounces *each* drained cooked black and pinto beans and 1 tablespoon minced fresh basil. Cook 3–4 minutes, until mixture is cooked through.)
Ratatouille (In medium saucepan, heat 1 teaspoon vegetable oil; add $^1/_2$ cup *each* cubed onion, green bell pepper, zucchini and eggplant and 2 garlic cloves, minced. Cook over medium-high heat, stirring frequently, 5 minutes, until vegetables are softened. Add 1 cup canned crushed tomatoes [no salt added] and $^1/_2$ teaspoon *each* dried oregano leaves and basil. Bring mixture to a boil; reduce heat to low. Cook, stirring frequently, until vegetables are very tender and flavors are blended.)
Iceberg Lettuce Wedge, with 1 tablespoon fat-free Thousand Island dressing
Fruit Salad, $^1/_2$ cup

SNACK

Cajun Popcorn (Lightly spray 3 cups hot-air popped plain popcorn with nonstick cooking spray. Sprinkle popcorn with $^1/_4$ teaspoon Cajun seasoning; toss to coat evenly.)

This menu provides: 2 Milks, 3 Fats, 2 Fruits, 15 Vegetables, 4 Proteins, 5 Breads, 30 Optional Calories.

Per serving: 29 g Fat, 30 g Fiber.

ASPARAGUS FRITTATA

Makes 4 servings

24 asparagus spears, cut into 1" pieces
6 egg whites
3 eggs
2$^1/_4$ ounces freshly grated Parmesan cheese
$^1/_4$ cup skim milk
2 tablespoons minced fresh chives
$^1/_4$ teaspoon salt
$^1/_4$ teaspoon freshly ground black pepper
1 tablespoon + 1 teaspoon olive oil

1. Preheat oven to 350° F.

2. In large pot of boiling water, cook asparagus 2 minutes, until just tender. Drain, discarding liquid; rinse with cold water. Drain again; set aside.

3. In large bowl, with wire whisk, combine egg whites, eggs, cheese, milk, chives, salt and pepper.

4. In large cast-iron skillet, heat oil; add asparagus. Cook over medium-high heat, stirring constantly, until coated; reduce heat to low. Pour egg mixture into skillet; stir quickly to combine. Cook 5 minutes, until edges are set.

5. Transfer skillet to oven; bake 10 minutes, until egg mixture is firm. Cut into 4 wedges.

Serving (1 wedge) provides: 1 Fat, 1 Vegetable, 2 Proteins, 5 Optional Calories.

Per serving: 218 Calories, 13 g Total Fat, 5 g Saturated Fat, 172 mg Cholesterol, 571 mg Sodium, 6 g Total Carbohydrate, 1 g Dietary Fiber, 20 g Protein, 281 mg Calcium.

BREAKFAST
Banana, $^1/_2$ medium
English Muffin, $^1/_2$ (1 ounce), toasted, with 1 tablespoon nonfat cream cheese and 1 teaspoon peach jam
Skim Milk, 1 cup
Coffee or Tea (optional)

LIGHT MEAL
Cheese Sandwich with Chutney Spread (In small cup or bowl, combine 2 teaspoons reduced-calorie mayonnaise and 1 teaspoon mango chutney; spread on 1 slice reduced-calorie whole-wheat toast. Top with 2 slices nonfat process American cheese, $^1/_4$ cup shredded Romaine lettuce leaves and 1 additional slice reduced-calorie whole-wheat toast.)
Cucumber and Carrot Sticks, 1 cup *each*
Sugar-Free Cherry-Flavored Gelatin, $^1/_2$ cup
Unsweetened Seltzer

MAIN MEAL
Asparagus Frittata, 1 serving (see recipe)
Corn-Tomato Salad (In small bowl, combine 1 cup torn iceberg lettuce leaves, 6 cherry tomatoes, halved, $^1/_2$ cup cooked corn kernels and 1 tablespoon fat-free Italian dressing.)
Roll, 1 small (1 ounce), with 2 teaspoons reduced-calorie tub margarine
Angel Food Cake, 2 ounces, with $^1/_4$ cup sliced strawberries
Iced Tea

SNACK
Double Blueberry Parfait (In stemmed glass, layer 1 cup aspartame-sweetened blueberry nonfat yogurt and $^1/_2$ cup blueberries.)

This menu provides: 2 Milks, 3 Fats, 2 Fruits, 8$^1/_2$ Vegetables, 3$^1/_4$ Proteins, 4$^1/_4$ Breads, 135 Optional Calories.

Per serving: 27 g Fat, 21 g Fiber.

BREAKFAST

Apricots, 3 medium
Mini Bagel, 1 (1 ounce), split and toasted, with
   1 tablespoon nonfat cream cheese
Skim Milk, 1 cup
Coffee or Tea (optional)

LIGHT MEAL

Pasta-Cheese Salad (In medium bowl, combine
   2 cups torn Romaine lettuce leaves, 1 cup cooked
   macaroni shells, 6 cherry tomatoes, halved,
   1^1/$_2$ ounces nonfat mozzarella cheese, diced,
   1 tablespoon minced fresh basil, 1 tablespoon
   fat-free Italian dressing and freshly ground black
   pepper, to taste.)
Celery and Carrot Sticks, 1 cup *each*
Breadsticks, 2 long
Sugar-Free Cherry-Flavored Gelatin, ^{1}/$_2$ cup, with
   1 tablespoon thawed frozen light whipped
   topping (8 calories per tablespoon)
Iced Herbal Tea

MAIN MEAL

Roasted Asparagus with Eggs and Parmesan Cheese,
   1 serving (see recipe)
Broiled Tomato (Cut 1 medium tomato in half.
   Sprinkle cut sides of tomato with 1 teaspoon seasoned dried bread crumbs each; dot each with
   1 teaspoon reduced-calorie tub margarine. Place
   onto nonstick baking sheet; broil until lightly
   browned.)
Italian Bread, 1 slice (1 ounce), with 2 teaspoons
   reduced-calorie tub margarine
Strawberries 'n' Creme (In stemmed glass, layer
   ^{3}/$_4$ cup sliced strawberries and ^{1}/$_4$ cup nonfat sour
   cream.)
Sparkling Mineral Water

SNACK

Chocolate-Almond Shake (In blender, combine
   ^{2}/$_3$ cup cold water, 3 ice cubes, 1 packet reduced-
   calorie chocolate-flavored dairy shake mix and 1
   teaspoon almond extract; purée until smooth and
   thick.)

This menu provides: 2 Milks, 3 Fats, 2 Fruits,
13^1/$_2$ Vegetables, 3 Proteins, 5 Breads, 100 Optional
Calories.

Per serving: 33 g Fat, 22 g Fiber.

ROASTED ASPARAGUS WITH EGGS AND PARMESAN CHEESE

Makes 4 servings

48 asparagus spears
3^3/$_4$ ounces freshly grated Parmesan cheese
1 tablespoon + 1 teaspoon olive oil
2 eggs
3 egg whites
^{1}/$_4$ cup minced fresh basil
^{1}/$_4$ cup minced fresh chives
1 cup diced plum tomatoes
Pinch salt

1. Preheat oven to 400° F. Spray 13 × 9" baking pan with nonstick cooking spray.

2. In large pot of boiling water, cook asparagus 2 minutes, until bright green and just tender. Drain, discarding liquid; transfer to prepared baking pan.

3. Sprinkle asparagus with 3 ounces of the cheese; drizzle evenly with 2 teaspoons of the oil. Bake 8 minutes.

4. Meanwhile, in small bowl, combine remaining ^{3}/$_4$ ounce cheese, the eggs, egg whites, 2 tablespoons of the basil, 2 tablespoons of the chives and 1 tablespoon water.

5. In small cast-iron skillet, heat remaining 2 teaspoons oil; add egg mixture. Cook over medium-high heat 5 minutes, until edges are set.

6. Transfer skillet to oven alongside pan with asparagus; bake 4 minutes, until egg mixture is firm and asparagus is heated through and cheese topping is crusty.

7. Meanwhile, in small bowl, combine tomatoes, salt, remaining 2 tablespoons basil and remaining 2 tablespoons chives.

8. Cut egg mixture into 4 wedges. Divide asparagus mixture evenly among 4 plates; top each portion with 1 wedge of the egg mixture and one-fourth of the tomato mixture.

Serving (1 wedge egg mixture, one-fourth of asparagus mixture, one-fourth of tomato mixture) provides: 1 Fat, 2^1/$_2$ Vegetables, 2 Proteins.

Per serving: 263 Calories, 16 g Total Fat, 7 g Saturated Fat, 127 mg Cholesterol, 608 mg Sodium, 11 g Total Carbohydrate, 2 g Dietary Fiber, 23 g Protein, 446 mg Calcium.

EGGPLANT PARMIGIANA

Makes 4 servings

³/4 cup plain dried bread crumbs
1¹/2 ounces freshly grated Parmesan cheese
2 cups sliced pared eggplant (¹/4" slices)
2 egg whites, lightly beaten with 1 tablespoon of water
2 teaspoons olive oil
¹/2 cup minced onion
2 cups crushed tomatoes (no salt added)
2 tablespoons minced fresh basil
¹/4 teaspoon salt
4¹/2 ounces skim-milk mozzarella cheese, grated

1. Preheat oven to 400° F. Spray nonstick baking sheet with nonstick cooking spray.

2. On sheet of wax paper or paper plate, combine bread crumbs and 1 ounce of the Parmesan cheese. One at a time, dip eggplant slices into egg white mixture, then into bread crumb mixture, turning to coat evenly. Transfer eggplant to prepared baking sheet; spray lightly with nonstick cooking spray. Bake 10 minutes; turn slices over. Bake 10 minutes longer, until golden brown and crispy.

3. Meanwhile, in large nonstick skillet, heat oil; add onion. Cook over medium-high heat, stirring frequently, 5 minutes, until softened. Add tomatoes, basil and salt; bring liquid to a boil. Reduce heat to low; simmer 5 minutes, until mixture is heated through and flavors are blended.

4. Spoon half of the tomato mixture into 11 × 7" baking dish; top with eggplant slices, then remaining tomato mixture. Bake, covered, 10 minutes; uncover. Sprinkle evenly with mozzarella, then remaining ¹/2 ounce Parmesan cheese; bake, uncovered, 5 minutes, until cheeses are melted.

Serving (one-fourth of eggplant mixture) provides: ¹/2 Fat, 2¹/4 Vegetables, 2 Proteins, 1 Bread, 10 Optional Calories.

Per serving: 283 Calories, 12 g Total Fat, 6 g Saturated Fat, 27 mg Cholesterol, 883 mg Sodium, 26 g Total Carbohydrate, 3 g Dietary Fiber, 18 g Protein, 463 mg Calcium.

BREAKFAST
Banana, ¹/2 medium
Mini Bagel, 1 (1 ounce), split and toasted, with
    1 teaspoon *each* peanut butter and grape jam
Skim Milk, ¹/2 cup
Coffee or Tea (optional)

LIGHT MEAL
Pasta 'n' Chick-Pea Salad (In medium bowl, combine
    2 cups torn Romaine lettuce leaves, 6 cherry
    tomatoes, halved, ¹/2 cup chilled cooked penne
    pasta, ¹/4 cup sliced scallions, 2 ounces drained
    cooked chick-peas and 1 tablespoon fat-free
    Italian dressing.)
Crispbreads, ³/4 ounce
Reduced-Calorie Chocolate-Flavored Pudding (made
    with skim milk), ¹/2 cup
Diet Ginger Ale

MAIN MEAL
Eggplant Parmigiana, 1 serving (see recipe)
Garlic Bread (Spread 1-ounce slice Italian bread with
    ¹/2 teaspoon minced fresh garlic or 1 roasted garlic
    clove; drizzle with ¹/2 teaspoon olive oil. Place
    onto nonstick baking sheet; broil until lightly
    browned.)
Arugula-Orange Salad (In medium bowl, combine
    2 cups torn arugula leaves, ¹/2 cup *each* orange
    sections and radish slices, and 1 teaspoon *each*
    olive oil and red wine vinegar.)
Sugar-Free Cherry-Flavored Gelatin, ¹/2 cup, with
    1 tablespoon thawed frozen light whipped topping (8 calories per tablespoon)

SNACK
Whole-Wheat Pretzels, ³/4 ounce
Hot Cocoa (In small saucepan, with wire whisk,
    combine 1 cup skim milk and 1 tablespoon
    unsweetened cocoa powder, blending until cocoa
    is dissolved. Cook over low heat, stirring constantly, until heated. Stir in sugar substitute to
    equal 4 teaspoons sugar and 1 teaspoon vanilla
    extract; pour into heated mug.)

This menu provides: 2 Milks, 3 Fats, 2 Fruits, 12³/4 Vegetables, 3 Proteins, 6 Breads, 105 Optional Calories.

Per serving: 29 g Fat, 23 g Fiber.

EGGPLANT, RICOTTA AND RED PEPPER ROLLS

Makes 4 servings

1 medium eggplant
2 tablespoons balsamic vinegar
2 teaspoons olive oil
$^1/2$ teaspoon granulated sugar
1 cup tomato sauce (no salt added)
$^1/4$ cup minced fresh mint leaves
$^1/2$ teaspoon salt
$^1/2$ teaspoon grated orange zest*
1 cup part-skim ricotta cheese
$2^1/4$ ounces freshly grated Parmesan cheese
1 egg
1 cup drained roasted red bell peppers, cut into strips

1. Preheat oven to 375° F.

2. Cut eggplant lengthwise into $^1/4$" slices. Select the 8 widest slices; wrap remaining slices in plastic wrap and refrigerate for use at another time.

3. In large shallow bowl, with wire whisk, combine vinegar, oil and sugar, blending until sugar is dissolved; add eggplant slices, turning to coat.

4. Place eggplant slices in a single layer onto nonstick baking sheet; bake, covered, 20 minutes, until soft.

5. Meanwhile, in 8" square baking pan, combine tomato sauce, 2 table-spoons of the mint, $^1/4$ teaspoon of the salt and the zest; set aside.

6. In medium bowl, combine ricotta and Parmesan cheeses, egg, remaining 2 tablespoons mint and remaining $^1/4$ teaspoon salt. Spread each eggplant slice with an equal amount of cheese mixture; top each with an equal amount of bell pepper strips. Starting at shortest end, roll eggplant slices to enclose filling; place eggplant rolls, seam-side down, into tomato sauce mixture. Bake, covered, 20 minutes, until heated through.

Serving (2 eggplant rolls, $^1/4$ cup sauce mixture) provides: $^1/2$ Fat, $2^1/4$ Vegetables, 2 Proteins.

Per serving: 240 Calories, 13 g Total Fat, 7 g Saturated Fat, 85 mg Cholesterol, 749 mg Sodium, 13 g Total Carbohydrate, 1 g Dietary Fiber, 16 g Protein, 408 mg Calcium.

The zest of the orange is the peel without any of the pith (white membrane). To remove zest from orange, use a zester or the fine side of a vegetable grater; wrap orange in plastic wrap and refrigerate for use at another time.

GRILLED SUMMER VEGETABLE PLATTER

During the summer, a platter of fresh grilled vegetables really hits the spot; here, the smoky flavor of the cheese is the perfect counterpoint to the radiant vegetable mélange. If you've never tried these miniature-size vegetables, you're in for an extra-special treat; available in green groceries and supermarkets throughout the country, their delicate texture and sweet flavor make this platter a feast for the eyes as well as the palate.

Makes 4 servings

24 thin asparagus spears
1 medium green bell pepper, seeded and quartered
1 medium yellow bell pepper, seeded and quartered
1 medium red bell pepper, seeded and quartered
Four 2-ounce zucchini, halved lengthwise
Four 2-ounce eggplants, halved lengthwise
Four 1-ounce leeks, halved lengthwise
1 tablespoon olive oil
6 ounces smoked mozzarella cheese, diced
Fresh flat-leaf parsley sprigs, to garnish

1. Preheat outdoor barbecue grill according to manufacturer's directions. Spray grill basket with nonstick cooking spray.*

2. Brush asparagus, green, yellow and red bell peppers, zucchini, eggplants and leeks on all sides with oil; arrange in prepared grill basket. Grill vegetables over hot coals, turning once, 5–10 minutes, until lightly browned and heated through.

3. Divide grilled vegetables evenly among 4 plates; serve each portion with 1^1/$_2$ ounces cheese. Garnish with parsley.

Serving (one-fourth of the vegetables, 1^1/$_2$ ounces cheese) provides:
5 Vegetables, 2 Proteins, 30 Optional Calories.

Per serving: 227 Calories, 13 g Total Fat, 6 g Saturated Fat, 33 mg Cholesterol, 171 mg Sodium, 18 g Total Carbohydrate, 3 g Dietary Fiber, 13 g Protein, 290 mg Calcium.

Using a grill basket makes it easy to turn vegetables during grilling. If desired, grill basket may be omitted and vegetables may be grilled directly on grill rack; spray grill rack with nonstick cooking spray before preheating.

BREAKFAST
Raspberries, ^{1}/$_2$ cup
Cornflakes, ^{3}/$_4$ ounce
Skim Milk, 1 cup
Coffee or Tea (optional)

LIGHT MEAL
Brown Rice 'n' Beans (Spray medium nonstick skillet with nonstick cooking spray; heat. Add ^{1}/$_4$ cup *each* sliced onion and red bell pepper; cook over medium-high heat, stirring frequently, 5 minutes, until vegetables are softened. Stir in ^{1}/$_2$ cup *each* cooked brown rice and green peas, 2 ounces *each* drained cannellini [white kidney] beans and pinto beans and 1 tablespoon minced fresh cilantro. Continuing to stir, cook 3–4 minutes, until mixture is heated through.)
Steamed Broccoli Florets, 1 cup
Tossed Green Salad, 2 cups, with 2 ounces drained cooked pinto beans and 1 tablespoon ranch dressing
Reduced-Calorie Chocolate-Flavored Pudding (made with skim milk), ^{1}/$_2$ cup
Sparkling Mineral Water

MAIN MEAL
Grilled Summer Vegetable Platter, 1 serving (see recipe)
Tomato Salad (In medium bowl, combine 1 medium tomato, diced, ^{1}/$_4$ cup sliced red onion, 3 tablespoons minced fresh flat-leaf parsley and 1 tablespoon fat-free Italian dressing.)
Italian Bread, 1 ounce, with 2 teaspoons reduced-calorie tub margarine
Watermelon, 3 × 2" wedge
Iced Tea with Lemon Wedge

SNACK
Plain Popcorn, hot-air popped, 3 cups
Skim Milk, ^{1}/$_2$ cup

This menu provides: 2 Milks, 3 Fats, 2 Fruits, 14^1/$_2$ Vegetables, 5 Proteins, 5 Breads, 75 Optional Calories.

Per serving: 32 g Fat, 36 g Fiber.

Grilled Summer Vegetable Platter

RICOTTA AND BROCCOLI PIE

Makes 4 servings

1 cup part-skim ricotta cheese
$^3/_4$ cup skim milk
1 egg
1 egg white
$2^1/_4$ ounces freshly grated Parmesan cheese
$^3/_4$ teaspoon grated orange zest*
2 teaspoons olive oil
3 garlic cloves, minced
One 10-ounce package thawed frozen chopped broccoli
$^1/_2$ cup minced fresh basil
4 ounces frozen phyllo dough† (about 6 sheets), thawed

1. Preheat oven to 350° F. Spray 9" pie pan with nonstick cooking spray.

2. In blender or food processor, combine ricotta cheese, milk, egg and egg white; purée until smooth. Add Parmesan cheese and zest; process just until combined. Set aside.

3. In large nonstick skillet, heat oil; add garlic. Cook over medium-high heat, stirring constantly, 1 minute, until fragrant. Add broccoli and basil; cook, stirring frequently, 2 minutes.

4. Line prepared pie pan with 1 phyllo dough sheet; spray lightly with nonstick cooking spray. Top diagonally with another phyllo dough sheet; spray lightly with nonstick cooking spray. Repeat with remaining phyllo dough sheets, spraying each lightly with nonstick cooking spray before placing the next. Fold edges of dough under to form a rim.

5. Transfer broccoli mixture to dough-lined pie pan; top evenly with cheese mixture. Bake 40 minutes, until crust is golden brown and filling is just set. Remove from oven; let stand 10 minutes. Cut into 4 wedges.

Serving (1 wedge) provides: $^1/_2$ Fat, 1 Vegetable, 2 Proteins, 1 Bread, 20 Optional Calories.

Per serving: 341 Calories, 17 g Total Fat, 7 g Saturated Fat, 86 mg Cholesterol, 582 mg Sodium, 27 g Total Carbohydrate, 1 g Dietary Fiber, 22 g Protein, 545 mg Calcium.

*The zest of the orange is the peel without any of the pith (white membrane). To remove zest from orange, use a zester or the fine side of a vegetable grater; wrap orange in plastic wrap and refrigerate for use at another time.

†Phyllo dough dries out quickly. To help keep it soft and pliable, keep sheets covered with plastic wrap until ready to use.

BREAKFAST

Banana, $^1/_2$ medium, sliced
Fortified Cold Cereal, $^3/_4$ ounce
Skim Milk, 1 cup
Coffee or Tea (optional)

LIGHT MEAL

Herb Scramble (In small microwavable bowl, combine $^1/_2$ cup egg substitute, 1 teaspoon minced fresh flat-leaf parsley and $^1/_4$ teaspoon *each* dried oregano leaves and basil; microwave on Medium-High [70% power], $1^1/_2$–2 minutes, stirring once or twice, until set.)
Vegetable Stir-Fry (In medium nonstick skillet, heat 1 teaspoon oriental sesame oil; add $^1/_2$ cup *each* snow peas, broccoli florets and red bell pepper strips. Cook over medium-high heat, stirring frequently, 3–4 minutes, until vegetables are just tender. Serve over $^1/_2$ cup cooked long-grain rice.)
Celery and Carrot Sticks, 1 cup *each*
Pineapple, $^1/_8$ medium
Chinese Tea

MAIN MEAL

Ricotta and Broccoli Pie, 1 serving (see recipe)
Cucumber, Tomato and Mozzarella Salad (In small bowl, combine 1 medium tomato, diced, $^1/_2$ medium cucumber, diced, $1^1/_2$ ounces nonfat mozzarella cheese, diced, 1 tablespoon minced fresh basil and 1 teaspoon *each* olive oil and balsamic vinegar.)
Roll, 1 small (1 ounce), with 1 teaspoon reduced-calorie tub margarine
Sugar-Free Berry-Flavored Gelatin, $^1/_2$ cup, with 1 tablespoon thawed frozen light whipped topping (8 calories per tablespoon)
Diet Cola with Lemon Wedge

SNACK

Nonfat Tortilla Chips, 2 ounces
California Dip (In small bowl, combine $^3/_4$ cup plain nonfat yogurt, 1 packet instant low-sodium vegetable broth and seasoning mix and 1 teaspoon dehydrated onion flakes.)

This menu provides: 2 Milks, 3 Fats, 2 Fruits, 11 Vegetables, 5 Proteins, 6 Breads, 50 Optional Calories.

Per serving: 35 g Fat, 21 g Fiber.

CHEESE AND VEGETABLE QUESADILLAS

Makes 4 servings

Eight 6" flour tortillas
4¹/2 ounces reduced-fat Monterey Jack cheese, grated
1 cup small broccoli florets
4 ounces drained cooked black beans
1 tablespoon fresh lime juice
¹/4 cup chopped drained canned green chiles
¹/4 cup minced fresh cilantro
2 tablespoons minced scallions
¹/2 cup mild or medium salsa
2 tablespoons nonfat sour cream

1. Preheat oven to 400° F. Spray eight 9" squares of foil with nonstick cooking spray.

2. Place 1 tortilla onto each of 4 prepared sheets of foil; sprinkle each with one-fourth of the cheese. Set aside.

3. In small saucepan of boiling water, cook broccoli 3 minutes, until bright green and just tender. Drain, discarding liquid; arrange broccoli on cheese-topped tortillas.

4. In small bowl, with fork, combine beans and juice, mashing beans to form a chunky paste; stir in chiles, cilantro, and scallions. Spread one-fourth of the bean mixture onto each portion of broccoli.

5. Top each portion of bean mixture with 1 remaining tortilla; top each with 1 remaining prepared sheet of foil, sprayed-side down. Crimp edges of foil together to seal; place onto nonstick baking sheet. Bake 7 minutes, until heated through.

6. Unwrap quesadillas. Place each onto plate; cut each into quarters. Top each quesadilla with 2 tablespoons salsa and 1¹/2 teaspoons sour cream.

Serving (1 quesadilla, with 2 tablespoons salsa and 1¹/2 teaspoons sour cream) provides: 1¹/4 Vegetables, 2 Proteins, 2 Breads, 5 Optional Calories.

Per serving: 294 Calories, 10 g Total Fat, 4 g Saturated Fat, 23 mg Cholesterol, 824 mg Sodium, 34 g Total Carbohydrate, 3 g Dietary Fiber, 18 g Protein, 366 mg Calcium.

BREAKFAST
Banana, ¹/2 medium, sliced
Bran Flakes Cereal, 1¹/2 ounces
Skim Milk, 1 cup
Coffee or Tea (optional)

LIGHT MEAL
Vegetable-Bean Soup (In small saucepan, combine ³/4 cup vegetable broth, 2 ounces drained cooked red kidney beans and ¹/4 cup *each* diced onion, green bell pepper and celery. Cook over medium heat, covered, until vegetables are tender.)
Torn Romaine Lettuce Leaves, 2 cups, with ¹/2 cup *each* sliced radishes and cucumber and 1 teaspoon *each* olive oil and cider vinegar
Breadsticks, 2 long
Reduced-Calorie Vanilla-Flavored Pudding (made with skim milk), ¹/2 cup
Iced Tea with Lime Wedge

MAIN MEAL
Cheese and Vegetable Quesadillas, 1 serving (see recipe)
Sliced Red and Green Bell Peppers, 1 cup *each*, with 1 ounce sliced avocado and 1 tablespoon fat-free Italian dressing
Whole Strawberries, 1 cup, with 2 tablespoons thawed frozen light whipped topping (8 calories per tablespoon)
Sparkling Mineral Water

SNACK
Hot Peanut-Cocoa (In small saucepan, combine ¹/2 cup skim milk and 1 teaspoon *each* smooth peanut butter and chocolate syrup; heat.)

This menu provides: 2 Milks, 3 Fats, 2 Fruits, 12³/4 Vegetables, 3 Proteins, 5 Breads, 100 Optional Calories.

Per serving: 29 g Fat, 20 g Fiber.

318
MOROCCAN TAGINE OF VEGETABLES AND CHICK-PEAS

Makes 4 servings

2 teaspoons olive oil
10 ounces new potatoes, pared and cut into $^1/_2$" pieces
2 cups cauliflower florets
1 cup parsnip chunks (1" pieces)
1 cup carrot chunks (1" pieces)
1 teaspoon ground coriander
1 teaspoon sweet Hungarian paprika
$^1/_2$ teaspoon ground cumin
$^1/_2$ teaspoon ground ginger
$^1/_2$ teaspoon freshly ground black pepper
1 pound drained cooked chick-peas
4 large prunes, pitted and chopped
1 tablespoon fresh lemon juice
$^1/_2$ teaspoon salt

1. In large nonstick skillet, heat oil; add potatoes. Cook over medium-high heat, stirring frequently, 5 minutes, until golden brown. Add cauliflower, parsnip, carrot, coriander, paprika, cumin, ginger and pepper; stir to combine.

2. Add chick-peas, prunes, juice, salt and 1 cup water to vegetable mixture; bring liquid to a boil. Reduce heat to low; simmer, covered, 20 minutes, until vegetables are tender and potatoes are cooked through.

Serving ($1^3/_4$ cups) provides: $^1/_2$ Fat, $^1/_2$ Fruit, $1^1/_2$ Vegetables, 2 Proteins, 1 Bread.

Per serving: 343 Calories, 6 g Total Fat, 1 g Saturated Fat, 0 mg Cholesterol, 309 mg Sodium, 63 g Total Carbohydrate, 10 g Dietary Fiber, 14 g Protein, 103 mg Calcium.

BREAKFAST
Apple, 1 small
Frozen Pancakes, 2, heated, with 2 teaspoons *each* maple syrup and reduced-calorie tub margarine
Skim Milk, $^1/_2$ cup
Coffee or Tea (optional)

LIGHT MEAL
Pineapple Cottage Cheese (In small bowl, combine $^1/_2$ cup nonfat cottage cheese and $^1/_4$ cup canned crushed pineapple [no sugar added].)
Carrot and Celery Sticks, 1 cup *each*
Aspartame-Sweetened Strawberry-Banana Nonfat Yogurt, 1 cup
Iced Coffee or Tea

MAIN MEAL
Moroccan Tagine of Vegetables and Chick-Peas, 1 serving (see recipe)
Cooked Couscous, $^1/_2$ cup
Green Bean and Red Onion Salad, 2 cups, with $1^1/_2$ teaspoons *each* olive oil and fresh lemon juice
Reduced-Calorie Vanilla-Flavored Pudding (made with skim milk), $^1/_2$ cup
Sparkling Mineral Water with Mint Sprig

SNACK
Oat-Bran Pretzels, $1^1/_2$ ounces

This menu provides: 2 Milks, 3 Fats, 2 Fruits, $9^1/_2$ Vegetables, 3 Proteins, 6 Breads, 70 Optional Calories.

Per serving: 22 g Fat, 25 g Fiber.

319
VEGETABLE SUKIYAKI

Makes 4 servings

1 cup pared butternut squash chunks ($^1/_4$" pieces)
1 medium carrot, halved lengthwise and cut into 1" pieces
2 cups quartered mushrooms
1 medium yellow squash, halved lengthwise and cut into $^1/_4$" slices
3 ounces linguine
$^1/_3$ cup reduced-sodium soy sauce
3 tablespoons firmly packed light or dark brown sugar
1 tablespoon mirin (Japanese cooking wine)
1 pound firm tofu, cut into 1" chunks
1 tablespoon cornstarch, dissolved in 2 tablespoons cold water
2 tablespoons minced scallions

1. In large pot of boiling water, cook butternut squash and carrot 4 minutes, until just tender. With slotted spoon, remove vegetables from water; set aside.

2. In same pot of boiling water, cook mushrooms and yellow squash 1 minute, until just tender. With slotted spoon, remove vegetables from water; set aside.

3. In same pot of boiling water, cook linguine 8–10 minutes, until tender. Drain, discarding liquid; set aside.

4. In large nonstick skillet, combine soy sauce, brown sugar, mirin and 1 cup water; bring to a boil. Reduce heat to low; add tofu, reserved vegetables and reserved linguine, tossing to combine. Return liquid to a boil; reduce heat to low. Stir in dissolved cornstarch; simmer 2 minutes, until slightly thickened.

5. Divide tofu mixture evenly among 4 bowls; sprinkle each with $1^1/_2$ teaspoons scallions.

Serving (2 cups) provides: 2 Vegetables, 2 Proteins, $1^1/_4$ Breads, 45 Optional Calories.

Per serving: 355 Calories, 11 g Total Fat, 2 g Saturated Fat, 0 mg Cholesterol, 826 mg Sodium, 46 g Total Carbohydrate, 3 g Dietary Fiber, 24 g Protein, 285 mg Calcium.

320

VEGETABLE PAPRIKASH

Makes 4 servings

6 ounces wide egg noodles
2 teaspoons olive oil
1 cup chopped onions
8 garlic cloves, peeled
2 cups diced turnips
2 medium carrots, cut into 1" pieces
3 cups quartered mushrooms
1 tablespoon sweet Hungarian paprika
$^1/_2$ teaspoon salt
$^1/_4$ teaspoon caraway seeds
1 pound drained cooked white beans
1$^1/_2$ cups chopped tomatoes
2 tablespoons tomato paste (no salt added)
$^1/_4$ cup light sour cream
2 tablespoons minced fresh dill

1. In large pot of boiling water, cook noodles 5–6 minutes, until tender. Drain, discarding liquid; set aside.

2. In large nonstick skillet, heat oil; add onions and garlic. Cook over medium-high heat, stirring frequently, 5 minutes, until onions are softened. Add turnips and carrots; stir to coat. Add $^1/_3$ cup water; bring liquid to a boil. Reduce heat to low; simmer, covered, 10 minutes, until vegetables are tender.

3. Add mushrooms to vegetable mixture; simmer, covered, 5 minutes, until mushrooms are tender.

4. Add paprika, salt and caraway seeds to vegetable mixture; stir to combine. Add beans, tomatoes and tomato paste; bring mixture to a boil. Reduce heat to low; simmer, covered, 3 minutes, until mixture is slightly thickened. Stir in sour cream and dill.

5. Add noodles to bean mixture; toss to combine. Cook, tossing constantly, until heated through.

Serving (2$^1/_4$ cups) provides: $^1/_2$ Fat, 5 Vegetables, 2 Proteins, 2 Breads, 20 Optional Calories.

Per serving: 469 Calories, 7 g Total Fat, 2 g Saturated Fat, 45 mg Cholesterol, 367 mg Sodium, 83 g Total Carbohydrate, 11 g Dietary Fiber, 22 g Protein, 189 mg Calcium.

BREAKFAST
Broiled Grapefruit (Sprinkle $^1/_2$ medium grapefruit with 1 teaspoon firmly packed light or dark brown sugar; place on nonstick baking sheet. Broil 2–3 minutes, until topping is bubbling.)
Tomato-Cheese Toast (Top each of 2 slices reduced-calorie whole-wheat bread, toasted, with $^1/_4$ cup nonfat cottage cheese and 2 tomato slices.)
Skim Milk, $^1/_2$ cup
Coffee or Tea

LIGHT MEAL
Eggplant Parmigiana Sandwich (Preheat oven to 350° F. Top 2-ounce slice Italian bread with $^1/_2$ cup cooked sliced eggplant, $^1/_4$ cup tomato sauce [no salt added], $^3/_4$ ounce skim-milk mozzarella cheese, grated, and 1 teaspoon freshly grated Parmesan cheese. Place onto nonstick baking sheet; bake until cheese is melted and sandwich is heated through.)
Escarole and Romaine Lettuce Salad, 2 cups, with 1$^1/_2$ teaspoons Italian dressing
Reduced-Calorie Vanilla-Flavored Pudding (made with skim milk), $^1/_2$ cup
Iced Tea

MAIN MEAL
Vegetable Paprikash, 1 serving (see recipe)
Cucumber Salad (In small bowl, combine $^1/_2$ cup cucumber slices, 1 teaspoon *each* vegetable oil and rice wine vinegar and pinch ground white pepper.)
Whole-Wheat Roll, 1 ounce, with 1 teaspoon reduced-calorie tub margarine
Raspberry Parfait (In stemmed glass, layer $^1/_2$ cup Sugar-Free raspberry-flavored gelatin, diced, and $^1/_2$ cup aspartame-sweetened raspberry nonfat yogurt; top with 1 tablespoon thawed frozen light whipped topping [8 calories per tablespoon].)
Sparkling Mineral Water with Lime Wedge

SNACK
Fresh Fig, 1 large
Chocolate "Float" (In tall glass, combine 1 cup diet chocolate soda and $^1/_2$ cup skim milk; add enough ice cubes to fill glass.)

This menu provides: 2 Milks, 3 Fats, 2 Fruits, 13 Vegetables, 4 Proteins, 6 Breads, 105 Optional Calories.

Per serving: 28 g Fat, 28 g Fiber.

BARBECUED VEGETABLES WITH CORN BREAD

Makes 4 servings

BREAKFAST
Grapefruit, $^1/_2$ medium
Cinnamon-Raisin Bread, toasted, 2 slices, with
  $^1/_4$ cup nonfat cottage cheese
Aspartame-Sweetened Vanilla Nonfat Yogurt, 1 cup
Coffee or Tea (optional)

LIGHT MEAL
PB&J Sandwich (Spread 1 slice reduced-calorie
  whole-wheat bread with 1 tablespoon peanut butter and 2 teaspoons raspberry jam; top with
  another slice reduced-calorie whole-wheat bread.)
Carrot and Celery Sticks, 1 cup *each*
Diet Ginger Ale

MAIN MEAL
Barbecued Vegetables with Corn Bread, 1 serving
  (see recipe)
Torn Romaine Lettuce Leaves, 2 cups, with $^1/_2$ medium tomato, sliced, and $^1/_4$ cup sliced red onion
  with 1 tablespoon fat-free Italian dressing
Banana Split (Scoop 4 fluid ounces vanilla sugar-free
  nonfat frozen yogurt into small bowl. Cut
  $^1/_2$ medium banana in half lengthwise; place
  halves on opposite sides of frozen yogurt. Drizzle
  yogurt and banana with 2 teaspoons chocolate
  syrup; sprinkle with $^1/_2$ ounce unsalted dry-
  roasted peanuts, chopped.)
Iced Tea

SNACK
Nonfat Process American Cheese, $1^1/_2$ ounces
Fat-Free Crackers, 7
Skim Milk, $^3/_4$ cup

This menu provides: 2 Milks, 3 Fats, 2 Fruits,
13 Vegetables, 5 Proteins, 6 Breads, 160 Optional
Calories.

Per serving: 35 g Fat, 24 g Fiber.

$^3/_4$ cup all-purpose flour
$^1/_2$ cup uncooked yellow cornmeal
$1^1/_4$ teaspoons double-acting baking powder
1 teaspoon granulated sugar
$^1/_2$ teaspoon salt
$^1/_4$ teaspoon baking soda
$5^1/_4$ ounces reduced-fat cheddar cheese, grated
$^3/_4$ cup skim buttermilk
1 egg
1 tablespoon + 1 teaspoon vegetable oil
1 cup tomato sauce (no salt added)
2 tablespoons firmly packed light or dark brown sugar
1 tablespoon cider vinegar
1 teaspoon Dijon-style mustard
$^3/_4$ teaspoon ground ginger
2 medium zucchini, thinly sliced lengthwise
2 medium yellow squash, thinly sliced lengthwise
2 medium red onions, thinly sliced and separated into rings

1. Preheat oven to 350° F. Spray 8" round cake pan with nonstick cooking spray.

2. To prepare corn bread, in large bowl, combine flour, cornmeal, baking
powder, granulated sugar, salt and baking soda; stir in cheese. In small
bowl, combine buttermilk, egg and oil. Add wet ingredients to dry; stir
just until combined. Transfer batter to prepared baking pan; bake 25 minutes, until golden brown and toothpick inserted into center comes out
clean. Remove to a rack to cool. Increase oven temperature to broil.

3. To prepare barbecued vegetables, in small bowl, combine tomato
sauce, brown sugar, vinegar, mustard and ginger. Add zucchini, squash and
onions; toss to combine. With slotted spoon, transfer vegetables to broiler
pan, reserving sauce mixture; broil 4" from heat, turning as needed and
basting occasionally with sauce mixture, 10 minutes, using all sauce, until
golden brown and cooked through. Serve vegetable mixture with corn
bread.

Serving (1 cup vegetable mixture; one-fourth of the corn bread) provides:
1 Fat, $3^1/_2$ Vegetables, 2 Proteins, 2 Breads, 45 Optional Calories.

Per serving: 431 Calories, 14 g Total Fat, 6 g Saturated Fat, 81 mg Cholesterol,
910 mg Sodium, 56 g Total Carbohydrate, 4 g Dietary Fiber, 22 g Protein,
527 mg Calcium.

CORN PUDDING WITH VEGETABLES

Makes 4 servings

2 cups evaporated skimmed milk
3 egg whites
2 eggs
1 teaspoon granulated sugar
1/4 teaspoon ground red pepper
2 cups canned cream-style corn (no salt added)
1 cup thawed frozen corn kernels
1 cup drained roasted red bell peppers, cut into strips
1 cup sliced scallions
3 ounces freshly grated Parmesan cheese
1 1/2 ounces reduced-fat cheddar cheese, grated
1/3 cup + 2 teaspoons plain dried bread crumbs

1. Preheat oven to 375° F. Adjust oven rack to divide oven in half. Spray 9" square baking pan with nonstick cooking spray.

2. In large bowl, with wire whisk, combine milk, egg whites, eggs, sugar and ground red pepper; fold in cream-style corn, corn kernels, roasted peppers, scallions, Parmesan and cheddar cheeses and bread crumbs.

3. Transfer mixture to prepared baking pan; place pan into larger baking pan. Place into oven; pour hot water into larger pan to come halfway up sides of smaller pan. Bake 1 hour, until just set.

Serving (one-fourth of pudding) provides: 1 Milk, 1 Vegetable, 2 1/4 Proteins, 2 Breads, 5 Optional Calories.

Per serving: 471 Calories, 13 g Total Fat, 7 g Saturated Fat, 136 mg Cholesterol, 866 mg Sodium, 60 g Total Carbohydrate, 3 g Dietary Fiber, 33 g Protein, 819 mg Calcium.

BREAKFAST
Blueberries, 3/4 cup
Reduced-Calorie Granola Bar, 1 (1 ounce)
Skim Milk, 3/4 cup
Coffee or Tea (optional)

LIGHT MEAL
Grilled Cheese and Tomato Sandwich (Split and toast one 2-ounce English muffin. Top one muffin half with 3/4 ounce reduced-fat cheddar cheese; top the other muffin half with 1/2 medium tomato, sliced. Place onto nonstick baking sheet; broil until heated through. Place cheese-topped muffin half onto tomato slices, cheese-side down.)
Tossed Green Salad, 2 cups, with 1 teaspoon *each* olive oil and balsamic vinegar
Peach, 1 medium
Diet Lemonade, 1 cup

MAIN MEAL
Corn Pudding with Vegetables, 1 serving (see recipe)
Chilled Cooked Broccoli and Cauliflower Florets, 1 cup *each*
Sugar-Free Strawberry Nonfat Frozen Yogurt, 4 fluid ounces
Iced Herbal Tea

SNACK
Graham Crackers, 3 (2 1/2" squares), with 2 teaspoons *each* peanut butter and apricot jam

This menu provides: 2 Milks, 3 Fats, 2 Fruits, 10 Vegetables, 3 1/4 Proteins, 6 Breads, 110 Optional Calories.

Per serving: 34 g Fat, 21 g Fiber.

323
BRUNSWICK STEW

Makes 4 servings

2 teaspoons olive oil
1 cup chopped onions
4 garlic cloves, minced
1 cup diced green bell pepper
$1^1/_2$ cups stewed tomatoes (no salt added)
1 cup tomato sauce (no salt added)
12 ounces drained cooked red kidney beans
1 cup thawed frozen baby green lima beans
$^1/_2$ teaspoon dried thyme leaves
$^1/_4$ teaspoon salt
$^1/_4$ teaspoon freshly ground black pepper
$^1/_4$ teaspoon hot red pepper sauce
1 cup thawed frozen corn kernels

1. In large nonstick skillet, heat oil; add onions and garlic. Cook over medium-high heat, stirring frequently, 5 minutes, until onions are softened. Add bell pepper; cook, stirring frequently, 5 minutes, until bell pepper is softened.

2. Add tomatoes and tomato sauce to vegetable mixture; bring liquid to a boil. Add kidney and lima beans, thyme, salt, black pepper and pepper sauce; stir to combine. Reduce heat to low; simmer 10 minutes, until flavors are blended. Stir in corn; cook, stirring frequently, 3 minutes, until mixture is heated through.

Serving ($1^3/_4$ cups) provides: $^1/_2$ Fat, $2^3/_4$ Vegetables, $1^1/_2$ Proteins, 1 Bread.

Per serving: 290 Calories, 4 g Total Fat, 0 g Saturated Fat, 0 mg Cholesterol, 199 mg Sodium, 55 g Total Carbohydrate, 10 g Dietary Fiber, 14 g Protein, 92 mg Calcium.

324
CAULIFLOWER AND POTATOES WITH TOMATOES AND SPICES

Makes 4 servings

15 ounces new potatoes, cut into $^1/_2$" chunks
2 teaspoons olive oil
3 cups cauliflower florets
3 garlic cloves, slivered
1 cup chopped tomato
2 tablespoons minced fresh cilantro
$^1/_2$ teaspoon salt
$^1/_2$ teaspoon ground ginger
$^1/_4$ teaspoon freshly ground black pepper
$^3/_4$ cup plain nonfat yogurt
1 pound firm tofu, cut into 1" chunks
$^1/_2$ cup fresh or thawed frozen green peas

1. Place potatoes into medium saucepan; add water to cover. Bring liquid to a boil; reduce heat to low. Simmer 10–15 minutes, until potatoes are tender. Drain, discarding liquid; set aside.

2. In large nonstick skillet, heat oil; add cauliflower and garlic. Cook over medium-high heat, stirring frequently, 7 minutes, until cauliflower is lightly browned. Stir in tomato, cilantro, salt, ginger, pepper and $^1/_2$ cup water; bring liquid to a boil. Reduce heat to low; stir in reserved potatoes.

3. Continuing to stir, gradually add yogurt; cook, stirring frequently, 7 minutes, until vegetables are tender and flavors are blended. Stir in tofu and peas; cook, stirring frequently, 3 minutes, until heated through.

Serving (2 cups) provides: $^1/_4$ Milk, $^1/_2$ Fat, 2 Vegetables, 2 Proteins, 1 Bread.

Per serving: 342 Calories, 13 g Total Fat, 2 g Saturated Fat, 1 mg Cholesterol, 347 mg Sodium, 37 g Total Carbohydrate, 5 g Dietary Fiber, 25 g Protein, 352 mg Calcium.

Pear, 1 small
Gingered Cottage Cheese (In small bowl, combine $^1/_2$ cup nonfat cottage cheese and 1 tablespoon chopped crystallized ginger.)
Crispbreads, $^3/_4$ ounce
Skim Milk, $^3/_4$ cup
Coffee or Tea (optional)

LIGHT MEAL
Deviled Egg Salad Sandwich (In small bowl, combine 1 hard-cooked egg, chopped, 2 tablespoons *each* chopped scallions and minced fresh flat-leaf parsley, 2 teaspoons reduced-calorie mayonnaise and $^1/_2$ teaspoon prepared mustard; spread between 2 slices reduced-calorie whole-wheat bread.)
Radishes and Celery Sticks, 1 cup *each*
Diet Lemonade, 1 cup

MAIN MEAL
Cauliflower and Potatoes with Tomatoes and Spices, 1 serving (see recipe)
Chilled Cooked Whole Green Beans, 1 cup, with 1 teaspoon *each* olive oil and balsamic vinegar and pinch dried oregano leaves
Carrot-Raisin Salad (In small bowl, combine 1 cup shredded carrot, 2 tablespoons raisins and 1 teaspoon *each* granulated sugar, reduced-calorie mayonnaise and fresh lemon juice.)
Breadsticks, 2 long
Aspartame-Sweetened Black Cherry Nonfat Yogurt, 1 cup
Decaffeinated Coffee or Tea

SNACK
Plain Popcorn, hot-air popped, 3 cups, with 1 teaspoon freshly grated Parmesan cheese
Diet Cola

This menu provides: 2 Milks, 3 Fats, 2 Fruits, 10$^1/_4$ Vegetables, 4 Proteins, 5 Breads, 80 Optional Calories.

Per serving: 34 g Fat, 33 g Fiber.

LIGHT MEAL
Italian Rice and Red Beans (In small saucepan, combine $^1/_2$ cup cooked long-grain rice, 2 ounces drained cooked red beans, $^1/_4$ cup tomato sauce [no salt added], 2 tablespoons chopped scallions and 2 teaspoons freshly grated Parmesan cheese; cook over low heat, stirring constantly, until heated through.)
Caesar Salad (In medium bowl, combine 2 cups torn Romaine lettuce leaves, $^1/_4$ cup packaged croutons and 1 tablespoon fat-free Caesar salad dressing.)
Sugar-Free Vanilla Nonfat Frozen Yogurt, 4 fluid ounces
Iced Herbal Tea

MAIN MEAL
Spaghetti with Creamy Blue Cheese Sauce, 1 serving (see recipe)
Steamed Broccoli and Cauliflower Florets, 1 cup *each*, with 2 teaspoons *each* olive oil and fresh lemon juice
Escarole and Arugula Salad, 2 cups, with 5 small pitted black olives and 1 tablespoon fat-free Italian dressing
Dutch-Apple Yogurt (In small bowl, combine $^1/_2$ cup aspartame-sweetened vanilla nonfat yogurt, $^1/_4$ cup unsweetened applesauce and $^1/_4$ teaspoon apple pie spice.)
Unsweetened Lime-Flavored Seltzer

SNACK
Oat-Bran Pretzels, $^3/_4$ ounce

This menu provides: 2 Milks, 3 Fats, 2 Fruits, 13$^1/_4$ Vegetables, 3 Proteins, 5$^1/_2$ Breads, 110 Optional Calories.

Per serving: 30 g Fat, 21 g Fiber.

SPAGHETTI WITH CREAMY BLUE CHEESE SAUCE

Makes 4 servings

6 ounces spaghetti
2 cups skim milk
2 tablespoons all-purpose flour
$^1/_4$ teaspoon salt
$^1/_4$ teaspoon freshly ground black pepper
Pinch ground red pepper
4$^1/_2$ ounces blue cheese (preferably Danish), crumbled
1$^1/_2$ ounces freshly grated Parmesan cheese
2 large dried figs, coarsely chopped
$^1/_4$ cup minced fresh chives

1. In large pot of boiling water, cook spaghetti 8–10 minutes, until tender. Drain, discarding liquid; place into serving bowl. Keep warm.

2. In large saucepan, with wire whisk, combine milk and flour, blending until flour is dissolved. Add salt and black and ground red peppers; cook over medium heat, stirring constantly with wire whisk, 5 minutes, until mixture is thickened.

3. Add blue and Parmesan cheeses to milk mixture; cook, stirring constantly, until cheese is melted. Stir in figs and chives.

4. Pour cheese mixture over warm spaghetti; toss to combine.

Serving (1 cup) provides: $^1/_2$ Milk, $^1/_2$ Fruit, 2 Proteins, 2 Breads, 15 Optional Calories.

Per serving: 404 Calories, 13 g Total Fat, 8 g Saturated Fat, 35 mg Cholesterol, 846 mg Sodium, 49 g Total Carbohydrate, 2 g Dietary Fiber, 22 g Protein, 493 mg Calcium.

FETTUCCINE CARBONARA

Makes 4 servings

1¹/₃ cups low-fat (1%) cottage cheese
1 cup evaporated skimmed milk
1 egg
¹/₂ teaspoon freshly ground black pepper
¹/₄ teaspoon salt
2 cups broccoli florets
6 ounces fettuccine
2 teaspoons olive oil
2 tablespoons minced shallots
2 garlic cloves, minced
¹/₂ cup finely diced red bell pepper
2¹/₄ ounces freshly grated Parmesan cheese
¹/₄ cup minced fresh flat-leaf parsley
2 tablespoons minced scallions

1. In blender or food processor, purée cottage cheese 1 minute, until smooth. Add milk, egg, black pepper and salt; process until combined. Set aside.

2. In large pot of boiling water, cook broccoli 3 minutes, until bright green and just tender. With slotted spoon, remove broccoli from water; set aside.

3. In same pot of boiling water, cook fettuccine 8–10 minutes, until tender. Drain, discarding liquid; set aside.

4. In same pot, heat oil; add shallots and garlic. Cook over low heat, stirring frequently, 2–3 minutes, until shallots are tender. Add bell pepper; cook, stirring frequently, 6–7 minutes, until bell pepper is softened. Add cooked broccoli; stir to combine.

5. Add cooked fettuccine and reserved cottage cheese mixture to vegetable mixture; cook, stirring constantly, until mixture is thickened and heated through. Add Parmesan cheese, parsley and scallions; toss to combine.

Serving (1¹/₂ cups) provides: ¹/₂ Milk, ¹/₂ Fat, 1¹/₂ Vegetables, 2 Proteins, 2 Breads.

Per serving: 409 Calories, 11 g Total Fat, 5 g Saturated Fat, 112 mg Cholesterol, 854 mg Sodium, 47 g Total Carbohydrate, 4 g Dietary Fiber, 31 g Protein, 512 mg Calcium.

BREAKFAST
Cooked Oatmeal, ¹/₂ cup, with 3 dried apple slices, chopped
Skim Milk, ¹/₂ cup
Coffee or Tea (optional)

LIGHT MEAL
French Onion Soup au Gratin, 1 cup
Tossed Green Salad, 2 cups, with ³/₄ cup sliced radishes and 1¹/₂ teaspoons *each* olive oil and balsamic vinegar
French Bread, 1 slice (1 ounce)
Reduced-Calorie Butterscotch-Flavored Pudding (made with skim milk), ¹/₂ cup
Unsweetened Lime-Flavored Seltzer

MAIN MEAL
Fettuccine Carbonara, 1 serving (see recipe)
Cucumber and Carrot Sticks, 1 cup *each*
Caesar Salad (In medium bowl, combine 2 cups torn Romaine lettuce leaves, ¹/₄ cup packaged croutons and 1 tablespoon fat-free Caesar salad dressing.)
Baked Apple (Preheat oven to 350° F. Pare 1 small apple halfway down from stem end; place into small baking dish. Sprinkle apple with 1 teaspoon granulated sugar and ¹/₄ teaspoon cinnamon; add ¹/₄" water to pan. Bake, covered, 30 minutes, until tender.)
Decaffeinated Coffee or Tea

SNACK
Chocolate "Float" (In tall glass, combine 1 cup diet chocolate soda and ¹/₂ cup skim milk; add enough ice cubes to fill glass.)

This menu provides: 2 Milks, 3 Fats, 2 Fruits, 16¹/₂ Vegetables, 3 Proteins, 5¹/₂ Breads, 145 Optional Calories.

Per serving: 32 g Fat, 20 g Fiber.

327
VEGETARIAN LASAGNA

Makes 4 servings

6 ounces curly or plain lasagna noodles (6 noodles)
1 tablespoon + 1 teaspoon olive oil
1 cup coarsely chopped onions
4 garlic cloves, minced
$^1/_2$ cup diced carrot
1 cup thinly sliced zucchini
1 cup sliced mushrooms
2 cups canned crushed tomatoes (no salt added)
$^1/_3$ cup minced fresh basil
$^1/_2$ teaspoon salt
$^1/_4$ teaspoon freshly ground black pepper
5 ounces skim-milk mozzarella cheese, grated
1 ounce freshly grated Parmesan cheese

1. Preheat oven to 350° F. Spray 9" square baking pan with nonstick cooking spray.

2. In large pot of boiling water, cook lasagna noodles 10–12 minutes, until tender. Drain, discarding liquid; set aside, keeping noodles flat and separate.

3. In large nonstick skillet, heat oil; add onions and garlic. Cook over medium-high heat, stirring frequently, 5 minutes, until onions are softened. Add carrot; cook, stirring frequently, 5 minutes, until carrot is softened.

4. Add zucchini and mushrooms to vegetable mixture; cook, stirring frequently, 4 minutes, until zucchini and mushrooms are softened. Stir in tomatoes, basil, salt and pepper; bring liquid to a boil. Reduce heat to low; simmer, covered, 3 minutes, until vegetables are tender.

5. Spoon 2 tablespoons vegetable mixture into prepared baking pan; top with a single layer of 2 cooked lasagna noodles, cut to fit. Spread noodles with one-third of the remaining vegetable mixture; sprinkle with one-third of the mozzarella cheese. Repeat layers of noodles, vegetable mixture and mozzarella cheese 2 more times; sprinkle evenly with Parmesan cheese. Bake 25 minutes, until heated through and bubbling. Remove from oven; let stand 5 minutes. Cut into quarters.

Serving (one-fourth of lasagna) provides: 1 Fat, $2^3/_4$ Vegetables, 2 Proteins, 2 Breads.

Per serving: 384 Calories, 14 g Total Fat, 6 g Saturated Fat, 26 mg Cholesterol, 778 mg Sodium, 47 g Total Carbohydrate, 4 g Dietary Fiber, 20 g Protein, 421 mg Calcium.

328

PENNE BOLOGNESE

A clever twist on a classic meat sauce, our version is made with richly flavored sun-dried tomatoes rather than beef. Make it today to enjoy tomorrow—it's even better a day later!

Makes 4 servings

16 sun-dried tomato halves (not packed in oil)
6 ounces penne pasta
2 teaspoons stick margarine
2 teaspoons olive oil
1 cup finely diced onions
1 cup finely diced carrot
1 cup finely diced or thinly sliced celery
1 cup canned whole tomatoes (no salt added), coarsely chopped
2 fluid ounces (1/4 cup) dry white wine
1 cup low-sodium vegetable broth
1 cup evaporated skimmed milk
Pinch freshly grated nutmeg
1 cup fresh or thawed frozen green peas
1 tablespoon + 1 teaspoon freshly grated Parmesan cheese

1. Place dried tomatoes into small bowl; add boiling water to cover. Let stand 30 minutes, until softened; drain, discarding liquid. Coarsely chop soaked tomatoes; set aside.

2. In large pot of boiling water, cook penne 13 minutes, until tender. Drain, discarding liquid; place into serving bowl. Keep warm.

3. Meanwhile, to prepare sauce, in medium nonstick saucepan, combine margarine and oil. Place over medium-high heat; cook until margarine is melted and mixture is heated. Add onions, carrot and celery; cook, stirring frequently, 5 minutes, until onions are softened. Add canned tomatoes, wine and soaked tomatoes; cook, stirring constantly, 5 minutes, until liquid is evaporated. Add broth, milk and nutmeg; bring liquid just to a boil. Reduce heat to low; simmer, stirring occasionally, 15–20 minutes, until vegetables are very soft, adding 1/4 cup water, 1 tablespoon at a time, if mixture becomes too dry. Add peas and 1/2 cup water; simmer, stirring occasionally, 5 minutes, until peas are cooked through.

4. Top warm penne with sauce; toss to combine. Serve sprinkled with cheese.

Serving (1 cup) provides: 1/2 Milk, 1 Fat, 4 Vegetables, 2 1/2 Breads, 30 Optional Calories.

Per serving: 376 Calories, 6 g Total Fat, 1 g Saturated Fat, 4 mg Cholesterol, 343 mg Sodium, 63 g Total Carbohydrate, 7 g Dietary Fiber, 17 g Protein, 283 mg Calcium.

BREAKFAST

Orange Sections, 1/2 cup
Cottage Cheese "Danish" (In small bowl, combine 1/2 cup nonfat cottage cheese, sugar substitute to equal 2 teaspoons sugar and 1/4 teaspoon cinnamon; spread onto 2 slices reduced-calorie whole-wheat bread, toasted.)
Skim Milk, 1/2 cup
Coffee or Tea (optional)

LIGHT MEAL

Swiss 'n' Egg Pita (Split 1 large [2-ounce] pita halfway around edge; open to form pocket. Fill pita pocket with 2 slices nonfat process Swiss cheese, 1 hard-cooked egg, sliced, 1/2 cup *each* spinach leaves and cucumber slices, 2 tomato slices and 2 teaspoons *each* reduced-calorie mayonnaise and prepared mustard.)
Carrot and Celery Sticks, 1 cup *each*
Reduced-Calorie Vanilla-Flavored Pudding (made with skim milk)
Unsweetened Seltzer

MAIN MEAL

Penne Bolognese, 1 serving (see recipe)
Cooked Broccoli, 4 spears, with 1 teaspoon freshly grated Parmesan cheese
Steamed Sliced Yellow Squash, 1 cup
Torn Romaine and Red Leaf Lettuce Leaves, 2 cups, with 1/2 cup sliced cucumber, 2 ounces drained cooked chick-peas and 1 teaspoon *each* olive oil and balsamic vinegar
Pear, 1 small
Sparkling Mineral Water

SNACK

Vanilla Wafers, 3
Skim Milk, 1/2 cup

This menu provides: 2 Milks, 3 Fats, 2 Fruits, 19 1/2 Vegetables, 4 Proteins, 6 Breads, 105 Optional Calories.

Per serving: 26 g Fat, 37 g Fiber.

329
PASTA WITH WHITE BEANS

Makes 4 servings

6 ounces small pasta shells
1 tablespoon + 1 teaspoon olive oil
$3/4$ teaspoon dried rosemary leaves, crumbled
5 garlic cloves, minced
1 medium carrot, cut in half lengthwise, then thinly sliced
1 cup thickly sliced mushrooms
$1/2$ cup crushed tomatoes (no salt added)
$1/4$ teaspoon salt
8 ounces drained cooked white beans
3 ounces freshly grated Parmesan cheese
3 tablespoons minced fresh flat-leaf parsley

1. In large pot of boiling water, cook pasta shells 8–10 minutes, until tender. Drain, discarding liquid; set aside.

2. Meanwhile, in large nonstick skillet, heat oil; add rosemary. Cook over medium-high heat, stirring constantly, 30 seconds, until fragrant. Add garlic; cook, stirring constantly, 1 minute. Add carrot and mushrooms; cook, stirring frequently, 7 minutes, until vegetables are tender.

3. Add tomatoes, salt and $3/4$ cup water to vegetable mixture; stir to combine. Stir in beans; bring liquid to a boil. Reduce heat to low; simmer, covered, 5 minutes, until mixture is thickened. Add cheese, parsley and cooked pasta; toss to combine.

Serving ($1 1/4$ cups) provides: 1 Fat, $2 1/4$ Vegetables, 2 Proteins, 2 Breads.

Per serving: 402 Calories, 12 g Total Fat, 5 g Saturated Fat, 17 mg Cholesterol, 598 mg Sodium, 53 g Total Carbohydrate, 5 g Dietary Fiber, 21 g Protein, 381 mg Calcium.

330

TORTELLINI IN RED PEPPER SAUCE

Makes 4 servings

80 cheese tortellini (5¹/₃ cups)
1 tablespoon + 1 teaspoon olive oil
3 garlic cloves, slivered
2 cups thinly sliced red bell peppers
1 cup thinly sliced onions
¹/₂ teaspoon grated orange zest*
¹/₂ teaspoon salt
¹/₄ teaspoon ground ginger
¹/₂ cup fresh orange juice
2 tablespoons tomato paste (no salt added)
2 tablespoons light sour cream

1. In large pot of boiling water, cook tortellini until tender. Drain, discarding liquid; set aside.

2. Meanwhile, in large nonstick skillet, heat oil; add garlic. Cook over medium-high heat, stirring constantly, 1 minute, until fragrant. Add bell peppers, onions, zest, salt and ginger; cook, stirring frequently, 5 minutes, until vegetables are softened. Add ¹/₄ cup water; bring liquid to a boil. Reduce heat to low; simmer, covered, stirring occasionally, 7 minutes, until vegetables are very soft.

3. Stir juice and tomato paste into vegetable mixture; bring liquid to a boil. Cook, stirring frequently, 4 minutes, until liquid is thickened.

4. Transfer vegetable mixture to blender or food processor; purée until smooth.

5. Return vegetable mixture to skillet; stir in sour cream. Cook over low heat, stirring constantly, just until heated through (do not boil). Add cooked tortellini; cook, stirring gently, just until heated through.

Serving (1¹/₂ cups) provides: 1 Fat, ¹/₄ Fruit, 1³/₄ Vegetables, 2 Proteins, 1¹/₂ Breads, 80 Optional Calories.

Per serving: 283 Calories, 10 g Total Fat, 3 g Saturated Fat, 26 mg Cholesterol, 480 mg Sodium, 41 g Total Carbohydrate, 3 g Dietary Fiber, 10 g Protein, 93 mg Calcium.

The zest of the orange is the peel without any of the pith (white membrane). To remove zest from orange, use a zester or the fine side of a vegetable grater.

BREAKFAST
Fresh Fig, 1 large
English Muffin, 1 (2 ounces), split and toasted, topped with 1 poached egg
Skim Milk, 1 cup
Coffee or Tea (optional)

LIGHT MEAL
Spinach-Mushroom Salad (In medium bowl, combine 2 cups torn spinach leaves, ¹/₂ cup *each* sliced mushrooms and sliced red onion, 1 hard-cooked egg, sliced, 2 teaspoons imitation bacon bits and 1¹/₂ teaspoons Italian dressing.)
Carrot Sticks, 1 cup
Roll, 1 ounce, with 1 teaspoon reduced-calorie tub margarine
Sugar-Free Grape-Flavored Gelatin, ¹/₂ cup
Unsweetened Lemon-Flavored Seltzer

MAIN MEAL
Tortellini in Red Pepper Sauce, 1 serving (see recipe)
Green Bean Salad (In small bowl, combine 1 cup chilled cooked green beans, ¹/₄ cup chopped red onion, 1 tablespoon minced fresh basil and 1 tablespoon fat-free honey-mustard dressing.)
Italian Bread, 1 slice (1 ounce), with 1 teaspoon reduced-calorie tub margarine
Aspartame-Sweetened Peach Nonfat Yogurt, 1 cup
Decaffeinated Coffee or Tea

SNACK
Strawberries, ³/₄ cup

This menu provides: 2 Milks, 3 Fats, 2 Fruits, 12¹/₄ Vegetables, 4 Proteins, 5¹/₂ Breads, 130 Optional Calories.

Per serving: 35 g Fat, 21 g Fiber.

BREAKFAST

Grapefruit, $^1/_2$ medium
Herbed Cottage Cheese (In small bowl, combine
   $^1/_2$ cup nonfat cottage cheese and 1 tablespoon
   each minced fresh flat-leaf parsley and chives.)
Mini Bagel, 1 (1 ounce), split and toasted
Skim Milk, 1 cup
Coffee or Tea (optional)

LIGHT MEAL

Three-Bean and Vegetable Salad (In medium bowl,
   combine 2 cups torn Romaine lettuce leaves,
   $^1/_2$ cup *each* cooked cut green beans, sliced mushrooms, diced tomatoes and sliced red onion,
   1 ounce *each* drained cooked chick-peas and red
   kidney beans and 2 tablespoons fat-free Italian
   dressing.)
Garlic-Herb Bread (Spread 1-ounce slice Italian
   bread with $^1/_2$ teaspoon minced fresh garlic or
   1 roasted garlic clove and $^1/_2$ teaspoon *each*
   minced fresh basil and oregano leaves; drizzle with
   1 teaspoon olive oil. Place onto nonstick baking
   sheet; broil until lightly browned.)
Reduced-Calorie Chocolate-Flavored Pudding (made
   with skim milk), $^1/_2$ cup
Unsweetened Black Cherry–Flavored Seltzer

MAIN MEAL

Orzo with Feta Cheese and Herbs, 1 serving (see
   recipe)
Grilled Bell Peppers (Preheat grill according to manufacturer's directions. Grill $^1/_2$ cup *each* sliced red,
   green and yellow bell pepper strips, turning as
   needed, until lightly browned and tender.)
Angel Food Cake, 2 ounces, topped with $^1/_2$ cup
   strawberries, sliced
Sparkling Mineral Water

SNACK

Plain Popcorn, hot-air popped, 3 cups, with 2 teaspoons reduced-calorie tub margarine, melted
Skim Milk, $^1/_2$ cup

This menu provides: 2 Milks, 3 Fats, 2 Fruits,
13$^1/_2$ Vegetables, 4$^1/_4$ Proteins, 5$^1/_4$ Breads,
125 Optional Calories.

Per serving: 29 g Fat, 25 g Fiber.

ORZO WITH FETA CHEESE AND HERBS

Makes 4 servings

4 sun-dried tomato halves (not packed in oil)
6 ounces orzo (rice-shaped pasta)
3 tablespoons balsamic vinegar
1 tablespoon olive oil
$^1/_4$ teaspoon salt
$^1/_4$ teaspoon freshly ground black pepper
4 cups packed washed trimmed spinach leaves, dried and torn into bite-
   size pieces
6 ounces feta cheese, crumbled
$^1/_4$ cup minced fresh basil
$^1/_4$ cup raisins
6 large black olives, pitted and coarsely chopped

1. Place tomatoes into small bowl; add boiling water to cover. Let stand
30 minutes, until softened; drain, discarding liquid. Coarsely chop tomatoes; set aside.

2. Meanwhile, in large pot of boiling water, cook orzo 9 minutes, until
tender. Drain, discarding liquid; place into large bowl. Add vinegar, oil,
salt and pepper; set aside until room temperature.

3. Add spinach, cheese, basil, raisins, olives and reserved chopped tomatoes to orzo mixture; toss to combine.

Serving (2 cups) provides: 1 Fat, $^1/_2$ Fruit, 2$^1/_2$ Vegetables, 2 Proteins, 2 Breads.

Per serving: 366 Calories, 14 g Total Fat, 7 g Saturated Fat, 38 mg Cholesterol,
747 mg Sodium, 47 g Total Carbohydrate, 4 g Dietary Fiber, 15 g Protein,
339 mg Calcium.

332

MINTED COUSCOUS TABBOULEH WITH CHICK-PEAS AND CHEESE

Makes 4 servings

6 ounces couscous (semolina)
10 ounces drained cooked chick-peas
12 cherry tomatoes, halved
$^3/_4$ cup minced fresh flat-leaf parsley
$^1/_2$ cup chopped scallions
$^1/_3$ cup minced fresh mint leaves
$2^1/_4$ ounces feta cheese, crumbled
3 tablespoons fresh lemon juice
1 tablespoon + 1 teaspoon olive oil
$^1/_2$ teaspoon Dijon-style mustard
$^1/_2$ teaspoon salt

1. Place couscous into large bowl; add boiling water to cover. Place a sheet of plastic wrap or foil over bowl and seal edges; let stand 10 minutes, until all water is absorbed. Add chick-peas, tomatoes, parsley, scallions, mint and cheese; stir to combine.

2. In small jar with tight-fitting lid or small bowl, combine juice, oil, mustard and salt; cover and shake well or, with wire whisk, blend until combined. Pour over couscous mixture; toss to combine.

Serving (2 cups) provides: 1 Fat, $^3/_4$ Vegetable, 2 Proteins, $1^1/_2$ Breads.

Per serving: 376 Calories, 10 g Total Fat, 3 g Saturated Fat, 14 mg Cholesterol, 485 mg Sodium, 57 g Total Carbohydrate, 5 g Dietary Fiber, 15 g Protein, 154 mg Calcium.

BREAKFAST

Banana Smoothie (In blender, combine 1 cup skim milk, $^1/_2$ medium banana, sliced, 2 ice cubes and 2 teaspoons honey; purée until smooth.)
Cinnamon-Raisin Bread, 2 slices, toasted, with 2 teaspoons reduced-calorie tub margarine
Coffee or Tea (optional)

LIGHT MEAL

Pineapple Cottage Cheese (In small bowl, combine $^1/_2$ cup nonfat cottage cheese and $^1/_4$ cup canned crushed pineapple [no sugar added].)
Torn Romaine Lettuce Leaves and Red Bell Pepper Strips, 2 cups, with 1 tablespoon fat-free Thousand Island dressing
Rice Cakes, 3
Diet Orange Soda

MAIN MEAL

Minted Couscous Tabbouleh with Chick-Peas and Cheese, 1 serving (see recipe)
Chilled Broccoli Florets, 1 cup
Cucumber Salad (In small bowl, combine $^1/_2$ cup cucumber slices, 1 teaspoon *each* vegetable oil and rice wine vinegar and pinch ground white pepper.)
Sugar-Free Vanilla Nonfat Frozen Yogurt, 4 fluid ounces
Sparkling Mineral Water with Lime Wedge

SNACK

Plain Popcorn, hot-air popped, 3 cups, with 1 tablespoon raisins
Chocolate "Egg Cream" (In tall glass, combine 1 cup diet chocolate soda and $^3/_4$ cup skim milk.)

This menu provides: 2 Milks, 3 Fats, 2 Fruits, $7^3/_4$ Vegetables, 3 Proteins, 6 Breads, 110 Optional Calories.

Per serving: 25 g Fat, 20 g Fiber.

333
INDIAN MILLET STEW

The seductive flavors of India permeate this healthful vegetarian stew.

Makes 4 servings

1 teaspoon vegetable oil
1 cup thinly sliced onions
1 tablespoon + 1 teaspoon grated pared fresh ginger root
$^3/_4$ teaspoon ground cumin
$^3/_4$ teaspoon ground coriander
$^1/_2$ teaspoon ground turmeric
$^1/_4$ teaspoon hot red pepper sauce
$4^1/_2$ ounces millet
2 cups chopped tomatoes
2 cups cubed pared acorn squash
1 teaspoon salt
$^1/_4$ cup minced fresh cilantro
2 teaspoons fresh lemon juice

1. In large saucepan or Dutch oven, heat oil; add onions and ginger. Cook over medium-high heat, stirring frequently, 5 minutes, until onions are softened. Add cumin, coriander, turmeric and pepper sauce; cook, stirring frequently, 1 minute.

2. Add millet to onion mixture; cook, stirring constantly, 1 minute, until millet is well coated. Add tomatoes, squash, salt and 3 cups water; bring liquid to a boil. Reduce heat to low; simmer, stirring occasionally, 30 minutes, until millet is tender. Stir in cilantro and juice.

Serving ($1^1/_4$ cups) provides: $^1/_4$ Fat, $1^1/_2$ Vegetables, 2 Breads.

Per serving: 198 Calories, 3 g Total Fat, 0 g Saturated Fat, 0 mg Cholesterol, 573 mg Sodium, 39 g Total Carbohydrate, 7 g Dietary Fiber, 5 g Protein, 48 mg Calcium.

BAKED CHEESE GRITS WITH MUSHROOM SAUCE

Makes 4 servings

2 cups evaporated skimmed milk
$^3/_4$ teaspoon salt
3 ounces fine hominy grits
$4^1/_2$ ounces reduced-fat cheddar cheese
2 eggs, separated
2 teaspoons olive oil
2 tablespoons minced shallots
1 cup thinly sliced shiitake mushrooms

1 cup thinly sliced white mushrooms
$^1/_2$ teaspoon ground dried sage leaves
$^1/_4$ teaspoon freshly ground black pepper
1 tablespoon all-purpose flour
2 tablespoons minced fresh flat-leaf parsley

1. Preheat oven to 375°F. Adjust oven rack to divide oven in half. Spray 2-quart soufflé dish with nonstick cooking spray.

2. To prepare grits, in large saucepan combine 1 cup of the milk, $^1/_2$ teaspoon of the salt and $1^1/_3$ cups water; bring mixture to a boil. Gradually stir in grits; continuing to stir, cook 15 minutes, until thickened. Remove from heat; let stand 5 minutes.

3. Add cheese to grits mixture; stir to combine.

4. In medium bowl, stir $^1/_2$ cup grits mixture into egg yolks, then stir yolk mixture into remaining grits mixture; set aside.

5. In small bowl, with electric mixer, beat egg whites until stiff but not dry; gently fold beaten whites into grits mixture. Transfer grits mixture to prepared soufflé dish, smoothing top; bake 35 minutes, until mixture is lightly browned and puffy.

6. Meanwhile, to prepare mushroom sauce, in large nonstick skillet, heat oil; add shallots. Cook over medium-high heat, stirring frequently, 2–3 minutes, until softened. Stir in shiitake and white mushrooms, sage and pepper; cook, stirring frequently, 5 minutes, until mushrooms are tender.

7. Sprinkle mushroom mixture with flour; with wire whisk, blend until flour is dissolved. Continuing to blend with wire whisk, gradually add remaining 1 cup milk, remaining $^1/_4$ teaspoon salt and $^1/_3$ cup water; cook, stirring constantly, until mixture is slightly thickened. Stir in parsley.

8. Divide grits mixture evenly among 4 plates; top each portion with one-fourth of the mushroom sauce.

BREAKFAST

Orange and Grapefruit Sections, $^1/_2$ cup
Breakfast Pizza (Top 1-ounce slice Italian bread with $^3/_4$ ounce nonfat mozzarella cheese, sliced, and $^1/_2$ medium tomato, sliced; broil until heated.)
Skim Milk, $^3/_4$ cup
Coffee or Tea (optional)

LIGHT MEAL

Chick-Pea–Potato Salad (In medium bowl, combine 2 cups torn iceberg lettuce leaves, 1 cup cooked cut green beans, 4 ounces diced cooked potato, 2 ounces drained cooked chick-peas and 1 tablespoon reduced-calorie mayonnaise.)
Carrot Sticks, 1 cup
Crispbreads, $^3/_4$ ounce
Sugar-Free Cherry-Flavored Gelatin, $^1/_2$ cup
Diet Ginger Ale

MAIN MEAL

Baked Cheese Grits with Mushroom Sauce, 1 serving (see recipe)
Endive and Watercress Salad, 2 cups, with 1 teaspoon *each* olive oil and fresh lemon juice
Breadsticks, 2 long
Sugar-Free Chocolate Nonfat Frozen Yogurt, 4 fluid ounces
Iced Tea

SNACK

Baked Apple (Preheat oven to 350° F. Pare 1 small apple halfway down from stem end; place into small baking dish. Sprinkle apple with 1 teaspoon granulated sugar and $^1/_4$ teaspoon cinnamon; add $^1/_4$" water to pan. Bake, covered, 30 minutes, until tender.)

This menu provides: 2 Milks, 3 Fats, 2 Fruits, 14 Vegetables, 4 Proteins, 5 Breads, 85 Optional Calories.

Per serving: 26 g Fat, 22 g Fiber.

Serving ($1^1/_2$ cups grits, $^1/_4$ cup mushroom sauce) provides: 1 Milk, $^1/_2$ Fat, 1 Vegetable, 2 Proteins, 1 Bread, 10 Optional Calories.

Per serving: 348 Calories, 11 g Total Fat, 5 g Saturated Fat, 134 mg Cholesterol, 841 mg Sodium, 36 g Total Carbohydrate, 1 g Dietary Fiber, 26 g Protein, 675 mg Calcium.

BARLEY SALAD

Makes 4 servings

BREAKFAST
Honeydew Melon, 2" wedge
Bagel, Cream Cheese and Red Onion (Split one
1-ounce mini bagel; spread bottom half with
1 tablespoon nonfat cream cheese. Top cheese
with $1/4$ cup sliced red onion and remaining bagel
half.)
Skim Milk, 1 cup
Coffee or Tea (optional)

LIGHT MEAL
Blueberry Cottage Cheese (In small bowl, combine
$1/2$ cup nonfat cottage cheese with $1/4$ cup blueberries.)
Red and Green Bell Pepper Strips, 1 cup *each,* with
1 tablespoon fat-free creamy Italian dressing
Roll, 1 ounce, with 2 teaspoons reduced-calorie tub
margarine
Mint Tea

MAIN MEAL
Barley Salad, 1 serving (see recipe)
Cucumber Salad (In small bowl, combine $1/2$ cup
cucumber slices, 1 teaspoon *each* vegetable oil
and rice wine vinegar and pinch ground white
pepper.)
Celery and Carrot Sticks, 1 cup *each*
Breadsticks, 2 long
Aspartame-Sweetened Strawberry Nonfat Yogurt,
1 cup
Diet Black Cherry Soda

SNACK
Apricots, 2 medium

This menu provides: 2 Milks, 3 Fats, 2 Fruits,
12 Vegetables, 3 Proteins, 4 Breads, 35 Optional
Calories.

Per serving: 26 g Fat, 22 g Fiber.

3 ounces pearl barley
1 tablespoon + 1 teaspoon olive oil
2 cups quartered mushrooms
$1/2$ cup diced carrot
8 ounces drained cooked chick-peas
1 cup diced tomatoes
1 cup sliced scallions
1 cup minced fresh flat-leaf parsley
$1/2$ cup low-sodium mixed vegetable juice
3 ounces skim-milk mozzarella cheese, grated
1 tablespoon fresh lemon juice
$1/2$ teaspoon salt

1. In large pot of boiling water, cook barley 15 minutes, until tender.
Drain, discarding liquid; place into large bowl. Set aside.

2. In large nonstick skillet, heat 2 teaspoons of the oil; add mushrooms
and carrot. Cook over medium-high heat, stirring frequently, 5 minutes,
until vegetables are softened; transfer to bowl with cooked barley.

3. Add chick-peas, tomatoes, scallions, parsley, vegetable juice, cheese,
lemon juice, salt and remaining 2 teaspoons olive oil to bowl with barley;
toss to combine.

Serving (1$1/2$ cups) provides: 1 Fat, 2$1/2$ Vegetables, 2 Proteins, 1 Bread.

Per serving: 307 Calories, 10 g Total Fat, 3 g Saturated Fat, 12 mg Cholesterol,
420 mg Sodium, 42 g Total Carbohydrate, 8 g Dietary Fiber, 14 g Protein,
222 mg Calcium.

POLENTA WITH TOMATO SAUCE

Makes 4 servings

$^3/_4$ cup yellow cornmeal

6 ounces freshly grated Parmesan cheese

2 teaspoons olive oil

1 cup chopped onions

3 garlic cloves, minced

1 cup diced red bell pepper

3 cups chopped tomatoes

$^1/_2$ cup minced fresh basil

$^1/_2$ teaspoon freshly ground black pepper

$^1/_4$ teaspoon salt

Pinch crushed red pepper flakes

1. Preheat oven to 375° F. Spray 11 × 7" baking dish with nonstick cooking spray.

2. In medium bowl, combine cornmeal and 1 cup water; set aside.

3. In large saucepan, bring 1$^1/_3$ cups water to a boil. Reduce heat to low; stirring constantly, gradually add cornmeal mixture. Simmer, stirring frequently, 10 minutes, until mixture is thickened. Remove from heat; stir in 3 ounces of the cheese. Transfer cornmeal mixture to prepared baking dish, smoothing top; set aside.

4. In large nonstick skillet; heat oil; add onions and garlic. Cook over medium-high heat, stirring frequently, 7 minutes, until onions are golden brown. Add bell pepper; cook, stirring frequently, 5 minutes, until pepper is softened.

5. Add tomatoes, basil, black pepper, salt and red pepper flakes to vegetable mixture; bring liquid to a boil. Reduce heat to low; simmer, covered, 5 minutes, until slightly thickened.

6. Spoon tomato mixture over cornmeal mixture; sprinkle evenly with remaining 3 ounces cheese. Bake 20 minutes, until heated through and bubbling.

Serving (1$^1/_2$ cups) provides: $^1/_2$ Fat, 2$^1/_4$ Vegetables, 2 Proteins, 1$^1/_2$ Breads.

Per serving: 370 Calories, 16 g Total Fat, 9 g Saturated Fat, 34 mg Cholesterol, 945 mg Sodium, 35 g Total Carbohydrate, 4 g Dietary Fiber, 22 g Protein, 659 mg Calcium.

BREAKFAST
Banana, $^1/_2$ medium
Mini Bagel, 1 (1 ounce), split and toasted, with
 1 tablespoon nonfat cream cheese
Skim Milk, 1 cup
Coffee or Tea (optional)

LIGHT MEAL
Pear-Cheese Salad (In small bowl, combine 1 small
 pear, cored and diced, and $^2/_3$ cup nonfat ricotta
 cheese. Line plate with 2 Romaine lettuce leaves,
 top with cheese mixture.)
Celery and Carrot Sticks, 1 cup *each*
Roll, 1 ounce, with 1 teaspoon reduced-calorie tub
 margarine
Sparkling Mineral Water with Lime Wedge

MAIN MEAL
Polenta with Tomato Sauce, 1 serving (see recipe)
Red Bell Pepper Strips, 2 cups, on 2 iceberg lettuce
 leaves with 1 tablespoon Italian dressing
Breadsticks, 2 long
Angel Food Cake, 2 ounces
Diet Cherry Cola

SNACK
Aspartame-Sweetened Black Cherry Nonfat Yogurt,
 1 cup

This menu provides: 2 Milks, 3 Fats, 2 Fruits, 11$^1/_4$ Vegetables, 4$^1/_4$ Proteins, 4$^3/_4$ Breads, 90 Optional Calories.

Per serving: 34 g Fat, 20 g Fiber.

Polenta with Tomato Sauce

BARLEY-VEGETABLE STEW

This rich stew is warming on a cold winter evening or at lunchtime after a morning of sledding.

Makes 4 servings

1 teaspoon vegetable oil
1 cup chopped onions
1 cup diced carrot
5 1/4 ounces pearl barley
2 cups sliced mushrooms
2 cups reduced-sodium vegetable broth
2 teaspoons minced fresh rosemary leaves
1/2 teaspoon salt
1/4 teaspoon freshly ground black pepper, to taste
1 cup chopped tomato
1/2 cup fresh or thawed frozen green peas
3 tablespoons minced fresh flat-leaf parsley

1. In large saucepan or Dutch oven, heat oil; add onions and carrot. Cook over medium-high heat, stirring frequently, 5 minutes, until onions are softened. Add barley; cook, stirring frequently, 1 minute. Add mushrooms; cook, stirring frequently, 1 minute, until mushrooms begin to release their liquid.

2. Add broth, 1 teaspoon of the rosemary, the salt, pepper and 1 1/2 cups water; bring liquid to a boil. Reduce heat to low; simmer, covered, stirring occasionally, 30 minutes.

3. Add tomato and peas to barley mixture; simmer, covered, stirring occasionally, 30 minutes, until vegetables and barley are very tender and mixture is thickened. Stir in parsley and remaining 1 teaspoon rosemary.

Serving (1 1/4 cups) provides: 1/4 Fat, 2 1/2 Vegetables, 2 Breads, 10 Optional Calories.

Per serving: 221 Calories, 2 g Total Fat, 0 g Saturated Fat, 0 mg Cholesterol, 331 mg Sodium, 45 g Total Carbohydrate, 9 g Dietary Fiber, 7 g Protein, 43 mg Calcium.

BREAKFAST
Grapefruit, 1/2 medium
Tomato-Cheese Egg-White Omelet (In small bowl, beat 3 egg whites and pinch *each* salt and ground white pepper until frothy. In small nonstick skillet, melt 1 1/2 teaspoons reduced-calorie tub margarine; add egg-white mixture. Cook, covered, over medium heat 4–5 minutes until mixture is firm. Top one side of omelet with 1/2 cup chopped tomato; sprinkle tomato with 3/4 ounce reduced-fat cheddar cheese, grated. With spatula, fold other side of omelet over cheese to enclose.)
Reduced-Calorie Multi-Grain Bread, 2 slices, toasted, with 2 teaspoons strawberry jam
Skim Milk, 1/2 cup
Coffee or Tea (optional)

LIGHT MEAL
Orange-Lentil Salad (In medium bowl, combine 1 cup torn Romaine lettuce leaves, 1/2 medium tomato, sliced, 1/2 cup *each* cucumber and jicama slices and orange sections, 4 ounces drained cooked lentils, 2 teaspoons red wine vinegar, 1 teaspoon olive oil and freshly ground black pepper, to taste.)
Flatbreads, 1 1/2 ounces
Reduced-Calorie Chocolate-Flavored Pudding (made with skim milk), 1/2 cup
Herbal Tea

MAIN MEAL
Barley-Vegetable Stew, 1 serving (see recipe)
Steamed Brussels Sprouts, 1 cup
Tossed Green Salad, 2 cups, with 1 tablespoon fat-free Italian dressing
Aspartame-Sweetened Lemon Nonfat Yogurt, 1 cup
Sparkling Mineral Water

SNACK
Graham Crackers, 3 (2 1/2" squares), with 1 tablespoon peanut butter

This menu provides: 2 Milks, 3 Fats, 2 Fruits, 14 1/2 Vegetables, 5 Proteins, 6 Breads, 85 Optional Calories.

Per serving: 28 g Fat, 45 g Fiber.

BREAKFAST

Cantaloupe, $^1/4$ small
Nonfat Cottage Cheese, $^1/2$ cup
Cinnamon-Raisin Bread, 1 slice, toasted, with 1 teaspoon reduced-calorie tub margarine
Skim Milk, 1 cup
Coffee or Tea (optional)

LIGHT MEAL

Egg Salad Sandwich (In small bowl, combine 1 hard-cooked egg, chopped, $^1/4$ cup *each* chopped celery and chopped red onion and 2 teaspoons reduced-calorie mayonnaise; spread between 2 slices reduced-calorie rye bread.)
Cucumber and Carrot Sticks, 1 cup *each*
Root Beer "Float" (In tall glass, combine 1 cup diet root beer and $^1/3$ cup skim milk; add enough ice cubes to fill glass.)

MAIN MEAL

Mexican-Style Risotto, 1 serving (see recipe)
Chilled Cooked Asparagus, 9 spears, with 1 teaspoon fresh lemon juice
Romaine and Red Leaf Lettuce Salad, 2 cups, with 10 pitted small black olives and 1 tablespoon fat-free Thousand Island dressing
Maple Yogurt (In small bowl, combine $^1/2$ cup plain nonfat yogurt and 1 teaspoon maple syrup.)
Light Beer, 6 fluid ounces

SNACK

Trail Mix (In small bowl, combine $1^1/2$ ounces pretzel sticks, 2 tablespoons raisins and 1 teaspoon sunflower seeds.)

This menu provides: 2 Milks, 3 Fats, 2 Fruits, $11^1/4$ Vegetables, 4 Proteins, $5^1/2$ Breads, 100 Optional Calories.

Per serving: 28 g Fat, 20 g Fiber.

338
MEXICAN-STYLE RISOTTO

Makes 4 servings

2 teaspoons olive oil
$^1/2$ cup chopped onion
1 teaspoon chopped seeded pickled jalapeño pepper
6 ounces Arborio or other short-grain rice
$^1/4$ cup fresh lime juice
2 teaspoons mild or hot chili powder
$^3/4$ teaspoon dried oregano
$^3/4$ teaspoon ground cumin
$^1/2$ teaspoon salt
$^3/4$ cup minced fresh cilantro
8 ounces drained cooked red beans
3 ounces reduced-fat Monterey Jack cheese, grated
$^1/2$ cup chopped tomato
$^1/4$ cup chopped drained canned green chiles

1. In medium saucepan, heat oil; add onion and pepper. Cook over medium-high heat, stirring frequently, 5 minutes, until onion is softened. Add rice; stir to coat. Add juice, chili powder, oregano, cumin and salt; stir to combine.

2. Add $^1/2$ cup water to rice mixture; cook, stirring constantly, until liquid is absorbed. Continuing to stir, add another $2^1/2$ cups water, $^1/2$ cup at a time; cook, stirring constantly after each addition, 18–20 minutes, until all liquid is absorbed, rice is tender and mixture is creamy.

3. Add $^1/4$ cup of the cilantro to rice mixture; cook, stirring constantly, 2 minutes. Add beans, cheese, tomato and chiles; cook, stirring constantly, until mixture is heated through and cheese is melted. Remove from heat; stir in remaining $^1/2$ cup cilantro.

Serving ($1^1/4$ cups) provides: $^1/2$ Fat, $^3/4$ Vegetable, 2 Proteins, $1^1/2$ Breads.

Per serving: 330 Calories, 7 g Total Fat, 3 g Saturated Fat, 15 mg Cholesterol, 519 mg Sodium, 52 g Total Carbohydrate, 4 g Dietary Fiber, 15 g Protein, 228 mg Calcium.

WALNUT-MUSHROOM RISOTTO

Walnuts add a wonderful crunch to this classic creamy risotto.

Makes 4 servings

3 cups low-sodium vegetable broth
2 teaspoons olive oil
1 cup chopped onions
1 garlic clove, minced
2 cups sliced mushrooms
1 cup finely chopped carrot
6 ounces Arborio or other short-grain rice
$^{1}/_{4}$ cup minced fresh flat-leaf parsley
1 ounce chopped walnuts, toasted*
$^{3}/_{4}$ ounce freshly grated Parmesan cheese

1. In medium saucepan, bring broth to a boil. Reduce heat to low; keep at a simmer.

2. In large nonstick saucepan, heat oil; add onions and garlic. Cook over medium-high heat, stirring frequently, 5 minutes, until onions are softened.

3. Stir mushrooms and carrot into onion mixture; cook, stirring frequently, 5 minutes, until mushrooms are tender. Add rice; cook, stirring constantly, 3 minutes.

4. Add $^{1}/_{2}$ cup hot broth to rice mixture; cook, stirring constantly, until liquid is absorbed. Continuing to stir, add remaining $2^{1}/_{2}$ cups broth, $^{1}/_{2}$ cup at a time; cook, stirring constantly after each addition, 18–20 minutes, until all liquid is absorbed, rice is tender and mixture is creamy. Stir in parsley, walnuts and cheese.

Serving (scant 1 cup) provides: 1 Fat, 2 Vegetables, $^{1}/_{2}$ Protein, $1^{1}/_{2}$ Breads, 15 Optional Calories.

Per serving: 305 Calories, 9 g Total Fat, 2 g Saturated Fat, 4 mg Cholesterol, 168 mg Sodium, 49 g Total Carbohydrate, 3 g Dietary Fiber, 8 g Protein, 104 mg Calcium.

*To toast walnuts, in small nonstick skillet, cook walnuts over low heat, stirring constantly, until golden brown; immediately transfer to heat-resistant plate to cool.

BREAKFAST

Raspberries, $^{3}/_{4}$ cup
Chive Omelet (In small bowl, beat $^{1}/_{4}$ cup egg substitute, 1 tablespoon water and 1 teaspoon minced fresh chives. Spray small nonstick skillet with nonstick cooking spray; heat. Pour egg mixture into skillet, tilting to cover bottom of pan. Cook over medium-high heat until underside is set, lifting edges with spatula to let uncooked egg flow underneath; fold in half.)
English Muffin, $^{1}/_{2}$ (1 ounce), toasted, with 1 teaspoon reduced-calorie tub margarine
Skim Milk, $^{1}/_{2}$ cup
Coffee or Tea (optional)

LIGHT MEAL

Mexican Pasta Salad (In small bowl, combine 1 cup cooked ziti macaroni, 4 ounces drained cooked black beans and $^{1}/_{2}$ cup *each* salsa and chopped green bell pepper.)
Nonfat Tortilla Chips, 1 ounce
Strawberries, 1 cup
Sparkling Mineral Water with Lime Wedge

MAIN MEAL

Walnut-Mushroom Risotto, 1 serving (see recipe)
Steamed Whole Green Beans, 1 cup, with 1 teaspoon reduced-calorie tub margarine
Italian Spinach Salad (In medium bowl, combine 2 cups torn spinach leaves, $^{1}/_{2}$ cup *each* sliced mushrooms and sliced red onion, 2 teaspoons imitation bacon bits and $1^{1}/_{2}$ teaspoons Italian dressing.)
Aspartame-Sweetened Blueberry Nonfat Yogurt, 1 cup
Iced Herbal Tea

SNACK

Vanilla "Egg Cream" (In tall glass, combine 1 cup diet cream soda and $^{1}/_{2}$ cup skim milk.)

This menu provides: 2 Milks, 3 Fats, 2 Fruits, 13 Vegetables, $3^{1}/_{2}$ Proteins, $5^{1}/_{2}$ Breads, 35 Optional Calories.

Per serving: 24 g Fat, 26 g Fiber.

BREAKFAST
Mango, $^1/_2$ small

Cheese 'n' Maple–Topped Waffle (Toast 1 frozen waffle; transfer to plate. Top waffle with $^1/_2$ cup nonfat cottage cheese and 2 teaspoons maple syrup.)

Skim Milk, 1 cup

Coffee or Tea (optional)

LIGHT MEAL
Hummus in Pita (In food processor, combine 4 ounces drained cooked chick-peas, 2 table-spoons *each* fresh lemon juice and tahini [sesame paste] and pinch garlic powder; purée until smooth. Split 1 small [1-ounce] whole-wheat pita halfway around edge; open to form pocket. Spread pita pocket with chick-pea mixture; top with $^1/_2$ cup *each* chopped tomato and shredded iceberg lettuce leaves.)

Whole Green Beans and Carrot Sticks, 1 cup *each*

Sugar-Free Grape-Flavored Gelatin, $^1/_2$ cup, topped with $^1/_4$ cup aspartame-sweetened vanilla nonfat yogurt

Iced Herbal Tea

MAIN MEAL
Carrot Juice, $^1/_2$ cup

Brown Rice–Dried Cranberry Salad, 1 serving (see recipe)

Chilled Cooked Broccoli and Cauliflower Florets, 1 cup *each,* with 1 tablespoon fat-free Italian dressing

Sugar-Free Vanilla Nonfat Frozen Yogurt, 4 fluid ounces

Sparkling Mineral Water

SNACK
Oat-Bran Pretzels, $1^1/_2$ ounces

Skim Milk, $^1/_2$ cup

This menu provides: 2 Milks, 3 Fats, 2 Fruits, 12 Vegetables, $4^3/_4$ Proteins, 5 Breads, 95 Optional Calories.

Per serving: 32 g Fat, 30 g Fiber.

340
BROWN RICE—DRIED CRANBERRY SALAD

The smoky taste of tempeh complements this salad's sweet-and-sour flavors.

Makes 4 servings

2 teaspoons olive oil
$^1/_2$ cup chopped onion
$^1/_2$ cup chopped celery
1 cup thinly sliced carrot
2 cups cooked brown rice
4 ounces tempeh (fermented soybean cake),* crumbled
$^1/_2$ cup dried cranberries
2 tablespoons cranberry vinegar
1 tablespoon fresh orange juice
$^1/_2$ teaspoon dried mint leaves

1. In medium nonstick skillet, heat oil; add onion and celery. Cook over medium-high heat, stirring frequently, 5 minutes, until vegetables are softened.

2. Add carrot and $^1/_3$ cup water to vegetable mixture; bring liquid to a boil. Cook, stirring frequently, 8–10 minutes, until carrot is tender and liquid is evaporated. Stir in rice, tempeh and cranberries; cook, stirring gently, 4 minutes, until mixture is heated through. Transfer to serving bowl.

3. Sprinkle rice mixture with vinegar, juice and mint; toss to combine. Let stand 10 minutes; serve warm.

Serving ($^3/_4$ cup) provides: $^1/_2$ Fat, 1 Fruit, 1 Vegetable, 1 Protein, 1 Bread.

Per serving: 254 Calories, 6 g Total Fat, 1 g Saturated Fat, 0 mg Cholesterol, 30 mg Sodium, 44 g Total Carbohydrate, 4 g Dietary Fiber, 9 g Protein, 54 mg Calcium.

Tempeh is available in most health-food stores.

Rice Frittata with Figs and Parmesan Cheese

It's easy to keep all these ingredients on hand, then prepare this simple recipe when you can't get out to the store but want to enjoy a wonderful meatless meal.

Makes 4 servings

$^1/_2$ cup finely chopped onion
$^1/_2$ small garlic clove, minced
2 eggs
3 egg whites
$^1/_2$ cup cooked long-grain rice
2 large dried figs, finely chopped
$^3/_4$ ounce freshly grated Parmesan cheese
$^1/_4$ teaspoon dried thyme leaves
2 teaspoons olive oil

1. Spray medium nonstick skillet with nonstick cooking spray; heat. Add onion and garlic; cook over medium-high heat, stirring frequently, 5 minutes, until onion is softened.

2. In large bowl, with fork, combine eggs and egg whites; stir in rice, figs, cheese, thyme and onion mixture.

3. In same skillet, heat oil; add egg mixture, tilting to cover bottom of pan. Cook over medium-high heat 3–4 minutes, until underside is set, lifting edges with spatula to let uncooked egg flow underneath. Slide frittata onto plate; invert plate and frittata into skillet. Remove plate; cook frittata 2–3 minutes, until browned on bottom. Transfer to serving platter; cut into 4 equal wedges.

Serving (1 wedge) provides: $^1/_2$ Fat, $^1/_2$ Fruit, $^1/_4$ Vegetable, 1 Protein, $^1/_4$ Bread.

Per serving: 164 Calories, 7 g Total Fat, 2 g Saturated Fat, 110 mg Cholesterol, 174 mg Sodium, 17 g Total Carbohydrate, 1 g Dietary Fiber, 9 g Protein, 111 mg Calcium.

BREAKFAST
Cantaloupe, $^1/_4$ small
Fat-Free Muffin, 1 (2 ounces), with 1 teaspoon reduced-calorie tub margarine
Skim Milk, $^1/_2$ cup
Coffee or Tea (optional)

LIGHT MEAL
Strawberry "Sundae" (Scoop 1 cup nonfat cottage cheese into small bowl; top with $^1/_2$ cup strawberries, sliced, and $^3/_4$ ounce crunchy cereal nuggets.)
Carrot and Celery Sticks, 1 cup *each*
Crispbreads, $^3/_4$ ounce
Diet Lemon-Lime Soda

MAIN MEAL
Rice Frittata with Figs and Parmesan Cheese, 1 serving (see recipe)
Pepper-Zucchini Sauté (In medium nonstick skillet, heat 1 teaspoon peanut oil; add 1 cup *each* sliced red bell pepper, onions and zucchini. Cook over medium-high heat, stirring frequently, 5 minutes, until vegetables are softened; sprinkle with 1 tablespoon minced fresh basil.)
Reduced-Calorie Vanilla-Flavored Pudding (made with skim milk)
Sparkling Mineral Water

SNACK
Cinnamon-Raisin English Muffin, 1 (2 ounces), split and toasted, with 2 teaspoons reduced-calorie tub margarine
Skim Milk, 1 cup

This menu provides: 2 Milks, 3 Fats, 2 Fruits, $10^1/_4$ Vegetables, 3 Proteins, $5^1/_4$ Breads, 100 Optional Calories.

Per serving: 21 g Fat, 21 g Fiber.

RICE PANCAKES WITH CHILI-VEGETABLE TOPPING

This updated version of the classic chili and rice makes an attractive presentation—it's a perfect entrée when guests come for dinner. Even your meat-and-potato-loving friends will savor this wonderful vegetarian dish!

Makes 4 servings

1 teaspoon vegetable oil
1 cup chopped onions
1 cup cubed zucchini
1 cup cubed yellow squash
4 ounces drained cooked black beans
1 teaspoon mild or hot chili powder
$^1/_2$ teaspoon ground cumin
1 cup canned whole tomatoes (no salt added), coarsely chopped
2 cups cooked long-grain rice
$1^1/_2$ ounces reduced-fat Monterey Jack cheese, grated
2 egg whites
2 tablespoons minced fresh cilantro

1. Line baking sheet with foil; spray with nonstick cooking spray. Preheat broiler.

2. In large nonstick skillet, heat oil; add onions. Cook over medium-high heat, stirring frequently, 5 minutes, until softened. Add zucchini and yellow squash; cook, stirring frequently, 7 minutes, until vegetables are lightly browned. Add beans, chili powder and cumin; cook, stirring frequently, 1 minute, until mixture is combined. Add tomatoes; bring liquid to a boil. Reduce heat to low; simmer, covered, 15–20 minutes, until mixture is thickened.

3. Meanwhile, in medium bowl, combine rice, cheese, egg whites and cilantro. Spoon four equal mounds of rice mixture onto prepared baking sheet; flatten with back of spoon to form 4–5" pancakes. Broil 4–5 minutes, until just firm and lightly browned.

4. Divide pancakes among 4 plates; top each pancake with one-fourth of the vegetable mixture.

Serving (1 pancake, $^1/_2$ cup vegetable mixture) provides: $^1/_4$ Fat, 2 Vegetables, 1 Protein, 1 Bread, 10 Optional Calories.

Per serving: 261 Calories, 4 g Total Fat, 2 g Saturated Fat, 8 mg Cholesterol, 220 mg Sodium, 44 g Total Carbohydrate, 3 g Dietary Fiber, 12 g Protein, 153 mg Calcium.

BREAKFAST

Bagel, Cream Cheese and Lox (Split one 2-ounce bagel; spread bottom half with 1 tablespoon non-fat cream cheese. Top cheese with $^1/_2$ ounce thinly sliced Nova Scotia lox [smoked salmon], $^1/_4$ cup sliced red onion, 2 tomato slices and remaining bagel half.)
Skim Milk, 1 cup
Coffee or Tea (optional)

LIGHT MEAL

Fruit 'n' Cheese Platter (Line plate with 4 iceberg lettuce leaves. Arrange $1^1/_2$ ounces reduced-fat cheddar cheese, cubed, and 1 small apple, cored and sliced, on lettuce.)
Roll, 1 ounce, with 2 teaspoons reduced-calorie tub margarine
Celery and Carrot Sticks, 1 cup *each,* with Russian Dressing (In small cup or bowl, combine $1^1/_2$ teaspoons *each* reduced-calorie mayonnaise and ketchup.)
Aspartame-Sweetened Black Cherry Nonfat Yogurt, 1 cup
Sparkling Mineral Water

MAIN MEAL

Rice Pancakes with Chili-Vegetable Topping, 1 serving (see recipe)
Torn Romaine and Bibb Lettuce Leaves, 2 cups, with $^1/_2$ cup *each* alfalfa sprouts and sliced radishes, 6 large pitted black olives and 1 tablespoon fat-free blue cheese dressing
Nonfat Tortilla Chips, 2 ounces, with Salsa-Cream Dip (In small bowl, top $^1/_2$ cup salsa with 2 tablespoons nonfat sour cream.)
Watermelon, 3 × 2" wedge
Iced Tea with Mint Sprig

SNACK

Frozen Raspberry Pop (Pour $^1/_2$ cup sugar-free raspberry-flavored drink into small paper cup; freeze until almost firm. Insert ice-cream-bar stick vertically into partially frozen drink; freeze until solid. Unmold.)

This menu provides: 2 Milks, 3 Fats, 2 Fruits, 16 Vegetables, $3^1/_2$ Proteins, 6 Breads, 75 Optional Calories.

Per serving: 30 g Fat, 21 g Fiber.

3 4 3
BROILED MARINATED TOFU

Makes 4 servings

$^1/_3$ cup reduced-sodium soy sauce
$^1/_4$ teaspoon grated orange zest*
$^1/_4$ cup fresh orange juice
2 medium scallions, chopped
1 tablespoon rice wine vinegar
1 tablespoon honey
2 teaspoons orange marmalade
2 garlic cloves, crushed
1 pound firm tofu, cut into 4 equal pieces

1. To prepare marinade, in gallon-size sealable plastic bag, combine soy sauce, zest, juice, scallions, vinegar, honey, marmalade and garlic; add tofu. Seal bag, squeezing out air; turn to coat tofu. Refrigerate at least 2 hours or overnight, turning bag occasionally.

2. Preheat broiler. Spray nonstick baking sheet with nonstick cooking spray.

3. Drain marinade into small saucepan; bring to a boil. Remove from heat. Place tofu onto prepared baking sheet; broil 4" from heat, turning once and brushing with some of the remaining marinade, 10–15 minutes, until tofu is browned and crispy.

4. Place fine sieve over small bowl; pour remaining marinade through sieve. Reserve liquid; discard solids. Place each piece of tofu onto a plate; top each portion with an equal amount of strained liquid.

Serving (1 piece tofu, 1 tablespoon strained liquid) provides: 2 Proteins, 30 Optional Calories.

Per serving: 214 Calories, 10 g Total Fat, 1 g Saturated Fat, 0 mg Cholesterol, 811 mg Sodium, 16 g Total Carbohydrate, 0 g Dietary Fiber, 19 g Protein, 245 mg Calcium.

The zest of the orange is the peel without any of the pith (white membrane). To remove zest from orange, use a zester or the fine side of a vegetable grater.

BREAKFAST
Mango Shake (In blender, combine 1 cup skim milk, $^1/_2$ small mango, pared, pitted and sliced, 3 ice cubes and sugar substitute to equal 2 teaspoons sugar; purée until smooth.)
Sesame Rice Cakes, 2
Coffee or Tea (optional)

LIGHT MEAL
Cheese-Pepper Quesadillas (Preheat oven to 350° F. Top each of two 6" flour tortillas with $^3/_4$ ounce nonfat cheddar cheese, grated, and $^1/_2$ medium roasted red bell pepper, sliced; place onto nonstick baking sheet. Bake 5 minutes, until cheese is melted.)
Celery and Carrot Sticks, 1 cup *each*
Marinated Mushrooms (In small bowl, combine 2 cups whole mushrooms and 1 tablespoon Italian dressing; refrigerate, covered, at least 2 hours or overnight.)
Pineapple, $^1/_8$ medium
Diet Lemon-Lime Soda

MAIN MEAL
Broiled Marinated Tofu, 1 serving (see recipe)
Cooked Soba Noodles, 1 cup
Grilled Vegetables (Preheat grill according to manufacturer's directions. Grill $^1/_2$ cup *each* sliced zucchini, sliced yellow squash, sliced green bell pepper, sliced pared eggplant, sliced red onion and sliced fennel, turning as needed, until lightly browned and tender.)
Sugar-Free Strawberry Nonfat Frozen Yogurt, 4 fluid ounces
Iced Tea

SNACK
Plain Popcorn, hot-air popped, 3 cups, with 2 teaspoons reduced-calorie tub margarine, melted
Chocolate "Egg Cream" (In tall glass, combine 1 cup diet chocolate soda and $^3/_4$ cup skim milk.)

This menu provides: 2 Milks, 3 Fats, 2 Fruits, 16 Vegetables, 3 Proteins, 6 Breads, 80 Optional Calories.

Per serving: 30 g Fat, 20 g Fiber.

344
BROILED TOFU AND VEGETABLES

Makes 4 servings

$1^1/_2$ cups crushed tomatoes (no salt added)
1 tablespoon + 1 teaspoon firmly packed light or dark brown sugar
2 teaspoons mango chutney
2 garlic cloves, peeled
$^1/_2$ teaspoon ground ginger
$^1/_2$ teaspoon ground cumin
$^1/_4$ teaspoon cinnamon
Pinch ground cloves
Pinch ground allspice
1 pound firm tofu, cut into 4 equal pieces
1 medium yellow squash, halved lengthwise and cut into 2" pieces
1 medium zucchini, halved lengthwise and cut into 2" pieces
1 medium red bell pepper, seeded and quartered
1 medium onion, quartered

1. Line broiler pan with foil. Preheat broiler.

2. To prepare sauce, in a blender or food processor, combine tomatoes, brown sugar, chutney, garlic, ginger, cumin, cinnamon, cloves and allspice; purée until smooth. Transfer to large bowl.

3. Add tofu, squash, zucchini, bell pepper and onion to sauce; toss to combine. Transfer mixture to prepared broiler pan; broil 6" from heat 12 minutes, until vegetables are cooked through and sauce is lightly browned.

Serving ($2^1/_2$ cups) provides: $2^1/_2$ Vegetables, 2 Proteins, 20 Optional Calories.

Per serving: 239 Calories, 10 g Total Fat, 1 g Saturated Fat, 0 mg Cholesterol, 198 mg Sodium, 22 g Total Carbohydrate, 2 g Dietary Fiber, 20 g Protein, 287 mg Calcium.

CURRIED VEGETABLES WITH TOFU

Makes 4 servings

$^1/_3$ cup boiling water

3 tablespoons shredded coconut

1 pound 4 ounces all-purpose potatoes, pared
    and cut into $^1/_2$" chunks

2 teaspoons olive oil

1 cup sliced scallions

2 garlic cloves, slivered

1 tablespoon minced pared fresh ginger root

1 teaspoon mild or hot curry powder

1 teaspoon sweet Hungarian paprika

$^1/_4$ teaspoon salt

1 cup diced red bell pepper

2 cups cauliflower florets

2 cups carrot chunks (1" pieces)

3 tablespoons fresh lime juice

2 teaspoons smooth peanut butter

1 pound firm tofu, cut into 1" pieces

1. In small bowl, combine boiling water and coconut; let stand 15 minutes.

2. Place potatoes into medium saucepan; add water to cover. Bring liquid to a boil; reduce heat to low. Simmer 10–15 minutes, until potatoes are tender. Drain, discarding liquid; set aside.

3. Meanwhile, in large skillet heat oil; add scallions, garlic and ginger. Cook over medium-high heat, stirring frequently, 4 minutes, until scallions are softened. Add curry powder, paprika and salt; cook, stirring constantly, 30 seconds. Add bell pepper; cook, stirring frequently, 5 minutes, until pepper is softened.

4. Add cauliflower, carrots and 1 cup water to vegetable mixture; bring liquid to a boil. Reduce heat to low; simmer, covered, 10 minutes, until vegetables are tender.

5. Meanwhile, place fine sieve over small bowl; pour coconut mixture through sieve, pressing with back of wooden spoon to extract as much liquid as possible. Reserve liquid; discard solids.

6. Add juice, peanut butter and reserved coconut liquid to vegetable mixture; stir to combine. Add tofu and cooked potatoes; cook, stirring frequently, 5 minutes, until tofu and potatoes are heated through and liquid is thickened.

BREAKFAST

Reduced-Calorie Whole-Wheat Bread, 2 slices, toasted, with 1 tablespoon strawberry spreadable fruit and $1^1/_2$ teaspoons peanut butter

Crunchy Honey Yogurt (In small bowl, combine $^3/_4$ cup plain nonfat yogurt and 2 teaspoons wheat germ and 1 teaspoon honey.)

Coffee or Tea (optional)

LIGHT MEAL

Chick-Pea Salad (In medium bowl, combine 2 cups torn Romaine lettuce leaves, 6 cherry tomatoes, halved, $^1/_2$ cup cooked cut green beans, 2 ounces drained cooked chick-peas, $^1/_4$ cup packaged croutons and 2 tablespoons fat-free Italian dressing.)

Breadsticks, 2 long

Unsweetened Seltzer

MAIN MEAL

Curried Vegetables with Tofu, 1 serving (see recipe)

Cooked Basmati Rice, $^1/_2$ cup

Cucumber and Radish Slices, 1 cup *each*, with 1 tablespoon fat-free creamy Italian dressing

Sugar-Free Strawberry Nonfat Frozen Yogurt, 4 fluid ounces

Non-Alcoholic White Wine, 4 fluid ounces

SNACK

Banana Shake (In blender, combine $^3/_4$ cup skim milk, $^1/_2$ medium banana, sliced, 3 ice cubes and sugar substitute to equal 2 teaspoons sugar; purée until smooth.)

This menu provides: 2 Milks, 3 Fats, 2 Fruits, 13 Vegetables, 3 Proteins, $4^1/_2$ Breads, 180 Optional Calories.

Per serving: 29 g Fat, 24 g Fiber.

Serving provides: 1 Fat, 3 Vegetables, 2 Proteins, 1 Bread, 10 Optional Calories.

Per serving: 389 Calories, 15 g Total Fat, 3 g Saturated Fat, 0 mg Cholesterol, 213 mg Sodium, 46 g Total Carbohydrate, 7 g Dietary Fiber, 24 g Protein, 302 mg Calcium.

346
BEAN ENCHILADAS

Makes 4 servings

2 cups evaporated skimmed milk
2 tablespoons all-purpose flour
3 garlic cloves, minced
$^1/_2$ teaspoon salt
$^1/_2$ cup minced scallions
$^1/_2$ cup minced fresh cilantro
1 pound drained cooked red kidney beans
Eight 6" flour tortillas
3 ounces reduced-fat Monterey Jack cheese with jalapeño peppers, grated
$^1/_2$ cup salsa

1. Preheat oven to 375° F. Spray 11 × 7" baking dish with nonstick cooking spray.

2. In large saucepan, with wire whisk, combine milk and flour, blending until flour is dissolved. Stir in garlic and salt; cook over medium heat, whisking constantly, 4 minutes, until thickened. With wire whisk, blend in scallions and cilantro. Remove from heat; set aside.

3. In small bowl, combine beans and one-fourth of the milk mixture; with potato masher, mash until almost smooth.

4. To assemble enchiladas, place tortillas onto work surface; arrange one-fourth of the bean mixture along center of each tortilla. Fold sides of tortillas over filling to enclose; place, seam-side down, into prepared baking dish. Pour remaining milk mixture evenly over filled tortillas; sprinkle evenly with cheese. Bake, tightly covered, 15 minutes, until hot and bubbling; serve with salsa.

Serving (2 enchiladas, 2 tablespoons salsa) provides: 1 Milk, $^3/_4$ Vegetable, 3 Proteins, 2 Breads, 15 Optional Calories.

Per serving: 467 Calories, 8 g Total Fat, 3 g Saturated Fat, 20 mg Cholesterol, 965 mg Sodium, 69 g Total Carbohydrate, 6 g Dietary Fiber, 31 g Protein, 657 mg Calcium.

347
RICE AND BEANS

Makes 4 servings

4 ounces regular long-grain rice
2 teaspoons olive oil
1 cup minced scallions
4 garlic cloves, minced
1 cup diced green bell pepper
1 cup diced red bell pepper
1 pound drained cooked red kidney beans
1 cup tomato sauce (no salt added)
$^1/_2$ cup minced fresh cilantro
$^3/_4$ teaspoon dried oregano leaves
$^1/_2$ teaspoon ground cumin
$^1/_4$ teaspoon salt
1 tablespoon fresh lime juice

1. In medium saucepan, bring $1^1/_2$ cups water to a boil; add rice. Reduce heat to low; simmer, covered, 17 minutes, until rice is tender and all liquid is absorbed. Remove from heat; set aside.

2. Meanwhile, in large saucepan or Dutch oven, heat oil; add scallions and garlic. Cook over medium-high heat, stirring frequently, 4 minutes, until scallions are softened. Stir in green and red bell peppers; cook, stirring frequently, 5 minutes, until peppers are softened.

3. Add beans, tomato sauce, $^1/_4$ cup of the cilantro, the oregano, cumin and salt to vegetable mixture; bring liquid to a boil. Reduce heat to low; simmer, covered, 5 minutes, until mixture is slightly thickened. Add cooked rice; stir to combine. Stir in remaining $^1/_4$ cup cilantro; cook, uncovered, stirring frequently, 2 minutes, until mixture is heated through. Add juice; stir to combine.

Serving ($1^1/_2$ cups) provides: $^1/_2$ Fat, $2^1/_2$ Vegetables, 2 Proteins, 1 Bread.

Per serving: 317 Calories, 3 g Total Fat, 0 g Saturated Fat, 0 mg Cholesterol, 158 mg Sodium, 59 g Total Carbohydrate, 7 g Dietary Fiber, 14 g Protein, 78 mg Calcium.

BREAKFAST
Strawberries, 1 cup
English Muffin, $^1/_2$ (1 ounce), toasted, with $^3/_4$ ounce reduced-fat Monterey Jack cheese and 1 teaspoon jalapeño jelly
Skim Milk, 1 cup
Coffee or Tea (optional)

LIGHT MEAL
Vegetable Omelet (Spray small nonstick skillet with nonstick cooking spray; heat. Pour $^1/_2$ cup egg substitute into skillet, tilting to cover bottom of pan. Cook over medium-high heat until underside is set, lifting edges with spatula to let uncooked egg flow underneath. Sprinkle $^1/_4$ cup *each* cooked chopped cauliflower and carrot evenly over one side of omelet; with spatula, fold other side over vegetables to enclose.)
Tomato, 1 medium, sliced, on 2 iceberg lettuce leaves, with 1 tablespoon ranch dressing
Reduced-Calorie Butterscotch-Flavored Pudding (made with skim milk), $^1/_2$ cup
Diet Orange Soda

MAIN MEAL
Rice and Beans, 1 serving (see recipe)
Nonfat Tortilla Chips, 2 ounces, with Salsa-Cream Dip (In small bowl, top $^1/_2$ cup salsa with 2 tablespoons nonfat sour cream.)
Tossed Green Salad, 2 cups, with $^1/_4$ cup packaged croutons and 1 tablespoon fat-free Thousand Island dressing
Sugar-Free Lemon-Flavored Gelatin, $^1/_2$ cup, with 1 tablespoon thawed frozen light whipped topping (8 calories per tablespoon)
Light Beer, 6 fluid ounces

SNACK
Ban-illa Yogurt (In small bowl, combine $^1/_2$ cup aspartame-sweetened vanilla nonfat yogurt and $^1/_2$ medium banana, sliced.)

This menu provides: 2 Milks, 3 Fats, 2 Fruits, 12 Vegetables, 5 Proteins, $4^1/_2$ Breads, 165 Optional Calories.

Per serving: 24 g Fat, 21 g Fiber.

348
BLACK BEANS AND YELLOW RICE

A snap to make, this hearty Cuban-inspired dish will become an instant family favorite.

Makes 4 servings

6 ounces brown rice
$^1/_2$ teaspoon ground turmeric
$^1/_2$ bay leaf
2 teaspoons corn oil
$^1/_2$ teaspoon ground cumin
1 medium green bell pepper, seeded and chopped
1 medium onion, chopped
1 medium carrot, diced
1 garlic clove, minced
1 cup low-sodium vegetable broth
8 ounces drained cooked black beans
2 tablespoons drained chopped pickled sweet red pepper (reserve 1 tablespoon juice)
1 teaspoon dried oregano leaves
$^1/_2$ teaspoon salt
2 tablespoons minced fresh cilantro
Hot red pepper sauce, to taste

1. In medium saucepan, bring 2 cups water to a boil; add rice, turmeric and bay leaf. Reduce heat to low; simmer, covered, 40 minutes, until rice is tender and all liquid is absorbed. Remove from heat; remove and discard bay leaf. Transfer rice to serving bowl; set aside.

2. Meanwhile, in medium nonstick skillet, heat oil; add cumin. Cook over medium-high heat, stirring constantly, 20 seconds, until fragrant. Add bell pepper, onion, carrot and garlic; cook, stirring frequently, 5 minutes, until vegetables are softened. Stir in broth, beans, pickled red pepper with juice, oregano and salt; bring liquid to a boil. Reduce heat to low; simmer, stirring occasionally, 5 minutes, until mixture is slightly thickened (for a thicker mixture, with wooden spoon, mash some of the beans before stirring them in).

3. Top cooked rice with bean mixture; sprinkle with cilantro. Serve with pepper sauce.

Serving (2 cups) provides: $^1/_2$ Fat, $1^1/_4$ Vegetables, 1 Protein, $1^1/_2$ Breads, 5 Optional Calories.

Per serving: 292 Calories, 4 g Total Fat, 1 g Saturated Fat, 0 mg Cholesterol, 344 mg Sodium, 55 g Total Carbohydrate, 4 g Dietary Fiber, 9 g Protein, 53 mg Calcium.

"REFRIED" BLACK BEAN CAKE WITH CORN SAUCE

Makes 4 servings

12 ounces drained cooked black beans
1 cup minced scallions
$^1/_2$ cup minced fresh cilantro
3 tablespoons fresh lime juice
2 tablespoons tomato paste (no salt added)
2 tablespoons plain dried bread crumbs
2 teaspoons olive oil
$^1/_2$ cup diced red bell pepper
$^1/_2$ cup diced green bell pepper
1 medium pickled jalapeño pepper, seeded and minced
2 cups canned cream-style corn (no salt added)
$^1/_4$ teaspoon salt
$1^1/_2$ ounces reduced-fat Monterey Jack cheese, grated

1. Preheat oven to 375° F. Spray nonstick baking sheet with nonstick cooking spray.

2. In large bowl, combine beans, $^1/_2$ cup of the scallions, the cilantro, 2 tablespoons of the juice, the tomato paste and bread crumbs; with potato masher, mash until mixture holds together. Form into 4 equal patties; place onto prepared baking sheet. Bake 20 minutes, until heated through and crispy. Remove patties from oven; leave oven on.

3. Meanwhile, in large nonstick skillet, heat oil; add remaining $^1/_2$ cup scallions. Cook over medium-high heat, stirring frequently, 2–3 minutes, until softened. Add red and green bell and jalapeño peppers; cook, stirring frequently, 5 minutes, until peppers are softened. Add corn and salt; stir to combine. Remove from heat; set aside.

4. Sprinkle patties evenly with cheese; bake 1 minute, until cheese is melted.

5. Add remaining 1 tablespoon juice to corn mixture; stir to combine. Spoon $^1/_3$ cup corn mixture onto each of 4 plates; top each portion of sauce with 1 baked patty. Top patties evenly with remaining corn mixture.

Serving (1 patty, $^1/_2$ cup sauce) provides: $^1/_2$ Fat, $1^1/_2$ Vegetables, 2 Proteins, 1 Bread, 15 Optional Calories.

Per serving: 298 Calories, 6 g Total Fat, 2 g Saturated Fat, 8 mg Cholesterol, 489 mg Sodium, 53 g Total Carbohydrate, 5 g Dietary Fiber, 15 g Protein, 159 mg Calcium.

BREAKFAST

Apple, 1 small
Poached Egg, 1
English Muffin, 1 (2 ounces), split and toasted, with 2 teaspoons reduced-calorie tub margarine
Skim Milk, 1 cup
Coffee or Tea (optional)

LIGHT MEAL

Cheese "Danish" (In small bowl, combine $^1/_3$ cup nonfat ricotta cheese, sugar substitute to equal 2 teaspoons sugar and $^1/_4$ teaspoon *each* cinnamon and ground nutmeg; spread onto 2 slices cinnamon-raisin toast.)
Iced Coffee or Tea

MAIN MEAL

"Refried" Black Bean Cake with Corn Sauce, 1 serving (see recipe)
Steamed Vegetable Medley (Place 1 cup *each* frozen artichoke hearts, cut asparagus and sliced leeks into steamer insert; steam over simmering water until tender. Serve sprinkled with fresh lemon juice.)
Tossed Green Salad, 2 cups, with 15 small or 9 large pitted black olives and 1 tablespoon fat-free blue cheese dressing
Rainbow Sherbet, $^1/_2$ cup
Unsweetened Lime-Flavored Seltzer

SNACK

Raspberry Yogurt (In small bowl, combine $^3/_4$ cup plain nonfat yogurt and $^3/_4$ cup raspberries.)
Graham Crackers, 3 ($2^1/_2$" squares)

This menu provides: 2 Milks, 3 Fats, 2 Fruits, $11^1/_2$ Vegetables, 4 Proteins, 6 Breads, 160 Optional Calories.

Per serving: 30 g Fat, 25 g Fiber.

"Refried" Black Bean Cake with Corn Sauce

350
Spicy Black Bean Stew

Makes 4 servings

2 teaspoons olive oil
2 medium red onions, cut into 1" chunks
1 medium pickled jalapeño pepper, seeded and minced
1 tablespoon minced pared fresh ginger root
4 garlic cloves, minced
1 cup diced seeded poblano chiles
2 cups diced butternut squash
1 pound drained cooked black beans
2 cups stewed tomatoes (no salt added), chopped
1 cup thawed frozen corn kernels
1/3 cup minced fresh cilantro
$^1/_2$ teaspoon salt

1. In large saucepan or Dutch oven, heat oil; add onions, pepper, ginger and garlic. Cook over medium-high heat, stirring frequently, 5 minutes, until onions are softened. Add chiles; cook, stirring frequently, 5 minutes, until chiles are softened. Add squash; cook, stirring frequently, 5 minutes, until squash is softened.

2. Add beans, tomatoes and $^3/_4$ cup water to vegetable mixture; bring liquid to a boil. Reduce heat to low; simmer, covered, 30 minutes, until vegetables are tender and mixture is slightly thickened.

3. Stir in corn, cilantro and salt; cook, stirring constantly, 2 minutes, until mixture is heated through.

Serving ($1^3/_4$ cups) provides: $^1/_2$ Fat, $2^1/_4$ Vegetables, 2 Proteins, 1 Bread.

Per serving: 309 Calories, 4 g Total Fat, 1 g Saturated Fat, 0 mg Cholesterol, 364 mg Sodium, 61 g Total Carbohydrate, 9 g Dietary Fiber, 15 g Protein, 137 mg Calcium.

BREAKFAST
Banana Smoothie (In blender, combine 1 cup skim milk, $^1/_2$ medium banana, sliced, 2 ice cubes and 2 teaspoons honey; purée until smooth.)
Reduced-Calorie Whole-Wheat Bread, 2 slices, toasted, with 2 teaspoons reduced-calorie tub margarine
Coffee or Tea (optional)

LIGHT MEAL
Mozzarella and Tomato Salad (Line plate with 4 Romaine lettuce leaves. Arrange 1 medium tomato, sliced, and $1^1/_2$ ounces nonfat mozzarella cheese, sliced, on lettuce leaves; sprinkle with 2 tablespoons minced fresh basil and 1 teaspoon *each* olive oil and balsamic vinegar.)
Garlic Bread (Spread 1-ounce slice Italian bread with $^1/_2$ teaspoon minced fresh garlic or the pulp of 1 roasted garlic clove; drizzle with $^1/_2$ teaspoon olive oil. Place onto nonstick baking sheet; broil until lightly browned.)
Diet Lemonade, 1 cup

MAIN MEAL
Spicy Black Bean Stew, 1 serving (see recipe)
Cooked Long-Grain Rice, 1 cup
Tossed Green Salad, 2 cups, with 1 tablespoon fat-free Italian dressing
Berry Parfait (In stemmed glass, layer $^1/_4$ cup *each* blueberries, raspberries and blackberries; top with 1 tablespoon thawed frozen light whipped topping (8 calories per tablespoon)

SNACK
Vanilla-Almond Yogurt (In small bowl, combine $^3/_4$ cup plain nonfat yogurt, sugar substitute to equal 2 teaspoons sugar and $^1/_2$ teaspoon *each* vanilla and almond extracts.)

This menu provides: 2 Milks, 3 Fats, 2 Fruits, $9^1/_4$ Vegetables, 3 Proteins, 5 Breads, 60 Optional Calories.

Per serving: 20 g Fat, 24 g Fiber.

351

HUEVOS RANCHEROS

Makes 4 servings

2 cups chopped tomatoes

8 ounces drained cooked black beans

$^1/_2$ cup minced red onion

$^1/_2$ cup thawed frozen corn kernels

$^1/_2$ cup minced fresh cilantro

1 teaspoon chopped deveined seeded jalapeño pepper (wear gloves to prevent irritation)

$^1/_2$ teaspoon salt

4 eggs

3 ounces nonfat tortilla chips

1. In large skillet, combine tomatoes, beans, onion, corn, cilantro, pepper and salt; bring liquid to a boil. Reduce heat to low; simmer, covered, 10 minutes, until flavors are blended and mixture is heated through.

2. Meanwhile, in another large skillet, poach eggs.

3. Divide tomato mixture evenly among 4 plates. Top each portion of tomato mixture with 1 poached egg; surround each with $^3/_4$ ounce tortilla chips.

Serving (1 egg, $^3/_4$ cup tomato mixture, $^3/_4$ ounce chips) provides: $1^1/_4$ Vegetables, 2 Proteins, 1 Bread.

Per serving: 278 Calories, 7 g Total Fat, 2 g Saturated Fat, 212 mg Cholesterol, 425 mg Sodium, 41 g Total Carbohydrate, 4 g Dietary Fiber, 15 g Protein, 115 mg Calcium.

352
VEGETARIAN MOLÉ

Makes 4 servings

4 large pitted prunes
1 tablespoon unsweetened cocoa powder
2 teaspoons granulated sugar
2 teaspoons mild or hot chili powder
$^1/_2$ teaspoon ground cumin
$^1/_2$ teaspoon cinnamon
1 tablespoon + 1 teaspoon vegetable oil
1 medium red onion, cut into 1" pieces
4 garlic cloves, minced
2 medium green bell peppers, seeded and cut into 1" pieces
1 cup diced pared butternut squash ($^1/_2$" pieces)
$^1/_2$ medium carrot, halved lengthwise and cut into $^1/_4$" slices
$^1/_2$ cup sliced yellow squash ($^1/_2$" pieces)
2 cups crushed tomatoes (no salt added)
8 ounces drained cooked black beans
8 ounces drained cooked chick-peas

1. In blender or food processor, combine prunes, cocoa powder, sugar, chili powder, cumin, cinnamon and $^1/_2$ cup water; purée until smooth. Set aside.

2. In large saucepan or Dutch oven, heat oil; add onion and garlic. Cook over medium-high heat, stirring frequently, 5 minutes, until onion is softened. Add bell peppers; cook, stirring frequently, 5 minutes, until bell pepper is softened. Add butternut squash and carrot; cook, stirring frequently, 7 minutes, until squash is just tender. Add yellow squash; stir to coat.

3. Add tomatoes, black beans, chick-peas and reserved prune mixture to vegetable mixture; bring liquid to a boil. Reduce heat to low; simmer, covered, stirring occasionally, 25 minutes, until vegetables are very tender and flavors are blended.

Serving ($1^1/_2$ cups) provides: 1 Fat, $^1/_2$ Fruit, $2^3/_4$ Vegetables, 2 Proteins, $^1/_4$ Bread, 10 Optional Calories.

Per serving: 324 Calories, 7 g Total Fat, 1 g Saturated Fat, 0 mg Cholesterol, 224 mg Sodium, 57 g Total Carbohydrate, 8 g Dietary Fiber, 13 g Protein, 130 mg Calcium.

BREAKFAST
Seedless Green Grapes, 20 small or 12 large
Mini Bagel, 1 (1 ounce), split and toasted, with 1 tablespoon nonfat cream cheese
Skim Milk, 1 cup
Coffee or Tea (optional)

LIGHT MEAL
Egg Salad Sandwich (In small bowl, combine 1 hard-cooked egg, chopped, $^1/_4$ cup *each* chopped celery and chopped red onion and 2 teaspoons reduced-calorie mayonnaise; spread between 2 slices reduced-calorie rye bread.)
Celery and Carrot Sticks, 1 cup *each*
Dill Pickle, 1 medium
Unsweetened Berry-Flavored Seltzer

MAIN MEAL
Vegetarian Molé, 1 serving (see recipe)
Herb-Scented Rice (In small bowl, combine $^1/_2$ cup cooked long-grain rice and 1 tablespoon *each* minced fresh oregano leaves and flat-leaf parsley.)
Papaya, $^1/_4$ medium
Light Beer, 12 fluid ounces

SNACK
Peanut Butter "Pudding" (In small bowl, combine 1 cup aspartame-sweetened vanilla nonfat yogurt and 1 tablespoon crunchy peanut butter; sprinkle with 3 tablespoons graham cracker crumbs.)

This menu provides: 2 Milks, 3 Fats, 2 Fruits, $9^3/_4$ Vegetables, 4 Proteins, $4^1/_4$ Breads, 125 Optional Calories.

Per serving: 30 g Fat, 20 g Fiber.

BREAKFAST

Banana, $^1/_2$ medium
Nonfat Cottage Cheese, $^1/_2$ cup
Cinnamon-Raisin Bread, 1 slice, toasted, with 1 teaspoon reduced-calorie tub margarine
Skim Milk, 1 cup
Coffee or Tea (optional)

LIGHT MEAL

Bean Tacos (Fill each of 2 taco shells with 2 ounces drained cooked black beans, 2 tablespoons salsa and $^1/_4$ cup shredded iceberg lettuce leaves.)
Apple, 1 small
Diet Cream Soda

MAIN MEAL

Three-Bean Salad, 1 serving (see recipe)
Chilled Broccoli and Cauliflower Florets, 1 cup *each*, with $1^1/_2$ teaspoons *each* olive oil and fresh lemon juice
Roll, 1 ounce
Sugar-Free Grape-Flavored Gelatin, $^1/_2$ cup, with 1 tablespoon thawed frozen light whipped topping (8 calories per tablespoon)
Decaffeinated Coffee or Tea

SNACK

Raisin Bran Cereal, $1^1/_2$ ounces, with 1 cup skim milk and 1 teaspoon granulated sugar

This menu provides: 2 Milks, 3 Fats, 2 Fruits, 10 Vegetables, 4 Proteins, $5^1/_2$ Breads, 55 Optional Calories.

Per serving: 27 g Fat, 26 g Fiber.

353
THREE-BEAN SALAD

Makes 4 servings

10 ounces all-purpose potatoes, pared and cut into 1" cubes
2 cups cut green beans (1" pieces)
2 cups julienned carrots (1" pieces)
4 ounces drained cooked chick-peas
4 ounces drained cooked red kidney beans
$^1/_2$ cup diced red bell pepper
$^1/_2$ cup julienned celery (1" pieces)
1 cup low-sodium mixed vegetable juice
2 tablespoons fresh lemon juice
1 tablespoon + 1 teaspoon olive oil
$^3/_4$ teaspoon dried oregano leaves
$^1/_2$ teaspoon salt
$^1/_4$ teaspoon freshly ground black pepper
2 cups torn Romaine lettuce leaves

1. Place potatoes into large pot; add water to cover. Bring liquid to a boil; reduce heat to low. Simmer 10–15 minutes, until potatoes are tender. With slotted spoon, transfer potatoes to large bowl; set aside to cool.

2. In same pot of boiling water, cook green beans and carrots 4 minutes, until green beans are bright green and vegetables are just tender; drain; discarding liquid. Transfer vegetables to bowl with potatoes; set aside to cool.

3. Add chick-peas, kidney beans, bell pepper and celery to bowl with cooked potatoes and vegetables; toss to combine.

4. In medium jar with tight-fitting lid or medium bowl, combine vegetable and lemon juices, oil, oregano, salt and black pepper; cover and shake well or, with wire whisk, blend until combined. Pour over potato mixture; toss to combine. Refrigerate, covered, until chilled.

5. Line each of 4 plates with $^1/_2$ cup lettuce; top each portion of lettuce with one-fourth of the potato mixture.

Serving ($1^3/_4$ cups) provides: 1 Fat, 4 Vegetables, 1 Protein, $^1/_2$ Bread.

Per serving: 247 Calories, 6 g Total Fat, 1 g Saturated Fat, 0 mg Cholesterol, 362 mg Sodium, 42 g Total Carbohydrate, 7 g Dietary Fiber, 9 g Protein, 94 mg Calcium.

354

MIXED BEAN CHILI

Makes 4 servings

2 teaspoons olive oil

I cup minced scallions

I cup diced green bell pepper

2 teaspoons mild or hot chili powder

I teaspoon ground cumin

I teaspoon ground coriander

$^1/_2$ teaspoon dried oregano leaves

8 ounces sweet potatoes, pared and cut into $^1/_2$" chunks

$I^1/_2$ cups stewed tomatoes (no salt added), chopped

8 ounces drained cooked black beans

8 ounces drained cooked red beans

$^1/_2$ teaspoon salt

$^1/_4$ cup nonfat sour cream

1. In large saucepan or Dutch oven, heat oil; add scallions. Cook over medium-high heat, stirring frequently, 4 minutes, until softened. Add bell pepper; cook, stirring frequently, 5 minutes, until pepper is softened. Add chili powder, cumin, coriander and oregano; stir to combine.

2. Add sweet potatoes and 1 cup water to vegetable mixture; bring liquid to a boil. Reduce heat to low; simmer, covered, 15 minutes, until potatoes are tender.

3. Stir in tomatoes, black and red beans and salt; return mixture to a boil. Reduce heat to low; simmer, stirring occasionally, until vegetables are very tender and mixture is thickened.

4. Divide bean mixture evenly among 4 bowls; top each portion with 1 tablespoon sour cream.

Serving ($1^3/_4$ cups) provides: $^1/_2$ Fat, $1^3/_4$ Vegetables, 2 Proteins, $^1/_2$ Bread, 10 Optional Calories.

Per serving: 283 Calories, 4 g Total Fat, 0 g Saturated Fat, 0 mg Cholesterol, 327 mg Sodium, 52 g Total Carbohydrate, 9 g Dietary Fiber, 14 g Protein, 128 mg Calcium.

BREAKFAST

Banana, $^1/_2$ medium

English Muffin, $^1/_2$ (1 ounce), toasted, with 1 teaspoon peanut butter

Skim Milk, 1 cup

Coffee or Tea (optional)

LIGHT MEAL

Stuffed Baked Potato (Cut one 4-ounce baked potato in half lengthwise; place, cut-side up, into small microwavable baking dish. Top potato with $^1/_2$ cup cooked chopped broccoli and $^3/_4$ ounce reduced-fat cheddar cheese; microwave on High [100% power] 2–3 minutes until cheese is melted and potato is heated through.)

Tossed Green Salad, 2 cups, with 1 teaspoon *each* olive oil and balsamic vinegar

Diet Cola

MAIN MEAL

Mixed Bean Chili, 1 serving (see recipe)

Nonfat Tortilla Chips, 2 ounces, with Salsa-Cream Dip (In small bowl, top $^1/_2$ cup salsa with 2 tablespoons nonfat sour cream.)

Cucumber Slices and Whole Radishes, 1 cup *each*, with 1 tablespoon fat-free blue cheese dressing

Seedless Green Grapes, 20 small or 12 large

Iced Herbal Tea

SNACK

Plain Popcorn, hot-air popped, 3 cups, with 1 tablespoon freshly grated Parmesan cheese and 1 teaspoon reduced-calorie tub margarine, melted

Skim Milk, 1 cup

This menu provides: 2 Milks, 3 Fats, 2 Fruits, $12^3/_4$ Vegetables, 3 Proteins, $5^1/_2$ Breads, 80 Optional Calories.

Per serving: 25 g Fat, 27 g Fiber.

355

LENTILS AND RICE WITH EGGPLANT AND GREEN PEPPER

Makes 4 servings

2 teaspoons olive oil
$^3/_4$ cup sliced scallions
2 tablespoons minced pared fresh ginger root
3 garlic cloves, minced
$2^1/_2$ cups diced pared eggplant
$1^1/_2$ cups diced green bell peppers
$^3/_4$ cup thinly sliced carrot
6 ounces lentils
4 ounces basmati rice
$1^1/_2$ cups low-sodium mixed vegetable juice
1 teaspoon salt
$^1/_4$ teaspoon ground allspice
$^1/_2$ cup minced fresh flat-leaf parsley

1. In large saucepan or Dutch oven, heat oil; add scallions, ginger and garlic. Cook over medium-high heat, stirring frequently, 4 minutes, until scallions are softened. Add eggplant, bell peppers and carrot; stir to coat. Stir in $^1/_2$ cup water; bring liquid to a boil. Reduce heat to low; simmer, covered, 7 minutes, until vegetables are tender.

2. Add lentils and rice to vegetable mixture; stir to coat. Stir in juice, salt, allspice and $3^1/_2$ cups water; bring liquid to a boil. Reduce heat to low; simmer, covered, 25 minutes, until lentils and rice are tender. Stir in parsley.

Serving (2 cups) provides: $^1/_2$ Fat, $3^1/_2$ Vegetables, 2 Proteins, 1 Bread.

Per serving: 327 Calories, 3 g Total Fat, 0 g Saturated Fat, 0 mg Cholesterol, 649 mg Sodium, 61 g Total Carbohydrate, 9 g Dietary Fiber, 17 g Protein, 92 mg Calcium.

VEGETARIAN BURGERS

Makes 4 servings

3 ounces lentils

1 cup shredded carrot

6 ounces firm tofu, mashed

$^1/_2$ cup tomato paste (no salt added)

$^1/_2$ cup minus 1 tablespoon all-purpose flour

$^1/_3$ cup + 2 teaspoons plain dried bread crumbs

$^1/_4$ cup minced fresh cilantro

1 egg

3 tablespoons fresh lime juice

1 tablespoon + 1 teaspoon reduced-sodium soy sauce

1 tablespoon + 1 teaspoon olive oil

$^1/_2$ small mango, pared, pitted and diced

$^1/_2$ cup diced red bell pepper

$^1/_4$ cup diced red onion

2 teaspoons honey

1. Place lentils into large saucepan; add water to cover. Bring liquid to boil; reduce heat to low and simmer 30–35 minutes until lentils are very tender. Drain, discarding liquid; place into large bowl.

2. Preheat oven to 400° F. Spray nonstick baking sheet with nonstick cooking spray.

3. Add carrot, tofu, tomato paste, $^1/_4$ cup of the flour, the bread crumbs, cilantro, egg, 2 tablespoons of the juice and the soy sauce to cooked lentils; combine thoroughly and form into 4 equal patties.

4. Place remaining 3 tablespoons flour onto sheet of wax paper or paper plate; one at a time, place each patty into flour, turning to coat.

5. In large nonstick skillet, heat 2 teaspoons of the oil; spread evenly to coat bottom of skillet. Add 2 patties; cook over medium-high heat, turning once, 8 minutes, until browned and crispy. Transfer burgers to prepared baking sheet. Repeat with remaining 2 teaspoons oil and 2 patties. Bake 10 minutes, until burgers are heated through.

6. Meanwhile, in small bowl, combine mango, bell pepper, onion, honey and remaining 1 tablespoon juice; serve burgers topped with mango mixture.

Serving (1 burger, $^1/_3$ cup mango mixture) provides: 1 Fat, $^1/_4$ Fruit, 2 Vegetables, 2 Proteins, 1 Bread, 20 Optional Calories.

Per serving: 360 Calories, 11 g Total Fat, 2 g Saturated Fat, 53 mg Cholesterol, 344 mg Sodium, 50 g Total Carbohydrate, 6 g Dietary Fiber, 19 g Protein, 157 mg Calcium.

BREAKFAST

Apple, 1 small

Open-Face Cheese and Tomato Sandwich (Top each of 2 slices reduced-calorie multi-grain toast with 1 slice nonfat Swiss cheese and $^1/_2$ medium tomato, sliced. Place onto nonstick baking sheet; broil until heated.)

Skim Milk, 1 cup

Coffee or Tea (optional)

LIGHT MEAL

Greek Salad (In medium bowl, combine 2 cups torn Romaine lettuce leaves, 1 large plum tomato, diced, $^1/_2$ cup cooked cut green beans, $^3/_4$ ounce feta cheese, crumbled, 3 large Greek olives and fresh lemon juice, to taste.)

Whole-Wheat Roll, 1 (2-ounce)

Cherries, 9 large

Unsweetened Seltzer with Mint Sprig

MAIN MEAL

Vegetarian Burgers, 1 serving (see recipe)

Pita Bread, 1 small (1 ounce)

Tossed Green Salad, 2 cups, with 1 teaspoon *each* olive oil and red wine vinegar

Sugar-Free Vanilla Nonfat Frozen Yogurt, 4 fluid ounces

Iced Decaffeinated Coffee

SNACK

Plain Popcorn, hot-air popped, 3 cups, with 1 teaspoon reduced-calorie tub margarine, melted

Chocolate "Egg Cream" (In tall glass, combine 1 cup diet chocolate soda and $^3/_4$ cup skim milk.)

This menu provides: 2 Milks, 3 Fats, 2 Fruits, 14 Vegetables, 4 Proteins, 6 Breads, 70 Optional Calories.

Per serving: 35 g Fat, 28 g Fiber.

357

HOPPIN' JOHN

This protein-packed, lightened version of the classic dish is a perfect vegetarian entrée.

Makes 4 servings

2 teaspoons olive oil

2 cups chopped onions

2 garlic cloves, minced

2 cups canned whole tomatoes (no salt added), drained and chopped

1 pound 4 ounces drained cooked black-eyed peas

4 cups cooked long-grain rice

$^1/_3$ cup minced fresh flat-leaf parsley

1 tablespoon + 1 teaspoon minced fresh rosemary or thyme leaves

1 teaspoon salt

Freshly ground black pepper, to taste

1 lime, cut into wedges

Hot red pepper sauce, to taste

1. In large nonstick skillet, heat oil; add onions. Cook over medium-high heat, stirring frequently, 5 minutes, until softened. Add garlic; cook, stirring constantly, 1 minute. Add tomatoes; cook, stirring frequently, 10 minutes, until slightly thickened.

2. Stir peas, rice, parsley, and rosemary into tomato mixture; cook, stirring constantly, 3 minutes, until mixture is heated through and flavors are blended. Sprinkle with salt and pepper; stir to combine. Serve with lime and pepper sauce.

Serving (2 cups) provides: $^1/_2$ Fat, 2 Vegetables, $2^1/_2$ Proteins, 2 Breads.

Per serving: 513 Calories, 4 g Total Fat, 1 g Saturated Fat, 0 mg Cholesterol, 761 mg Sodium, 101 g Total Carbohydrate, 17 g Dietary Fiber, 19 g Protein, 126 mg Calcium.

BREAKFAST

Cooked Oatmeal, $^1/_2$ cup, with 2 tablespoons raisins and 1 teaspoon reduced-calorie tub margarine

Skim Milk, $^1/_2$ cup

Coffee or Tea (optional)

LIGHT MEAL

Vegetable Cottage Cheese (In medium bowl, combine $^1/_2$ cup nonfat cottage cheese and $^1/_4$ cup *each* chopped scallions, cucumbers, celery and carrot.)

Breadsticks, 2 long

Nectarine, 1 small

Unsweetened Seltzer

MAIN MEAL

Hoppin' John, 1 serving (see recipe)

Sauteed Collard Greens and Onions (In medium skillet, heat $1^1/_2$ teaspoons vegetable oil; add $^1/_2$ cup chopped onion and 1 garlic clove, minced. Cook over medium-high heat, stirring frequently, 5 minutes, until onion is softened. Add 1 cup chopped collard greens; cook, stirring frequently, until wilted.)

Roll, 1 ounce, with 1 teaspoon reduced-calorie tub margarine

Aspartame-Sweetened Strawberry-Banana Nonfat Yogurt, 1 cup

Iced Tea

SNACK

Butterscotch Parfait (In stemmed glass, layer $^1/_2$ cup reduced-calorie butterscotch-flavored pudding [made with skim milk] and 3 tablespoons graham cracker crumbs; top with 1 tablespoon thawed frozen light whipped topping [8 calories per tablespoon].)

This menu provides: 2 Milks, 3 Fats, 2 Fruits, 7 Vegetables, $3^1/_2$ Proteins, 6 Breads, 50 Optional Calories.

Per serving: 23 g Fat, 25 g Fiber.

BREAKFAST

Honeydew Melon, 2" wedge

Cinnamon-Sweet Cottage Cheese (In small bowl, combine $^1/_2$ cup nonfat cottage cheese, sugar substitute to equal 2 teaspoons sugar and $^1/_4$ teaspoon cinnamon.)

Reduced-Calorie Rye Bread, 2 slices, toasted, with 2 teaspoons reduced-calorie tub margarine

Skim Milk, 1 cup

Coffee or Tea (optional)

LIGHT MEAL

Cooked Linguine, 1 cup, with $^1/_2$ cup marinara sauce and 1 tablespoon freshly grated Parmesan cheese

Italian Bread, 1 slice (1 ounce)

Torn Romaine Lettuce Leaves, 2 cups, with 1 tablespoon fat-free Caesar salad dressing

Sugar-Free Pineapple-Flavored Gelatin, $^1/_2$ cup, with 1 tablespoon thawed frozen light whipped topping (8 calories per tablespoon)

Iced Tea with Mint Sprig

MAIN MEAL

Vegetable Chowder, 1 serving (see recipe)

Oyster Crackers, 20

Celery and Carrot Sticks, 1 cup *each*

Sliced Jicama and Alfalfa Sprouts, 1 cup *each,* with 1 tablespoon fresh lemon juice

Blueberries, $^3/_4$ cup, with $^1/_4$ cup nonfat sour cream

Sparkling Mineral Water

SNACK

Frozen Raspberry Pop (Pour $^1/_2$ cup sugar-free raspberry-flavored drink into small paper cup; freeze until almost firm. Insert ice-cream-bar stick vertically into partially frozen drink; freeze until solid. Unmold.)

This menu provides: 2 Milks, 3 Fats, 2 Fruits, 15$^1/_2$ Vegetables, 3 Proteins, 5$^3/_4$ Breads, 110 Optional Calories.

Per serving: 25 g Fat, 26 g Fiber.

358
VEGETABLE CHOWDER

Makes 4 servings

10 ounces all-purpose potatoes, pared and cut into $^1/_2$" cubes

2 cups small broccoli florets

1 cup diced carrot

2 teaspoons olive oil

1 cup diced red bell pepper

3 garlic cloves, minced

3 tablespoons all-purpose flour

4 cups skim milk

1 pound drained cooked white beans

$^3/_4$ teaspoon dried marjoram leaves

$^3/_4$ teaspoon salt

$^1/_2$ teaspoon freshly ground black pepper

$^1/_4$ teaspoon ground red pepper

1. Place potatoes into large pot; add water to cover. Bring liquid to a boil; reduce heat to low. Simmer 10–15 minutes, until potatoes are tender. With slotted spoon, remove potatoes from pot; set aside.

2. In same pot of boiling water, cook broccoli and carrot 3 minutes, until broccoli is bright green and vegetables are just tender. Drain, discarding liquid; set aside.

3. In large saucepan or Dutch oven, heat oil; add bell pepper and garlic. Cook over medium-high heat, stirring frequently, 5 minutes, until bell peppers are softened. Sprinkle with flour; stir quickly to combine. Continuing to stir, gradually add milk; bring liquid to a boil. Reduce heat to low; simmer, stirring frequently, 5 minutes, until thickened.

4. Stir beans into milk mixture; cook, stirring frequently and mashing some of the beans with back of spoon, until mixture is heated through. Stir in marjoram, salt, ground black and red peppers and cooked potatoes, broccoli and carrot; cook, stirring frequently, until heated through.

Serving (2 cups) provides: 1 Milk, $^1/_2$ Fat, 2 Vegetables, 2 Proteins, $^3/_4$ Bread.

Per serving: 384 Calories, 3 g Total Fat, 1 g Saturated Fat, 5 mg Cholesterol, 577 mg Sodium, 67 g Total Carbohydrate, 9 g Dietary Fiber, 24 g Protein, 457 mg Calcium.

SPLIT PEA SOUP WITH HERBED DUMPLINGS

Makes 4 servings

4¹/₂ ounces dried split peas, rinsed
¹/₂ cup chopped onion
¹/₂ cup sliced carrot
¹/₂ cup minced fresh dill
2 tablespoons tomato paste (no salt added)
4 garlic cloves, slivered
1 teaspoon salt
1 cup evaporated skimmed milk
¹/₃ cup + 2 teaspoons all-purpose flour
¹/₂ teaspoon double-acting baking powder
Pinch ground red pepper
2 teaspoons stick margarine, cold
1¹/₂ ounces reduced-fat cheddar cheese, grated
1 tablespoon minced fresh flat-leaf parsley
1 tablespoon minced scallion

1. To prepare soup, in large saucepan combine split peas, onion, carrot, ¹/₄ cup of the dill, the tomato paste, garlic, ³/₄ teaspoon of the salt and 4 cups water; bring liquid to a boil. Reduce heat to low; simmer 40 minutes, until split peas are tender.

2. Transfer split pea mixture to food processor; purée until smooth. Add ³/₄ cup + 1 tablespoon of the milk; process until combined. Return mixture to saucepan; set aside.

3. To prepare dumplings, in large bowl, combine flour, baking powder, pepper and remaining ¹/₄ teaspoon salt; with pastry blender or 2 knives, cut in margarine until the mixture resembles coarse crumbs. Add cheese, parsley, scallion and remaining ¹/₄ cup dill; toss to combine. Stir in remaining 3 tablespoons milk, 1 tablespoon at a time, until a soft dough forms.

4. By scant tablespoonfuls, drop dough into large pot of simmering water, making 8 dumplings; cook, covered, 7 minutes, until dumplings have risen to surface and are firm.

5. Cook soup over medium heat, stirring frequently, until heated through. Divide soup evenly among 4 soup bowls; with slotted spoon, transfer 2 dumplings to each bowl.

Serving (1¹/₄ cups soup, 2 dumplings) provides: ¹/₂ Milk, ¹/₂ Fat, ³/₄ Vegetable, 2 Proteins, ¹/₂ Bread.

Per serving: 278 Calories, 5 g Total Fat, 2 g Saturated Fat, 10 mg Cholesterol, 809 mg Sodium, 42 g Total Carbohydrate, 3 g Dietary Fiber, 18 g Protein, 382 mg Calcium.

BREAKFAST

Peanut Butter–Banana Smoothie (In blender, combine 1 cup skim milk, ¹/₂ medium banana, sliced, 2 ice cubes and 1 teaspoon smooth peanut butter; purée until smooth.)
English Muffin, ¹/₂ (1 ounce) with 1 teaspoon strawberry jam
Coffee or Tea (optional)

LIGHT MEAL

Cooked Cheese Tortellini, 20, with ¹/₂ cup tomato sauce (no salt added)
Green and Yellow Bell Pepper Strips, 1 cup *each*, with 2 tablespoons fat-free ranch dressing
Sugar-Free Lime-Flavored Gelatin, ¹/₂ cup
Unsweetened Seltzer

MAIN MEAL

Split Pea Soup with Herbed Dumplings, 1 serving (see recipe)
Red and Green Leaf Lettuce Salad, 2 cups, with 1¹/₂ teaspoons *each* olive oil and red wine vinegar
Flatbreads, 1¹/₂ ounces
Reduced-Calorie Chocolate-Flavored Pudding (made with skim milk), ¹/₂ cup
Decaffeinated Coffee or Tea

SNACK

Watermelon, 3 × 2" wedge

This menu provides: 2 Milks, 3 Fats, 2 Fruits, 10³/₄ Vegetables, 4 Proteins, 5 Breads, 175 Optional Calories.

Per serving: 28 g Fat, 21 g Fiber.

BREAKFAST

Fresh Fig, 1 large
Cooked Oatmeal, $^1/_2$ cup, with 1 teaspoon firmly
   packed light or dark brown sugar
Skim Milk, 1 cup
Coffee or Tea (optional)

LIGHT MEAL

Italian Spinach Salad (In medium bowl, combine
   2 cups torn spinach leaves, $^1/_2$ cup *each* sliced
   mushrooms and sliced red onion, 2 teaspoons
   imitation bacon bits and $1^1/_2$ teaspoons Italian
   dressing.)
Breadsticks, 2 long
Sparkling Mineral Water

MAIN MEAL

Tomato-Vegetable Soup with Tortellini, 1 serving
   (see recipe)
Italian Bread, 1 slice (1 ounce)
Carrot and Celery Sticks, 1 cup *each*
Seedless Green Grapes, 10 small or 6 large
Decaffeinated Coffee or Tea

SNACK

Strawberry-Nut Yogurt (In small bowl, combine
   1 cup aspartame-sweetened strawberry nonfat
   yogurt and 1 ounce dry-roasted unsalted peanuts,
   chopped.)

This menu provides: 2 Milks, 3 Fats, 2 Fruits,
13 Vegetables, 3 Proteins, $4^1/_2$ Breads, 110 Optional
Calories.

Per serving: 35 g Fat, 20 g Fiber.

TOMATO-VEGETABLE SOUP WITH TORTELLINI

Makes 4 servings

80 cheese tortellini ($5^1/_3$ cups)
3 cups low-sodium mixed vegetable juice
1 cup fresh orange juice
1 teaspoon granulated sugar
$^3/_4$ teaspoon ground ginger
$^1/_2$ teaspoon salt
$1^1/_4$ cups thinly sliced carrots
$1^1/_4$ cups julienned well-washed leeks
$^1/_2$ cup diced turnip
2 tablespoons minced fresh dill

1. In large pot of boiling water, cook tortellini until tender; drain, discarding liquid. Set aside; keep warm.

2. In large saucepan, combine vegetable and orange juices, sugar, ginger, salt and 3 cups water; bring to a boil. Add carrots, leeks and turnip; return liquid to a boil. Reduce heat to low; simmer, covered, 10 minutes, until vegetables are tender.

3. Divide warm tortellini evenly among 4 large soup bowls; top each portion with an equal amount of juice mixture. Serve sprinkled with dill.

Serving (20 tortellini, $1^1/_2$ cups soup) provides: $^1/_2$ Fruit, 3 Vegetables, 2 Proteins, $1^1/_2$ Breads, 75 Optional Calories.

Per serving: 579 Calories, 11 g Total Fat, 4 g Saturated Fat, 62 mg Cholesterol, 951 mg Sodium, 98 g Total Carbohydrate, 5 g Dietary Fiber, 22 g Protein, 248 mg Calcium.

361

MINESTRONE SOUP

Makes 4 servings

2 teaspoons olive oil
1 cup chopped onions
3 garlic cloves, minced
1 cup thinly sliced carrot
10 ounces all-purpose potatoes, pared and diced
2 cups shredded cabbage
2 cups chopped tomatoes
1 1/2 ounces elbow macaroni
1/2 cup minced fresh basil
1/2 teaspoon salt
1/4 teaspoon freshly ground black pepper
8 ounces drained cooked white beans
1 cup cut green beans (1" pieces)
3 ounces freshly grated Parmesan cheese

1. In large saucepan, heat oil; add onions and garlic. Cook over medium-high heat, stirring frequently, 7 minutes, until onions are golden brown.

2. Add carrot and 1/4 cup water to onion mixture; bring liquid to a boil. Reduce heat to low; simmer, covered, 4 minutes, until carrot is just tender. Add potatoes, cabbage, tomatoes and 3 3/4 cups water; bring liquid to a boil. Reduce heat to low; simmer, covered, 20 minutes, until potatoes are tender.

3. Add macaroni, basil, salt and pepper to vegetable mixture; cook 7 minutes. Add white and green beans; cook, stirring occasionally, 4 minutes, until macaroni is tender. Remove from heat; stir in cheese.

Serving (2 cups) provides: 1/2 Fat, 3 1/2 Vegetables, 2 Proteins, 1 Bread.

Per serving: 363 Calories, 10 g Total Fat, 4 g Saturated Fat, 17 mg Cholesterol, 706 mg Sodium, 52 g Total Carbohydrate, 8 g Dietary Fiber, 20 g Protein, 451 mg Calcium.

BREAKFAST

Strawberries, 1 cup
Herb Scramble (In small microwavable bowl, combine 1/2 cup egg substitute, 1 teaspoon minced fresh flat-leaf parsley and 1/4 teaspoon *each* dried oregano leaves and basil; microwave on Medium-High [70% power], stirring once or twice, 1 1/2–2 minutes until set.)
English Muffin, 1/2 (1 ounce), toasted, with 2 teaspoons reduced-calorie tub margarine
Skim Milk, 1 cup
Coffee or Tea (optional)

LIGHT MEAL

Cheese and Tomato Sandwich (Layer 1 medium tomato, sliced, and 1/4 cup part-skim ricotta cheese between 2 slices reduced-calorie whole-wheat toast.)
Tossed Green Salad, 2 cups, with 1/2 cup red bell pepper strips and 1 tablespoon fat-free Italian dressing
Reduced-Calorie Chocolate-Flavored Pudding (made with skim milk), 1/2 cup
Diet Cream Soda

MAIN MEAL

Minestrone Soup, 1 serving (see recipe)
Caesar Salad (In medium bowl, combine 2 cups torn Romaine lettuce leaves, 1/4 cup packaged croutons and 1 tablespoon fat-free Caesar salad dressing.)
Garlic-Herb Bread (Spread 1-ounce slice Italian bread with 1/2 teaspoon minced fresh garlic or 1 roasted garlic clove and 1/2 teaspoon *each* minced fresh basil and oregano leaves; drizzle with 1 teaspoon olive oil. Place onto nonstick baking sheet; broil until lightly browned.)
Kiwi Fruit, 1 medium
Red Wine Spritzer (In wineglass, combine 1/2 cup *each* unsweetened seltzer and non-alcoholic red wine.)

SNACK

Graham Crackers, 3 (2 1/2" squares), with 2 teaspoons raspberry jam
Skim Milk, 1/2 cup

This menu provides: 2 Milks, 3 Fats, 2 Fruits, 14 1/2 Vegetables, 5 Proteins, 5 1/2 Breads, 145 Optional Calories.

Per serving: 32 g Fat, 28 g Fiber.

BREAKFAST

Banana Yogurt (In small bowl, combine $^3/_4$ cup plain
    nonfat yogurt, $^1/_2$ medium banana, sliced, and
    sugar substitute to equal 2 teaspoons sugar.)
Skim Milk, $^1/_2$ cup
Coffee or Tea (optional)

LIGHT MEAL

Tropical Cheese Delight (In small bowl, combine
    $^1/_2$ cup nonfat cottage cheese, $^1/_2$ small mango,
    pared, pitted and diced, and 1 teaspoon shredded
    coconut.)
Celery and Carrot Sticks, 1 cup *each*
Torn Iceberg Lettuce Leaves and Sliced Radishes,
    2 cups, with 1 tablespoon fat-free Thousand
    Island dressing
Flatbreads, $^3/_4$ ounce
Diet Ginger Ale

MAIN MEAL

Asian Tofu-Noodle Soup, 1 serving (see recipe)
Carrot and Celery Sticks, 1 cup *each*
Bell Pepper Strips with Ginger Vinaigrette (In small
    jar with tight-fitting lid or small bowl, combine
    2 teaspoons *each* vegetable oil and red wine vine-
    gar and pinch ground ginger; cover and shake well
    or, with wire whisk, blend until combined. Pour
    over $^1/_2$ cup *each* red, green and yellow bell pepper
    strips.)
Rice Cakes, 2
Reduced-Calorie Vanilla-Flavored Pudding (made
    with skim milk), $^1/_2$ cup
Green Tea

SNACK

Reduced-Calorie Granola Bar, 1 (1 ounce)

This menu provides: 2 Milks, 3 Fats, 2 Fruits,
18 Vegetables, 3 Proteins, 4 Breads, 85 Optional
Calories.

Per serving: 31 g Fat, 22 g Fiber.

362

ASIAN TOFU-NOODLE SOUP

Makes 4 servings

3 ounces angel hair pasta (capellini), broken in half
1 tablespoon + 1 teaspoon oriental sesame oil
1 cup thinly sliced carrot
1 cup thinly sliced mushrooms
1 cup sliced scallions
2 tablespoons minced pared fresh ginger root
4 garlic cloves, minced
3 tablespoons reduced-sodium soy sauce
3 tablespoons rice wine vinegar or cider vinegar
1 pound firm tofu, cut into 1" pieces
2 cups watercress leaves
1 cup halved snow peas
$^1/_4$ cup minced fresh cilantro

1. In large pot of boiling water, cook pasta 3 minutes, until tender. Drain, discarding liquid; set aside.

2. In large saucepan, heat 2 teaspoons of the oil; add carrot, mushrooms, scallions, ginger and garlic. Cook over medium-high heat, stirring frequently, 5 minutes, until vegetables are softened. Add soy sauce, vinegar and 4 cups water; bring liquid to a boil. Reduce heat to low; simmer, covered, 5 minutes, until vegetables are tender.

3. Add tofu, watercress, snow peas and cilantro to vegetable mixture; return liquid to a boil. Reduce heat to low; simmer, uncovered, 2 minutes, until mixture is heated through.

4. Stir reserved pasta and remaining 2 teaspoons oil into tofu mixture; cook 1 minute, until pasta is heated.

Serving (1$^3/_4$ cups) provides: 1 Fat, 3 Vegetables, 2 Proteins, 1 Bread.

Per serving: 340 Calories, 15 g Total Fat, 2 g Saturated Fat, 0 mg Cholesterol, 491 mg Sodium, 32 g Total Carbohydrate, 4 g Dietary Fiber, 24 g Protein, 308 mg Calcium.

Savory Bread Pudding

Makes 4 servings

2 cups small broccoli florets
2 cups skim milk
1 cup nonfat cottage cheese
1 1/2 ounces freshly grated Parmesan cheese
2 eggs
2 egg whites
2 teaspoons Dijon-style mustard
1/4 teaspoon ground red pepper
Pinch ground nutmeg
2 tablespoons minced fresh flat-leaf parsley
2 tablespoons minced fresh dill
6 slices white bread, toasted and quartered

1. Preheat oven to 350° F. Spray a 9" square baking pan with nonstick cooking spray.

2. In large pot of boiling water, cook broccoli 3 minutes, until bright green and just tender. Drain, discarding liquid; rinse with cold water. Drain again; set aside.

3. In food processor, combine milk, cottage cheese, 3/4 ounce of the Parmesan cheese, the eggs, egg whites, mustard, pepper and nutmeg; purée until smooth. Add parsley and dill; process just until combined.

4. In prepared pan, combine toast quarters and cooked broccoli. Top with cottage cheese mixture; sprinkle evenly with remaining 3/4 ounce Parmesan cheese. Let stand 15 minutes; bake 35 minutes, until golden brown and set.

Serving (one-fourth of pudding) provides: 1/2 Milk, 1 Vegetable, 1 1/2 Proteins, 1 1/2 Breads, 10 Optional Calories.

Per serving: 308 Calories, 8 g Total Fat, 3 g Saturated Fat, 122 mg Cholesterol, 800 mg Sodium, 33 g Total Carbohydrate, 3 g Dietary Fiber, 26 g Protein, 418 mg Calcium.

BREAKFAST
Banana, 1/2 medium
Reduced-Calorie Granola Bar, 1 (1 ounce)
Skim Milk, 1 cup
Coffee or Tea (optional)

LIGHT MEAL
English Muffin Pizza (Split and toast one 2-ounce English muffin. Top split side of each muffin half with 2 tablespoons tomato sauce [no salt added], then sprinkle each with 3/4 ounce nonfat mozzarella cheese, grated, and 1/4 teaspoon dried oregano leaves. Place onto nonstick baking sheet; broil until heated.)
Celery and Carrot Sticks, 1 cup *each*
Tossed Green Salad, 2 cups, with 2 ounces drained cooked chick-peas and 1 tablespoon fat-free Italian dressing
Unsweetened Seltzer

MAIN MEAL
Savory Bread Pudding, 1 serving (see recipe)
Arugula and Sliced Tomato Salad, 2 cups, with minced fresh basil
Orange Sections, 1/2 cup
Decaffeinated Coffee or Tea

SNACK
Vanilla–Peanut Butter Parfait (In small bowl, combine 1/2 cup reduced-calorie vanilla-flavored pudding [made with skim milk] and 1 tablespoon crunchy peanut butter; in stemmed glass, layer pudding mixture and 3 tablespoons graham cracker crumbs.)

This menu provides: 2 Milks, 3 Fats, 2 Fruits, 14 Vegetables, 3 1/2 Proteins, 5 1/2 Breads, 75 Optional Calories.

Per serving: 26 g Fat, 22 g Fiber.

Savory Bread Pudding

POACHED PEARS STUFFED WITH GORGONZOLA CHEESE

Makes 4 servings

Two 3 × ¹/₂" strips lemon zest*
¹/₃ cup fresh lemon juice
3 tablespoons granulated sugar
³/₄ teaspoon ground ginger
6 whole black peppercorns
1 bay leaf
4 small Bartlett pears, pared, cored and halved lengthwise
2 teaspoons Dijon-style mustard
2 cups watercress leaves
1¹/₂ cups sliced Belgian endive
6 ounces Gorgonzola cheese, crumbled
2 tablespoons Neufchâtel cheese
1 tablespoon sherry wine vinegar
¹/₄ cup slivered celery
¹/₄ cup minced scallions

1. In large nonreactive skillet, combine zest, juice, sugar, ginger, peppercorns, bay leaf and 1¹/₄ cups water; bring liquid to a boil. Reduce heat to low; add pears, cut-side down. Simmer, basting pears occasionally with poaching liquid, 15 minutes, until pears are tender but still hold their shape. With slotted spoon, remove pears, zest, peppercorns and bay leaf from skillet. Discard zest, peppercorns and bay leaf; set pear halves and poaching liquid aside to cool.

2. Transfer cooled poaching liquid to large bowl; with wire whisk, add mustard, blending until combined. Add watercress and endive; toss to coat.

3. Divide watercress mixture evenly among 4 plates; top each portion with 2 pear halves, cut-side up.

4. In small bowl, with fork, combine Gorgonzola and Neufchâtel cheeses, vinegar and 1 tablespoon water, beating until smooth. Fit pastry bag with decorative tip; add cheese mixture.† Fill core cavity of each pear half with an equal amount of cheese mixture; top evenly with celery and scallions.

Serving (2 stuffed pear halves + one fourth of greens) provides: 1 Fruit, 2 Vegetables, 2 Proteins, 55 Optional Calories.

Per serving: 318 Calories, 16 g Total Fat, 10 g Saturated Fat, 43 mg Cholesterol, 691 mg Sodium, 38 g Total Carbohydrate, 5 g Dietary Fiber, 11 g Protein, 280 mg Calcium.

BREAKFAST

Orange Sections, ¹/₂ cup
Herb Scramble (In small microwavable bowl, combine ¹/₂ cup egg substitute, 1 teaspoon minced fresh flat-leaf parsley and ¹/₄ teaspoon *each* dried oregano leaves and basil; microwave on Medium-High [70% power], stirring once or twice, 1¹/₂–2 minutes, until set.)
English Muffin, ¹/₂ (1 ounce), toasted, with 2 teaspoons reduced-calorie tub margarine
Skim Milk, 1 cup
Coffee or Tea (optional)

LIGHT MEAL

Confetti Salad (In medium bowl, combine 2 cups torn Romaine lettuce leaves, 1 medium tomato, diced, ¹/₂ cup *each* cooked corn kernels and cooked long-grain rice and 2 ounces drained cooked black beans.)
Flatbreads, ³/₄ ounce
Unsweetened Seltzer

MAIN MEAL

Poached Pears Stuffed with Gorgonzola Cheese, 1 serving (see recipe)
Cherry Tomatoes, 6, with 1 tablespoon fat-free ranch dressing
French Bread, 1 slice (1 ounce), with 2 teaspoons reduced-calorie tub margarine
Reduced-Calorie Chocolate-Flavored Pudding (made with skim milk), ¹/₂ cup
Sparkling Mineral Water with Lemon Wedge

SNACK

Plain Popcorn, hot-air popped, 3 cups, with 2 teaspoons reduced-calorie tub margarine, melted
Vanilla "Egg Cream" (In tall glass, combine 1 cup diet cream soda and ¹/₂ cup skim milk.)

This menu provides: 2 Milks, 3 Fats, 2 Fruits, 9 Vegetables, 5 Proteins, 6 Breads, 115 Optional Calories.

Per serving: 34 g Fat, 26 g Fiber.

*The zest of the lemon is the peel without any of the pith (white membrane). To remove zest from lemon, use a zester or vegetable peeler.

†If pastry bag is not available, cheese mixture may be spooned evenly into pear halves.

365

CHEESE SOUFFLÉ

Makes 4 servings

1 cup evaporated skimmed milk
3 tablespoons all-purpose flour
2^1/$_4$ ounces freshly grated Gruyère cheese
1^1/$_2$ ounces freshly grated Parmesan cheese
2 eggs, separated
2 tablespoons minced chives
^{1}/$_2$ teaspoon salt
^{1}/$_4$ teaspoon freshly ground black pepper
Pinch ground red pepper
3 egg whites

1. Preheat oven to 350° F. Adjust oven rack to divide oven in half.

2. In medium saucepan, with wire whisk, combine milk and flour, blending until flour is dissolved. Cook over medium heat, stirring frequently,
5 minutes, until thickened. Add Gruyère and Parmesan cheeses; stir until
melted. Remove from heat.

3. In small bowl, with wire whisk, lightly beat egg yolks; continuing to
beat, gradually add ^{1}/$_4$ cup of the milk mixture. Beat yolk mixture into
remaining milk mixture; place over low heat. Cook, beating constantly,
2 minutes, until thick. Remove from heat; stir in chives, salt and black and
ground red peppers. Place a sheet of wax paper directly onto top of milk
mixture to cover completely; set aside until room temperature.

4. In medium bowl, combine all 5 egg whites; with electric mixer, beat
until stiff but not dry. Stir one-fourth of the egg whites into cooled milk
mixture; gently fold in remaining egg whites. Spoon mixture into 5-cup
soufflé dish, smoothing top; bake 35–40 minutes, until mixture is lightly
browned and puffy. Serve immediately.

Serving (1^1/$_4$ cups) provides: ^{1}/$_2$ Milk, 2 Proteins, ^{1}/$_4$ Bread.

Per serving: 326 Calories, 11 g Total Fat, 6 g Saturated Fat, 135 mg Cholesterol,
671 mg Sodium, 13 g Total Carbohydrate, 0 g Dietary Fiber, 20 g Protein,
511 mg Calcium.

INDEX